HERNÁN CORTÉS

Conqueror of Mexico

HERNÁN CORTÉS

From an oil painting in the Hospital de Jesus Nazarene,
City of Mexico

SALVADOR DE MADARIAGA

HERNÁN CORTÉS
Conqueror of Mexico

HENRY REGNERY COMPANY
CHICAGO, 1955

First published 1942
Second edition 1955

PRINTED IN GREAT BRITAIN

To
SIR JOHN C. SQUIRE

My dear Squire,

When you read my book on Columbus
you wrote to me: "I'm not sure you
oughtn't to do another."

Here it is.

S. de M.

CONTENTS

PROLOGUE

CHAPTER   PAGE

I. THE RETURN OF QUETZALCOATL 3

PART I

SELF–DISCOVERY

II. HERNÁN CORTÉS LANDS IN THE NEW WORLD . 19

III. THE NEST OF HAWKS 33

IV. CORTÉS WATCHES TWO MEN FAIL AS CONQUERORS 44

V. LOVE AND REVOLT IN ESPAÑOLA . . . 57

VI. CORTÉS WATCHES TWO MORE MEN FAIL AS CONQUERORS 70

PART II

CORTÉS CONCEIVES THE CONQUEST

VII. CORTÉS RISES TO LEADERSHIP 87

VIII. A PORTRAIT OF THE MAN 102

IX. FROM SPANISH KNIGHT TO MEXICAN GOD . . 113

X. CORTÉS FOUNDS VERACRUZ AND BREAKS AWAY FROM VELÁZQUEZ 126

XI. CORTÉS "BURNS" HIS SHIPS 140

CONTENTS

PART III

THE FIRST CONQUEST

CHAPTER		PAGE
XII.	VICTORY OVER TLAXCALA	161
XIII.	VICTORY OVER HIS OWN ARMY	179
XIV.	THE MASSACRE OF CHOLULA	198
XV.	AT THE GATES OF THE CITY OF MEXICO	216
XVI.	THE MEETING OF THE TWO WORLDS	233

PART IV

CORTÉS THROWS AWAY HIS CONQUEST

XVII.	THE SEIZURE OF MOTEÇUÇUMA	253
XVIII.	MOTEÇUÇUMA GIVES AWAY HIS SOVEREIGNTY	268
XIX.	CORTÉS THROWS AWAY HIS CONQUEST	279
XX.	NARVÁEZ COMES TO AVENGE VELÁZQUEZ	294
XXI.	THE DEFEAT OF NARVÁEZ	305

PART V

THE SECOND CONQUEST

XXII.	THE MASSACRE OF MEXICO	321
XXIII.	THE FLIGHT FROM MEXICO	335
XXIV.	RISE AFTER THE FALL	346
XXV.	CORTÉS PREPARES THE SIEGE OF MEXICO AND ENTERS INTO LEGEND	359
XXVI.	THE SIEGE AND FALL OF MEXICO	374

CONTENTS

PART VI

SELF–CONQUEST

CHAPTER | PAGE

XXVII. THE CONQUEROR CONQUERED BY HIS CONQUEST 395

XXVIII. CAPTAIN GENERAL AND GOVERNOR OF NEW SPAIN 412

XXIX. CORTÉS GOES TO LAS HIBUERAS AND LOSES MEXICO 430

XXX. THE MARQUESS OF THE VALLEY . . . 445

XXXI. THE MARQUESS VS. THE VICEROY . . . 460

XXXII. BEYOND THE CONQUEST 474

NOTES

I. ACKNOWLEDGMENTS 489

II. SPELLING OF NAMES 490

III. PORTRAITS 491

IV. BIBLIOGRAPHY 492

V. NOTES TO THE CHAPTERS 498

GENERAL INDEX 543

SPECIAL INDEX ON HERNÁN CORTÉS 552

ILLUSTRATIONS

HERNÁN CORTÉS . . . . Frontispiece
  From an oil painting in the Hospital de Jesus Nazarene,
  City of Mexico

PAGE

MAP OF PART OF MEXICO, SHOWING THE ROUTE OF CORTÉS
  FROM VERA CRUZ TO THE CITY OF MEXICO 158

LAGOON OF THE CITY OF MEXICO WITH ITS SEVERAL CITIES . 392

PROLOGUE

CHAPTER ONE

The Return of Quetzalcoatl

IN THE year 4-House of the eighth sheaf of years of the Mexican era the Emperor Moteçuçuma the Younger had a great fright. We know this year as 1509. The Mexicans counted their time in "sheafs" of fifty-two years, and in order to designate them without error or ambiguity, a system had been adopted which can be best understood by reference to a pack of cards: as if we were to call our years one of spades, two of hearts, three of diamonds, four of clubs, five of spades, six of hearts, seven of diamonds, eight of clubs, etc. It is clear that the series or "sheaf" would begin again every fifty-two years. The Mexican calendar divided the fifty-two years of a "sheaf" into four sets or "colours" of thirteen years, i.e., rabbits, reeds, flints and houses. (1)

Moteçuçuma was *Uei Tlatoani* of Mexico, that is senior Lord, literally, *the one who speaks*; and as such, he was entitled to the utmost respect from everyone in the Empire, beginning with the second highest dignitary in the State, who proudly bore the title of *Ciuacoatl* or Serpent-Woman (a combination formidable enough). Wherever Moteçuçuma went, streets were carefully swept before he passed, though he never actually set foot on them, for he was conveyed·in a litter or, if he walked, it was over carpets which protected his august feet from the touch of mother earth; powerful magnates covered their rich garments with rough, cheap wraps before being admitted to his presence. No one was allowed to look him in the face. If such a man had a fright it could only be caused by the fear of supernatural powers.

He was a keen observer of the religious tenets of his people, and when, on the death of the Emperor Ahuitzotl, the twelve electors

3

had chosen him out of sixteen possible candidates, though he was but sixth in the line of descendants from Emperor Axayacatl (2) his father, their choice may have been guided not only by his military exploits (which gave him the right to wear his hair plaited in the manner of those who had caught at least six prisoners alive for the sacrifices to Uitzilopochtli, the war God) (3) but by the fact that his piety had already earned him the position of head of the priesthood. King Nezahoalpilli, of Tetzcuco, one of the chief magnates of the Empire, seems to have played a leading part in this election which had taken place in the year 10-Rabbit. (4) "The twelve of the Empire, having come to an agreement, prepared a brazier, a fire, and copal-incense, close to the chimney [. . .] And a bodkin of tiger-bone and another one of lion-bone, and the incensory, an invaluable wrap, very rich, loin-cloths, golden greaves, and the crown which they called *xiuhhuitzolli*, which was a half-mitre worn on the forehead and tied at the back of the head." This done, the electors went to fetch the new Emperor at the *Calmecac* or Monastery of the noblemen where he lived. They "made him sit on the throne and then they cut his hair in the regal way and bored a hole through his nose-partition in which they set a thin and subtle tube of gold which is known as *acapitzactli*. Then, from his waistband they hung a small *tecomatl* or gourd, to imply or mean that he was to carry *picietl* (5) or snuff in it, that is, grit for the journey, and they put on him gold earrings and gold lip-ornaments, and a wrap of blue netting, like a thin shawl with many small and valuable stones and expensive loin-cloths, thin blue greaves and the crown of lordship. This done, they incensed him and the two kings hailed him Emperor of Mexico-Tenuchtitlan."

This was no sinecure, as the two kings immediately went on to explain with as much eloquence as prolixity. From Uitzilopochtli, who required to be "served, worshipped, revered in praises and sacrifices," and whose service was such that "it allowed no sleep," down to "the old men and women," to be treated "with much love, giving them what was necessary for their upkeep," the Emperor had to attend to all persons, things and duties; and, not content with seeing to it that the roads were clean and swept, "particularly where the sacrifices of blood-penitence are to be made," he had also to keep watch over the stars, for he was told: "At dawn, known as *tlahuizcalpan teuctli,* you must bathe and do sacrifice, paint your face black and pierce your ears, arms and legs, to draw blood from them, then, with the incensory, offer incense to the ninth heaven, looking at it."

As if to prove that he was willing and ready, the new Emperor at once "asked that two bodkins should be brought to him very sharp, one made of tiger-bone and one of lion-bone, and again and again he pierced his ears, arms and legs. He then took two quails, cut their heads off and sprinkled the blood on the fire. He then ascended the temple of Uitzilopochtli and, having kissed the earth with his finger, at the feet of the god, again pierced his ears, arms and legs. Then he seized a few quails, cut off their heads and sprinkled the blood on the temple. Then he took the incensory and incensed the god Uitzilopochtli and the four parts of the temple and, having bowed deep, he went down to the royal palaces with the kings and lords who accompanied him. After their meal was over, they all went up to the temple again, stopping short of the four highest steps, on which the god image stood, just at the round stone known as eagle-dish, *cuauhxicalli,* blood brazier and duct. As the stone was pierced through, it swallowed much blood and the whole could hold many human hearts, and there he made another sacrifice and beheaded more quails." (6)

* * *

"He was"—says the Canon of Mexico, Cervantes de Salazar, writing shortly after his death—"a man of average stature, with a certain gravity and royal majesty which plainly showed who he was even to those who did not know him. He was thin, light-bodied, of a yellowish brown colour, as of a parrot, in the manner of all persons of his nation; his hair was long, very black and shiny, almost down to the shoulders; he had a sparse beard, with a few black hairs some inches long; his eyes black, his glance grave, and over his face a certain affability along with a royal majesty, such that those who looked at him felt drawn to love and revere him. He was a fairly strong man, lithe and light; he was a good archer, a good swimmer and proficient in all warlike exercises; he was good-natured, though strict as a judge, and this he was in order to be loved and dreaded, for on account both of what his predecessors had told him and of what he had learned from personal experience, he knew that his subjects were such that they could not be governed nor kept within the bounds of justice otherwise than by rigorous and stern ways [. . .] He spoke well and wittily when there was occasion for it; yet most prudently; he was very fond of women and used to take drugs to strengthen his virility; he treated them well and enjoyed them in the utmost secrecy; he was fond of feasts and pleasures, though, owing to his gravity, he was sparing in the use of them. In his religion and worship of his vain gods, he was most careful and devout; in offering sacrifices, most assiduous; he ordered that all laws and statutes concerning religion should be respected with the utmost rigour; for nothing was he less lenient than for an offence, however slight, to the divine worship. In the punishment of larceny and adultery, to which he saw his people especially addicted, he was so severe that no friendship or entreaty was enough for him to stay the execution of a law. Towards his own people, he behaved with such majesty, that, no matter how great the person, he allowed no one to sit down in his presence or to wear shoes or look at his face, save such and such a person and they had to be great lords and of royal blood.

"He was always very trim and, in his way, richly dressed; he was marvellously clean, for every day he took two baths; he seldom left his apartment, save for meals; he did not receive many visitors; most business was transacted through the members of his council, and they or one of them came to report to him, but even this only through two or three interpreters, though they all spoke the same language. He went through his house to the sacrifices which were offered in the chief temple of Uitzilopochtli, where, at some distance from the great of his realm, he showed much devotion; he came out downcast, wrapped in thought, speaking to no one." (7)

*   *   *

This was no doubt the mood in which he was cast when, on that fateful year 4-House of the 8th sheaf, he heard one evening the yells and wails of his subjects and, coming out on the terrace of his palace, beheld a meteor in the sky which confirmed his worst fears. For it had fallen to his lot to govern in a most unhappy era. The *tonalpouhque* or astrologers of Mexico held that the world in which they lived would fare no better than the three worlds which had preceded it: the first, called *Atonatiuh,* or Water-Sun, had been swallowed by a deluge; the second, known as *Tlalchitonatiuh,* or Earth-Sun, had been quartered and disjointed by earthquakes; the third, *Ecatonatiuh,* or Wind-Sun, had been swept away by a hurricane, leaving nothing alive but a number of female monkeys. The fourth, Moteçuçuma's world, was known as *Tlatonatiuh,* or Fire-Sun, and the astrologers knew for certain that it would be destroyed by fire. Nor was this destructive madness altogether devoid of method; for the Mexicans held that the end of the world was to come in the future, as it had done in the past, on one of the 2-Reeds years, i.e., one of the years in which they "tied up the sheaf" (8), the fifty-second or last of a cycle. Moteçuçuma could still remember the last time—just two years earlier—in which he had passed with his people through the ordeal of doubt: is it to be this time, or have we still another fifty-two years to live? The omens had been most unfavourable right through the year: eighteen hundred Mexican warriors had been drowned in a river; "the Sun had been eaten" (i.e., there had been an eclipse) (9), and there had been an earthquake. No wonder that, from the Uei Tlatoani himself to the humblest of his subjects, all Mexicans had trembled for months, weeks, days, till the last hour of the cycle had come; no wonder that the ceremony of the rekindling of the fire had been that year exceptionally grave and moving.

Moteçuçuma had directed that in that year's fights, his warriors should endeavour to catch alive a generous and noble enemy, whose name should be specially connected with the ceremony; a soldier, named Itzcuin, had been fortunate enough to seize in battle a captain of Vexotzingo, known as Xiuhtlamin, and as *Xiutl* means *year,* the Emperor considered this a sufficient indication that the prisoner would be a welcome victim for the exacting gods. At last, the dreaded, yet longed-for period set in, and the Mexicans began to prepare for the day of doubt. With the nihilism of approaching death, they threw into the lagoon on which the town was built their domestic utensils and ornaments, the small stone-mills with which the housewife made flour out of her maize, together with the wood or stone images of their familiar gods; then, after carefully sweeping and cleaning their empty houses, on the day so much sighed for, they put out all their fires. The five "empty days," *nemontemi*, which came at the end of every year, were this year devoted to fasting and prayer. Nothing in the whole empire was then allowed to burn or raise a flame. The fire was dead. And until the "Master of the Science of the heavens" or, in Mexican, *Ilhuicatl Tlamatilizmatini*, announced that the world did go on rotating, no fire was necessary.

No fire would be necessary, for if the stars did not continue to turn the priest would not be able to kindle a new fire, and the world would come to an end. The Sun would not return; the night would stay for ever, and in its permanent darkness the monstrous *Tzitzimitles* would fall upon them and devour them all. So, they all ran up to their terraces, after locking up the pregnant women who, were the stars to stay their course, would be sure to turn into ferocious *Tzitzimitles* and devour every human being within their reach; the children had to be kept awake by all possible means, for if they ever fell asleep they were sure to turn into mice, as everybody knew might have happened on any of the previous seven sheaf-years. All Mexico, tense and trembling, watched from the terraces of the town the hill of Uixachtecatepetl where the new fire—if any—was to be kindled.

Meanwhile, the priests had donned their masks and ornaments, which made each of them a living image of the god whose servant he happened to be, and had begun the long, solemn procession which by carefully calculated steps was to bring them to the hilltop just at midnight. The priest entrusted with the duty of lighting the new fire walked along practising with the two pieces of wood, a spindle and a plank, with which he was to raise the life-giving sparks and, close to him, marched the unfortunate prisoner Xiuhtlamin, on whose breast the fire was to be kindled. A vast concourse of people followed the grim procession, while by other roads and in canoes more crowds converged on to the slopes of the hill of Uixachtecatepetl.

There, on a small temple on the very top, the *Ilhuicatl Tlamatilizmatini* anxiously watched the Pleiades as they approached the Meridian, crossed it and went on in their unperturbed motion; he observed also the three stars in Taurus which stand close to the Pleiades and which the Mexicans identified with the fire-kindling instrument, whose name, *mamalhoaztli* (10), they had given them. As soon as these stars had passed the Meridian, gazing from afar on the obscure worshippers who made of their serene light a signal for bloody rites, the *Ilhuicatl Tlamatilizmatini* announced the fact to the other priests who, possibly less anxious than the crowd of their faithful in the plain, awaited in darkness within a lower temple. The last minute had come for Xiuhtlamin; he was quickly seized by five priests, laid helpless on the sacrificial stone and stabbed by the chief priest just above the heart with a sharp obsidian knife which at one stroke severed all his chief veins and arteries. His heart was plucked out and raised, still throbbing, towards the bloodthirsty deity and on his gory chest the fire-kindling priest laid his wooden *mamalhoaztli* and feverishly turned the sharp spindle into the dry, hot hole of the plank. A dust of wood flour rose from the plank and fell on the victim's body— but suddenly, a fleeting spark, then another and another ignited the dust; the priest pressed home his advantage and soon a steady flame illumined the gaping wound of the victim's body and the eager faces of the priests. On this new fire, the victim's heart was thrown, the first fuel of the new era, and gradually his whole body was made to feed the flame.

Presently, a flaming brazier was brought out of the temple into the cold night, teeming with an anxious human sea. The sight of the flames was the signal for the rebirth of joy, of life and of its thousand minor activities. Every man and woman present, on seeing that light, had pierced his ears with *maguey* thorns and sprinkled the blood drawn from their wounds in the direction of the fire. Round the brazier, the local priests of all the towns and villages in the valley endeavoured to kindle their pine-torches at the newborn flame and, this done, ran downhill as quickly as they could; the light of a new hope went running here and there in the dark night, to kindle new ritual fires in the temples, bonfires in the squares, hearth fires in every home, so that soon after midnight, such was the speed and eagerness of all, there were enough fires everywhere to illumine the whole valley with a light almost as clear as the light of day. (11)

*   *   *

Moteçuçuma remembered that memorable day. He knew that his people had outlived that doubt and fear. And yet, he had remained in mortal dread of fate. The gods were hard. He was a youth of nineteen when, in the year 8-Reeds, his predecessor Ahuitzotl, elected Uei Tlatoani the year before, had dedicated a new temple to Uitzilopochtli, in whose honour he had sacrificed twenty thousand prisoners from Maçatlan, Tlapan, Tzicoac, Uaxtepec, Xolochiuhyan, Tzapotlan, Cuauhnauac and Yoaltepec. During four days, in fourteen temples, the victims stood in queues, miles long, waiting for the hour when their turn would arrive. They were painted over with chalk, except for a black band across the eyes; they wore eagle feathers on the head; on their brows, a fillet of bark-paper tied with down tassels; a collar, waistband and loin-cloth, also of paper; they held a paper flag in their right hand and in their left a mock shield made of reeds adorned with five eagle-down feathers. On arriving at the temple, the victim was led up the steps or dragged by the hair if too feeble or too strong to walk to his death; and once at the top, he was seized by five priests and thrown on his back upon the *techcatl;* two priests held his legs; two his arms; and a fifth held his head back by a wooden yoke under his throat. The sacrifice was then performed in the usual way, by opening the victim's breast with a swift stroke of an obsidian knife and tearing his heart out to be offered as food to the sun. The gory priests had to take turns to relieve one another when exhausted by the physical effort.

Heart after heart was poured into the eagledish; body after body was hurled down the steps of the temple to the yard; the *cuacuacuiltin,* old men told off for this gruesome work, took them away and had them flayed and cut up. (The choice parts went to the table of the Uei Tlatoani; the rest to that of the warrior who had caught the slave.) (12) Never in the history of Mexico had such a human holocaust been offered to the god of war. Moteçuçuma, gloomy with foreboding, might well reflect that, during his reign, no such proof of faith and devotion had been raised towards the gods. An old tradition announced the return to Mexico of one of the most powerful of them, Quetzalcoatl or Serpent-with-Precious-Feathers, god of the wind: "a man of good appearance, of a grave countenance, white-skinned and bearded; dressed in a long white garment." This man "whom they called Quetzalcoatl, and others Huemac, owing to his great virtues," had come to the land of the Mexicans and "taught

them by word and deed the way of virtue, saving them from vice and
sin, giving them laws and good doctrine; and to restrain them in their
lusts and lewd ways, had instituted fasting amongst them [. . .]
But seeing how little fruit his doctrine brought forth, he had gone
away by the same road he had come, which was to the East, vanish-
ing on the Coast of Coatzacoalco, and as he parted from them, he had
said to them that at a future time, on a *Ceacatl* [1-Reeds] year, he
would return, and then his doctrine would be received, and his sons
would be lords and owners of the lands, while they [the Mexicans]
and their descendants would undergo many calamities and persecu-
tions . . ." (13) Moteçuçuma, as a thoughtful statesman and as
the upholder of the worship and tradition of his folk, could not but
be alive to the signs and portents which might foretell the fulfilment
of this prophecy, for the return of the white-skinned and bearded
prophet from the Orient would bring in its trail calamities and per-
secutions for his race. Now on that fateful year 4-House of the 8th
sheaf, not one but several portents came to disturb him deeply: One
night, "a big comet appeared in the sky, on the East side of it, which
looked like a big flame of fire, very bright, and which threw forth
fire-sparks. This comet was in the shape of a pyramid, wide at its
lower part, and becoming narrow as it rose, so that it ended in a
point; it could be seen in the middle of the Orient; it began to appear
shortly after midnight and persisted till the morning; and the light
of the sun covered it so that when the sun was out it was no longer
to be seen."

Hardly had the Mexicans recovered from the fright, when the
Cu, or temple, of the god of war Uitzilopochtli, was seen ablaze
"without any human reason for it, and the flames came from the
beams outwards; the priests shouted for water to put out the fire,
but the more water was thrown on it, the more it burnt." "The next
portent was the lightning stroke which, without purpose or thunder,
hit the Cu of the God of Fire, known as *Xiuhtecutli*. This Cu had a
straw roof, and the lightning struck it and burnt it out. All held it
to be a miracle, for there was no thunder, though it rained a little."
"The fourth portent was a comet which, by day, while the sun shone
in the sky, ran from the west of Mexico to the east, throwing off hot
coals and big sparks; it had a very long tail, and everybody began
to yell, all at once, for it looked like a thing of terror and as such it

was held." "The fifth was that the lagoon of Mexico, without any wind whatsoever, rose; it seemed to boil and the water leapt up high, and there was a great storm on the lagoon, and the waves beat on the houses near by and brought down many of them. The Mexicans held it as a miracle for there was no wind." "The sixth portent was that in those days voices were heard in the air as of a woman who went about weeping and said: 'Oh my children, the days of our end are at hand!' And at other times she said: 'Oh my children, whither shall I take you?'"

We may imagine how these voices would echo in the prophetic soul of Moteçuçuma, so full of forebodings. For, of all the signs and portents of nature, those that speak reach deepest into our inner self, such is the power of the human voice. Hence, Moteçuçuma would, no doubt, feel most grateful for the discretion of the eighth portent, to wit, "men with two heads" which at that time "appeared in many places"; for "they were led to Moteçuçuma's palace for him to see them, and once he had seen them, they vanished without saying anything." But the worst of all these portents which filled Moteçuçuma with fear and horror was the seventh: "a bird in size and colour like an eagle, which had a mirror on the crown of its head." "The fishermen or water-hunters" who caught it "took it to Moteçuçuma, who was in his palace, in a hall known as Tlillan Calmecac. This was in the afternoon, and Moteçuçuma looked at the bird and looked at the mirror which it had on its head, which was round and very polished, and glancing at it he saw the stars of heaven, the 'Little Masts' or *Mamaloaztli,* and Moteçuçuma was frightened at this and looked away, with the face of a frightened man; and, having looked again into the mirror on the bird's head, saw in it men on horseback who came all together and armed."

This was a pretty direct hint. So the unfortunate Emperor "summoned the soothsayers and astrologers and men learned in matters of portents, and asked them: 'What is this which I have seen here? What does it mean?' And while they were all thus frightened the bird vanished." (14)

It was, it must be owned, a pretty poor situation for all these astrologers and soothsayers; indeed, a dangerous one, for Moteçuçuma was not used to being disappointed and he had a somewhat heavy hand with those who defrauded him of his expectations. Unfortunately for his augurs, the era was rich in portents and their powers were soon to be put to even harder tests.

One morning, the priests who watched by night the temple of Tetzcatlipoca, King of the gods, came to report to the Emperor that towards midnight they had seen a column of white smoke in the east; it was so white that it shone with as much light as if it were midday, "and it rose from the earth till it almost touched the sky, and seemed as if it came forward walking like a great white giant." Moteçuçuma said to them: "Be sure you were not half asleep, or perhaps you have dreamt it." But upon their insistence, Moteçuçuma spent the next night watching for it, and it did come out, "whiter than snow, and it came forward, thickening, so that it looked as if a very tall man were approaching through the air, close to the sky." The Emperor summoned his necromancers and magicians and asked them: "What have you seen by day or by night, watchmen for the people as you are?" At which the unfortunate necromancers and magicians answered: "Sir, we have seen nothing at all, either by day or by night." Moteçuçuma was wroth and had them taken to jail and walled up so that they should starve to death. He then summoned Nezahoalpilli, the aged King of Tetzcuco, one of the neighbouring states which acknowledged his imperial authority, and for whose experience and virtue he had the utmost respect. The old king, who had not been taken unawares by the portent, said to Moteçuçuma: "It is the will of our gods that this should come to an end; what can I say? As for me, my lord and beloved grandson, I shall not see it, because I am going to lie down, and this is my farewell." Moteçuçuma wept; he wept both for his old granduncle and for himself; and in a new fit of wrath had his necromancers strangled. (15)

Nothing daunted by the death of their interpreters, portents followed portents so that Moteçuçuma saw how the very acts of piety which he performed to placate the gods became for the gods but new occasions to haunt him with their gloomy omens. The pious Emperor bethought himself of the fact that in his lifetime he had done nothing to perpetuate his memory; so he called the Serpent-Woman and imparted to him that he had decided to have a huge round stone cut in honour of Uitzilopochtli. The Serpent-Woman thought well of this and took adequate measures thereto. But when the huge stone was ready, no effort was sufficient to persuade it to

B

come down to the spot in the city for which it had been prepared. In vain long strings of slaves pulled with all their might at the ropes; the ropes broke and the stone did not budge; in vain did the priests sacrifice quail after quail, to smear the stone with innocent blood and so propitiate it; not only did the stone remain motionless, but it went so far as to express its determination in unmistakable terms. After a few dark and premonitory utterances, the stone was good enough to say: "Tell Moteçuçuma it is too late. He should have thought of it earlier. His end is at hand." The Emperor, nevertheless, gave orders that priests should cajole it by smearing it again with the blood of quails, and that copal-incense should be burnt in its honour and old men should go to dance and sing to it, to induce it to move. It looked at first as if this treatment were to be successful, for the stone did move; but as they arrived halfway across the bridge of Xoloco, "which was made of big cedar planks seven hands wide and nine hands thick," "the stone spoke again and said: 'Up to here it shall be and no farther,' saying which, the bridge broke." The stone fell into the water. Next day Moteçuçuma in person directed operations for rescuing it; but though he chose the hour of midday when water is at its clearest, and though the weather was so fine that he had to protect his majestic person with a parasol, and the stone was huge, it could not be found. It was presently discovered on top of the hill whence it had come so unwillingly. (16)

Hardly recovered from this episode, Moteçuçuma one day, as he paced a terrace above his palace, saw a white cloud rising towards the sky over Tetzcuco. This is what had happened. A peasant was working on his land, upon the small hill of Quetzaltepetl, when suddenly an eagle seized him by the hair and took him away across space into a hall "the best he had ever seen." The peasant then saw no eagle but a great lord who said to him: "Come here; fear not; take this rose and this perfume-sprayer; enjoy yourself. But see, behold here Moteçuçuma lying helpless, dead drunk. Wound him in a thigh." After some hesitation, the peasant did so, and the great lord then spoke again: "Do you see how he lacks all sense, being too far gone with drink? Go back now to the world and tell him all, and how I made you wound him in his thigh, and tell him to give up what he is now doing, for his end is at hand." "And the same eagle brought the peasant back to his land with the rose and the perfume-sprayer.

The peasant went straight to Moteçuçuma and told him all. The Emperor called his steward Petlacalcatl and said to him: 'Take this drunkard out of my sight and let him die stoned or beheaded or walled up.' " But, when the peasant had gone, he called Petlacalcatl again and complained of a sharp pain in his thigh; and though his wives found remedies for it, he remained impressed with this revelation after so many others. (17)

There could be little doubt that this last warning came direct from Huecmac himself, and so we find Moteçuçuma at this time so much obsessed by the powerful and mysterious lord that he dreamt—whether asleep or awake—of giving up his dangerous and exalted functions and taking refuge in Zincalco, the Paradise of Huecmac, where one never dies, "where there are all kinds of food and drink, and all kinds of roses and of fruit-trees." (18) He had four slaves sacrificed to Uitzilopochtli and flayed so that the skins should be sent as presents to Huemac. His thoughts evidently went back to this Huemac, Huecmac or Quetzalcoatl, the Feathered Serpent, whose ancient prophecy predicted a return of white, bearded men as conquerors from the East. He gave orders that priests, old men, women and his *calpixques,* or provincial stewards, should report whatever dreams were dreamt in his dominions; and soon enough, dreams of bad augury began to pour in: he had the dreamers put to death. But the worst augury was no dream: it was a vision of reality.

One day a *mazehual,* or man of humble station, came to see him: "Lord and King of ours"—he said—"forgive my daring: I come from Mictlan Cuauhtla; I walked to the seashore and I saw a kind of mountain or big hill moving about in the midst of the sea, without touching the shore, and this we had never seen, and as watchmen of the seacoast, we are always on the alert." Said Moteçuçuma: "Let it be. Go and rest." "And this man who came to see him with the news had no ears for he was earless; nor had he any toes, for they had been cut off." In his usual way, Moteçuçuma had the messenger locked up in the wooden prison. Yet he sent trusted men to find out whether his report was true. The trusted men came back saying that "it was true that two towers or small hills were moving about on the sea." Two of Moteçuçuma's high dignitaries went then to the coast: they hid in the thick foliage of the tree and observed this last portent; then went back to the imperial city and "repaired straight to the palace of Moteçuçuma to whom they spoke with the reverence and humility which were his due. They said: 'Lord and King of ours, it is true that there have come we know not what people and have arrived at the shore of the great sea; where they have been fishing with rods, and others with a net which they throw into the water, until, having fished till quite late, they entered a small canoe and boarded the two big towers and climbed into them. This people might be about fifteen persons, wearing some kind of red bags, and others blue, brown or green, and others of a dirty colour, as ugly as our *ychtilmatl*, others crimson, and on their heads some wore red cloths, others big headcovers like pans, perhaps to protect themselves from the sun; and their flesh is very white, whiter than ours, but most of them have long beards, and their hair comes down to the ears.' Moteçuçuma was downcast and spoke not a word." (19)

Quetzalcoatl had returned. His name was now Hernán Cortés.

PART I

SELF-DISCOVERY

CHAPTER TWO

Hernán Cortés Lands in the New World

FERNANDO, Hernando or Hernán Cortés
was born in 1485, 6-House of the eighth sheaf as the people he was
born to conquer would have said. He was born in Medellín, a small
town of Extremadura, "one of the best provinces of Spain" (1), the
land which lies north of that Puerto de Palos in which the discovery
of America was prepared, and which, very aptly, gave birth to the
most famous conquerors of it. Here is a most felicitous view of
Extremadura by one of the greatest contemporary masters of English
prose: "The Spanish landscape, particularly in these stretches of it
whence man is almost absent, gives out an impression of endurance
as does nothing else I know. One says to oneself: The well watered
countries of the North have changed perpetually and are changing
before our eyes to-day; the men of the North riot in experiment,
triumph, failure, achievement and failure again. The desert also
beyond the sea, beyond Atlas, is utterly unchanging, but unchanging
after a different fashion, for no man seeks a habitation there nor
thinks of it in terms of a mortal polity. But Spain—these great
steppes of Spain—have something of both the changing and the
unchanging, and yet resemble neither. It is land habitable enough
and breeds famous races of men. From this very countryside of
which I speak here came certain of the mighty Conquistadores, the
like of whom was never known before their time or has been known
since, riders of horses and dominators of the world. [. . .] It is
everywhere a land of challenge, and, what is more, a land provoking
worship of something symbolised by those wave-like mountainsides.
Indeed, these sweeps of the bare Iberian land, almost treeless, almost

19

untenanted, resemble and recall the sea, but a sea upon a scale more than titanic, a sea moved by gales such as our world never knows." (2)

*   *   *

His father was Martín Cortés de Monroy, and his mother Doña Catalina Pizarro Altamirano. "Both," adds Gómara, "were *hidalgos*. For all these four lineages Cortés, Monroy, Pizarro and Altamirano are very old, noble and honoured." Yet Las Casas—who did not like Cortés, but, all the same, knew him well—is content to say: "He was the son of a squire whom I knew, very poor and humble, though an old Christian and, so they say, an *hidalgo*." It is, at any rate, significant, that Gómara himself, chaplain to Cortés in his days of later splendor, while giving a *Doña* to the Conqueror's mother, gives no *Don* to his father. (3) This would by no means exclude Martín Cortés from the "squirearchy" in which Las Casas places him, yet would suggest that the maternal side of Hernán Cortés was of higher rank than the paternal in the social landscape of those days.

Martín Cortés de Monroy had taken part as the captain of fifty horsemen in the campaign waged against Queen Isabel by Alonso de Monroy, *Clavero* or Warden of the Military Order of Alcántara. This war had been one of the curious episodes of the struggle through which Ferdinand and Isabel had succeeded in taming their rebellious aristocracy. Monroy—who, despite the coincidence in their names, cannot have been related to Martín Cortés de Monroy, for otherwise Gómara would certainly have trumpeted it—was one of those noblemen who resented the Queen's wise policy of conferring on her own husband the King the masterships of the four powerful military orders as they came to fall vacant; and, being, as Warden or *Clavero*, second only to the Master in the Order of Alcántara, he rebelled against the Queen. Nor was it the least shrewd of Isabel's moves to set against him Don Alonso de Cárdenas, who was Master of the Order of St. James. Martín Cortés had therefore taken arms in a rebellious war. Yet he does not seem to have fared any the worse, either in the Queen's reign or in the reign of Charles V when he had often to act in Court as the ambassador and advocate of his brilliant son.

We may well imagine him living in his out-of-the-way Medellín,

in a still retreat
Sheltered, but not to social duties lost,

for his life cannot have differed much from that of the hidalgos whom
we can see living in the pages of Cervantes. He was, to be sure, "one
of those hidalgos with a spear in a rack, an old leather-shield, a
thin horse and a swift greyhound. A stew of something more beef
than mutton, meat-salad most evenings, ham and eggs on Saturdays,
lentils on Fridays and perhaps a pigeon on Sundays, would account
for three quarters of his revenue. The rest was spent in a broadcloth
frock, velvet breeches for festivities, with slippers of the same, and
on week ends he would honour himself with clothes of the finest
wool." His house was, no doubt, "spacious as village houses are;
with his arms displayed, though rough-hewn, on the stone above the
street door; the bodega in the courtyard; the cellar off the hall, and
many large earthen jars around" (4)—one of those houses in which
Spanish summers can be spent in quiet delight, in the shade of thick
walls and the fresh aroma of watered earth.

In such a house the early years of Hernán Cortés were spent.
We are told by one of his biographers that "his parents gave him to
a wet-nurse for her to feed him, with less pomp than in later years
the courage of his person conquered for him." (5) But Cortés was
never touchy, still less in those early days. As an hidalgo's son, he
would find the pleasures of his boyhood in riding his father's horse
and chasing hares with his father's greyhound, and now and then in
leading—for he would certainly lead—other local youngsters in the
usual pranks wherewith new generations initiate their protest against
the world which they find established on their arrival into it. His
health, however, was not very good. We know from Gómara that
"he grew up so ill that he was often on the verge of death." (6)
This is often the case with men of great spirit, for with them in the
early days the bodily vessel lacks the necessary consistence to withstand without painful strain the tensions which develop within it.
The remedy sought by the family seems to have been a special devotion towards St. Peter. Why St. Peter? it may be asked, and the
ingenious and imaginative may cast about for reasons and no doubt
find excellent ones, yet not the actual cause of the choice which was
chance; for "his parents, pious and devout people, drew lots to see
which of the twelve apostles was to be his patron saint, as is still

B*

done amongst us in our families, and the lot fell on St. Peter, which was the motive of the special devotion which he professed for this saint during all the rest of his life, to whose protection he believed he owed that robustness which stood him in such good stead in the long series of hardships which it was his lot to undergo." (7)

Cervantes de Salazar would have the child-conqueror's wet-nurse instead of the law of probabilities as the active agent in this important episode: "They say that his wet-nurse, being a very devout worshipper of the Apostle St. Peter, offered herself to him with certain sacrifices, worthy of a Christian woman; and so it is piously believed that the child recovered his health because the pious woman had taken the Saint as her intercessor and advocate." This version, however, is not as satisfactory as the first; for it was meet that both St. Peter and chance should stand at the gates of the life of Hernán Cortés; St. Peter among the apostles stands for the art of government and the craft of supreme power for which Cortés was predestined; while on the road thereto, the frail boy of Medellín was often to allow his destinies to be guided by the star of luck which was to protect him constantly in his adventurous career—to protect him especially against his worst enemy, who was of course to be Hernán Cortés himself. Nor was he averse to gambling in the usual form. "He played all kinds of games without any of the ways of the professional gambler, showing as good a face to losses as to gains." (8)

*   *   *

He was fourteen when he was sent to Salamanca. The famous University, then one of the four great seats of learning in Christendom, was not only an educational but a social centre of the utmost importance for an ambitious youth; for there, in the turbulent colleges and in its now quiet and studious, now overactive and rowdy halls, the poor but proud squire's son could meet on an equal footing the sons of the greatest. The University was governed under democratic rules, allowing much power to the students, including that of electing their own professors. Young Cortés went to Salamanca in 1499. Seven years earlier, while at the age of seven he was playing in his native Medellín with childish toys and, in his struggle with his unwilling body, he sought the patronage of St. Peter, a Genoese visionary of Spanish-Jewish origin had discovered a new world. In 1499, the cosmographers of Salamanca, agog with the dramatic change in the field of their studies which this discovery implied, could hardly guess that, lost in the crowd of students in the faculty of law, there was a boy of fourteen who would one day impart its true meaning to the discovery by conquering a resplendent exotic empire in that new world dreamt of and never really found by Colón.

How much he studied in Salamanca and how far he went up the ladder of academic achievement and why he gave up his studies and returned home are points on which his biographers are somewhat at variance. Las Casas, who knew him, says that "he was a Latin scholar . . . for he had read law in Salamanca and was a bachelor of law"; Bernal Díaz del Castillo, who knew him even better, says: "He was a Latin scholar and I heard that he was a bachelor of law, and when he spoke with scholars or men who knew Latin, he answered in Latin." But three other authorities deny that he graduated at all, and, on this concrete point at any rate, two of them happen to be of more weight than either Las Casas or Bernal Díaz. Cervantes de Salazar says: "When he was fourteen, his parents sent him to Salamanca, where in a short lapse of time he read Grammar, for he was very able; his parents wanted him to devote himself to the study of law, but as his fortune called him for so important an enterprise, leaving his studies owing to some quartan fevers, from which he recovered in a few months [. . .] he returned home . . ." The unknown but well informed author of the Latin chronicle of his life and doings says: "Sent to Salamanca at the age of fourteen on account of his studies, he spent two years studying grammar, lodged in the house of his aunt Inés de Paz, wife of Francisco Núñez Valera. Whence owing both to boredom with his studies and to expectation of bigger things (for the highest, indeed, had he been born) he left and returned home. His parents were bitter and impatient at this, for they had put all their hopes on him, their only son, and they wished him to take up the study of the science of law, which is everywhere held in such high honour and esteem." Finally, Gómara, who no doubt heard from Cortés himself his own version on the matter, says: "He returned to Medellín, surfeited, or having changed his mind as to studying, or possibly for lack of money. His parents were much put out by his return; they showed him their displeasure because he had given up his studies; for they wished him to read law, a rich faculty, and honoured over and above any other; for he was of a very good mind and able for everything." (9)

Gómara is probably right, save that we may take as actual causes the three which he gives as mere alternatives; for a couple of years studying grammar in the University, under the wary eyes of his no doubt devout and disciplinarian aunt, young Hernán Cortés would feel at the same time surfeited (*harto*), sorry to have chosen the path of learning instead of the path of war, and short of funds—for in Salamanca, with so many princely friends about, a poor squire's son had to live through many a hard quarter of an hour. And so, young Cortés, aged sixteen, left Salamanca and letters for good and all. The chief impulse was already the ambition of the man of action, which drove him to move on, to move away from the cloisters of learning and to seek more wealth, that is, more radius of action for his life—for material ambition in the man of action is but the form which the hunger for space takes in his powerful soul. Yet in all these testimonies from his contemporaries we perceive a rival force at work, which might have retained young Cortés on the path of learning: he was made for it, at least as much as for action. He was keen-minded, able in the art of mastering mental concepts, no less intelligent than brave. The detail given by Bernal Díaz del Castillo is most eloquent, particularly if, following Gómara, we take the view that Cortés remained two years only in Salamanca and would not wait to become a bachelor of law: he was a good Latin scholar and answered in Latin speeches made in Latin to him. This shows that he possessed exceptional gifts as a student. Cortés would, then, be a representative man of his time in that he had been placed by nature at the parting of the ways between letters and arms; capable of comparing the two walks of life with the impartial eye of a man who knew he could succeed in either of them. This parallel between arts and letters was to fascinate another man—no less illustrious than Cortés—who followed now one and now the other path, and won signal glory in both, though no wealth in either; for in the frequent allusions to the subject which Cervantes puts into the mouth of Don Quixote we hear the voice of Cervantes himself.

Whether he was a bachelor of law or not, therefore, we shall see Cortés evince throughout his adventurous career an equal aptitude for letters and for arms; an astonishing capacity for being always *present*—presence of will in action, presence of mind in thought; a masterly hand with men; a masterly mind with things; a gift for expression, in action by doing the right thing, in thought by saying the right thing, always at the right time; and last but not least, the swift eye and powerful claw of the eagle, but also the devious, sly and, if need be, tortuous ways of the serpent—thus uniting in his complex personality the eagle and the serpent, symbolical of the people he was destined to conquer, and of the God Quetzalcoatl—the Feathered Serpent whom they believed at first he impersonated.

* * *

Meanwhile Quetzalcoatl, aged sixteen, returned to face his angry parents in his native Medellín. "He used to give and take much annoyance and to make much noise in the house of his parents, for he was turbulent, haughty, restless and fond of arms." (10) Fond of "arms," as will be seen anon, in more senses than one. The young man must have been a somewhat difficult person for his parents to handle in their small town, for, in spite of their natural attachment to their only son, they consented to let him follow the perilous profession of arms, which, for a Spaniard in those days, meant Italy or the Indies. Hernán hesitated between enlisting under the banner of Gonzalo de Córdoba, known to Spain as *the* Great Captain, then at the zenith of his glory in Italy, and following in the wake of the Spaniards who then flowed to the Indies, lured by the gold which came from them. While he was pondering, with his usual forethought, "which of the two voyages would suit him best," (11) a powerful fleet of thirty ships was being prepared to convey the new Governor General, appointed by the King and Queen to the Indies. This new Governor Don Frey Nicolás de Ovando, Commander of Alcántara, appointed on September 3rd, 1501, (12) was staying at the time in Cáceres, not far from Medellín; and he seems to have been on terms of acquaintance, if not of actual friendship, with the Cortés family. The career of young Hernán was therefore settled: he would sail to the Indies in the suite of the new Governor—and the Indies were surely big enough for him.

But it was not to be; for "meanwhile, once, as he was walking on other people's roofs, for he had a love affair with a young lady, he fell from a ruinous wall. While half buried, he would have been run through the body by a man, if an old woman,(this man's mother-in-law), on whose door the small iron shield of Cortés had crashed with much noise, had not prevented him, who had rushed out on hearing the same noise, and begged him to do the stranger no harm till he had found out who he was."(13) As Ovando sailed from Sanlúcar on February 13th, 1502, and this tragi-comic disaster prevented young Hernán from sailing with him, the precocious Don Juan was then at most seventeen. His fall confined him to bed, and in his bed his old quartan fever came back to visit his aching body and prey on it. The illness, says Gómara, lasted a long time.

As soon as he was on his feet again, he resolved to seek fortune in Italy. The Great Captain was still there, as fascinating as ever to a young man's imagination: "and to go thereto, he set foot for Valencia." (14) We have seen him on the road, for Cervantes seems to have written one whole page of his great book, with an eye on this boy of eighteen going to Italy with no money in his pocket, but with a treasure of wealth and glory in his eyes. "A little farther they came upon a youth who was pacing along in front of them at no great speed, so that they overtook him. He carried his sword over his shoulder, and slung on it a budget or bundle, apparently of his clothes, evidently his breeches or trousers, and his cloak and possibly a shirt; for he had on a short jacket of velvet with glimmers of satin about it, and had his shirt out; his stockings were of silk and his shoes square-toed after the fashion of the court. His age might have been eighteen or nineteen; he had a gay face and evinced great nimbleness of body. He went along singing *seguidillas* to beguile the wearisomeness of the road. As they came up with him, he was just finishing one:

> I'm off to the wars
> Out of sheer need.
> But if I had money
> I would not indeed.

The first to address him was Don Quixote, who said: " 'You travel very airily, Sir Gallant; whither bound, may we ask, if it is your pleasure to tell us?' To which the youth replied: 'As for travelling so airily, the heat and poverty are the cause of it; and as for whither bound, I am going to the wars.' 'How poverty?' asked Don Quixote; 'the heat one can understand.' 'Sir,' replied the youth, 'in this bundle I carry velvet trousers to match this jacket; if I wear them out on the road, I shall not be able to make an honourable appearance in them in the city, and I have not the wherewithal to buy others; and so for this reason, as well as to keep myself cool, I am making my way in this fashion to overtake some companies of infantry that are not twelve leagues off, in which I shall enlist [. . .] I would rather have the King for a master and serve him in the wars, than serve a low-born one at court.' ' [. . .] there is nothing on earth'—said Don Quixote—'more honourable or profitable than serving, first of all God, and then one's King and natural lord, particularly in the profession of arms, by which is to be won, if not more wealth, at least more honour than by letters, as I have said many a time; for though letters may have founded more great houses than arms, still, those founded by arms have I know not what advantage over those founded by letters, I know not what splendour which puts them above all others.' " The youth listened to Don Quixote about one century after young Cortés followed the same road in nearly the same attire and frame of mind on his way "to the wars"; but nothing could be more fitting to the situation of young Hernán Cortés than this allusion to the dilemma of arts and letters from which he had just escaped, unless it were the parting words with which the noble knight of La Mancha said farewell to his preincarnation on the road: "And bear in mind what I am about to say to you, for it will be of great use and comfort to you in time of trouble; do not let your mind dwell on the adverse chances that may befall you; for the worst of all is death, and if it be a good death, the best of all is to die." (15) The conqueror of Mexico lived up to this stoic advice with a fidelity which makes it sound as if it had been inspired by his life.

Yet, at the time, Cortés did not reach Italy but wasted a year in adventures which he seems to have covered with a veil of discretion, for of all his biographers, the only one who refers to them, his own confidant and chaplain Gómara, passes over them with a haste not altogether devoid of a touch of disapproval: "Yet he did not cross over to Italy, but wandered wantonly, though not without much need and hardship for nearly a year." (16) That is all. Hernán, born a man of action, was completing his studies as a man of action in the University of experience.

Despite the silence of his biographers, no great effort of imagination is needed to guess where the youthful Cortés had wandered so wantonly. Imagine a child, usually kept at home, who knows that a most brilliant pageant is filing past his windows. Where is the child? ask his parents. Where can he be but at the window? Could Cortés, born in Medellín, a small inland town of Extremadura, let loose in Southern Spain keep away from the seashore at the time when Seville, Cádiz, Sanlúcar and Palos, all the harbours of the South, were teeming with the most glorious pageant that history had ever seen? The incoming caravels, radiant with the light of the New World: captains, pilots, adventurers, monks, soldiers of fortune, Indian caciques, now stark naked, now dressed in exotic attire with golden rings and headdresses of silver and plumes; slaves, men, women, children, shivering and hungry; gold, gold, gold, tales of monstrously big grains, as big as a pea, as a nut, as a good Castillian loaf, as a church bell, which had enriched So-and-so in one day; and So-and-so, himself, disembarking, his face gaping with a smile of success, his hat gorgeous, his gold necklace resplendent, and slaves galore; and now and then, the discoverer himself, passing through the streets of Seville at the head of one of his carefully organized processions, richly decorated with popinjays, glittering with golden chains and golden masks of strange design and profile; or perhaps by contrast, clad in the dark brown frock of a penitent monk of St. Francis, or even in iron chains, as a proud, shipwrecked, sullen prisoner; waves upon waves of excitement; new lands; banks of pearls; islands to be had for the asking. A crowd of discoverers-to-be, Vicente Váñez, Hojeda, Bastidas, Guerra, Alonso Niño, Nicuesa, Pedrarias, Balboa, Ponce de León—keen, eager, anxious, watching one another—coming and going from the offices of the Royal Chancery to the offices of Bishop Fonseca, the dignitary in charge of Indian affairs, to secure a charter, a slice of the earth to be combed for gold or pearls, possibly a subsidy for caravels, perhaps an appointment as Adelantado or Governor of the lands-to-be-discovered; thence to the quays of Seville and Cádiz to recruit sailors and youths eager to make a fortune or die, to find a pilot or shipmaster ready to risk his ship and his skin for so many shares in the gold and slaves to be had—everywhere the tension of that fantastic new world pulling at the old Iberian oak and tearing from it roots, branches and foliage to feed the fire of discovery . . . Such was the sight which filled the eyes of young Hernán Cortés when in his eighteen-nineteenth year, he wandered wantonly we know not where but we may safely guess in Seville, Cádiz and other harbours beaten by the waves of new world life. That is why "he came back to Medellín determined to cross over to the Indies. His parents gave him their blessing." They also gave him money for the voyage.

*   *   *

At last, in the early part of 1504, Cortés, aged nineteen, sailed from Sanlúcar de Barrameda towards his high destinies. His ship, master, pilot and crew were of Palos, the little harbour from which, but twelve years earlier, Colón had started on his expedition of discovery. There were five ships in the convoy, which was of a purely commercial character. The master of the ship, one Alonso Quintero, seems to have been a strange sort of person, devoured by a keen and low cupidity. The crossing to La Gomera, a kind of compulsory first stage in the voyage for the none too experienced pilots of the day, was uneventful.

In La Gomera, "after having prayed to St. Mary of the Passage," (17) they re-stocked their hulls with food and water; then Quintero, eager to steal a march on the other shipmasters in order to sell his goods at a higher price in Santo Domingo, sailed away unobserved; but before he had even reached the Island of Hierro, westernmost of the Canaries, the wind, which in its supreme freedom and wanton anarchy works for justice and virtue whenever it thinks fit, rose with so much fury against the inconsiderate mariner that it broke his mast, which crashed on deck dragging down the crossyard, sails and rigging. There were no victims because most of the passengers and men happened just then to be abaft, "eating the preserves and jams which Cortés had brought on board for his own stores." (18) He was nineteen, but he was already evincing that generosity which was in later years to be one of the causes of his hold on men. Food on board ship in those days was no mean possession; as the ocean was soon to remind all the travelling companions of Cortés.

Much disappointed, Quintero returned crestfallen to La Gomera, where he begged the other shipmasters to wait for him while he had his mast repaired. Strange to say, though he deserved it precious little, the four shipmasters decided to wait; and yet, they were sure to know the Spanish saying "he who makes one basket makes one hundred," and had every right to suspect that it was not for the pleasure of their company that Quintero asked them to wait for him, but to be able to leave them behind again, the moment favourable conditions turned up anew. That is exactly what he did a few days later, as the five ships were sailing together in mid-ocean. Impelled again by his cupidity, he spread all his sails in the night to a fresh wind which soon spirited him away out of sight of his long-suffering companions, while in the dark, the little winds and zephyrs which fly here and there, and now are in the Indies, now in Spain, now in the present, now in the future, laughed in their wings (they have no sleeves), thinking of the disappointment that awaited the avaricious mariner.

Virtue had to prevail, and Quintero had to be punished. The pilot—not the wind—was this time in charge of immanent justice; nor was he, be it said in his honour, a willing minister thereof, for the higher powers, who no doubt know best, chose to trust his ignorance rather than his righteousness. He was one Francisco Niño, of Palos, of that family of Niños who have no less a claim on American History than that of having been the owners of one of the three caravels of the Discovery, *La Niña*, by name, and of having piloted her to the New World. Withal, this particular offshoot of the famous family does not seem to have carried his illustrious name with as much assurance as others, for he actually lost his way. "The sailors were astonished, the pilot was sad, the passengers wept and no one knew the way they had come nor the way they had to go. The shipmaster threw the blame on the pilot, the pilot on the shipmaster; for, as it turned out, they were at loggerheads. By then, food was getting scarce and there was no water: for they drank none but that which they collected when it rained; and they all confessed [each other, and forgave each other, adds another chronicler whom we may readily believe]. Some cursed their fortune; others asked for mercy, awaiting death, which some had swallowed already, or expecting to land on lands inhabited by Caribbeans, where they eat men." (19)

In this desperate plight, at nightfall on Good Friday, a dove came circling softly round the mast "undisturbed by the laments of the navigators. For a long time, it seemed to them not that it flew round the mast, but that it remained motionless; then it sat on the mast and appeared to them without doubt as an omen of good fortune [. . .] They wept for joy, raised their hands to heaven, thanked the most merciful God, lord of all things. One said that land could not be far away, another one that it was the Holy Ghost which in the form of that bird had deigned to come to comfort the sad and afflicted. Wherever the dove flew, there followed the ship." (20)

There followed the ship, with her cargo of faithful and believing men, ready to trust their fate either to natural laws or to supernatural protection. For to their pious minds, that dove might just as well be a bird in search of food, flying to or from a nest on land, as the reincarnation of that Holy Ghost which in their native parish church they had always seen represented as a pigeon, his white wings spread over the hoary head of God the Father in a halo of golden light. Cortés might have read yet another symbol in this visitation, for he was the first great conqueror to take flight in the sky of the New World in the wake of that *Colombo*, whose name, whether in Italian or in his original Catalan *Colom*, meant "dove," and it was meet that a dove should guide his ship upon his first arrival. As a further hint of fate, the man who on the fourth day after the visit of the "Colom" or dove, saw land and shouted the exhilarating word in triumph, was called Cristóbal, like the great discoverer; that his surname was Zorzo is neither here nor there. The joy on board may be imagined. Francisco Niño recovered at once all the self-assurance which had so sadly forsaken him during the crossing. It was the Coast of the Fig Trees and the Promontory of Samana, on the island then known as Española. "If it be not so, he said, cut my head off, and throw my body to boil into that cauldron on the fire." And for once, despite the obstinate opposition of the Quintero clan, he was right. Four days after seeing land, they entered the harbour of Santo Domingo. There, to his dismay, Quintero found the other four ships which had preceded him and presumably taken from him the cream of the market. (21)

The Governor General was not in the town, but one of his secretaries, Medina, a friend of Cortés, much relieved no doubt at the arrival of the young man whom they all thought lost at sea, came on board to see him, and explained to him "the laws of islands and conquerors"; on the strength of which, he advised his young and inexperienced friend to register and settle as a citizen in order to enjoy the privileges of conquerors; this meant some land for farming and a plot in town for a house, plus the assurance that he should soon be the lord of a few Indians; after five years of residence in the island, without ever leaving it save on special authority from the Governor, he would be able to please himself and go where he wished. Young Hernán Cortés listened courteously, then made answer: "Neither in this Island nor in any other of this New World, do I wish or mean to stay for so long." (22)

This pleased not Medina.

CHAPTER THREE

The Nest of Hawks

WHEN Cortés, aged nineteen, arrived in Santo Domingo, the new world was just beginning to emerge from the mythical and nebulous "Indies" of Colón's imagination and taking historical shape as the American Spanish Empire. Discovery, conquest, subjugation of the "Indians," economic development of the new countries and political organization of the colonies were proceeding apace, though far from harmoniously. It is necessary to disentangle the several strains which made up the turbulent life of those busy days, in order to understand events and developments otherwise inexplicable. The purest and most admirable of all these strains is the Christian zeal of the best spirits of the Spanish nation. This zeal was genuine. No impartial and well informed student of the period will doubt that Queen Isabel and her immediate advisers, men like Hernando de Talavera, Archbishop of Granada, and Cardinal Ximénez de Cisneros, both chosen by her not only as political advisers but as confessors, took their religious duty in earnest and considered the salvation of the "Indians" as the first call upon the Spanish Crown. This strain is well represented in America during those first years when the tumultuous waves of the conquest break into the Unknown Continent like a sea shaken out of its basin by a geological upheaval. It is doubtful whether any nation ever gave to the cause of human charity and equality a galaxy of more devoted, active and fearless servants than those Spain then gave forth. These men—Las Casas, Motolinia, Mendieta, Sahagún, Montesinos, and many more—defined the principles of conduct in the name of which many Spanish conquerors and settlers have been condemned, most of them, though not all, deservedly. But the principles which they laid down are of such sterling value that to this day they stand far above the level of performance in any colonial enterprise known to history.

Las Casas, one of the leaders of this line of thought, "stood un-compromisingly for the true Christian attitude: the Indies belonged to the Indians; it was their home as determined by God and all that was found in it, mineral, vegetable and animal, was their property. The Spaniards had no title whatever to be there, except the Gospel. For Las Casas, as for every European in those days, the Christian religion was truth and all the rest was error. But unlike most other Europeans, Las Casas *meant the truth to live*. His dilemma was inescapable: either the Christians behaved in the Indies like Chris-tians or they had no business to be there at all. In many passages of his *History* he defines the policy which the Spaniards should have followed in the Indies as one of the patience, service and evangelisa-tion, for the ultimate benefit of the Spaniards themselves. 'There is no legitimate reason for Spaniards to enter these realms and lands other than to spread news and knowledge of the one and true God and of Jesus Christ'—he says boldly." (1)

Thanks to this invaluable element, the Spanish Conquest was immediately followed by the foundation of educational centres, both monasteries and parish churches, for it is as such that we must think of these religious houses. Born and bred in a century in which the Church has been divorced from the remaining civic collective activ-ities, and confined to a kind of limbo for which an idle Sunday, meaningless and disconnected with anything that matters, has been set aside, we moderns are apt to think of monasteries and parish churches as spiritual luxuries, thoroughly uneconomic and mostly useless or at any rate irrelevant. But in those days religious life was the core of all life; dissenters were not known; sinners there were, but the worst of them acknowledged the only truth there was. Monasteries and parish churches were therefore the nerve centres of the community; from them came the light in which men walked to their occupations and against which they sinned. Nor were they yet considered as they too often are nowadays as the mere fore-runners of a State which behind the missionary sends the merchant and the soldier; colonisation in our sense of the word, the opening up of a "backward" country for the benefit of the home country, had not emerged yet. The new lands became just more "kingdoms" for

the King of Spain in line with Castille, León, Aragón, Sicily, for that
King of Spain whose duty it was to watch over the spiritual and
material interest of his new subjects. The very vehicle of unified
nationalism as known to us, the language, was not even recognised
as in any way a predominant feature of the conquest: in most cases
the Spanish monks and priests learned the native vernaculars in
order to convey to the "Indians" the universal truth of the Gospels
in the language they could best understand.

*   *   *

The second strain was the political. Seldom if ever was a State
confronted at so early a time with so vast a problem as was the
Spanish State on receiving the fabulous Indies the very year when,
by the conquest of Granada, it achieved its own political unity.
Spain had just come of age—one might well say, Spain had just
been born—on January 2nd, 1492, when Cristóbal Colón (2) discovered a new Empire for her on October 12th of the same year. The
political task which this windfall implied was titanic. It was further
complicated by the exorbitant privileges which Colón had secured
for himself in his Capitulations with the Crown, since those Capitulations made him Viceroy and Governor General by right and granted
to his heirs the privilege of succeeding him. After a brief period in
charge of political affairs in Española, Colón proved his incapacity
as a governor and was removed. His successor, Don Francisco de
Bobadilla, governed the island till 1502. At the time of Cortés'
arrival, the Governor was Don Frey Nicolás de Ovando, Chief Commander of the Military Order of Alcántara. He was, says Oviedo,
who knew him well, "very devout and a great Christian; and most
charitable and liberal with the poor; mild and well spoken with all;
and with the insolent he had the prudence and stern ways which were
needed; he favoured and helped the weak and humble, and showed
the haughty and proud the severity which is required towards all
transgressors of the royal laws. He punished [the guilty] with the
temperance and moderation which were necessary; and as he held the
island in good justice, he was loved and feared by all. He protected
the Indians greatly; and as for the Christians who here lived under
his authority, he treated them all like a father, and he taught them
all to live uprightly; being a religious and very wise gentleman, he

held the country in great peace and quiet." Las Casas, poles apart
from Oviedo on the Indian labour question, endorses this portrait
with one single and important reservation: "This gentleman was a
most prudent man and worthy of governing many people, but not
Indians, for, with his ways of governing, he inflicted on them incal-
culable wrongs." (3)

These governors sent by Spain to the New World had a singularly
difficult task: the object or matter of their government was ever-
changing and fluid; it was also new. Imagine a sculptor whose clay
turns to water. Such was the plight of these colonial statesmen
handling a community in which traditions and ways conflicted on
the edge of two races and melted away in the wilderness of hardly
conquered spaces. The mother country sent caravel after caravel
of new settlers to islands inhabited by aborigines of an entirely different mode of life; lands had to be distributed; towns, founded; roads,
opened; harbours, provided; labour, organized; revolts, suppressed;
the King's fifth on all gold mines, collected, guarded and sent home;
quarrels, settled; and information, secured on events in neighbouring islands and the mainland.

The centre and head of the colonial administration was Santo
Domingo or Española (now Haiti), a choice determined by Colón's
preference for this island, and confirmed by its fairly central geographical situation, though Cuba, explored later, would have been
preferable from this point of view. Oviedo devotes a whole chapter
of his History to showing how the island was a much better country
than either Sicily or England, "two of the biggest and best islands
of the Christians," an opinion which he maintains by extolling its
mineral wealth and by recalling how generously it had responded to
the efforts of its new colonists, multiplying a thousandfold every seed
and animal brought over from Spain. He mentions settlers with as
many as thirty-two thousand head of cattle "and if I were to say
forty-two, there is one who has them, a widowed lady, an honoured
gentlewoman known as María de Arana." He writes in 1547, in the
year of Cortés' death, but the figure may do as an indication of the
growth of economic wealth in what after all was, for all intents and
purposes, a new country. (4)

The transition between the conqueror and the settler is well
brought out by Oviedo when, referring to an Indian revolt under a

native cacique known as Enrique who held the Spaniards in check
for a long time, he recalls the early days when three hundred
Spaniards held sway over the island then full of natives: "I must
say what was the cause of this: when the Christians, being few, beat
and destroyed the Indians (who were many), they slept on their
shields and scutcheons, with their swords in hand, and kept watch
over their enemies. When Enriquillo did all these things, the Christians slept in good and soft beds, wrapped up in their sugar-cane
farms." (5)

                    *   *   *

This observation registers the triumph of the colonising over
the conquering strains. The King and Queen had endeavoured to
populate their Indies with the best kind of people. (6) They sought
to ensure quality according to the lights of the time, by selecting their
settlers amongst the families best known to them, and particularly
in their own household. Yet no class or rank will ensure complete
uniformity of tone and behaviour—still less in new circumstances
like those of the Indies, in which every man was thrown back on his
own resources. And so, on arriving in Santo Domingo, each chose
his path according to his inner voice: some became farmers; others
went in search of gold; others just waited like hawks perched on a
branch, watching for a better prey.

There is little doubt that, in spite of the wealth which it invariably brought with it, the first path, that of the farmer, was at a discount amongst the gentry that came from the Court. The good
monks, who observed life at close quarters, constantly complain of
the tendency of the Spaniards to seek adventures farther on instead
of remaining where they were and working on the land. But even
these goods monks can wax satirical at the sight of the comfortable
gentleman farmer too well served: "See how reluctantly a Spaniard
rises from his soft bed, and many a day is turned out thereof by the
light of the sun, and at once dons a dressing-gown (so that the wind
does not touch him) and asks to be dressed, as if he had no hands to
dress himself, and so he is dressed as if he were armless, and while
he is buttoning himself, he is praying, you may imagine how attentively; and because he feels a little cold or wind, he draws close to
the fire while they clean his coat and cap; and as he feels so weak

from the bed and the fire, he cannot comb his hair, so that someone else must come and do it; then, while his shoes or slippers and his cloak are brought, the church bell rings for mass, and at times he goes after breakfast and the horse is not quite ready; you may imagine in what guise he goes to mass; but, provided he comes in time to see God, or that the priest has not taken communion yet, he is pleased, rather than to have to do with a priest who perchance may say mass somewhat slowly, and make his knees hurt. There are some who have no scruple about it, even on Sundays or holidays. Then, back home, his dinner must be most punctual, otherwise there is no patience; and then, he rests or sleeps. Now tell me whether the remainder of the day is enough to deal with affairs and accounts, and to see about his mines and farms; and before all this business is over, it is supper time, and at times he falls asleep at table unless he puts off sleep by means of some game . . ." (7)

Yet, for all his defects, and his neglect of church, this kind of settler who was content to live and let live was perhaps the backbone of the new communities which were at the time developing here and there in the islands and mainland; and his very tendency to comfort, satirised by the hard-living monk, was the best guarantee against the curse of the age—the ill-treatment of the native by the get-rich-quick sort of adventurer who came in search of gold.

* * *

This gold-myth had haunted the European imagination at any rate since the days when Marco Polo had fascinated it with his tales of oriental splendour. It rose to a pitch of obsession in Cristóbal Colón, who made of it almost a fetish or a divinity, steeped as he was in Old Testament literature, and full of visions of Solomon walking in his priestly-royal splendour through golden halls. Oviedo records a quaint detail which illustrates this religious colour which the Admiral of the Indies had imparted even to gold-prospecting. When he explored Cibao, a region in Española on which he had laid great hopes, he found that the Indians kept away from their wives whenever they set out to find gold. This habit struck him deeply, and, adds Oviedo, when "he saw that the Indians gathered gold in the water of their brooks and rivers without digging, with the ceremony and religion I have just mentioned, he did not allow Christians to go gold-gathering without first confessing and taking communion. And he said that since the Indians kept twenty days apart from their women (or any women), and fasted, and said that when they came to their wives they never found gold; therefore, since those bestial Indians observed all that solemnity, it was even more meet that Christians should keep away from sin and confess their guilt, for, being in God's grace, He would more fully grant them temporal and spiritual gifts. Such sanctimony was not to the taste of all, for they argued that as to their wives they could not be more apart from them since their wives were in Spain; and as for fasting, that many Christians were dying of hunger and ate roots and other poor kinds of food, and drank water." (8)

But for most of the youthful adventurers who crossed over from Spain, gold was no such symbol of religion and chastity; it was what it still is and will always be for most human beings: the standard of social power, the instrument for securing dominion over less fortunate men and women, the ladder of social success. And the fabulous reputation which Colón had deliberately given to his discovery as an Eldorado—a reputation which was not fully justified till Pizarro conquered Peru—acted on Spanish manhood like a powerful magnet, and created a migratory movement not always of the best. Much should, however, be discounted in what has been written on the subject. The pro-native monks, Las Casas in particular, impressed as they were by the cases of inhuman treatment inflicted on the Indians by unscrupulous gold-diggers, are reliable enough in the description of what they saw; but we know from others that the growth of crop and livestock wealth in Española was prodigious in the years preceding the discovery of Peru, so that, while it cannot be doubted that the gold-obsession of the first settlers acted as a disturbing factor on the economic development of the colony and as a disastrous and demoralising force on the relations between the two races, it was by no means the main reason for the retrogression which Oviedo observes when he compares the state of Santo Domingo in 1547 with that in 1525.

The capital of the Indies was already a beautiful town, "so well built that there is no township in Spain generally better constructed leaving aside the illustrious and very noble city of Barcelona"; it boasted of a cathedral, "made of beautiful and strong stonework," beautiful gardens and avenues, three monasteries, many stone houses, "beautiful streets well planned and wide," "a very good hospital, well built and provided with a good income wherein the poor are cured and helped, in which God is very well served," and last but not least, a college, the first University founded in the new Continent. (9)

* * *

But, Oviedo observes, the beautiful town, amidst its orange-groves, was less populated than in 1525; and he provides the reason: "Many who made a fortune returned to Spain; and others went to settle in other islands or on the mainland, for most of the Indies have been discovered, settled and supplied from here, this island being the head and mother and nurse of all the other parts of this empire." (10) The fact is that, simultaneously, while monks preached, christened and taught, governors administered, gentlemen farmers waxed fat on the rich land and gold-seekers squeezed gold out of the unfortunate Indians, conquerors and explorers and adventurers went on, swarmed forth into a vast world, ever vaster behind and beyond what was already known. "Like a flight of hawks" the conquerors landed in Española from their creaky and tired caravels, but only for a brief stay, and a fresh flight again on to newer shores. This gives its full value to the answer which Cortés gave Medina on his arrival in Santo Domingo: "Neither in this Island nor in any other of this New World, do I wish or mean to stay for so long."

Notice the strong individual accent. Of course, it is the voice of Cortés, an exceptional personality; but he was just nineteen, an age at which most men still talk the language of the community which has reared them. The fact is that Spain was then a thoroughly democratic country, in which every man was his own master. At the root of the political conceptions—or rather tenets and assumptions—of the day, there was again a religious culture. God above all, but God was supreme Goodness and it was open to every righteous man to walk in His light by the light of his own reason. This was consciously or subconsciously translated into political terms to the effect: The King above all; but the King was the incarnation of law, and every wise man knew what the law was and therefore had a right to have a say in the application of it. In the following century, the greatest religious dramatist of Spain and of Europe was to write amidst general approval (11):

> In all that is not just law
> He must not obey the King.

This was already a reaction against a hardened monarchy, which had sadly forgotten the democratic vigour of its earlier days; but in the days of Cortés, the monarchy was the fountain of liberty and individual rights, being the dispenser of equal rights for all, and every Spaniard felt the right to cooperate with the King by advice (freely granted), by criticism and even, in cases of emergency, by disobedience, if only temporary. Such is the background on which may be read the often recurring saying, "The King's order was obeyed but not carried out," in which no irony should be seen, no display of humour, but the subtle distinction which the citizen made between his general recognition of the King's authority and his own right to judge as to the wisdom of carrying out a particular order therefrom at a given place and time. Thus, Oviedo: "And when he presented his commission to the Chief Commander, he [the Chief Commander] obeyed the [Royal] order, and as for its being carried out, he made answer that he would report to the Catholic King, and in the end all would be done according to His Highness's wishes." (12)

The bright side of this individualistic sense was its creative vigour. This was shown not only in the rapid development of the economic resources of the island and in the swift succession of expeditions of discovery, but also in the healthy growth of democratic, municipal institutions, which were founded almost as soon as the first stockades and ditches had marked out the new settlement on watershore or forest-edge. The *Cabildo,* meeting of the *neighbours* or burgesses, convened by the chief of the expedition, at once recorded its own legal constitution and elected its *regidores* or councillors and its Alcalde or chief magistrate in charge of both executive and judicial functions. Thus the State reproduced itself in its own image, by relying on the political initiative of all. And, by a kind of transfer from the political to the military spheres, we witness a remarkable development of democratic habits even in the armies and fleets which here and there pierce the veil behind which lurks the continent still for the most part unrevealed to its adventurous invaders.

* * *

But the free, democratic and individualistic sense of this society had also its unsavoury side. The native race stood defenceless before the inrush of a crowd of men most of whom, by a kind of natural selection, were unscrupulous men of action, intent on seeking their own material ends at whatever cost to the native. Even when we discount the passionate exaggerations which render Las Casas so unreliable—particularly in what concerns figures—enough remains of what he has recorded to show that the plight of the native during these first years of the Spanish conquest was tragic beyond words. The colonial State was still too inchoate and weak, the mother-State too far away—and, in fact, too young also—to oppose a sufficient obstacle to the unruly ambitions of the gold-hunters; and the very principles and underlying assumptions which ruled the theoretical behaviour of the whites toward the natives were still the subject of ardent disputes. From the saintly friars, who upheld the view that the Spaniards had no right to set foot in the Indies save as bearers of the Christian light, to the gold-hunter who—whatever he *thought* —took the Indian for a beast of all work for his own profit, a balance had to be struck by life; and an empirical solution had to be found: this was the *repartimiento,* a form of apportionment of labour amongst the settlers which laid on the Christian the responsibility of enlightening the Indian's soul while granting him the privilege of utilising the Indian's body.

Las Casas has exposed the abuses to which this system gave rise, not the least of which was the granting of Indians to powerful officials in Spain who had never seen the Indies otherwise than in their dreams. Ferdinand's own secretary, Conchillos, and Bishop Fonseca, the kind of Colonial Secretary of the day, were amongst those who benefited by this scandalous abuse. The monks reacted energetically and without fear. They faced their congregations at church and boldly denied them the right to "own" Indians, even though "granted" by the King; they travelled to Court, waited in the King's anterooms, fought, begged, argued and wrote; and through their admirable persistence succeeded in gradually extirpating the worst abuses and in setting in a trend of thought which was to culminate in the magnificent *Laws of the Indies*. (13) Yet, time will exact its toll from all human endeavours and while this movement benefited the evolution of the Spanish Empire in general, the Antilles could not be saved and their native population was wiped out. (14)

* * *

The chief activity of the Spanish captains, pilots and adventurers who swarmed round the main island was then discovery and conquest. This period, during which Cortés ripens as a leader of men on the border of two worlds, facing the still unknown, unexpected and unconquered continents, saw the first episodes of that era of discovery and conquest which has never been equalled before or since in the annals of the world. "To appreciate the total achievement," writes an American authority, "it is necessary to remind the reader that Spain was not a rich country, that her area was about equal to that of New England, New York, Pennsylvania and Ohio combined, that her population at the end of this period was somewhat smaller than that of New York today, and somewhat larger than that of Pennsylvania. Most of this work, however, fell to natives of the Kingdom of Castille, whose population was probably half a million less than that of Pennsylvania. Taking up first the extension of geographical knowledge, we have to record the exploration of the Atlantic coast line from Nova Scotia to Cape Horn and of the Pacific coast line from the Straits of Magellan as far north as Oregon. The Pacific had been crossed both north and south of the equator going west; and the proper eastward road, after repeated failures, was discovered in 1565 by Urdaneta. The empires of Mexico and of the Incas had been conquered, and their wealth had become the support and the stimulus to the most arduous and heroic overland explorations of modern times." (15)

CHAPTER FOUR

Cortés Watches Two Men
Fail As Conquerors

AT THE time of Hernán Cortés' arrival in his dominions, Ovando was governor not only of Española but of a vague and expanding region known as "The Indies," including the islands already discovered, one of which, Cuba, was still believed by many to be the mainland, as well as several hundreds of leagues of mainland coast, still believed by many to be islands. These curious notions were the flower of all the errors which Colón had sown out of his fertile imagination. The domains of the King and Queen of Castille which Ovando governed for them, changed every day, were enlarged, explored and gradually brought down from dreams into reality, by the simultaneous efforts of the Crown and of the free captains and sailors who, at their own expense and risk, came to the new continent in search of fame and wealth.

During the short time between Colón's third voyage and the arrival of Cortés in Santo Domingo, the little colony had taken a greater or lesser share in a number of expeditions—either as a first-row spectator or, more frequently, as a purveyor of men and food, and even as the nurse and comforter of not a few failures. In May 1499, Alonso de Hojeda, one of Bishop Fonseca's favourites, sailed from Cádiz at the head of a privately owned expedition, attracted by the discovery of some pearl fisheries which had just been reported by Colón. Hojeda had on board two men famous in the annals of American discovery: the great cosmographer Juan de la Cosa, author of the oldest map of the New World, and Américo Vespucci, the astute Florentine who, realising the value of publicity, secured for himself the glory of naming the new continent less by his compass

44

than by his pen. Hojeda, a brave and even a foolhardy adventurer, lost much time in minor skirmishes within Española, where a kind of endemic civil war or rebellion threatened the authority of Colón; yet before returning to Spain he discovered and mapped out the coast of what is now British Guiana, and the country he himself called Venezuela or Little Venice.

At about the same time Pero Alonso Niño, one of the Niños of Palos, leaving Palos after Hojeda, reached the northern coast of South America before him (having a lesser taste for civil wars) and returned wealthy. In November of the same year, Vicente Yáñez Pinzón, who had sailed in Colón's first voyage, and was the greatest Spanish pilot of the time, sailed from Palos and was the first to touch the New World south of the equator; he discovered the coast of Brazil on January 20th, 1500, and carefully explored and studied two thousand miles of the coast, including the mouth of the Amazon; meanwhile Diego de Lepe (possibly with Americo Vespucci on board) sailed from Palos and saw the Brazilian coast, reaching beyond Cape St. Augustine. Finally, Rodrigo de Bastidas, deserting his law practice in Seville, sailed in October 1500 with Juan de la Cosa and explored the coast from Venezuela to Panama, returning to Cádiz in September 1502. (1)

This relatively short period had therefore sufficed for the sailors of Spain to discover, explore and map out about three thousand miles of the coast of what is now South America, from Cape St. Augustine to Panama. The quest of the Indies, which had been one of the driving impulses of Colón's adventure, had lost none of its incentive; for, if there were growing signs that, despite Colón's illusions, "the Indies" were not India, the thought was gaining ground that there was a passage somewhere which would enable the Spanish caravels to steal a march on the Portuguese which sailed round Africa. Bartholomeu Diaz had discovered the Cape of Good Hope in 1486, while Colón was still offering his grand discovery to the Spanish Crown; and Vasco da Gama had sailed round it from Lisbon to India in 1497–8, while Colón was still dreaming over Cipango and Quinsay. In 1500, Cabral, on his way to India, met with a "diplomatic" storm which carried him to the coast of Brazil. The rivalry between the two sister nations was rapidly turning into a race towards the Spices —Islands of the East. The Castillians hoped to win this race by dis-

C

covering the Straits. But life dealt fairly with both sister-nations: it granted the first arrival in the coveted islands to Portugal and the discovery of the Straits to Castille, and as if to show the two countries the path of union, it decreed that this last historical discovery should be made by Castillian ships under a Portuguese navigator—Magellan.

But that was still to come. Meanwhile, in 1502–3, aloof and unaware of the real import of his own discovery, Colón tried for the fourth and last time to break through to the Grand Khan. The little colony of Santo Domingo saw his ships, off the coast of the island which he had discovered, denied access to the harbour in which his own brother had founded Santo Domingo, the oldest town in the Continent, and condemned to wander about in search of the passage through to the West, finally to be left derelict in Jamaica, with his ships too worm-eaten to sail. The colony learnt with surprise and admiration that two of the Admiral's men, Diego Méndez and Bartolomé Flisco, had succeeded in crossing over from Jamaica in a small canoe, in search of supplies; and all in the island had watched with mixed feelings how Ovando allowed the matter to drag on through the summer and the autumn of 1503, without a single word or deed of help or comfort, beyond the sending of a small ship to inspect the position, in command of one of Colón's enemies. Public opinion in the island, none too favourable to Colón, took up his case; and the broadcasting system of those days—the Sunday sermons—were loud in their condemnation of the callous Governor. (2) Cortés, who landed in Santo Domingo towards Easter in 1504, must have heard some of these sermons of criticism. Possibly to meet this opposition, and ultimately to yield to it, Ovando returned to his capital and there met the ambitious young man who "having kissed his hand and told him that he came from Extremadura, gave him some letters of introduction." Ovando received him "graciously" but gave him nothing beyond words. The young hidalgo seems then to have spent a period of want, for, we are told, he and two other friends had only one cloak between them with which to go out to the market. Yet, he launched forth into the world and began to seek a livelihood in gold mining. While he was thus engaged, Colón passed through Santo Domingo on his way back to Spain. The future conqueror of Mexico may have cast a meditative eye on the now aged and saddened Discoverer Errant, whom Ovando treated with outward deference but with scanty respect for his viceregal authority and privileges, and who, on the eve of his departure for Spain from those "Indies" which he had discovered and which he was never to see again, was a living and moving witness to the vanity of human glory. (3)

The first rise in the fortunes of the future conqueror seems to have been due to "letters" rather than to "arms," for we find him as Public Notary or *Escribano Público* in the small town of Azúa, not far from Santo Domingo. It is true that Gómara and other chroniclers present this appointment as a reward for his valour in a war against the Indians, but dates are not as pliant as chroniclers, and it so happens that the war in question took place in 1503, while Cortés landed in the island in 1504. (4)

We have then to be content with an appointment due to favour rather than to service and military exploit, and to imagine the future conquistador in his new post of Notary Public of Azúa, a young, active, light-bodied, strong-willed, quick-witted person in his early twenties, settled as a gentleman farmer in a "town" which, but for its church, its fortress and one house or two was little more than a village. Ovando had given him enough Indians to keep manual work at the distance which then passed for dignity. Cervantes de Salazar records that "he then remained six years devoted to farming and discharging his official duties to the satisfaction of the whole town." (5) That may be so, for he was a clear-minded man and could express himself well, while both his native talent and his Salamanca training made him able and possibly willing to enter fully into the game of legal fictions, expressions and complications which a Notary Public could freely practise in the rising colony, with its constant changes in ownership, and its continuous strife between the budding order of colonisation and the stormy disorder of conquest. Cortés was made for both worlds, capable of conceiving law and order, yet rich in the unruly rigour of disorder which is wont to manifest itself in love as in war; so that, while he waited for war, he seems to have fought bravely in the fields of love: "I heard it said," writes Bernal Díaz, "that as a young man in Española he was somewhat sportive about women and that several times he was at daggers drawn over this with brave and seasoned men and always was victorious; and he had a knife scar close to the lower lip, which could be seen by those who looked attentively, though he covered it with his beard, which scar he had received when he went about in those quarrels." (6)

All this, we can readily believe of the youth who at seventeen had already been at the point of death for having sought to reach his lady-love by trespassing over his neighbour's roof. Yet Ovando, the Governor and virtual dictator of the island, was a stern ruler in such matters. "He had," said Las Casas, "a very good way for keeping everyone in order [. . .] If he knew of anyone who was a disturbing factor or who gave a bad example, and especially if he happened to be told that such a person set eyes on a married woman, even though his information went no further than that the man in question passed by her street several times and that this aroused some suspicion in the town, [. . .] he had the man summoned with much tact and he received him with a pleasant countenance and asked him to dine as if he intended to grant him new favours. He asked his guest about the other neighbours (in the place whence he came) and their business, and about how they got on together and other things which he feigned to want to know; the newcomer was led to believe that the Chief Commander had summoned him because he thought him more virtuous and wanted to show him more affection and to have him for his confidant and give him more Indians and that he would thus favour him. And as he always summoned such persons when there were ships in the harbour, when they were on the point of sailing, he would say to his guest: 'So-and-so, see which of these ships will do for you to sail to Castille.' And the other man, now pale, now red, said: 'Sir, why so?' He answered: 'Think now of nothing else.' [. . .] And it must be known that to exile a man to Castille in those days was worse than death." (7)

It is, therefore, short of miraculous that young Cortés, as keen a love-poacher as ever roamed in Ovando's well kept preserves, was not among those exiled back home from the delights of Española. Punishment, however, seems to have come to him not from Ovando but from subtler forces hidden in nature. "At this time," writes Cervantes de Salazar, "he meant to sail over to Veragua, a land famous for its wealth; he was not able to do so owing to an acute pain in his leg. His friends said that it was the buboes for he was always fond of women and Indian women infect those who come to them with this disease more than Spanish women do." (8)

It was the second time that his love-activities had thwarted his war-prowess. Yet, it is impossible to tell whether any particular event is lucky or unlucky in the general composition of a man's life. Laid up in Azúa, drinking possibly of that *guayacan* which, Oviedo tells us (9), the Indians had already found to be a precious cure for syphilis, Cortés missed the disastrous expedition of Nicuesa-Hojeda in which another great Conquistador, Francisco Pizarro, was to play a prominent part. (10) What luck! say in different terms all his biographers. But, again, how did they know that, with Cortés on board, things would not have happened otherwise?

* * *

This expedition, in which Cortés might have taken part, provides a number of clues to the understanding of later events in his adventurous career. Diego de Nicuesa was no ordinary person. "He had," says Las Casas, "served as carver to Don Enrique Enríquez, uncle of the Catholic King," and was "a very wise person and courtly and of gracious speech, a great lute-player and above all a great horseman, who, on a mare which he had, for few horses had as yet been born in those days, did marvels. In short, one of those men gifted with human graces and perfections to be found in Castille; all he had (against him) was that he was but middle-sized, yet he was of good strength, so much so that when he played at reed-spear tournaments the strokes of his reed-spear on the shield hurt deep down into the bones." (11)

Hojeda was no less gifted in perfections and human graces, and had fully deserved to be chosen by Colón himself to command one of the caravels in his second voyage; for he was a "young man whose courage and quickness was then believed to exceed that of many men, be they as quick and brave as they might." (12) Las Casas relates a striking example of his coolness: "When Queen Doña Isabel went up to the tower of the Cathedral in Seville, wherefrom the men below seem as dwarfs, he walked out on the plank which juts twenty feet out of the tower and measured it with his feet quickly, and then, at the outside end of the plank, he put one foot out into the void and wheeled round (on the other) and with the same speed returned to the tower, so that it seems impossible that he should not have fallen and smashed himself to pieces." "This," adds the bishop, "was one of the most signal temerities that a man could have done, for anyone who has seen the tower and the plank and ponders over the act, must needs tremble in his body." (13)

In one point, however, did Nicuesa and Hojeda differ considerably—for while Nicuesa had amassed a fortune in Española, by methods which Las Casas, in his Christian zeal, condemns severely, Hojeda was always panting after his debts and organising expeditions of conquest in order to pay for his past failures with his future successes. Both seem to have had friends at Court where both worked to be appointed governors in the new-discovered mainland of Veragua, attracted "by the scent of the news of its wealth which the Admiral [Colón], the first who had discovered them, had spread abroad." (14) Fonseca sent them both away, each with a good share of the mainland "to govern," including most of the Atlantic coast of what is today Colombia and Panama, while the island of Jamaica was set aside as their base. They had not yet left Santo Domingo when the two governors fell out as to who was to have the land of Darien within his domains, for the charts and maps of the time were far from fool-proof while Don Diego Colón, the great Admiral's son and heir to his claims, incensed at all these governorships so lightheartedly granted in the face of his hereditary rights and determined to thwart the enterprise of the two would-be governors at least in what concerned Jamaica, sent thither a gentleman of Seville, Juan de Esquivel, "to populate it" and "as his lieutenant there." To whom Hojeda, on the point of sailing, made bold to say that he swore that, "if Esquivel landed in Jamaica, he would cut his head off." Such were the methods used in those days in order to spread the Gospels among the benighted natives. (15)

Having uttered his ominous warning, Hojeda left Española on the 10th or 12th of November 1509 with two ships and two brigantines, three hundred men and twelve mares; while Nicuesa tarried in Santo Domingo, detained by cunning legal obstacles thrown across his path by the friends of Don Diego Colón, so that even at the very end, when his seven hundred men and six horses and his captain general were already at sea, leaving just a brigantine behind for him to join them later, as he was about to sail, the law-court ushers were on him again for a caution of five hundred castillians; he was, however, able to dodge this last trick of his enemies through the generosity of an onlooker who put down the money, and in the end he sailed away to his governorship which was to be his doom, leaving behind instructions to have one thousand sides of bacon made from five hundred of his pigs—and, adds Las Casas, "I saw them made in the town of Yáquimo, and they were of the big and beautiful sides of bacon which I have seen in my life." (16)

Hojeda had taken advantage of his ten days' advance to pack as much disaster as possible into them. He had hardly arrived in Cartagena when, against the advice of the great cosmographer Juan de la Cosa, who had financed his expedition and was his captain general, he decided to attack the fierce Indians of that region known for their skill in the use of poisoned arrows. He lost seventy men, had to leave Juan de la Cosa dying of poisoned wounds and owed his own life to his swiftness and to his luck, for he was found by his men hiding in a thicket with no fewer than three hundred impacts on his shield. But the unkindest cut of all for the beaten commander was to hear that Nicuesa's fleet was in sight.

Hojeda decided to remain in hiding till his men had ascertained how Nicuesa would react on hearing the news. Nicuesa, however, was a gentleman and, much surprised at Hojeda's suspicions, brushed aside past differences and put all his forces at the disposal of his beaten rival, who, thus reinforced, avenged his setback with the cruelty usual in those days, as in ours. In the course of this "punitive expedition," "they came across the body of Juan de la Cosa tied to a tree, looking like a hedgehog bristling with arrows; and as, owing to the poisonous herb, he was probably swollen and misshapen, and showing some frightful ugliness, the Spaniards were so greatly scared that no one dared remain there that night." (17)

No wonder that the first town founded by Hojeda in his governorship should have been given the name of St. Sebastian, a heavenly protector against arrows, poisoned or otherwise, though, as Las Casas points out, St. Sebastian took no heed to protect or cure them because "God and his Saints do not usually help injustice and iniquity." (18) Hojeda built a fortress there and took it as a base for gold and food raids against the fierce Indians, who proved too much for him and finally compelled him to remain practically besieged in his fortress,

watching his troops gradually dwindle as hunger and disease took
man after man. Yet, sinners as they all were, they must have prayed
fervently for help, for the Lord, in his inscrutable way, sent them
unexpected relief, choosing as His emissary one Bernardino de
Talavera who, wishing to make himself scarce in Española, where
he was coveted as a desirable guest by the prison authorities, stole
away with seventy comrades in a ship full of bread and meat, over-
looking the fact that the said ship belonged to some Genoese merchants whose ideas on how to come by other people's goods were more
elaborate.

When the hungry garrison saw the white sail against the blue
sky and realised that it was true and not a hallucination of their
transparent bodies, and better still, when Talavera declared himself
—for a consideration—ready to hand over his bread and meat, they
all revived and began again to attack their besiegers. The Indians
were anxious to wound the leader, whose impulsiveness in attack
and swiftness and luck in avoiding injury had so far baffled them;
and by means of a stratagem, they succeeded in wounding him right
through the thigh. Hojeda, who despite his rashness had never been
wounded in his life, "ordered at once that some iron sheets should be
heated white, and when white-hot, he ordered his surgeon to apply
them to the wounded leg; the surgeon refused, arguing that he was
sure to kill him with that fire; Hojeda threatened him with a solemn
vow to God that if he did not apply them he would have him hanged.
Hojeda did this because it is known that the arrow-herb is poisonous
if allowed to grow cold. The surgeon, to escape being hanged, applied
the white-hot iron sheets, one on each side of the thigh, in such a
way that not only did he burn through the thigh and the leg and the
fire conquered and expelled the evil of the herb, but it penetrated his
body to such a degree that they had to consume a whole barrel of
vinegar imbibing sheets and wrapping his body in them. Hojeda
went through it all of his own will, without being held nor tied—a
signal proof of his great spirit and outstanding courage." (19)

Nicuesa and his fleet left in search of their own fate; Hojeda
revived; Talavera's bread and meat were eaten away and hunger
returned: faithful hunger which, like a shadow, stalks ever behind
man's body wherever it breathes. Hojeda's men were muttering,
conspiring, mutinous. He suggested to them that he should sail to

Santo Domingo for help in Talavera's ship and if he had not returned within fifty days, they should be free to do as they pleased with the brigantines he left behind. As their leader, he would leave Francisco Pizarro, the future conquistador of Peru. The plan was accepted, and Talavera and his companions decided to return with Hojeda.

They were of low quality and lacking in heroic metal. But who knows what life has in store for him? Of the unbelievable odyssey of these men, Las Casas writes: "Truly, though the hardships to which the Spaniards have submitted themselves in these Indies, in search of wealth, have been the direst and cruelest which ever men had to endure in the world, these which Hojeda and those who went with him had to suffer, were of the greatest." (20) They landed in Cuba, grounded the ship and decided to walk towards the east, to draw closer to Española. The island was not yet "populated," and in this no-man's-land, the Talavera faction made Hojeda their prisoner. Natives of the warlike variety attacked them; whereupon, they decided to free Hojeda because "he was worth more than half of them for war." (21) In this unruly and precarious way they walked more than four hundred miles, when they strayed into a bog which they crossed for thirty days, walking sometimes knee-deep, sometimes up to their necks in filthy mud; of the twenty men, half the number died of hunger or thirst, or were drowned in the swamp; wherever they could, they climbed into mangrove trees to snatch a few hours of sleep. In these moments of rest, Hojeda drew out from his sack "an image of our Lady, most devout and marvellously painted, made in Flanders," (22) and the distressed troop prayed for Her intercession. Finally, with the help and charity of some peaceful Indians, they were able to send a canoe to Jamaica, and eventually Hojeda was rescued by a caravel commanded by a captain who was to play a leading part in the life of Cortés—Pánfilo de Narváez, who took them all to Jamaica. There Hojeda was most chivalrously housed by that Juan de Esquivel whose head he had sworn to cut off. Talavera was hanged, and Hojeda went back to Santo Domingo, there to die in hospital, without a farthing to pay for his funeral.

* * *

C*

Meanwhile, the men left on the mainland under Francisco Pizarro, having waited for fifty days, decided to leave the inhospitable land; this, however, was no easy matter, for they numbered about sixty and there was not enough space in the brigantines for all of them; so that it was agreed to wait till "hunger, disease and the Indian arrows had reduced their numbers to those the brigantines could hold." (23) They did not have to wait long, and having killed for meat the four mares they had kept alive for safety to frighten the Indians with, they at last sailed away from Urabá six months after landing, in their two brigantines, one of which sank with all the men on board soon after they put to sea. Francisco Pizarro, in command of the one which remained, took refuge in Cartagena, and as he entered the bay, he saw a ship arriving there at the same time. It was the relief expedition of Anciso, Hojeda's partner, arriving many months too late. Anciso brought one hundred and fifty men, food, artillery, ammunition, twelve mares, a few horses, pigs, and last but not least, hidden inside an empty barrel, Vasco Núñez de Balboa, who had thus spirited himself away from the island of his debts in search of Darien and that South Sea which it was his fate to discover.

Despite the earnest entreaties of the sorely tried men under Pizarro, Anciso, who had sway over them as Hojeda's *Alcalde Mayor*, forced them all to sail back to Urabá, only to see his ship smashed to pieces by the angry waves against a treacherous bank; the men just saved their bodies; mares, horses and pigs, all perished. Hunger and poisoned arrows again. But this time, there was Balboa. He remembered, he said, that across the gulf there was a great river, good food and Indians who did not use poisoned arrows. And so the adventurous troop discovered Darien and founded a town which, in fulfilment of a vow they had made when in dire need—for who makes vows in good weather?—they christened *Santa María del Antigua del Darien*. Vasco Núñez de Balboa seems to have then begun to feel the itch of ambition, and to have set about to undermine Anciso's authority on the ground that they had gone beyond the borders of Hojeda's governorship. Anciso himself did the rest by forbidding any dealings in gold with the Indians under pain of death. He was deposed and the rank and file elected two alcaldes, one of whom was Balboa.

In this way, the colony managed to split into three factions: those who felt that they owed allegiance to Anciso; those who thought they should go over to Nicuesa, into whose lands they had strayed; and Balboa's party. One morning, they heard repeated gun reports. They answered with their own artillery, and presently two new ships appeared in the bay. They were led by one Rodrigo de Colmenares, a lieutenant of Nicuesa, who came from Española with food and ammunition and, puzzled at finding no trace of Hojeda, had fired his guns in the hope of being heard by him. With the prestige which good hams give their owner and dispenser amidst a hungry crowd, Colmenares persuaded the majority of the settler-soldiers to acknowledge the authority of Nicuesa.

But where was Nicuesa? His tribulations were not less tragic than those of Hojeda. Owing to a more or less sincere misunderstanding, his captain general, Olano, had failed to meet him after a temporary separation and he had been left with one caravel only which he lost in the usual way, by a combination of sea-fury, uncharted harbours and bad seamanship. Walking, hungry and dejected, along the burning coast, under the menace of unfriendly Indians, he found himself, with most of his men, stranded on a small, sterile island, to which he had crossed in the caravel punt, thinking it to be the opposite side of a mainland bay, while his four sailors, tired of suffering, rowed away in the night, in the hope of at least finding Olano and bringing back help. They did find him, in a scarcely less grave plight than that in which they had left Nicuesa, and persuaded him to send a ship with some palmitos and fresh water to revive the stranded men. When Nicuesa, thus relieved, returned and rejoined the rest of what remained of his expedition, he could hardly restrain his fury and, but for the insistent entreaties of his men, he would have hanged Olano there and then. Yet worse was to come; for unable to secure food except by hazardous raids against a mobile and dangerous enemy, the Spaniards came to such a desperate state of hunger that thirty of them, having found a dead Indian, ate the corpse and died of it.

Nicuesa decided to try again somewhere else, and sailed away in a caravel which Olano had made his men build with the wood they had saved from the lost ship; and in this improvised craft he followed the coast eastwards, till seeing a spot which seemed to him fit for a settlement, he said, "Let us stay here in the name of God." And such was the origin of the colony of *Nombre de Dios*. Ruthlessly, he set his weak and hungry men to work to build a fortress, and to those who complained, he answered: "Begone, to the dying-place." (24) Of 785 men whom he had brought over, he had 100 left, towards December 1510, while he was building this fortress. Things went from bad to worse, and they were all so weak that there was no one left to keep watch by night.

This was the state of the Governor of Golden Castille (Castilla del Oro) when Colmenares came to inform him that there were sixty men in Darien who sought the honour of being his subjects. His joy at the sight of a roast hen was so great that, remembering his carver days, he carved it in the air. His spirits went up so high that he swore he would punish his new subjects for having amassed gold without his authority. And, as if intent on engineering his own destruction, he sent forward the caravel with the news, remaining behind in a sloop.

When he appeared before Darien, the colony was up in arms against him. He proved neither energetic nor shrewd enough to meet the crisis, and, despite Balboa's efforts and advice, he was taken a prisoner, and sent in an old sloop to Española with seventeen of his friends. No one ever heard of him again. (25)

*   *   *

While two of his neighbours in Española were destroying over twenty thousand pesos and over a thousand human lives in two sense-less expeditions, Hernán Cortés stayed in Azúa, nursing his love-wounds. "One afternoon, as he had fallen asleep, he dreamt that suddenly, having shed his old poverty, he saw himself covered with rich cloth and served by many strangers who addressed him with words of great honour and praise [. . .] and though, as a good Christian, he knew that one must not give credence to dreams, withal he was elated, for his dream had been most fitting to his thoughts, which most wisely he concealed for fear of being taken for a mad-man." And "he said to his friends with a new and not yet seen satisfaction that he would either eat with trumpets or die in the gallows." (26)

CHAPTER FIVE

Love and Revolt in Española

ON JULY 10th, 1509, a fleet more ornate and colourful than usual anchored in Santo Domingo bay. The second Admiral of the Indies, Don Diego Colón, son and heir of the Discoverer, had at last succeeded in vindicating his hereditary right to be Viceroy and Governor General of the Indies, and he landed in his overseas fief "very well accompanied, and his household peopled with gentlemen." He brought over with him his two uncles, the Adelantado Don Bartolomé, who had founded the town, and the parson-like Don Diego, who had erected a gallows at each end of it on which to hang unruly Spaniards while he governed it; and his bastard brother Don Fernando, who was to write it all down for posterity. But, if Cortés was present, which is quite possible, he probably bestowed his keenest attention on yet another feature of the new Viceroy's establishment; for the Vicereine, Doña María de Toledo, a niece of the Duke of Alba, brought over in her household "a few ladies and noble maids, and all or most of those who were young were married in this city and in the island with persons of rank and wealth who lived here, for in truth there was great need of such women from Castille; and though there were some Christians who married Indian women of good families, there were many more who would on no account take them in matrimony, owing to their incapacity and their ugliness." (1) Now, if Cortés was there and watched the graceful cargo of Spanish girls unloaded on the island, demurely hiding their curiosity under a shyness which protected them from the hungry masculine eyes waiting on the shore, he was sure to have beheld amongst them the woman who was to be his

57

wife and the cause of more than one dramatic adventure in his career.

*   *   *

Don Diego Colón, then in his thirtieth year, "was a man of high stature, like his father, of fine looks and of well proportioned limbs; his face was long and his head raised, showing lordship and authority; he was of a good temper and heart, simple rather than cautious or cunning." He was as clannish as his father had been, and when, after the usual social and official duties arising out of the change-over had been performed, he provided a fleet for the return home of his predecessor, he thought it quite natural to put it under the command, not of the venerable old man himself, but of his stripling of a brother, Don Fernando, then twenty years of age, a tactless deed which, Las Casas records, provoked not a little comment. (2)

The new Viceroy organised first the conquest and settlement of the island of Borinquen, which the Spaniards christened San Juan, now Puerto Rico. This conquest does not seem to have interested Cortés. It was, nevertheless, most dramatic, particularly after the Indians had ascertained that the Spaniards were not immortal, which they did in a most scientific manner by inducing a young man named Salcedo, to travel in their company for some distance and to allow himself to be conveyed across a river on the shoulders of a native who, with the help of twenty others, interested in the experiment, promptly drowned him. Drowned? That was precisely the point. Could a Spaniard die? They laid the motionless body on the bank and for two days came now and then to speak to him: "Señor Salcedo," they said, "do forgive us; for we all fell together; let us walk on." Not till the body showed unmistakable signs of death, did they consider the experiment as final. (3)

Cortés' absence from the Puerto Rico wars would tend to strengthen the view—contrary to that usually adopted—that he was content at first with a pleasant life as an amorous gentleman-lawyer-farmer; since, had he been impatient of military prowess, this was no doubt an excellent moment to show it. Furthermore, when the time comes at last for his second emigration, his voyage to Cuba, we are to see him appointed, not in a military but again in a civilian capacity, though the enterprise was decidedly of a warlike character.

Cuba was then hardly yet explored. Shortly before his recall, Ovando had sent an expedition under a Captain Sebastián de Ocampo, with the task of ascertaining whether it was an island, as most people believed, or the mainland, as Colón had made his crews swear it was. But beyond finding that it was an island, Ocampo had done little to improve the Spanish hold on it. In 1511 Don Diego Colón decided to have it conquered and settled, choosing as the leader of the enterprise one of the chief gentlemen and captains in Española, known as Diego Velázquez, "the wealthiest and most esteemed among the old settlers of this island." Velázquez had belonged to the household of the Adelantado Don Bartolomé Colón. Las Casas, in his inimitable style, always an uncompromising enemy of the conquest, gives a bittersweet description of his qualifications: "He was wealthier than any other; he had much experience in shedding or helping to shed the blood of this unfortunate people; he was much loved by all the Spaniards who lived under his authority, for he had a merry and human disposition and all his talk was on pleasures and festivities, as between rather unruly young men, though when necessary he knew how to assert his authority and wished it respected; he had his lands in Xaraguá, and in those parts close to the harbours facing Cuba. He was very handsome in body and face, and therefore the more liked; he was growing fat, yet had lost but little handsomeness; he was wise, though believed to be somewhat thick-minded, yet he belied this fame." (4)

Such was the man who, towards the close of 1511, left the town of Sabana in Española to conquer Cuba with three hundred men. The campaign was not long nor very difficult, for the Cuban natives seem to have been soon demoralised by the superiority of the invaders in armament and in physical strength. Reinforcements of a voluntary character were sent from Jamaica under a man who, next to Velázquez, was to play an important part in the life of Cortés: Pánfilo de Narváez, a lieutenant of Juan de Esquivel, Governor of Jamaica. He was, says Las Casas, "a man of impressive mien, tall, somewhat fair, almost red-haired, honest, of good sense, though not very cautious, of good conversation, a good way of life, and brave against Indians, possibly also against other peoples, but he had over it all this failing, that he was most careless; of whom"—he adds most aptly—"there is much to be related anon." (5)

Though the reinforcements brought over by Narváez were not impressive—thirty Spaniards, bowmen, well trained in handling this native weapon—Velázquez made him his chief captain, a kind of second in command. Presently, a new character appeared on the scene, at Velázquez' own request: this was Bartolomé de Las Casas himself, who later, as bishop of Chiapa, was to write it all down in shame and grief, but who, in those days, as a young priest, accompanied Narváez, softening, whenever he could, the onslaught of the Christians on the nearly defenceless Indians. Narváez, with Las Casas at his elbow, carried out most of the conquest, for Velázquez was too fat for warlike activities, which, though not of the most arduous and heroic which the Spanish conquerors had to face in the Indies, were strenuous enough. Las Casas relates one of the most dangerous episodes of the campaign, when careless Narváez woke up one night to find his twenty-five men surrounded by several thousand Indians, eager not so much for Spanish blood as for Spanish clothes; for ever since they had seen the Spaniards, the natives coveted their clothes and wanted to go about dressed. The din and the noise of the invading crowd and, more directly, the impact of a big stone on his chest and stomach, awoke the drowsy captain who had his mare —the only cavalry present—quickly harnessed and leapt on it in his nightshirt. But the mere tinkling of the bells of the mare's harness put so much terror into the natives that they all fled in the night. (6)

How about Cortés? If we are to believe his Latin chronicler, he took a prominent part in the campaign, having come over to Cuba at the insistent request of Velázquez, who "begged him many a day to accompany him, promising him seas and mountains if Cortés would help him in that war, and as he was not very fitted for war owing to his obesity, he made Cortés his associate and adviser in all his decisions." We are also told that "he behaved so bravely in war, that in a short time he became the most experienced of all." (7)

But there is no trace whatever of such excellence in the texts of those who were closer to the facts; there is indeed, for once, a curious agreement on this point between Las Casas, who actually lived all this chapter of Cortés' life, and Gómara, Cortés' personal chaplain and historiographer, both of whom show him at this time on the civilian side of Velázquez' activities: Las Casas as one of Velázquez' two secretaries and Gómara as treasurer for the expedition, on behalf of

"Miguel de Pasamonte, the King's Treasurer in Española, to keep account of the fifth due to the King and of the royal estate; and Diego Velázquez himself begged him to do so, for he (Cortés) was able and active." (8) There is no reason whatever, therefore, for dismissing Las Casas' opinion here since his usual pro-Indian bias is not at stake and his invaluable authority as a personal witness is strengthened by that of Gómara writing under Cortés' own inspiration. Moreover, it fits the facts much better than the hero-worship legends of the Latin chronicler. At this time, we must see Cortés as Las Casas sees him: "He was cunning and cautious, though he did not show himself yet as wise and able as he was to prove in later days and in arduous things." Indeed, we may for once believe his admiring Latin chronicler when he says: "After he went over to Cuba with Velázquez, there was nothing to which Cortés devoted more care than to winning the good graces of his chief." (9)

This is a valuable sidelight, particularly valuable since it comes from quarters friendly to Cortés, and very much needed in view of the all too frequent tendency to distort the early years of famous men by forcing on them the perspective of their later doings. Cortés was a great captain in the field, and his bravery was, as a matter of coldly ascertained fact, truly heroic; but he was also a born diplomat, a cunning negotiator, a shrewd craftsman in the art of handling men, and this feature, rather than the former, was the chief instrument of his rise in the early days of his marvellous ascent.

He was twenty-six when he became Velázquez' secretary and the King's Treasurer in the island. While paying his main attention to conquering the Governor's good graces, he did not neglect the rest of the colony, for he knew too well that governors come and go but the governed remain, and, in the curious anarchical-democratic conditions of the nascent community in the Indies, a man's opportunity might come just as well from below as from above. He was thus gradually led to an attitude of open opposition to the Governor. The game was dangerous, and Cortés met the danger, faced it and eventually—such was ever to be his style—came through, not only unscathed, but stronger and more powerful than at the outset.

This phase of his estrangement from Velázquez is intricate and somewhat obscure, for his several chroniclers are neither clear nor agreed as to motives and events. There are two strains in the story:

one political and one, of course, amorous. Juan Xuárez of Granada, one of the settlers who had come over from Española to Cuba with Velázquez, had brought with him "three or four sisters and his mother who had gone to Santo Domingo with the Vicereine Doña María de Toledo in 1509 with the intention of marrying rich men there; for they were poor, and there was one of them, Catalina, who in all earnestness used to say that she was sure to become a great lady, either because she had dreamt it or because she had been told so by some astrologer. They were beautiful. For which reason, as well as owing to the scarcity of Spanish women at the time, they were much sought after." (10)

Cortés conquered Catalina's good graces and, having succeeded beyond his expectations, he was somewhat remiss as to honouring his promises of marriage. But it so happened that Diego Velázquez developed an interest of the same kind in another of the Xuárez girls; and the sister wooed by the Governor, watching over the affairs of the sister wooed by the secretary-treasurer, put official pressure on Cortés to exact from him payment in marriage for love-favours granted on account.

Gómara goes so far as to say that the recalcitrant lover was put in prison as a result—direct or indirect—of his obduracy. "In the end, he married her, though he first had a few quarrels over it and went to jail." (11)

But Cortés seems to have given the Governor a better opportunity for putting him in jail than his amorous adventure. His Latin chronicler and Gómara endeavour to throw the blame of these events on some envious enemies of Cortés, who sedulously cultivated ill-feeling between the Governor and his chief secretary; but there is little doubt that the attractive, even commanding, personality of Cortés was beginning to act as it was always to do in later days, as a focus for any human activities which might be wandering aimlessly about him for want of leadership. The newfangled Governor was gradually reaping the harvest of power—every action of his made one ungrateful friend and nine resentful enemies. If he did not give Indians or land to So-and-so, he was a tyrant; if he did, he was a crafty fox who had given so few Indians and such poor land when the other fellow could boast of twice as many hands and much better fields. So wagged many a tongue, flashed many an eye, shook many a fist. And at night, under the cloak of darkness, the swords of conspiracy met in Cortés' house. The conspirators soon learnt with satisfaction—possibly through Cortés himself who would be amongst the first to know, owing to his official position—that Judges of Appeal had arrived in Española to keep control over the actions of the Executive; and they decided to write down at length all their complaints against Velázquez and to send them to the Judges of Appeal. But who was to take on the dangerous duties of courier, and brave not merely the wrath of the Governor but the fury of the sea as well? "And they found no one hardier and bolder in the face of any danger, for he had to go across to this island (Española) in a canoe or native boat, with such high seas, and usually so stormy, than Hernándo Cortés." (12)

Whether Cortés conspired out of a sense of justice over the abuses committed by Velázquez or because he was incensed at his chief's attitude in the matter of his love affair, it is difficult to say. Velázquez seems to have had no qualms about it, for having had wind of the plan at the moment when Cortés was going to embark in his canoe full of reports and complaints, he had him arrested. His first decision was to have his secretary hanged. Where was the gallows from which would have hanged the finest leader of men that Spain has known, the destiny of a continent and the tale most splendid and fertile in legends that the West has ever lived? For a few days, the fate of Cortés and of the conquest of Mexico hung not indeed on the rope of that gallows, but on the thread of Velázquez' own humour. The fat Governor, however, "was of a good disposition and his bad temper never lasted long"—a peculiar grace with which obesity is wont to lighten the spirit of those whose body it overloads. (13)

So Cortés was not deprived of his life; yet he lost his liberty, and while he had dreamt of a dangerous cruise to Española followed by a skilful negotiation in the political and legal waters which he navigated with so much confidence, he found himself in a dungeon, with iron rings round his ankles. He was not the man to stay there long. What combination of skill, daring and diplomacy he performed to regain his freedom is a problem difficult to solve, for the facts are reported in different ways according to the bias of the writer. Gómara sums them up by saying that "he broke the lock of the stocks; he

seized the sword and buckler of the fortress warden; he opened the
window and let himself down from it, and he took refuge in the
church." It is difficult to see how a prisoner in a fortress could do all
this without the connivance of his keeper, particularly when keeper
and prisoner slept in the same room; and so we read in the Latin
chronicler that the keeper "Cristóbal de Lagos, if we are to tell the
truth, feigned to have heard nothing out of fear, not out of friendship as has been imputed untruly." (14) But whether Cristóbal de
Lagos contrived his escape through friendship or fear, the net yield
is the same: Cortés had already enough following amongst the
Spanish islanders to outweigh the authority and power of the Governor in the mind of an official presumably trusted, as the keeper
of the fortress was bound to be when there was only one fortress to
keep.

The Governor was angry and "scolded Cristóbal de Lagos,
accusing him of having let Cortés out for money and bribes"; and he
tried to get hold of the rebel either by persuasion or by force; "but,"
as Gómara puts it, "Cortés saw through the words, and withstood
force." (15) Yet Velázquez was the stronger, for he had on his side
the greatest possible lure for a man like Cortés—he had space. How
could Cortés remain for long besieged in a small church? Space
moreover is full of all kinds of things, including women, to whom
Cortés never was indifferent; and it seems that at this stage, whether
by accident or by guile, Catalina, the very lady whom he had
refused to marry, was dangled before his no doubt bored eyes. He
came out to talk to her, and was seized by a squad of soldiers who
were in hiding. Cortés fought hard against their leader—one Juan
Escudero—who, during those hot seconds when in a stubborn
embrace he held in his arms the struggling body of the future lord of
Mexico, might perhaps have seen through a tear in the veil of time
a distant scene in which he was to hang from the gallows erected by
the man he was at that moment arresting. (16)

This time, Velázquez had his prisoner locked up on board ship,
and, no doubt, wishing to get rid of so turbulent a character, he made
up his mind to have him sent over to Española. But Cortés might
then have put his case as the lover in the two first lines of the Spanish
love song:

When I wanted, you did not;
Now that I don't want, you do.

He would gladly have gone to Española as a witness against
Velázquez, but he would not go as his prisoner. Here again, his
escape must have been the outcome of a combination of luck, daring
and an astute ability for securing accomplices; he succeeded in
squeezing his foot out of his stock, not without acute pain; then, at
night, having changed clothes with his servant, he coolly went up on
deck and loafed about, watching a group of sailors round the kitchen
fire, without being recognized; seeing that conditions were so favourable, he then let himself down into the ship's boat, and rowed away
in the night. Yet, he first rowed towards one other ship lying in the
harbour and untied the rope of her boat so that the sea should wash
it away and it might not be available if and when his own flight came
to be discovered. This done, he endeavoured to row towards land,
but the river was too strong for him and he made up his mind to
swim. Here shines yet another glimmer of his double-edged personality: at that hour of danger, "he undressed, and with a kerchief
he tied up over his head a number of papers which he held as notary
of the Municipal Council and as an officer of the Treasurer, and
which told against Diego Velázquez" (17); here is a clear case of a
pen-and-sword man. This feature will remain constant right through
his life: always ready to fight if need be, Cortés is always readier
still to make a case. At that moment, with his bundles of legal papers
tied to his head, he plunged into the shark-infested waters of
Baracoa Bay and swam in the night. Hardly was he safe from the
perils of shark and sea before the perils of men and land were
threatening him; for in the night he heard the voices of a number of
soldiers; he hid in the bush, away from the road, and then, across
country, he went straight for the house of Juan Xuárez.

This decision may appear strange at first sight. Stranger still in
that no biographer of Cortés has either raised the problem or suggested its obvious solution. Why should Cortés seek the home of
the very man whose sister he refused to marry, thus providing
fuel of a private nature for the fire which his public behaviour
had raised in the Governor's soul? But the narrative of Gómara
suffices to suggest the answer. "Cortés married Catalina Xuáres

because he had promised it and to live in peace." (18) It follows that Cortés went to see Xuárez precisely to tell him that he was ready to marry Catalina and thus end his feud with the Governor. Cautious to the end, however, he again sought refuge in the church, pending Velázquez' decision; Xuárez acted as friendly negotiator between the two suitors of his two sisters; his task was obviously easier, now that Cortés had consented to be married, and it seems that the reconciliation between the Governor and his secretary was quick and cordial. Velázquez was out of town, on a warlike expedition against the Indians; Cortés turned up one evening with Xuárez, ready with spear and bow to help in the fray. The Governor was reading an account book. "Hullo, gentlemen," said Cortés through the window. "Here is Cortés who greets his brave Captain." The rebel was forgiven. He fought well in the campaign and was rewarded with many Indians by his grateful chief. (19)

Velázquez seems to have borne him no grudge, for he went so far as to stand him godfather to a daughter which Cortés then had. "I do not know whether by his wife or not," says Las Casas (20); but Cortés had no children by his first wife, while we know that he had a daughter "by a Cuban Indian woman whose name was Doña Hulana Piçarro," (21) no doubt baptized under his auspices and called after his own maternal family name, for such was the custom with Spaniards who christened Indians. This fact shows how successful Cortés had been in recovering the Governor's good graces. "He was unremitting in serving and pleasing him and in never crossir.g him whether in big or in small things, as he was most astute, so that he won him over again and put him off his guard, as he had been before." And to give his one-time secretary a fresh proof of his renewed confidence Velázquez made him alcalde, or Magistrate, of the town of Baracoa, which soon after became Santiago. (22)

No special effort of imagination is needed to see in these changes other factors than those accurately observed by Las Casas. A winning way was ever one of the leading forces which shaped Cortés' life. He had a golden tongue; indeed, he was gifted with that most precious yet most rare of combinations: presence of will with presence of wit, an irresistible, double-edged weapon for the fights of daily life. But along with this asset, he surely found his way back to favour because on the one hand he was able both for office and for field work; and on the other because Velázquez was shrewd enough to realize that he had better have Cortés for a friend than for an enemy.

*   *   *

It is worth noticing how, at this early stage, the young treasury official evinced signs of that sound economic sense which he was to show later as a statesman, for we hear of his spirit of enterprise both as a mine owner and as a farmer. "He bred cows, ewes and mares and was the first who had herds of cattle and sheep there," says Gómara; and his Latin biographer adds that he was the first also to prospect for gold in Cuba and to breed cattle from all kinds of breeds which he brought over from Española. (23)

These reports convey a tradition of spirit and enterprise so consonant with later activities that they must carry conviction. Las Casas puts in his usual criticism in typically uncompromising and even picturesque terms: "Cortés put great haste and diligence into making the Indians whom Diego Velázquez had given him, get for him a great quantity of gold, which was then everybody's hiccup, and so they dug out for him two or three thousand pesos of gold, which for those days was great wealth; those who died, God knows the number of them better than I." For once we catch the good bishop letting himself go to the prejudice into which his otherwise admirable pro-Indian bias betrayed him. He had seen so many cases of ill-treatment of the native by greedy gold-diggers that he took for granted that all wealth acquired in the Indies was raised on Indian lives. Yet, *pace* Las Casas, Cortés cannot have been a hard master to his Indians. All his political views and economic sense were against it. There is a dramatic moment of his life at this precise time which would tend to show that the natives liked him. He had gone out, as was his wont, to visit his Indians, and was returning in a canoe from Bani to Baracoa when a nasty wind made him lose all hope of reaching land before night; indeed, when darkness fell, he found himself still at sea, fighting hard against wind and wave, tired and unable to control his canoe which finally capsized. He was saved by some Indian shepherds, and his Latin biographer, though always prone to make extravagant claims about his hero's prowess, recognises that he owed his life to those natives who took timely measures to save him. It is not credible that a man known in the countryside for his harsh treatment of his Indians should owe his life to the very Indians whom he maltreated. (24)

* * *

This was then for Cortés a period of growth, experience and formation. The colony was developing apace. As for the Governor, he was growing with the colony and acquiring a sense of his own dignity and importance as the apex of power over a world of men which the sea and distance made a kind of world apart. He "was human and affable in conversation, but when necessary and if he was angry, those in his presence trembled, and he demanded to be always treated with the utmost reverence, and no one sat down in his presence, not even knights." (25) In short, Velázquez considered himself as a kind of viceroy or local king, with his court, his favourite ministers, his captain general (Narváez), his courtiers and even his jester, for as we are to see anon in one of the scenes most vividly set down by Bernal Díaz, Velázquez had a kind of fool who, in the tradition of the day, addressed him with the utmost liberty of both form and substance; that the name of this fool was Cervantes is but another of those caprices which the Muse of History—the most pince-sans-rire of the nine—allows herself under the mask of gravity.

It is therefore but natural that Diego Velázquez should have endeavoured to secure for himself some degree of permanency in this position, for not in vain did he come from that Castille which has coined the proverb "Better be head of a mouse than tail of a lion." His island was small and undeveloped, but he was King of his island and wealthy at that—as one would say, again in Castillian parlance, honey over cake. And so the good Governor made up his mind to work in Spain over the head of the very Admiral Don Diego to whom he owed his governorship, in order to have his appointment securely confirmed direct by the King. "And he managed things so well and secured the help of such intermediaries to put his case before the Catholic King, with the friendship which united him to the Treasurer of this Island [Española] Miguel de Passamonte, who enjoyed great credit [at Court], that even if the Admiral had wished to remove Diego Velázquez from the governorship, he would not have been able to do so." (26)

This Miguel de Passamonte was precisely Cortés' chief as Treasury official. There is here more than a suggestion that the official relations between his ambitious and enterprising secretary and the powerful Treasurer of Española, whom he needed as a way of access to the King, may also have influenced Velázquez' leniency towards Cortés. There is indeed in the whole affair a smack of astuteness and even of intrigue which leads one to suspect that Cortés may have shared in the negotiations. At any rate, he watched them closely and was bound to have observed their outcome for the jovial, fat and successful Governor.

Successful? Oviedo, who relates the whole story, goes on to say: "Diego Velázquez showed no more courtesy to the Admiral Don Diego Colón, in keeping for himself, against the Admiral's will, the governorship of Cuba with his secret ways and manœuvres, than Hernándo Cortés showed to Diego Velázquez when he left him out and kept for himself the post of New Spain." And the honest chronicler concludes: "Thou shalt kill and killed shalt be; and killed shall be your killers." (27)

CHAPTER SIX

Cortés Watches Two More Men Fail As Conquerors

THERE is at first sight something unpleasant and unsavoury in this tale of infidelity and insubordination which recurs again and again in the early days of the Spanish conquest, till it becomes a kind of pattern of the story; yet, without in any sense losing any of its value as a feature in the character of this or that individual conquistador, its very recurrence reveals it to be a kind of biological process whereby European life spreads over the Indian territories. The mother-cell of Española gave forth the cells of Jamaica, San Juan (Puerto Rico), Castilla del Oro, Andalucía, Florida, New Spain (Mexico), Peru and others, through this tendency of the Iberian to cut himself loose from the main authority; and the aggregate stands as an impressive monument to the strength of the monarchical principle of Spain in those days, for, despite the corrupt practices of some of the Crown's chief officers at home and despite the uninterested, ungrateful and at times unenlightened attitude of Charles V, none of the spirited and unruly conquistadores ever dreamt of setting up an empire of his own in the distant and unclaimed lands which they made theirs.

Most of the expeditions were of a spontaneous and popular growth, strongly imbued with equalitarian and, as we would say nowadays, democratic ways—I say "ways" advisedly, for while they were far stronger and more vital they were also less conscious than principles. It is idle to follow Las Casas and believe that these expeditions were all animated with a desire to rob, kill or kidnap the unfortunate natives. They sprang straight from the settlers, and their character depended on the character of those who conceived

70

them; some were undertaken by small men, with the limited ambition of re-stocking their mines and farms with that human livestock which ill-treatment, smallpox and no doubt also deep sorrow for liberty lost, decimated; others sought to attain fame and wealth by discovering new lands which, of course, like all undiscovered lands, were fabulously wealthy. It is difficult for us to imagine what the mind of our ancestors was, for ours has its frontiers neatly mapped out and closed up by concrete knowledge, while theirs had a whole side open wide towards an unknown continent, never more fascinating and promising than during those first years of the sixteenth century when it was already known to exist but was still unknown in its outline and depths, nature and secrets. This was moreover the time when the romances of Chivalry were rapidly rising to the zenith of their vogue, when from the Emperor-King Charles V down to the last of his soldiers and kitchen boys, every man and woman in Spain read, enjoyed and often believed in the adventures of *Amadis de Gaul,* and possibly also of *Tirant lo Blanch* and of *Palmerin de Oliva,* the three first Knights to gallop over the fields of extravagance.

What lay behind the mystery of that Continent which every conquest revealed as more spacious and every discovery as more unknown? The men of those days were not limited in their expectations as we are nowadays, by a more precise framework of general knowledge to which we know in advance nature will adjust itself. Why should the new world be like the old? Not only had they been led by Colón's extravagant imagination (and shrewd propaganda) to expect splendid oriental wealth—for that West was still a kind of super-East—but they were subconsciously ready for any extra-, infra- or super-natural revelations, or rather, should we say, for any revelations which would widen and transfigure the meaning and scope of what was "natural"—trees that could move, men that could fly, forms of life still unimagined, marvellous or dreadful, till then concealed from the old world.

It was in these oceans of Fancy that Florida was discovered. "Then it was," says Oviedo, "that the fable of a fountain which made old men recover youth and become young men again was divulged; this happened in the year 1512. And it was so much divulged and certified by the Indians of those parts that the Captain Johan Ponce and his men and caravels were lost and suffered much hardship for six months, in among those islands, in search of that fountain; which was much mockery for the Indians to tell of such a fountain and a still greater folly for the Christians to believe in and to waste their time in looking for it. But he heard of the Mainland and saw it and gave a name to a part of it which goes out into the sea for one hundred leagues in longitude and for quite fifty in latitude and called it *Florida*." (1)

* * *

The epilogue of Nicuesa's expedition was still agitating the colony of Veragua where Balboa had stood beholding for the first time—silent, upon a peak in Darien—the most longed-for South Sea, a prize for which Fate was to make him pay but four years later when his successor Pedrarias, jealous of his achievement, beheaded him. In that same year (1517) a few of the men who had conquered the land with Balboa returned to Cuba because "there was nothing left to conquer, for Balboa had conquered it all and the land is of itself very short." (2) The man who wrote these words was to share in all the expeditions set up to explore and conquer Mexico; and sixty years later, when over eighty-four years of age, he was to set it all down with so much simplicity, sincerity and sheer genius for expression that to this day he stands as the greatest of Spanish chroniclers.

His name was Bernal Díaz del Castillo, and he had been born in Medina del Campo, in 1492, the very year of the discovery, of a family in which the men, as he himself proudly claims, "were ever servants of the royal crown." In 1514, "wishing to resemble them," he sailed to Darien with Pedrarias, and in 1517, on his return to Cuba, he entered upon his New Spain adventures. His straightforward, earnest, brave, modest yet proud, religious yet ironical and unsuperstitious character will shine at every step in Cortés' life, as we again and again go to his vivid pages for a true light on past events. He wrote, he says, because "I have no wealth to leave my sons and descendants but this my truthful and notable narrative"; but as he was already well on in his tale, of which he had set no less than seventeen chapters on paper, he came upon the histories devoted to the same subject by learned men such as Gómara, Illescas, Jovio, and felt dismayed at his "rude words, without daintyness"; yet, as he read on, he was so incensed by what he read that he decided to proceed with his narrative for the sake of truth, since, he says, those fine authors "put down eighty thousand as easy as eight thousand, and as for those slaughters of which they speak, when we were but four hundred and fifty soldiers and it was just as much as we could do to defend ourselves not to be killed or utterly defeated, for had the Indians been tied up we would not have killed as many." Grammar he had not much, nor did he need more of it to make his narrative one of the most enjoyable that ever were penned, and so true that, though he wrote in ever watchful opposition to Gómara's constant eulogy of Cortés and in ever watching care for the fame of the humbler folk of conquistadores to whom he belonged, Cortés comes out greater by far from his homely narrative than from the courtly pages of his learned private chaplain. (3)

Bernal Díaz tells how "one hundred and ten companions, some of them back from the Mainland, and others of those who in Cuba had no Indians, decided to agree with a gentleman known as Francisco Hernández de Córdoba, who was a wealthy man and owned a *pueblo* of Indians in that Island, for him to be our captain, for he was capable enough for it, in order to go at our own risk to seek and discover new lands and occupy our persons in them, and to this effect we bought three ships." (4) In these simple and moving words we catch an invaluable glimpse of the creative process of the discovery. We see it as the overflow of surplus youthful energies, the urge for activity and the hunger for risk on the part of young men of action with time on their hands, for as Bernal Díaz says, in order to explain how the scheme arose, "three years had gone by [. . .] and we had done nothing worth telling." (5) Their general was wealthy and, if we are to believe Las Casas, he had two other partners who were able to contribute between fifteen hundred and two thousand castillians each; yet most of the "gentlemen and persons of quality" who were associated in the business-adventure were poor, and one of the three ships had to be borrowed from the Governor. This was fortunate for us, because it gave Bernal Díaz an opportunity to let us see how things were done—or not done—in the Indies in those days: "The other one was a ship which we borrowed from the Governor Diego Velázquez, on condition that before he let us have her, we were to bind ourselves to sail with the three ships to some small islands which lie between Cuba and Honduras, now known as the Guanaxes Island, and that we were to go on a war footing and to load our ships with Indians from those Islands and pay the ship with Indians to be used as slaves." It will be seen that Diego Velázquez tried to solve his labour problem in the easiest possible way for a man given to obesity; but how did the young, lean and brave soldiers take to the proposition? "As we the soldiers saw that what Diego Velázquez asked of us was not just, we answered him that what he said was not commanded by either God or the King, [namely] that we should make free men slaves." So this small group of men bound together by the hope of achieving some conquest in common were already a kind of small republic with a democratic opinion which could make itself felt and heard. The Governor, despite his local omnipotence, respected their views, and helped them to complete their purchases of food, munitions and goods; and finally on February 8th, 1517, they sailed away, "having commended ourselves to God our Lord and to the Virgin St. Mary, our Lady, His blessed mother." (6)

They sailed westwards—"towards our luck," says Bernal Díaz—"in the direction where the sun sets, knowing nothing about banks, nor currents, nor the winds which usually hold sway over those parts," and led by a pilot Antón de Alaminos, who, though one of the early companions of Colón, seems to have been more cantankerous and quarrelsome than skilful. But after a dangerous storm which shook them for two days and two nights, and an otherwise uneventful voyage of yet another nineteen days, they saw not only land but, about two leagues inland, a town of such size and solidity as no one had ever seen yet in the new world. The delighted Spaniards immediately gave it as a name the Great Cairo. (7)

Why Cairo? There is no mystery about it. The people who lived in that town were not Christians; people who are not Christians are infidels; infidels are "Moors"; and Cairo is a big "Moorish" town; anyhow, it was near enough for devout soldiers of a race which had waged war for eight centuries against the Moors and who often referred to the pagan temples of the new world as "mosques."

The Great Cairo was a small town—possibly a big village—close to Cape Catoche, in the Peninsula of Yucatán. The natives surrounded the three Spanish ships with their canoes, and about thirty were received on board and presented with glass beads; their chief seemed very anxious that the Spaniards should visit his "town" in their canoes; the Spaniards hesitated, yet in the end decided to land, though in their own boats, and with fifteen bows and ten muskets, they walked on, surrounded by Indians; suddenly the cacique began to shout, and swarms of armed Indians came forth from the woods and attacked the Spaniards, wounding fifteen of them; a battle ensued in which the Spaniards were saved by the moral effect of gunpowder. They went on, and came upon "a small square, in which there were three stone-houses, which were *cues* and temples where they had many earthen idols, with faces some like devils, some like women and some like other bad figures." The Spaniards were very much elated to have discovered such a land; and while they fought, the priest of the expedition bagged the idols and all the gold which he could find and took it on board. The gold was not of good quality, but the fight had yielded something better than gold—two Indians, who were christened Julian and Melchior, both cross-eyed, as if nature had predestined them to look both ways, for they were to be the first interpreters between their nation and their nation's conquerors.

Alaminos was certain that Yucatán was an island. "Islands," by the way, seem to have been the King Charles' head of the navigators of those days. But the fleet was then less busy with geography than with dear life, for they had no water owing to some defect in their barrels, for "as our fleet was one of poor men, we had had no money to buy good barrels." They tried several times to land and dig for water but several times thought it wiser to withdraw, being heavily outnumbered, till at last they had to face this battle which they had sought to avoid; they had landed to refill their barrels, when, after a night of doubt and ominous signs, they were attacked at dawn, at such close quarters, that at the outset eighty of them were wounded. It was for the most part a hand-to-hand fight. Hernández de Córdoba was wounded ten times and went on fighting though "bleeding freely in many places"; fifty soldiers were killed; most of them wounded two or three times, including Bernal Díaz who had felt an arrow, as he puts it, "pass into the hollow of my body"; two had been carried away alive, to be sacrificed to the god of war. In this grave plight, they "decided with stout hearts to break through the native battalions" and take to their boats, which they did, and so, some in the boats, some hanging from them, some swimming, they found themselves exhausted on board their three ships. Thirst and those wounds—many of them in the throat—were the torment of the small band of conquered conquerors; the captain was much weakened by both. It was thought best to return home; but the pilots thought it safer to return by way of Florida, where Alaminos had gone with Ponce de León; and while the Indians of Florida proved no less dangerous and accounted for yet another wound of the already much perforated Bernal Díaz, the fleet was able to secure provisions of water, and thus refloated, not without the usual dangers and sufferings of seafaring folk in those days, returned to Habana, if not richer in wealth, richer no doubt in fame and even more in hopes and in delusions.

Hernández de Córdoba died of his wounds in Sancti Spiritus whither he went straight from Puerto de Carenas (as Habana was then named); but when the ships arrived in Santiago and reported to the Governor and showed their idols and their gold, albeit not very fine, "there was a great fame about it." (8)

* * *

Diego Velázquez was not long in preparing another expedition to establish his prior right as the discoverer and settler of the new lands. He added two ships of his own to the two left available by the first adventure, and provided also, says Bernal Díaz contemptuously, "a certain amount of cheap merchandise for bartering, such as beads and other odds and ends like vegetables"; the bulk of the food, cassava bread and bacon, was provided for each ship by the captain; finally every one of the two hundred and forty soldiers who volunteered, lured by the news of "houses of masonry" and of gold, provided also food, arms and ammunition out of his own pocket. Here again, we perceive the thoroughly democratic character of the enterprise, so typical of all Spanish life; and as a final touch of Spanish colour, here is a lively detail from Oviedo: "the mainstay of their barter-stock was very good wine of Guadalcanal, for it was known from the first voyage of Hernández that the Indians of that land are fond of it and drink it willingly; nor do I mean those of that land only, because all Indians from most of these Indies, as soon as they have tasted it, desire it more than anything which the Christians can give them, and drink it till they fall backwards if they are given enough." (9)

The three captains were to be prominent figures in the conquest. The chief of them was Pedro de Alvarado. "He was then about thirty-four; well proportioned; and he had a very merry face and countenance and in his glance was very loving, and because he was so handsome the Mexican Indians nicknamed him Tonatio, which means 'the Sun'; he was very agile and a good horseman; and above all very liberal and of a good conversation; and in his dress he was most courtly and fond of rich and expensive clothes; he wore a thin gold chain round his neck with a jewel, and a ring with a good diamond"; the second captain was Francisco de Montejo, "somewhat middle-sized, and his face merry, and he was fond of rejoicings and a businessman, and a good horseman; when he came over [to Mexico] he might have been about thirty-five: and he was liberal and he spent more than his income warranted"; the third, Alonso Dávila, "was of a good body and a merry face, and his talk was expressive, very clear and in good reason, and he was very bold and courageous; he might be thirty-four when he came over, and he had another quality, that he was liberal with his companions, but he was haughty and fond of commanding others and not to be commanded and somewhat envious and he was proud and turbulent." Each of these three men, so vividly painted by Bernal Díaz, was in command of one of the four ships. (10) The fourth was under the direct command of the captain general of the expedition, a kinsman of Velázquez named Juan de Grijalva.

Las Casas seems to have had a liking for this particular conquistador, a somewhat wistful, good-natured, and ineffective though very brave and attractive figure. "He was a handsome young man" and dressed richly; as for his moral qualities, "he was of such a natural condition that in point of obedience and even of humility and of other qualities, he would not have made a bad monk. I knew him well and spoke often to him and knew he was bent on virtue, obedience and a good way of living." (11)

The final arrangements were concluded in Santiago de Cuba, then the capital of the island, and having blessed the banners, and (after reconciling themselves with one another) heard a Holy Ghost

D

mass, the troops marched down to the ships to the sound of pipes and drums. Fat Velázquez had marched down with them—no small sacrifice on his part—and on the waterfront, having embraced the four captains, spoke to them words as high-sounding in their form as they were shrewd in their substance. "Gentlemen and my friends, servants and connexions," he began,. extending over them a wide mantle of patronage and ownership. "You may have gathered before now that my chief aim and motive, in spending my capital in such enterprises as this, has been the service of God and of my natural King, who will (both) be well served if with our industry new lands and peoples are discovered, so that with our good example and doctrine, once brought over to our holy faith, they may come to be of the herd and flock of the elected. The means towards this end are: that every man should do his duty, regardless of any interest at the time; for God, for whose sake we launch out on this important and difficult task, is sure to favour you in such a manner that the least He will give you will be temporal wealth." Some of the soldiers, "gentlemen and persons of quality" who heard this oration may have grinned and exchanged glances of intelligence and irony, particularly those who knew that the instructions which Velázquez had given Grijalva were: "to acquire by barter as much gold and silver as possible and if he saw that a settlement was advisable or dared to settle, to do so, otherwise to return to Cuba." (12)

Thus comforted with the Governor's words, the fleet left Santiago on January 25th, "not without tears from those who remained and from those who said farewell with much noise of music and shots from the ships," sailing round the northern coast to Matanzas, which was then a more important centre than Habana and where they loaded more bread and pork; then on to San Antón, the westernmost point of the island, where, "after they all had confessed, they cut their hair short, the first time the Spaniards did so in the Indies, for till then they prided themselves on their long hair, and they did so because they thought that long hair would be in their way in battle." (13)

On May 1st they sailed away. Within three days, they saw the island of Cozumel, off the east coast of Yucatán. Juan de Grijalva and his three captains went ashore, and as the boats touched land the Captain General, bidding the others wait, landed alone, knelt on the new-discovered earth and "made a brief and secret prayer to the Lord," after which, with all legal solemnity, and the Castillian banners well displayed, he took possession of "the island and of its annexes and lands and seas and all the rest that belonged or might belong to it in the name and on behalf of the Queen Doña Juana and her son Don Carlos." (14)

Indians, they saw none. All had fled; and though, here and there, a canoe approached, parleyed and disappeared, Grijalva seems to have been unable or unwilling to come to any definite relation— either peaceful or otherwise—with the natives of Cozumel, which he soon left behind in his desire to explore Yucatán.

They came within sight of it on Friday the 7th, very much elated to see clusters of houses made of masonry and "a town or pueblo so big that even the city of Seville could not be better nor bigger; and one could see a very big tower in it." (15) But Grijalva did not allow the excitement of his companions to disturb his cautious tactics, and he returned to Cozumel for water, of which he had run short. He had, no doubt, in mind the disastrous experience of his predecessor Hernández de Córdoba, and he observed disquieting signs of enmity and preparedness in the Indians, particularly the recurrence of fires on prominent points of the coast. Grijalva was beginning to feel his troops restive and disaffected. He had given them strict instructions on the way they were to deal with the Indians, the gist of these being that he was to control and direct all negotiations of every kind, and that the army was to maintain a severe discipline— all most abhorrent notions for his adventurous and equalitarian troops; his pilot Alaminos had claimed the right not to be interfered with in the discharge of his expert duties, a claim which Grijalva seems to have granted rather meekly. On the morning of Tuesday May 11th, the Captain General missed one of his caravels; he feared first that she might have run aground; but, having come close to her in his own ship's boat, he found that she had stayed to pick up a Christian who had been running along the coast for two leagues in sight of the fleet; the "Christian" turned out to be a Jamaican Indian young woman—"of good looks," notes Bernal Díaz sixty years after the event, with the memories of his early twenties still fresh in his evergreen soul. She told them she preferred the Christians to the Indians of Yucatán, where she had stayed with other Jamaican

natives, who had perished. This episode made Grijalva more cautious, particularly as she told him that the men of Yucatán had all
vanished out of sight. But, though cautious, he was no coward; and
on seeing a tower white against the sky he conceived the idea of saying mass in that pagan temple. They landed, and Grijalva marched
his men to the temple; but the priest, though duly forewarned, was
not ready, having forgotten to bring over his ornaments from the ship;
and Grijalva "scolded him with more temper than was reasonable,
addressing him with some harsh words which were repelled and condemned by all the men." There was a good well close by, and Grijalva decided to camp round the well. The Indians then came forward
and repeatedly requested the Spaniards to leave; Grijalva demurred,
parleyed, spoke of friendship and peace, but did not embark. At
last the patience of the natives was exhausted, and they expressed it in
their own way, by lighting a brazier of odorous gums in front of the
camp, and explaining that as soon as that fire had gone out they
would attack the intruders. The intruders were not to be outdone
in point of symbolism and solemnity: Grijalva summoned his fleet
notary and officially demanded of the Indians the right to wait in
peace till the whole fleet had provisioned its full complement of water,
"a thing which no nation could refuse another nation when no enmity
pre-existed." But the brazier had gone out and the Indians show-
ered arrows on the camp; a battle was inevitable. It was bloody for
both sides: the Spaniards lost seven killed and sixty wounded; as for
the Captain, he was wounded several times, but particularly, owing
to his harsh words to the priest, "it seems that God allowed that,
fighting with the Indians, he should be hit on the mouth with an
arrow which knocked out three of his teeth, and had he not had his
mouth shut at the time, as he himself confessed, the arrow would have
run through his mouth." What would have happened if he had not
merely opened his mouth unintentionally, but opened it in order to
utter more harsh words to that priest, bears no thinking. But, of
course, Grijalva could take a hint, and so "having realised that it was
all due to his sinful action, since he had offended the priest publicly,
so, publicly, giving an example of a man who repents, he asked his
forgiveness." (16) This self-denial made him recover enough sympathy from his followers for them to suggest to him that, since he
was so badly wounded, he should withdraw to the ship with those who

were dangerously wounded, while the able-bodied ones should enter the Indian town and do as much harm as possible; but Grijalva gratefully rejected this fair offer, declaring that "he had not come to avenge injuries nor to fight against the Indians, but to discover that land and plant the Catholic faith in it." This said, he officially took possession of the land in the presence of his overworked notary, and, having embarked all his troops, he left it—for a stronger man.

He was leading his fleet round the northern and western coast of Yucatán, still uncertain as to whether it was an island or not; the bay known to this day as Puerto de Términos still records the error of Alaminos the pilot, who insisted that Yucatán was an island which ended precisely there. Yet the fleet went on, and Yucatán, despite Alaminos, went on also; and they discovered Tabasco, where they heard the noise made by busy wood cutters, and at once knew that fortresses and palisades were being prepared to resist them, should they venture to land. (17) Grijalva landed all the same, closely watched by a strong native force in their canoes, with flags and drums. But the Spanish chief was genuinely desirous to avoid bloodshed, and he gradually attracted a number of native warriors by showing them green beads and small mirrors, not to speak of "blue diamonds," and when he had got together an audience worth the trouble, he explained to them, through his two "tongues" Julianillo and Melchiorejo (the Indians caught by Hernández de Córdoba) such obvious things as that he and his men "came from far-off lands and were vassals of a great emperor who called himself Don Carlos, who had many great lords and caciques as his vassals and that they [the Indians] should take him as their Lord and they would do very well under him": a message strange enough in itself but no doubt stranger still in the form in which, transmitted through the "tongues," it must have reached the bewildered natives. Yet the gist of it seems to have been conveyed to the natives clearly enough by the strangers' acts if not by their words, for, having declared that they already had a lord and needed none, they made it known to the strangers that they were ready to fight if they were not left in peace. There was peace and an exchange of mutual offerings, and the natives intimated to the Spaniards that though they were poor in gold, there was more of it in Culúa, by which they meant Mexico. So, Grijalva made up his mind to sail away "because the ships were in much danger owing to the north wind, and also to come closer to the places where they said there was gold." (18)

They were now in the month of June, in thé tropics, and one morning, as they had entered a wide bay to explore it, their astonished eyes beheld the eternal snows on the heights of Mexico. They knew by that unmistakable sign that they had struck a spacious country. Presently, however, a fresh sign, this time not of spaciousness but of power and wealth, came to add to their wonder and joy; at the mouth of a river, a fleet of canoes was awaiting them, crowded with Indians, who showed flags made of white cotton wraps hanging from long poles. The captain sent a strong force under Francisco de Montejo, who was courteously and peacefully received. Grijalva then landed, was no less well received, treated to excellent food and to almost religious ceremonies, and given as much gold as could be found. Yet he left again, unable to see the real import of what was happening: through all these salaams, Moteçuçuma's envoys were watching and studying him in order to report to their master on the strength and purpose of the newcomers.

They had no doubt instructions to assume that the bearded white men were the vanguard of Quetzalcoatl; it is difficult to interpret otherwise this strange interlude of peace, good grace and humble offerings on the part of the natives in such contrast with the policy of steady and constant defiance and armed resistance to the whites followed before and after. When Grijalva landed, says his chaplain, "the Indians brought green branches for him to sit on, and so all, including the captain, sat down; they gave him some reeds with perfumes similar to storax and benzoin and then some food, much ground maize [. . .] and cakes and hen pies very well made"; now—the irony of it!—this foreign god, offered religious food, abstains because of his own religion—"and as it was Friday, they were not eaten," a quaint case of two worships at cross purposes. The chaplain goes on to say: "They brought many cotton wraps very well painted with various colours, and we were here ten days, during which the Indians were to be seen before dawn on the shore making branch bowers so that we should be in the shade; and if we did not come soon they were offended, for they felt very friendly to us and they embraced us and made up to us most eagerly [. . .] The cacique

presented to our Captain a youth of about twenty-two, and he would
not have him [. . .] When we were leaving, the Indians embraced
us and wept because we left; and they brought an Indian girl to the
Captain, so well dressed that, had she been clad in brocade, she
would not have been as sumptuous." (19) Those cotton wraps very
well painted with various colours were the books and records of the
Mexicans. In them, the envoys of Moteçuçuma had no doubt
recorded events of Mexican life, possibly the particular traditions
and prophecies referring to Quetzalcoatl, for they had every right to
think that, if those white, bearded men were his men, they were sure
to recognise his story. The reaction was pitiful. "The captain said
that all we wanted was gold." (20) This would appear to the Mexicans a rather easy-going god, used as they were to offering panting
hearts to their deities; and, to be sure, they tried to gather as much
gold as possible for the white gods, even though these gods had been
unable to make head or tail of their hieroglyphs. But the situation
could no doubt have been turned to a better account had Grijalva
possessed a shrewder way with men.

Grijalva had missed his tide. His bread was rotting; his men
were tired or wounded and, in any case, not numerous enough to
settle in what by then he was sure was the mainland; there was
enough gold on board to impress the Governor. So, he decided to send
Alvarado to Velázquez for help. This may well have been a compromise on his part with those who wanted to return altogether, for,
despite Gómara's aspersions, we have Bernal Díaz' positive testimony
in favour of Grijalva, of whom he says that "he always proved a
spirit worthy of a brave captain"; and moreover, after Alvarado's
departure, he sailed on along the coast, till Alaminos refused to pilot
him further and both Dávila and Montejo opposed him in his desire
to settle in the land. The fact is that there was no longer any spirit
in the adventure. True, the Spaniards had of late seen some gruesome
sights; young boys still panting on the threshold of death, their
breasts opened, their hearts plucked out as an offering to the god of
war; bones, corpses, blood, all the sinister apparatus of the Mexican
worship which filled their souls—none too tender—with pity and
horror. But, as events were soon to show, they were not the men to
stand back for fear of such dreadful sights and of all they implied
in the nation which they had set their hearts to conquer. What made

them fail then was the lack of the peculiar quality of leadership in their leader.

The land was still to lure them by two further portents: the Indians of Coatzacoalco and near-by districts used to carry about some very showy and shiny golden hatchets; the Spaniards bartered for over six hundred of them, joyful in the thought that, though they were not very fine, they were heavy; let alone the fact that if it came to using gold for making hatchets, the land was sure to be fabulously wealthy. The other sign was even more definite: "This day, late in the evening, we saw a very great miracle, and it was that a star appeared over our ship after sunset and moved away throwing out rays of light till it set on that big village or *pueblo,* and it left a track in the air which lasted for three long hours; and we saw moreover other clear signs whereby we realised that God wanted us to settle in that land for His service." (21) Yet none of these signs were of any avail. Whether, as Las Casas would have it, because he had orders not to "settle," or because he was unable to withstand the opposition of Dávila and Montejo, as Bernal Díaz says, Grijalva did not pursue the advantage he had thus far acquired, and he returned to Cuba in that twilight which covers men who will neither succeed nor fail. "He lacked good fortune to become the lord of that land." (22)

PART II

CORTÉS CONCEIVES THE CONQUEST

CHAPTER SEVEN

Cortés Rises to Leadership

WHILE GRIJALVA came and went, toying with his own fate, as is the way of most men, Velázquez worried over the absent fleet more than a fat man could bear, for worry feels at home only in men of a lean body who can carry it as straight as a pole and not spill it this way and that. In the end, he was unable to worry on and do nothing, for he was most liberal with other people's exertions, and so he decided to send a caravel to enquire into the whereabouts and doings of his missing Captain General. As a captain of this second expedition, he appointed one Cristóbal de Olid, who was to play a prominent part in the conquest, and whom Bernal Díaz thought worthy of a portrait by his own masterly pen: "Had he been as wise and prudent as he was spirited and courageous in his person, whether on foot or on horseback, he would have been an outstanding man; but he was not fit to command but only to be commanded, and he was about thirty-six, born close to Baeza or Linares, and as for his presence and size he was of a good body, very thick-set and a big back, a good waist; he was somewhat fair-haired and had a handsome presence in his face and he had his lower lip kind of slit as it were with a crack. In his talk he spoke with a somewhat thick and frightening voice, and he was of a good conversation and had other good qualities (such as) being liberal, for he had nothing of his own which he did not give away." (1)

The Governor instructed this good soldier to follow the course of Hernández de Córdoba until he found Grijalva; but the wind would have none of it, and when off the coast of Yucatán the caravel, in a deadly fight with it, had to cut her cables and leave her anchors at the bottom of the sea, Olid thought best to return to Cuba and to leave Grijalva to his fate. For the third time, a captain had tried his fortune at Mexico and had failed. (2)

But at this juncture Pedro de Alvarado arrived in Santiago Bay with the wounded, indeed, but also with the gold, much of it, though not very fine; and as it was not just in bars which can be tested, but in jewels, some of them of a fine workmanship, it astonished the colony and gave an added impetus to the wings of fame which had already proclaimed the "Island" of Yucatán as the "Rich Island." Velázquez showed his gratification in public tournaments, including reed-spear tournaments; but while his people indulged in pleasure he did not neglect business. It was imperative to forestall any attempt on the part of some gentleman influential at court "to steal the blessings from him." The precaution was by no means superfluous. The young King of Spain, just arrived in his dominions from his native Flanders, unable to speak Spanish, inexperienced and well-meaning, was liberally handing round the plums of State and Church to a host of Flemish friends, and had given the measure of his truly insensate ignorance of Spain by giving the venerable (and wealthy) see of Toledo, just fallen vacant on the death of the great Cisneros, to a youth of nineteen, a nephew of his Flemish chancellor. So if Toledo, why not Yucatán? And sure enough, there was an eager Flemish potentate who, on the ground of being the Admiral of Flanders, obtained from King Charles the island of Yucatán which the petulant young King gave him "as if he gave him a meadow to put his cattle on." Presently the said Admiral, having first taken the advice of Las Casas at lunch ("for such is the manner and habit of the Flemish when they wish to negotiate"), brought over five ships from Flanders to Sanlúcar loaded with peasants wherewith to people Yucatán; they ultimately died in Spain or returned ruined, because Don Diego Colón, duly warned by Las Casas, upheld his rights and insisted on allowing no other Admiral but his father's son to settle or ruin men in the Indies. (3)

Knowing all this to have happened or to be possible, Velázquez sent his chaplain Benito Martín as emissary to King Charles' court, then in Barcelona. The young King had just been elected Emperor of Germany. He had had to bleed his subjects and to run into debt in order to buy his seven Electors. The news of those outlandish discoveries must have struck him as somewhat irrelevant, but when the priest from overseas began to produce piece after piece of the gold which Alvarado had brought over to Cuba, his heart must have beat quicker, for he was in dire need of wealth, being the mightiest and neediest man in the world. The priest seized his opportunity and obtained the title of Adelantado for his chief and of Abbot of the "Rich Island" for himself. (4)

Velázquez was therefore relentlessly pursuing his policy of shaking off the authority of the Admiral Don Diego Colón, with regard both to his appointment in Cuba and to his activities as the discoverer of Yucatán. But even as he was obtaining these victories over the Admiral, another overseas governor and court-navigator was stealing a march on him. Francisco de Garay, Governor of Jamaica, who had been one of the first companions of Colón, under the pretext of an exploring expedition which he had sent to Pánuco, on the tracks of Grijalva, asked and obtained from the distracted King-Emperor the title of Adelantado of those lands—as vaguely described as known—and Charles V granted it in the same year, 1519, while still in Barcelona. Thus were the seeds being sown of the trouble which was to make Cortés' task even more difficult and his ultimate success more astonishing. (5)

Grijalva meanwhile did not return, nor did Olid, and Velázquez began to worry again. Events here are somewhat confused, partly owing to Bernal Díaz' lapses of memory, partly, no doubt, because documents and statements conceal as much truth as they convey. Bernal Díaz says that Velázquez "after Juan de Grijalva's return to Cuba, and seeing that the lands were wealthy, ordered a good fleet to be sent, much bigger than the previous one." But the instructions given by the Governor to the Captain General of that fleet—no other than Hernán Cortés in person—prove him wrong. The text of these instructions shows beyond dispute that Velázquez organised this expedition before the return of either Grijalva or Olid and, ostensibly at any rate, to rescue them from any danger into which they might have strayed. Point 15 of these instructions bids Cortés enquire about Juan de Grijalva's fleet and Cristóbal de Olid's caravel. But this document must be read with the utmost caution, and carefully set in its psychological context. It is, in my opinion, a diplomatic and plausible paper, which covers more than it says, as shown by the

fact that the fleet for which it was drafted, though ostensibly organised to find Grijalva and rescue him, sailed after Grijalva's arrival,
strengthened by four of Grijalva's own ships and most of his men,
including our invaluable Bernal Díaz. (6)

Unless this document is considered as a mere screen, this fact,
as well as a number of other features, of the historic expedition,
remains inexplicable. There is, let it be said in passing, one telling
and picturesque detail in it sufficient to betray the grain of salt with
which it was dictated by Velázquez to his Notary Escalante: the
second injunction which Cortés, the gallant Cortés, the lady-killer
Cortés, received from Velázquez—the godfather of his natural
daughter—is to the following effect: "In order that you máy the
better serve the Lord on this voyage, you shall not tolerate any public
sin, nor persons publicly living in concubinage; nor that any of the
Spanish Christians in your company have carnal intercourse with
any woman outside our faith, for it is a sin most hateful to God, and
the laws, divine and human, forbid it, and you shall act with the
utmost severity against whosoever may commit such sin or crime
and you shall punish it according to the laws." (7) Admirably self-
controlled as he was, Cortés must have found it difficult to keep a
straight face at this.

The avowed aims of the expedition were: to find Grijalva and
Olid; to find six Christian captives who were vaguely believed to
have remained in the hands of some natives somewhere, probably as
an epilogue of Nicuesa's disaster; to explore the country and learn
all that could be known about the inhabitants, their features, animals,
plants and mineral wealth, not forgetting gold; to enquire into the
quality of the people, "for it is said that there are persons with big
and wide ears and others with dog-faces, and also to find out where
dwell the Amazons who, as these Indians going with you say, are
near there"; to find out all that pertained to the religion of the land;
and, of course, to barter for gold and silver. What about "settling"?
The matter has been one of the many in which partisans of Velázquez
and partisans of Cortés have argued at length. But here again the
document is obscure, no doubt deliberately. There is no passage in
it which may be read as a definite order either to settle or not to settle
in the lands to which Cortés is being sent. Cortés is to take possession
of all the island discovered, in the presence of his notary and of many

witnesses and with the utmost solemnity; he is to be most cautious
and watchful whenever he accepts invitations to land; and not to
allow the natives to mix with the Spaniards; and he is to induce the
natives to accept the Christian faith and to become vassals of the
Crown of Spain. It is easy to see that these instructions allowed
Cortés to consider himself either limited to exploration and barter
or permitted to land and "settle," according to whichever interpretation suited him. Furthermore, there was a general clause allowing
Cortés to take practically any decision he wished "in the best service
of God our Lord and of their Highnesses," in accordance with his
instructions, if possible, and with the advice of "some prudent and
wise persons who go with you and in whom you put trust and confidence." (8)

The vagueness of this document, its shiftiness in fact, suggests
that it was drafted by several pens with several intentions, not all
the same nor in harmony with one another. First, there was
Velázquez: he had every reason to fear that Grijalva and Olid were
stealing a march on him and trying to keep the conquest for themselves. "The thief thinks every man a thief," says a Spanish proverb,
and Velázquez knew how it could be done, since he had himself
applied this method for getting rid of the authority of Don Diego
Colón. His first thought in deciding to send this new fleet must, no
doubt, have been to see that neither Grijalva nor Olid passed him
over. Then there was Don Diego himself. He had no lack of friends
in Cuba, in Española or at Court. Therefore it was necessary to
present things in such a way that his privileges were not outwardly
and blatantly invaded. Don Diego was then in Spain, and Española,
as well as "the Indies" in general, was governed by a Committee of
three Jeromite friars, residing in Santo Domingo. (9) Diego
Velázquez applied to them for permission to explore the land and to
barter in it, but nothing more. (10) That, however, does not mean
that Velázquez was not thinking of settling there at all, as shown by
Bernal Díaz, who says that though his instructions did not mention
settling, his propaganda did; but as shown better still in the letter
which Velázquez wrote on November 17th, 1519, to Rodrigo de
Figueroa, then acting Governor of Española and all "the Indies,"
complaining of Cortés' insubordination, in which he says, "for I
intended to bring over all those peoples to the knowledge of our holy

faith, and to put them under the royal Crown with the least possible detriment and injury to them." (11) This is, therefore, a definite avowal of double-dealing or, at any rate, of concealed aims on the part of Velázquez. But why conceal in the paper what was not only meant but published as well, at any rate within the island? The answer is simple: Velázquez' legal title to settle in Yucatán was not good, not until it was officially granted in Barcelona towards the beginning of the summer of 1519; while, on the other hand, nothing short of a definite plan for settling would have attracted enough soldiers and young captains whose ambition was not to be satisfied with just one more bartering expedition, and required new lands in which to win fame and wealth.

Then, there was Cortés. It is a curious fact that, to my knowledge, none of his biographers or critics has ever raised this point: why had he remained passive all these years, while Hernández de Córdoba and Grijalva tried their hand and failed where he was to succeed? The amount of things that are tacitly taken for granted in the lives of great men is one of the strange features of history. Cortés was thirty-three. He was strong, prosperous, healthy, influential, Alcalde of Santiago, a prominent figure in the Island. His vigour, enterprise, imagination, winning ways, power of leadership, no one can doubt. How are we to believe that he felt all these qualities suddenly born in him on the day Velázquez gave him the command of the fleet? Abstention in a man like Cortés is but another form of action, as positive, as deliberate, as action itself. Men of his age, captains such as Alvarado, Olid, Dávila, Montejo, who were to serve under him but two years later, were boarding the adventurous caravels which sailed away towards Yucatán. Are we to believe that he remained behind out of sheer indolence or absent-mindedness, unable to realise what was going on under his eyes? He had intended in his youth to accompany Hojeda and Nicuesa; why should he not have tried now to join Hernández de Córdoba, Grijalva or Olid? The answer to these questions flows from the facts: no man in Spanish history ever possessed a steadier purpose, a longer glance than Cortés. The conquest of Yucatán must have been the quiet goal of his ambition ever since the return of the first expedition, and his passive refusal to share in either Grijalva's or Olid's voyages goes far to show that he preferred to hold himself untouched by events till his hour had struck.

He was bound to know what kind of men were these leaders who were being sent over to the Rich Island—Hernández de Córdoba, Grijalva, Olid and the rest. As good a judge of men as ever was, living as he did in the highest official circles of what was after all but a small community in which everybody knew everybody else, he was sure to have a definite opinion as to the powers and gifts of all the men available for the conquest. The natural view, therefore, is that he deliberately remained in the background, sparing his energy, influence and friends for the moment when these pioneers would have prepared the ground for him by their failure in a task which he was the only man big enough to undertake.

To be sure no one was then in a position to gauge the gigantic difficulty of that task; but, as events were to show, there was in Cortés such a store of latent energy, such a magazine of will power, that even he may have felt somewhat impatient at the return of Olid, defeated by the sea, and of Grijalva, defeated by his own lack of persistence. Grijalva's return, moreover, must have impressed him deeply in more ways than one. To begin with, it gave rise to much merriment in the island because the famous hatchets turned out to be made of humble copper, "and there was much laughter and talk over the hoax and the barter." (12) Now Cortés was not the kind of man to expose himself to such a risk, for his inward estimate of his own destiny and powers was high above mere barter for gold, as he was soon to show both in words and deeds. Bernal Díaz records how at the beginning of his voyage, during what was for him a phase of exploration but for most of his companions just another barter-for-gold adventure, his "Tongue," a Spaniard who knew the district, tried to induce him to fight his way into the country for gold "and Cortés answered laughingly that he had not come for such small things but to serve God and the King." (13) He was from the outset intent on conquest and settlement, and he can but have been strengthened in this design by the strange reception extended to Grijalva by Velázquez; for, while pleased at some of the results—after all, along with the hatchets, there were about twenty thousand pesos of gold— and even more at the prospects, the Governor reproached Grijalva for having come back without "settling," that is for having remained faithful to his instructions or even (if we follow Las Casas' version of these instructions) for not having broken them! (14) This fact is well established and should be given its due weight when Cortés' own decisions in similar circumstances come to be considered. The strange behaviour of Velázquez towards Grijalva, at this crucial stage when Cortés' expedition was being organised, must have released active psychological forces in Cortés and in his men, contributing to loosen their ties of duty and of discipline towards the Governor of Cuba.

* * *

All these factors should be borne in mind in their bearing both on Velázquez' instructions to Cortés and on the knot of contradictory statements recorded on the financial side of the expedition. Prescott somewhat naively observes that the "instruction" "is often referred to by writers who never saw it, as the Agreement between Cortés and Velázquez. It is, in fact, really the instructions given by this latter to his officer who was no party to it." (15) He was a great scholar, too pure and undefiled by affairs to know that most people who receive instructions manage to draft part if not most of them. Cortés could have been a far less shrewd and cunning handler of men than he was and yet not have cared to set out on so important a mission without having some say in the charter on which his power was to be based. It is safe to assume that both what the instructions say and what they do not say, both what they set down clearly and what they nebulously suggest, had been carefully pondered over by the man to whom they mattered most—a man moreover who was as skilful with his pen as with his sword.

Cortés was, of course, on the best of terms with Velázquez' secretarial staff. In fact, one of the most striking features of this singular man is that he was on the best of terms with everybody, so that, though, eaglelike, he could fall upon his prey and overpower it, he preferred to coil himself like a crafty serpent round friend or foe. The masterpiece of these tactics was his successful manœuvre to be appointed leader of the Mexican fleet by this same Velázquez who knew his turbulent and ambitious nature, at the very moment when the mistrustful Governor had turned down another candidate for fear that he might do precisely what Cortés was to do later: "There were," says Bernal Díaz, "many debates and cross-purposes because some gentleman said that our Captain should be one Vasco Porcalla, a relative of the Count of Feria, and Diego Velázquez feared that he would revolt with the fleet, for he was bold." (16)

This masterpiece of court-intrigue was achieved through Cortés' ability in winning over to his side the two chief officials in the Governor's Chancery: the secretary, Andrés de Duero, "as tall as an elbow, but wise and very silent, and he wrote well"; and the accountant, Amador de Lares, "a most astute man and who had spent twenty-two years, I heard him say, in Italy and had been butler to the Great Captain, which shows he was not slow-witted, when the Great Captain gave him such a post when he was small even in body and could neither read nor write, yet his wisdom and cunning out-weighed his shortcomings." Las Casas who pens this portrait adds a delightful sidelight on international psychology: watching the astute accountant come and go, he himself used to say to Velázquez: "Sir, beware of twenty-two years of Italy." (17)

There is ample evidence to show that Cortés had entered into some sort of secret pact with the secretary and the accountant; Bernal Díaz defines it most neatly: "The two confidants of Diego Velázquez were to see that Hernando Cortés was appointed Captain General of all the fleet and the three were to divide the share of Cortés in gold, silver and jewels." Things can hardly have been as simple as that; Bernal Díaz, though a close observer and shrewd within his lights, was not a match for Cortés, and now and then, to use a telling Spanish phrase, Cortés span thinner than Díaz could see; this seems to be one of such cases, for the honest soldier-chronicler goes on to explain that "secretly Velázquez was sending [Cortés] to barter and not to settle"; now whatever we may think of Velázquez' intentions—far from clear at that—they mattered less than those of Cortés himself, and these were so ambitious that the idea of dividing the spoils with Duero and Amador de Lares cannot even have occurred to him; he was moreover quite able to buy them over to his cause without in any way binding himself beforehand to such an extent.

On whatever basis it was concluded, the pact existed and bore fruit; Cortés was elected to command the expedition, and Bernal

Díaz, confirming the conclusions which our own reading of the instructions had led us to anticipate, adds: "The Secretary Andrés de Duero drafted the Instructions, as the proverbial saying goes 'in very good ink' and just as Cortés wished them." (18)

Mere cleverness and astuteness, however, even if applied with the balm of human sympathy, in which Cortés was rich, could not account for so much success. There was another important feature, possibly the chief factor in men's fortunes, the readiness to take risks in the gamble of life, a generous hand with the grain for seed sown liberally in the hope of the harvest. Cortés was not as wealthy as Velázquez, but, whatever the actual figures may turn out to be if and when they are known, he was certainly more liberal and generous in expenditure and provision than his covetous and sedentary chief. This is the main impression to be gathered from the writings and documents of the period. Velázquez' agent Benito Martín, in a petition to the King-Emperor against Cortés, says that the seven ships had been sent "entirely at his [the Governor's] expense"; yet Velázquez himself, in his letter to Rodrigo de Figueroa, does not go beyond cleverly suggesting this, "after having sent it [the fleet] very abundant and provided with all that was necessary"; and in the rest of the letter, a long complaint against the rebel, he puts forward no claim on account of his own financial loss. This fact should suffice to drive out of court those writers who, like Las Casas, in his bitterness against Cortés, refuse to take the reasonable view: Velázquez was a fairly well-meaning, easy-going, good-natured governor; but he was not averse to getting results out of other people's exertions and purses. Indolent and, if not precisely avaricious, at least slow in spending as he was slow in moving, he let eager Cortés take the initiative both in action and in expenditure. Cortés in his turn was quick to realise that, in the circumstances, a good financial stake in the fleet was bound to strengthen his position as Captain General of it. He spent liberally and borrowed boldly. (19)

*　　*　　*

Like all men who see deep, he was fully alive to the value of surfaces and appearances. "He began," says Bernal Díaz, "to polish and adorn his person, much more than he used to, and he donned a plumed hat, with a gold medal and chain, and a coat of

velvet sown all over with gold knots." So much for the chief. Now
for the banner: "He ordered two standards or banners to be made,
embroidered in gold, with the royal arms and a cross on each side,
with a scroll which read 'Brothers and companions, let us follow the
sign of the Cross with true faith and in it we shall conquer.' " Then,
the hope of gain: no restraint, no dissimulation about the object of
the expedition; the crier promised a share of "gold, silver and any
wealth which there might be," as well as Indians in trust, to every
one who would enlist to "conquer and settle" in the newly discovered
lands. Note the shrewdness of this action: in thus forcing the issue
by making his secret public, he made Velázquez his accomplice;
either Velázquez agreed that Cortés had in fact authority to settle
in Mexico or, if he refused that authority, Cortés could accuse him
of double dealing with his men. The combination of the obscure and
elastic "Instruction" with this bold public recruiting "to conquer
and settle" gave Cortés a powerful weapon which he was to put to a
most effective use.

This very energy and efficiency of the brand-new Captain
General, his active search for arms of all kinds, his purchases of
food and barter-goods, his choice of distinguished companions, may
well have disquieted the indolent governor. Velázquez had formed
the habit of going down to the harbour to watch the progress of the
work on the fleet, followed like a petty king by a numerous court,
with Cortés on his right hand "to honour him." This petty king
had a petty fool, by name Cervantes, and one day, on their way to
the harbour, Cervantes began to put forth all kinds of jokes and
hints on Cortés and his designs: "Oh, Diego, Diego," he said in his
familiar way to the Governor, "what a Captain thou hast taken,
soon thou'lt be by him forsaken, for he comes from Medellín, out
thou goest and he comes in." Andrés de Duero was alarmed and
exposed the method in the fool's madness, saying, "Be quiet, you
drunkard, for we all know that all that mischief does not come from
you"; for, as Bernal Díaz explains, Cortés' enemies had bribed him
to speak as he had done; but, bribed or not, his words sank deep
into Velázquez' suspicious and uneasy heart. (20)

A group of his own kinsmen—Velázquez also by name—were the
leaders of the anti-Cortés faction, advised by an old man named
Juan Millán, "known as the astrologer, and it was even said that he

had a twig of madness." This group worked on the Governor's
mind and nursed the seed of suspicion sown in it by the fool (whom
they themselves had prompted); but Cortés knew all through his
two confederates Duero and Amador de Lares, though, as Las Casas
points out, "in order to realise the situation he needed hardly more
than glance at Diego Velázquez' countenance with his astute shrewdness and worldly wisdom." (21)

How did Cortés react? In a manner which was by no means
simple, impulsive, or unexpected; but on the contrary, subtle, complex, meditated and so deeply consonant with his steady character
that we shall see it recur again and again as an oft repeated *pattern*
of his style in action. He was suave in manner, strong in fact.
"Cortés never left the company of the Governor and showed himself
his great servant, and used to say to him that, God permitting, he
would make him most illustrious and wealthy in a short time"; (22)
but while he thus tried to allay the qualms of the suspicious Governor,
he forged ahead at full pace with his preparations, having made up
his mind to leave, not merely as soon as possible, but in an abrupt
and unexpected way. One night, he ordered all his men and captains
on board; and by a final stroke of that combination of foresight and
boldness which was typical of his character, he forced the man in
charge of the town meat supply, one Hernando Alfonso, to surrender
all his stock to him; which again suggests, as so often in Cortés'
life, some kind of secret acquiescence on the part of Alfonso, for, let
alone the fact that he would not lack means to warn the Governor
of such an extraordinary action, and the further fact that delivery
could be neither easy, quick, nor secret, he asked to be compensated
for the fine he would have to pay; whereupon Cortés gave him the
gold chain he was wearing round his neck. This done, Cortés gave
orders for the fleet to leave. It was dawn. The fat Governor rushed
to the port panting with emotion. Cortés came forward, to meet
the danger, wisely ready for any emergency, in a boat well provided
with muskets and bows (the artillery which Las Casas mentions
seems a touch of ecclesiastical imagination) and, note the two telling
touches, with "the soldiers he trusted most and his stick as Alcalde";
thus prepared, he came forward to within a bowshot from land.
"What, *cofather*!" asked the Governor. (They were "cofathers"

according to Spanish ways, since Velázquez was the godfather of
Cortés' daughter.) "Is that the way you leave, without saying farewell to me?" And Cortés answered in words true to his style and to
the occasion: "Sir, forgive me, but such things must be done rather
than thought." (23)

Velázquez was nonplussed and chose to bow before the inevitable.
We know too much about him to imagine that he receded for lack
of character. His attitude plainly shows that he felt weak before
his rebellious subordinate; possibly because he did not possess a
sufficient financial hold over the fleet. Boldness, moreover, and positive action always win the day, and the fleet must have felt on that
early morning of November 18th, 1518, that they had at last found
a real leader. (24)

* * *

Cortés had sailed away somewhat prematurely, without all the
men and all the provisions he wanted; but he wisely thought that
there were other harbours than Santiago in the island, and that the
farther he was from the capital the more powerful he would be. He
sailed to Trinidad, a harbour on the southern coast of Cuba, where
he lodged in the house of Juan de Grijalva, in front of which he
raised his banners, and he had his criers promise fame and wealth to
all who would join him. Trinidad brought him some of his most
famous captains, and particularly the four Alvarados, youthful
Sandoval, second to none but Cortés himself in quality of leadership, Juan Velázquez de León, a kinsman of the Governor who was
to play many a dramatic part in the conquest, Cristóbal de Olid, who
was to be his chief of staff and rebel against him and die of it, and
an illustrious nobleman, Alonso Hernández de Puertocarrero, who
was to be privy to his innermost thoughts and whom he always distinguished and sought to please. The brave and genial leader is here
seen at his best, conquering men and mastering things: "with tasty
words and offers, drawing to him persons of quality" and coming
forward with his usual generosity wherever there was need for it;
Puertocarrero had no horse; he bought his friend a mare, giving for
it one of the golden knots which he wore on his velvet coat; a man
Juan Sedeño turned up with a ship full of food which he was going

to sell at some gold mines farther on, and "after some talks he bought the ship on credit and persuaded Sedeño to join us. We had thus eleven ships and everything turned out prosperous for us." (25)

Cortés was Alcalde of Santiago. The Alcalde of Trinidad was one Francisco Verdugo, brother-in-law of Diego Velázquez. While Cortés was still in his city, Verdugo received letters from the Governor announcing that Cortés had been revoked, and that he was to be taken a prisoner and sent back to Santiago. In order to strengthen his position, Velázquez had also written to one Diego de Ordás, a man of his own household, whom he had sent as one of Cortés' captains to watch over him. Such was Cortés' ability that he used Ordás to persuade Verdugo to leave Velázquez' orders unheeded, while, of the two trusted messengers sent by the Governor, he won over and enlisted one in the fleet, and the other he sent back with a most cordial letter to the Governor in which he expressed his surprise at Velázquez' action and assured him again that he had no wish but to serve God and the King. (26)

Thus the iron of his will and the oil of his skill kept the wheels of his fortune moving smoothly. After ten days of constant activity, he left for San Cristóbal de la Habana (not the present Habana), on the south coast. On his way there, his ship disappeared from sight of the others; during the five days of his absence, the usual intrigues arose about who was to command and step into his shoes; his return —his ship had run aground—put an end to all the trouble, but he took note of the fact that Diego de Ordás had been one of the ringleaders, and so, to keep him busy and away, he sent him with a ship to Guaniguanico, to load cassava bread and pigs and to await there the arrival of another ship along the northern coast. His thoughtful activity saw both to appearance and to realities; Bernal Díaz records that it was then, while in Habana, that Cortés began "to treat himself as a lord"; while he organised his artillery with the utmost attention to technical details and saw to it that his sixteen horses were distributed in all the ships. Bernal Díaz gives a detailed account of all the sixteen horses, which he judges and describes with his usual impartiality; and being a poor foot soldier he cannot refrain from extolling the wealth of Juan Sedeño, whose mare gave forth a foal on board ship. "He was the wealthiest soldier of the fleet, for he brought his own ship and the mare and a negro and cassave bread and bacon, for in those days neither horses nor negroes could be had save for their weight in gold." (27)

When Diego Velázquez heard that his brother-in-law Verdugo and his servant Ordás had gone over to the enemy, he was wroth and, says Bernal Díaz, roared with fury. (28) Stubborn in his belated opposition, he sent another message to Pedro Barba, his lieutenant in Habana, and letters appealing to his friends in the fleet, and in particular to his kinsman Juan Velázquez de León. Cortés had wind of it through Fray Bartolomé de Olmedo, the friar who represented spiritual interests in his expedition, who heard the news from another friar of his Order in the service—so to speak—of the Governor. He had no difficulty in weathering this last storm. Juan Velázquez de León was easily won over and, as for the rest of the men, Bernal Díaz is most definite: "We would all have laid down our lives for Cortés." So, Pedro Barba wrote to the Governor that "he had not dared arrest Cortés because he was very strong with soldiers," while Cortés wrote also "with words so good and with offers, which he knew very well how to put, and that the next day he would sail and that he remained his servant." (29)

CHAPTER EIGHT

A Portrait of the Man

O N FEBRUARY 10th, 1519, after mass, the nine ships sailed towards the point of San Antón to meet the two other ships which were sailing along the northern coast, one of which, in charge of a pilot named Camacho, had on board Pedro de Alvarado with sixty soldiers, amongst whom was Bernal Díaz. Camacho, no doubt unacquainted yet with the kind of captain he had, sailed on regardless of his instructions and arrived in Cozumel several days before the fleet, time enough for Alvarado, who had more blood than judgment, to frighten away the natives, and take from them forty hens and several objects without much value, as well as two men and a woman. Then, Cortés arrived on the scene. Camacho was immediately put in irons for his disobedience—an obvious hint at Alvarado, who was the real culprit, yet possibly too powerful for Cortés to inflict such a punishment on him at so early a date in his command. Cortés, however, did not allow him to go scot-free either and severely reprimanded him, arguing that "such was not the way to pacify any land"; he made restitution to the natives for everything taken from them and wished that no harm should be done to them. "Here in this island," says Bernal Díaz, "Cortés began to command very much indeed, and our Lord gave him grace, for wherever he laid his hand it turned out well, particularly in pacifying the peoples and natives of those lands." (1)

What sort of man was he, and what was in his mind? There he was, on the threshold of his mighty adventure, at the head of eleven ships, five hundred and eight soldiers and captains, one hundred seamen including pilots and masters, sixteen horses, ten bronze guns, four falconets and thirteen shotguns. (2) He was their leader less by law than by nature, the man who had conquered them and was to prove able to reconquer them everytime they would have to be reconquered; he was far and away the best man in the fleet, both in point of "letters" and in point of "arms"; he had a mind as well as a will, and a purpose behind both. What kind of man was he, and what was in his mind at this decisive moment in his life?

"He was," says Bernal Díaz, "of a good height and body and well proportioned and of strong limbs and the colour of his face was somewhat ashy and not very merry and had his face been longer he would have been handsomer and his eyes had a somewhat loving glance yet grave withal; his beard was dark and sparse and short and the hair, which in those days was worn [long] the same as the beard, and his chest was high and his back of a good shape and he was lean and of little belly and somewhat bowlegged and his legs and thighs well set and he was a good horseman and skilful with all weapons on foot or on horseback and knew very well how to handle them, and above all a heart and a courage which is what matters [. . .] In everything, in his presence as well as in his talk and conversation, in his table and his dress, in everything he showed signs of being a great lord. The clothes he wore depended on the time and purpose and he cared nothing for silk and damask, but they were very plain and very clean, nor did he wear heavy gold chains but just a thin chain of gold of simple pattern and a trinket with the image of our Lady the Virgin Saint Mary with her precious son in her arms and with a legend in Latin on our Lady's side and on the other side of the trinket the Lord St. John the Baptist with another legend; and he also wore on his finger a very rich ring with a diamond, and in his cap, which in those days was worn of velvet, he wore a medal, the figure of which I forget, and on the medal a letter thereon. Later on, he always wore a wool-cloth cap without a medal. He had himself served richly, like a great lord, with two butlers and stewards and many pages and all the service of his household most complete and great dinner sets of gold and silver. He ate well and he drank a good cup of wine mixed with water, about a pint, and he also took supper and he was not in the least lickerish nor fond of delicate and expensive food, save when he thought it necessary to spend and offer them; he was of a most affable disposition with all his captains and companions [. . .] and he knew Latin and I heard it said that he was a bachelor at law and when he spoke with scholars or men versed in

Latin he answered in Latin. He was a bit of a poet; he made songs
in metre and in prose. And what he had to say he always said most
quietly and with much urbanity; he prayed every morning with a
[book of] Hours and heard mass with devotion; he had for his
protector the Virgin Mary our Lady (whom all Christians must hold
as our intercessor and protector) as well as the Lord St. Peter and
St. James and the Lord St. John the Baptist; and he was fond of
giving alms. When he swore he said 'on my conscience' and when
his anger was aroused by some soldier, one of us, his friends, he said
to him 'may you live to rue it!' and when he was very angry a vein
in his throat and one in his forehead grew swollen, and even at times
when very angry he threw up a lament to heaven and he never said
an ugly or offensive word to captain or soldier and he was most long-
suffering for there were rude soldiers who addressed him in inconsiderate words and he made no proud or ill answer though there was
cause for it and the most he would say would be 'Be quiet' or else
'Go, go with God and mind what you say, for another time you might
pay dearly for it'; and he was most stubborn particularly in war
matters [. . .] and when we began to build the fortress [of Vera-
cruz] the first man to dig and carry earth for the foundations was
Cortés; and I always saw him in battle stepping in along with us
[. . .] I do not wish to speak about many other feats of prowess
and brave deeds of the Marquess Don Hernando Cortés because they
were so many and so varied that I would not soon have done relating
them [. . .] he was very fond of cards and dice and when playing he
was very affable in the game and said certain idle words which dice-
players are wont to repeat: and he was overfond of women and
jealously guarded his Indian ones (3); he was most careful in all our
campaigns, even by night, and many nights he went round the camp
and challenged the sentinels and he entered into the tents and
quarters of us men and if he found one unarmed and his sandals off
he scolded him and said that the low-bred ewe finds her wool too
heavy." (4)

*　　*　　*

Such was the man as seen by one of his soldiers. Cortés stands
out in these pages first and foremost as one of the conquistadores.
He was one of the gentlemen-adventurers who were then hurling

themselves, their persons, fortunes, lives, at the unknown continent;
of the same historical lineage which had given Hojeda and Nicuesa,
Pedrarias and Balboa, Pizarro and Solís, vigorous centaurs of the
Discovery-conquest, who galloped over the unknown continent, lured
by gold and ambition, fearless of native's arrow, nature's inhospitable
and cruel ways and their own Christian rivals; until native, nature
or Christian foe brought their adventurous life to an untimely end;
like them, Cortés was moved by an unexpressed, inarticulate ambition, born of the mere existence of unknown though known-of lands,
of the tension between the untapped vitality within and the unlimited
scope without, a tension which acted on all, for it was in the air, yet
which energised everyone in proportion to the quality of his own
metal.

These merely natural proclivities had acquired a definite historical shape during the seven centuries of Moorish wars which had
ended when Cortés was six years of age. During those seven centuries, the only profession which a spirited Spaniard thought worthy
of him was that of fighting against the Infidel. But mark the point:
this fight against the Moor was not so much a religious crusade as an
economic occupation. Any poor squire knew that there over the
hills, ten, fifty, a hundred miles from his dry, skinflint land, there
were Moorish towns and estates which he could "gain" by a courageous raid, and thus become a wealthy landowner whom the King
would instantly ennoble. The national epic, the *Cantar de Mio Cid*,
conveys this economic aspect of the age-long crusade in a few lines
of magnificent simplicity. The Cid, exiled and poor, conquers
Valencia and therefore becomes rich; he brings his wife and two
daughters from Castille to join him in his prosperity; then, the
Moors counter-attack and the Cid mounts his horse, seizes hold of
his spear and says:

> My wife and my daughters will now see me fight.
> They will see how homes are made in these foreign lands.
> With their own eyes, they will see how one earns one's bread.

These words, carved into the granite of early Castillian, expressed
the tradition of conquest as a profession which had evolved in Spain
as a result of seven centuries of frontier life, facing a people outside
the pale of Christendom. Cortés and all the conquistadores sprang

from this tradition. They went to the new world to make new homes and to earn their bread with their spears, and they doubted no more about the ethics of it all than a corporation shareholder doubts today about the ethics of his dividends or a skilled worker about the ethics of his high salary. It was an established form of life, a recognised though unwritten law, that a gentleman fought for his living, fortune and lineage. Work was not dishonourable as such; far from it: a good craftsman was everywhere esteemed. Work was dishonourable only for the gentleman in that it implied a lack of courage to make a living and even a fortune by more dangerous ways. Therefore, the conquistadores, scions of twenty generations of conquerors of Moors, went to the new world imbued with the absolute certainty that they had both the right and the duty, as gentlemen, to gain new homes and earn their bread in the foreign lands of the new heathen.

And then, they also felt that they had the same right and duty not only as gentlemen, but as Christian soldiers also. As Cortés used to repeat, so far as he was concerned, "I have no thought but to serve God and the King." What did he mean by serving God? He was a man of his century, deeply imbued with faith, indeed of the very stuff of faith. How can we, for whom faith is a lottery won or lost as the luck of the soul will have it, how can we understand that age in which faith was like air and light, one of the very conditions of existence, the very breath with which people spoke? Cortés breathed the faith of his day. "He prayed every morning in a [book of] Hours," says Bernal Díaz, "and heard mass devoutly." This faith was simple and rested on the unshakable rock of unity and truth. It was true, therefore one; one, therefore true. Luther was born already but was not yet vocal, at any rate, in the new world. All men, whatever their colour and nation, were either Christians, infidels, or liable to being enlightened and brought into Christianity. The service of God meant one or other of these two simple things: to bring into the fold the unconverted, ignorant peoples still outside the faith; or to make war against the infidels who refused to be converted and were the enemies of God and His Church. That is what Cortés meant to do in the unknown lands which lay to the west of his ships: if the "Indians" were ready to listen to his friar, to be christened and to become subjects of the Emperor of Christendom, peace; if they proved obdurate, war.

This service to God was also a service to the King-Emperor. After all, was not the Emperor the minister of God on earth? This was a central idea in Spanish political philosophy, and he was sure to have heard it expounded in Salamanca: the King was to be obeyed not as king but as the minister of God. Cortés would therefore be serving the King by the mere fact that he would be conquering for Christendom the good will of a new Empire.

And then, of course, State and religion, faith and civilisation were one in those days, so that the service of God and the service of the King were but one in yet this other sense that conversion was, in the eyes of the century, less a religious-individual than a political-collective act. *Cujus rex eius religio* was the principle of the era, not merely then, when the Reformation was not yet dreamt of, but even later when the Reformation had made this principle, so strange in our eyes, a matter of much concern to all Christendom. This explains both that Cortés should launch forth into his adventure with five hundred soldiers and but one friar, and that he and all his companions should have felt so certain of the holiness of their cause —for, once their power established over the land and its people "pacified," i.e. subdued, conversion was a foregone conclusion. There was no tyranny implied; the conclusion was foregone because their faith was true and, for them, shone as the only truth, in a way which no free eyes could fail to see.

Nor should we wonder at their attitude nor smile superciliously, for the men of our day think and act in a like manner with regard to their religion, the so-called Western Civilisation; which is also supposed to be a boon every man in his senses is bound to accept at sight, yet is made to accept by conquest in the name of progress and liberty. The words have changed but the tune is the same. We are unfair to the men of our day and to those of Cortés' time when we read hypocrisy into their actions. Some of them are now, and were then, hypocrites and low-minded egoists; but many are now as they were then, conscious of no contradiction or disharmony between their aims and their methods. Cortés was certainly one of those sincere conquerors. When he spoke of serving God and the King he meant what he said; he was speaking of his part as the Christianiser and civiliser of heathen souls and of a barbarous State.

To be sure, it was no easy matter to incarnate a religion so absolute in its standards. The Captain, no less than his soldiers, was bound to find at times that the armour of a soldier of Christ was far too rigid for the free movements which life demands of humble human beings. At these moments, Cortés sinned, or found an "elastic joint" in his conscience between the absolute of the gospel ideal and relative reality. Thus we shall see him accepting Indian women, freely given him as presents by his Indian friends, though not without first having them baptised; but as for the conquest itself, Cortés will appear throughout as a conqueror persuaded of his inherent right to take over those heathens into the Christian fold, yet conscious of his duty never to have recourse to arms unless he has exhausted all other means to obtain their allegiance. That such an attitude was due not merely to his desire to spare his scanty troops but also, and mainly, to a theoretical view based on his religious conception, is proved by his quaint habit of making his notary formally put on record his thrice repeated offers of peace and their rejection by the adversary whom he is about to attack. (5)

This ceremony was for him no empty formality. Nor does he seem to have been aware of the spiritual contradiction which—at any rate for us—exists between his aim and the astute methods which he applied with insuperable skill to secure his dominion over the Indians by exploiting their feuds. Cortés was no less illogical in this than many a great Empire-builder of our age, whose Christian faith was no less staunch yet whose methods for spreading his country's hold over simple people were no less astute. He was a highly developed political genius and he went ahead on his creative adventure by gigantic steps from victory to victory, due no doubt to his stout heart, yet even more to his agile brain.

* * *

And then, of course, he was ambitious. He had it in him to rise to his inherent level. He felt greatness within, and this inner greatness craved for its outward forms. Gold, land were for him mere vehicles of power. A gold chain was a fit mark of rank but even more useful to buy meat for an army in an emergency. At the time when he was borrowing money and goods to finance his exploits, Bernal Díaz says "he was in debt and poor, though he had good Indians in trust and got gold out of his mines, but he spent it all on his person and on his wife's dresses [. . .] and on guests who came to him for he was of a good conversation and friendly." (6) This generosity of Cortés has not always been understood, owing to his sharp eye for gold. Two factors are usually overlooked in this connection. The first is that, while struggling towards his conquest, Cortés had to justify the somewhat dubious origins of his authority; nothing but success could do it; and, pending a final victory and the offer of yet another crown to the already overcrowned Charles V, gold was the only yardstick of success. The second is even weightier: the gold that his soldiers made out of their expedition was theirs; the fifth which was sent to the King-Emperor went to quench the ever thirsty creditors of the unfortunate monarch who never saw the bottom of his bottomless debt; but Cortés' own fifth did not merely serve to pay for his household and to maintain his dignity—it was also the only exchequer for the rising State which was taking shape within the conquering army. Cortés was the only man in the army with a sense of statesmanlike responsibility. The epoch had not yet clearly discriminated between the official finances of the State and the personal finances of the prince, between the Nation's State and the King's Estate; but even if it had, Cortés' establishment as that of a mere chief of a small troop of adventurers more or less legally connected through Velázquez to the Spanish Monarchy, could not be but personal. It was his own private fortune which stood behind the enterprise, and therefore it was for him a matter of life and death that at every moment the conquest as such should be self-supporting. His endeavours to this end were bound to take on an air of selfish acquisitiveness, since there was no enterprise, no company, no State, no firm, no army, nothing but Cortés to answer for everything. His was the responsibility; his had to be the means wherewith to discharge it. He was not merely a man, a soldier, a captain; he was a State.

This political vision is the gift which from the outset puts Cortés in a category of his own, not merely over and above his companions in the New Spain adventure but over and above all other conquistadores. Both in his strategy and in his tactics, Cortés is constant, methodical, careful, purposeful, knowing where he is going and how he is going. And, of course, as is the case with men of action, he is a keen gatherer of information but a spare supplier of it;

E

so that his plans are never fully understood until they are unfolded
by time in all their import. In this masterpiece, the first conquest,
i.e. his swift march and successful entry into Mexico, we are to see
him develop an unmistakable style of his own, in which two forms
of action recur with a constancy that makes of them regular patterns
of behaviour: the first is that combination of suavity in manner and
forcefulness in matter which we have already noticed in his relations
with Velázquez; the second is a sly sense of cooperation with his
democratic army which leads him to achieve the boldest deeds by a
kind of fecundation of his army with ideas secretly sprung in his
fertile brain but sedulously disseminated amongst his soldiery to
make them appear born in their midst. An ever watchful attention
to essentials and to details, readiness to act at every moment, a forward attitude, no matter what the odds, maintained throughout the
years with astonishing perseverance down the valley of strife and
over and beyond the crest of success; the genius for being present
where he is most wanted, the refusal to bow before obstacles, combined with an adequate recognition of their importance, both in the
study and in the field, and above it all the crowning grace of good
humour and a delightful imagination which knew how to combine
business with pleasure—these are the chief features which make
of Hernán Cortés one of the greatest and one of the most attractive
captains in history.

* * *

Bernal Díaz reveals how one of the most important advantages
which Cortés enjoyed in his campaign—a competent and above all a
trusted interpreter—was due to the captain's watchful initiative.
It was quite at the beginning of their stay in Cozumel: "As Cortés
put great diligence in everything," says the good soldier, "he called
me and a Biscayan known as Martín Ramos." These two men had
taken part in Hernández de Córdoba's expedition, and Cortés wanted
to ask their opinion about the words "Castilan, Castilan" which the
natives used to repeat to them at the time. "I have often thought
about it," added Cortés, "and wondered whether there may be some
Spaniards in the land." Cortés had guessed right. He had one of
them rescued, while the other one chose to remain. Why the difference? *Cherchez la femme*. Aguilar, the one who returned and

became his interpreter, had a church vocation, and had even taken minor orders. His eight years of slavery had been rich in adventures, from spending a few weeks in the back yard of a cacique, fattening for his master's table, to becoming the war-leader of a native tribe; he had finally conquered the confidence of yet another cacique by resisting a temptation which this astute Indian chief had laid to test his Christian slave; he had sent the slave to spend a night by a lake shore with a lovely Indian girl instructed to stop at nothing to conquer his, so far, untouched virtue. Aguilar resisted. This self-denial kept him in spiritual contact with the Christian community from which he was severed—for ever, so far as he knew—until Cortés' messages found him. His cacique let him go, not without sorrow; but, as a good Christian, Aguilar went farther inland, first to rescue his comrade Gonzalo Guerrero, a common sailor of Palos: "Brother Aguilar," said Guerrero, "I am married and have three sons, and they hold me as a cacique here and a captain when they are at war; go with God for I have my face all tattooed and my ears pierced; what would the Spaniards say if they saw me? And then see my little ones, how pretty they are; give me those green beads for them." (7) And he remained happy in his new fatherland. So much so indeed that, according to Aguilar, it was this Guerrero who had instigated the Indians to attack the Spaniards of Hernández de Córdoba—a memory by the way which may have strengthened his refusal to return to Christendom. (8)

We owe to Bernal Díaz two details of this stay in Cozumel, both most illuminating:

Some sailors had stolen a few sides of bacon belonging to a soldier; the soldier complained to Cortés, who summoned the sailors; they denied their guilt on oath; further enquiry showed that the sailors had perjured themselves. Cortés had them flogged, and the requests for clemency made to him by several captains were of no avail. Cortés was punishing the perjury, not the theft.

The second episode was of more moment. The Spaniards attended a native service and listened in silence to a "sermon" delivered by a native priest, clad in long cotton wraps, his hair, in the ritual way, uncombed and unwashed since he had entered the priesthood, a mass kept solid by hardened human blood. Cortés asked Melchior the Indian interpreter to translate and then made him explain to the natives that "if they wanted to be our brothers they were to remove those idols which made them go astray and to put instead in their temples an image of our Lady and a Cross which he gave them." The Indians demurred for fear of their own gods and challenged the Spaniards to do so themselves, when they would soon find that the gods destroyed them at sea. Cortés thereupon had the idols broken up and thrown down the steps; he had the church cleaned, purified from the thick layers of human blood which defiled its walls, and whitewashed; and he had an altar built on it for an image of the Virgin, which he had decorated with branches and flowers. "The Indians watched with much attention." (9)

This will seem, no doubt, a most unscientific action to many an archaeologist; and there will be some sceptic rationalists who, brandishing the Inquisition, will declare Cortés' religion no better than that of the natives and therefore the swapping of idols without any significance whatever for mankind. Yet the sober-minded observer will, on reflection, think otherwise. No one can read the page in which Bernal Díaz records this episode without feeling the fragrance of the new faith and legend which comes to fill up the void created by the destruction of the old; the mother and child, symbols of tenderness and weakness, of promise and self-denial instead of the terrible, bloodthirsty gods. Cortés was no doubt led to this symbolic action by his somewhat naive and simple faith—the only naive and simple feature in his highly sophisticated character—but also by a sound instinct of the value of concrete, tangible acts and objects in the government of peoples. The destruction of the idols was to become one of the legendary scenes in his life once his unheard-of achievements had turned him into a heroic figure overgrown with flowery legends; and rightly so, for a legend is an act whose truth lies in the realms of symbols; and Cortés was more than once to perform again this highly symbolic and creative act which alone could have raised the natives of New Spain from their dismal cannibalistic rites to a higher level of civilisation. How ready the natives were for the change is shown indirectly by Bernal Díaz, who records that the fleet having had to come back unexpectedly after it had sailed away for good, owing to some damage to one of the ships, they found "the image of our Lady and the cross very clean and incense burning before it," and adds, "We were very glad." (10)

CHAPTER NINE

From Spanish Knight
to Mexican God

O N MARCH 12TH, 1519, the
fleet arrived in Tabasco at the mouth of the river which Grijalva had
discovered, and to which he had given his name. (1) The natives of
the district were ready for war. The neighbouring tribes had
reproached them for their friendly attitude towards the Grijalva
expedition and held them in contempt for it as cowards. Cortés made
Aguilar talk to their chiefs and explain that he wanted peace; but
the more Aguilar spoke the more warlike the Tabasccans grew. He
had to prepare his men for battle; when all was ready, his boats full
of armed soldiers ready to land by force, "Cortés gave order to stop
for a while and not to shoot with either bow, musket or artillery, and
as he wished that all his acts should be fully justified, he summoned
the natives again before the King's notary, whose name was Diego de
Godoy, and through Aguilar's tongue, he demanded that they should
let us land and make provision of water and speak to them on matters
pertaining to God and to His Majesty and that if they should wage
war on us and if in self-defence we caused them deaths or other losses,
this would be their fault and responsibility." These "summons" were
no improvisation on the part of Cortés; they were the outcome of a
deliberate policy defined by the Council of the Indies in order to
provide a basis of law to the Spanish conquest. The conquistadores
carried in their baggage a copy of the official document which had
been approved to that effect, and which had been drafted by Dr.
Palacios Rubios, one of the members of the Council. It was of a
truly disarming simplicity. God had made one man and one woman;
their offspring had scattered over the whole earth; God had put

113

St. Peter at the head of them all; one of St. Peter's successors had given "these Islands and the Mainland of the Ocean Sea" to the King and Queen of Spain; therefore, the Indians were requested to think it over and "take as much time for it as might be fair" and accept the Christian religion and the sovereignty of Spain; if so, the King and Queen of Spain would grant them many favours and privileges; if not, war and slavery. (2) This document makes Las Casas angry and Oviedo merry; after a useless attempt at "putting it over" to the Indians of Darien, Oviedo, who was in charge of the precious text, said to his captain: "Sir, it seems to me that these Indians do not wish to listen to the theology of this summons; nor have you anyone to convey its meaning to them; order it to be put away till we have locked up one of these Indians in a cage so that he can learn it at leisure and His Grace the Bishop explain it to him." Yet, for all its incredible naivety, this document witnesses to the hold which ideas of right and wrong had upon the Spanish State. (3)

Cortés' formal summons raised rather than abated the warlike spirit of the Indians, who shot a volley of arrows at the Spaniards. The Spaniards landed nevertheless—Cortés lost his shoes in the mud —and after much fighting—in which, as Bernal Díaz repeatedly records with obvious satisfaction, the natives fought most bravely and "never actually turned their backs on us till we reached a big courtyard where they had large living houses and three temples"— Cortés thought wise to stop and allow his adversaries to run away. Here he drew his sword and slashed the trunk of a ceiba tree three times to signify that he took possession of that country in the name of His Majesty; then he looked round, and said that if there was anyone who would challenge him, he was ready to stand by his action with his sword and buckler. His soldiers declared themselves ready to back him in this, and the notary drew up a deed. Yet those in the fleet who were of Diego Velázquez' faction liked it not. (4)

*   *   *

The next day, he lost his native "tongue" Melchior, who ran away to Nakedland leaving his Christian clothes—very likely all the Christianity he had ever donned—hanging from a tree. The natives were still defiant. Two scouting expeditions sent by Cortés met with heavy fighting; there were ominous signs of war in the whole plain. Cortés

gave orders to land the horses, which for a whole day were awkward
and shy on land after so many days on board ship. He personally
took command of the cavalry (thirteen in all) entrusting his infantry
to Diego de Ordás—a shrewd move on his part, and often repeated,
for this Ordás was the chief of Velázquez' men in his company; his
artillery was in command of one Mesa. Thus formed in battle order,
the five hundred Spaniards marched across the flat plains to a place
called Ciutla, where the chief force of the enemy was mustered, and
in fact was also marching towards them: an impressive crowd of
painted and plumed warriors beating on their noisy drums and sounding their small shell trumpets, well armed with bows and arrows and
huge swords made of hard wood with edges of obsidian as sharp as
razors; as for their numbers, they covered the whole plain. Their
first onslaught wounded seventy Spaniards, Bernal Díaz said to the
Captain, Ordás, "I believe we can fight breast to breast with them
for they feel the edge and point of our swords and that is why they
keep off"; but Ordás thought this most unsound because they were
three hundred to one. Nothing could have saved them but the horses.
Presently, though terribly late owing to the marshes which had forced
them to take a roundabout way, they suddenly appeared on the
scene, and the Indians, seeing what they thought to be a new kind
of human being on four legs, fled, though not without wounding three
riders and five horses. This sudden arrival of the horsemen gave rise
to a legend, which Gómara put in circulation, to the effect that the
first horseman to appear was St. James, or possibly St. Peter. "That
might be," says Bernal Díaz, "and yet, I, as a sinner, was not worthy
of seeing it; what I then saw and recognised was Francisco de Morla
on a chestnut horse who was coming along with Cortés." And he
quietly records how, as it was late and they were tired of fighting and
they had had no dinner, they buried three soldiers who had died of
throat and ear wounds and they cured men and horses by burning
their wounds with fat from a dead Indian whom they opened up for
the purpose. (5)

Having won respect for his force, Cortés bethought himself at
once of negotiating. He sent some Indian prisoners to explain again
his good will and peaceful intentions; the Indians sent first a batch of
fifteen low-class slaves painted as for battle, with presents of hens,
roast fish and maize; but Cortés sent them back displeased, and made

it understood that he expected ambassadors of more weight. Meanwhile, says Bernal Díaz, "as Cortés was always most alive to everything, he said laughing to us soldiers who were by him: 'You know, gentlemen, I do believe that these Indians are very much afraid of the horses and maybe they think that it is the horses who do the fighting, and also the lombards; I have devised something to make them think it still more: let Sedeño's mare, the one who foaled a few days ago on board ship, be brought here and be tied up here close to where I am, and then let the horse of Ortiz the musician be brought also, for he is very lewd and he will smell the mare.' " This was done and a lombard set up and loaded. The caciques sent as ambassadors arrived towards midday, smoked copal before Cortés and his soldiers and spoke of repentance; Cortés looked grave and displeased, yet had Aguilar explain that he would nevertheless have peace, but if they misbehaved again he would let loose some of his "irons" and kill them all. While he said this, he had the lombard fired; the day was clear and the stone ball made the air and hills reverberate with its rebounding thunder. The caciques were most frightened, yet worse was still to come; for Ortiz's horse was then brought on the scene whence the mare had been withdrawn just before the arrival of the natives; the horse took no notice of the copal-incense but picked up the scent of its own species: it began to rut loudly and to stamp the floor, and goggle most terrifically at the Indians—or so they thought, terror-stricken. Cortés, who was kind-hearted withal, got up from his chair and went "to talk to the horse and explain that the Indians were now peaceful" and sent the beast away, blissfully ignorant of the historical role it had filled for a brief moment of its humble existence. (6)

This stratagem, which so aptly illustrates Cortés' character, playful and imaginative even when positive and businesslike, bore instant fruit: the caciques hurried away and presently came back with new, abundant offerings—of which more hereafter. Cortés, while gracefully accepting their presents, asked the native messengers for two more substantial tokens of peace and friendship: the first was that within two days their women and children should be brought back and peacefully settled again in their homes, whence they had been spirited away by their warlike menfolk, "for in this he would recognise true peace"; the second was that they should give up their bloodthirsty rites and worship before an altar of the Virgin and Child. Here again, as in Ciutla, close by, an altar was made and a Cross erected, and Fray Bartolomé de Olmedo, the friar, said mass, with the two caciques present, whose thoughts over the mystery of the Virgin Birth must have been somewhat recondite. Five days were necessary to allow the wounded to recover, during which Cortés "attracted the caciques with good words" and explained to them the might and majesty of his King-Emperor with so much success that the men of Tabasco declared themselves his vassals—feeling perhaps that this white lord had the advantage of being farther away than the Mexican Emperor. "These," says Bernal Díaz, "were the first vassals who in New Spain gave their obedience to His Majesty." (7) The next day was Palm Sunday. Cortés made the Indians bring their wives with them to a solemn religious ceremony during which the fierce natives, wont to identify religion with bloody death, saw the dreaded bearded whites, who had beaten them in the field, kneel before the image of a woman and child and kiss the Cross, filing past afterwards in a procession each carrying in his hand, instead of the deadly sword, a peaceful branch cut from a tree.

The next Monday morning, the Spaniards sailed away.

*   *   *

The repentant caciques of Tabasco had brought Cortés "a present of gold, to wit, four diadems and a few lizards and two kinds of small dogs and earrings and five ducks and two Indian faces and two soles of gold as those in their *cotaras* and other things of little value [. . .] and the whole present was as nothing compared with twenty women, and amongst them one very excellent woman who was named Doña Marina when she was christened."

Enter Doña Marina, one of the chief figures in the conquest. Notice that *Doña*. In those days it was no common title. None of Cortés' men—not even the leader himself—had the use of *Don*. It was the mark of nobility. The fact that it was granted to this Indian woman from the first should therefore be given its due weight. Doña Marina was a Mexican, and "from her childhood was a great lady and *cacica* of villages and vassals." Her stepfather had given her away to the Tabascoans, but the Spaniards knew from them that she was a great lady. The Spaniards, very naturally, read their own institutions into those of the Mexicans. A lady might be Indian; she was a lady for all that. In Spain, a lady was styled Doña. On being christened, the cacica became therefore Doña Marina. This seemingly unimportant detail proves to what an extent the subconscious attitude of the Spaniards was one of racial equality and assimilation. The twenty girls had been brought to them as a present. Cortés had them first catechised and baptised, then he gave them to his captains, and "this Doña Marina, as she was good-looking and meddlesome and enterprising, he gave to Alonso Hernández Puertocarrero," a man Cortés specially nursed.

Doña Marina knew the languages of both Mexico and Tabasco, while Aguilar knew only that of Tabasco. This intelligent woman, shrewd, energetic and, in course of time, most loyal to Cortés, was therefore a godsend for Cortés at the time when he was beginning to organise his ascent to the high tableland over which ruled Mote-çuçuma. (8)

*   *   *

It was a fine day, and the sun shone on the Mexican shore which the boats followed closely on their way to San Juan de Ulúa. There were several men on board who knew the coast well, and for whom such a point, such a river, such a cocoa-planted valley brought definite memories of fortunes or misfortunes, gold won or blood lost. Bernal Díaz was one of them, for he had been a companion of Grijalva and of Hernández de Córdoba; and in the usual democratic way of Spain, these soldiers of the first expeditions kept pointing out to their chief the landmarks of their past adventures: the broken rock, the river of Alvarado, where that headstrong chief had strayed inland against Grijalva's wish; the river of the flags, "where we bartered for sixteen thousand pesos [of gold]," the Green Island, and the Island of Sacrifices; the chief looked on and kept silent. But Puertocarrero then spoke words of great import in language of great poetical power for the imagination of Spanish soldiers. "It seems to me, sir, that these gentlemen have been saying to you,

> " 'See there France, oh Montesinos,
> See there Paris the great city,
> See the waters of the river
> Where they go to meet the sea.'

And I add,

> " 'See these lands how rich they are
> And know what is best for thee.' "

Bernal Díaz, who records this invaluable scene, goes on significantly to say: "Cortés understood full well the intention with which these words had been said and he answered,

> " 'Let God give us luck in arms,
> As he did the Knight Roldán,'

and for the rest, having you and other gentlemen as my friends, I shall manage things for the best." (9)

This scene is so full of the life of the day and so much instilled with the "arms and letters" spirit of Cortés that it must be considered as one of the many episodes of his life directly or indirectly inspired by him. In his usual roundabout way, Cortés is beginning to sow the seeds of his thought amongst the soldiers and captains who surround him. He is thinking of seceding from Velázquez and of setting up a separate Spanish establishment depending directly on the King. The operation is the more delicate in that a strong minority of his troops are Velázquez' men. He must walk warily, trying the ground as he proceeds. He has the idea mooted by a man of great prestige in the fleet, one whom he has specially nursed, and who is often going to be his unofficial mouthpiece; and the idea appears first in the vague, if beautiful, attire of one of the popular ballads which every Spaniard knew then by heart. The language, therefore, was one that could be understood by everyone. Nothing concrete had been said, nothing the other side could seize upon as treacherous; but Cortés had found the right answer by taking up the cue in the spirit of the ballad itself and by putting all his trust in his "gentlemen." (10). The plumed serpent was gradually charming his men. What an atmosphere of collaboration, association, opinion and suggestion do we feel constantly alive round Cortés! Nothing of this in the accounts we have of other expeditions, not even when they come from the same lively pen of Bernal Díaz. With Cortés we feel, from the very beginning, a continuous interchange of influences going from the chief to the men and from the men to the chief; and that the small fleet and army is already a city.

On Good Thursday, after midday, they arrived in San Juan de Ulúa.

*　　*　　*

News that there were strange ships about was already abroad in Mexico in the year 13-Rabbit. But when in the first third of the year 1-Reeds the Emperor learnt that they had appeared on the northern coast, he was most impressed. His worst fears were confirmed. He seems to have experienced contradictory feelings: certainty that the newcomer was Quetzalcoatl; doubt that it was so; a fatalistic surrender to the returning god; a refusal to let him come; fear of his arrival; elation at his return. His hesitation and his weakness seem to be due to this havoc played on his mind by the awful event, rather than to any inherent lack of character. He had Mexican food prepared in great abundance to send to the strangers and said to his messenger: "And if you see that they eat all this, truly will he be the one we are waiting for, Quetzalcoatl; and if they will not eat of all this, then we shall know he is not Quetzalcoatl. And should he wish to eat human flesh and eat you, so much the better, for I will take charge of your house, wife and sons; doubt it not." (11) So says the chronicler Tezozomoc, adding that the messenger, one Tilancalqui, was to take with him Cuitlalpitoc "and should they eat him, that is what we bought him for, as the slave he is." This tallies with Sahagún's own report: "Moteçuçuma gathered a few sorcerers and augurs and small chiefs and sent them to the harbour to see that the Spaniards lacked neither food nor anything they might wish to have; and to look around with sharp eyes and report to him on all that might occur; and with them he sent a few captives to be sacrificed before the god who was coming, should they think it suitable and should [the Spaniards] ask for blood to drink." (12)

This report is particularly valuable owing to the incomparable knowledge of Mexican ways which Father Sahagún had acquired by the time he wrote his history. His version is the more satisfactory for the illuminating remarks he makes on the rich presents which Moteçuçuma sent Cortés. Of all the chroniclers who mention these highly elaborate jewels and ornaments, Sahagún is the only one who, rightly, understands their religious character: "The ornaments or insignia of Tezcatlipoca [the Mexican Jupiter] which were a headdress made of rich feathers, hanging over the back down to the waist, studded all over with gold stars [. . .] Also the ornaments or insignia of the god known as Tlalocantecutli which were a mask with its feathers and a flag . . . Other ornaments [. . .] were those of Quetzalcoatl himself: a tiger-hide mitre, and hanging from it a long cape made of leather-feathers . . ." And, recording Moteçucuma's instructions to his messengers, Sahagún makes him say: "See, they say that our Lord Quetzalcoatl has arrived: go greet him and hear what he may say with great attention; see you forget nothing of what he says; see these jewels which you will present to him on my behalf, and which are the priestly ornaments which befit him." (13)

Thus loaded with presents for Quetzalcoatl, in case it was the God himself who had returned, the messengers left for the coast. But, from the narrative of Bernal Díaz, the closest not only to the facts but to the impressions of those days, it would appear that the question of the real identity of Cortés and his men was never fully clarified in the minds at any rate of some of the Mexicans, and in particular of Moteçuçuma. Upon the arrival of the Christians in San Juan de Ulúa, the Indians sent some of their men on board to find out who they were, and Cortés, blissfully ignorant of his godlike condition, modestly answered that "they came to see them and trade with them and they would do them no harm"; next day, Good Friday, he landed his horses and placed his artillery on some sand dunes and on the following day the messengers arrived. Cuitlalpitoc was there, for he becomes Pitalpitoque in the inimitable style of Bernal Díaz, who adds this delightful touch: "Later on we called him Obandillo," probably, though he does not say so, because in his ways or looks the Mexican slave turned "Governor" in the eyes of the Spaniards, reminded them of the solemn Ovando, Governor General of the Indies. (14) This way of disguising slaves as personages was a trick often played by the Mexicans on the Spaniards for obscure reasons, one of which may well have been fear on the part of the real native governors who preferred to act behind a straw man whom they could afford to have "eaten" by the unaccountable foreigner.

The situation was in effect a real comedy of errors as complex as any of the numerous ones which enliven the pages of the discovery and conquest of America. Teuhtile, the local Governor, (15) and "Pitalpitoque" presented Cortés with the food prepared for him by

Moteçuçuma, in order to find out whether he was Quetzalcoatl. But, as the Spanish proverb has it, "The horse is thinking one thing and the man who is saddling him, another." Cortés thanked the Mexicans and embraced them, but before partaking of the repast he had an altar erected and had high mass said by Fray Bartolomé de Olmedo, "who had a fine voice," in the presence of Teuhtile and Pitalpitoque who, had it been possible for them even to misunderstand the Holy Sacrifice, might have compared a religion in which god ate man with one in which man ate god. To us, however, this action of Cortés appeals as wiser than mere supercilious critics might judge it; for it is obvious that the direct impact of a religious service of song and symbol on a people whose religion was steeped in blood, was the most efficacious, indeed the only way, to convey to them the new spirit.

After mass, the chief Mexicans and Cortés met at lunch, and there the Spaniard spoke to the Mexicans about the King-Emperor and how that distant Majesty longed for the friendship of Moteçu-çuma (of whom he had never heard), and how he wanted to have Moteçuçuma for a friend and to trade with him; and finally asked point-blank where it was Moteçuçuma's pleasure to see him. By this time Teuhtile and Pitalpitoque must have been in a state of complete bewilderment, for this story of strange and far-off things, intricate in itself to their secluded minds, reached them moreover through a double cascade of interpretations; Cortés' flow of Spanish words fell on Aguilar's ears; Aguilar's Tabascoan words fell on Doña Marina's ears; and Doña Marina's Mexican words (God only knows what she made of Emperors and Christians) fell on Teuhtile's ears, conveying to them a tale no doubt but faintly related to the original tale uttered by Cortés. Whatever he made out of the story, Teuhtile seems to have come to the conclusion that this bearded white man was not Quetzalcoatl; for on hearing Cortés' desire to see Moteçuçuma, "he answered somewhat haughtily: 'You have hardly arrived and you already want to speak to him.'" He nevertheless proceeded to pre-sent Cortés with the ritual presents which Moteçuçuma had sent for him, and, if we are to believe Sahagún, they dressed him with some of them. Cortés failed to realise the religious value of the ceremony, which could but confirm Teuhtile in his opinion that he was not Quetzalcoatl, and, as a mere gentleman, he presented Moteçuçuma, through his messenger, with a carved armchair, a crimson cap with a gold medal of St. George on it, and other lesser offerings. All these happenings were carefully recorded by a scribe-painter in Teuhtile's suite. The Mexicans had a kind of written language consisting in actual pictures of the objects combined with conventional symbols for certain abstract ideas such as numbers: a purse, for instance meant 8,000 and a feather 400; the Spaniards noted the work which this scribe-artist was painting in bright colours on cotton sheets; Cortés lost no time in realising the value which this record had for him: it was necessary to impress Moteçuçuma, for whom no doubt the record was meant, by making it as eloquent as possible on the strength and powers of the Spaniards: he had his guns fired, echoing and re-echoing in the surrounding hills, and he made his horsemen gallop on the shore, led by Alvarado on a "swift and restless mare." None of this was lost either on the artist or on Teuhtile, though, if we are to judge by the specimens of these pictures which remain, the horse was too much of a puzzle for the Mexican artist who drew it as an uncouth hybrid of cow, ass and dog, while the moustache of the Spaniard is wont to migrate from his upper lip to the middle of his cheek. (16)

This Teuhtile seems to have been anything but shy, as Bernal Díaz, with his eye on the human detail, does not fail to point out; and, noticing that one of the soldiers had a gilt helmet, "though rusty," asked to see it, "for it looked like one they had which had been left them by their ancestors and lineage and it was worn by Witchywolves"; whereupon, Cortés let him have it, requesting that, as a matter of mere curiosity, it should be sent back full of grains of gold. Each side was, to use another Spanish saying, drawing the hot coals to his own sprat, and while Cortés, with an eye to expenses and success, sought to acquire some gold, Teuhtile was still wondering, despite his first negative conclusions, whether after all that helmet was not one with the helmet of Quetzalcoatl.

This seems to have been the opinion of Moteçuçuma when he saw the helmet. Bernal Díaz says that "as soon as he saw the helmet and that which his Witchywolves wore he felt certain that we were of those who, his ancestors had said, would come and hold sway over the land." (17) But the honest soldier does not seem to have been equally well informed when he adds that "the Great Montezuma was dumbfounded and on the other hand felt great contentment"; for

Sahagún, whose contact with the Mexican side and traditions was incomparably closer, gives a version far more consonant with the situation, with Moteçuçuma's character and with later facts. "During the time these messengers came and went, Moteçuçuma could neither eat nor sleep, nor put his mind to anything; but was very sad and sighed constantly; he was in deep anguish; no pastime gave him pleasure [. . .] and he said: 'What will become of us?' [. . .] His heart suffered great affliction and torment, and he said: 'Oh Lord, whither shall I go? How shall I escape?'" When the messengers arrived, he was in bed, at night. He would not hear the news in his bedroom; he had the messengers sent to a state room, "and then had several captives smeared all over with clay to have them sacrificed and the messengers and Moteçuçuma went to the state room and there in the presence of the messengers, the captives were killed and the messengers anointed with their blood. This ceremony was performed because they had seen great things and had seen the gods and talked to them."

Then the messengers spoke. They showed him the picture and commented upon it: the noise and power of the cannon balls, the size, swiftness and power of the horses, the valour and strength of the white men, "their white faces, their blue eyes, their red hair, their long beards, and how some amongst them were black with curly black hair," for some of the Spaniards had negro slaves with them. "When Moteçuçuma heard this report, he was frightened and he began to fear and to feel dismayed and anguished." (18)

The unfortunate Emperor sought the help of the only powers he thought strong enough to oppose to those godly beings: nature and man, he felt, were not equal to the newcomers: it was necessary to rely on supernatural powers. He sent for "diviners, augurs and necromancers to see whether they would not be able to perform some witchcraft or enchantment against the Spaniards to make them fall ill or die or go back." (19) This tallies tolerably well with Bernal Díaz' account, for the return of Teuhtile, as told him, describes ceremonies of an undoubtedly magic character. There is even in Bernal Díaz a detail, not to be found in Sahagún, which enhances the magical nature of the manœuvre which Moteçuçuma in his despair seems to have tried on Cortés and his men. The chief messenger in this second, magical embassy, had been chosen to resemble Cortés, whose features were known to Moteçuçuma thanks to the skilful brushes of his artist-scribe. This personage, whose unknown name Bernal Díaz transfigured into Quintalbor, had so strong a likeness to Cortés that the Spaniards called him Cortés." (20) Mexicans were adepts at this kind of magic by impersonation or likeness. Their priests always sought to resemble the god they served. Quintalbor, says Bernal Díaz, "kissed the earth and with braziers made of earth, which they brought with them and their incense, they incensed him and all the soldiers who happened to be there with him." But the incantation was lost on the Spaniards, who, unaware of what was going on in the minds of the Indians, took all that incense burning as a matter of course, waited as patiently for the ceremony to end as the Mexicans had waited for the end of their own high mass, and "showed them much love" when they had done.

Evidently the magicians thought it wise to have recourse to other equally (or more) magical if less esoteric means. And so Quintalbor had some thick cotton sheets spread on the ground and unpacked his load of presents; their splendour was abundant proof of the fear which possessed the soul of Moteçuçuma: first, a disc of gold "as big as a cartwheel" on which was engraved the sun—a Mexican calendar; and another wheel just as big and thick, made of silver, and no doubt a representation of the moon-calendar of the Mexicans. These two planets, shining in the tropical sun, dazzled the Spaniards with their sheer intrinsic value, and astonished them by their workmanship. They were surrounded by constellations of other presents of gold, silver, leather, precious stones and cotton, all of them valuable witnesses of a civilisation both wealthy and highly developed in the arts and crafts of luxury.

This revelation acted as a powerful incentive on Cortés. But Moteçuçuma's messengers had strict orders to insinuate to him that there could be no question of his coming up to Mexico. Evidently Moteçuçuma had hoped that these presents would satisfy the strangers, should his magicians fail to render them innocuous. Cortés, fully alive to the value of the land he had struck and, no doubt, realising that the spirit of Moteçuçuma was possessed with fear, made answer to the messengers that he would go and see the Emperor wherever he might be, and with small offerings "from the poverty which we had brought over," as Bernal Díaz says, he sent the messengers away. (21)

CHAPTER TEN

Cortés Founds Veracruz and Breaks Away from Velázquez

THE MOMENT had come for Cortés to prepare in earnest for his visit to the mighty Emperor. Now, after the event, we are apt to think of this moment as if Cortés were then the man he soon became through his success. But at that time he was no more than an adventurous captain who had left Cuba just a few weeks earlier, breaking loose from the authority of Diego Velázquez, in deed though not in words. He was on a barren, sandy, hot shore, in an unknown country, facing a mysterious civilisation, with eleven ships, about five hundred men, thirteen horses and a few guns, at the foot of a steep wall twelve thousand feet high, challenging a monarch who could dazzle him with a golden sun and a silver moon later to be admired by all Europe. What was his base? He had no base. He was in alien territory and, as for the help or supplies to be drawn from Cuba, he could have no illusions: from Cuba, he could expect nothing but vindictive enmity. He was soon to prove himself capable of a courage none too cautious, when circumstances demanded daring rather than prudence; but there was no point in taking risks that could be avoided. Bold he was, but not foolhardy. At this moment, his methodical mind seems to have struck on two ideas: he would go and see for himself this Moteçuçuma and his Empire; but he would leave a force somewhere on the coast to keep his sea door open. And, of course, underlying both, the secret plan of cutting himself loose from Velázquez at the first opportunity.

The sandy shore on which they had made a temporary camp was not a good site for a permanent settlement. It was barren and infested with mosquitoes. He therefore sent Montejo to reconnoitre the coast, under the advice of the cantankerous pilot Alaminos. While Montejo was thus engaged, Teuhtile came back from Mexico. He brought more presents for the Emperor of the Christians, and in particular some valuable *chalchivitls,* green, opaque stones held in high esteem amongst the Mexicans, less perhaps for their intrinsic worth than for their conventional value as a sign of social rank. These presents were the sugar coating the bitter pill of Moteçuçuma's stern refusal to receive Cortés. But Cortés was not the man to take a refusal, and so, beholding the precious *chalchivitls,* he turned to his men and, in his usual, quiet way, he merely said: "Truly, he must be a great lord and rich; and if God wishes it so, some day we shall go and see him."

The sun was setting and the camp bell struck the air repeatedly to call the men to Evensong; Teuhtile and his companions were puzzled to see all those dreaded white warriors go on their knees and bow their heads before a Cross which they had erected on one of the sand dunes; the last words of the Ave Maria had just been said and the men had stood up again when Teuhtile asked the Spaniards "why they humbled themselves before that pole, and as Cortés heard it and the friar of the Mercy was present, he said to the monk: 'This is a good moment, father, as we have a good ground for it, for us to explain to them through our tongues the matters of our holy faith.' " Fray Bartolomé lost no time in giving the Mexicans "so good a reasoning, for such a moment, that good theologians would not have done it better." But if we are to judge by the effect which theology has on our own European minds, in our own language, we could hardly blame Teuhtile and his companions for their bewilderment on hearing it through the two tongues, even though one of them was that of a man ordained in minor orders. (1)

It is difficult to resist the conclusion that Cortés' faith was an inconsistent feature in his character as a man of action. For the first time, though not for the last, we see him led astray by his desire to spread the faith which for him was the only truth, into undoing the work which his shrewdness and even his Machiavellism were otherwise so successfully achieving; for while all his conscious and logical efforts aimed at raising the prestige of the Christians and the awe they inspired in the Mexicans, his Christian humility in worship, utterly beyond the ken of the Mexicans, was bound to create in them the impression that these so-called gods were no such gods after all.

Whether owing to this circumstance or to more recondite reasons, including a possible change of policy on the part of Moteçuçuma, Pitalpitoque began to neglect supplies, and the camp to feel hungry. The neighbouring Indians no longer came to the camp with their maize and hens; the soldiers fell back on fish which the Spanish sailors caught and sold to them for gold which they bartered from the Indians with their usual trifles, beads and bells. Now this business of bartering for gold was traditionally considered as a monopoly of the chief of the expedition, in the interest of his principal and of the King. But, unlike Grijalva, who had strictly forbidden it to his soldiers, "Cortés was pleased at it and turned a blind eye on it, though he saw it, and it had been reported to him by Velázquez' friends and members of his household." The party of Velázquez, led by Juan Velázquez de León, one of his relations, was getting restive; they argued that Velázquez had not sent Cortés in order to allow all the gold to leak away by way of the soldiers, and that Cortés should have the crier announce that bartering for gold was thenceforward forbidden. This was Cortés' opportunity: he agreed, and declared himself ready to appoint any person as treasurer that the Velázquez party might suggest. The Velázquez party appointed one of their group, Gonzalo Meiía, for this unpopular post; whereupon Cortés, having thus "put them on the map" as the unmistakable leaders of the movement against the interests of the common soldier, turned a "displeased face" on them and reproached them for their attitude. "Our companions," he said, no doubt in their presence, "are undergoing great hardship, having nothing to eat, and that is why we ought to let them alone, the more so as their bartering is but a misery, compared to that which with God's help we shall obtain. Now that we have forbidden them to barter, as you wished, we shall see how we are going to eat." (2)

Cortés had manœuvred in his usual long-sighted way. Any other simpler commander, reacting automatically under impulses of habit and greed, would have sternly forbidden all indiscriminate bartering for gold. He saw the gold-dealings and let them develop, guessing that they might lead to a situation which he could exploit to his advantage. The Velázquez party had fallen into the commander's trap. They now stood as the selfish enemies of the common soldier, whose interests and needs found support in the generous Cortés. Things were ripening for the astute commander, but were not yet quite ripe. The choice of a new site for a base provided another opportunity which Cortés was quick to seize.

After a dramatic and, at times, dangerous voyage lasting twelve days, Montejo returned with but an indifferent report. He had followed the coast as far as Pánuco, and, feeling unable to weather the stormy seas which he had met with, he had decided to return; about twelve leagues from San Juan de Ulúa, where Cortés was at the time, Montejo had found a small Mexican town with a fortress, named Quiahuitzlan, (3) and close to it a good harbour, fairly sheltered from the north wind and surrounded with lands rich in rivers, wood and building stone. The camp was getting tired both of inaction and of mosquitoes and bad food. The Velázquez faction urged a return to Cuba. (4) Cortés suddenly announced his decision to transfer the Spanish settlement to the site which Montejo had discovered. Montejo was of the Velázquez group; Cortés, with his usual eye on every detail, had chosen him for this expedition precisely because he was a member of the opposition: he had kept him away while he was preparing the ground for his conquest of his own army and, by the same occasion, he had put the group in the invidious position of having to refuse to move to the spot selected by one of their friends.

The Velázquez faction, however, expressed their opposition in unmistakable terms: there was no food; thirty-five soldiers had already died of wounds, illness or hunger; the land was big, the cities populous; the Mexicans would wage war; it was better to take stock of the gains secured and to return to Cuba with the golden sun and the silver moon and the helmet full of grains of gold. To which Cortés answered that it was not wise to go back before having gone forward, that it was usual to die in war, that it was necessary to find out all about the land, and that while the Indians had food the Spaniards' hands would be very weak indeed before they went hungry. (5)

This calmed the faction for the time being, and Cortés went ahead with his plans, which he had matured with the brothers Alvarado, Cristóbal de Olid, Alonso Dávila, Juan de Escalante, Francisco de

Lugo and others, but particularly with his confidant Puertocarrero. Thanks to Bernal Díaz, we are in a position to watch a scene of his actual canvassing, worthy of any modern democracy in electioneering times: "One night, past midnight, Alonso Hernández Puertocarrero and Juan de Escalante and Francisco de Lugo, who was more or less a relation of mine and of the same country, came to my hut and said to me: 'Hullo, Sir Bernal Díaz del Castillo, come out with your arms, to go the rounds, we will accompany Cortés who is going the rounds'; and as soon as I had walked away from my hut, they said to me: 'See here, sir, keep secret this we want to tell you, which is a weighty matter, and let it not be known to the companions in your hut, for they are of Diego Velázquez' party'; and what they told me was: 'Do you approve, sir, that Cortés should have brought us here under false pretences, and having had it cried in Cuba that he came to settle, now we learn that he has no power to do so, and they want us to go back to Cuba with all the gold we have had so that we shall all be the losers and Diego Velázquez keep the gold? See, good sir, you have come three times already, spending your own money, and have remained in debt, and risked your life so many times, with so many wounds. We are telling you all this so that the move goes no farther, and there are many gentlemen whom we know to be friends of yours determined to have this land settled in the name of His Majesty, and in that of Cortés in his royal name, and to have it made known in Castille to our King and lord as soon as we can; see, sir, that you give him your vote so that we all elect him as captain by a unanimous will, for it is a good service to God and our King.' " (6)

Bernal Díaz promised his vote, and the canvassers went "from soldier to soldier" until the matter reached the ears of the Velázquez group, for Francisco de Montejo was watching. The opposition lost no time in unmasking the scheme and accusing Cortés of intriguing to secure the new land for himself, and they summoned him to return to Cuba, since he had neither men nor supplies to "settle." Cortés was too shrewd to oppose them, thus exhausting his forces in a breast-to-breast fight. As was his wont, he managed to draw forward the rest of the men by merely feigning a retreat. "Without showing any displeasure, he said he was content, he would not run counter to his instructions which he had from Diego Velázquez, and he had his crier announce that the following day everybody should embark, each in the ship in which he had come." This order promptly roused those who wanted to settle; they argued Cortés into agreeing with what he had always thought and forced him to carry out what he had always intended. "And though he took much requesting, it all was as with the proverb: 'You beg me to do what I want as much as you.'" But the astute leader had so managed things that he now was in a position to exact a good price for what he always had longed to possess: he yielded, but on condition that he should be made Captain General and Chief Justice, and that he should be entitled to a fifth of the gold after the royal fifth had been deducted.

The trick was played. Yet not quite. All had been settled but the form; and form, despite what shallow creatures imagine, is of the essence of things. Here the "letters" of Cortés came to the help of his "arms." The procedure followed bears the stamp of his unmistakable style. The soldiery, having decided that the best service of his Majesty required it, summoned Cortés to stop bartering for gold, to found a city with authorities for the administration of justice and to appoint alcaldes and councillors. Cortés gave himself one day for reflection, the better to simulate that he did by force of circumstances and popular pressure what he had carefully planned to do; next day he bowed before public opinion, as every good democrat does when he is elected, pointing out, again like every good democrat, that he was sacrificing his personal interests, for he was entitled to seek in bartering for gold an adequate return for his outlay. He therefore reluctantly acquiesced in his own design, and founded the *Rich Town of the True Cross*, a lovely name which recalled both the business of gold and the pleasure of the gospel. As alcaldes thereof he appointed his friend Puertocarrero and Velázquez' friend Montejo, whom he thus compromised in the deed even if, as events were to show, he did not fully win him over. This meant that the expedition had become a Spanish municipal community, governed democratically by its *Cabildo* or Chapter, which was duly sworn in by Cortés in the name of the King. (7)

But now, Cortés was no longer in a no-man's-land, as the captain of an expedition sent by Diego Velázquez under definite instructions. Now Cortés was a citizen of a Spanish community (more or less) duly constituted. The next day, the Chapter solemnly met and summoned Cortes before them, asking him to show them the powers and instructions which he held from Diego Velázquez, which Cortés instantly did, for he was most respectful of all democratic institutions which he had packed with his friends. The Chapter studied them to the best of their ability and found—without undue surprise—that they could no longer be held as valid, whereupon they decreed that Cortés was no longer either Captain or Chief Justice. This put the newborn Spanish community in a serious predicament, inasmuch as it is well known that the administration of justice and the command of the public force are two indispensable functions of state for which a person of outstanding gifts is always required. Fortunately the Chapter struck on the happy idea of appointing Cortés to fill up the two vacancies which the lapsing of his powers had just created; and having secured his acceptance of those new responsibilities, the Chapter had him sworn in with all the ceremonies usual in such unusual cases. (8)

Thus was Diego Velázquez, Governor of Cuba, elegantly ousted from the enterprise. What, the Chapter might ask, was Cuba to them, or they to Cuba? They were a Spanish municipal community known as the Rich Town of the True Cross, as wealthy (in hopes) as pious (in intentions), or else they would have chosen a less long name, like that "ugly name" which Montejo had given to the harbour he had discovered and which not even Bernal Díaz, despite his fairly free language, dares print. They were free Spaniards, empowered by the traditions of their democratic country to found a town wherever they wished, even in a camp where, as a matter of fact, there was no town; for events had rushed ahead of Cortés' timetable and, seeing that swift action was necessary, he had decided to found his little republic before he began to build the town, which he did not do till later, when, after settling to his satisfaction what he would nowadays call his constitutional position, he moved his camp across to the vicinity of Quiahuitzlan and actually built the town of the True Cross or Veracruz. (9)

The Velázquez party, however, despite the loss of Montejo, were not beaten yet; they were, in fact, rather incensed, and Bernal Díaz records that the friends of Cortés were hard put to it to prevent them from running amok and revolting in arms. (10) They seem to have failed to realise the deep difference in the status of Cortés' authority which the setting up of the Chapter implied. Cortés was no longer

under any obligation to compromise with his enemies. He was duly
elected by the rank and file: he struck hard. Juan Velázquez de León,
Diego de Ordás, Escobar and Juan Escudero, the ringleaders, were put
in irons and imprisoned in the ships; as for the rank and file of the
opposition, he handled them in his usual way; he announced that any
one wishing to return to Cuba could do so, and he sent away most of
them on a foraging expedition which he put under the command of
Pedro de Alvarado. There were, of course, no candidates for Cuba;
Cortés knew only too well that if the bulk of the expedition remained
in Mexico, the dissenters would not go back, if only for fear of cutting
a sorry figure while their comrades conquered wealth and laurels.
As for Alvarado's men, they found many bloody traces of human
sacrifices but little food for Christians; though when his soldiers
came back to the camp each came, says Bernal Díaz, "loaded with
hens and other vegetables" (11): a shrewd anticipation of vegetari-
anism, as it is actually practised. Bernal Díaz is an invaluable store-
house of details on Cortés and on the workings of his mind; we learn
through him that Alvarado returned without causing any more harm
to the Indians (other, he means, than the taking away of the "hens
and other vegetables" from their vacated houses) because he had
orders to that effect from Cortés who still remembered his lieutenant's
high-handed ways in Cozumel—ways which were to be the chief
cause of the great conqueror's later sorrows.

Cortés meanwhile had lost no time in healing the wounds he had
inflicted on his enemies. "Gifts break rocks," says a Spanish proverb, aptly quoted by Bernal Díaz at this juncture. By means of gifts
and what another Spanish telling phrase describes as "beak syrup"—
the singular persuasive force of his words, behind which there was
of course the inherent attractiveness of his person—Cortés won over
all his adversaries, some of whom, in particular Juan Velázquez de
León, became his staunchest friends. Nor is this winsome grace the
feature of the conqueror's character most to be admired on this occasion. The most admirable feature here shown by Cortés is his
capacity for remaining aloof from the quarrel between man and man
which this division in his camp implied; his ability to discriminate
between Cortés the man and Cortés the leader; the steadiness with
which he keeps his eye on the enterprise and brushes aside his personal feelings when estimating the action to be taken with regard to

the rebels and adversaries of to-day, the friends and useful soldiers of to-morrow. This serene control of his own feelings, this complete subordination of the self to the work in hand, is one of the chief qualities of Cortés; it contributes to make of him one of the great men of action whom history has known.

* * *

Meanwhile, he and his troops were facing dangers which would have made even their hot and brave Spanish blood curdle, had they but known them. Moteçuçuma had been awe-struck on seeing the picture-report brought him by his messengers. He called the wise old men of Chalco, Cuitlahuac and Mizquic and asked them what kind of men were to come and hold sway over Mexico: the Chalco wise men said that the newcomers would be known as Tezocuilyoxique, or, for short, Zenteycxique, "men with one foot only, with a large foot-palm wherewith they shade themselves, and they have their heads on their chest." Moteçuçuma, somewhat annoyed, pointed out that this did not tally with his picture—so he sent for the men of Xochimilco and in particular for a wise man known as Quilaztli, who assured him that the newcomers would be known as Coayxeequee, and would have faces like snakes or like big fish, and would come in big hills moving on the sea, in which they lived and ate and slept; and others riding *tenacamazatl*, that is very big deer or something to that effect; with white faces and bodies and long beards and clothes of many colours. This was near enough for Moteçuçuma to exhibit his picture; and the comparative study of the two documents, the new in Moteçuçuma's hands and the old in Quilaztli's, left in the unfortunate Emperor's heart the conviction that here were men amongst whom perhaps Quetzalcoatl might not be, but who certainly were meant to conquer his Empire.

He feared the worst. Yet he tried again the effect of magical powers. "There are many necromancers in the Hot Land, and for instance in Quahnahuac, Yauhtepec, Huaxtepec, Ayacapichtlan, Xohuitotc, Ocuilan, Malinalco, and Tenantzinco, great sorcerers and enchanters, who eat the hearts of living men and take them away o' nights on their shoulders under a spell." The Emperor had all these worthies summoned to his presence and made them a long speech to the effect that they were to hinder the newcomers from advancing inland, by exerting their powers over them so that they should be seized by fear and would go back; he was good enough to suggest some definite action, such as that the magicians should take the strangers away on their shoulders and throw them down some rocky ravines, or that they should eat the strangers' hearts.

So the magicians, who, despite their impressive powers, were obedient and loyal subjects of Moteçuçuma, repaired to the Spanish camp and attacked it, taking it between two fires so to speak, and in the utmost secrecy. Each group of sorcerers went about his business according to his specialty. Those whose talent it was to turn into wild beasts said, "We want to try our fortune and if we fail we shall eat their hearts." But they tried in vain, for instead of hearts they could only find in them ashes and smoke (by then, perhaps, some of the Spaniards had acquired the Cuban custom of smoking tobacco, which might explain the smoke, though not the ashes); then it was the turn of the magicians who turn into snakes and scorpions, but they also failed, indeed, it may be that some of them died of having bitten the Spaniards; then came the sorcerers who eat legs and in particular that part thereof not inadequately known as the calf; but they were nonplussed to find that, so it seemed to them, the Spaniards had no calves in their legs, though a legion of mosquitoes were trumpeting to the contrary throughout the sultry air, and one could hear the scratchings to the accompaniment of the grinding of the flinty shore combed by the waves. Finally, the sorcerers who were to put them to sleep and spirit them away to dash them down a rocky ravine, were also powerless because while some Spaniards slept others watched over them. In short, the poor helpless magicians returned crestfallen to Moteçuçuma, for whom their defeat was but another sign of his oncoming doom. (12)

* * *

Whether as a result of these unsuccessful efforts to get rid of the Spaniards by magical means, or for more matter-of-fact reasons, one morning Pitalpitoque disappeared without warning and the usual supplies of food or gold were not forthcoming. Since Bernal Díaz explains the fact as the outcome of direct advice given to Moteçuçuma "by his idols," particularly by "Witchywolves, god of war," and "Tezcatepuca, god of Hell," we may infer from this hint that the magicians had something to do with the change of policy. Cortés interpreted it as, at any rate, a danger of war, and held himself in readiness.

One day, Bernal Díaz, who with another soldier was on sentry duty on some sandy stretches near the camp, saw five Indians coming towards them; their attire was different from that of the Mexicans; they wore ornamental blue stones set in wide holes on their lower lips and ears; their manner was courteous and friendly, and they asked by signs and gestures to be allowed to go to the camp. On arriving there, led by Bernal Díaz himself, it was found that neither Aguilar nor Doña Marina understood their language; Doña Marina asked them whether they spoke *nahuatl*, the language of Culúa or Mexico, and two of them who knew it were then able to explain that they were Totonacs, sent by their chief, the cacique of Cempoal; the Totonac messengers informed Cortés how Moteçuçuma tyrannised over them and exacted heavy taxes from them. The cacique of Cempoal seemed anxious to receive the visit of Cortés. (13)

This visit was a revelation for Cortés; coming as it did precisely at the time when he was trying to persuade a strong part of his army to engage in the arduous conquest of a still unknown land, it must have shone in his eyes like a light from on high. For it meant that these Indians, whom he had made up his mind to subjugate, were divided amongst themselves, and that Moteçuçuma had enemies on whom the stranded strangers might lean in the struggle against him, if it came to that.

Cempoal was on the way to Quiauitztlan; the fact must have decided Cortés to leave for his newly chosen quarters by land, while sending his stores by sea. They marched along the hot sand under the burning sun of July, with the blue sea on one side and on the other the mountains, "very beautiful and amongst them one which overtops the others by a great height, and it is so white that we believe it to be snow, and so the natives say it is, though as we have not seen it thoroughly, though we have been quite near, and as this land is so hot, we are not positive about it." (14) They walked on, amidst the gorgeous sights of nature and the gruesome sights of men, passing empty villages in which the blood of human sacrifices was still fresh on the temples; "and there we slept and there was nothing for supper," says Bernal Díaz without further comment (15); the landscape gradually became greener; there were green meadows and deer too swift for even Alvarado's mare, and the thousand scents and colours of tropical lands fecundated by abundant water; the next night they slept in another village also marred by recent traces of human sacrifices. In the morning, having duly warned the cacique, the army left for Cempoal. Cortés, even though on a visit to a friend, would leave nothing to chance; he organised his troops so as to be ready for any emergency: everybody on the alert and his scouts wide awake. But when they were about one league from the town, they saw a walking garden advancing towards them—twenty prominent Cempoalans were coming to greet them with bunches of roses which they offered Cortés and his cavaliers. The Spaniards were much elated to find so happy a land, and so peaceful, looking like an orchard, with well built streets of neat houses and colourful gardens, and they praised God for having allowed them to discover such lands. They were so delighted with Cempoal that they called it Seville, than which there was no higher praise. "There," shouted one, "isn't that like the house of the Duke of Medina?" "And there," said another, "that of the Duke of Arcos?" (16) The long stay on the hot sands of San Juan de Ulúa must have set their imagination athirst, and at the first exhilarating draught of colour and happiness, some of them seem to have become intoxicated; for the scouts who had gone ahead to the main square where the houses were resplendent under the sun in their new coats of whitewash, rushed back to tell Cortés that the natives had houses coated with silver. "Doña Marina and Aguilar said it was probably plaster or lime and we had much fun out of their silver and frenzy."

The cacique had sent those roses by way of an apology, explaining that he was too fat to come out to greet his host. He had the good-humoured, life-loving temperament which every thoroughgoing, honest to God, fat man ought to have: and so he gave Cortés and his men comfortable quarters and excellent food, and, as a man who knows what food means to mankind, he waited patiently till the Spaniards had eaten before asking to call on Cortés. He was met with the usual courtesies and embraces and treated to the usual explanations on the holy faith and on the mighty power of the King-Emperor of Spain; to which the fat cacique listened with but a distracted ear and a downcast eye, for he had his own troubles, which now and then bubbled up from his ample chest in the form of sighs, and finally came out in a torrent of lamentations and complaints against Moteçuçuma, who had of late reduced him to subjection, taken away his treasure and crushed him under heavy taxes. Cortés listened to this with the utmost attention and promised to attend to his new friend's affairs as soon as he had settled in Quiauitztlan.

The next morning, the fat cacique put about four hundred *tlamemes* at the disposal of the army, men whose duty it was to carry loads (about twenty-two pounds for about twenty miles). This for the Spaniards was a welcome discovery. The Mexicans had not yet invented the wheel, nor had they any domesticated animals which they could load; transportation was done on human backs, and, as Bernal Díaz says, the soldiers had to carry their own kit bags, for only five or six of them had brought Indians from Cuba. (17)

Thus relieved of their baggage—no small relief in those hot lands—the Spaniards, the next day, climbed the steep hill to Quiauitztlan, a small town erected amidst fierce rocks, a kind of natural fortress, "and had there been any resistance, difficult to take." But there was no resistance; the Indians, afraid of the cannon and horse, had vacated it, all but about fifteen of them, who were awaiting the invaders in one of the temples, and who received them with much smoking of incense and other magic ceremonies. Hardly had Cortés time to explain to them his two favourite themes—religion and empire—when the fat cacique turned up, of course in a litter, conveyed by prominent Indians; and there, in the presence of the men of Quiauitztlan, and with their moral support, he enlarged on his own theme, the tyranny and oppression of Moteçuçuma, and, with tears and sighs, spoke of their sons and daughters taken away to be sacrificed; their harvests lost, their wives and daughters raped by Moteçuçuma's taxgatherers. The Spaniards were moved to pity; their chief, no doubt also, yet more still to action, particularly when he was told that Moteçuçuma's men were thus terrorising a wide region, the whole Totonac district, covering more than thirty small towns. This, for a wide-awake general, meant many thousands of warriors in the field. It was therefore imperative that he should secure a definite alliance with the men of Cempoal. Time was an all-important element. The legal fiction of Veracruz, a town founded in spirit but, as yet, lacking even a body, was but an empty form which only success could endow with life. It was imperative for Cortés to show results before the aggrieved Velázquez should destroy his precarious position by making use against him of the strong friendships which the Governor of Cuba had at Court.

The chief obstacle was the dread of Moteçuçuma's power which paralysed the heart of the men of Cempoal. Cortés seems to have clearly sized up the situation and realised that it was necessary to bring the Cempoalans out into open rebellion against Moteçuçuma. But he seems to have seen more than that; for after all he was not yet fully informed as to the power of the much dreaded Emperor, save that he was strong enough to frighten the Cempoalans with his arms and to dazzle the Spaniards with his treasures. Therefore, while it was imperative to manœuvre the Cempoalans into open rebellion, it was no less imperative to remain on good terms with Moteçuçuma, for he must, if he could, avoid a trial of strength with the mighty monarch, even while getting ready for it in case it was unavoidable.

These are no doubt the thoughts which he brewed in his busy head while his captains and soldiers listened with moved indignation to the tale of woe which the fat cacique was unfolding before them. The scene was suddenly brought to an end by the hurried arrival of some Indians who excitedly imparted some news to the caciques of Cempoal and Quiauitztlan. The news was grave, for the caciques grew pale and shook with fear. Five of Moteçuçuma's taxgatherers had just arrived.

So fate, after all, was playing into Cortés' hands—as it always does into the hands of the strong. (18)

CHAPTER ELEVEN

Cortés "Burns" His Ships

THE MEN of Cempoal and of Quiauitztlan on hearing of the arrival of the powerful *calpixques*, or agents of Moteçuçuma, rushed out of the room, leaving Cortés alone; alone with his meditations. What kind of allies were these? How far would he be able to trust them? How much of his own spirit would he have to instil into them before they could be counted upon to stand up to that Moteçuçuma towards whose tyrannous agents they were so subservient? There they had gone, from tears and sighs and complaints to smiles and bows and greetings; and when he hoped they might be thinking of preparing for a war of resistance, there they were preparing lodgings and ordering a sumptuous meal for their unwelcome visitors.

While thus brooding over the situation, the neglected Spaniards saw the five calpixques pass under their very eyes, full of pride and self-assurance, indifferent to the presence of the strangers, clad in rich embroidered wraps, their shiny hair tied up on top of the head, a curved stick in the right hand "in the manner of the Alguacils of the Crown of Aragón," a nosegay of roses in the left, protected against the sultry weather by feather fans which their servants waved by their sides, and followed by a subservient crowd of local chiefs. In this dignified manner, the Mexican calpixques went to their lodgings and took the meal prepared for them by the terrorised Totonacs; after which, they summoned the fat cacique, his eyes still wet with the tears of woe poured before Cortés, and severely upbraided him for having given hospitality to the bearded whites, in punishment for which, they demanded twenty men and women to sacrifice to Uitzilopochtli. (1)

140

There was the poor fat cacique between the devil of Moteçuçuma and the deep sea of Cortés. Hardly had he left the presence of the dreaded calpixques when he had word that the white chief wanted to see him; by whom he was told that he was on no account to yield to the tyrannous demands of Moteçuçuma's men, since he was now under the protection of the King of Spain. The distracted cacique heard with dismay that he was now protected enough to dare to imprison the calpixques. Cortés had to repeat his suggestion, for at first it terrified the Totonacs as much as the bullying of the calpixques had done. Still, encouraged by Cortés' calm, the Totonacs dared the undarable and put the five calpixques into a kind of "stocks" consisting of a pole with straps tied round the neck, arms and legs, known amongst the Spaniards as "friend's foot." (2)

The effect of this measure was almost magical, and the Spaniards, who were known to be the origin of the new strength, were henceforward held as gods—*Teotl* or, as Bernal Díaz says, *teules*. This exalted position, by the way, lasted but three years, for the friars taught the Indians to realise that there was only one God, much to the annoyance of some of the dethroned teules, "some silly Spaniards," says Father Motolinia, "indignant against us because, they said, we deprived them of their name, and this they said in dead earnest, without realising, poor wretches, that it was they who usurped the name of God." (3) But for the time being the Spaniards were admitted to the benefit of a divine nature established on the basis of their having dared to oppose the might of Moteçuçuma.

Or, at least, so the Totonacs believed. In fact, matters were far more complex. For the Totonacs, the position was quite simple: the thing to do with the prisoners was to sacrifice them straight away. This course had two advantages in their eyes: the calpixques would not be able to escape and report their plight and the rebellious action of the Totonacs to Moteçuçuma; while the gods would no doubt be sensitive to so choice a selection of victims. Cortés, however, vetoed this elegant solution, having views of his own both on worldly and on divine matters, and in fact had the prisoners guarded by his own men. This action saved the life of the calpixques, who were much surprised by it. But their surprise was to soar higher still when, at midnight, two of them were released and taken in secret to the presence of Cortés. The astute captain had seen to everything, even

F

to instructing his soldiers that the men to be released were to be "the two most diligent in your opinion."

He showed himself quite ignorant and uninformed. "Who are you?" he asked them. "Why are you arrested?" "What is your country?" With an earnest, aggrieved face, he heard their story and assured them that he was sorry about it; he begged them to waste no time in going to Mexico and reporting the situation to Moteçuçuma, assuring the Emperor that he was his friend and would watch over his interests and, in particular, over the safety of the three remaining calpixques. The two men were much pleased at this, yet were afraid to move unprotected in Totonac territory; whereupon, Cortés had them conveyed by sea twenty miles towards the southeast, and landed safely on loyal Mexican territory.

Next morning the Totonacs, missing two of their prisoners, were determined to sacrifice the remaining three. Cortés, however, prevailed upon them not only to do nothing of the kind, but, showing great annoyance at the flight of the two others, to hand the three calpixques over to him; he had them chained and finally conveyed to one of his ships, arguing that they would be in safer custody there. But no sooner had they disappeared from the curious eyes of the Totonacs, than the calpixques, walking from surprise to surprise, found themselves set free on board ship, and told in courteous words that the captain would send them back to Mexico as soon as possible.

The Totonacs meanwhile realised two things: they had broken with Moteçuçuma, who was not a man to take their rebellion passively; they were not in a position to resist the onslaught of Moteçuçuma's retaliation without the help of Cortés. They therefore conveyed to the "tongues" their desire to acknowledge their allegiance to the King of the *teules*. As soon as Cortés heard this, he sent word to his notary public, who, armed with paper and ink, set it all down in black and white.

The Totonacs were full of joy at having shaken off the yoke of Moteçuçuma. And Cortés was full of joy having secured a powerful ally, without necessarily having broken with his hidden adversary. (4)

* * *

Cortés may have had by now more detailed information about the enemies of Moteçuçuma. (5) He was a keen searcher for news and information of all kinds, and must by then have gathered at least enough on Moteçuçuma's enemies to feel confident about the enterprise. It was clear to him by now that the vicinity of Quiauitztlan was, from the political point of view, a favourable zone for his base. This explains the fact that all his chroniclers register the actual foundation of Veracruz immediately after his alliance had been well established, not merely with the Cempoalan cacique, but with all the Totonacs. (6)

There is a detail in Bernal Díaz which throws a flood of light on Cortés and well explains his success as a leader. "Cortés," he says, "was the first who began to carry earth and stone on his back and to dig the foundations." Bernal Díaz is writing his book as a rank-and-file protest against Gómara's tendency to attribute all the glory of the enterprise to Cortés; moreover, there was no lack of man-power, for the army was still nearly five hundred strong and they had an unlimited number of Indians at their disposal; but Cortés was in a hurry and he wanted good work. By putting his own shoulder to the wheel, he set the pace for the others: "all the captains and soldiers were constantly at it," says Bernal Díaz. (7) This leader of men, who had already "won his election," and need not therefore have sought the favours of the crowd, was merely showing his keen sense of equality with his men when an important piece of work had to be performed; just as in battle he was the first in action, so in work he was the first in toil.

And yet he discharged to the full his responsibilities as a leader, for the decision to build the town there and the general plan of it are his: the church and the square, the two first ideas which we see to this day from Patagonia to San Francisco and Savannah as the pattern of Spanish town building, were the first features to be drawn on the still virgin soil of the plain, about half a league down from the Quiauitztlan; then, the chapter-house, for it was meet that the chapter of that Rich Town of the True Cross which had so far lived a purely spiritual life should at last be housed with dignity; then a prison, for next to the law must be housed the breakers thereof; then "the arsenal, the store, the slaughterhouse and other buildings suitable for the good government and ornament of the town." (8)

While the Spaniards and their Indian friends were engaged in the building of Veracruz, another embassy from Moteçuçuma was announced. The Mexican Emperor was very well informed of what was going on in his dominions. He was soon aware of the new attitude of defiance adopted by the Totonacs, and, of course, realised that it was due to the support of Cortés. He seems to have been much incensed at this and to have prepared a punitive expedition to be sent against the rebels, without regard to their foreign allies. But as the Mexican army was getting ready for this campaign, the two calpixques released by Cortés arrived in Mexico with their strange tale. There is no ground for believing that Moteçuçuma was taken in by Cortés' astute ways. In point of shrewdness, a Mexican is a match for any European, and Moteçuçuma was no fool. Whatever he thought of the ins and outs of this business, he chose tactics curiously resembling those of his foe: he sent him two of his nephews with presents of gold and wraps "worth about two thousand pesos"; his message was as hot-and-cold as Cortés' own had been; thanks for having set his stewards free; complaints for the support given to the rebellious Totonacs and threats to send an army against the rebels, which he refrained from doing out of deference for Cortés who was still their host.

This was of course a language in which Cortés was past master. He assured the ambassadors that he was and always had been Moteçuçuma's friend; that the remaining three calpixques were safe—thanks of course to him—and would be instantly released, which was done on the spot; but that he was not pleased at the behaviour of Pitalpitoque, Moteçuçuma's representative, who had left San Juan de Ulúa without warning, leaving them without supplies; this had forced Cortés to seek the hospitality of the Totonacs. Moteçuçuma must forgive them for what they had done in the past; and as for the future, inasmuch as the Totonacs had agreed to acknowledge the authority of the King of Spain, the matter had better be left for negotiations when Cortés should have the pleasure and the honour of meeting Moteçuçuma. This said, he gave glass beads to the Emperor's nephews and had his horses gallop about under their impressed eyes. It was all a masterpiece of diplomacy and "presentation." When the arrival of the ambassadors had been reported to him, Cortés had ordered a chair to be brought, on which he sat, surrounded by all his captains, bareheaded, with two pages and an *alférez*, or flag-bearer, in attendance; and he made the messengers wait until they received orders to appear before his presence. (9) This was no vanity; the man who sat in princely majesty on that chair and made the Mexican ambassadors wait had been carrying stones and earth on his shoulders possibly that very morning. It was one of those touches of human artistry which Cortés managed to put into everything he did. Nor had he to wait long for his reward; for the Totonacs, who had expected a violent Mexican vengeance, were overawed to find that instead of an army, Cortés received an embassy loaded with gold, which moreover he kept waiting.

Those Spaniards were indeed *teules,* gods.

*   *   *

Cortés did not fail to perceive the state of mind which his victories had created in the Totonacs, and he soon exploited it for purposes of both business and pleasure. The fat cacique came to seek his help against the Mexican garrisons in Cingapacinga, a land eight or nine leagues away, which raided the Cempoalans and took away their food and women. Cortés turned to his companions and said laughing: "You know, gentlemen, I do believe that in these lands . . . they think we are gods or something like their idols; I have a mind that, to make them believe that one of us is enough to defeat the warriors, their enemies, who, they say, are in their fortress, we should send old Heredia." Heredia was no beauty: "for he was a Biscayan and had an ugly countenance in his face and a big beard and the face all cut about, and one eye blind and he was lame of one leg." Cortés had him summoned, and said: "Go with these caciques down to the river and there stop to drink and wash your hands and fire once with your musket, when I will send for you . . . for I do it so that they may believe we are gods and as you are so ugly they are sure to think you are an idol." Then, turning to the Totonac caciques: "Here is a brother of ours I am sending with you; he will kill all those Mexicans and bring back to me as prisoners all those who resist." The caciques were nonplussed and "looked at Cortés watching whether he changed his face," but as Cortés kept a straight face through it all they took the Spanish *teul* away, and believed in his powers. Nor would Cortés allow the matter to go so far as to leave poor Heredia shorn of his divine prestige; for, on hearing the signal, he had him recalled and explained to the caciques that he had determined to take the matter in hand himself, and asked for *tlamemes* for his artillery. (10) He meant to leave the following day. But, though a god, he was not omnipotent; for gods are only omnipotent in their relations with men; as between god and god, one omnipotence cancels the other; and the Spaniards were all gods. So, when the army was on the point of leaving, seven gods of the Velázquez persuasion loudly and insolently declared that they were determined to go on no campaign whatever, for what they wanted was to return to Cuba, and they demanded that Cortés should put a ship at their disposal as he had promised to do. "True I promised," said Cortés quietly, "yet you do not do well in leaving unmanned your captain's banner." And, this said, he had a ship prepared and provided with food for their return, and then waited. He did not have to wait long; for the alcaldes and councillors of the Rich Town of the True Cross were watching, and they came to Cortés and demanded him to forbid any man to desert, under pain of death—which demand could hardly find Cortés unprepared since he had secretly contrived to have it made. As in previous cases, and not for the last time, Cortés managed to have his inner decisions sanctified by the authority born of all. (11)

*   *   *

The Spanish Olympus being now pacified—at any rate for the time being—the army left for Cingapacinga, passing first through Cempoal where they were joined by two thousand Indian soldiers. The next day, at Vespers, they arrived in Cingapacinga, a stiff climb through fortified rocks. The caciques and priests came forward and explained to Cortés "weeping with their eyes" that the Mexican garrisons had left after the imprisonment of the calpixques; and that the real reason for the raid was an old grudge which the Cempoalans nursed against them; they begged Cortés not to allow the Cempoalans to enter their territory and plunder it. Cortés instantly gave orders to prevent the advance of the Cempoalan force; but the Spaniards were not quick enough and found the Cempoalans helping themselves liberally in the farms of their enemies. Cortés was wroth, not only at the plundering but also because he felt he had been used as a tool—the thing which the habitual tool-user hates most. He forced the Cempoalans to disgorge their loot—slaves of both sexes, and hens—which was returned to the owners, and "with a very furious face" he ordered them out of the camp.

This attitude greatly increased the authority of Cortés, and won for him the formal allegiance of the Cingapacinga people; he lost no time, however, in effecting a reconciliation between them and the men of Cempoal, for his policy obviously was to unite his friends and to disunite his enemies..(12) And, moreover, with him passions and emotions were never allowed to outlive their utility with one exception only.

He was soon to give another touching example of this rule and a striking example of this exception. On their way back, a soldier stole two hens from a native house. Cortés happened to see it. He had the soldier instantly hanged, in the presence of the whole army, and as they all were watching the knot slip to its deadly grip, Alvarado, who stood beside Cortés, drew his sword and cut the rope. Alvarado knew his chief well and realised that he was thereby releasing not only the soldier from death but the captain from an awkward situation, and that Cortés would be relieved to find that justice had been satisfied without loss of life. (13)

The men of Cempoal, though defrauded of their expectations of loot, conceived a high opinion of the Spaniards and offered them food, lodging and a present of eight of their daughters, one of whom was a niece of the fat cacique whom the grateful chief begged Cortés himself to accept. The girls were dressed in rich native chemises, wearing gold necklaces and earrings, and accompanied by servant maids. Cortés received them graciously but, as for accepting them, he explained to the fat cacique and to his friends that it was first necessary for the Cempoalans to give up their idols, their human sacrifices, their cannibalistic practices, and their sodomite ways. This was his exception, the only point on which Cortés was never ready to compromise. He had achieved a masterpiece, the peaceful penetration and diplomatic conquest of vast territories for the Crown of Castille; all that, he was now ready to put to the arbitrament of war because the men of Cempoal refused to give up their idols. The Spaniards, incensed at the appalling sights they had beheld, were ready for everything. Cortés, on his side, appealed to them to be ready to die, for he was determined to dash the idols down to the ground. The fat cacique sized up the situation and called for his troops; but the determination of the Spaniards, the arguments acutely supplied by Doña Marina, who reminded the Cempoalans of Moteçuçuma, awaiting his vengeance, and possibly the debonair proclivities of the fat cacique made the Indians acquiesce with horror in what they could not avoid, and as soon as caciques and priests had covered their faces, fifty Spanish soldiers ran up the steep steps of the temple and dragged down the monstrous figures which fell in pieces down the very steps over which so many gory human bodies before them had been precipitated in their honour.

The temple was cleaned, whitewashed, adorned with roses and plants and put in charge of an old soldier and eight native priests who were made to cut off their heavy manes, thick with victims' blood. An image of the Virgin and Child was put on an altar, and a tall Cross on a stand. The Indians were taught how to make wax candles and told to keep some always burning before the Virgin. Father Olmedo said mass. The girls were brought from their parents' houses, where they had remained while they were still heathen, and were christened; the most beautiful, Doña Francisca, Cortés gave to his friend Puertocarrero, as he had done with Doña Marina; the fat cacique's niece was named Doña Catalina, "and she was very ugly; she was given to Cortés, and he received her with a good face"; Cortés gave the others to his chief captains; and as the girls were now Christian, the Spanish felt free to live with them in mortal sin. (14)

* * *

Upon his return to the Rich Town of the True Cross, Cortés found that a caravel which he had bought in Santiago de Cuba and left behind in dry dock had arrived in the harbour. It was commanded by Francisco de Salcedo, known as The Polished, for he was most finical about his elegance. He brought with him food, ten soldiers and a captain, one Luis Marín, "who was most valuable," says Bernal Díaz; one horse and one mare, which was even more valuable; and finally news: Diego Velázquez had been appointed Adelantado of Cuba and had received powers to barter and settle in Yucatán. (15)

This new fact meant a fresh stimulus to the Velázquez faction, still turbulent below the surface, as events were soon to show; it was therefore imperative to take bold and rapid decisions. Cortés took them—three, all as bold as was to be expected of his stout heart and subtle brain; but, in his usual manner, he manœuvred to have them put forward by his rank and file. These decisions were: (a) to go to Mexico either by ruse or by force or by both; (b) to send a ship straight to Spain with all the wealth he and his men had amassed whether in the form of presents from Moteçuçuma and other caciques or through bartering; (c) to "burn" his ships.

The first two decisions are recorded by Bernal Díaz in simple words which reveal their true origin with disarming candour: "Most of us, soldiers, told Cortés [. . .] that we had stayed more than three months in that land and that it might be a good thing to go and see what kind of thing was the great Montezuma and seek our life and our luck, and that ere we took to the road we should send [messengers] to kiss his Majesty's feet and to render him an account and a report of all that had happened since we had sailed from Cuba, and it was also discussed that we should send his Majesty all the gold we had acquired either by bartering or as presents sent by Montezuma, and Cortés answered that it was an excellent decision and that he had already been discussing it with a certain number of gentlemen."

Not content with hearing from his soldiers exactly what he wanted to hear, Cortés, in his scrupulous respect for the democratic forms, organised a regular plebiscite for which he appointed as both canvassers and tellers precisely two of the leaders of the Velázquez faction, i.e. of the opposition—for there is nothing new under the sun. These two, Diego de Ordás and Francisco de Montejo, went from soldier to soldier requesting them all to sign—of course if they so wished—that, as the other captains and soldiers had signed before them, they agreed to give up their share of gold in order to swell the present which was sent to the Court. The vote was of course unanimous, and the Chapter appointed as "procuradores," i.e. representatives of the commonwealth, Alonso Hernández Puertocarrero and Francisco de Montejo, a curious coincidence, it must be owned, for Puertocarrero happened to be Cortés' intimate friend and confidant; while Montejo, one of Velázquez' chief men, had just received from Cortés about two thousand pesos of gold. (16)

F*

The two representatives were given a paper signed by all the men in the army—at least all but those who sided with Velázquez—addressed to the King and Queen (for Joan of Castille, though unable to reign, was still officially the Queen of Spain). (17) In this letter, the Chapter of Veracruz summed up the history of the attempts made before Cortés to secure a footing in Mexico; reviewed the events, up to date, of Cortés' own expedition; recorded the foundation of Veracruz and the appointment of Cortés as Captain and Chief Justice "until your Majesties decide whatever is best for their service"; described the land and its peoples, their ways, and the need in which they stood to be converted to the Holy Faith; laid stress on the fact that Velázquez had contributed but one-third to the expenses of the fleet, and even that only "in wines and clothes and the things of little value which he sold us here at a much higher price than he had paid for them"; and begged their Majesties to grant no authority to him and to confirm the appointment of Cortés till the whole country was conquered and at peace. (18)

This letter was of course written under the influence of Cortés—due to sheer intellectual superiority, for, so far, he had not chosen to use the all but unlimited power which his double authority as Captain and Chief Justice gave him; but though written for him it was not written by him, as an examination of its style suffices to show. The letter was indispensable, not as a kind of "progress report" to the King-Emperor, since Cortés wrote at length himself, (19) but as an "independent" testimonial in his favour on the part of the army. It is likely that he had seen rough drafts of it when, at his request, the Chapter showed it to him. On reading the high praise bestowed upon him by his soldiers, he was very much pleased and thanked them, even though he wished they had not mentioned the promise of a fifth which they had made him nor the two previous attempts made by his predecessors, Grijalva and Hernández de Córdoba. This was promptly seized upon by one of the minor gods who surrounded him: "there was no lack of a person to tell him that we cannot leave out anything in what we report to our lord the King." (20) Yet Bernal Díaz himself, who never leaves out any shadow in his portrait of Cortés, provides the detail which shows that, in this observation to his soldiers, Cortés was not ungenerous but merely cautious and shrewd. All—save the Velázquez group—

were interested in securing Cortés' position at Court; the letter was not a historical document, written for scientific information, but a political paper, intended to achieve specific results: the time had not come for them to speak of Grijalva and of Hernández de Córdoba; "he said that now, at this moment, it would have been better to have left that out." And there is not the slightest doubt that he was right. Nor did he think the matter grave enough to insist—and the letter was left as it stood. (21)

As arguments of more weight in his favor, Cortés sent all the treasures which the army had accumulated, headed by the famous golden sun and silver moon. Not without difficulty, he obtained from the fat cacique four young men and two young women from the wooden cages in which they were being fattened for their symbolic sacrifice to the gods and effective consumption by the faithful, and the ex-victims were also sent to Spain. Finally the presents to the King contained a number of pictorial records on cotton of the events of native history.

Cortés gave his messengers his best ship, his chief pilot and three thousand castillians of gold for expenses as well as another three thousand for his father, no doubt to be spent in manœuvres at Court. He instructed them to sail through the Bahama Canal, straight to Spain, and above all not to touch Cuban soil.

They left San Juan de Ulúa on July 26, 1519. (23) They did touch Cuban soil. Rivers of blood were to flow from their disobedience.

*   *   *

With the departure of Puertocarrero, Doña Marina lost her *de facto* husband. She became Cortés' companion and bore him a son. This fact does not seem to have aroused any special interest, and Bernal Díaz records it without the slightest comment. (24) She was handsome and intelligent, "and had much being" (25) as Bernal Díaz says with his inimitable strength; she came to be so prominent a feature in his armies that the Indians gave her the name *Malintzin*, made up of Marina (the sound *r* being unknown to the Mexicans, who imitated it, like the Chinese, with *l*) and the suffix *tzin*, conveying rank or nobility. And she enjoyed the unique distinction of having given her own name to her master, for the

Indians took the habit of referring to Cortés himself by the name of his gifted interpreter-mistress, Malintzin, which the Spaniards turned into *Malinche*; yet Cortés failed to see her merits at first and passed her on with hardly a glance to his friend Puertocarrero and yet again, as soon as Puertocarrero left for Spain, he took her to himself and made her the mother of one of his sons, to whom he gave his father's name; and yet again, four years later, in 1523, he married her to one of his captains, "an hidalgo whose name was Juan Xaramillo." (26)

There are a number of observations to be drawn from these curious yet undisputed facts. The first bears on the background. We should go badly astray were we to draw the conclusion that the attitude of the Spanish captains to those Indian girls, who were presented to them generally by the girls' own parents, was one of sexual indulgence and no more. There was in Spain an institution which endeavoured to combine the sanctity of monogamous marriage and the polygamous proclivities of the race: the *barragania*. The *barragana* was a kind of recognized and admitted concubine. It is only fair to assume that, explicitly or tacitly, the Spanish captains who took to them one or more of the young *cacicas*, looked upon them as *barraganas*, i.e. wives in all but the sacrament. We have seen how they decorated them with a Spanish *Doña*, outward symbol of nobility which implied respect and deference on the part of the rank and file; they were *ladies*, not slaves. When, as we shall see anon, Cortés conquered the friendship of Tlaxcala, the chief cacique, Xicotencatl, gave him his daughter, whom Cortés gave to Alvarado. She became Doña Luisa; "the greatest part of Tlaxcala recognised and held her as their lady, and by her Pedro de Alvarado, unmarried, had a son who was named Don Pedro and a daughter whose name is Doña Leonor, wife, now, of Don Francisco de la Cueva, a good nobleman, a cousin of the Duke of Albuquerque." As for Cortés, his son Don Martín Cortés, whom he had by Doña Marina, became Knight Commander of the Order of St. James. (27) The attitude of the Spanish captains towards the Indian women of rank was therefore of a complex nature; we cannot even be certain that the reason why they did not marry them was one of stand-offish superiority, since this would have worked equally strongly against their half-caste offspring; their studious care to remain celibates seems to have been due to ambition, for they all hoped that their wealth and glory would enable them to enter into a matrimonial alliance with the ducal houses of Spain—as Alvarado and Cortés actually did. But, short of marriage, the Spaniards granted their Indian mistresses every other possible honour and privilege, implying on their part the most genuine social and racial equality.

This is the background on which we must endeavour to see Cortés' attitude to Doña Marina. There can be no doubt as to his feelings towards her: he had a high opinion of her ability, but he was by no means smitten with love for her. Indeed, there is no getting away from the fact that Cortés chose to make her his bedfellow just during the period when her loyalty was vital to him, and that he was quite content to see her mated to other men both before he realised her usefulness as a political tool and after she ceased to be, if not useful, at any rate indispensable as such.

This conclusion dovetails with two features of his character: the real nature of his amorous life on the one hand and, on the other, his attitude towards the passions in general. His amorous life was both precocious and active; but his almost unlimited polygamy and a certain readiness to share a woman with other men, at any rate in the course of time, as shown in the case of Doña Marina, point to a love-activity fed almost exclusively on animal spirits. Cortés was a splendid, healthy, strong animal. He delighted in all kinds of activity and was nearly untirable. His love campaigns were just another form of life, as were his war campaigns. The particular woman on whom his vitality was spent did not matter—of course within certain limits of quality and taste. His polygamy was frankly and openly opportunist.

It was moreover severely kept under his iron will. We have seen him twice passing the choicest peaches of the Mexican orchard to his friend Puertocarrero, and receiving "with a good face" that Doña Catalina, niece of the fat cacique, who, Bernal Díaz ruthlessly tells us, was very ugly. In these scenes, so clearly recorded, Cortés shows himself a man of action, in complete control of his own desires, capable of subordinating everything that is personal to the high endeavour in which he is engaged. This was a constant feature in his character. He was no puritan, no abstainer. He loved and hated, enjoyed his pleasure and gave vent to his fury—but all these motions of the soul were like so many dogs sporting themselves under his ever serene eyes. At the slightest call to work, everything fell back into order. Seldom if ever was Cortés hampered by any passion, pleasant or unpleasant, in the fulfilling of his coolly formed decisions. And in at least one case, that of his intimacy with Doña Marina, he used his passion to fasten to his service a being whose loyalty was of paramount importance for the success of his plans.

Four days after the departure of the Chapter representatives; at midnight, one Bernardino de Coria asked to see Cortés, and with much fear and trembling confessed to him that he wanted to back out of a conspiracy formed by a group of Velázquez' followers to steal a ship and return to Cuba, to report to the Governor about Cortés' doings and the departure of his messengers with a ship full of wealth. Cortés was shocked to hear that the conspirators were ready to sail that very night. He obtained from Coria a list of the culprits, gave swift orders to deprive the stolen ship of her compass and rigging, and seized the conspirators. This time, punishment was swift and stern. Escudero and Cermeño, who seem to have been the leaders, were hanged; Escudero happened to be the alguacil who had overpowered him and taken him to jail in his youthful days; Cermeño, says Torquemada, "could scent land fifteen leagues away"; and he drily adds, "though he did not scent that death"; a pilot known as Umbria had his feet cut off, and two sailors were flogged.

Judged by the standards of military discipline, not merely of his day, but of any day up to about one hundred years ago, Cortés' sanctions were mild; and all authors record that he turned a blind eye on many culprits "of more quality, because circumstances forced him to excuse them," as was the case with the priest Juan Díaz. This is a clear occasion in which Cortés, given time and circumstances, and bearing in mind current standards, showed himself capable of the utmost restraint in the use of severity. (28)

Moderate though it was, this act of authority does not seem to have been easy for him; as soon as he had signed the death sentences "with much sighing and feeling," (29) he galloped away to Cempoal, giving orders that two hundred soldiers should join him there; whether this was in order to be out of reach at the hour of clemency or for other reasons is not clear: but, as he had instructed Alvarado, whom he had sent foraging with two hundred soldiers, to meet him also at Cempoal, it is plain that he meant to leave the smallest possible garrison in Veracruz—at most about eighty men. This again was a carefully calculated move on his part; for in his plan of events the time had come to run the ships aground, and the operation would be made easier if most of the men were away at the time.

For this is the culminating moment in the life of this heroic man. Not in vain has the world made of this action a symbol of man's determination to conquer fate, and transfigured a fact into a legend by making Cortés burn his ships. He had conceived the thought of conquering Moteçuçuma's Empire: a few days earlier, he had written to Charles V: "I shall have him a prisoner, or dead, or a subject of the royal Crown of your Majesty." (30) This he was determined to do. But what about his troops? Though heavily punished, the Velázquez faction still hankered after their farms and wives in Cuba, and there were men amongst his soldiers who thought it a folly for five hundred men to attempt the conquest of an Empire rich and highly civilised in its technique. The idea of being some day fattened for Moteçuçuma's table, as they had seen other prisoners fattened for lesser tables, may well have added to the objections raised to so rash a conquest by the more prudent members of the army. These were the thoughts that were revolving in Cortés' mind at the time of the Escudero revolt. A less spirited captain would have taken the revolt as a danger signal and prepared the return of the fleet; for Cortés, it was but the last stimulus which spurred him to carry out his bold decision: "And as, over and above those who, being friends and servants of Diego Velázquez, wanted to leave this land, there were others who, seeing it so big and so full of people and such peoples, and how few we Spaniards were, were of the same opinion, I, bearing in mind that if I left the ships there they would revolt (and sail away) with them, and that [. . .] I would have remained alone [. . .] contrived, under pretence of the ships being unfit for sea service, to run them aground, so that the men lost hope of leaving the country and I took to the road feeling safer." (31)

"I contrived," said Cortés. It was a piece of work after his usual style, one in which astuteness and courage were inextricably mixed, indeed, which began in tortuous, underground manœuvres but ended in a daring stand and the victory of the spirit. The complete picture can be obtained only by combining the elements supplied on the one hand by Cortés and his chroniclers and on the other by Bernal Díaz. Cortés began by "planting" some friends to suggest to him that it might be best to get rid of the ships, because there were about one hundred seamen who would be better employed in war than idling in the port. This was just casually mooted in a group of friends while at Cempoal. Some objected; others pointed out that this would finally do away with the danger of further conspiracies to sail away to Cuba. Having thus prepared the ground amongst his friends, Cortés called in the pilots, took them into his confidence, promised them "seas and mountains," gave them gold, and finally half bamboozled, half bullied them into accepting responsibility for the deed: they bored holes in the ships and came to report to him that the ships were no longer seaworthy as they were eaten up with sea-worm. Cortés pulled a long face, looked at the men in whose presence the sad news had been imparted, and waited for several of them to feel that they had found the right solution—to have the ships run aground. As soon as the popular instinct had hit on the course of action to take, Cortés, always true to his democratic feelings, followed the clue. He sent Juan de Escalante to Veracruz to see that everything useful was landed out of the ships and that the empty hulls were grounded.

But here he or Escalante made a mistake: either for technical reasons, which are unknown, or because of that kind of resistance to destruction which lies hidden in most of us, only five of the ten ships were run aground at first; the army took it as an unavoidable calamity. When, however, a few days later, four other ships were run aground, there was a deep emotion in the rank and file; what they might have accepted as a great calamity had it all occurred on the same day, awoke their suspicions when done piecemeal; they guessed the secret intentions of their sly captain and felt mutinous— indeed, if we are to believe Las Casas, murderous.

Cortés was too farsighted not to have foreseen this danger. That morning, after mass, he called his men together and spoke to them with that effective, simple yet elegant eloquence which time and again calls forth the admiration of Bernal Díaz; far from running away from the cause of the trouble—the feeling his men had that by destroying the ships he had cut off their retreat and left them to conquer or die—he dwelt on it: he told them how they would now have to fight not only for God and King as ever, but for dear life as well "and about this he told many comparisons and heroic deeds of the Romans." To the faint-hearted, he offered the one ship that remained—and his contempt.

They accepted neither, and he ran aground that last ship also. (32)

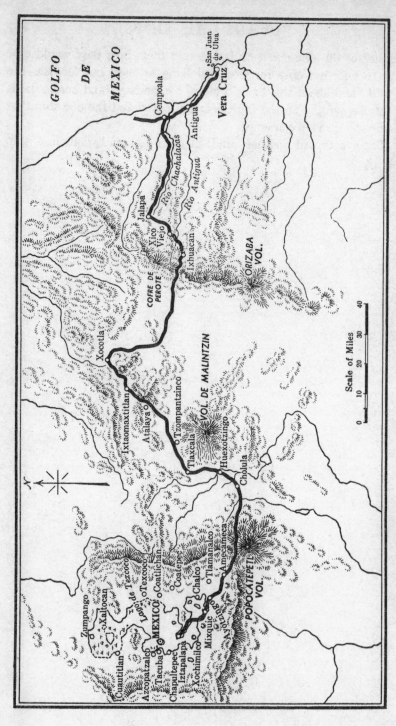

Map of part of Mexico, showing the route of Cortés from Vera Cruz to the City of Mexico

PART III
THE FIRST CONQUEST

CHAPTER TWELVE

Victory over Tlaxcala

THERE is nothing like it in history, not even the crossing of the Rubicon; for Caesar, by this act, while symbolically cutting himself adrift from Republican Rome, was materially marching in strength towards it; if, politically, he turned away, actually he returned to that city of which he was a prominent citizen, in which he had so many friends; a city which he could reasonably expect to master. But Cortés destroying his ships deliberately cut himself off, not merely from the State of Spain, as represented by Velázquez, but from the only base from which he could expect eventual help and supplies; and he turned his face towards an Empire which, barbarous though it was, could outnumber him by possibly one thousand to one, so far as he knew, in a virgin country of which he had no map and but scanty information. His decision was truly heroic. The small circle of captains and soldiers who knew of it, and who helped him to impose it on the rest of the army, are entitled to a share of admiration, but the decision was his; it sprang from his heart in the awful solitude of leadership, the most desolate peak accessible to the human soul.

Now they had to turn resolutely inland. Till that fateful day, they were all attached to Cuba by that channel of subconscious attention and tension which our memory keeps open at the back of the soul and which, hidden in the inner dark through the days, and gleaming under the moon of dreams through the night, connects us with our immediate past. His men, even the most determined, walked light-footed on a land in which they felt but the guests of time and luck; there, round the corner of their thoughts, Cuba waited, their

161

farms, their tame Indians, their cows, their comfortable houses, for
some their wives and families, for all the sedate life of a prosperous
settler, a community in which the Spaniard was the lord.

Cortés ran all that aground with the ten ships. Cuba, to be sure,
was still there, in the blue sea, with its farms, its cows and its tame
Indians; but the way to Cuba was no longer through sunny blue
waves, rocked in soft idleness, oblivious of danger and endeavour;
it was through Moteçuçuma's Court, which had to be conquered by
ruse, by force, or by both; through a sea of warlike Indians who ate
their prisoners and donned their skins as trophies; at one stroke of
their chief's masterly hand, the five hundred men had lost that flow
of vital memories and hopes which linked up their souls with their
mother-island; at one stroke, their backs had been withered and had
lost all sense of life. Henceforward, for them, all life was ahead,
towards those forbidding peaks which rose gigantically on the horizon as if to bar all access to what was now not merely their ambition,
but their only possible aim—Mexico, mysterious and powerful behind
the conflicting tribes.

Cortés' back was not oversensitive. He was one of those men
who are born with a forward impulse, whose whole vitality is gathered
up in the senses and organs which cut through time and space: eyes
that see, hands that work, heart that propels, brain that steers. He
had been intent on the conquest from the outset. (1) For him, the
vital link with Cuba had been severed on the day when he had made
up his mind that he would achieve what both Hernández de Córdoba
and Grijalva had left undone, and that, to that end, he would break
away from Velázquez. The impulse which drove him forward was
vigorous enough to carry him on, over the mountain wall, the bloody
battlefields, the net of Indian civil wars, the traps laid for him by
crafty Moteçuçuma, on and on till he had caught the heathen
Emperor dead or alive, and brought his barbarous Empire into the
Christian fold of Charles V and to the light of the faith which for
him was holy. The decision to destroy his ships, heroic in our eyes,
was in his probably a mere measure of prudence, rather obvious and
ordinary, for by then he was already too much immersed in his
enterprise to realise the size of the actions which his mighty endeavour led him to achieve.

And yet, such is the irony of fate, Cortés, the only man in the army for whom the recent past was dead, was the only one also who was not allowed by fate to forget the world that lay behind his back, as he prepared to ascend the heights that led to Culúa. There, in Cuba, Diego Velázquez nursed his grievance and was sure to be preparing something against him. Of his two representatives, one was loyal, but the other one, Montejo, was only attached to him by chains of gold; and Cortés knew only too well that gold could undo what gold had done, particularly in the case of a man who spent more than his income warranted (2); Cortés could not feel certain that the world behind his back would not avenge itself, not until he had had news of the outcome of his message to the King-Emperor. Moreover, Diego Velázquez was only one of the agents of fate lurking behind his back. No one knew better than Cortés how many men there were in the Islands of the Indies and in the harbours of Spain ready to stake their all for any Empire that might be in the offing as a temptation to unemployed conquerors; they were on the edge of the world; the Spanish State was not in a position to organise the discovery and conquest of the New World, any more than, in our own lifetime, the powerful nations of the West have proved able to organise the conquest of the air upon the discovery of aviation; that historical task fell to the lot of individual adventurers, who rushed to it in picturesque eagerness and disorder; the offices in Seville and in the itinerant chancery of the Crown of Spain were utterly unable—and some of the officials were unwilling—to follow with more than a fitful, cursory and incompetent attention these tumultuous and far-off events; governors, adelantados, captains, were vaguely appointed to nebulously known territories for more or less defined dates, and while the solemn and verbose papers crossed the ocean in the slow caravels, other captains invaded by force of arms and by virtue of their free initiative the preserves which the court-intriguer had tried to carve for himself; the captains fought against the Indians with gunshot and powder, and against one another with paper and ink; but they all knew that in those days, in the Indies, the only safe road to success was success itself

*   *   *

Such was the situation which, no doubt, occupied the mind of Hernán Cortés in Cempoal when, having destroyed his ships, he was preparing his departure for Mexico. He had left Veracruz, as he thought, for good. His instinct told him that it was best to keep his men away from that sea on which many of them were not to cast eyes again, and that their determination to venture inland would thrive better in Cempoal than in the harbour full of memories where the ships' broken hulls still lay, like the carcasses of their dead hopes. He had left in Veracruz one of his trusted men, Juan de Escalante, with a garrison of between fifty and one hundred Spaniards, mostly seamen and more or less disabled soldiers, and had urged the friendly caciques to keep on good terms with him and help him to build the church, fortress and houses. Taking Escalante by the hand, in the presence of all the caciques: "This is my brother," he had said; "whatever he tells you to do, you must do."

One day, while Cortés was still in Cempoal, Juan de Escalante saw a ship cruising off the coast. He made bonfires and displayed white flags, he rode along the shore wrapped in a red cloak; but the ship paid no attention to him, though his endeavours to be seen could not have passed unnoticed. This coyness aroused the suspicions and curiosity of Escalante, who in one of the ships' punts—the only sea-craft which remained available—took to the sea and came within speaking distance of the ghost-ship, whose occupants told him that "they were of Francisco de Garay, lieutenant and governor of Jamaica, and that they came to discover." Escalante explained that Hernán Cortés "had already 'peopled' this island in the name of His Highness and had built a town about one league away from where the ships were now and that they might sail thereto and inform him of their coming." But though he offered to help in every possible way, and even to act as a pilot for them, and though the newcomers agreed to come, they did not do so and remained hovering about the coast, in their ghostlike manner, sailing hither and thither —aimlessly, it would seem.

Such was the gist of a letter which Cortés received in Cempoal from his Veracruz lieutenant. While he was busy preparing for his march forward, the world behind pulled him back. He lost no time. We are going to see him, throughout his life, always turn instantly towards the spot where the stakes are highest and most urgent, always present at the summit of action. He left Alvarado in command at Cempoal, and galloped away towards Veracruz with four horsemen, giving instructions for fifty soldiers to follow him. They were to be "of the swiftest," says Bernal Díaz; and he adds not without pride, "There and then he himself chose us."

When Cortés arrived in Veracruz, he found that the ships—three of them—had been located close to a river, three leagues down the coast, and that no one had landed from them, so far. Thither he went at once with an escort—"before we had even eaten a bite," says Bernal Díaz. Escalante, who perchance had had no lunch either, advised his chief to rest, offering to go himself. "A lame goat sleeps no siesta," dryly remarked Cortés, and rode away. About two-thirds of the way, he met three of Garay's men, three soldiers—one might think, three conquerors, ready to subdue a whole Empire with their heroic prowess? Not in the least. One of them was a notary, Guillén de la Loa, who, armed with a deadly inkpot and a sharp and poisonous quill, came to take possession of the land on behalf of a Captain Alonzo Alvarez Pineda, whose fleet was anchored in Pánuco River; the other two were his witnesses: Andrés Núñez, shipwright, and Master Peter of the Harp, whose trade is not known, though, if trade and name go together, he might be a musician. The notary informed Cortés how Pineda had discovered that land—a land, of course, can bear any amount of discovering without the quivering of a twig—and wished to "people" it, and therefore summoned him to draw up the border between their respective discoveries. Cortés was first curious to learn what was Pineda's title to discover, for he knew full well that there were fellows about who set out to "discover" and even to "conquer" with titles that did not bear close scrutiny, and he was very keen that discoveries and conquests should not be undertaken on flimsy bases. Guillén de la Loa, being a man of law, knew of course all about his principal's titles. He was good enough to explain that when Garay, in his distant Jamaica, had wind of the twenty thousand pesos brought back from Yucatán by Grijalva and his companions, he was seized with such an irresistible eagerness to spread the Holy Christian Faith in those gold-yielding lands that he had sent his steward Torralba to Spain; and, as he was on good terms with Bishop Fonseca, he had been appointed Adelantado of all he might discover towards the north; whereupon, he had sent Alvarez Pineda with three ships, two hundred and seventy soldiers, supplies and horses.

Considering that he himself had five hundred men and sixteen horses, Cortés cannot have thought much of Pineda's legal titles, and so, with his usual swiftness and economy of useless stages, he asked "with loving words" whether it would be possible for him to get hold of the ship which was close at hand. Guillén de la Loa, being a man of law, was not in the least put out by this extraordinary proposal, and very reasonably answered that he and his two companions would try to signal her with their cloaks, which they did, though without success. This is what Bernal Díaz, who was present, tells us. Cortés, however, wrote to Charles V that he offered his services and suggested a conversation in Veracruz, but that Loa answered that "on no account would the captain [Pineda] or any of his people meet me on land or wherever I would happen to be"; and, suspecting that this attitude was due to some harm which they had done in the land, he changed his tactics. Here Cortés is embellishing his own part in the episode. Much as he tries to picture himself to the Emperor as the embodiment of law and order, Cortés is still on no better a footing than Pineda. He is still in the wilderness of pioneering, and he knows he can only prevail by some audacious stroke. An offer to negotiate may, indeed, have been made; but his "loving words" to enquire how he could get hold of the ship ring true to life.

Whatever the motive, the fact is that Cortés resolved on a stratagem. He made the notary and witnesses change clothes with three of his men, and he, with his troops, ostensibly marched away along the coast, as though they were returning to Veracruz, and then hid in the woods till past midnight, when after the moon had set they returned to the spot from which the ship could be seen. At sunrise, the three disguised soldiers signalled to the ship; a boat was sent to fetch the stranded men; there were about a dozen of Garay's soldiers in the boat, but suspecting the look of things, only four landed who were promptly seized by Cortés, not without danger, for one of them, who happened to be the master of the ship, would have killed Escalante with his musket, "but that Our Lord wished that the wick did not catch fire." Cortés had to return to Veracruz leaving this matter unsettled. Yet he did not sleep over it, and, knowing that the ambition of Garay aimed at Pánuco, he devoted special care to cultivating the caciques of the district, who seem to have sided with him. But Garay was to remain one of the ghostly dangers in the world which threatened him behind his back. (3)

* * *

On August 16th, 1519, Cortés left Cempoal for Mexico at the head of an army composed of four hundred Spaniards, thirteen horses, six or seven small pieces of artillery and one thousand *tlamemes*, or native carriers, for transporting food, ammunition and artillery; for, as for soldiers' baggage, as Bernal Díaz points out, "none was needed, for our own arms, our spears and muskets and bows and bucklers and all other kinds, we slept with them." (4) A number of Cempoal persons of quality accompanied Cortés all the way; as well as some of Moteçuçuma's local chiefs, who deliberately led Cortés through the bad passes, through rough and broken lands, of different climates, some of them very hot, "so that, with the roughness of the roads and violent changes of the weather, our men should fall ill and die, and so their arrival in Mexico should be avoided." (5) Cortés may have had an inkling of this; at any rate, he seems to have split his forces during the first day or two, for Cervantes de Salazar records that on arriving in Xalapa, Cortés and Alvarado met, for they had marched separately "to avoid troubling the villages they were to cross." In this first day of their journey, they lost a foal; the young stranger was adopted by a herd of wild deer and found eighteen months later, when it was made to return to civilisation—and to war. (6)

They marched three days in lands of Cempoal and other communities inimical to Moteçuçuma, by a circuitous route which endeavoured to climb the forbidding height turning first northwest, towards Xalapa, then almost dead east, towards Tlaxcala. They had left behind the swampy, hot lowlands, "where," says Torquemada, "the horses sink down to the belly," and were climbing through drier slopes, sunny and gay. On his way up, Bernal Díaz still notes "many vines of grapes of the country," but not for long, because soon after crossing a pass they found themselves on a bleak deserted plain beaten by frozen winds, and had to withstand a hail and rain storm on empty stomachs. Some of their Cuban Indians died of cold; the Spaniards "though feeling the frost through their armour, which was all they had to keep them warm," (8) suffered the weather with the usual adaptability of the Iberian; they were marching on a level of over seven thousand feet, having left behind them natural and human obstacles enough to put fear into the bravest heart; but they marched on mesmerised by their brave captain, even though "very much on our guard and in very good order" towards that enigmatic Mexico of their dreams. After crossing another pass, they beheld a plain which showed signs of good cultivation; the air was soft; the people seemed poor to Cortés: but after wandering two leagues in search of the town they came upon it and were surprised and pleased to find that it surpassed Cempoal, "for the houses were all of masonry and very well built and there were in them many and very great halls and many rooms very well decorated." Cortés calls this place Caltanmi, and Bernal Díaz, Cocotlan; some Portuguese soldiers were reminded of their native Castilblanco, and the army seems to have adopted that name; it has been identified as Tlatlanqui-tepec, which might suffice to answer the question: what is in a name? (9)

The cacique, Olintetl (which Bernal Díaz turns into Olintecle), received them very well, if we are to believe Cortés. But we gather from other sources that his attitude was, to say the least, mixed. Cortés had sent him two Cempoalese to announce his arrival; Moteçuçuma had also sent a message to Olintetl, instructing him to be courteous and hospitable—in form at any rate. Olintetl complied —according to his lights: he sacrificed fifty men just before the arrival of the Spaniards, so that they should find the blood still fresh; but on the other hand he gave them "to eat little and with a bad will." (10) Evidently Moteçuçuma was following tactics similar to those of Cortés—friendly in form but inimical in substance; and it is only on the assumption of such tactics on the part of Moteçuçuma that Olintetl's attitude can be understood. He was a fat man— fatter even, it would seem, than the lord of Cempoal, for when carried by the young men his body shook with the movement; and the Spanish soldiers nicknamed him "The Shaker." He was also shrewd, and seems to have made special efforts to impress Cortés with the power of Moteçuçuma. "Are you his vassal?" asked Cortés. Olintetl kept silent so long that the sands of Cortés' patience ran out and, as he was going to ask again, the cacique, sure now of his effect, answered with another question: "And who on earth is not

Moteçuçuma's vassal?" This brought out Cortés' usual speech on the great Christian Emperor who had for his vassals kings and potentates more powerful than Moteçuçuma could be. But Olintetl insisted on the strength and impregnability of Mexico, and how it was built on water, and only accessible through three easily defended causeways, so that, says Bernal Díaz, "we were astonished hearing him and all he told about its strength and bridges, and as we are of such a quality, we Spanish soldiers, we wished we were already trying our luck." Meanwhile, the sly, fat cacique went on laying it on as thick as possible, for "Montezuma was so great a lord that all he wished to possess he mastered and that he [Olintetl] did not know whether Montezuma would be pleased to have had us there and given us food and lodging without his permission." Whereupon Cortés again spoke of the King of Spain and how he, Cortés, had come on his instructions, to tell Moteçuçuma he was to stop sacrificing men and eating human flesh and indulging in sodomite practices; and, gradually rising to higher spheres, "he declared many more things touching upon our faith." Olintetl and the other caciques kept silent, feeling no doubt out of their depth in theology. They had wasted their time; the strangers were not impressed by their tales of Moteçuçuma's might, and, for some reason which they could not fathom, these unaccountable men objected to human sacrifices and sodomite ways. There was a deadlock. Cortés had an idea—it was by no means new; he turned to the soldiers and captains who were present and said: "It seems to me, gentlemen, that, since we can do nothing else, we had better erect a cross."

The soldiers all agreed that this might be a good thing; but the friar was not of the same opinion. "It seems to me, sir," argued Father Olmedo, "that it is too soon to leave a Cross to these peoples, for they are shameless and fearless and, as they are Montezuma's vassals, they might burn it or do some evil thing, and this which we have told them will do till they have a better knowledge of our holy faith." Cortés was content to rely on the advice of his spiritual expert, but other means had to be found to impress the natives with the power of the Christian civilisation; so the Spaniards again displayed their swift horses, and their noisy guns and even a hound about which the Indians asked whether it was a tiger or a lion. These methods gradually established their reputation as *teules,* and on the strength of this divine essence they obtained a few presents of gold, "all of it of low standard," and four Indian women "who were very good for grinding bread." Yet, despite this exalted position, many a Spanish god must have shivered uncomfortably in the depths of his mortal flesh, at the sight of the skull store, in which there were rows and rows of neatly arranged human skulls and crossbones "which might be one hundred thousand, and I say again one hundred thousand." (11)

* * *

Nothing daunted, however, by such gruesome sights, the army, always in good order and ready for any emergency, marched on a couple of leagues into the valley to settle in another town and fortress known as Ixtacamaxtitlan (which Bernal Díaz humanises into Xalacingo) where, well received by the natives, Cortés chose to remain while some messengers he had sent to Tlaxcala returned with an answer. His Cempoalan friends had suggested to him that these Tlaxcalans, good fighters and deadly enemies of Moteçuçuma, should be won over as his allies, and Cortés, who had learnt to trust the Cempoalans, chose as ambassadors four of their own. They took as a present a Flanders beribboned red hat and as their credentials a letter, which, precisely because the Tlaxcatecs would be unable to read it, would show them that it came from people who wrote such things, and therefore from the now famous *teules*.

In the international customs of the world of Aztec and kindred nations, ambassadors were sacred and marked out for special deference and respect by distinctive clothes and insignia. "They wore a thin cotton wrap slanting round the body, so as to cover the navel, with two knots on the back, so that from each knot there should hang a hand's length of wrap." Lest these arrangements might fail to impress their ambassadorial rank on people who went about displaying their unimportant navels, they wore yet another wrap of thick cotton rolled up and tied over the chest and shoulders by means of a thin string; in the right hand, each carried a dart, with the point between the fingers, the feathers upwards, and in the left, a small round buckler and a netting bag containing their food for the journey.

When the four ambassadors sent by Cortés arrived in Tlaxcala, they were, of course, recognised at once for what they were and received as befitted their function by the officials of the republic, who took them to the community house; after luncheon and a rest, they proceeded to the house of government, with great composure, in silence, as if rehearsing in their minds the message with which they had been entrusted, carrying bunches of roses in their left hands, now free from the buckler and food bag; and there, with quiet and solemn step, and their eyes cast down—for it was insolent to look great persons in the face—they entered the presence of the Council of four, which governed the city and nation, taking great care to cover their bodies with the thin cotton wrap. Tlaxcala was a republic composed of four federated groups, each represented in the Council by a speaker, or *tlatoani*. It was a kind of Sparta to the Mexican Athens; blockaded by Mexico and thereby deprived of things as necessary as cotton, cocoa and salt, it nevertheless resisted the claims to domination made by the Mexicans and maintained an all but permanent warfare with them, mostly in the interests of the god of war, for the warfare was meant to produce a regular supply of live prisoners to feed his sacrificial stones. The four tlatoanis waited, seated on low stools, known as *ycpallis*. The ambassadors entered the hall, bowed low and advanced halfway towards their hosts, then knelt on the ground, sat on their feet and legs, well held together, and drew the wraps towards them to cover themselves fully. There was a silence; then Maxixcatzin, one of the tlatoanis of Tlaxcala, beckoned the ambassadors to speak. In a low voice, as courtesy demanded, one of the Cempoalese, with a great flourish of eloquence, yet with motionless mien and cast-down eyes, began to develop their message. (12) He spoke of the new men, bearded, red-haired, white-skinned and blue-eyed, who had come from the east in big *acatl* (boats), and who were so powerful that they had helped the Totonacs to shake off the yoke of the Mexicans; he added that, mainly owing to their advice, for they were of Cempoal, the strangers were ready to strike an alliance with Tlaxcala and to pass through its territory on their way to Mexico. The four tlatoanis had listened in silence, with the utmost attention, their heads bowed very low, so that their mouths touched their knees. There was again a silence, if only for the sake of courtesy—for poor was the message that could be answered without reflection—and then Maxixcatzin spoke a few

words of welcome and sent the ambassadors away till the Council
had deliberated over their message.

The Council of the four tlatoanis discussed the situation straightway. Maxixcatzin, who was the first to speak, was in favour of
granting the strangers a friendly passage, for if they were *teules* they
would be able to pass in any case, and if not they were at any rate
enemies of Moteçuçuma and they should be received as such.
Xicotencatl, however, whose old age and experience gave him great
authority, pointed out that these new people, if one were to believe
public reports on them, were not men but monsters, sprung from
the sea-foam, who galloped about on huge and swift deer, eating
earth, seeking gold, sleeping on cotton wraps, enjoying all kinds of
delights; and that no doubt the sea, unable to stand them, had thrown
them up onto the land; therefore it would be a grave error to admit
them into the Republic; this deadlock was solved by another tlatoani
who answered to the harmonious name of Temilutecutl though other
authors say his name was only Tlehuexolotzin: let ambassadors, he
suggested, be sent to the strangers inviting them to come to Tlaxcala,
where they would be well received, and meanwhile let Xicotencatl
junior, son of old Xicotencatl, try his hand at them with his Otomies
—a warlike tribe which fought under Tlaxcalan banners; in this way,
if young Xicotencatl beats them, all is well; if he is beaten, we will
throw him over and put the blame on the barbarous Otomies. This
advice, which showed the high degree of civilisation attained by the
Tlaxcalans, was of course followed unanimously. (13)

* * *

Cortés waited and waited, and his messengers did not return. It
was of course part of the game. But Cortés grew impatient, and
having talked matters over with the men of Cempoal, who again
assured him that Tlaxcala would be an excellent ally, he gave orders
to go forward. The army took to the road on August 31st. He had
but to follow the river, for he was already in the valley, the only
outlet or gate of the Spartan Republic, towards the East. Cortés
rode in front of the army with six horsemen, fully half a league in
advance, because, as he himself explains, he liked to be the first to
know anything that might happen, so that he might prepare his
men for all emergencies. So, he was the first to see the wall which

Tlaxcala had erected across this valley, to close up its only gate. It was a formidable wall, of excellent masonry, "difficult to pull down with iron picks"; nearly three yards high and twenty feet wide, with a parapet one and one-half feet wide to fight from above; with only one winding passage ten steps wide. The army halted for a while to look at it; and, says Bernal Díaz, "it gave us much to think about." Cortés did not fail to observe the effect of this fortress on his troops. In its eloquent language of stone, it said to them: "Here is strength and here is industry. Pass this wall if you dare, strangers; but, before you pass it, think whether you will be able to pass it back again." So, at the foot of the stone wall, which threw such a mighty physical and moral obstacle across his path, he said to his men: "Gentlemen, let us follow our flag, which is the sign of the holy Cross, for with it we shall conquer." And they all answered as one man: "Let us by all means, for God is the true strength."

On they passed. Cortés had the banner displayed by the alférez Corral; he talked to his men all the while, keeping their minds on the war; how the horsemen were to charge and return at a hard gallop, in groups of three, so as to help one another, with their lances held somewhat short, and how when they broke through the enemy formations they were to hold their lances at the level of the enemy's faces, without stopping to give thrusts. (14) Perchance someone came to point out that there was no enemy in sight; for Cortés—so Bernal Díaz records—went on to say: "Consider, gentlemen companions, that we are but few; we must always be as ready and on our guard as if we were right now seeing our enemies come to the fight, and we must not merely see them come, but imagine that we are actually in battle with them." This was the language of a captain to soldiers who were his friends and companions, of a leader ever on the alert, who knew that his men would rise higher in achievement if kept on their mettle. While he talked to them in this way before the battle, he took great care to add: "For when we are fighting I know full well you need no advice, for I know that, well as I may endeavour to say it, you will do it much better and more bravely." (15)

He rode ahead of the army as was his wont. Had he chosen the right path? While his men beheld the forbidding wall, he had ridden along it for a couple of miles, to study its length and purpose;

G

Yztacmichtitlan, the cacique of the valley, had tried to induce him
to go south, and proceed by way of Cholula; Mamexi and his
Cempoalan friends had warned him to beware of Cholula, treacherous
peoples, in conspiracy with Moteçuçuma. He had had to make up
his mind alone, guided only by his instinct and by his courage, in a
land so strange and unknown to him, amidst people whose secret
thoughts and intentions he could not fathom. He chose the Tlaxcala
road because, he writes the Emperor, he had a better idea of the
Cempoal men than of the others; possibly also because, had he
changed his mind at the foot of that wall, he would have seemed to
lack spirit, and the moral effect of his decision might have been
disastrous. (16)

Yet, while he rode ahead, seeing at every step lands on which
no European eyes had rested before his, he might well have wondered
what lay in store for him in those virgin spaces of his future, now
slowly coming towards him at the steady pace of his chestnut horse.
As he was possibly thinking this, his ever watchful eyes beheld a
strange sight. They had entered a thick pine forest and they found
their road crossed and recrossed by threads bearing mysterious
papers: it was like a thin and light imitation of a wire entanglement.
They paid no attention to it; these threads and papers were charms
laid there by the sorcerers and magicians of Tlaxcala to halt the
Spaniards by the only means which seemed adequate to them. (17)

Teules, after all, the Spaniards conquered that danger, the more
easily for their being unaware of it, and rode on; then, as Cortés
and four of his horsemen were coming near the top of a hill on the
road, they saw the two other horsemen of the vanguard, who were
riding in front of them, rush back to inform them that about fifteen
Indian warriors, with swords and bucklers and a profusion of coloured feathers on their heads and shoulders, who had obviously been
there waiting for them, had run away on seeing them. As the scouts
were arriving on top of the hill, " a dog scented spies and barked";
Lares, an excellent horseman, rushed forward and saw the Indian
group; he killed two of them, a fact which should suffice to explain
the flight of the others. Cortés galloped forward and signalled them
to come back, but the Indians ran on and so did Cortés with his
six horsemen; then, as the Spaniards closed upon them, the fifteen
Tlaxcatecs turned and attacked with such courage and skill that

they killed two horses, and wounded three horses and two men; but men in Cortés' army matter much less than horses. The fight, despite the advantage the horses gave the Spaniards, was becoming dangerous, for while on Cortés' side there were by now eight horsemen and the two dismounted riders, numerous reinforcements estimated by Cortés at four or five thousand, and by Bernal Díaz at three thousand Tlaxcatecs, appeared in the field; for a while the small band of Spanish cavalry must have longed for St. James; but this time he did not turn up, and it was lucky for them that, on a hint from Cortés brought by a horseman, the infantry and cavalry hurried to the scene and the Tlaxcatecs withdrew, though in good order and with no signs of panic. They had lost seventeen men; the Spaniards had had four wounded, whose wounds were cured "with the grease of a fat Indian of those we had killed, whom we opened, for we had no oil"; and having supped of some Indian dogs which they found in the houses in the village, and set their watches and sentinels, keeping the horses ready in full harness, they took a well earned rest. (18)

Just after the battle, a number of messengers from the local caciques came to see Cortés, accompanied by two of the four ambassadors he had sent to Tlaxcala; they explained that they regretted what had happened—which, no doubt, was literally true—and that it had all been due to some independent action on the part of undisciplined tribes, which was perhaps less true; they declared themselves well disposed towards Cortés and ready to pay for the horses. Cortés feigned to believe everything, answered courteously and waived all indemnities on the ground that plenty of horses would soon be forthcoming. He can hardly have spent a carefree night. Next morning, the other two ambassadors arrived, weeping. In violation of all international usages, the Tlaxcatecs had tied them up in order to kill them, and they had succeeded in escaping through the night. Cortés was still listening to their pitiful tale, when the Tlaxcatec army appeared in strength, a mass of colour and a sea of sound, feathers and banners waving in the air torn by the shrill peals of the horn trumpets and booming with the stubborn beat of the *teponaztles,* or wooden drums. There were about six thousand warriors in the field. The Spaniards were about four hundred, and had with them fifteen hundred Cempoalese and three hundred men of Ixtacamaxtitlan, of whose loyalty they could hardly be certain.

Cortés began by putting himself right with the law. Which law? The law of nations, yes, the law of the world commonwealth which then existed and later disappeared into the jungle of unlimited sovereignties. He sent the Tlaxcatecs three prisoners, taken the day before, to explain that the Spaniards wanted peace and friendship, and instructed Diego de Godoy, "one of our soldiers who was his Majesty's notary, to watch well all that happened and give witness of it, if necessary"; but the Tlaxcatecs, possibly mistaking all these scruples for lack of heart, sent volleys of arrows as their only answer. "St. James and at them," said Cortés.

One onslaught was enough to make the Indians recede, though in good order; in fact, in much better order than the Spaniards advanced, for the crafty Tlaxcatecs succeeded in drawing them into a narrow ravine, in which neither cavalry nor artillery could be used to any account; and when, after fighting every foot of their way, the Spaniards saw at last the open plain beyond, their eyes beheld so vast an army that Cortés estimated it at one hundred thousand men, and Bernal Díaz at forty thousand. The Spanish battalion had to fight in serried ranks. The native sword, a heavy weapon, made of a wooden blade three and a half feet long and four inches wide, with a number of obsidian razors set on its two edges, was so formidable that Pedro de Morón had his mare beheaded at one stroke and was only saved from the *cuauxicalli,* or eagle-cup of sacrifice, by the stubborn protection of his brave comrades. In the end the Tlaxcatecs withdrew; "and we," says Bernal Díaz, "were not sorry, nor did we pursue them because we could not stand on our feet, we were so tired." As for the Tlaxcatecs, they took away their men as soon as they were wounded, so that the Spaniards were not able to count their dead. (19)

*   *   *

The army settled down for the night of September 1st, (20) close to the village of Tecoacinco, round a native temple which they later christened Victory Tower, and as there were many men and horses wounded and their bows and arrows needed attention, they spent a day which, though busy, was peaceful. But next morning things began to happen again. This time, Cortés took the initiative, and in characteristic fashion, a double-edged one; on the one hand, he sent an embassy to the Tlaxcatecs, explaining again that he sought their friendship and was not, as they feared, in alliance with the Mexicans against them; on the other, "so that it was I who started the fight," he explains to the Emperor, he left the camp at dawn with the horsemen, one hundred infantry and the three hundred Indians from Ixtacamaxtitlan—no Cempoalese, since he meant to attack their Tlaxcatec friends—and raided the valley, coming back with about four hundred prisoners, men and women. On his return, Pedro de Alvarado, whom he had left in command, informed him of the outcome of his peace effort: the Tlaxcatec answer was: "Come all to Tlaxcala and then we shall make peace by offering your hearts and blood to the gods, and feasting on your bodies." "We did not think this a good thing," says Bernal Díaz, "tired as we were with our past battles." Cortés went on gathering information: both from his messengers and from his prisoners—"partly by making up to them, partly by torture"—he learnt that Xicotencatl the Younger was ready to attack him with the whole army of the confederacy, at least fifty thousand men, well equipped and fighting in good order under their respective banners, above which would rise the heron and rock of Xicotencatl himself." "As we are men," writes Bernal Díaz, "and we feared death, many of us, and even all the rest, confessed ourselves with the Father of the Mercy and with the priest Juan Díaz, who were the whole night hearing our sins."

With a light conscience but a heavy heart, the army saw the light of dawn rise on a plain full of enemies. "As though there were some big fields two leagues wide and as much in length and in the midst of them four hundred men, so was the plain full of them." Bernal Díaz is less generous than usual to the native contingents who fought bravely by their side, but even this contingent came to fewer than two thousand men. Cortés had mustered all his forces, even the wounded that could walk; the wounded horses were also made to serve. Strict orders were issued to the troops to keep together, and in true Cortesian style the army moved out to meet the foe. The Tlaxcatecs were a mass of colour and a sea of noise: feathers and banners, *teponaztles* and horn trumpets; the gold and copper of their war attire and the obsidian razors of their swords shining murderously in the brilliant sun. The battle was "perilous and doubtful." The sun was darkened by a hail of darts before the armies joined issue; the serried ranks of the Tlaxcatecs were mowed down by cannon balls and by the inrush of the thirteen horsemen, but closed every breach as soon as it was opened. At one time the Christian battalion was all but dispersed, which would have meant death; Cortés' shouts were of no avail, so great was the cloud of Indians that fell upon them; "but miraculously by dint of sword play we forced them to allow us to reform our ranks." This resistance of the valiant troop no doubt brought out the internal trouble which so far had lain concealed under the apparent unity of their enemies; Xicotencatl junior fell out with another young blood, son of Chichimecatecuhtli and lost a whole captaincy, soon followed in its inaction by that of Guaxocinco. Xicotencatl seems to have lost heart at this, and his men with him. The Spanish cavalry challenged them and would have pursued them had they themselves felt less close to utter exhaustion. The Spaniards had won. (21)

CHAPTER THIRTEEN

Victory over His Own Army

THIS was the turning point in the conquest, or at any rate one of the main turning points, on an uphill road to victory, in which there was no lack of nerve-racking bends. Despite the well meant advice of the Cempoalese, the Tlaxcatecs had proved obdurate to Cortés' blandishments, and the Spanish captain had been constrained to win their alliance on the battlefield. Had he failed to do so, this would have meant his own destruction and sacrifice on the altars of Uitzilopochtli or, at best, an advance through inimical Cholula with defiant Tlaxcala on his flank. He was now in a position to appreciate the formidable power of the native at war, his fearlessness, and his skill in the handling of weapons comparable with the Spanish weapons actually at his disposal, particularly when numbers were so unequal; he was not yet able to realize that much of his success was due to the tradition which set military prowess in catching enemies alive for sacrifice above killing them. He saw in his victory the protecting hand of that Lord whose interests he was devoutly sure of fostering, sinner though he knew himself to be. So that, not yet alive to the crucial character of his victory, which later events were to reveal, and too realistic to attribute the merit of it to his own exertions, mighty as they had been, he gave no more than eight lines of his long report to the Emperor to this eventful day, explaining the victory because "Our Lord wished to help us."

But he was too experienced a captain to feel that the fruits of his victory could be allowed to ripen of themselves: despite the terrible exertions of the day, he was afield the next day before dawn, and with his horsemen and one hundred infantry he raided ten villages and small towns, some of them with as many as three thousand houses; meanwhile, in his usual double-edged manner, he sent some of his chief prisoners to Tlaxcala, to explain again that all he wanted was to be allowed to cross their territory in peace. The four tlatoanis were this time less averse to listening, for they were puzzled and could not make out the actual nature of the strangers. They had been by no means remiss in seeking information, having even had recourse to methods of an experimental sort. The day after his second raid, Cortés received messengers from Tlaxcala; they brought good words, five fattened Indians, copal-incense and feathers, hens, maize-bread and cherries. "If you are a flesh-and-blood-eating god," they said, "eat these Indians and we shall bring you more; if you are a mild god, here are copal incense and feathers; if you are a man, here are hens, bread and cherries." Cortés simply answered: "I and my companions are men just as you are; and I very much desire that you should not lie to me, for I shall always tell you the truth, and in truth I say to you that you must be sensible and not fight." (1) It is obvious that Cortés did not attach much importance to the part of this message which revealed the doubt as to his real nature still lurking in the Tlaxcala mind, for in his letter to the Emperor this well authenticated episode appears simplified in the extreme; yet the Tlaxcatecs were still puzzled, for though the Spaniards said they were men—thus showing that, if proud, the Spaniard has no vanity—their prowess at war, and their haunting likeness to the men spoken of in the prophecies, made the Tlaxcatecs hesitate, particularly as the Cempoalese, to serve their own ends, had sedulously induced them to believe that the Spaniards were *teules* who ate Indian hearts and behaved generally as gods. The Council of tlatoanis called on their magicians and necromancers and handed the puzzle over to them. This consultation, unlike many of its kind in which Moteçuçuma had wasted much time and expense, led to some positive results: the magicians and necromancers were of opinion that the Spaniards were men, and that they ate mere hens and dogs and bread when available, and even, at a pinch, prickly pears; but that, inasmuch as they were the offspring of the sun (which, after all, was true) they were invincible by day, while in the dark they lost their spirit and could be beaten. This advice ran counter to military tradition, which in Tlaxcala had been from time immemorial set against fighting by night; but the Tlaxcatec military experts were bound to see in the idea an excellent way for neutralising the disadvantage at which they had to fight against horses and artillery; thus, the church provided spiritual ammunition for the army, as it has often done in barbarous and backward nations.

The upshot of it all was that groups of innocent-looking Indians began to frequent the camp, bringing hens and vegetables to sell. One morning, when upwards of fifty of them were wandering about in the camp, looking here and poking there, Teuch, the Cempoalese chief, who had always remained faithful to Cortés, came to him and warned him that these Indians were spies, drawing his attention to the fact that they spoke in sly undertones with the men of Ixtacamaxtitlan. In his swift, forcible and—when in danger—ruthless way, Cortés obtained confirmation of Teuch's suspicions from some of the spy-visitors; he reminded them of his injunction not to lie to him and sent them all back to Xicotencatl, their wrists bleeding, handless. Some authors try to gloss this action over; but who but a hopeless romantic would mistake Cortés for Parsifal or claim that the conquest of the most bloodthirsty—literally bloodthirsty—Empire in the world could be achieved without blood? Moreover, what responsible commander, having regard to all the circumstances (his own danger, the sanguinary and hardened nature of his foe) would condemn for this grim decision a captain who till that very day had proved time and again his forbearance and his constant desire to reduce violence to a minimum? To look away is hypocritical; to pretend to be horrified is even more hypocritical, for history—even yesterday's—abounds in pages far less defensible.

That very night, Xicotencatl followed the advice which the necromancers had given him and stealthily drew near the camp. Cortés was watching. He had had the horses harnessed with bells, so that the horsemen should know where they were in the dark. He would not let the Indians come too near, knowing full well that in the weird moral atmosphere of darkness, initiative, creative initiative, can invent a victory before the soldier has had time to fight for it; he sallied out with his horsemen and put them to flight through the maize-fields, where they left their food bags in order to run quicker. Cortés, as usual, immediately after his victory sent yet another embassy of peace to the stubborn Tlaxcatecs.

G*

For several days, he kept close to the camp, beating off minor skirmishes; but this was not the kind of tactics that would appeal to Cortés. He was ill with some kind of malaria, and probably slept little, having a good deal to think about. From the teocalli where he dwelt, on top of the hill, he used to watch the plain, in which the secret of his destiny lay hidden. The smoke of village fires and of camps attracted his trained eye; they enabled him to size up the importance of villages and towns; he gazed for long at a spot, some sixteen miles away, which looked as if it might be a large town; he decided to go and see. The night was dark. He left the camp with one hundred Spanish soldiers, all the horsemen and a contingent of Indian allies; a sharp wind, iced by the snow-covered mountains whence it came, made them tremble. One horse fell; Cortés ordered it to be ridden back to camp; the troop walked on in the night. Another horse fell; Cortés was informed of the fact by voices somewhat less assured; he gave the same order again; his voice was set; the hearts of some of his soldiers sank. A third horse fell. "Sir," cried a voice, "do bear in mind that this is of ill omen; let us at least wait till dawn, and we shall see where we are going." But, in the black night, the quiet, set voice rose again, from a self-anchored soul: "Why do you believe in auguries? I shall not give up this raid, for I fancy much good is to come out of it tonight, and the devil puts these obstacles in the way to hinder it." So says one of the soldiers present; but he, to the Emperor: "And though all my soldiers begged me to return, for it [the falling of the horses] was of ill omen, nevertheless, I went forward, bearing in mind that God is above nature."

Then Cortés' own horse fell, and yet one more. He sent the five fallen horses back to camp, dismounted the remaining riders and made the whole troop walk silently in the dark, towards that smoke he had seen from the teocalli. They lost their way, were guided back to the right direction by two natives and, before dawn, fell on two pueblos "in which"—he writes to the Emperor—"I killed many people." It is clear that he had no qualms whatever about killing those natives; his position was firm and unmoved; he came as a Christian conqueror, ready to enter everywhere in peace and to establish his Cross and banner by conversion and persuasion; he had invited the Tlaxcatecs to peace, time and again; they had chosen

war. He made war. The rest is pious whitewashing, which was not
to his taste.

But, though always ready if need be to make the weight of his
arms felt, he was readier still to return to politics. At dawn they
arrived in Tzimpanzingo or Zimpanzingo, a town of twenty thousand
houses; the Spaniards broke in by surprise; the unfortunate natives
ran out of their houses, naked; "fathers did not wait for sons," says
Bernal Díaz. "I began to do them some harm," writes Cortés to
the Emperor; but as they opposed no resistance he accepted their
offers of peace, and presently the Christian troop enjoyed a rest and
breakfast close to a fountain outside the town. As soon as the sun
shone on them, Cortés climbed a hilltop "to discover land" and saw
the big town of Tlaxcala, dazzling white between the blue horizon
and the red earth; to his soldiers, whom he had just pulled back from
the hot pursuit of the defenceless natives, he said quietly: "See, what
would have booted killing a few Indians here, when there are such
multitudes there?" He went down again to his breakfast, "and so"—
he wrote to the Emperor—"I left them at peace." (2)

*   *   *

Having conquered and pacified his enemies, Cortés now had to
conquer and pacify his friends. His absence from the camp had
evidently given rise to fears lest he had suffered a fatal reverse. These
fears may have been, in part at least, the outcome of wishful feeling
—a psychological reality no less pertinacious than wishful thinking.
The drive of the man was so powerful that it must have provoked
strong reactions in his more reluctant followers; when would an
Indian arrow or obsidian sword rid them of the overbearing chief
who was leading them to superhuman deeds against their sluggish
leanings?

On his return to camp with a rich booty of hens and Indian
women (for labour, rather than for pleasure), he found a situation
which he describes to the Emperor in his quiet and terse style, but
which Bernal Díaz depicts with a delightful abundance of telling
phrase and of felicitous detail. There were "small circles and talks"
over the grave dangers which the Spaniards were running in that
strange and powerful country. The movement was led by those who
had left houses and Indians in Cuba, and in particular, says Bernal

Díaz, by "seven of them whom I do not wish to name here, for their honour's sake." Cortés was apprised of the situation by his friends. One night, as he was going the round of the camp, to keep his sentinels on the alert, he overheard his name in a tent. He stopped in the dark and listened: "If the Captain is mad, let us be wise, and let us speak out and say he must look out or we will leave him alone." "Those who dare say so," observed Cortés to his watch-companions, "will dare do it." Next day, whether called by him or unbid, the grumblers came to his tent, and one of them addressed the chief with some assurance and even with a certain petulance. He reminded Cortés of the fact that fifty-five men had already lost their lives and the rest, many of them wounded, ill, thin, underfed, were constantly on the alert, and sure to be sacrificed some day to the idols; he advised a return to Veracruz, there to build a ship to be sent to Cuba for help; he complained of the destruction of the ships; pointed out that the men went about in a worse plight than beasts of burden, for they were never unloaded; and argued that in no history of the Romans or of Alexander could it be read that a captain ever dared destroy his own ships and march inland completely surrounded by warriors. (3)

Cortés, though noticing the lack of respect in the tone of this address and in the bearing of those who were of the same way of thinking, answered quietly. This was, we know, his usual way—not for lack of spirit and temperament, far from it, but because he was hardly ever caught out in the careful watch over himself which was one of his most prominent features. Moreover, he was thoroughly in sympathy with the fears thus expressed; indeed, he would have been not merely foolhardy but a fool had he not realised the appalling disproportion between his means and his task; and in his letter to the Emperor he records his own fears along with those of his companions in a sentence which does great honour to his sincerity and to his respect for his men: "I assure Your Majesty that there was not one amongst us who did not feel much fear seeing we were so far inland, in the midst of so many people and such people, and so completely without hope of help from anywhere."

This feeling must have softened the tone of his answer to the undisciplined group which came to protest against his plans. He began by flattering them: no Spaniards had ever been known to fight better, and when he remembered the enemies they had encountered and beaten he was seized with fear; nor would anyone be able to say he had been slow to meet the dangers himself—whereupon Bernal Díaz puts in, "And he was right in saying it, for in truth in all the battles, he was among the first"; but as God had helped them in the past, so he would in the future, since they preached and "settled." His doctrine wherever they went; and he believed that the war in Tlaxcala was over because Xicotencatl had been thrice beaten. He passed quickly over the lost ships but reminded the complaining party that there were gentlemen in the camp who held other opinions, and that therefore it would be best to walk in the service of God; as for the Romans and Alexander, true, he said, they never achieved deeds as great as ours, that is why, henceforward, God willing, the histories which will be written about us will have more to tell than those on our forefathers. Therefore, he concluded, there is no sense in going back, for the very stones would rise against us, and from *teules* and gods we should become cowards in their eyes. As for the fifty-five men who had lost their lives, and their being few and ill and wounded, his answer was terse: "Let God give us the strength of many, for it is well known that wars waste both men and horses." In fine, the Captain reminded them that they were soldiers and gentlemen, advised them to give up all thought of Cuba, and concluded: "After God, our help must come from our valorous arms."

There were still some soldiers who dwelt again on the dangers of the march on a city as strong as Mexico and on the exhausted state of the Spanish troop. This time Cortés was less patient, and there was a gruffness in his voice when he retorted that it was better to die as good men than to live without honour; this brought out his old guard of friends, who openly sided with him and advised him to pay no heed to "small circles and talks." (4)

*   *   *

It is most fortunate that this scene has been so vividly painted by Bernal Díaz, precisely the man who wrote under the grievance that Gómara and the other courtly authors brought out the deeds of their hero to the detriment of the rank and file; for, under his pen, Cortés appears as the real moving spirit of the enterprise. The men who advised a cautious retreat had a strong case, indeed, an unanswerable case had the army still been in a position to choose. The only argument in reason which Cortés could put forward was that, having gone so far, there was less risk in daring than in caution—even though the risk in daring was desperate enough. Cortés did not fail to put this argument to his men and to develop it with much cogency; crises such as this, however, are not solved by the brain but by the heart; "and above all courage and heart, which is what matters," says Bernal Díaz when enumerating the gifts of Cortés. He was bound to know the gigantic nature of his task in a more complete and concrete way than any man in his army; he was shrewd, all-seeing, well informed and cautious; he felt then—so Bernal Díaz says—confident that he had broken the resistance of the Tlaxcatecs; but his men were tired out; the moral effect of horse and gun over the natives was wearing thin if it had not altogether disappeared; and every new experience or scrap of information strengthened his conviction that the Mexican nation was altogether different from the savage or semi-savage Indians of the islands and of the coast of Veragua, and was a well organised State, comparable—but for its cannibalism—at any rate for war purposes, with a European nation. If, therefore, despite the overwhelming hostages which he gave to fortune, he found in his stout heart the strength which silenced all opposition and led his men forward to Mexico, it is only natural to expect that a man so well balanced who, though brave to the pitch of heroism, was not foolhardy, was able to draw on sources of spiritual strength at least as powerful as the dangers he was facing. Any other conclusion makes of Cortés an irresponsible man, which he by no means was. With all his spontaneous gifts, his humour, his sallies, his resourceful, quick reactions to the challenges of a life full of incident and accident, Cortés is one of the steadiest, most calculating, careful men of action known to history. When, therefore, despite odds which he had accurately sized up, he made up his mind to march on, what were the forces which made him feel equal to the mighty deed he had set his heart on achieving?

We know them, for he recorded them when relating this scene to the Emperor. The first was an unbounded faith in Spanish valour. This feeling, which was to last in Spain till the battle of Rocroi, was of course entirely subjective and untranslatable in terms of reason. The only similar example which comes to mind is the feeling of unbounded, matter-of-course assurance of the British Navy in our days. But, curiously enough, in the Spanish armies and navies, it might be thought to have arisen precisely out of the fabulous conquests of Cortés himself and of his handful of men; here we see it already breathing powerfully before these conquests achieved the dramatic success which made them world-famous. Cortés' own words suggest a kind of accumulated glory shining from the luminous year 1492, which saw both the conquest of Granada and the discovery of the New World, over the armies and navies of the great young Emperor, monarch of most of the Old World and of this New World, gradually unfolded to the admiring eyes of men by soldiers who knew how, beyond the seas, in Italy, the Great Captain Gonzalo de Córdoba was brilliantly laying down new standards of strategy, of tactics and of valour. "And I," writes Cortés to the Emperor, "encouraged them, asking them to bear in mind that they were vassals of Your Highness and that never were Spaniards anywhere found to fail." (5)

Next to this confidence in his men, that faith in victory without which no victory is possible, Cortés felt the call to conquer vast territories and peoples for the Christian Empire whose soldier he felt himself to be. For him, the spread of the faith and that of the banners of Spain were one and the same thing—and a thing so obvious as to admit neither doubt nor discussion. And so he writes how, in order to encourage the hesitant amongst his troops, he reminded them also "that we were in a position to win for Your Majesty the greatest realms and dominions in the world. And that moreover we were, as Christians, bound to fight against the enemies of our faith, and in this way we would earn the glory of the other world, and in this world we would achieve the greatest pride and honour ever won before our day by any generation." (6) These words show how inseparable the national and the religious motives were in his mind, a fact which should not surprise us in a man of his day, whatever his nationality, still less in a Spaniard, used by the protracted war against the Moorish invader to identify foreigners with infidelity and faith with patriotism.

Finally, Cortés relied on the help of God. The narrative of

Bernal Díaz is here most precious, in contrast with that, much shorter and more chastened, of Cortés himself; for while the soldier, despite his boisterous tendency to bring forward the rank and file, is led by the sheer beauty of quiet courage to emphasize the merit of Cortés—from whose unmoved soul, he makes us feel, radiates all the courage of the army—Cortés himself points quietly to heaven for the strength he imparts to his men, in words the very simplicity of which convey the aroma of heartfelt sincerity: "And they were to bear in mind that we had God on our side, and that to Him nothing is impossible, and that they should see this to be so in the victories we had won, in which so many of our enemies had lost their lives, and none of us." (7) That this reliance on the help of God was a steady, living force in him is borne out by a scene recorded in Tapia's narrative. Cortés had been seeking advice and information from the natives whom he could trust. There was one in his camp, Teuch, the Cempoalese, "a wise man, and, as he said, grown up amidst their wars. This Indian said to the Marquess [Cortés]: 'Sir, do not waste your effort in trying to go forward beyond this place, for I was in Mexico in my youth, and am an old hand at war, and know you and your companions to be men and not gods, and that you suffer from hunger and thirst and fatigue just like men; and I must tell you that, past this province, there are so many men that one hundred thousand may fight against you first and, when dead or beaten, as many more will come; and so they will be able to die and replace themselves by the hundred thousand, and you and your men, even though you may be unbeatable, will die of sheer exhaustion after so much fighting, for, as I have told you, I know you are men; nor have I more to say but that you ponder over what I have said, and if you make up your mind to die I shall go with you.' The Marquess was very grateful and told him that withal he would go forward, for he knew that God who had made Heaven and Earth would help them, and that he [Teuch] should be sure of it." (8)

These were the living forces which fed his courage. They were not new in him. They had from the very first imparted to his denser ambitions a light and an inspiration without which he would not have been able to maintain his hold over the soldiers and captains who swarmed impatiently round him, like stinging wasps. But, though animating him from the first, there is little doubt that they grew in power and in intensity as he went on from ordeal to ordeal and from victory to victory amidst dangers which would have broken his courage had it been solely rooted in animal vitality.

*   *   *

Events could but feed with their broken wood of facts the fire of this faith which burnt in the Captain and which illuminated his troops, all, even the grumblers and dissenters among them. In skirmish or in battle, by night or by day, the white, bearded men held their own. The drive of the small but powerful band of strangers was beginning to impress the leaders of Mexicans and Tlaxcatecs, in spite of the warlike spirit which animated both these brave peoples. Moteçuçuma was still hesitating as to the best course to take. While Cortés fought the Tlaxcatecs, all was well for him; but, if the white chief were either to beat Tlaxcala or to come to terms with it, what would become of Mexico? He sought the advice of his kinsmen, Cacama, ruler of Tetzcuco, and Cuitlahuac, ruler of Ytztapalapan. "Put your business in council," says Sancho Panza, "and some will say it is white and others will say it is black." This Spanish proverb held sway in Mexico before the Spanish conquest. Cuitlahuac advised him to send a friendly embassy to Cortés, with many and valuable presents, but with the request not to proceed to Mexico; Cacama was of opinion that the Spaniards should be well received in Mexico and allowed to deliver their message, for, should they try to overstep the bounds of what they owed to Moteçuçuma's majesty, the Mexicans were in a position to give a good account of themselves. Moteçuçuma took the advice of Cuitlahuac, not so much because Cuitlahuac was his brother as because his brother's advice happened to suit his procrastinating tactics. (9) One day, while the Spaniards were still fighting hard against the Tlaxcatecs, a bright procession entered their camp, headed by six proud Mexicans with about two hundred men for their service; they brought Moteçuçuma's friendship and such expressions of peace and amity as, translated from Aztec into Castillian, led Cortés to believe that the Uei Tlatoani of Mexico wished to become a vassal of the King of Spain. This misunderstanding astride an ocean was nevertheless solidly built on the promise of a yearly tribute of gold, silver, pearls, precious stones, slaves, cotton and everything in Moteçuçuma's giving, on condition that Cortés did not carry out his intention to visit Mexico. (10)

It is difficult to imagine a message more calculated to spur Cortés on to his chief goal; facing his sturdy faith in his men and in his God, he felt but a faltering faith which durst not face the encounter. Whatever the material forces which this historical duel was pitting against each other, the spiritual forces were evidently unequal. Moteçuçuma was neither a coward nor a fool; he had been chosen to lead his people by methods which compared very favourably with those of our democracies and autocracies in ensuring that neither cowards nor fools could rise to the summit of power; yet, in this hour of need, Moteçuçuma was unable to draw either on his courage or on his wisdom because both wisdom and courage are but the ministers of faith; and the unfortunate Monarch had lost his faith.

Cortés received the Mexican envoys gracefully and thanked them for the presents of gold and cotton clothes which they had brought him; then, with his usual diplomatic acumen, he made them linger in the camp till he had settled the Tlaxcalan war. This would enable the Mexicans to see for themselves how the Spaniards could handle the native warriors. Meanwhile, Cortés had given strict instructions to his men to respect the Mexican Ambassadors as the representatives of a great and friendly monarch. (11) While the Mexican Ambassadors were in the Spanish camp, the impetuous Xicotencatl attacked it with three of his squadrons. Cortés, still suffering from quartan fever, had taken a purge, "some camomilles which are found in the island of Cuba and are very good for those who know how they should be taken." "He asked for a horse, without regard for the purge, and riding it, went out and fought bravely in person for a long time, both as captain and as soldier." The next day, his purge had its expected effect. Torquemada, who was minister provincial of the Order of St. Francis in Mexico, and an authority in theological matters adds: "The Doctor said that nature had stayed its course owing to the new emergency and I add that it was the work of God, so that this work of the conquest should be carried out and put through for the salvation of so many souls as since have in effect been saved." Yet, it is only fair to point out that Cervantes de Salazar, who was a bachelor of canon law and a doctor of theology, definitely says: "It was not a miracle, but nature stayed its course owing to the new emergency." In view of which discrepancies the matter must remain, perhaps for ever, an unsolved problem in the life of Cortés. (12)

The main thing, however, was that this attack had failed, and that the victory this time had the double advantage of impressing Moteçuçuma's envoys, who witnessed it from the tower of the teocalli round which Cortés had built his camp, and, owing to this very circumstance, of giving bitter food for thought to the Tlaxcatecs. What was best for them? To persist in their war policy, at the risk of bringing about an alliance against themselves between the old enemy Moteçuçuma and the new enemy Cortés, or to forestall this alliance by accepting the repeated offers of friendship which Cortés, though invincible, never failed to dangle before them? Their priests and magicians had proved themselves wrong: the white strangers were as unbeatable by night as by day; that was the fact, so far as they could judge, for the Tlaxcatecs were not in a position to guess the terrible fears which many a Spanish heart was then undergoing at the sight of "so many people, and such people."

The Spaniards meanwhile were in similar ignorance about the intentions of their enemies. "As we were in our camp," says Bernal Díaz, "not knowing that they were going to come to offer peace, though we desired it very greatly, some preparing their weapons, others making arrows, each busy in whatever he had to attend to towards the war," the horsemen who were guarding the road came to announce that many Indians of both sexes were advancing towards the camp, stopping to rest now and then. "Cortés and all of us were very glad of this news, for we thought they came for peace, as it turned out to be, and Cortés gave orders that there should be no noise and no feeling shown, and that we should keep out of the way in our huts." (13) This was the first embassy sent by the Tlaxcatecs with the real intention of making peace. The chief ambassador was Tolimpanecatl Tlacatecuhtli. Cortés received him and his companions in the presence of the Mexican envoys; he had placed himself in such a position that the two Indian States were bidding for his favour. Before the Tlaxcalan had had time to deliver his message, the chief Mexican ambassador, Atempanecatl burst forth: "Why do you come here? What is your message? Who is responsible for the revolts and feuds which have occurred in Huitzilhuacan, Tepatlaxco, Tezmolocan, Teotlatlzinco, Tepetzinco, Ocotepec, Tlamacazquicac, Atlmoyahuacan, Zacayaloacan, and in all the region down to Chololan? Let us see what you are going to treat about with Cortés, for I want to see and hear everything."

Tolimpanecatl had listened unmoved; when his foe was silent at last, he turned towards Doña Marina and said: "I should like to answer my kinsman the Mexican here, in the presence of our father the Captain Cortés." What better luck could Cortés wish than this strife and division within the people he had to conquer, or die? Whether because she saw a light in his eye or because by now she did not even need to look into his eyes to guess her master's thoughts, Doña Marina simply said: "Proceed with your challenges and answers." At this the Tlaxcalan turned to the Mexican and asked: "Have you any more to say?" "I have said enough," curtly answered the Mexican, whereupon the Tlaxcalan overwhelmed him with a cataract of similar accusations, while Cortés looked on. (14)

Having settled his kinsman—at any rate, in words—the Tlaxcalan turned to Cortés and explained how his countrymen had fought against the Spaniards in the belief that they were in conspiracy with Moteçuçuma, and how the first warriors who had attacked them had been unruly Otomies; but now Tlaxcala knew its error and was ready to make amends; they offered their good will and steady supplies of food. When their chief had spoken, all the Tlaxcatecs laid their hands on the earth and lowered their heads. Cortés feigned to be still incensed at their obduracy, the better to hide his joy; he recalled his past endeavours to win their friendship and asked for a bigger and more important embassy as a proof of the earnestness of their peaceful intentions. With this answer, Tolimpanecatl Tlacatecuhtli left for Tlaxcala, leaving behind a number of servants and abundant food for his new friends. (15)

In exacting a more impressive embassy, Cortés was acting with an eye both on appearances and on realities: he raised the value of his friendship and the prestige of his cause both in Tlaxcalan and in Mexican eyes; and by the same occasion, he gave himself time to obtain and mature more guarantees of security from his new friends. The Tlaxcatecs were not slow in giving him satisfaction and, rightly guessing what was in his mind, chose as their next

ambassador Xicotencatl the Young, the chief person in the Republic
after the four tlatoanis—so much for prestige—and the captain general of their armies and chief partisan, till then, of the warlike policy
of Tlaxcala—so much for security and guarantees. "This Xicotencatl," says Bernal Díaz, "was tall and of wide shoulders and well
made, and his face was long and kind of hollow and robust, and
he might be as old as thirty-five and in his countenance he showed
much gravity." (16) Surrounded by a brilliant suite of fifty prominent Tlaxcatecs, he explained to Cortés how they were besieged by
Moteçuçuma and denied access to supplies of salt and cotton, which
made them a poor country, but what they had they offered with a
good will. The young captain begged his rival to enter Tlaxcala and
settle in it.

Cortés received his enemy with a most chivalrous grace but did
not at once fall in with Xicotencatl's invitation to go to Tlaxcala. As
he explains to the Emperor, he dared not trust them yet; moreover,
it was obviously to his advantage to raise the price of his friendship,
and he lingered on till—he writes—"all the lords [of Tlaxcala] came
to beg me to come to their city." The Mexican ambassadors did not
fail to sow distrust in his mind: "As soon as Xicontega had taken
his leave," says Bernal Díaz, "Moteçuçuma's ambassadors asked
Cortés half laughingly whether he believed in those offers made in
the name of all Tlaxcala, for it was all a fake and should not be
believed for they were all treacherous and deceitful words." And
though Cortés answered with feigned coolness that he cared nothing
whether the Tlaxcalans meant true or false, for if they betrayed him
he would punish them harder, he agreed with the Mexicans' suggestion to await in the camp the return of two of their number who
were being sent to Moteçuçuma. (17)

*　　*　　*

That week in the camp, after Xicotencatl's visit, must have been
a period of relative rest for Cortés, enabling him to look before and
after, and to throw over his field of action one of those all-embracing
glances by which the mind seeks strength in the past and guidance
for the future. He was poised between two uncertainties: far away,
behind the sea, Diego Velázquez, behind whom farther away still
and far more powerful, lurked the awe-inspiring Majesty of the

Emperor. What had become of his messengers Puertocarrero and Montejo, entrusted with the difficult task of explaining to a hostile Court his cleverly disguised rebellion against Velázquez? Uncertainty. Closer to him, ahead of him, another Emperor just as awe-inspiring in the eyes of the Indians as Charles V was in his eyes; a city and a State of which everyone, friend or foe, gave him most glowing accounts, revealing a strength which even he was bound to feel formidable and out of proportion with his little troop. What would be the outcome of this final step he was taking against the advice of many of his soldiers and of his trusted Indian allies? Uncertainty again.

If, weary of contemplating these two dangers which blocked his two horizons, he sought rest in the brighter sides of his landscape, he could behold himself raised from the position of an adventurous "discoverer," painfully negotiating with coastal chiefs over the right to fill up his barrels with fresh water in order to sail on to another shore, to that of a General dreaded by all the natives but loved by many of them, who commanded a force of four hundred Spaniards, of whom he was the elected leader, and of several thousand natives who saw in him an invincible man, if not a god. His camp was like the capital of a potentate, to which ambassadors of rival states sought access vying with each other for his favours; and, every now and then, the most dreaded of the native potentates spontaneously presented him with gold and clothes, thus strengthening his hold over his Spaniards who expected from him, not merely glory, but wealth as well.

When in this mood, he was entitled to consider as one of his great achievements the fact that his long line of communications between the camp and his coast base Veracruz, was absolutely safe—a triumph of political wisdom, of diplomatic skill, possibly also of personal charm. The thousand small details, the stern discipline over his soldiers, the thoughtfulness in keeping local chiefs happy and content, the watchfulness over those inclined to betray him, which this fact implies, have not perhaps been sufficiently noticed. His revolt against Velázquez and the destruction of the ships had transfigured Cortés' enterprise from a military campaign into a heroic gamble without any base whatsoever; yet the safety of his communications with Veracruz remained necessary because Veracruz

was itself in many ways an important supply base for his army—
let alone reasons of prestige and others which were still unrevealed
in the bosom of time.

It was while in this camp that Cortés wrote to Escalante, his
commander at Veracruz, to inform him of the victories he had
achieved. But that is not the way he put it: we have Bernal Díaz'
version to the effect that "in the said letters he let him know the
great favours which Our Lord Jesus Christ had done us in the
victories we have had in the battles and fights we have had from
our entry in the province of Tlaxcala, where they have now come
to seek peace, and [said] that they all were to thank God for it;
and that he was always to favour the Totonacs our friends and that
he was to send by post two jars of wine which Cortés had left hidden
underground in a certain spot in his house . . ." Rather a come-
down, one might think, for a commander who is so watchful about
his policy (favour the Totonacs) and so devout and worshipful in
offering to the Lord the glory of his victories, thus to ask for two
jars of wine which he had—rather meanly?—hidden underground in
his rooms at Veracruz. But stay. Read on: ". . . two jars of wine
[. . .] and that he was also to send hosts of those we had brought
from Cuba, for those we had brought over for our campaign had
all been consumed." That wine was not for revels, and it had not
been hidden from the thirsty troops to quench the general's thirst:
that wine was required for the mass, and it had been put away in
order to ensure the continuous ministration of the Holy Sacrament. "In those days in our camp, we put a Cross, very tall and
sumptuous; and Cortés ordered the Indians at Cingapacinga, and
those who dwelt close to the camp, to have it whitewashed and well
kept." (18)

*   *   *

Meantime, the Tlaxcatecs saw with dismay that Cortés lingered
on in his uncomfortable camp and delayed his entrance into Tlaxcala,
where he was eagerly awaited. The Mexican ambassadors were still
in the camp. The local Tlaxcatec chiefs came to the camp with hens
and prickly pears, and would take no payment from their Spanish
friends, whom time and again they begged to come and settle in
Tlaxcala. Cortés, however, as he had promised, awaited the return

of the two men whom the Mexicans had sent to Moteçuçuma. They returned with even richer presents: three thousand pesos of gold in jewels, two hundred garments of cotton, and featherwork; under this sugar coating, there came a pill to the effect that Cortés was to put no trust in the Tlaxcatecs, who would rob him of all he had, for they were so poor that they could not afford even a cotton wrap—which was true enough, and Moteçuçuma knew it only too well, since he was the cause of their poverty. Cortés was unmoved by the warning, though moved by the rich present, and at this point in the proceedings the arrival of the four Tlatoanis of Tlaxcala was announced.

This was a master stroke of Cortés' diplomatic strategy. By making them each wait for the other, he had put both Mexicans and Tlaxcalans in such a state of mutual distrust and tension that now he was in a position to force the Mexicans to wait while he received —not an Embassy—but the very Government of Tlaxcala, which came to invite him to go to their capital. Cortés turned to the Mexican ambassadors "and begged them to wait for three days for the answers to their Lord, for he had now to speak and decide about the past war and the peace they [the Tlaxcatecs] now are seeking."

They came, some on foot, some conveyed in hammocks; at the head of the procession, Xicotencatl the Old, Maxixcatzin, Tlehuexolotzin and Citlalpopocatzin, followed by a numerous suite. (19) They arrived before Cortés and bowed three times before him, while copal-incense was burned in his honour; they then touched the earth with their hands, and Xicotencatl the Old spoke for them: " 'Malintzin, Malintzin,' he said, 'many times have we sent you messages asking to be forgiven for having waged war against you, and we have already explained to you that it was because we thought you were on the side of evil-minded Moteçuçuma, for had we known what we know now, we would have swept the roads for you and would have gone to fetch you to the sea-edge; and now we beg you to come to us, for we shall serve you with our persons and goods and do not believe the falsehoods and lies of the Mexicans, for we understand that is why you have not come to our city.' " (20)

Cortés thanked his visitors and tactfully explained that he would willingly have gone to Tlaxcala had he been able to transport his guns. "As soon as the Tlaxcalans heard this, they were so pleased that we saw it in their faces," says Bernal Díaz, and he adds that in less than half an hour there were five hundred *tlamemes* at the disposal of Cortés.

The next day, early in the morning, Cortés and his army left the camp for Tlaxcala. Cortés took the Mexican ambassadors with him. They were going to the capital of their enemies under the protection of the Spanish general. They must have felt like prisoners. (21)

CHAPTER FOURTEEN

The Massacre of Cholula

ON SEPTEMBER 23rd, 1519, Cortés entered the city of Tlaxcala in triumph. As soon as they had seen the camp train move towards the city, the five chiefs had left hurriedly, in order to have everything ready for their guests' arrival. The Spanish army advanced in the strictest military order, amidst their friends as if they had been enemies, for such was the firm rule laid down once for all by the Captain, and presently, when they could already see the town sprawling on the horizon over a width which filled them all with admiration, and possibly with awe, the chiefs appeared on the road again, coming out to greet them, each of the four wards of the federation displaying its colours on its rough henequen wraps, neatly painted and decorated. Behind the colourful crowd, came the priests, carrying small braziers in which copal-incense was burning, clad in long white robes, and capes "which wanted to look like those worn by canons," their hair long, unkempt and thick with blood, their ears still bleeding from their latest self-sacrifice in thanksgiving for the newly conquered peace; they came with heads low, in sign of humility, and the nails of their fingers were very long. (1)

The Spanish army had to cut its way through an eager and joyous crowd, which thronged streets and terraces to drink their fill of the strange vision—the horses above all, the men afterwards, the guns, the small firearms, the metal swords, the steel armours and helmets. All the horsemen were offered bunches of roses, and through the streets, humming with comment and excitement, the leaders guided the happy warriors to the Great Cu or Temple, where quarters had been prepared for them.

198

"The said city is so big," Cortés wrote to the Emperor, "and so much to be admired that though I leave out much of what I might say of it, that little which I will say is, I believe, almost incredible, for it is very much bigger than Granada and much stronger and with as many good buildings, and far more people than Granada had when it was won, and very much better supplied with things of the land, to wit: bread and fowls and venison and fish of the rivers, and other vegetables and very good things which they eat." Cortés goes on to extol the abundance of goods of all kinds to be found in their market and notes that they have barbers' shops; he praises the beautiful husbanding of the valleys which surround the city and, noting their ordered ways, concludes: "They are people of much reason and sense and such that the best in Africa do not equal them." He was struck by their excellent police system, for, on his complaining to Maxixcatzin about a theft of gold from the Spanish camp committed by one of the natives, the culprit was quickly found and brought to him for punishment; he, characteristically enough, left the matter in the hands of the local authorities; the Tlaxcatecs thanked him for it and, having paraded the thief with a public crier who announced his guilt, they had him executed in the market place. (2)

With his usual thirst for accurate information, he had an inspection made to find out the population of Tlaxcala; according to this study the republic (including Guaxocingo) was made up of 150,000 heads of families. (3) He was therefore in the capital of an important State, inhabited by a hardy race, whose respect and friendship he had conquered in the battlefield. His first thought was to ensure that nothing should be done on the Spanish side to impair this friendship. He dictated strict orders setting bounds to his men: "And he gave orders," says Tapia, "that we were not to pass beyond nor go outside [such bounds] and so truly we did, for we would not go to a brook a stone's throw out of bounds without asking for his permission." Not in vain says Bernal Díaz that "there never was in the world a captain obeyed with as much respect and punctuality." He had enjoined on his men that "no one was to dare to take [from the natives] more than he was given, nor cause any unpleasantness, however slight," which was the least he could do in view of the generous hospitality he and his men were enjoying: a Spaniard had

but to tear off a strip from his coat and give it to a native and with
this strip of Spanish cloth for a voucher the native could obtain
anything which the Spaniard might wish from the Tlaxcatec community house. As for food, it was served daily and abundantly, "and
in twenty days during which we stayed there we had always more
than we wanted." (4)

This friendship, however, did not in the least induce Cortés to
abate his military discipline nor the watchfulness which he exacted
from his men and from himself. The camp was as strictly regulated
as if they were in the midst of enemies; day and night, they set their
scouts, their watchmen and their sentinels. A captain, during a watch
in charge of these three services, finding them no doubt irksome,
bethought himself of their superfluousness, for otherwise, he would
hardly have troubled to criticise: "It seems to me, sir," he said to
Cortés, "that they are quite at peace; we hardly need to guard ourselves and keep on the watch as strictly as we usually do." "Look,
gentlemen," answered Cortés, "I see that what you say is so, but as
a matter of good habit, we must remain ever ready; for though they
may be very friendly, we must not believe in their peace, rather must
we act as if they wished to make war on us and as if we saw them
coming, for many captains have been destroyed through too much
trust and carelessness [. . .] particularly we, being so far from home,
and having been warned by Moteçuçuma, for it may be untrue and
made up, yet should we be on the alert." (5)

The Tlaxcatec chiefs did not fail to notice this cautious attitude
of the Spanish army in their midst, which hurt them deeply. They
called on Cortés and complained of his mistrustful ways, which they
attributed to the poisonous advice of their Mexican enemies; they
offered their lives in the service of the Spaniards and, in order to
conquer the full confidence of Cortés, declared themselves ready to
put into his hands any hostages he might wish to have. "Cortés and
all of us," says Bernal Díaz, "were astounded at the grace and love
with which they said it." Cortés found a tactful explanation which
removed the sting yet allowed him to remain ready for any emergency: it was, he said, the inveterate tradition of Spanish soldiers to
camp in peace exactly as if they were at war. This answer, in fact,
enhanced the prestige which the Spaniards already enjoyed with the
virile and warlike Tlaxcatecs. (6) But the shrewd captain was not

content with this success, and feeling, no doubt, that the stiffness of his military arrangements needed a constant corrective, he devoted his stay in Tlaxcala to cultivating the good graces of the prominent men of the State, whom he invited to come and talk to him separately and privately. In these visits, which soon became a coveted honour amongst the Tlaxcatec chiefs, Cortés obtained much useful information about both Tlaxcala and Mexico, and conquered the good will of his new allies by his presents and by the grace of his winsome and courtly ways. (7)

*   *   *

Peace and amity were beginning to bear fruit. The Tlaxcatecs were pleased to discover that these men who had come to them preceded by a dreadful godlike reputation—for the native gods were terrifying—were after all easy-going and friendly beings, well behaved provided they were not attacked. Many of the natives, says Tapia, came over to live with the Spaniards and liked the Spanish way of life. (8)

This drawing towards the Spaniards may well have begun on the part of the most defenceless of the population. Bernal Díaz records a pathetic episode to this effect: the Spaniards "found in Tlaxcala wooden houses, made of trelliswork, and full of Indian men and women whom they [the natives] held as prisoners, fattening them up till they were fat enough to be eaten and sacrificed; which prisons," he adds, "we broke up and destroyed so that the prisoners in them should go free, and the sad Indians dared go nowhere but stayed there close to us, and so they saved their lives." Bernal Díaz goes on to say how the first thing Cortés did wherever he went was to break up such prisons and to free the captives, and that he angrily scolded the Tlaxcalans for their cruelty and made them promise that they would no longer kill and eat men. But he adds that in his opinion it availed but little for, as soon as the Spaniards turned away, the same cruelties continued. (9)

The humble folk must have felt drawn to the newcomers by such acts as these. It is probable that Indian women entered into friendly relationship with the soldiery, though this was very much against the grain of the responsible Spaniards so long as the Indians remained unchristened. The Tlaxcatecs do not seem to have done things by halves: while at war, they fought like lions; but now, in peace, there was nothing they would not give to their new friends. One morning, the Tlatoanis came to see Cortés; they brought more than three hundred women waiting to be sacrificed and five Indian maids, "and for Indians, they were of good looks"; each girl had another young girl for her service, and all were daughters of prominent men. Xicotencatl took one by the hand and said: "This, Malintzin, is my daughter. She is a maiden. Take her for you; the others are for your captains."

Cortés gracefully thanked his Tlaxcatec friends and declared that he received them as his; "yet," he added, "let them remain for the present in the house of their parents." The Tlaxcatec leaders were nonplussed, and asked to know the reason of Cortés' strange answer. This started Cortés on his favourite theme: he first wanted to do what God demands; the Tlaxcatecs must forsake their idols, cease their human sacrifices and believe in the one and only God. Bernal Díaz assures us that it was all very well explained to them "because Doña Marina and Aguilar, our Tongues, were already very experienced in it"; yet he goes on to say that the bewildered Tlaxcatecs were shown "an image of our Lady with her precious son in her arms, and they were given to understand that that image is the figure of our Lady, called St. Mary, who is in the high heavens, and is the mother of our Lord, who is that child Jesus whom she has in her arms, and that she conceived him by grace of the Holy Ghost, remaining a Virgin before childbirth, in childbirth and after childbirth"; (10) and as the Spaniards, moreover, capped this cryptic statement by declaring that they would not take the five girls to them until they had been converted to the worship of the Virgin Mother, the scene must have caused the most devastating effects on the Tlaxcatecs, one of whose aims in giving their daughters to the white captains was to draw a powerful offspring from that new, invincible stock. (11)

We can but surmise the waves of mutual incomprehension and misunderstanding that the sudden meeting of the two civilisations raised in both Indians and Europeans. Granted that Aguilar and Doña Marina, gifted as they both were, succeeded in rendering a tolerably adequate transfiguration of the Christian faith and dogmas not merely into the language but into the idiom of the Tlaxcatecs, how could these Indians' minds assimilate the dogma of the Virgin Birth unless they attached to it some immediate, positive meaning, as in the case of their own gods? These and other thoughts of a similar nature must have been working obscurely in their minds, while the Tongues went on explaining that if they gave up their idols and sacrifices they would find health and prosperity in this world and eternal glory in the next, whereas if they persisted "they would go to hell where they would burn for ever in living flames," as Bernal Díaz says magnificently. This threat, so terrifying in those days for any Christian, failed to impress the Tlaxcatecs, who were not a whit less devout, brave and loyal than their Spanish invaders, and after having explained that a change such as that which was suggested to them took some thinking over, they signified in unmistakable terms that they would die rather than forsake their gods.

Were it possible to relate now how Cortés, being a wise and enlightened man, thought best to let sleeping dogs lie and abide his time, this would make a most neat and logical picture. But life cares not a brass farthing for neatness and logic—and it flourishes with a logic of its own which it challenges us to understand and interpret. The scene did end in wisdom and compromise, but not owing to Cortés, who, had he not been advised by wiser persons *on this point,* might have undone many months of political sagacity by a few seconds of religious intemperance. Here is Bernal Díaz' story: "And as soon as we saw their answer, and how truly given, and how fearlessly, the friar of the Mercy, who was a capable man, and a theologian, said: 'Sir, think not of importuning them any more on this, for it is not fair that we should make them Christians by force, nor should I like it to be done as we did in Cempoal, casting down their idols, till they have acquired a knowledge of our holy faith. What boots taking away their idols from a Cu or house of worship, since they can move them on to another one? Let them gradually feel our admonitions, which are holy and good, so that they later come to realise that our advice is sound.' " Whereupon three gentlemen of his army said to Cortés: "The friar has spoken very well, and your lordship has done his duty and let these caciques be left in peace on this matter." (12)

Such are the facts, and they tally only too well with events which happened both before and after to be questioned. At first sight, they would appear to jar with the general lines of Cortés' character, and in particular with his astuteness, his wisdom, his diplomatic skill, his insight into situations. Yet it is surely a superficial view which sees man's qualities as uniform layers covering without fault the whole area of his life; rather must we see our gifts, tendencies and shortcomings as qualified by the context into which life is apt to force them. These "faults" in human characters are almost inevitable in the case of men of great integrity, and in particular in the chief virtue which makes up their integrity, for it is natural that the fault should occur where the tension is highest. "I am but mad north-north-west" is the way Shakespeare put it, and, of course, it cannot be bettered. The man who is always and consistently brave is sure to be timorous in some odd way, along a certain direction of the compass; the man who is always and consistently wise, will have a north-north-west of folly through which the winds and storms of nature blow right into his otherwise quiet soul.

Cortés was mad north-north-west. Wise though he was, astute, cautious, foreseeing, patient in action, mild in words, he was always spurred to instant action and to an abrupt breaking off of negotia-tions as soon as the faith which illumined him and fed his courage was checked in its triumphant progress. His faith was both the chief source of his strength and the main cause of his weakness. And it is another confirmation of the sincerity and depth of his religious impulse, that this impulse should have been the only one which succeeded in bursting through the steely armour of his self-control, and in obscuring and leading astray his otherwise clear vision of both immediate and far-off realities.

In this case, however, the advice of his friar and captains pre-vailed, though the Indians were "ordered by entreaties" to clear one of their *Cues* which was whitewashed and transformed into an altar on which a Cross and an image of Our Lady were placed. Mass was said in the presence of the caciques, and the young ladies were baptised. Here again, Cortés declined to keep any of the youthful and graceful presents for himself. The chief of them in point of rank was Xicotencatl's daughter, whom the proud and brave Tlaxcatec had offered to his victorious rival; Cortés gave her to Alvarado; she was now Doña Luisa, and her sons and daughters became Spanish

Grandees; a daughter or niece of Maxixcatzin was named Doña Elvira, "and she was very beautiful"; Cortés gave her to Juan Velázquez de León; two others were given to Alonso Dávila and Cristóbal de Olid; the last to a youthful captain, who was to play a part in the conquest second only to that of his chief—Gonzalo de Sandoval. (13)

*   *   *

Marriage in the Christian sense of the word was of course wholly unnecessary in Tlaxcatec eyes, and the deference shown by the Spanish captains to their Indian concubines, whom they treated as their equals and had served as ladies not only by their Indian, but also by their Spanish, servants, cemented a friendship which the mutual esteem born on the battlefield had established on solid human grounds. Cortés profited by this situation to give his troops a respite of about twenty days—a niggardly holiday indeed for an army which had gone through such an ordeal—and to acquire as much information as possible about his chief adversary. His friends told him that Moteçuçuma could easily put 150,000 warriors into the field, as they knew only too well; and with this force "he and his Mexicans usurped other dominions and widened and extended their empire every day, inflicting great cruelties when they conquered, so that the other peoples should surrender and submit to their empire, for fear of undergoing a similar cruelty; and they were so evil-hearted that they never kept their word, nor kept a secret, nor remembered good works done to them, however weighty." "Things which might have made another man's beard tremble." (14) Yet Cortés asked his Tlaxcatec friends how it was that, being so powerful, Mexico had never knocked out Tlaxcala in one hundred years of war. This was precisely the question which one of Cortés' soldiers, Tapia, was later to ask Moteçuçuma in person, who answered thus: "We could easily do it; but then we should have no way of exercising the persons of our young men, save too far away; and moreover, we wanted always to have people to sacrifice to our gods"; an answer, it must be owned, which reveals a highly evolved conception of war and of the precious and indispensable utility of a good enemy. The Tlaxcatec answer to Cortés was not quite as neat and, amongst other reasons, included the lack of enthusiasm for battle shown by many of the

H

troops of Moteçuçuma, made up of peoples he had subdued. The Tlaxcatecs were most eloquent in extolling the power of Mexico; the wealth and majesty of Moteçuçuma; the magnificence, military strength and vast resources of his capital, built on a lagoon, accessible only through three causeways carried over numerous bridges (any one of which, being raised, could entirely isolate the town from inimical strangers) and made up of innumerable houses with terraces built so as to provide shelter for their warriors; the water supply which came from Chapultepec, two miles from the city, in specially built ducts; the weapons of his Mexicans, arrows which passed through all (cotton) armour, "flint" spears (they were made of obsidian, and really formidable, as Cortés knew too well) and swords to be brandished with both hands. The Tlaxcatecs showed their guest pictorial records of their past battles with the Mexicans, in which their way of fighting was clearly seen.

Cortés, with a number of his captains and soldiers (for Bernal Díaz seems to have been present), followed this narrative with great attention till it came to armament and tactics, when, as his native friends were teaching him nothing new, he changed the subject abruptly, asking them how they, the Tlaxcatecs, had come to settle there. This brought out the story that the earlier inhabitants of the land had been some giants whom the Tlaxcatecs had beaten; in proof of which the natives produced a thigh bone of gigantic proportions—had it been human, which, of course was not the case. "I think," said Cortés to his soldiers, "that we had better send this big bone to Castille for His Majesty to see." Meanwhile, the Tlaxcatecs, thrown back on their past, revealed to the Spaniards the prophecy of Quetzalcoatl: "an idol," says Bernal Díaz, "of whom they were very devout, had told them that there would come men from the parts where the sun rises and from far-off lands, to subdue them and to rule over them; that if we were such men, they would be glad, since we are so brave and so kind; and when they treated with us for peace, they remembered this that their idols had told them; that is why they give us their daughters, to have kinsmen to defend them against the Mexicans." This revelation dumbfounded the Spaniards, who kept wondering whether it could possibly be true. Cortés, however, wisely chose to remain as close as possible to the facts and neatly answered: "The Spaniards undoubtedly come from where the sun rises and, for that reason, the King has sent us to make of the Tlaxcatecs our brother, for he has news for you, and may God give us grace so that by our hands and intercession, you may be saved." To which all the soldiers present said: "Amen." (15)

* * *

Cortés was a man who meant what he said. He was therefore bound to draw his own conclusion from this pledge he had given his Tlaxcatec friends. It was now more necessary than ever that he should leave his comfortable quarters in Tlaxcala, to lead his troops and his allies to Mexico itself. He quickly felt the advantage of having in front of him such a clearly outstanding capital: for it was enough for him to secure that capital to prove his victory unmistakably to friends, foes and rivals. On to Mexico, was then the order of the day.

He began by sending a scouting expedition under cover of an embassy to Moteçuçuma. His emissaries were Pedro de Alvarado and Bernaldino Vázquez de Tapia. These two captains left for Mexico with just one servant; which shows that Cortés felt by now confident enough in his own strength to send away two of his captains without any escort. The two emissaries returned without having reached Mexico; Tapia fell ill with fever and Alvarado decided to return, whether because, in Iztapalapan, he was told by Moteçuçuma's officials that he was not to proceed farther, as the Emperor had a headache, or because Cortés had him recalled on representations from his soldiers, who objected to the risk run by their captains. (16)

Cortés' decision to march on to Mexico was soon known in the camp, where it did not fail to raise some opposition amidst the rich soldiers of the "Cuban" party; this was promptly put down by the resolute attitude of "us, poor soldiers"—says Bernal Díaz—"who at all times had already offered our souls to God who made them, and our bodies to wounds and hardships till we died in the service of Our Lord and of His Majesty." There was also some opposition on the part of Xicotencatl and Maxixcatzin, who feared for the Spaniards in the midst of those Mexicans who, for them, were the incarnation of treachery. This brought out the most subtle reaction on the part of Cortés. He brushed aside the danger, but his sharp mental ear detected an undertone of incipient mistrust in the advice of his Tlaxcatec friends, and this he at once set out to meet: he gave the two leaders rich presents from the stores he had received from Moteçuçuma, and in particular cotton clothes, the most coveted luxury in blockaded Tlaxcala; and he went even as far as to suggest that it might be a good thing if they were to conclude a peace with the Mexicans, so that they could trade freely and import cotton and salt.

Xicotencatl and Maxixcatzin rejected this idea as being beyond the bounds of possibility, owing to the lack of good faith of the Mexicans; and were shocked to hear that Cortés was determined not only to go to Mexico, but to go by way of Cholula, a city-republic in alliance with Moteçuçuma, from which, as they had often told Cortés, treacherous attacks had often been launched against them. The way of Cholula had been advised by the Mexican ambassadors, who had remained close to Cortés right through his stay in Tlaxcala. The Tlaxcatecs advised the road through Guaxocingo, a community which was allied to them. Cortés made up his mind to go by Cholula, because it was a big town, well supplied, in which he could tarry while devising how to enter Mexico without waging war; he went so far as to fix a day to the Mexican ambassadors. This decision came to the knowledge of the Tlaxcatecs, who hurried to Cortés to inform him of the danger he was running: Moteçuçuma had sent to Cholula fifty thousand men who were lying in wait for the Spaniards two leagues outside the town; the regular road was closed, and another had been opened, with traps for the horses; the town itself was prepared for war, some streets were walled off, the house terraces well provided with stones; finally, as a proof of the ill will of the Cholulans, the Tlaxcatecs pointed out to him that they were the only people in the vicinity who had sent no deputation to greet him. (17)

This struck Cortés deeply, and he at once suggested that the Tlaxcatecs should provide messengers to summon the leaders of Cholula to his presence. The Cholulans sent an embassy, of sorts. The Tlaxcatecs warned Cortés that this embassy was a mockery, common people unfit to be received by him. Cortés nevertheless spoke to them: he told them that an embassy to so high a prince as the King of Spain should not be entrusted to men such as they; and he summoned the leaders of Cholula to come within three days to declare their obedience to His Majesty, warning them that, should they refuse to come, he would attack and destroy them. All of which he moreover gave them in writing, duly signed by himself and by his notary. This brought the Cholulan leaders the next day; (18) they explained their remissness in coming to greet Cortés on the ground of unsafety, for Tlaxcala was enemy territory; begged Cortés not to believe the tales against them which he might have heard from the Tlaxcalans and declared themselves "vassals" of the King of Spain, whatever they made of the nation and of the monarch—all of which, again, Cortés had taken down by his notary.

This done, he finally chose to go by Cholula, "so as not to show weakness," he writes to the King. (19)

*   *   *

On October 13th, 1519, the army left for Cholula, in the strictest order. The Spaniards were accompanied by their allies the Cempoalese, about five hundred strong, and by the whole Tlaxcatec army, which Cortés estimates at one hundred thousand—though this is hardly credible. He had—he says to the Emperor—done his best to dissuade them from following him, arguing that he did not need them. But the Tlaxcatecs may have had reasons of their own for entering the territory of their enemies in such excellent company. This, however, did not suit Cortés, and when they had arrived within two leagues of Cholula, "by dint of my importunity, they went back, though five or six thousand of them remained in my company." He determined to stay the night there, by a brook, for he wished to avoid any disturbance in the city and does not seem to have felt quite at ease about those Tlaxcatecs. The Cholulans sent them food for the evening, and the next morning came out to receive them with music, more religious than military, "singing as they do in their mosques." Leaders and priests came to them peacefully, and the priests brought their braziers with them in which they burnt copal-incense—whether to honour or to exorcise the strangers is not clear. The Cholulan leaders explained that they did not think it fair that their enemies the Tlaxcatecs should be allowed to enter their town in arms. Cortés had noticed many a sign on the way which made him fear the Tlaxcatecs had warned him only too truly: the regular road was closed, and there were some traps on the one which they had had to follow; yet, he was struck by the force of the argument of the Cholulans; he decided to have a kind of public explanation about it; he ordered the army to stop and gather round him and there and then, as he was, on horseback, summoned the Cholulans and asked them to state their case; the Cholulans then put forward their official explanation: they had not gone to Tlaxcala, not for lack of good will towards Cortés, but because it was an enemy city; they asked Cortés to keep the Tlaxcatecs out of the town. Cortés thereupon instructed his second in command, Pedro de Alvarado, and his field-master, Cristóbal de Olid, to order the Tlaxcatecs to camp outside the town, and to allow no natives to enter Cholula other than the Cempoalese soldiers and the Tlaxcatec *tlamemes* who were carrying the artillery.

This decision calmed the Cholulans, and when Cortés saw them in a more receptive mood, he addressed them with his usual message: he was sent by a powerful monarch to ask them to give up their idols, to make them stop their human sacrifices and their sodomite ways and to make of them his brothers. He asked them to let him pass on his way to Mexico, and, as others had done before them, to give their allegiance to the King of Spain. The Cholulans refused to give up their idols, but were content to give their allegiance to "that King you speak about," though Bernal Díaz notes that they said so merely "by word of mouth and not before a notary." He was eminently fair, and since the Cholulans betrayed this allegiance soon after they had promised it, the honest Spaniard does not fail to point out this undoubtedly extenuating circumstance. Cortés, however, was this time content to let the destruction of the idols abide its time, and the army moved on towards the town. He was well advised, because Cholula was a kind of Mecca for all the peoples who followed the religion of Anáhuac, and in particular, for the cult of that Quetzalcoatl who had prophesied his coming and whom, in the eyes of many, he reincarnated. There were three hundred and sixty teocallis in Cholula (just as many as there are churches today), and an ancient pyramid on which stood the great teocalli dedicated to Quetzalcoatl. Cholula was supernaturally defended against unbelieving armies, both by thunder and by lightning, which Quetzalcoatl was sure to unleash in case of such a danger, and by torrents of water which, in such an emergency, would burst forth from the walls of the pyramid. That is why, if any part of this wall came to fall unexpectedly, it was imperative that the priests should at once stop the gap—which they did with a special cement made with lime and the blood of children sacrificed for the purpose. (20)

It would not have been reasonable to expect the Cholulans to give up the worship of so powerful a deity. The Spanish army, how-ever, though undoubtedly unbelieving from the Cholulan point of view—for, alas, nothing is more relative than infidelity—were not marching on the town as aggressors but as guests; and they were received accordingly, not by thunder and lightning but by the rumours and smiles of a crowd eager to behold the strange men and their still stranger beasts. While thus advancing through the human river to the quarters assigned to them, the horsemen, from their point of vantage, observed that some streets were walled off, and that there were holes in the streets and suspicious-looking barricades. Cortés noted moreover that there were fresh messengers from Moteçuçuma in the town, but evidently not sent to him, for they did not come to his presence though they spoke much with the Mexican Ambassa-dors who had been part of his establishment since leaving Tlaxcala, and who had advised him to come to Cholula; nor did the fact escape his attention that when these new messengers left Cholula, they took with them the chief of the ambassadors attached to him.

All this was very disquieting, particularly as, after the departure of these Mexican messengers, supplies became scarcer and services more casual on the part of the Cholulans. One day, at dinner, Diego de Ordás commented on all these evil signs of both Mexicans and Cholulans and concluded: "Sir, I like these people's looks not at all, and I believe I am not mistaken." Cortés banged the table and, simulating anger, he exclaimed: "Heavens alive, Diego de Ordás, what a lot of fear you do have! what could these people or the other people do to us, were they never so many?" (21) He was concerned, withal. He tried to gain information from the chief Cholulans, but they refused to come, even though he tried to nego-tiate with them through two priests whom he won over by presents of *chalchivitls*. Three Cempoalese came to see him, and revealed that they had found hidden holes in the streets round the camp, with

sharp-pointed pickets; that the terraces were full of stones and barricaded; while in a street near by there was a barricade of big wooden
beams; they were still speaking when eight Tlaxcatecs of the army
left outside the town rushed in. "Malintzin," they said to Cortés,
"this town is in a bad mood; last night they have sacrificed seven
persons, five of them children, to the god of war; and they
are sending out their clothes and women and children." Cortés sent
them back with a message to their captains to be ready for a call at
any time.

That night, Cortés took special precautions round his camp; he
had every man ready and armed and every horse saddled and harnessed, for he fully expected a combined attack of the Mexicans
and Chololtecs. He held an informal council of war with his captains
and some of his trusted soldiers, such as Bernal Díaz. Some of his
companions held the view that it would be better to give up the
route of Cholula and to go to Mexico by way of Guaxocingo; others,
that it was safer at any rate to return to Tlaxcala; but the view which
prevailed was the bolder course of attacking the Chololtecs in their
town, for if they once tolerated such betrayals they would be lost
for ever.

While the soldiers deliberated, an old lady of Cholula, accompanied by a youth, both showing signs of wealth and power, called
on Doña Marina in the still of night. She was the wife of one of the
Chololtec captains, and she came with her son to warn Doña Marina
of the deadly risk she was running. Seeing her rich and young and
good-looking, the good Chololtec lady had conceived the idea of
marrying her to one of her sons, and she revealed to her that the next
morning, by order of Moteçuçuma, the Spaniards would all be either
killed or taken to Mexico, to feed the sacrificial stone of Uitzilopochtli. "Mother," answered Doña Marina, "I am very grateful to
you and I would fain go with you straightway, had I any one whom
I could trust to carry my wraps and gold jewels. Could you and your
son wait by me? At present, these *teules* are watching, and they
would be sure to see us trying to escape." The old lady remained
and, of course, talked on. The plan was three days old; Moteçuçuma
had sent her husband a golden drum as a reward for his part in it,
and other valuable presents to other captains. "Wait here a
moment," said Doña Marina. "I will begin to bring my things little

by little." And as her heart belonged to Cortés, she went away and told Aguilar.

Cortés lost no time; he quietly seized hold of one of the leading Cholulans, who seemed particularly busy, and pointing a dagger at his heart, asked what was afoot. He obtained a fairly full confession. The lady, her son and the prominent Cholulan were retained under a close watch; meanwhile the dawn was breaking, and the soldiers noticed the bustle and the excitement which went on between the leaders, the priests and a thick swarm of armed Chololtecs who had invaded the camp, on the ground that Cortés himself had asked for two thousand of them to accompany him to Mexico. But the Spaniards had not been caught napping; soldiers with sword and buckler were at the gates to prevent any of the Chololtecs that had entered the camp from leaving it alive; Cortés had summoned as many leaders as he was able to find and had locked them up in a room; he was now on his horse, in the midst of his troops; he cast a glance on the Chololtec warriors who with leers and jeers of ill omen thronged the vast courtyard, and said to his soldiers: "How eager these traitors are to see us in the ravines to eat their fill of our flesh! The Lord will do things better." From his horse, he then addressed the Cholulans in the camp: he told them that he knew all; that he had only wanted to be their friend, but they had planned to destroy him and his companions, and vowed to sacrifice twenty of them to their idol, as they had already done seven of their own, for which their idol had promised them a victory; "but," he added, "as he is a false and bad idol, he holds no sway on us, and all these betrayals and crimes are now to fall back on you." Doña Marina put this speech into *nauatl*, and the Chololtecs, very much impressed, threw all the blame onto Moteçuçuma. But Cortés did not accept this excuse and gave them this characteristic answer: "Such treasons, it is ordered in the royal laws, cannot remain unpunished. You must die." And he had a musket fired. This was the agreed signal, and, he writes to the Emperor: "In two hours more than three thousand men died."

The Spaniards had to fight hard, for the Chololtecs were no cowards, and though "they were easy to defeat, for we took them by surprise, particularly as they had no leaders," they were more than ready, and had fortified many streets and towers, "where they

H*

defended themselves and attacked us." The fight lasted for five hours, the last three of which were harder for the Cholulans owing to the arrival on the scene of their enemies the Tlaxcatecs, whose destructive zeal Cortés had to check with the utmost energy; he sent Cristóbal de Olid to bring him all the Tlaxcatec captains and ordered them to take their men out of the town at once; he, moreover, forced them to give up the captives they had made—we know for what purpose captives were made in native wars—"but," says Bernal Díaz, "they remained wealthy this time in gold and wraps, and cotton and salt and slaves."

Meanwhile, some of the "heads of the opposition," Cholulan chiefs who disagreed with the policy recently adopted by their City State, called on Cortés to ask for clemency; they explained that the traditional policy of Cholula had been one of alliance with Tlaxcala and Guaxocingo against the Mexican Triple Alliance (Tenochtitlán or Mexico proper, Tetzcuco and Tlacopan), while of late, owing to the other party, the City had shifted its allegiance. Cortés immediately seized this opportunity to establish peace not merely within Cholula but between Cholula and Tlaxcala as well. The new city leaders, appointed by him, brought back the population which, within a few days, had recovered its normal life; and he succeeded in restoring the good relations that had prevailed between the two cities until Moteçuçuma had recently sown discord between them.

This quick work in the healing of the wounds inflicted by his arrival in the country must be borne in mind when discussing the tragic days of Cholula. It is barely possible that the Tlaxcatecs helped to create a misunderstanding; but the first warning did not come from them; it came from the Cempoalese, who were utterly indifferent to the Tlaxcatec-Cholula feud. It is again possible that another man in exactly the same circumstances might have found a better solution. Yet, it is difficult to see what else Cortés could have done—*once the premise of the conquest is accepted as a fact*. True, Sahagún, whose knowledge of Mexican affairs always commands respect, definitely says that "the Chololtecs had no defensive nor offensive weapons" and implies that while they were cold and distant to the Spaniards, they meant no treason. But he came onto the stage much later, and his information on a point on which the natives themselves · differed was bound to be influenced by the particular source in which he sought it. Bernal Díaz, who defends his companions against the accusations of Las Casas, points out that the Franciscan Friars investigated the facts upon their arrival in New Spain and, after talking to the same Cholulan priests who had taken part in the events, found that they had happened in accordance with his narrative. He mentions in particular the saintly and strongly pro-Indian Motolinia. (22)

That Cortés was perfectly capable of falling on an unarmed population is proved by the fact that he did so, as he himself narrates it, on his night raid in Tlaxcala territory. But that is precisely why he, and his companions Tapia and Bernal Díaz, should be believed when—writing separately and without knowledge of one another's writings—they concur on the main facts: *there was a conspiracy, and the Cholulans were armed.* This is one of the cases in which Las Casas, in his passionate desire to blacken all the conquistadores, is caught red-handed—though only with red ink, of course. He denies the conspiracy and attributes to Cortés a most callous and cruel attitude, all by hearsay. "The 'massacre' at Cholula," writes a contemporary American authority, "*was* a military necessity to one warring as Cortés was." (23)

It is moreover consonant with Cortés' legalistic mind, and with his almost pedantic scruple, that while he thought himself free to wage war even on an unarmed village, after the State to which it belonged had refused to allow him a peaceful admittance, he should have considered himself bound to respect the hospitality of Cholula, even to the point of excluding from it his allies the Tlaxcatecs, until fully convinced of the Chololtec betrayal; and, on being sure of this, that he should have told the "traitors" that such a crime could not be left unpunished as required by the royal laws. Yet events have a logic of their own; and, though justified in his eyes, the Cholula massacre was to sink into the army's memories and give rise to an action in the same style, prompted no doubt by this precedent: a rash outburst of preventive violence on the part of Alvarado which was to be one of the two chief tragedies of the conquest.

CHAPTER FIFTEEN

At the Gates of the City of Mexico

CORTÉS handled the Cholulan episode with characteristic subtlety, so far as Moteçuçuma was concerned. He could not entertain the slightest doubt as to the responsibility of the Mexican Emperor in the whole affair; but he was not in a position to enter Mexico as an enemy, or at least, he preferred to enter Mexico as a friend. He could not therefore, publicly and officially, take the view that the Emperor had betrayed him; and so, when the Cholulan caciques had come to implore his mercy, he called in Moteçuçuma's ambassadors and made the Cholulans repeat before the Mexicans how the plot had been engineered by Moteçuçuma; but he took no notice of this and answered the Cholulans that "though the whole city deserved to be destroyed, he would forgive them out of respect for Moteçuçuma whose vassals they were." However, once the city had been pacified, Cortés again called the Mexican ambassadors and bitterly reproached them for their master's betrayal and announced that he had changed his mind: instead of entering Mexico as a friend, he would enter it on a war footing and do as much harm as he could. (1)

The Mexican ambassadors asked and easily obtained leave for one of them to go to Mexico, report and come back. Cholula is about eighty miles from Mexico. Moteçuçuma was still stubbornly hoping to keep Cortés off, arguing through his ambassadors that the land was almost inaccessible (a word meaningless for a Spaniard) and poor and sterile (a view robbed of all authority by Moteçuçuma's own gorgeous presents to Cortés). One day, in Cholula, the Mexican ambassadors, at a loss for fresh arguments, pointed out to Cortés

216

that "Moteçuçuma had many and very fierce tigers, lizards, lions and other dreadful and wild animals which in one hour would be able to kill all the men who came against him." Cortés laughed and hid his anger, for he did not want to break with Moteçuçuma. (2)

This happened before his victory over Cholula, which increased his prestige still further over all Anáhuac. The leaders of Tepeaca sent him a present of thirty slaves and some gold—which decided those Spaniards who hesitated to follow Cortés on to Mexico; (3) Guaxocingo also sent a valuable present. The destruction of the great temple of Quetzalcoatl in Cholula had shaken the faith of the natives in the power of their gods. (4) Moteçuçuma's messengers came back to Cholula with yet more presents, with lame explanations about the Cholula episode and with one more request, after so many —that Cortés should not come to Mexico.

Cortés' answer was typical of his firm character and suave ways. "I answered that the journey to his country could not be excused, for I had to report to your Majesty about him and it; [. . .] that, therefore, since I would not fail to come and see him, he was to take it in good part and not to plan anything else, for it would be to his great harm and I should be sorry for any that might befall him." (5) The arrival of this second message produced devastating effects on the unfortunate Emperor, and he sought religious advice. He ordered many human sacrifices to be made, and remained for days locked up in the Great Teocalli, fasting and praying and drawing blood from his ears, arms and legs in search of inspiration. He seems to have received it and in a pretty concrete form, though we are entitled to harbour doubts as to the channel through which it reached him: "The Devil to whom he used to confide his affairs spoke to him and told him not to fear, for the Christians were but few and he was the Lord of many and of brave men and he would be able to do whatever he wanted with the Christians; he was not to discontinue human sacrifices, so as not to expose himself to some disaster; and he was to keep his idols Uitzilopochtli and Tezcatlipoca in a propitious state." (6)

This encouragement from his own inner consciousness or devil may have been due to quite a different experience from that recorded here by Torquemada. Moteçuçuma had as a kind of Governor of the Northern Coast a nobleman known as Quauhpopoca, Lord of

Coyohuacán, who resided in a town not far from Veracruz, known
by the Mexicans as Nauhtla and by the Spaniards as Almería. The
troops of Quauhpopoca had an encounter with some Spanish soldiers;
the chief motive seems to have been Quauhpopoca's desire to supply
Moteçuçuma with a live specimen of a Spaniard. He caught one
dead and one alive, though badly wounded, and both were sent to
the Emperor, but as the wounded man died on the way, the messengers—let it be remembered that all transport was then done on the
backs of human beings—cut the two heads off and left the bodies on
the way. One of the men, Argüello, "had a very big head, and the
beard black and curly, and he was very robust in his countenance and
a youth of great strength." When the two heads were put before
the Emperor, he beheld them in silence for a long while, pale and
downcast, then said: "These are not immortal men, but to judge by
their faces, they are brave." And the gruesome sight confirmed his
belief that the white bearded men were those who, according to the
old prophecies, would come from the East and rule the lands. (7)

This revelation led him to a change at any rate in tactics. He
sent six messengers to Cortés inviting him to come to Mexico, where
he would be well received. Cortés "gave them a good answer and
very loving"; sent back three of them with it and kept the remaining
three as guides for the journey. Not very reliable guides, one would
think, and as it turned out, altogether fatal, had not Cortés guessed
the plans of his no less astute adversary. The insistence of the
Mexican ambassadors on the choice of a particular road awoke his
suspicions, and at this point—he writes to Charles V—"as God has
always devoted great attention to guiding Your Majesty's affairs
ever since Your Majesty's childhood, and as I and my companions
were marching in Your Majesty's royal service, He showed us
another road, though somewhat steep, not as dangerous as that by
which they intended to lead us." (8)

*   *   *

From time immemorial, when the Lord wants to impart something to men, he is wont to have recourse to a column of smoke. This
was precisely the way He signalled to Cortés, then in danger, while
engaged in His service and that of His chief agent on earth, Charles
V. When in Tlaxcala, the Spaniards had noticed a column of smoke

"as big as a big house" (9) rising from the summit of the mighty hill which the natives called Popocatepetl; it rose straight in the sky, for the strong winds that blew over the mountaintop had no power over it. They noted the fact, with the curiosity of men of their time, and asked the natives about it. The natives thought it quite natural that a mountain known as "The Hill That Smokes" for that is what *Popocatepetl* means, should live up to its name. They were moreover full of religious fears about it, for Popocatepetl and his wife Iztaccihuatl or the White Woman (the equally majestic peak which rises near it), were connected in their minds with the spirits of the dead. Many would no doubt associate the activity of Popocatepetl with the arrival of the white *teules* in their midst. The Spaniards, of course, knew that, if the hill smoked, this meant that in the mind of God something was brewing which would be sure to redound to His glory and to that of His white servants.

But the ways of the Lord are inscrutable, and He ordained that Cortés should take heed of His meaning by the roundabout way of scientific curiosity; "and as I always have desired," he writes to the Emperor, "to report most particularly to Your Majesty on every one of the things of this land, I wished to know the secret of this one, which seemed to me somewhat marvellous." It so happened that this captain Diego de Ordás—one of Velázquez' men—wanting to show the Indians that there was nothing a Spaniard could not do, came to ask Cortés to be allowed to climb to the top of that smoking mountain. Cortés gave him nine other men "such as were required for this kind of business" and a few natives as guides and carriers, and let him go. (10) It was, of course, no easy matter, for Popocatepetl rises to nearly 18,000 feet above sea level. They had first to cut their way through a thick forest; then to climb up the usual crags and over the usual precipitous paths wherewith earth's giants defend their proud solitudes. The natives of the party had foretold that the Spaniards would not be able to go more than halfway, owing to the flames, stones and ashes which the huge crater ejected; they, in any case, would not go beyond the *Cues* which had been erected on the hillside in honour of the local gods. That is exactly where they remained, bound by some impassable taboo; the Spaniards went on and soon found themselves walking on snow, then on ice, struggling with all the now well-known difficulties of mountaineering.

But when, close to the crater, they might have thought that their labours were at last to be crowned by success, the Popocatepetl rumbled furiously and clouds of hot, sulphurous smoke screened off its top from the adventurous strangers.

Ordás and his companions decided to return; they brought snow and icicles to show the height they had reached, and stories enough to satisfy the objective curiosity of their respected chief and the less critical curiosity of his soldiers and Indian auxiliaries. Cortés writes to the Emperor that they were not able to reach the top—a fact which dissatisfied him both as a general and as an enquiring mind, and led him to organise a second and more successful expedition two years later; but Bernal Díaz reports that Ordás and his companions —whom he reduces to two—on seeing the flames and smoke, "remained motionless, without stepping forward, for about an hour, when they felt the flames had abated and the volcano threw up less cinders and smoke, and then they climbed to the top, which was very round and wide and as wide as a fourth of a league"; and he adds that they all admired it greatly, "for in those days we had not seen such a thing nor heard of it, as now when we all know what it is and many Spaniards have climbed to the mouth, even Franciscan friars." (11)

Cortés evidently kept the relative failure of the expedition to himself, judging that Ordás' bragging, backed by his icicles and snow, was good material for impressing all and sundry with the mettle of the Spaniards; and in itself this result was worth the trouble and expense. But Ordás had brought him excellent news as well, i.e. the message which God meant to convey to him by means of this self-important and noisy volcano. On the way up, they came across a good road; Diego de Ordás asked where it led. "To Culúa" (i.e. Mexico), answered the Indians, and they added it was a better way than the one the Mexicans were offering Cortés. Presently, Ordás and his companions were able to cast eyes on the glorious sight of the lagoons with the Aztec Venice poised on its crystalline blue water, on the edge of which other smaller towns repeated the pattern of houses, bridges and causeways. The Spaniards were overjoyed at the sight. (12)

Cortés meanwhile was actively serving this Lord so attentive to his dangers. He began by breaking up the wooden cages in which the Cholulans kept a store of men and boys to fatten for sacrifice, ordering the captives to return to their respective towns and exacting from the Cholulans a promise—which the sceptical Bernal Díaz deems useless—to give up the habit of eating human flesh. He then called together the priests and leaders of the republic and made them the usual request to forsake their faith in their false idols, feeling on stronger ground now than on the evening before he entered the city, since now he could argue that their god had not been able to prevent their defeat. He was not very successful; and Father Olmedo intervened to point out that "it was useless, at the beginning, to take away their idols." A compromise was found: the great Teocalli was turned into a church, and a cross of masonry was erected on it which could be seen from the whole valley and sufficed to show that a change had come over the land—for ever. (13)

* * *

Everything was now ready for the final march to Mexico. The Tlaxcatecs heard the news of Cortés' decision with some dismay; they feared that the Spaniards would not be able to escape alive from the land of Moteçuçuma; but their decision was all to their honour: they offered ten thousand men with valiant chiefs and supplies. Cortés made answer that he was grateful but did not think it fair that he should enter Mexico with so many warriors; he accepted one thousand men to carry his artillery and help on the roads. This answer was not merely chivalrous; it was shrewd as well. Cortés, by now, knew from the events of Cholula how difficult it was to hold in check a body of native warriors on enemy territory. (14) He was, to all appearances at least, entering Mexico as a friend, for his warlike language to the ambassadors was just a diplomatic manœuvre; he would therefore wish to avoid arousing suspicions, even at some risk to himself.

The Tlaxcalans promptly sent him the thousand men he required; but on the same day he lost his faithful Cempoalese. They came to him and explained that, in their opinion, if they went on to Mexico they would all die—and Cortés also; they seem to have been overwhelmed by their own responsibilities in initiating the revolt against the power of Mexico; Cortés assured them that, since they would be of his company, their safety would be complete; he promised them that

he would make them wealthy—but the men of Cempoal did not want
to be wealthy, they wanted to be alive. "God knows," said Cortés,
"that we would never want to keep with us by force these Indians
who have served us so well." And he sent them away loaded with
presents, not forgetting his old friend the fat cacique. (15) He had
received a letter from Escalante on the death of the four Spaniards
trapped by Quauhpopoca, about which he said nothing to anyone.
He answered it, and dispatched his answer with his Cempoalese
friends, and left for Mexico at the head of his four hundred and fifty
Spaniards and four thousand natives, on November 1st, 1519.

* * *

They marched as usual in strict formation and, as Bernal Díaz
says, "the beard on the shoulder." (16) The first night, they camped
in Calpan, in the lands of Guaxocingo, allies of the Tlaxcalans. They
were cordially received and offered humble presents, for the land
was poor, though rich in advice: the natives told them that there
were two ways to Mexico; one was closed by order of Moteçuçuma,
who had had it barricaded with tree trunks; the other was
clean and ready for them, but it led to some broken passes in
which the Mexicans were awaiting to destroy them all. Cortés took
note.

The next day, they passed between the Popocatepetl and the
Iztaccihuatl, and were able to verify what their Calpan friends had
told them about the two roads, the clean, and the closed. Cortés
asked the Mexican ambassadors why this was so: they explained
that the clean road led through Chalco, while the other had been
closed because it was longer and led through no town big enough
to receive the army. Cortés showed no sign of mistrust—but chose
the closed road. It was no easy road, to be sure; for while nature
itself had made it difficult, man had increased its difficulty by barring
it with barricades of gigantic trees; and moreover, it was covered
with snow. Here, on the cold, pure, heights, the Spaniards cast eyes
for the first time on the Mecca of their adventurous pilgrimage.
Suddenly, the plain with its two lakes, and its thirty cities, sprang to
view in the bright sun, calling forth in their minds visions of the
enchanted cities they had read or heard of in the books of Chivalry.
Compared to what it became in Spanish days, Mexico was then but

a big village; but its adobe houses were spotlessly white with plaster and shone like silver in the pure air of the high tableland, while its teocallis rose above them with the quiet majesty of their-cubic lines. The chief impression was one of power and greatness, unlike anything that the Discovery had as yet revealed. For the first time, the dreams of Colón came true. The eager and hungry expressed their high hopes in typical Spanish language: "This is the promised land." To which in no less typical Spanish others commented: "The more the Moors, the better the spoils." But "the opposition" grumbled and, awed by the immensity of what they saw, their hearts sank in dismay. "We are tempting God," they said, "if we let ourselves into that danger, so few of us in the midst of so many." Cortés noticed the state of mind of his men. Promises here and appeals to Spanish valour there, soon calmed the fears of the less brave, and the army marched on, knowing now for certain that if the stakes were vital the prize was glorious. (17)

That night, the Spaniards were able to camp in far more comfortable quarters than they expected, in a place called Quauhtechcatl, which they christened El Patio, and which happened to be a hostel for travelling merchants. Here Cortés received a strange embassy. It arrived in the big square preceded by wave upon wave of rumours that Moteçuçuma in person was coming to greet Cortés, showing his good will towards him in thus coming out of his capital. The pomp and majesty of the visitors and the wealth of the presents which they brought with them, the deference shown to the chief amongst them by all his suite, everything was calculated to lend a colour of reality to the sensational rumour. The camp was agog. Cortés, however, refused to yield to the general excitement and, feeling no doubt that such a visit would have been out of keeping both with Moteçuçuma's dignity and with the reserved attitude which the Mexican Emperor had so far maintained, he quietly ascertained that his visitor was one of the Emperor's men, named Tzioacpopoca. The rumour, however, remained a subject of curiosity for his enquiring mind, and he rightly guessed that it emanated from the Mexicans themselves. He received his haughty visitor with his usual grace, and, observing his important mien, he asked him whether he was Moteçuçuma; the Mexican answered that he was. Whereupon, Cortés, turning to his Tlaxcatec friends, asked, "Is this Moteçuçuma?" and they answered: "No. It is Tzioacpopoca, one of his men." Cortés dismissed the ambassador with an angry frown. (18)

This curious episode is generally explained as a kind of experiment made by Moteçuçuma to find out the intentions of Cortés regarding his person. Despite the favourable reports brought by his messengers, who assured him that Cortés was sincere in his desire to strike a friendly arrangement with him, and that, far from harbouring designs of prison or death against him, they came to Mexico in mortal dread of perishing at his hands, which was indeed the case, the Emperor, seized with fear of the white strangers, decided, we are told, to simulate this visit so that the Spaniards, believing they had Moteçuçuma at their mercy in the camp, away from Mexican forces, should show their hand. That may be so. Yet, the scene smacks of the magical ways to which the Emperor-Priest was so much addicted. This Tzioacpopoca, especially chosen because of his likeness to Moteçuçuma, brings to mind that "Quintalbor" sent to Cortés because of his likeness to Cortés. Though not identical, the scenes have a family air, and may well have been dictated by considerations of magic, the meaning of which escapes us.

Who knows the messages, incantations and charms which Tzioacpopoca was conveying there and back while impersonating his Master? It is, at any rate, significant that, according to the two authorities on which this episode is based, Moteçuçuma, having heard his messenger's report, summoned his sorcerers and necromancers and asked them to provide the means whereby to stop the advance of the foreign invaders. They promised to do their best, and a strong force of them sallied forth to meet the Spaniards; but on the way, as they were climbing the hill of Tlalmanalco, they saw a vision coming towards them which filled them with holy terror. To the uninitiated it was just a peasant of the land of Chalco, "possessed by the four hundred rabbits," i.e. drunk. The spirit of wine, *Centzontotochtlin* (in English, "four hundred rabbits"), was playing havoc with him, and he came downhill towards them, all overrun with rabbits, hands, fingers, mouth, eyes, nose and hair; his naked chest was girded by eight ropes of hay, and he gesticulated wildly. As he saw the sorcerers and necromancers, he stopped dead, barring the way. The sorcerers and necromancers fell on their knees, muttering prayers, and feverishly fumbling in their bags for their maguey thorns to bleed themselves in sacrifice: they had instantly recognised Tetzcatlipoca, the chief of the gods of Anáhuac.

"What do you want?"—shouted the god, mastering his four hundred rabbits at one stroke of his omnipotent will. "Why do you come again? What is Moteçuçuma's mind? Is it now that he wakes up? Now, that he begins to fear? Too late, too late! Too many deaths, too much deceit and mockery!" The sorcerers and necromancers were overwhelmed. With their own bleeding hands, they built up a mound of earth and covered it with green grass for the god to sit on it as on an altar. But the god neither sat down nor even looked at his wretched worshippers; indeed, the uninitiated might perhaps have thought that, exhausted by his first oratorial effort, he had yielded to a fresh attack of the four hundred rabbits. Yet if that were so he quickly mastered it and, irritated at the puerile ceremonies of the sorcerers and necromancers, he thundered on: "You need not have come; never again shall I give heed to Mexico; I shall leave you for ever. Away! What you desire cannot be. Turn round and cast your eyes on Mexico!"

They obeyed and their eyes saw such a vision that their throats dried up and gasped for air. Mexico was burning. The Cues, the Calpullis, the Calmecacs, all the noble buildings which they knew well, were in flames. Unable to bear the sight, they turned back to the god with appealing eyes. The god had vanished.

With slow, sad steps, they returned home, and told Moteçuçuma their terrible experience. He grew infinitely sad, and spoke not. He sank onto the ground and buried his head in his hands. There was a long silence. Then, the Emperor spoke: "What can we do if our gods forsake us? We have already swallowed our death. Let us not climb to our mountains nor run away. We are Mexicans. Let us await what may come for the sake of Mexican honour; I grieve for the old and for the children, who have neither feet nor hands to put up a fight. Where shall their parents and kinsmen take them? What shall we do? We were born: let come that which may come." (19)

*   *   *

Cortés must have been puzzled at the strange embassy he had received. He was nearly always on a different plane from that of his adversary, and therefore constantly misunderstood him. He had reacted to the pretence of Tzioacpopoca from the point of view of categories such as prestige, knightliness, and the like, all probably foreign to Moteçuçuma, who in his turn lived in a world of magical forces utterly foreign to Cortés. The upshot of it all, in a man of Cortés' cautiousness, was bound to be an added mistrust of the Emperor's intentions. He was continually warned by his Tlaxcatec friends against the bad faith of the Mexicans. Tapia relates that Cortés grew uneasy at the number of people he noticed in the forest; he evidently suspected their intentions. He called some of their leaders and said to them: "You must know that those men who come with me do not sleep by night; if they sleep at all, it is just a little by day; and by night they are armed, and whomsoever they see walking about or coming close to them, they kill him on the spot; and I can do nothing to avoid it; therefore, let your people know it and tell them that no one is to come near us after sunset, for he would die, and I would be sorry for the dead." (20)

He gave orders in that sense to his sentinels and watchmen, and several spies were found dead next morning about the field—amongst which dead, he himself might well have lain, for in his eagerness to leave nothing to chance that he could master and control with his ever present will, he went out to test his own sentinels in the still, dark night, when a soldier, Martín López, having heard and half guessed a man in the blackness, covered him with his bow and was on the point of shooting his arrow, when Cortés challenged him—and saved his life. "Next time, sir," admonished Martín López, with Spanish plainness, "do speak from a longer distance." (21)

While in Calpan he received yet another propitiating embassy from the unfortunate Moteçuçuma, with the usual presents of gold and requests to turn back on the ground that Mexico was poor in food and built on water. Moteçuçuma offered to pay a yearly sum which he declared himself ready to deliver on the seacoast. Cortés reports his answer to the Emperor with astonishing candour: "I received them well and gave them some things of our Spain, which they valued very much [. . .] and answered their message that, were it in my power to turn back, I would do it to please Muteczuma, but that I had come to this land by order of Your Majesty, and that the main thing on which Your Majesty had ordered me to report had been the said Muteczuma and his great city, of which and of whom Your Majesty had had notice for a long time; and that I begged him to take my coming in good part, for no harm, rather advantage, would follow from it both for him and for his country; and that, if after our meeting he did not wish to have me in his company, I would return; and that he and I would best discuss together the way in which he was to serve Your Highness than through third persons, even though they were such as to deserve the greatest credit." This to the Emperor, whose only knowledge of the mere existence of Moteçuçuma came from the letters of Cortés. (22)

This embassy gave the Spaniards much to think about. It showed a stubborn opposition to their advance, which might at any time spring disaster on their small troop. On November 3rd, 1519, they began their descent towards Amecameca; "and as we are men," says Bernal Díaz, "and feared death, we never ceased thinking about it, and we marched by small stages, commending ourselves to God and to His blessed Mother Our Lady." (23)

In Amecameca they were well received and housed. The white chief was by now preceded by so much prestige that there were deputations waiting from several towns, congregated there to conciliate his help and sympathies against the exactions of Moteçuçuma. They brought modest presents in order to be received as friends, and "Cortés welcomed them with great love and offered himself to them, and as soon as he saw them together, he asked the Father of the Mercy to admonish them on the things of our faith, and about giving up their idols and the things we used to say everywhere, and to all of it they answered that it was very well said and they would look into it presently." Thus Bernal Díaz, though as devout as any man of his day, quietly registers the protest of common sense against the Quixotic crusading spirit of his chief; with a recondite—possibly subconscious—humour enhanced by what follows: "They were also given to understand the great might of the Emperor our Lord, and that we came to undo injuries and thefts, and that such was the reason why he had sent us to these parts—and as soon as they heard this, all those peoples, secretly, and out of hearing of Monteçuma's ambassadors, made many complaints against Monteçuma and his tax collectors who robbed them of all they had, and raped their wives and daughters in their presence, if they were beautiful and before their husbands, and made them all work like slaves [. . .] and took their lands [. . .]" (24)

Cortés was thus gradually realising that the might of Moteçuçuma's empire rested on tyranny and 'oppression; and, being a statesman as well as a soldier, he no doubt felt the stronger in the trial of strength which he felt coming. He "comforted them with loving words, which he knew very well how to say," and promised them his help for a more fitting occasion; he then asked them to send a few men to verify whether the road which had been cleaned and swept for them was in effect barricaded and manned by ambushed Mexicans, but the Indians answered: "Malinche, there is no longer any need to do so; the road is now quite clear [. . .] We know that their Witchywolves has advised them to let you pass and as soon as you enter Mexico, they will kill you all there." The Indians asked him to remain with them in Amecameca. But Cortés answered: "Neither the Mexicans nor any other nations have the power to kill us. Only the God in whom we believe can take our life." And he asked them to let him have twenty of their number to enter Mexico in his suite. (25)

This was no mere whim. It was a constant feature in his policy. Wherever he passed, he attached some of the prominent natives to his suite; he seems even to have kept some Cempoalese, for even after the Cempoal contingent left him on the eve of his departure from Cholula, there is a mention of Cempoalese members of his expeditions in all the records, including his own. His idea, no doubt, was to impress upon Moteçuçuma the fact that the native population was all at one with him. The fact would no doubt be duly noticed by a number of messengers sent to Amecameca by Moteçuçuma to see that the Spaniards were properly attended to and, it may be surmised, to inform their master about it all.

On November 6th, 1519, the army left Amecameca towards the lake of Chalco. Moteçuçuma had called a council again, to advise him, even at this eleventh hour, on what was to be done. But the positions had remained the same: Cuitlahuac, Moteçuçuma's brother, expressed the view of those who did not want to allow the Spaniards into Mexico; while Cacama, the youthful ruler of Tetzcuco, was of opinion that they should be received as ambassadors, and therefore as sacred men; for, were they to overstep their functions, they would be destroyed by the power of Mexico. What was actually decided was a compromise between the two views: Cacama was sent to try to induce Cortés to turn back, and failing this, to receive him. (26)

Meanwhile, Cortés had arrived in Ayotzinco, on the lake of Chalco, just cut off from the view of Mexico by the spur of Iztapalapa, which all but severed the lake of Mexico from the lake of Chalco. It was a small pueblo, half of it built on wooden piles on the water. Cortés found disquieting signs of treason the first night, "save that, as it turned out, they wished to do it in all safety to themselves and to fall upon us by night, when we were not watching." Thus Cortés to the Emperor, and he adds with most felicitous phrase: "And as I was so much on my guard, they found me standing in front of their thoughts." (27)

Next morning, early, when the army was on the point of leaving for Mexico, one of the scouts came to announce that a great number of Mexicans were approaching in a peaceful way, all richly clad. Cortés gave orders for the army to stand by, and presently four prominent Mexicans appeared before him and, with deep obeisance, begged him to await the arrival of Cacamatzin, a nephew of Moteçuçuma, King of Tetzcuco. "And he did not tarry." The Spaniards then beheld a sight of splendour and greatness which must have compensated them for their past dangers and hardships. The young prince, "of as much as twenty-five years," came towards them, carried in a chaise resting on the shoulders of eight Mexicans whose own dress, mien and attire suggested wealth and authority. The chaise was a thing of beauty, in which silver, gold, precious stones and green featherwork were skilfully wrought in imitation of trees and forests. As they came close to the house where Cortés waited, the eight bearers helped the prince to descend from the chaise and swept the path he had to tread; then with great show of deference and respect they led him to the Spaniard. "Malintzin," said the prince, "I and these men come to serve you and accompany you to our city, for so we have been commanded to do by Moteçuçuma, who soon will be able to show you his good will to serve your Lord; yet I beg you still, if possible, to turn back, for otherwise you will suffer much hardship and want and Moteçuçuma will be much ashamed to be unable to provide for you as he would wish." This message was repeated to Cortés by the prince's suite, with so much

vigour that, he writes to the Emperor, "nothing remained for them
but to add that they would defend the road against me, if I insisted
in going thither." But, of course, Cortés, who had refused to listen
to such messages when he was still on the coast, was not the man
to turn away from his prey when it lay before him in the morning
sun, placidly poised on the blue lake. Yet, though firm in his decision, he was, as always, courteous and suave in his manner, and sent
the prince away with a few presents and assurances that no harm
should come to them from the coming of the Spaniards. (28)

As soon as the prince had left, Cortés and his men began their
next march, in the direction of Iztapalapa. The road followed at
first the coast of the Chalco lake; they passed and visited Mizquic,
a tiny Venice built on the lake, and marched on till the road ventured
straight across the water towards the isthmus on which Iztapalapa
stood facing Mexico itself. It was a road "as wide as a horseman's
spear," says Cortés, admirably built of stone and cement. The crowds
which had come to behold them, so thick that at times they were a
hindrance, and at times, Cortés had thought, a danger, now thronged
the water in canoes which on both sides approached as closely as
possible . . . when the horses had passed. The natives were dumbfounded; but the Spaniards no less so; "and as we saw," says Bernal
Díaz, "so many cities and towns settled on the water, and on land
other great habitations, and that causeway, so straight and so level,
leading to Mexico, we were struck with admiration and we said that
it was all like those things of enchantment which are told in the book
of Amadis—those big towers, and *cues* and buildings which they had
on the water, all made of masonry, and there were some soldiers who
even asked whether all that they saw might not be a dream . . ."
(29) A truly Spanish reaction, this doubt whether life is a dream
or dreams are life. And who knows?

Thus the little army dreamt themselves into a gem of a town
which shone, silver on turquoise, between the coast and the isthmus
—Cuitlahuac, "the most beautiful, though small, we had yet seen."
The Spaniards were well received, and the local chiefs begged Cortés
to spend the night there, but the representatives of Moteçuçuma
who accompanied Cortés advised him to proceed to Iztapalapa, the
seat of Moteçuçuma's brother, also named Cuitlahuac, the one who
had always advised against his being allowed to enter Mexico. (30)

This first causeway had led them to the mainland, on the opposite shore of the lake of Chalco, the isthmus which divided the salt- from the fresh-water lake. The road, skirting first the southern shore of the isthmus, crossed over towards the North and led into Iztapalapa, a city of between twelve and fifteen thousand houses, built half on land, half on the water. Wonder and admiration grew constantly in the Spaniards. This town was so beautiful! Cuitlahuac, who, with the ruler of Coyoacan, came forward to meet Cortés, had some houses "as good as the best in Spain," says Cortés; and Bernal Díaz extols the woodwork ("cedar and other good aromatic woods"), the spacious patios and halls with cotton-covered walls; the garden was no less marvellous, with its fruit trees, its roses and other flowers; its pool beautifully built in stone and brick, covered with stucco and painted over with pictures "which had much to be praised," alive with the gay confusion of all kinds of waterfowl. "I stayed looking at it, and I thought that nowhere in the world could there be lands discovered such as these." Note that "discovered." It suggests the vast reservoir of marvels which, for the men of those days, was still untapped in the undiscovered world. (31)

Cuitlahuac and his companions gave Cortés a hearty welcome; they offered him "three or four thousand castillians [of gold] and a few women and clothes." But though Iztapalapa was good, Mexico was better, and the next morning the Spanish army left for the last day of their historic march. It was November 8th, 1519. The road went straight across the water, for Tenochtitlán, the city proper of Mexico, was right in the lake, and only accessible through artificial causeways. This one, which the army was now following, was "as wide as two spears, and very well built; eight horsemen can ride on it abreast." Yet, though wide, it was thick with the crowds which had gathered to witness what was to be one of the most famous scenes in the history of man; cues, towers, terraces were black with people; the lake had disappeared under a solid mass of canoes. "And as we saw such admirable things," writes Bernal Díaz, "we did not know what to say to ourselves or even whether what we saw was true; for on the one hand, on land, there were great cities, and on the lagoon many more, and we saw it all full of canoes, and on the causeway, many bridges from stretch to stretch, and ahead of us the great city of Mexico, and we were hardly four hundred men, and we had present in our memories the talks and warnings of the men of Guaxocingo, Tlaxcala and Tlalmanalco and many more, warning us not to enter Mexico, for they would kill us [. . .] Let the curious readers see whether there was not much to ponder over in this which I venture to write and whether there were ever in the universe men who had such daring." (32)

CHAPTER SIXTEEN

The Meeting of
the Two Worlds

THE Spanish army
walked in a tense excitement, suspended in the mid-air of their souls,
between wonder and fear, their spirit wrapped in faith and hope,
their bodies immersed in the breath of strange multitudes, feeling
upon them the glances of thousands of eyes like so many sharp
arrows. It was November 8th—for the Mexicans, the second of the
month of Quecholli in their civilian or astronomical calendar, and
the eighth of the sign of Ehecatl, in the religious, or astrological calendar. The month of Quecholli was the Month of the Flamingo, a
bird known as Teotlquechol, or bird of the gods, which in that part
of the year used to come from Florida to Anáhuac. It was the month
of lovers; in the course of it many maids were sacrificed in honour
of love, and wanton women came out openly and offered themselves
for sacrifice or, accompanying the soldiers to the battlefield, threw
themselves in the midst of the fight, in search of death, cursing themselves and hurling insults at honest women. The month of Quecholli
was also the month of effeminate men. (1)

The Spanish army arrived in Mexico on the second day of the
month, one of the first five days during which there was no religious
ceremony "and all was quiet in everything that concerned the service
of the gods." (2) Within four days everybody would be busy cutting
arrows from reeds to offer to Uitzilopochtli. It was also, in the complicated time-reckoning of the Mexicans, the eighth day of the sign
Ehecatl, particularly ill-fated in their astrology "because it was under
the sway of Quetzalcoatl, the lord of winds and whirlwinds." The

arrival of the white Quetzalcoatl on a day governed by the gods whom
for many Mexicans, not altogether excluding their Emperor, he
incarnated, must have been one of the supernatural factors which
shaped the strange historic events of that day. The men born under
this sign were sure to be sorcerers, necromancers and given to all
kinds of witchcraft. The dreaded witch-brigands known as *Temac-
palitotique* or *Tepupuxaqueirique* sallied forth to their nocturnal
robberies displaying before them the Ehecatl sign and the image of
Quetzalcoatl; thus protected, fifteen to twenty of them went dancing
into the night, under the leadership of one who brandished the left
arm of a woman dead in childbirth. On arriving at the house of
their prospective victims, the leader struck the threshold, with the
dead woman's arm; this caused all the house dwellers to fall into a
trance which made them unable to do anything in self-defence. The
thieves treated the women abominably; loaded their backs with gold,
silver, stones, feathers and cotton wraps and went away in safety,
unless, on the way, one of them happened to sit down, for then, he
could no longer rise again and the robbery was found out. (3)

This was the month, the day, the sign, that lived behind the
thousands of eyes which on that sunny Mexican morning were drinking in the sight of Quetzalcoatl's arrival. Quetzalcoatl, meanwhile,
followed by his four hundred men, was riding with his twelve
companions along the wide causeway which led across the lake from
Iztapalapa to Tenochtitlan; dreaming himself into his undreamt-of
victory. Half a league from the city, the Coyoacán causeway joined
the Iztapalapa causeway; a stronghold with two towers closed the
entrance; here, a brilliant crowd of about a thousand prominent
citizens came out to receive Cortés. On the copper-coloured skin of
their lithe bodies stood out the bright reds, blues, greens and yellows
of their *maxtlatl* or loincloths and of their rich wraps; feather plumes
rose over their heads, and ornaments of gold and chalchivitls shone
round their necks and wrists and even on their ears, nose or lips.
The progress of the army was halted for nearly an hour, till every
one of these prominent persons had performed the same gesture of
homage and friendship before Cortés: to touch the ground with the
hand, then kiss it. (4)

The ceremony over, the Spaniards passed through the one
entrance door in the fort. It is natural to imagine that their leader's

thoughts would then go back but a few weeks to that day when he had decided to pass through the gate of the Tlaxcala great wall, towards a mystery similar to that which now confronted him. But the dice were cast, and this was in any case—so he had the right to think—his last gamble with fate. Closer to the city they passed a long bridge, ten steps long, he says to the Emperor, with the accuracy of a man whose eye is on the details that matter; for he notes that this bridge is not only necessary to allow the water to flow from one lake to the other, the salt lake having a kind of regular tide, "but also invaluable to defend the city, for the long, wide beams which form the bridge can be removed wherever they wish." And he adds: "And of these bridges, there are many all over the city."

Past this bridge, the road became "a wide, straight beautiful avenue, two-thirds of a league in length, with very good and big buildings on both sides, dwelling houses and mosques." (5) Two long lines of "Mexican lords" were advancing towards them, close to the street sides, their eyes on the ground, dressed in rich colourful attire, but all bare feet. They preceded the Emperor himself whose litter borne by noblemen could be seen in the distance, advancing at a solemn pace under a pallium of green feather cloth, with a rhythm, a pomp and a wealth of gold and jewelry which was bound to call forth in the Spaniards memories of the religious processions of their fatherland. Moteçuçuma was very richly dressed, as was his wont, and he had on his feet *cotaras* with soles of gold. As the litter arrived close to where Cortés waited, Moteçuçuma descended on the rich cotton wraps laid on the ground for him and advanced towards his guest. Some of his courtiers came first, carefully sweeping the ground; then other courtiers, laying cotton wraps to protect his feet from touching the earth; then three heralds with gold sticks held high, a symbol of his authority; finally, grave and solemn, the Emperor walked between his two kinsmen Cacama, King of Tetzcuco, on his right, and Cuitlahuac, ruler of Iztapalapa, on the left, and followed by the lords of Tlacopan and Coyoacan, all richly dressed, but barefooted.

Cortés alighted from his horse and walked smiling towards the great Emperor. Then, at last, they looked into each other's eyes.

*   *   *

They were the two spearheads of the two mutually strange civilisations, confronting each other for the first time after centuries of separate history; behind each of those two men, there stretched a world of human spirit separated from the other far more deeply than by the accident of language, living, thinking, hoping, weaving itself into time and space by the threads of individual lives and deaths in patterns as different from the patterns of the other as if each had been incarnated on a different planet of the vast sky which covered them both. They had nothing in common but the flesh—for, even though different enough in shape and colour to keep each wondering at the other's looks, the animal bodies of their two races were born of the same stock and sought each other in the embraces of fertile love, as do all bodies within the same species. But once the glances of either had ceased wandering over the solid walls of the other man's body and sought to enter the inner chambers of the other man's being through the ethereal gates of his eyes, everything was new, strange, inscrutable and inexplicable; in the vast ocean of the white man's eyes, all the thoughts of the Mexican sank like worm-eaten canoes; in the lofty and secluded lakes of the Aztec Emperor's eyes, the Cross-hallowed caravels of the Spaniard were paralysed and sank as if smitten by an evil spell.

Spells, incantations, sortileges and witchcraft shone in the black flashes of Moteçuçuma's eyes. His people were still in that period of collective evolution in which the sense of good and evil is not yet born in man, so that the only social restraints on his individual caprice are those that flow from divination, sacrifice or taboo. Over and above their day-to-day life, the Mexicans felt another life governed by the gods, spirits hardly distinguishable from past leaders either of their own or of other tribes from whom they had borrowed them; these gods were traditionally believed to require certain sacrifices in exchange for which certain benefits were expected from them: human hearts offered to Uitzilopochtli ensured victory in arms (though in actual fact it was the other way round), children sacrificed to Tlaloc, the god of rain, ensured rain at the right time, and the more the children cried on the way to sacrifice the more rain was sure to fall. In a world without right or wrong, there could be no notion of last Judgment. Human beings went to Hell, "a place without light or windows," to Paradise, an evergreen place in which

summer is perpetual, or to Heaven, the dwelling of the Sun, in which
the dead turn into bright-coloured birds, according not to their
deserts, but to the cause of their death; those who died of usual
diseases or of old age went to Hell; those killed by lightning or
drowned or dying of contagious diseases, such as leprosy, went to
Paradise; those who fell in battle or were sacrificed by the enemy
to the gods, went to Heaven. Men born under an evil sign were
unlucky; men born under a good sign were lucky; space was crowded
with ghosts, and time woven with premonitions. At night, there
were phantasms without feet or head which made all but the boldest
soldiers run away; the dwarfish woman known as Cuitlapanton came
at dusk to announce the impending death of those who saw her;
ghosts in the form of a dead man's skull stuck to one's leg and went
noisily knocking against the stones of the road as one walked on,
ran on, in the vain hope of detaching one's trembling body from the
evil things. Ill omens kept one awake, and they were numerous:
a wild beast's roar, an old woman's cry, an owl's hoot, heard at night;
a rabbit entering the house (which with us is bad omen for the
rabbit) or the sight of a special kind of mouse known as *Tetzauhoui-
michtin.* (6)

The *Tonalpouhque,* or sorcerers, and the priests were the natural
leaders of such a society. They were not in a position to interpret a
consistent human law—whether based on revelation or on reason—
and therefore could not be expected to lead their people in a conscious
way along a line of progress marked out and lit up by such a law.
And yet, there were two aspects of reality which, sooner or later,
would have led the Mexicans, (7) as they had led the whites who
were then conquering them, out of the premoral era into the era of
the moral law: one was the marvellous order of the stars; the other,
the order immanent in all human societies which gradually compels
men to bow to reason.

The knowledge of astronomy revealed by a detailed study of the
Mexican calendar is astonishing. One of the best authorities cal-
culates at 0.01136 of a day, i.e. just over one hundredth of a day,
the error at the end of the Mexican sacred cycle of two hundred and
sixty years. (8) Whether they owed this science to other races or
whether their priests had evolved it, the fact remains that so accurate
a hold over the reality of the stars allows the retrospective prophecy

I

that the Mexicans would have risen above the premoral civilisation in which they were found by Cortés. This forecast is confirmed by their institutions. True, these institutions were almost exclusively shaped by a warlike conception of life; but, whether we find their practice to our taste or not, the Mexicans had understood the principle that all aristocracy must be based on service to the community, and their education of the young and their standards of social prestige were grounded on a sound view of the importance of character.

Yet this warlike—nay, sanguinary and fearless—race, living in everyday companionship with blood and death, was then helplessly giving up its historical evolution into the hands of a handful of white strangers. How often have we been told that this victory of Cortés was due to the superiority of his weapons, to his gunpowder and his horse. We know now that this explanation will not do. We know that Morón's horse had been decapitated at one stroke of the two-handed obsidian-edged wooden sword of a Mexican warrior, and surely the Mexicans would not remain for ever in dread of mere noise. The reason why the Mexicans gave in was that their faith gave way before a firmer faith.

That man standing before Moteçuçuma with courteous, bowing gesture and smiling eyes was the living incarnation of the Christian faith. He also came from a nation which in the remote past had known human sacrifices, as Torquemada, with Christian humility, takes great care to point out. (9) But between that dreadful past and the glorious present in which he lived—which, in fact, he was creating—there had died in Palestine the Son of Man in whose light he walked with steady, firm steps. That sacrifice had washed away the sins of the world and abolished all other sacrifices; it had made of man a universal spirit and of the earth a human home; it had blotted out colour barriers and opened to all men the gates of equality through conversion to the faith. This Faith had come to him through Rome, the sacred, universal, supranational city, twice the metropolis of the world, as the seat of the Holy Father now, but in older days as the seat of the Roman Emperor whose spiritual descendant was Charles V, his august master. The language of Rome had been throughout the centuries the lifeblood not only of the Faith of Christ, which made all men one in their hearts, but of the Reason of Socrates, which made all men one in their brain. In Salamanca he had received the direct impact of this age-long tradition of reason, transmitted through the scholastic centuries, and turned into orthodox doctrine by the Fathers of the Church and by the great monks and bishops of Europe: Isidore of Seville, Roger Bacon, St. Thomas Aquinas. Cortés was a typical European, a man of faith in matters "above the roof," as the Spanish saying goes, a man of reason in matters of this world; in action, cold, objective, impartial, detached; in thought, curious, anxious to learn and register everything about man, animal, plant, sea, rivers, mountains, roads, with a mind ever open to true knowledge; in passion, disciplined, controlled, generous and harnessed to his higher purpose. Behind him, his troops were the vanguard of Europe's great quest for knowledge of man and planet, the forerunners in action of the great adventure of the Renaissance; in fact, true "apostles" of that Renaissance *in partibus infidelium*.

In their brave and eager souls, there lived all the forces which were shaping Europe: their ambition and thirst for gold and land was the first direct manifestation of that colonial capitalism which was to dominate three or four centuries of European history and to act as the most potent factor in the spread of Western civilisation. Their simple faith, in which there still lingered many a superstitious belief from their own premoral, anthropomorphic era, was to act as a useful bridge between the sacrificial faith of the natives and the purely spiritual Christianity whose highest light was soon to shine in their own countryman St. John of the Cross. Their enterprise and forward spirit was the very spirit of the European Renaissance turned to action, the urge to go and see, to discover, to settle, to populate, that is, to expand the life of newborn Europe into all the confines of the Earth.

Thus on that fateful Tuesday November 8th, 1519, third day Quecholli, 8th Ehecatl of the year 1-Reeds of the eighth sheaf, the two men stood before each other, looking into each other's eyes. But the eyes of the Mexican were closed lakes, soon to dry up under the sun of another knowledge; while in the eyes of Cortés there lived the endless sea.

*   *   *

The Spaniard stepped forward and opened his arms; it was the gesture which that tense moment dictated to his body—at that moment but the incarnation of a world-spirit which, facing another world-spirit, reacted in harmony with its own inner sense. The Christian world opened its arms to the unknown, in a gesture both of fraternity and of absorption. But the two princes stretched their hands forward, and checked the Christian gesture. The Emperor was too sacred to be touched; the Mexican world was too rigid and vigorous to be so readily absorbed. And yet, this world so stiff and so distant was ready for courtesy and even for reverence towards the mysterious strangers; the two princes first, the Emperor himself afterwards, touched the ground and kissed their hand. "Oh, Lord of ours," said the Emperor, "be welcome: you have arrived in your land, among your people, and in your house Mexico: you have come to sit on your throne and on your chair, all that I have owned in your name for a number of days, other Lords, now dead, had it all before me. All of us have carried on our shoulders your republic and your vassals. The dead can no longer see or know what is now happening. Would to God for whom we live that one of them were alive and these things which come to pass in my presence came to pass in his: they are gone. Lord of ours, I am neither asleep nor adream: with my own eyes do I see your face and your person; I had been expecting this for days; for days had my heart being watching the parts whence you have come; you have come from the clouds and mists, places hidden to all. This is, indeed, what had been told us by the bygone Kings: that you would return to rule these lands, and that you would sit on your throne and chair. Now I see what they had said to us was true. Be welcome: You must have suffered many hardships in your long journey; rest now: here are your house and your palaces; take them and rest in them with all your captains and companions."

Cortés said to Doña Marina: "Tell Motezuzoma to be of good cheer and fear nothing, for I love him well and so do all these who come with me; he will be harmed by no one; we have been very happy to see him and to know him, which we have wished to do for many a day and our wish has been fulfilled. We have come to his house, Mexico; we shall see him and speak to him at leisure." (10) Cortés was wearing a necklace of "margarets," glass beads with

coloured patterns, threaded with gold and perfumed with musk; he
took it off and put it round the Emperor's neck. All the prominent
men who had come with Moteçuçuma passed then before Cortés and
performed the ceremony of kissing the earth; and this done, the
Emperor walked away towards his city with Cacama his nephew,
while, on his instructions, Cuitlahuac his brother was left behind to
accompany Cortés. They walked thus for a while, the Emperor and
his nephew in front, Cortés a short distance behind them, hand in
hand with Cuitlahuac, "who did not allow anyone, whether Castillian
or Indian, to approach him and this was the highest honour which
Moteçuçuma could have bestowed on Cortés"; (11) and then, a
messenger arrived and put a packet in the Emperor's hand. Moteçuçuma came back to Cortés and threw over his neck "two necklaces
made of red shells which they hold in much estimation and from
each necklace there hung eight golden shrimps of much perfection,
several inches long." (12) These necklaces were the insignia of
Quetzalcoatl. Evidently Moteçuçuma had ratified his premonition
as to the identity between Quetzalcoatl and Cortés on seeing his
guest, and the present confirmed the address with which he had
received Cortés-Quetzalcoatl.

Thus, by quiet though dramatic steps, both men were building
up in the crowd of onlookers the prestige and moral power of the
white captain. The meeting, the courtesies, the exchange of necklaces, and in particular the symbolical fact, that Moteçuçuma, who
came to meet Cortés carried in his sumptuous litter, went back with
him on foot, must have made a deep impression on a people less
used to reasoning than to drinking in life through their senses. No
one was bold enough to look on while the Emperor was passing (an
admirable habit for which all rulers should envy Moteçuçuma);
but once he had passed, thousands rushed to street and terrace to
wonder at the strangers. "Gods they must be," said the young, "for
they come from where the sun rises." And the old shook their
pessimistic heads and sighed: "These must be the men who were
to come and hold sway over our persons and lands, for, though so
few, they are so strong that they have beaten so many." (13) This
admiration of the crowd would be sure to rise to its highest pitch on
seeing Moteçuçuma lead the white strangers to the most revered,
spacious and luxurious building in the city, which had been set aside

as their abode: the palace or "houses" of his own father, Emperor Axayacatl, which was then a temple, a convent of priestesses and the Imperial Treasurer House. This building or set of buildings was so spacious that the Spaniards with their two thousand native auxiliaries and the host of women whom they brought in their service, were all well provided for. There were some rooms big enough to accommodate one hundred and fifty Spaniards; all were scrupulously clean, polished, carpeted and adorned with facings of cotton or feather cloth of many colours. The Spaniards were given mat-beds in the Mexican national fashion, for, as Bernal Díaz says in his quaint, elliptic style, "they give no beds, however great a lord you may be, because they do not use them." There were braziers burning in every room, which in November, in high Mexico, is not unpleasant, and we may take the fact that incense was burnt in them as a proof of the delicacy of the Mexican nostrils receiving the impact of a crowd of much travelled Spanish soldiery. Swarms of servants everywhere "were an eloquent proof of the greatness of that prince." (14)

Moteçuçuma took Cortés by the hand and led him to the central hall, facing the large courtyard through which they had entered the palace. There, Moteçuçuma made his guest sit on a rich seat wrought in gold and precious stones, which Cortés says had been built for the Emperor himself, and said: "You are in your house. Eat, rest and enjoy yourself: I shall return presently." Cortés bowed low, and the Emperor, with all his suite, left the palace. (15)

But Cortés was not the man to eat and rest and enjoy himself before he had attended to his business. He set out at once to reconnoitre the dwelling which had been assigned to him and to his troops. He must have been satisfied, for the palace, with its buildings and surrounding walls, afforded a good base for defence, provided it were well stocked with food. He allocated the several halls and buildings to his captaincies, and emplaced his artillery in a commanding position; then, having given strict orders for every man to be on his guard and ready to serve, he allowed his men to enjoy the "sumptuous dinner" which had been prepared for them by their Mexican hosts. "And this," says Bernal Díaz, "was our happy and bold entry into the great city of Tenustitlan; let us thank our Lord Jesus Christ for all, and though I may have not expressed

other things which I should have said, let your Signiories forgive
me for not knowing how to say it better for the time being." (16)

* * *

The Spaniards were enjoying a well-earned rest after their
"sumptuous" meal when there was a general stir, and the Emperor
was again announced. Cortés and his captains went out to meet him.
Moteçuçuma came in great state, followed by a brilliant suite. Seats
were brought, made of gold, "very rich and wrought in many ways,"
and when both the captain and the Emperor had sat down, Moteçuçuma made "a very good speech." He declared himself pleased
to have in his house and kingdom gentlemen as brave as Cortés and
his companions, and told his visitor how he had heard about the
two earlier expeditions, which had greatly excited his curiosity; the
pictures which had been sent him of the battles won by Cortés on
his way had confirmed him in his belief that the white strangers
were the men whose return from the parts where the sun rises had
been so often foretold in their prophecies. Cortés assured the
Emperor that he and his friends did come from the parts where the
sun rises, which he could do without sinning, and added that he had
been sent by Emperor Charles V to see him and to beg him to
become a Christian, "with other very good things which he would
hear anon." The Mexican Emperor then had presents brought up:
rich jewels for Cortés, gold presents for the captains and numerous
loads of cotton clothes for all. Nor was the present given without
that joy which is the hallmark of the true generous giver; "in everything," says Bernal Díaz, "he showed himself a great lord." (17)

Moteçuçuma then asked Cortés whether all the Spaniards present
were brothers and vassals of the same Emperor; and he answered
that they were all brothers in love and friendship, and important
persons and servants of the King. The question was by no means
idle. It revealed at this early stage that a certain doubt was already
arising in Moteçuçuma's mind as to the unity of that force which
had come to overpower him; this doubt was to emerge again and
again to the surface of his mind. For the moment, however, he
accepted Cortés' somewhat formal and general answer, and after
giving his men orders to keep the Spaniards well supplied with food

and service, he left the palace, accompanied by all the Spaniards to the street gates. (18)

Next day, November 9th, 1519, having first sent word of his intention, Cortés repaid the Emperor's visit. He was most careful in the choice of his companions: four captains—Pedro de Alvarado, Juan Velázquez de León, Diego de Ordás and his youthful commander Gonzalo de Sandoval—but also five soldiers, for his army was a democratic institution, and this was the culminating moment of the conquest. Moteçuçuma came out to receive them halfway through the spacious hall. He lived in a palace more modern than that which he had set aside for Cortés: twenty doors gave access to it from the four streets which bounded its precincts; three large courtyards gave it air and light; a beautiful ornamental fountain centralised its water service; there were in it many large halls, one hundred rooms twenty-five to thirty feet square, one hundred baths. The wood framework was most elaborate yet without nails at all, which astounded the Spaniards; the walls were made of ordinary stone or of marble, jasper, porphyry, "a black stone with red veins like blood," white stone and alabaster; the ceilings were of cedar, cypress, palm, pine and other woods, skilfully carved into animal or other shapes; the rooms painted and covered with carpets, their walls faced with rich cotton, rabbit-hair or feather cloth. The Spaniards marvelled at these splendours and were struck by the contrast of all these lovely and luxurious standards with the poverty and discomfort of the beds, just thin coverlets of cotton over flat matting, spread on the bare boards. (19)

The Emperor was accompanied by some of his nephews, the only persons allowed into his inner apartments. He took Cortés' hand and made him sit on his right side, then made the other Spaniards sit down also. This time, Cortés thought necessary to enlarge upon his favourite theme: "how we were Christians and worshipped one only God known as Jesus Christ, who suffered death and passion to save us [. . .] and resuscitated on the third day and is in heaven, and it was He who made the sky and the earth and the sea and the sands, and created everything which is in the world and gives us the waters and the dews and nothing ever happens in the world without His holy will [. . .] and those they hold as gods are not so, but only devils, which are very bad things and if their looks are bad their deeds are worse; and that they could find out how little value there was in their gods considering that wherever we had raised our Crosses they dared not appear."

The words are in the simple, quaint, but vivid and telling style of the soldier; yet how clearly we can see through them the earnest, persistent effort of the Christian Captain! Bernal Díaz registers that at this point Cortés entreated the Emperor to be particularly attentive: he explained ("very well put," says the soldier) "the creation of the world and how we are all brothers, children of one father and one mother, named Adam and Eve; and that as such a brother, our great Emperor, grieving for the loss of so many souls, for many were those whom their idols took away to Hell where they burn in living flames, sent us to remedy this of which he had heard [this lie in the midst of his homily!] and he added that in the course of time, our lord the King would send men who amongst us live most saintly lives, better men than we are (this humility on the day of his triumph!) to explain it all to him."

At this point, Cortés, turning to his companions, said: "With these remarks we have done our duty, for they are only the first touches." Thus he revealed the earnestness of his preoccupation, always to consider it his first obligation to put forward the interests of his faith. Moteçuçuma answered: "Malintzin, I know your arguments and talks about the three gods and the Cross, from my servants and other peoples to whom you have explained them. As for us, we worship our gods and hold them to be good, as no doubt yours are also, so you need not trouble to raise this matter again." This was pretty final. Neither the Mexican Emperor nor the Spanish Captain was in a position to realise that they were discussing from two different stages of man's development, fencing so to speak on two different storeys of the fencing club. For Cortés, God was the self-revealed light which reveals all else, the one and only Creator, alpha and omega of things, surrounded by the beautiful mysteries of the Trinity, the Incarnation and the Virgin Birth as the sun loves to be surrounded with clouds to shine not the less but the more and the more beautifully. For Moteçuçuma, the gods were spirits of the past and of nature, not unlike what they were to the Greeks and Romans, men left in a state of mid-air life, invisible but omnipresent though hovering only over the people whose dreams they were. The ever-

I*

longing religion of the Christian, open to all, was as incomprehensible to the closed-in religion of the Aztec as the infinite sea would have been to the two Mexican lofty but landlocked lakes.

Cortés had the good sense to leave the matter there for the present. The Emperor went on speaking in his dignified way, with few and noble gestures yet with a good-humoured, almost merry countenance; this was probably the moment when Bernal Díaz' mental camera was snapshooting him for us: "Of good stature and well proportioned, and lean, of little flesh, and the colour not very dark, but the very colour and shade of an Indian, and he wore his hair not very long, just enough to cover his ears, and dark, not thick, the beard, well placed and sparse, and the face somewhat long, and gay, and the eyes of a good appearance and in his person he showed, in his glance, sometimes love, and when necessary, gravity." He spoke on, and Doña Marina translated it all. He went back to the other two captains, Grijalva and Hernández de Córdoba. They also had said they were the servants of that great King. The Emperor wanted to know if they were all one people. Cortés again assured Moteçuçuma that they were all brothers and servants of the same great King and that the first two captains had come to pave the way for him—which was true in fact, though not in intention. Here, Moteçuçuma was good enough to explain why he had opposed the advance of the Spaniards; "It had been very much against his will, but his vassals were frightened because they had been told that we thrust thunderbolts and lightning, and with our horses we killed many Indians, and that we were ferocious gods, and all kinds of childish notions, while now he saw we were of flesh and bones and of much reason, and he knows we are brave." His anxiety to put himself right on this score was but natural; yet his explanation did not tally with the magic efforts he had made to arrest the progress of Cortés. He laughed outright: "Malintzin," he said, "I know the Tlaxcatecs, your dear friends, have told you that I am a kind of god or *teotl* and that all things in my houses, the walls, the carpets, were made of gold and silver and precious stones. I am sure that you know too much ever to have believed it. My houses, as you see, are made of stone and plaster and wood"; he then raised his arms, baring his lithe, copper-coloured body: "my body, see, is made of flesh and bones as yours and as everybody's and I must die and I can be touched." With his hands, he seized his own arms and body: "See how they have lied to you. True, I have some wealth, gold which has been left me by my ancestors, but not the follies and lies they have told you, which you must not believe any more than I do your thunder and lightning." Cortés laughed also: "Enemies," he said, "will always tell lies about those they dislike; as for me, I do not expect ever to meet a more magnificent lord anywhere; not in vain are you so well known to our Emperor."

Presents of gold and cotton garments were then brought and distributed, and as it was past midday, Cortés said: "The lord Moteçuçuma has taken the habit of overloading us with favours. It is time for him to be left to eat in peace." The Emperor answered that Cortés' visit was the true favour, and on this the Spaniards left. "We went away," says Bernal Díaz, "conversing over his good manners and breeding, and how we were to show every deference to him, and to take off our caps wherever we passed him." (20)

* * *

On Cortés' strict instructions, the Spaniards had kept within the four walls of their quarters. This was by no means a hardship for them since, within those four walls, there were spacious gardens which they could enjoy. With his usual caution, he wished, no doubt, to avoid incidents of any kind and meanwhile to take the air of the city and feel his way in the new world he had discovered and easily—all too easily!—conquered. After four days of this self-denying confinement, he thought, however, that some sign of life became necessary, and he sent his "tongues" to Moteçuçuma: Doña Marina, Aguilar and a page, by name Ortega (known to the soldiers by the friendly diminutive of Orteguilla), who was assiduously learning the *nauatl* language. The three "tongues" were to convey to Moteçuçuma his intention to visit the Great Teocalli of the capital. The Emperor can hardly have been pleased at this; we know how ardently devout he was towards his gods and how ruthlessly he was wont to punish the slightest offence against their worship; yet he turned a good face to the bad weather, as his guests would have said, and made arrangements for the Spaniards to be admitted and accompanied on their visit by some of his courtiers and priests, while he himself, fearing perhaps some violence or insult to Uitzilopochtli, had himself conveyed in state to the temple, preceded by his three gold-sticks-in-waiting.

In no lesser state, and with every measure of military preparedness, the Spanish Captain left his headquarters on horseback, followed by all his cavalry and most of his infantry, in good order. They turned northwards, towards Tepeyac (the present Guadalupe), along one of the main avenues, till, not far from the northern edge of the city, their guides made them turn slightly west; suddenly their astonished eyes beheld the *Tianguiz* (*Tianquiztli*) or market, a buzzing hive, swarming with human bees. So much life and so much order was more than they had expected; every trade and commodity had its separate alley or street, just as in Bernal Díaz' own town, Medina del Campo, the home of the greatest fairs in Spain. Gold and silver wares, feather-cloth and cotton-cloth, slaves "brought to be sold in that big square, as the Portuguese bring their Guinea blacks, and they brought them tied to long poles by means of neckbands so that they should not run away, and others loose"; cocoa; ropes; sweet-roots to eat; skins of tigers, lions, otters, jackals, deer and other animals; badgers and wild cats, tanned or untanned, beans, sage, and other vegetables; hens, turkeys, rabbits, hares, venison, geese, small dogs, fruit, cooked food of all kinds, pottery from big jars to small pitchers, honey and honeycakes and other sweets such as nut pasties, wood, planks, wedges, beams, blocks and benches, firewood—"what shall I say," adds Bernal Díaz in admiration; "but, speaking with due respect, they sold canoes full of human excrements to make salt or to tan leather, for without it, they said it was not good"; paper, small tubes full of liquidamber, of tobacco, or other of yellow ointments; cochineal; herbs of all kinds; salt; fish; obsidian knives; hatchets made of brass, copper, tin—not iron which was a metal unknown to Anáhuac—all this world was moving and living in perfect order, watched over by policemen and ruled by three permanent market judges, within a square of stone arcades not unlike the Plaza Mayor of the towns of their native Spain.

The Spaniards left the Tianquiztli and passed on to the contiguous square of the Teocalli. As they were almost on the border between the two, they noticed the gold-merchants who brought gold as it came from the mines to sell it in the market; the samples shown inside goose quills which allowed buyers to judge the value of the metal. They were now in the vast Cu-yard, "bigger, I think, than the big square in Salamanca," paved with large white stones, very smooth, or else whitewashed and polished and so clean that there was not one straw nor speck of dust to be seen. This, the great Teocalli of Tlatelolco (the northern district), was at least as big as that of Tenochtitlan, which rose in the centre of the town, close to the Spanish quarters. It was built on the same pattern, in the form of a truncated pyramid, with a base 350 feet square and a top of about 150 feet square. Two chapels of unequal height crowned this pyramid, and 124 steep steps led to these two chapels, consecrated one to Uitzilopochtli the other to Tetzcatlipoca.

As the Spaniards were seen below from the chapels, where Moteçuçuma was worshipping with his priests, six priests and two courtiers hurried down the interminable steps; the thoughtful Emperor was sending them to hold his guest by the arms up the one hundred and fourteen steps, as was done in his own case. Cortés refused the honour and the help, and, preceded by the Mexicans and followed by his own men, climbed the stairs with a brisk step —an exhausting exercise, for they were extremely steep. The Spaniards saw the *cuauhxicallis* or sacrificial stones, still fresh with newly shed blood; the Emperor came out of one of the chapels and with great courtesy said: "Malintzin, I am sure you must be tired after having climbed all the way to our temples"; whereupon, Cortés in a quiet outburst of calculated bragging: "Neither I," he said, "nor these my friends ever get tired by any exertion."

The Emperor took his hand and showed him the town at their feet. It was a glorious sight: a living map, the white and yellow chessboard over the blue and muddy canals; the bridges; the three causeways to the north, that of Tepeyac to the south, that of Iztapalapa, by which they had arrived in the town; to the west that of Tacuba, which was to be their tragic, bloody way of escape into safety for some, into death for most of them; the coming and going of the canoes; the thousands of houses with their crenelated terraces; the cues and fortresses, so easy to defend, so formidable as bases for attack; the seething, strange crowd, so big that "the mere rumour and buzz of their voices and words could be heard more than a league away"; the lakes, so pleasant in peace, so dangerous in war . . . The Captain looked on, pensively. We know him too well by now to have any doubts as to what he was thinking: he was taking in the incredible dangers of his situation, the trap in which his own faith in his destiny and in the protection of the Lord had enclosed him and his men. That is what was in his mind; but this is what he said: "What do you think, gentlemen, of this great favour which God has granted us? After having given us so many victories over so many dangers, He has brought us to this place, from which we can see so many big cities. Truly, my heart tells me that from here many kingdoms and dominions will be conquered, for here is the capital wherein the devil has his main seat; and once this city has been subdued and mastered, the rest will be easy to conquer." (21)

PART IV

CORTÉS THROWS AWAY HIS CONQUEST

CHAPTER SEVENTEEN

The Seizure of Moteçuçuma

ORTÉS turned to Father Olmedo and said: "Methinks, Father, that it might be a good thing if we now sounded Montezuma about building a church here." His line of thought was clear and steady: conquer to convert, convert to conquer. The wise friar turned the proposal down as premature. Checked in this direction, Cortés' urge for action came out in an unexpected request; he asked Moteçuçuma to let them have a look at the gods; the Emperor, after consultation with his priests, agreed, and the Spaniards were admitted into Uitzilopochtli's chapel. Their impressions have been vividly recorded by Bernal Díaz: "On each altar there were two statues, as of giants, and very fat, and the first, on the right side, they say, was that of Witchywolves, their god of war, and his face and front were very wide, and his eyes out of shape and horrible, and so many rich stones and gold and pearls and pearl seed stuck to his body with sticking paste that all his body and head were covered with it; and girded to his body some kind of big snakes, made of gold and rich stones; and in one hand a bow, and arrows in the other. And another small idol close to him, who, they said, was his page, was holding a short spear for him, and a round buckler, very rich of gold and stones; and, round his neck, the said Witchywolves was wearing some Indian faces and some hearts of Indians, some of gold, some of silver, with many blue stones; and there were many braziers with their incense, which is copal, and with the hearts of three Indians which they had sacrificed that day and

253

were burning [. . .] and the walls of that chapel were so steeped black with crusts of blood, and the floor also, that it stank very badly."

The Spaniards were then shown Tetzcatlipoca and Bernal Díaz records his visit in no less forcible terms: "The other big image, as tall as Witchywolves, had a face like a bear, and eyes that shone, made of their mirrors, which they call *tezcat,* and the body stuck all over with rich stones just like that of Witchywolves, for, they said, the two were brothers and this Tezcatepuca was the god of hell and he was in charge of the souls of the Mexicans; and close to his body he had some figures like small devils with tails like serpents; and on the walls so much blood and the floor soaked in it that in the slaughterhouses of Castille the stench was not worse."

There was a third god in the highest part of the Cu, richly carved and gilt; this was the god of seeds and fruits; his image, half man, half lizard, was kneaded with all the seeds of the land and, of course, with human blood; and there was a huge drum which "when played upon, the sound was so dismal that it was a truly hellish instrument, and could be heard two leagues away." The sight of yet more traces of fresh sacrifices, the butchery, the stench, made the soldiers desirous to leave the unholy place. "Sir," said Cortés, half laughing, "I cannot understand how so great a lord and wise a man as you are has not yet thought it out that these idols are not gods, but very bad things known as devils, and so that you may come to know them as such, and all your priests see it clearly, grant me as a favour that we set up a Cross on top of this tower, and we shall set aside one part of these chapels, where Witchywolves and Tezcatepuca now are, for an image of Our Lady, and you shall see the fear these idols [. . .] will then feel." Moteçuçuma's priests did not hide their anger. Somewhat upset, he said: "Malintzin, had I known that you would utter such an insult, I would not have allowed you to see my gods." Cortés, with a good-humoured face, retorted, "It is time we should all be going"; but Moteçuçuma explained that he had to remain and to atone for the visit which he had allowed and for the insult his gods had had to endure. "If that be so," said Cortés, "forgive me, sir." And he led his men down the one hundred and fourteen steps. "Some of our soldiers, who were ill with the boobies or other humours complained of pains in their thighs." (1)

*   *   *

The scene must have given Cortés much food for thought. It had put the whole complex, glorious yet dangerous situation before his eyes. The Emperor was the ruler of a powerful and rich land: the Spaniards were in admiration at the lavish scale and standards of his establishment; the populous harem of noble ladies; the ante-rooms thronged with prominent men; the humble ways of those who came to visit him; the countless dishes for his table, all set on braziers, for him to choose and suit his fancy; the four beautiful girls who served at table; the fifty jugs of frothy cocoa brought to him which he, after tasting it, gave over to his hunchback jesters; the thousands of meals served daily for his women, friends and retainers; his armoury, full of the most valuable and artistic weapons; his aviaries, swarming with the most varied, fascinating, coloured birds, aquatic and otherwise, each fed on fish, meat or grain as fitted its tastes; his wild beasts, housed and fed in similar fashion, some of which were given to eat those parts of the body of sacrificed victims not acceptable to prince or priest; his goldsmiths, silver-smiths and jewellers; featherworkers; painters and woodcarvers; weavers and garment-makers; dancers, jugglers of all kinds; car-penters, masons; his gardens and orchards, tended by an army of expert gardeners, with their enchanting nooks and corners wherein to trap fleeting, happy moments of life—all these sights gradually revealing themselves to the somewhat austere Spaniards, impressed them not merely as signs of wealth but as signs of power. "And there was so much to see in these gardens as in everything else," says Bernal Díaz, "that we could never feel surfeited to behold his great power." (2)

With his keen mind, Cortés would naturally dwell on the person who, for the time being, incarnated this power. Moteçuçuma was no longer in any doubt about the mortal, human nature of the Spaniards; he remained, however, convinced that they were the men whose coming had been foretold in the cycle of prophecies connected with Quetzalcoatl. This name, moreover, evoked one of those figures ever hovering in an ill-defined zone bordering on history, legend and heavenly regions; he was a god for priests and people, a legendary hero for the wise, a man possibly for the studious who could read and interpret the old pictorial records. The Spaniards were at first admitted into this intermediate zone, from which they had emerged into plain history, owing mostly to their human, all too human ways. Cortés therefore, particularly since his last interview, felt that though he could no longer play the god, he was still able to benefit from the prophecy which made of Charles V the real lord of Anáhuac, coming at last into his own.

His simple and intense faith enabled him to give a rational and universal meaning to this prophecy, for he was sure to see in it a deliberate design of God to ease the path of his servant in that heathen land. This thought was bound to enhance his religious zeal, that most exalted of his passions, the only one which could at times drive him astray from the path of his steady judgment. It so happened that Moteçuçuma's chief passion was also his faith, and there is a curious parallel in the patterns of the Conqueror and the Conquered, for in Moteçuçuma also we find his religious zeal as an odd feature which upsets the logic and harmony of his attitude. It is indeed strange that he, who was but a few days later to give a dramatic proof of his utter surrender to Cortés as the man foretold by Quetzalcoatl, should have remained obstinately faithful to the gods whom the man foretold by Quetzalcoatl bade him forsake. This contradiction, dictated by religious faith, was even more illogical in him than in Cortés; for the Spanish captain, carried by his faith from victory to victory, could excusably, in moments of impatience or exaltation, spread the sails of his soul to the wind of that faith; while Moteçuçuma had repeatedly tasted the bitterness of seeing his gods defeated and their temples destroyed by the very man whom one of his gods had announced.

These, however, are thoughts for our time. On that November morning of the year 1519, Cortés could not in the least have dreamt of a parallel between the two faiths. All he would retain of the brilliant and barbarous scene on top of the teocalli would be a strong feeling of physical loathing, coming to strengthen his steady purpose to abolish the worship of the Mexican devils and to set up instead that of the Christian Trinity and of the Mother and Son. This spiritual ambition was incarnated in the material ambition of

acquiring dominion over the land which enabled this mighty
Emperor to live in so gorgeous a state. His boldness had been
justified. He was the first Conquistador to conquer anything worth
conquering.

But he had not conquered it yet. The stubborn resistance of
Moteçuçuma to his religious suggestions was a disquieting sign: it
meant that the Emperor's assurances that Mexico was in truth
Cortés' own kingdom, country and "throne" were either insincere
or hedged round with dangerous limitations. Cortés was bound to
remember the repeated warnings he had received from Tlaxcala and
Cempoal as to the treacherous character of the Mexicans; and how
his experience at Cholula had led him to put implicit trust in the
advice of his Tlaxcala and Cempoal friends. He was told by his
soldiers that there were disquieting signs, not unlike those which had
heralded the Cholulan conspiracy; the stewards of Moteçuçuma in
charge of the Spanish supplies were noticed to grow insolent and to
reduce the rations; two Tlaxcatecs told Aguilar the interpreter that
the attitude of the Mexicans did not seem reassuring; Cortés knew
his Spaniards too well to feel very confident about their own good
behaviour in such a tempting city, and had every reason to fear the
ill consequences of an incident. In his mind, moreover, steeped in
the monarchical ideas of his time and continent—for in this he was
not merely a Spaniard but a European—there lived the conviction
that, once the Monarch had been secured, the country was already
subjugated, for what was a country but a body politic of which the
monarch was the head? All these meditations led him to a bold and
most spectacular decision: he would make Moteçuçuma his prisoner. (3)

*   *   *

Let us pause a moment to behold this act. It is, we find, true to
Cortés' unmistakable style: when in danger, to run the highest risk
and thus avoid it and all the smaller ones as well; when the weaker,
to strike at the adversary's head. It was the style of the "burning"
of the ships. It will be the style of his victory over Narváez. Nor is
it merely so in substance, for in form also he remains faithful to himself. Having made up his mind to this bold course, he manages to
have it suggested to him by some of his own men. The Spaniards had
built a church within the precincts of their headquarters. Thither,
the day after the visit to the teocalli, four captains, Juan Velázquez

de Léon, de Ordás, Gonzalo de Sandoval and Pedro de Alvarado, with twelve soldiers of the inner circle of his friends, took Cortés in order to confide to him their fears about the situation. It is easy to see through the honest narrative of Bernal Díaz, who was one of the soldiers present, that the whole scene had been carefully prepared by Cortés, for he heard from his soldiers arguments which were then in his mind, together with the conclusion at which he had arrived. "Don't believe, gentlemen," answered Cortés, "that I am asleep. But where is our strength for so much daring?" Whereupon the captains, who were in his confidence, revealed his own plan: "With good words, to bring him from his dwelling to our quarters, and to tell him he must be a prisoner and if he were to become agitated or to shout, he would pay with his person." (4)

Cortés had thought it all out, including the pretext which would enable him to broach so unheard-of a subject to the Emperor. More than one of his historians has emitted solemn moral sermons on this pretext: "to deceive his own conscience," says one; "the most bare-faced action seeks to veil itself under some show of decency," says another. (5) But Cortés was not in need of a *moral* justification; he merely sought a diplomatic springboard, a psychological basis for his demand. All this ink spent in defending and in attacking him on this occasion has been wasted; as a matter of fact, he has left the clearest and most sincere account of it all in his letter to the Emperor: "I thought that in the interest of the royal service and of our security it was advisable that that lord should be in my power, and not wholly free, so that he should not change the purpose and good will which he evinced to serve Your Highness; particularly since we Spaniards are somewhat importunate and unruly, if angry, he might do us much harm, and so much that there would be no memory left of us, such is his great power; and also because, having him under my control, all the other lands subjected to him would come round more quickly to the acknowledgment and allegiance of Your Majesty." It will be noticed that he does not even mention an actual change for the worse in the mood of the Mexicans, found in other accounts, such as that of Bernal Díaz, probably exaggerated by later historians in order to "justify Cortés." His report is concise, clear and frank. It is wholly *political*. (6)

There was no reason why a man in his position, in his day, should entertain any doubts as to his right to seize the body of the Emperor, if he thought it expedient or wise. As for his pretext, it was in his hand: the letters of Juan de Escalante, which he had received in Cholula, pointed to Moteçuçuma as the initiator of Quauhpopoca's treason. Cortés spent the night "thinking of all the forms and manners to observe so that he could be arrested without scandal or disorder"; he remembered this incident. The way was open for one of those operations of diplomatic boldness of which he was past master. It was to be the boldest of his life; and his faithful soldiers, says Bernal Díaz, spent "the whole night praying God that all should happen for the best in His holy service." (7)

Early in the morning, two Tlaxcatecs came to him in secret and brought him news from Veracruz which must have clinched his resolution and even led him to believe in some definite message from Providence; Juan de Escalante had been killed in battle by Moteçuçuma's allies and the whole coast was in revolt against the Spaniards. Cortés put these letters into his pocket and, having given notice of his coming, set out to visit the Emperor.

He took with him five of his captains, and a number of soldiers, including the two men, Bernal Díaz and Tapia, who were later to record it in their writings. They were all armed; he had moreover left orders to the rest of the army to be ready for any emergency. Cortés entered Moteçuçuma's rooms with about thirty Spaniards, leaving some more at the door and in the main courtyard, while special forces were held in readiness at chief street crossings. Moteçuçuma was expecting trouble, for he seemed to have had news, though not all the news, of the Veracruz events, and he received Cortés with less assurance than usual. He was good-humoured and gay. He offered Cortés some jewels and one of his daughters; he offered other noble girls to the captains who had come with Cortés. Then, Cortés came to business. He went about it in his usual, diplomatic and subtle way: he did not mention the second battle, for a defeat is never a good recommendation; but, concentrating on the events of Nauhtla, or Almería, he pointed out that Quauhpopoca excused himself on the ground that he had acted on Moteçuçuma's orders and that while he, Cortés, did not believe such a thing, it was necessary to have the guilty parties brought to Mexico to probe the truth of the matter. Moteçuçuma agreed at once and on the spot sent messengers, to whom he gave a small stone seal he carried tied round his arm, to bring Quauhpopoca and his accomplices over to Mexico. When the messengers had left, Cortés thanked the Emperor and then explained that, in order to give a full account of the death of those Spaniards to the King, it was necessary that Moteçuçuma should move to his residence until the matter had been cleared up. Moteçuçuma was very much upset and, with much gravity, said: "My person is not such as to be in prison; and, even if I were willing, my people would not tolerate it." Cortés then explained that the Emperor would not be a prisoner; he would enjoy a complete liberty, nor would the exercise of his authority and dominion be hindered in any way; he was to choose whichever apartments suited him in the house where Cortés resided, and he might be certain that all the Spaniards would serve him obediently. Arguments and expostulations went to and fro during four hours; but Cortés was as patient as stubborn. Velázquez de León, however, was stubborn but not patient; and in his rough, thick voice, he exclaimed: "What is your Lordship doing there with so many words? Let him come or we will run him through the body." The Emperor asked Doña Marina what the captain was shouting; but the shrewd "tongue" answered: "I advise you to move without noise, for they will honour you as what you are, while if you remain, you will die here and now." "Malintzin," said the Emperor, "I have one son and two daughters." He meant legitimate ones. "Take them as hostages, but spare me this insult." Cortés remained adamant, and finally the Emperor gave in.

He sent his servants to prepare apartments for him in what, after all, was his father's palace, and presently several lords, bare-bodied, their wraps under their arms, and barefoot, raised him on a litter "not very well adorned," and they conveyed him to his new, enforced quarters. They walked in silence, weeping. (8)

* * *

There was some emotion in the city—"it began to stir," says Cortés—but Moteçuçuma calmed it down. Cortés gave strict orders that the Emperor should be treated with the utmost respect; "and in this he gave the best example, for whenever he went in to visit him, he bowed once and many times down to the ground, which seemed greatly to ease his mind." His establishment in his new quarters was just as regal as in the old; his women, his baths, his elaborate meals; his retinue of courtiers, twenty of whom were constantly in attendance; his official audiences, all the sumptuous life of an oriental potentate to which he was used was most faithfully respected, so that "he became reconciled to being a prisoner without showing any grief about it"; yet, needless to say, on the day he had accepted to become his guest's enforced guest, he had lost his moral authority; from that fateful day, despite the tragic episodes which were still in store for the Spaniards, the true Emperor of Anáhuac was Hernán Cortés. (9)

The confusion created in Moteçuçuma's mind by Quetzalcoatl's prophecies was one of the chief factors which led to this extraordinary situation; yet Cortés could not expect that prophecy to yield the rich results it did for him when he took the decision to arrest the Emperor; the deed remains one of the boldest in conception and one of the ablest in execution which history has known. Not the least able feature of this masterpiece of military politics is the tact and deference which—with one carefully calculated exception—Cortés maintained throughout in form towards that monarch whom in substance he had decapitated. One of the Spanish soldiers set by Cortés as the Emperor's guard missed two native women of his service: he claimed them from the Emperor, who promised him that inquiries would be made; two days later the soldier asked for his women again, and Moteçuçuma shook him off somewhat curtly; the Spaniard answered back insolently; Moteçuçuma kept silent and dismissed the incident from his mind; yet the story reached the ear of Cortés and he sentenced the soldier to be hanged. The Emperor, who was magnanimous, saved the soldier's life, but was not able to save him from the whip. (10)

Moteçuçuma was settling down to live as a chained King when, twenty days after his imprisonment, Quauhpopoca arrived. He came in great state, carried on a litter borne on the shoulders of his servants, and followed by his son and fifteen other prominent men. As he arrived before the gate of the Palace, he alighted, changed his clothes for poorer and rougher ones, took off his sandals, and thus barefoot, his eyes on the ground, he was admitted to the presence of Moteçuçuma. The forms of submission and respect for power had—as they often do—survived the power in the presence of which they were assumed; nothing is known for certain about this interview, which must have been dramatic. Torquemada makes Moteçuçuma take the offensive and severely accuse Quauhpopoca of having killed the Spaniards and of having thrown the blame upon the Emperor, adding that this action deserved the punishment meted out to traitors; whereupon Quauhpopoca tried to exculpate himself, but the Emperor would not listen. (11) Though this version cannot be altogether ruled out, it does not ring true; it smacks of a Spanish interpretation of Aztec mind-twists and workings very different from ours; it is perhaps more likely that Moteçuçuma should have said to Quauhpopoca: "I am grateful to you for having caught those Spaniards, and even more so, for having sent me their heads, which were an invaluable piece of information; I should like to reward you for it; and so, as the White Bearded One is furious with us and probably will want some human sacrifice to placate his Anger-God, I have decided that you shall have the honour to be the victim for my sake." Whereupon, Quauhpopoca would leave the room overwhelmed with gratitude and ready to die ten times for such a magnanimous monarch.

This "version" of the meeting between Moteçuçuma and Quauhpopoca, though entirely my own, is quite as likely to represent the truth as that of Torquemada; it would appear at any rate to fit Aztec ways better and more closely. In their interpretation of the Indian mind, the Spaniards had the defect of their chief quality, which I take to have been an uncompromising belief in the fundamental unity of man, flowing from their solid faith in the Word and therefore in Adam and Eve; since all men were the offspring of Adam and Eve, all men were brothers—by no means in a sentimental or even in a charitable sense; but, merely in the bare sense of being identical, all men are "much of a muchness"; it follows that their mental processes and reactions must be identical, and that, therefore, if they are not, there is something wrong with *the other* fellow. That is why Quauhpopoca died.

Moteçuçuma had delivered him over to Cortés, along with his son and the fifteen prominent men who were also held to be responsible for the murder of the two Spaniards. They were all tried and, having confessed their guilt, were sentenced to death. When asked whether Moteçuçuma had given them orders to attack and kill the two Spaniards, they all answered in the negative, but, says Cortés, "as the sentence was on the point of being carried out, all to a man said that it was true that Muteczuma had sent orders for them to do it, and that it was on his orders that they had done it." This, though asserted by Cortés himself, does not ring true; it does not tally with Quauhpopoca's proud bearing and undoubtedly brave nature. There is no need, however, to conclude that Cortés was deliberately screening his ruthless action behind a fake confession of guilt: all that the accused said—more or less clearly, at that, even in their language—reached Cortés through two other tongues (and minds); and moreover, the events themselves as interpreted above, were somewhat complex precisely on this point of Moteçuçuma's responsibility; for the odds are overwhelming in favour of the view that all the local governors were in possession of standing instructions to try to seize some Spaniards alive for at least three reasons: (a) the traditional habit of the Mexican to catch live prisoners for sacrifices; (b) magic defence; (c) "information" in our sense of the word. Add the subconscious attitude of Cortés, all in favour of finding Moteçuçuma guilty the better to hold him, and the upshot of it all would be that the more or less complicated answers given by the accused on this point would fatally be "boiled down" to the desired conclusion. (12)

Moreover, we must not fall into the error of attributing to Cortés standards of ethics *in public matters* which in those days were practically unknown. Hernán Cortés was not a man of our time, or rather, should we say, was not an intellectual of our time; it is surely a mistake to measure his acts by the standards of reactions of a sensitive soul of the contemplative species; he was pre-eminently a military chief engaged in a masterpiece of creative action; the standards by which he must be measured are those of political-military creative statesmanship. What he was asking himself at the time was certainly not "How am I to handle this business so as to pass muster before my biographers and their readers?" but "How am I to exploit this incident to tighten up my hold over this empire, considering I only have four hundred soldiers and a few vague prophecies on my side?"

From this point of view—his and not ours—we must now try to see the situation. Cortés had to consider: (a) the coast in revolt;

(b) the capital, uneasy and critical about Moteçuçuma's wisdom in submitting so meekly to Cortés; (c) the powerful armament stores which he had been able to inspect in the teocalli and in Tlatelolco; (d) his own situation in a town completely surrounded by water. As for this last point, he decided to build two brigantines with the rigging and other sailing material he had carefully saved in Vera-cruz; he had amongst his soldiers one Martín López, who, beyond being certified as "a good soldier for war" by no less an expert than Bernal Díaz, was a master shipwright as well. Moteçuçuma was asked to provide the wood and the carpenters. But this was long-term action. (13) The situation on the coast could only be retrieved by swift, impressive and dramatic action; this meant the death of Quauhpopoca and of all his fifteen accomplices. Nothing less drastic could impress a people so familiarised with blood and death as were the Mexicans. But how were they to die? Here again, chopping their heads off meant nothing for Mexicans who saw panting hearts plucked out of their victims' chests as we see priests take communion on Sunday. Cortés' imagination supplied the answer: they were to die at the stake, in the square in front of Moteçuçuma's palace, so that all the city should see the sight and be impressed by it. But if a stake was to be made big enough to consume sixteen or seventeen victims, why not bank it up with the arsenal of bows, arrows, spears and obsidian-edged wooden swords which he had seen in the teocalli? The plan was now complete. Cortés "had all the arms that could be found brought out of the stores, and they were about rather more than five hundred cartloads, and he had them burnt and with them, Qualpupoca, and he said he burnt them in order to burn him"—so says Tapia, one of his own soldiers, in a phrase studiously balanced, which leaves open the question whether the real cause of the fire was the guilty chief or the arsenal of dreaded weapons. (14)

The city witnessed the sight in utter silence, dumbfounded at this assertion of sovereign power by a stranger in their midst; as a further precaution, Cortés had fetters set round Moteçuçuma's ankles during the execution, "at which he felt no little terror," (15) a last touch of audacity not the least striking in this astonishing man. But as soon as all was over, he called on his humiliated victim, in great ceremony, with five of his captains; he found the Emperor in deep misery, surrounded by kinsmen and retainers, sad, some in tears kneeling before him, squeezing thin cotton wraps between the irons and his ankles, to protect his skin. Cortés, who had left him in irons with a great show of indignation, came back with a good grace; and then from his heart, no doubt released from the rigid discipline of his brain, came the healing gesture; he, the victor, knelt on the ground and released the royal feet from their dishonourable fetters.

The Spaniard was in his winsome mood. The eagle had passed the work on to the serpent. He told Moteçuçuma that he held him not merely as a brother but as the lord and king of many lands and peoples, and that if he could he would conquer more for him; he went even so far as to offer to let him return to his own palace. Moteçuçuma listened with tears in his eyes; he knew by now that Cortés could "smile and smile and be a villain"; this offer was merely a screen to spare the "face" of the Emperor in public; but in private, Cortés had instructed Aguilar to "reveal" to Moteçuçuma that, if Cortés suggested a return to his Palace, he was to decline the offer, because the remaining captains and soldiers would prevent its being done. And so, the unfortunate monarch "answered with great courtesy that he thanked him, though he fully realised that these words of Cortés were mere words," and that for the present it was better that he should remain there a prisoner for fear of trouble in the city. Whereupon Cortés embraced him (this time no one dared stop the sacrilegious gesture) and exclaimed: "Not in vain, Lord Montezuma, do I love you as much as myself." (16) Which, if I remember right, is one of the ten commandments.

There remained the coast. Quauhpopoca's execution was, no doubt, a powerful deterrent against further high-handed action threatening the Spaniards left in Veracruz—a mere handful as they were. But, with Escalante's death, Cortés had lost a true and loyal friend and a brave captain. At this stage, Cortés passed through one of the accesses of overconfidence which from this time on are now and then to obscure his judgment, even though only for a brief span. He chose as Escalante's successor in Veracruz one Alonso de Grado— "because," writes Bernal Díaz, "he was a very clever man and of a good conversation and presence, and musical and a very good writer." None of these qualifications, save possibly the first, were especially required for the post; but Bernal Díaz adds yet another detail which makes the choice still stranger: "This Alonso de Grado was one of those who always were adversaries of our Cortés and against our coming to Mexico, and for returning to the Rich Town, and when there were small circles in Tlaxcala, he it was who moved it all." So sure does Cortés feel now of his success that he sends one of his adversaries to Veracruz; we have, of course, often seen him trusting important missions to men "of the opposition"; yet, in this case—as events were to show—he had gone too far in his self-assurance. Bernal Díaz caps his narrative with a delightful scene, to which we owe a glimpse of Cortés' true intentions in this choice; the good soldier-chronicler, who could put a point with both aptness and charity, says of Alonso de Grado that, "if he had been as good a man for war as he was a man of wit, the whole together would have helped him along nicely." Then he tells his story: "When our Cortés gave him the post, as he knew his condition, for he was no man to stand up to anything, and Cortés was witty in what he said, he told him: 'Here you are, Señor Alonso de Grado, your wishes are fulfilled, for you are now going to the Rich Town, as you wished, and you will have to see to the fortress; and mind you do not go sallying forth as Juan de Escalante did, and get killed'; and as he said this he winked to us, the soldiers who were present, so that we got his meaning, for he knew that even if he were to order him to go out raiding on pain of punishment for disobedience, Alonso de Grado would not do it." (17)

This little comedy is full of information. Not only does it confirm the playful character of Cortés and the atmosphere of pleasant comradeship which he kept in his army, but it affords proof that, in selecting Alonso de Grado, what Cortés had sought was to secure a state of peace between his Veracruz garrison and the surrounding district, which in turn strengthens the view that Escalante's own spirit, his "blood in the eye," must have been for something in the incident for which Quauhpopoca was to die—and he also.

But, of course, man's capacity for making mistakes is so rich and varied, so irrepressible also, that though the new governor of Veracruz did not raid Indian villages, as Escalante had done, he found plenty of other fields over which to display his faults. He probably left Cortés in a mood of secret resentment, for, on being selected from the ranks to succeed Escalante as governor of Veracruz, he had dared ask Cortés for Escalante's succession also as

Alguacil Mayor, or Chief Constable, a highly confidential post which Cortés had wisely bestowed on his favourite captain, Sandoval. Cortés had sent him away with good words and promises; but the disgruntled governor proved an utter failure: he alienated the Spaniards by assuming a lordly style of living and the Indians by sending constantly for gold and young women to the close-by settlements— more than thirty of them—which were on friendly terms with the Spaniards; he thought of nothing but eating and gambling, and was foolish enough to say "to his friends and to those who were not his friends" that if Diego Velázquez came or sent some captain, he would give the land over to him.

On hearing this, says Bernal Díaz, Cortés was much annoyed with himself; (18) this time, he gave the matter more thought and sent as governor his trusted friend Gonzalo de Sandoval, one of the youngest men in his army. "He was," writes Bernal Díaz, "very brave; and when he came over he might be twenty-four; in his body and stature, he was not very tall, but rather well-proportioned and of strong limbs; his chest high and wide, and also his back; somewhat bowlegged and a very good horseman; and his face was inclined to be robust; and his beard and hair, then worn [long] was chestnut and curly; and as for his voice, it was not very clear, but somewhat frightening, and he lisped a little. He was not a man who knew letters, rather was he simple and plain; nor was he covetous save of renown and of behaving like a good brave captain, and in the wars we had in New Spain, he always took account of the soldiers who seemed to him to do things like men and he favoured and helped them. He was not a man who went about richly dressed, but very plainly [. . .] This Gonzalo de Sandoval was the captain of whom the Marquess Cortés said to his Majesty that of all the stout soldiers he had in his company, who were so brave that they might be counted amongst the best in the world, above all stood this Sandoval, who was already his colonel for many armies and a man of words and deeds. He was from Medellín, and a hidalgo. His father had been the Alcalde of a fortress." (19)

CHAPTER EIGHTEEN

Moteçuçuma Gives Away His Sovereignty

Cortés gradually settled down as de facto ruler of Anáhuac. Moteçuçuma was his prisoner. At first, his subjects tried all kinds of ways to free him, and he participated in at least one—and the most desperate—of these attempts. "If it had not been for the particular care which was taken," says Torquemada, Moteçuçuma's kinsmen "would have taken him from Cortés, for many made holes in the walls and tried other devices thereto, and one day he tried to throw himself over from a terrace, fifty feet high, for his friends to receive him; but one of the Castillian watchmen who happened to be close by prevented it." (1)

This mood, however, seems to have given way to a kind of resignation, which, as later events were to show, was rooted in a faith as simple and unquestioning as that of Cortés himself. Cortés did all in his power to make this situation bearable by keeping and forcing his men to keep all the forms of deference to the sovereign. The Uei Tlatoani himself seems to have striven to seek compensation for his humiliated state in a lavish distribution of presents for his captors, and a kind of ostentation of his regal attributes. All the Spanish chroniclers abound in picturesque details on this generosity of the now fallen monarch, but none can vie with our inimitable Bernal Díaz, in his wide range from the courtly to the homely. Cortés, with a number of captains, called on the Emperor every morning after prayers—by then they could no longer say mass for lack of wine, "for as Cortés and other captains and the friar were ill during the Tlaxcala wars, they had gone through the wine which we had for our mass very quickly." (2) They spent the morning in conversation, often in arguments on religious matters, which were wont to turn on the respective merits of their Gods; or at games, and particularly one known as *totoloque* which Cortés played with Moteçuçuma, throwing small discs or balls of gold onto pins also of gold. Cortés' score was kept by Alvarado and Moteçuçuma's by one of his nephews. Alvarado invariably scored one point more in favour of Cortés than Cortés had made, which made Moteçuçuma exclaim one day that *Tonatiuh*—as the Mexicans called the red-haired Spaniard —was a cheat and a liar, much to the delight of the soldiers present. The sin turns out to have been a courtesy, since the stakes, jewels and gold, were distributed by the winner: if Cortés, to the Mexican courtiers; if Moteçuçuma, to the Spanish captains and soldiers. And though these windfalls from Moteçuçuma's gains at totoloque seem to have been fairly frequent "he never let a day pass," says Bernal Díaz, "without giving us presents of gold and garments." "He was so kind that he gave jewels to us all, wraps and lovely girls. As in those days I was a youth, and whenever I was on duty or had to pass by him, I took off my war-cap with great respect, and the page Ortega had told him how I had twice come over to discover this New Spain, before Cortés, and I had spoken to Orteguilla of my intention to beg Moteçuçuma for the favour of a very lovely girl, and as Moteçuçuma knew of it, he summoned me and said: 'Bernal Díaz del Castillo, I am told that you are in *motolinea* [Mexican for need] of garments and gold, and I will have a fine girl given you. Treat her well, for she is the daughter of a prominent man, and you will also be given gold and wraps.' I answered him with great respect that I kissed his hands for so great a favour and that may God our Lord make him prosperous, and it seems he asked the page what it was I had answered and the page told him and I believe Montezuma said: 'Bernal Díaz must be of a noble nature.' " (3)

But, of course, all the Spanish soldiers were not equally noble, and it was lucky that Orteguilla was available to make the Emperor "understand the quality of every one of the soldiers, which of them was a gentleman and which not." "I remember," says Bernal Díaz, "that there was on duty a soldier very tall in his body, and handsome, and very strong, whose name was Truxillo, and he was a seaman, and when he took on the night watch he was so lacking in manners that, speaking here with all respect for the honourable readers, he

K

behaved in a boorish way, so that Montezuma heard it, and as he was so exalted a King of these lands, he held it to be bad manners and lack of respect that in a place where he might hear it, such a thing should come to pass, regardless of his person, and he asked of his page Orteguilla who was that churlish, dirty man, and Orteguilla answered he was a man who used to go about on the sea and who knew nothing about courtesy or manners [. . .] As soon as day came, Montezuma summoned him and asked him why he was of such a condition and without regard for his person did not observe the respect due to him, and he gave orders for a jewel to be given him, worth five pesos. And Truxillo cared nothing for what Montezuma had said to him, and another night, on purpose, thinking he would be given another present," he did the same. This ingenious exploiter of his own shortcomings was removed from the service by Juan Velázquez de León, but Cortés does not seem to have heard of the story, possibly owing to some charitable discretion on the part of those who knew it. (4)

Cortés was very much impressed by the cost of the imperial establishment. There seemed to be no limit whatever to the expenditure of that lavish household. Over and above its normal expenses, there was now added the upkeep of Cortés' army, in which every Spanish soldier had two or three *naborias* or slaves for his personal service—all a charge on Moteçuçuma's budget. Cortés sought to lighten the burden of his royal prisoner by decreeing that no Spaniard should keep more than one Indian woman to cook for him; whereupon Moteçuçuma reproached him for it as a slight on his greatness and gave orders that the naborias were to be given better quarters and double ration. It is difficult to explain this decision otherwise than as a reaction of his depressed spirits. Cortés thanked him for it and, no doubt, took note of the fact as a further proof of the wealth of a land which could bear so much extravagance. (5)

They were by now on excellent terms, and the Emperor, though strictly guarded by Spanish forces, was given a fairly long tether to move about. The first time he had felt the need to communicate with "his Witchywolves," Cortés gave in to him but warned him that he was sending enough captains and soldiers to run him through the body, if he tried to run away or to raise trouble: he also asked him to abstain from human sacrifices. The Emperor left in great pomp, preceded by his three gold-sticks-in-waiting, followed by four Spanish captains and one hundred and fifty Spanish soldiers, and accompanied by the friar of the Mercy, to prevent any human sacrifices. But when the Spaniards arrived at the Cu of "Witchywolves," they found that four victims had already been sacrificed during the night in expectation of the royal visit.

The completion of the brigantines afforded Moteçuçuma yet another welcome distraction from the contemplation of his now futureless destiny. He was delighted to see the swift sails fleeting over his erstwhile quiet lagoon and at once expressed a desire to be conveyed in them to the Rock of Tepepolco, where he had a secluded hunting lodge; to which Cortés readily acquiesced; Moteçuçuma took a numerous suite with him, accompanied by two hundred soldiers, under Velázquez de León, Alvarado, Olid and Dávila, all men, as Bernal Díaz points out, "with blood in their eye." These hunting expeditions were naturally considered by the Spaniards as one of the attributes of royal greatness, like that liberality which they had already noticed in the Emperor. (6)

*   *   *

Thus were things gradually evolving towards some kind of peaceful common enjoyment of life by the Emperor and his captors. But the increasing hold of the Spaniards over Moteçuçuma had shaken the authority of the Uei Tlatoani over his fellow princes, and opposition to his policy of resignation came from Cacama, the ruler of Tetzcuco. (7) The young prince, however, was not very fortunate in his followers; and he seems to have made his first mistake in seeking the advice of two of his brothers, both too ambitious to be loyal; he did, however, obtain some definite pledges from the leaders of Coyohuacán and Matlatzinco, Moteçuçuma's kinsmen both, as also from Tocoquihuatzin, lord of Tlacopan and from Moteçuçuma's brother Cuitlahuac, who ruled over Iztapalapan. The conspiracy, weakened by internal dissensions, reached the ears of both Moteçuçuma and Cortés; but the Emperor took Cortés into his confidence and revealed to him more facts than the Spaniard knew; Cortés' advice was that he should be given enough Mexican forces to go to Tetzcuco and seize the rebel; but Moteçuçuma demurred. Cortés then tried twice to negotiate with Cacama, urging him to cease his activities "against the interests of our lord and King," meaning of course, Charles V; to which fiery Cacama answered that "he knew no such King and wished he had never known Cortés." (8)

The young man held a council of war in which he declared himself ready to destroy the Spaniards in four days, for, he said, they were not immortal, nor their horses either, and they had all seen the head of the dead *teul* and the body of the dead horse; he would destroy them all, and they would eat their bodies; as to his uncle, he was a hen, or else the whites had chilled his heart with their sorceries and the great woman whom they put on their altars. In short, war. (9)

Then, on the advice of Cortés (says Bernal Díaz) or on Moteçuçuma's initiative (says Cortés), it was decided to seize the rebel by treachery, for Moteçuçuma, writes Cortés to the Emperor, "had in Cacamazin's country many prominent people in his pay." (10) The young prince was advised by these false friends to attend a conference in one of his own houses built on the lake, beneath which Moteçuçuma's men had a number of canoes waiting for their prey. The rash young man was seized and brought to Mexico—"where," writes Cortés, "he was hoisted onto a litter as his state and their tradition required and brought to me; I put him in fetters and under a strong guard." In agreement with Moteçuçuma, Cacama was deposed and his brother Cuicuitzcatl, or Swallow, was appointed King. This Swallow was christened and received the name of Don Carlos: "and he was most obedient in all that I ordered him to do on behalf of Your Majesty." Cortés soon obtained from the Emperor the imprisonment of Cacama's main accomplices, Tocoquihuatzin, Cuitlahuac and the leader of Coyohuacán. He had instructed his blacksmiths in Veracruz to make a big iron chain from the material salvaged from the ships; a detail which throws a curious light on his foreseeing ways; and now the use of this chain was at last revealed; it was a chain for kings. Cacama, Cuitlahuac and the others were chained to it. (11)

*   *   *

"See how great a lord he was," says Bernal Díaz of Moteçuçuma, "that even when a prisoner, he was thus so well obeyed." (12) But how are we to explain the fact that, being sure of so much outside obedience, he should have acquiesced in his miserable subservience, to the point of sacrificing his own nephew Cacama and his own brother Cuitlahuac?

The answer is beyond dispute: a religious prepossession. Moteçuçuma was not merely the Commander in Chief of his troops; he was the Chief Priest of his religion. Now we know from Bernal Díaz, an eye and an ear witness, that the reason why he remained a prisoner, even after Cortés, more or less sincerely, dangled offers of liberty before him, was his conviction that this situation had been prescribed for him by his gods. The process whereby he reached this state may be followed in the pages of Bernal Díaz as one of self-suggestion; which, in the case of a man in the position of Highest Priest would appear from this example to be particularly easy. Moteçuçuma began by bringing in Uitzilopochtli as a convenient screen to hide his impotence on the day Cortés bullied him into accepting his own imprisonment; hardly had he consented, after a four hours' discussion, to a course with which he strongly disagreed, when he answered his kinsmen and courtiers "that he was pleased to be a few days with us of his own accord, and not by force [. . .] and they were not to stir nor grieve for it, for all this which happens is welcome to Witchywolves, and so he was told by certain priests who know it for they talked it over with their idol." Time went by, and when he asked Cortés for permission to go to worship in the teocalli, he explained that this should help him to make his impatient kinsmen "believe that it is so, just as he had told them and as has been ordered him by his god Witchywolves"; (13) finally, when he tried to calm down Cacama, he sent him a message to the effect that, "as for his being in prison, Cacama must not worry, for had he wished to shake off his fetters he might have done so time and again and Malintzin has told him twice to go back to his palace, but he does not wish to, for he must obey the orders of his gods, who have told him to remain a prisoner, and that if he were not to, he would be killed, and that he has been told this many days ago by the priests who are in the service of the idols." (14)

What began as a plausible pretext ended in a kind of inspiration; whether owing to the intervention of some of his priests or, on the contrary, to some outward projection of his own decision not to resist, at any rate for the time being, Moteçuçuma made of his imprisonment

a god-ordained fact. This led him therefore to accept, not merely
the prison itself, but all its consequences, including the sacrifice of
his brother and nephew. It led him further still—to the formal recognition of his submission to the King of Spain.

This act of formal submission, in a solemn and official assembly,
before a royal (Spanish) notary, was a strange ceremony which
bears all the stamp of Cortés. His Salamanca days, his "letters"
side, his legalistic turn of mind, his implicit belief in a universal
commonwealth of men of reason, within which things must happen
according to recognized rules, are all alive behind this advice which
he gave Moteçuçuma, and which Bernal Díaz records with disarming
candour: Cortés, he says, "told Montezuma, that twice, he [Monte-
zuma] had sent him [Cortés] messages to the effect that he wished
to pay tribute to His Majesty and that [. . .] therefore it might be
well if he and all his vassals now gave their allegiance to His Majesty,
for such is the general custom, that first allegiance is given, then
tributes are paid." Just as he would not take any native girl to his
private rooms before she had been christened, so he would not
"accept" the wealth and power of the Empire he had conquered until
the visible head of that Empire had signed away his own independence before the royal notary of the Christian Emperor whose
crown symbolised the unity of all mankind.

Such is the psychological background on which we must imagine
that historic day, in order to form an adequate estimate of its meaning. On that day, the Christian world acquires a new dominion;
the Middle Ages, or in other words, the Roman Empire baptised in
the Jordan, opens out a window onto a different sector of mankind,
and, historically, the Renascence begins: the Christian widens into
man. The experience was, as usual, saddened by grief, for man cannot rise one step up the steep teocalli of history without covering
with blood and tears the step he has just left behind. Nothing is
more moving perhaps in the whole vast book of history than the
narrative of this scene by two eyewitnesses: Bernal Díaz and Cortés
himself.

When Moteçuçuma heard of Cortés' desire to register his allegiance and that of his "vassals," he summoned all the leaders of
Anáhuac to a conference at which no Spaniard but Orteguilla was
present. He put to them the same arguments with which he had

sought to justify his passivity in his own eyes and in those of his countrymen: the men who were to come from the east; their identity with the Spaniards, about which, says Bernal Díaz, "he understood from what his gods had told him, that we were these men, and that the priests have [again] asked Witchywolves for guidance, but he does not want to answer as he used to, though they sacrifice to him about it, and the most that their Witchywolves will say is that they are to believe what he has told them already, and that he wants no more questions"; "so that," Moteçuçuma concluded, "let us give our allegiance and tribute to the White Emperor, until we get a better answer from Witchywolves." Here again, Moteçuçuma repeated his statement as to the true cause of his acceptance of prison: "and if now at present our gods permit that I should be detained here, I should not stay, were it not that, as I have told you many a time, my great Witchywolves has ordered me to." (15)

Save for some of the magnates, who had refused to come to the Uei Tlatoani's summons, agreement was general, though far from enthusiastic; and the official ceremony was fixed for the following day, some not yet ascertained date in December 1519. It took place in one of the great halls of Axayacatl's palace, in which both Cortés and Moteçuçuma were living at the time. Moteçuçuma was surrounded by a brilliant array of magnates; Cortés, by his captains and many soldiers; his private secretary, Pero Hernández, acting as public notary.

Moteçuçuma addressed his countrymen in terms which we know through Cortés' own narrative to the Emperor—therefore inevitably transfigured by their passage through another, and a very different, mind. "Brothers and friends," he said, "you know that for a long time you and your forefathers have been subjects and vassals of my ancestors and mine, and have always been well treated and honoured by them and by me, while you on your part have done all that good and loyal vassals are bound to do towards their natural lords; and I also believe that you must have memories from your ancestors to the effect that we are not native of this land, and that they came hither from a far-off country, brought over by a lord whose vassals they were and who led them here; which lord came back much later and found our ancestors settled and established in this land and married with the women thereof, and they had a great multiplication of children; so that they refused to go back with him, and he went away, and he left word that he would return or send somebody with enough power to force and attract them to his service." This *force* and *attract*, *arms* and *letters*, *eagle* and *serpent* is obviously a touch of Cortesian colour with which he subconsciously dyes Moteçuçuma's words. "And you know well how we have always been expecting him, and, to judge by what the Captain has told us of that King and lord who has sent him here, and the part of the world whence he comes, I hold as certain, and so must you, that this is the lord we were expecting, particularly since he says that over there they knew about us. And since our ancestors did not behave as they were bound to do towards their lord, let us do so ourselves, and let us thank our gods for the coming in our time of that which had been awaited for so long. And I beg you instantly that, just as hitherto you have held me as your lord and obeyed me as such, henceforward you hold as your lord and obey the said great King, since he is your natural lord, and, in his stead, this Captain; and all the tributes and services you rendered me, render and give them to him, for I myself will have to contribute and serve in every way I may be told; and besides thereby doing all that you are bound to do, you will afford me great pleasure." Moteçuçuma delivered this pathetic speech, "with the greatest tears and sighs which a man could show," says Cortés. Tears ran also down the manly, lean faces of all the Mexicans present. "And I certify to your Majesty," writes Cortés, "that there was not a single Spaniard who heard his argument but felt the deepest compassion." "We had so much affection for him," says Bernal Díaz, "and from the bottom of our hearts, that on seeing him weep, our eyes grew tender, and there were soldiers who wept as much as Montezuma, such was our love for him." On which, Oviedo, none too tender for the rights of the Indians when the spread of Christianity is concerned, comments: "The allegiance which is given to a prince is usually granted with laughter and songs, and a diversity of music and joy as tokens of pleasure, and not in mourning, tears and sobs, nor with the giver of the allegiance in prison, for as Marcus Varro says, 'That which is given under duress is no service but just theft.'" (16)

An honest, free criticism of Cortés' action, precious as an indication of the wealth of opinion which from the very outset was laying the foundation of the Spanish Empire. Farther away still from the conquistador, Las Casas stood for the uncompromising Christian view that the gospel could only be preached by love and never by war. "Holding conversation with him," he says of Cortés, "as I asked him with what justice and conscience he had apprehended that great King Moteczuma, and usurped his kingdoms, he admitted in the end that I was right and said: *Qui non intrat per ostium fur est et latro*. Then I said plainly to him: 'Let your ears hear what your mouth says,' after which all ended in laughter, though I wept inwardly, seeing his insensibility, holding him to be an unfortunate man." (17) Three Spaniards of the conquest; three voices; three attitudes; the conqueror, the friar, the historian-settler; each trying to size up the events which they thought were living, but which were in reality living in and through them. Cortés and Las Casas, two mutually incomprehensible absolutes, agree apparently that "he who does not enter by the door is a thief and a robber," because, of the two, Cortés was the more mundane and knew how to yield graciously in conversation—but it all ended in laughter, the merry wind that takes away the unyielding swords and allows the hands, left empty, to clasp each other. Oviedo himself does not delve deep enough, for Moteçuçuma was not a prisoner of Cortés' military force: in fact, he was not a prisoner of Cortés at all; he was a prisoner of his own self. It was his faith that delivered him, hand and foot, into the hands of the Spaniard, and it was the faith of his compatriots which made them all accept Moteçuçuma's proposal of surrender. Had they wished or, rather, had their faith allowed them to wish it, the Mexicans could have made mincemeat of the Spaniards (nor would this saying have ever been an apter way of putting it); but they were held in sway, not by Cortés' horses and guns, but by "Witchywolves" and his "orders."

Opposite them, a similar faith—similar in its integrity, though not in its tenets—made the Spaniards as sure of their right to exact the allegiance of the Mexicans as the Mexicans were of their duty to grant it. But both sides were men; both knew what a deep tragedy it is for a man to give up his power into a stranger's hands; both felt the awe of the occasion, because they realised that both were the instruments of bigger powers than either. When Moteçuçuma gave his throne away in tears, he wept because he was powerless before the gods; and when the Spanish soldiers wept out of love for him,

K*

their tears were shed over the misery of man, the toy of higher, hidden powers.

On no other basis can we explain the compassion for the victim felt at the time not merely by those of the soldiers who actually wept, but by all the soldiers and captains and by Cortés himself. He was still a dry-eyed man. Grief had not searched him yet to the fountain of tears; but no one can read his narrative of the scene in his letter to the Emperor without perceiving the aroma of genuine compassion in his manly heart—for whom? For the man whose grief he was causing. And as hypocrisy must be ruled out—for no man ever was less hypocritical than Cortés—it follows that he had remained capable of feeling the higher unity of all men above the plane of strife on which he was a protagonist.

And then, there was the pity of it all, the sheer waste of human life not merely of that life which flows in blood and rots away with the killed flesh, but of the life of the spirit which was pitting against each other two civilisations planted, grown and come to blossom in two different soils, under two different skies, yet out of the same seed and under the same heaven; and which could find no other way to live side by side and mutually fecundate each other than this tragic, human, all too human, spiritual oppression. That scene in Mexico, when the men of Cortés shed tears for Moteçuçuma, is one of the most moving moments in the discovery of man by man; a moment of profound unity, achieved not as the Christian dogmatically asserted in the belief in a common origin, but in the grief and shame of common failure before the challenge of life. On that day, man wept over himself and history wept over history. One may feel the tragedy of that sad, yet noble, day ring with other forms of the perennial grief of man, in this line, perhaps the loveliest, of Camoëns (18):

Time, time itself, over itself doth weep.

CHAPTER NINETEEN

Cortés Throws Away His Conquest

THE recognition of Charles V's authority by the chief of the Mexican State put Cortés at rest as to the legitimacy of his absolute power over that land. Incredible as it seems even now, and even taking into full account the religious prepossessions which had hampered Moteçuçuma and most of his followers, Cortés had conquered Mexico with just over four hundred men, thirteen horses, a number of small guns which could be counted on the fingers, and—hardly any fighting; for his Tlaxcala campaign had been most dangerous but very short. This conquest was, and remains, the chief masterpiece of economy in the use of military power known to history. Dangers no doubt there remained, but the skill and daring which had overcome the much greater dangers of the past could be relied upon to deal with them victoriously. For the present, Cortés was the undisputed lord of the whole Anáhuac.

He began to look around, and to take stock of his gains. His activities seem then to have concentrated on three chief points: gold; economic and strategic survey; religious matters.

Gold was the most important of the three. For a normal conqueror, the economic exploitation of the land acquired is, no doubt, the chief asset of the conquest; but this is a fruit which takes time to grow and mature. A conqueror whose adventure begins somewhat irregularly is in a hurry about immediate results; his conquest must justify itself without delay. Cortés had to meet: the claims of his soldiers, all of whom had come to "conquer" and "discover" in the

279

expectation of wealth; his own requirements as an ambitious man having to pay for the expenses of a now great household; the maturing claims of the captains and others whom he had loaded with promises during one or other of the many crises his expedition had had to weather since their departure from Cuba; and the loyal tributes to be sent to Madrid—an official fifth for the King's treasury and God knows how much unofficial good will for the King's servants.

One night, while Cortés was turning over in his mind the plan for taking Moteçuçuma a prisoner, pacing, like a lion in its cage, the hall in which he dwelt, Juan Velázquez de León and Francisco de Lugo, two of his favourite captains, came at this unusual hour to inform him that Alonso Yáñez, the army carpenter-mason, who had been looking around for a good wall on which to build the altar for the Virgin, had noticed a spot on which there were signs that a door had been walled up, whitewashed and covered with stucco; which made him suspect that behind that door, recently sealed, there might be the famous treasure-hall of Emperor Axayacatl, in whose house they were living. Cortés decided to have the door secretly opened; "and when he and the captains went in and saw so much gold in jewels, ingots and slabs, and so many chalchivitls and other very great riches, they were dumbfounded." The Spaniards called this secret store the Jewel Shop. There were also innumerable stores of cotton garments, in boxes as high as the beams of the hall, and so wide that in later days, when through Moteçuçuma's generosity, they had been emptied of their contents, two Spanish soldiers lodged in each of them. Cortés allowed all his men to visit this hidden splendour, then had it all walled up again. (1)

This, of course, did not mean that he gave up all hope of getting hold of that fairy-tale room; he was no fairy-tale captain himself! It meant that Cortés was nothing if not a most punctilious stickler at forms, and an immediate seizure of the treasure, which many of his captains and soldiers—men such as Velázquez de León or Alvarado, though certainly not Bernal Díaz—would have been unable to resist, appealed to him as a coarse and ungentlemanlike sort of action. He preferred to abide his time. (2)

So, one day, when he was quietly conversing with Moteçuçuma, he told him that "the Castillians are most turbulent; and as they will not keep quiet, while looking around in the house, they had taken away some gold and other things which they found in some halls. See what is your pleasure about it." "That," said Moteçuçuma, fully realising that it all was a tactful way of informing him that the Treasure had been discovered, "belongs to the gods; but leave the feathers and all that is not made of gold or silver, and the rest you can keep for yourself and for them, and if you want some more, I shall give it also." (3)

Though vouched for by Tapia, who was an eyewitness of the events, and by Torquemada, who explicitly bases his narrative on that, now lost, of another eyewitness, Alonso de Ojeda, this story of the spontaneous gift of his Treasure to the Spaniards by Moteçuçuma must, in my opinion, be rejected as an attempt to whitewash the conquerors. Curiously enough, it has been generally accepted without demur, even by authors ever ready to censure and condemn Cortés. There are a number of reasons why it should be rejected. The first is that it does not tally with all we know of the Uei Tlatoani's profound piety that he should give away the Treasure belonging to the gods. The second is that the idea of leaving the feathers and taking the gold, i.e. of destroying beautiful pieces of craftsmanship for the sake of the metal, would come to many a Spanish soldier but not to the refined and highly fastidious taste of the Emperor, so that the words put into his mouth by Tapia and Ojeda sound like an attempt at fastening on him the vandalish treatment inflicted on many of his jewels by the soldiery. The third is that Bernal Díaz, as good an eyewitness as Ojeda or Tapia, gives an entirely different version of this act of "liberality" of "the Great Montezuma" as he calls him. According to Bernal Díaz, the gift of the Treasure of Axayacatl was Moteçuçuma's own contribution to Emperor Charles V: after offering Cortés all the gold brought from the country as a tribute for the Emperor, and excusing himself for the small size of the offering, on the ground of lack of time, Moteçuçuma adds: "What I have set aside for the Emperor is all the Treasure which I received from my father, which is in your power, in your dwelling, for I know full well that soon after your arrival, you opened up the house and saw everything and had it shut up again as it was before." (4) These words, pronounced in the presence of Bernal Díaz, suffice to show that the story repeated by Tapia and Torquemada cannot be correct, since, according to these two authors, Cortés had informed

Moteçuçuma of the discovery of the Jewel Shop by some "turbulent" soldiers.

In my opinion, it is necessary to link up two events which have so far been related independently: the discovery of the "Jewel Shop" and the imprisonment of Moteçuçuma. All the narratives, whether those which attribute the discovery to Cortés himself or those which record that it was first discovered by the carpenter-mason Yáñez, present one curious common feature: in all of them, the discovery of the Jewel Shop immediately precedes the decision to imprison Moteçuçuma, with such clockwork precision as to amount to a subconscious confession of the author's personal conviction that the relation was one of cause and effect. (5)

No better proof, short of a definite statement by Cortés himself, could be adduced to satisfy us that the discovery of the treasure of Axayacatl was one of the deciding factors in the imprisonment of Moteçuçuma. But, when dealing with Cortés, special caution is needed, for his motivations and his actions are apt to be subtle and complex. In my view, due weight must also be attached to yet another feature of all the narratives, save perhaps that of Bernal Díaz: in all of them, Cortés is shown deeply concerned with the safety of his army and meditating Moteçuçuma's seizure, before the discovery of the Treasure, so that this discovery is inserted by all between the conception and the execution of the plan. Now this fits in beautifully with Cortés' character and style, and enables us to reconstitute the actual sequence and motivation of these events: Cortés with his usual caution and foresight began to ponder over the situation as soon as he arrived and made up his mind to seize Moteçuçuma; but it was necessary to carry his men with him; they were impressed by the Emperor's power, fearful of what might happen to them if the town "stirred," and possibly also mollified by the Emperor's really spontaneous gifts. When the discovery of the Treasure was announced to him, and he was able to experience on his own self the effect of this accumulation of gold and jewels, he bethought himself of the value which the mere sight of the Jewel Shop would have as a stimulant towards his secret plan; with his characteristic astuteness, he let all the soldiers see it and undergo the effects of its diabolic magnetism, then had it walled up again and said nothing. He had meanwhile "planted" in some of his privy captains arguments in favour of seizing Moteçuçuma—of course, for purely military reasons!—and so the underground relation which the astute leader had tacitly established between the one and the other event oozes out in all the chronicles and is acknowledged in none.

There is always in him a mixture of caution and gambling. In this case, he gambles not merely by his unheard-of seizing of the very monarch whose guest he was—for, after all, theoretically he passed himself off as the Ambassador of Charles V on a mission of friendliness and acquaintance—but also in awakening the cupidity of his captains and men by an exhibition of precious things of which he says himself to the Emperor, that "beyond their mere value, they were such and so marvellous that, considered in their novelty and strangeness, they had no price, nor is it to be believed that any of the princes of the world of whom there is any knowledge could possibly own any like them or of such a quality." As time went by and as the Mexican Emperor showed himself more reconciled to his fate, the Spanish soldiery grew more and more impatient with the situation, and in the end they broke into the Jewel Shop. (6)

There are several hints here and there which suggest the demoralising effects of unchecked power on the Spanish conquerors. What else could we expect in the circumstances? All their past hardships and privations, all their past fears, also all their past repressed hungers now opened their greedy mouths and spread forward their grasping hands towards the incredible booty which they thought theirs because they had fought and suffered for it. To us, reading it coolly in the mild climate of our comfortable homes, hothouses for the most delicate flowers of ethics, the sight of these rude soldiers feverishly breaking up the feather-and-gold jewels of Moteçuçuma to pocket the gold and drop the feathers, and throwing higgledy-piggledy into the melting pot priceless masterpieces of native craftsmanship to make good, solid, square ingots, is one of the saddest scenes in history. They were not thinking of our museums, but of their wives and children at home.

Sadder still than the soldiers' failure to live through their success unscathed, is that of some of the chiefs close to Cortés, and in particular of Pedro de Alvarado, that red-haired, merry captain whom the Mexicans called Tonatiuh—the Sun—and of whom the Spaniards say he was always laughing. He seems to have been afflicted by a rapacity not usually connected with the merry type. Torquemada relates how three hundred natives in the Spanish service (probably Tlaxcatecs, though he does not say so) broke one night into one of Moteçuçuma's cocoa-stores and took away a considerable amount of cocoa, a precious commodity, used by the Mexicans not only as a food but also as money. Alvarado had wind of what was going on; he turned up with fifty Indians of his own and took away as much as he could. He was to do much worse still. Sent by Cortés to collect the gold "offered" by Cacama, as King of Tetzcuco, he ordered Cacama to be tortured by pouring hot tar on his naked body. These facts, important in view of later events, raise the question of Cortés' relations with his captains, and in particular with Alvarado, whom he implicitly treated as his second in command. Alvarado does not seem to have deserved this confidence, save in point of bravery, a quality which could hardly single him out in the company in which he was. The cocoa-store affair had ended in Cortés having to bottle up his indignation on finding Alvarado mixed up in it, though he had not failed to tell him in private what he thought of it. From the days of Alvarado's initial insubordination on leaving Cuba, numerous incidents suggest that Cortés did not feel strong enough towards his chief captain, who moreover had three brothers in the company. (7)

This relative weakness of Cortés towards his army remained a prominent feature of the conquest throughout its many vicissitudes. Such is, in particular, the case with the distribution of gold, forced upon Cortés by the eagerness of the soldiery. The gold dollar or sterling value of the total gold and silver put together, counting Moteçuçuma's treasure and the gold received from the provinces, has been calculated at six million three hundred thousand dollars or one million four hundred and seventeen thousand pounds, i.e. over three thousand pounds sterling per man. (8) But the distribution could not possibly be so simple. The deep loyal feelings of the army to the Crown may be seen in the promptness with which the royal fifth is set aside. Then Cortés claimed the fifth which had been promised him in Veracruz. Then, Bernal Díaz grumbles, Cortés set aside sums for the expenditures he had made towards the expedition, and for Diego Velázquez' expenditures and for the procurators sent to Castille, and for the men left behind in Veracruz, and a double share for the horsemen; and in the end the common soldier found his share so small that many shouted they would not receive it. (9)

So far Bernal Díaz. He reflects as usual, the way of thinking of the rank and file and, in this particular case, he is most bitter against Cortés. Yet Cortés' case cannot have been as bad as the disgruntled soldier says; we gather that he divided the spoils with a somewhat mixed criterion in which may be discerned the following elements: (a) the desire to save as much of the artistically valuable treasure as possible by setting it aside for the Emperor, in a kind of separate heap, not to be counted within the royal fifth, possibly to forestall a demand from the soldiery that it be melted; this royal museum was estimated by Cortés at one hundred thousand ducats; (b) his own requirements, which were great, particularly as he felt he had to prop up his somewhat faulty political structure with discreet golden props here and there, both in Mexico and in Spain; (c) his arrangements with his captains, of which we know nothing save that they existed—particularly with such men as Velázquez de León; (d) the feeling that gold, if too soon distributed, would demoralise his men, many of whom had helped themselves before any distribution had taken place. (10)

That is exactly what happened both with the soldiers and even with some captains; Bernal Díaz tells of one Pedro Valenciano who made perfect playing cards with the skin of a drum, and the camp gave itself to gambling; while Velázquez de Léon had a dispute with Mexía, the treasurer, who claimed from him the royal fifth on some gold which the captain maintained he had received from Cortés; from words they passed to deeds, and as both were brave they inflicted two wounds on each other; Cortés put them both in chains. If we are to believe Bernal Díaz' story—and it bears all the accent and flavour of truth—Cortés handled the situation with his usual "serpentlike" sinuous ways: he quietly sent word to Velázquez de León to be patient, and freed Mexía, who as the King's Treasurer needed special treatment; but Moteçuçuma heard the noise of the chain which Velázquez de León dragged about in a room close to his apartment, and asked who was in prison there, and when Cortés came to pay homage to him, he asked why so brave a soldier as Velázquez de León had been put in chains; whereupon Cortés explained that he was a bit mad and wanted more gold and for fear he would go about in the country importuning people for it, he had been put in jail. Moteçuçuma then begged Cortés to free him and offered more gold; Cortés accepted as a compromise to send him in exile to Cholula, but first reconciled him with the Treasurer.

This was but part of the process of disintegration and reconstruction which his army underwent as a result of the sudden influx of wealth. The grumblings over the distributing of the gold went on in the rank and file. He felt he had to face the issue squarely: he told his soldiers that all he had was theirs; he there and then renounced his own fifth, keeping only his share as Captain General; and pointed out to them that all that booty was but "a little air" when there was so vast and wealthy a country before them. He promised that if any soldier were in need of anything, he would see to it that he got it. And Bernal Díaz, deeply disgruntled though he is, owns that he carried the whole army with him. Now, an army of hardy soldiers disgruntled over a booty of gold, cannot be easily won over by mere "mellifluous words." There is little doubt that, in the words of their leader, the soldiers felt the weight of reason and justice. (11)

*   *   *

Gold was the bait which he used also for sending groups of Spanish soldiers and captains here and there to "enquire into the secrets of the lands within the dominions of this Muteczuma, as of other neighbouring lands." "He begged Moteçuçuma to tell him and show him the mines where he and his subjects obtained gold and silver. He answered it was his pleasure to do so, and straightway appointed eight Indians, four silversmiths and experts in mining and four experts in the land," to accompany the Spaniards. (12)

Cortés put the quest for gold mines first, but he asked the men he sent to bring him back "a true and long report" on "the things of the land." He had been told by Moteçuçuma that gold came from Zozolla or Zulula (which he spells Culula), a district now in the State of Oaxaca; and thither he sent Umbría, the pilot whose feet he had cut off as a punishment for rebellion; the fact did not escape Bernal Díaz who, recording the return of the expedition, adds: "And, as we could gather and see, Umbría and his companions came back wealthy with much gold and having done well, for that is why Cortés

had sent him, to make a friend of him, owing to the past scores."
There was another gold-producing district to the north of the first,
in the areas inhabited by the Chinantecs and the Zapotecs, all of
them to the southeast of the Capital. Moteçuçuma had warned
Cortés that these peoples did not obey him; Cortés, nevertheless,
sent thither an expedition which can hardly have impressed the warlike mountaineers; true, it was commanded by a youthful captain,
whom Cortés treated as a kinsman, and whose name, Pizarro, sounds
intimidating enough; but, as Bernal Díaz drily points out, "In those
days, there was no fame of Peru nor were any Pizarros talked about."
Under this young conqueror, Cortés had sent four soldiers, two of
whom were "Heredia the Old," "lame in one leg and blind in one
eye," and Cervantes the jester. This choice suggests the high degree
of self-confidence which Cortés had achieved. The Pizarro expedition met with a mixed reception on the part of the local chief; he
declared himself ready to admit the White Bearded Ones but not
the Mexicans; and Pizarro, after a glance at his variegated, if scanty
company, took the risk. He was well treated, and received a present
of gold and promises of friendship and collaboration, as well as many
complaints against the Mexicans. Pizarro came back with just one
soldier and reported all this to Cortés, who was much elated at the
present and still more so at the prospect of yet another powerful
alliance against Moteçuçuma, if it ever became necessary. Then he
asked about the four other soldiers. Pizarro explained that the land
was so rich that he had instructed them to remain there and set up
big farms for growing cocoa, maize, cotton and poultry; and meanwhile to explore the rivers for gold. Cortés listened and said nothing,
for in fact the idea in itself was excellent; yet it was, of course,
premature and even dangerous, for he needed his soldiers for fighting; and so, in private, he reproached his kinsman for having gone
beyond his instructions, and, characteristically, told him that "it was
not fitting for men of quality to engage in rearing fowls and planting
cocoa fields"; and he sent another soldier to fetch the four men. (13)

In spite of which, he took the hint and, as he himself relates to
the Emperor, he begged Moteçuçuma to build an estate for the King
of Spain in the province of Malinaltepec which Pizarro had also
explored, and the Uei Tlatoani took it so much to heart that in less
than two months six *hanegas* (about ninety acres) were sown with

maize and ten with beans, and there were two thousand feet of cocoa, not to speak of several houses and a pool with five hundred ducks for feather farming, fifteen hundred hens and other riches the total of which was estimated by the Spaniards at twenty thousand gold pesos. (14)

Cortés was most anxious to find some good anchorage on the coast, and he asked Moteçuçuma about it; the Emperor, having first confessed his ignorance—for this curious Empire, which knew all about the stars, or at any rate, had an excellent calendar, felt no curiosity whatever about the sea—promised him that he would have the coast painted on a cloth. This picture was by no means a map; yet it enabled Cortés to spot the Coatzacoalco River as a zone worth exploring. Thither he sent Diego de Ordás with ten soldiers and pilots, who reconnoitred the coast of Chalchiuhcuecan from San Juan (the present Veracruz) to Coatzacoalco; there, the local chief Tochintecuhtli, barred the way to Moteçuçuma's men, but received Ordás and his Spaniards and gave them every help. Ordás' report was so favourable that Cortés sent Velázquez de León with one hundred and fifty men to build a fortress and to found a town. (15)

This winter of 1519–20 is therefore for Cortés a period of statesmanlike activity. While dealing with the instant everyday problems raised by his precarious situation in the midst of a foreign nation, his glance never loses that power for steady long-distance accommodation, that foresight, that care for the development of permanent creations which raises him above all his companions. He remains, in the midst of urgent tasks and instant dangers, a statesman.

*   *   *

All seemed to be taking shape in a favourable way, and though difficulties and dangers remained, there was no need for a man of his resource to fear the future. He was the lord of Anáhuac. He was wealthy, and he could build himself a fleet, seek more men in Santo Domingo or even in Cuba, and impress the Court in Spain by the sheer power and splendour of his conquest. He was living like a potentate. He had a household of Spanish and Indian servants; he had even a kind of harem, composed mostly of natural daughters of Moteçuçuma, presented to him by their father. " 'Here, Malintzin,' " said Montezuma to him. " 'I love you so much that I want

to give you one of my daughters, very beautiful, for you to marry her
and hold her as your legitimate wife.' And Cortés took off his cap
in acknowledgment of the favour, and said it was a great favour
Montezuma granted him, but that he was a married man and had
a wife, and that with us we cannot have more than one wife, and
that he would have her in such conditions as a daughter of so great
a lord deserved, but that she must first become a Christian [. . .]
and Montezuma was content." (16)

It is a curious fact that Bernal Díaz goes on from this to relating
how Moteçuçuma went on sacrificing human victims despite the
insistent requests to the contrary which Cortés kept making. This
is a constant feature of Bernal Díaz' narrative: invariably, the offer
of native girls—through the necessity of christening them before the
Spaniards can have access to them—leads them to the human sacrifices and to the efforts at conversion. It seems to reveal a kind of
desire for union between the conqueror and the conquered checked
by the difference in faith, and above all by the most repugnant feature in the native worship.

Cortés made repeated efforts to convert Moteçuçuma. They can
hardly have been adequate to the task. He was far too distant in
mind and spirit and lacked the necessary mental and linguistic bridge
to have access to the recondite mind of the Aztec Emperor. At any
rate, it is a significant fact that, though Cortés himself realised the
vain quality of the Mexican idols, many of his soldiers, including
Bernal Díaz, and not a few chroniclers, such as Torquemada, Cervantes de Salazar and Gómara believed in their actual existence and
in their capacity to "speak" to Moteçuçuma and to his priests no
less (possibly more) than the Mexicans themselves. Their religion
was no less able than Moteçuçuma's to absorb other gods, thanks to
the protean virtues which it recognised in the Devil, the most active
ingenious, intelligent, ubiquitous and imaginative of the creations of
human mythology. For the simple Christians of those days, for the
soldiers and for a good many of the friars—even of the scholarly
ones—the Devil it was who impersonated "Witchywolves," Tetzcatlipoca and the other monstrous figures worshipped by the Mexicans;
a fact which transfigured these statues from mere empty stone forms
representing nothing but vain dreams of an undeveloped race into
living creations with a will and a language of their own; a fact which

made the conversion of the natives something like a spiritual conquest of God's soldiers over the spirit of the Evil One.

We are in a position to compare the popular mind and the mind of Cortés himself in this respect by collating Cortés' own narrative of his now famous destruction of the gods of the Great Teocalli with that of Andrés de Tapia. Cortés writes with his usual conciseness and (if the combination does not sound strange) with matter-of-fact elegance. In his references to both native gods and the One universal God of the Christian faith, he speaks a clean, intelligent, one might say purely rationalistic language—wholly modern. "The statues and bodies of the idols in which these people believe," he writes to the Emperor, "are much bigger than the body of a big man. These are made of a dough of all the seeds and vegetables which they eat, ground and mixed together and kneaded with blood of human hearts [. . .] For each thing, they have an idol specially dedicated, as was the way with the gentiles who in antiquity worshipped their gods." "The chief of these idols, [. . .] I myself knocked down from their seats and I had them thrown down the steps, and I had the chapels, in which they were, cleaned, for they were thick with blood from the human victims sacrificed, and I put images of Our Lady and of the Saints in them, at which Muteczuma and the other natives grieved not a little, and begged me not to do it, for if it were known by the people, they would rise against me, for they held that those idols granted them all their temporal goods, and that, if they allowed them to be maltreated the gods would be angry and would give them nothing and would deprive them of the earth's fruits and the people would die of starvation. I made them understand with the tongues how deceived they were to have put their hope in those idols, which were made by their hands, and of unclean things, and that they were to know that there was only one God, universal lord of all, who had made Heaven and Earth and all things, and that He was without a beginning and immortal . . ." (17)

This is the language of a clear intellect, far above not merely his soldiers, who had not passed through Salamanca, but even many a friar trained in the university who possibly, in point of scholarship, surpassed Cortés. He has sized up the religion of the Mexicans with the eye of a man of the Renascence—albeit a devout believer in the Dogmas of what was then the Church Universal for all Europeans alike. But there was another quality in him which he does not let pass into his cool, informative letters to the Emperor; under his clear mind, there was a hot, religious heart, which explains that violent action against the native gods, so coldly told in his own narrative; and this trepidating, questioning Cortés has been transmitted to us in Tapia's narrative, even though somewhat warped by the personal vision of the narrator. He explains how, when Cortés went to the teocalli, he had few of his men in Mexico because they were in the country, collecting the gold-tribute; "and walking in the courtyard, he said to me: 'Go up to that tower and see what there is in it'; and I went up [. . .] and I saw a curtain made of many folds of hemp, with many metal bells; and as I tried to enter, the bells made so much noise that I thought the house would fall down. The marquess went up, just to pass the time, with eight or ten Spaniards, and as the curtain made the hall very dark, we put it out of the way with our swords; [. . .] All the inside walls were made up of stone images [. . .] of idols, and in their mouths and bodies they had much blood, as thick as two or three fingers, and he uncovered the idols of precious stone work and saw through them all that could be seen, and he sighed having grown sad, and said, for we all heard it: 'O God! Why dost Thou allow the Devil to be so much honoured in this land?'" This was no doubt his mood, but can hardly have been his language in view of what he himself writes to the Emperor on the idols. And the soldier-chronicler goes on to say that Cortés exclaimed also, still in his sad questioning mood: "Accept, O Lord, that we may serve Thee in this land." By this time many priests and others had come upon the scene, warned by the noise of the bells; Cortés said to them: "God who made Heaven and Earth made you and us and all, and created that whereby we live, and if we are good He will take us to Heaven, and if not, we shall go to Hell, as I shall explain at more length when we can understand each other better; and I desire that, here where you have these idols, there shall be the image of God and of his blessed Mother, and bring water to wash these walls and we shall remove all this from here.' They laughed, as if it were an impossible thing, and said: 'Not only this city, but the whole land, as one, hold these as their gods, and all this is here by the power of Witchywolves, whose creatures we are; and everyone holds his parents and children as nothing compared to this god, and would rather die; and mind that on seeing you come up here, they have all run to arms and wish to die for their gods.' The Marquess told a Spaniard to go and see that Muteczuma's person was well secured and that thirty or forty men came to support him, and answered the priests, 'I shall be ever so happy to fight for my God against your gods, who are nothing,' and before the Spaniards he had sent for had arrived, he was angered by some words he heard and, taking hold of an iron bar which happened to be there, he began to smash the precious stone idols: and I pledge my faith as a gentleman, and swear to God that it is true that I can see now how the Marquess leapt up in a supernatural way, and swung forward holding the bar midway till he struck the idol high up on its eyes, and thus broke off its gold mask, saying: 'We must risk something for God.' " (18)

This remarkable narrative confirms in every way our reading of Cortés' character. He was at the time the virtual, undisputed owner of an Empire which he had conquered by a masterpiece of foresight, caution, shrewdness, patience and astuteness. And one morning, "as a pastime," he went to see the Great Teocalli. He sees the idols, and the gruesome traces of their inhuman worship, and he grows sad, wonders, questions God, offers to serve Him by freeing the land from that abomination; then, he argues about it with the priests; hears their resolution to die for their gods, and the cautious captain in him rapidly takes a few *tactical* precautions. But, does he change his strategy? Does he for one second reflect that in one minute he may destroy the magnificent success of a whole winter of hardship, courage and intelligent perseverance? Does he think of his gold now safely stowed, of his power now safely established? Not for a second. He seizes an iron bar, even before the Spaniards he has sent for have arrived, and leaps on the idols to smash them to pieces before the dumbfounded priests.

Tapia, and no doubt also his companions, saw him greater than himself, rising in space as high as the gigantic idols he was challenging and destroying. He *was* greater than himself. "I consider that God is above nature," Cortés had written once to the Emperor. So, now, drawn always upwards by God, Cortés rose "supernaturally." The march begun on the swamps of Veracruz, higher and higher and ever higher up the slopes of the Cordillera to the very heart of lofty

Mexico, had to end in this highest of all ascents—on the top of that tower of the Chief Teocalli, where Cortés hit Uitzilopochtli between the eyes. That morning was the culminating moment of the conquest. It was the triumph of man's yearning for ever higher things over his contented enjoyment of the ordinary; of ambition and endeavour over success, of faith over reason. Had he been a less reasonable man, his action might have to be discounted as that of a hothead, below the standard which man must reach to be fully grown to manhood; but no. Cortés was caution and reason incarnate. His action was not below reason, but above reason. And that is why it is legendary, as are all those acts whereby man rises above men.

CHAPTER TWENTY

Narváez Comes to Avenge Velázquez

NOT long after the day when Cortés destroyed the images of the gods with his own hands, and when the two altars, one with the image of the Virgin and another with an image of St. Christopher ("for," says Tapia, "we had no other images available") were set up, some Indians came to the teocalli, and showing the Spaniards a few handfuls of poor, lifeless maize, exclaimed: "Since you took away our gods, to whom we prayed for water, see that your God gives water to us, for our crops are in danger." Cortés assured them that it would rain soon—a not infrequent occurrence after a long drought—and begged all the Spaniards to pray God for water; the next day, the Spanish contingent went in procession to the teocalli, and mass was said, under a bright sun; but on their way back, it rained so hard that the Spaniards had to wade through the flooded yard of the teocalli, much to the wonder of the Indians. (1)

This seems to have been more than "Witchywolves" was disposed to stand. That a foreign captain should smash his golden mask with a bar of some low-caste metal was bad enough; but that a mere woman and child, without even demanding a drop of blood, should equal and even surpass him in his interference with the weather, was something which a self-respecting god could not tolerate. And so, Orteguilla came one morning to Cortés with a very long face and a message from Moteçuçuma to the effect that the Emperor desired to import some weighty news to his Spanish guest. Orteguilla explained that Moteçuçuma had spent the whole night and part of the day with some chief priests and captains, talking over matters which the young interpreter had been unable to grasp. "I like not this novelty," said Cortés, "God grant it may be for the best." He took with him Cristóbal de Olid and four other captains, with his two tongues, and went to hear what the Emperor had to say. (2)

"Malintzin," said Moteçuçuma, "how sorry I am about the answer we have had from our gods; it is that we are to make war on you and kill you and make you go away to the sea and beyond; and I gather that, before war begins, you had better leave this city and none of you remain here. Do this in any way convenient to you, for otherwise, you will all be killed." (3)

We are well informed about the reasons which led to this change in the situation. Gómara gives three, two of which we can dismiss: the pressure of opinion in the Mexican nation against Moteçuçuma's subservience; and the fickle condition of Moteçuçuma. Though both may have contributed to the new situation, it is obvious that neither created it. The third cause is the true one, and it happens to be the only one mentioned by Bernal Díaz: "It seems that, as on their big Cu we had placed an altar with the image of Our Lady, and a Cross, and mass and the holy gospel were said, Witchywolves and Tezcatepuca spoke to the priests and told them that they wanted to go away from that province, since they were so maltreated by the [Spanish] *teules*, and that they would not stay wherever those images and Cross were allowed to remain, unless the Mexicans killed us, and that was their answer and they need not wait for any other." There is even some evidence to show that this Witchywolves and his compeer Tezcatlipoca were emanations of the Christian Devil (I assume that *our* Devil is entitled to the adjective Christian) for Torquemada points out that the two gods, arguing with their priests, based their case for refusing to remain in the same Cu with the Virgin and Cross on the fact that "two contraries cannot live in the same house, whereby the accursed Devil took advantage of the sentence of Christ Who says of Himself to men that no one can serve two masters." (4)

Whether backed by such excellent arguments or not, the anger of the gods was evident; and, in any case, comes to confirm our analysis of Moteçuçuma's attitude towards the Spanish invader. The Mexican Emperor had remained faithful to Cortés in the midst of the most trying and dramatic episodes—the death of Quauhpopoca;

the deposition of Cacamatzin—owing to a belief, more or less self-manufactured, in a divine ordination to the effect that he was to surrender to Cortés and to his distant and mythical Master; on the day Cortés, by his heroic action against the gods, destroyed this psychological fabric in Moteçuçuma's mind, his fate was sealed; the resentment of the whole nation against the high-handed foreigners was free to manifest itself in a new dispensation of the gods—and Witchywolves decreed his extermination.

Cortés was not a little disturbed at the dramatic change in the situation. Perceiving, no doubt, in Moteçuçuma's words the accent of determination, his immediate reactions were characteristic: he showed no concern whatever, and took the change in the Emperor's attitude as if it were the most natural thing in the world; he quietly sent an urgent message to the Spanish headquarters to be ready for any emergency, "for their lives were at stake," this, in case things turned suddenly for the worse there and then; (5) and he answered Moteçuçuma that, as the ships had been destroyed in Veracruz, it was necessary to build other ships; therefore, he begged him to restrain his priests and captains till the ships were built, for otherwise they would all die if they made war against the Spaniards. This was the kind of calculated bragging which he used in order to impress the Mexicans with his apparent assurance, for lack of more substantial forces; but he can hardly have entertained any illusions about the danger he was running. With that superb self-control which was his chief quality as a man of action, he went on even to explain to Moteçuçuma that, while he was willing to go, it was to be clearly understood that Moteçuçuma himself was to accompany him so that the Christian Emperor should see him, which plunged the unfortunate Mexican into the deepest sadness.

The Spaniards were not in much better spirits when they left the Uei Tlatoani. Cortés had obtained from him that the priests and captains should be ordered to keep the city quiet, and Moteçuçuma had been good enough to add that he would try to calm Witchywolves with sacrifices—though not with human sacrifices, adds Bernal Díaz, not very convincingly. But they were all in deep anguish, and had a rude awakening from the days of their undisputed sway over Mexico and the whole Anáhuac, and though poor Orteguilla was the only one young enough to find relief in tears, all the soldiery were in deep concern. Cortés sent Martín López, his shipwright, to Veracruz, to build three ships. (6)

What was it that had so deeply altered their situation? Nothing whatever in the material world. Nothing in the military or even in the economic situation. All that had changed was that Cortés had smashed Witchywolves' face; and those men who had given him their daughters and their gold, their territory and their State, declared war on him as soon as their gods were threatened. Such is man. Nothing really matters to him except the immaterial. Nor was Cortés himself entitled to feel surprised at this, for he also had destroyed his brilliant material situation with one bold stroke of immaterial ambition.

He was, moreover, fully aware of his responsibility in the new situation which had arisen. This can be safely assumed, for not only was he especially gifted in the art of appraising situations but we have his discreet silence over the whole episode in his letter to the Emperor as a proof that he did not consider it the kind of story to be told. As Don Quixote wisely observed less than a century later, "actions which neither alter nor change the truth of the story need not be written down if they are to tell against the lord of the story." (7)

Cortés was too much a man of action to be given to introspection, and therefore he probably meditated about the event in so far as it required fresh efforts and watchfulness—but no more. Yet, by some coincidence of fate, the two weak points in his situation, both due to his own character rather than to external events, revealed themselves almost simultaneously and challenged his admirable powers of recuperation. His religious enthusiasm had already made his stay in the capital precarious: his undisciplined attitude towards Velázquez, that seed of trouble which he had sown in his path at the very outset, now suddenly bore bitter fruit which he had to eat with blood and tears.

*　　*　　*

About a fortnight after Martín López and his carpenters had been sent to cut wood for the ships, Cortés went in his usual way to see Moteçuçuma "to hold palace to him," as Bernal Díaz quaintly says. (8) He found the Uei Tlatoani unusually gay and in excellent spirits. They exchanged their courtesies, for they had remained throughout most punctiliously attached to the formalities of the Mexican Court, and then Moteçuçuma waited. He seemed to be expecting some important news from Cortés, particularly as this was the Spaniard's second visit on the same day. But nothing came from the Spaniard, and so the Mexican, after turning things over in his mind for a while, gave some orders to his men, and a roll of cotton cloth was brought in and exhibited to Cortés. It was one of the pictorial records which did the work of letters and reports in the Mexican world; and it showed eighteen ships, five of which were depicted aground and broken on the coast. "Malintzin," said the Uei Tlatoani, "I have just this minute received messengers informing me that, in the harbour in which you landed, there have arrived eighteen ships and more, and many men and horses; everything is painted in these cloths, and as you had come to see me twice to-day, I thought you came to tell me about them; now you no longer need to build those ships; and as you did not speak to me, I was annoyed with you for hiding it from me, yet I was glad also of the arrival of your brothers for now you will all be able to go back to Castille." (9)

Cortés scrutinized the pictures closely and showed much satisfaction: "Let us thank God," he exclaimed, "Who has provided what was needed when it was the best time for it." And his men, taken in at first by this admirable self-control of their Captain, could not withhold their joy; the horsemen galloped about and the artillerymen shot salvoes. All the army gave itself to the joy of deliverance. But Cortés, as soon as he left the presence of Moteçuçuma, grew silent and concerned; and this mood, soon noticed by his captains and by the soldiers of his inner circle, gradually pervaded the army, after the first outburst of joy.

He was not a man to waste time over mere moods. He enquired for Andrés de Tapia, an officer he trusted, and was told he had just arrived from Cholula and Tlaxcala, where he had been sent to adjust the claims of conflicting local caciques—for such was already the authority of the budding Spanish State in Mexico. Without giving him any rest, he sent his trusted man to Veracruz, and instructed him to travel as fast as possible and not by the usual road. Tapia walked by day and had himself conveyed by night on the back of an Indian; in this way, he reached Veracruz in three and a half days. He found that Sandoval had already sent Cortés a report together with three Spaniards of the newly arrived fleet, whom he had seized. (10)

The fleet was under the command of "an hidalgo named Pánfilo de Narváez, a man tall in body, and thick-set, and he spoke in somewhat high tones, as under a vault, and he was born in Valladolid, and married in Cuba to a lady, a widow, known as María de Valençuela, and he had good pueblos of Indians and was very rich." (11) This captain came as lieutenant of Diego Velázquez, who, though now no longer fat, for Cortés' success had worried all his fat out of him, still kept from his happier days the habit of preferring other people's exertions to his own. The unfortunate Governor of Cuba had received the news of his rebellious rival's first good fortune through Montejo's disobedience. The ship conveying Puertocarrero and Montejo to Spain had strict orders not to touch at any Cuban harbour; but Montejo seems to have been unable to resist a desire to visit his estate in El Marien, close to San Cristóbal de la Habana, and so the ship stole into that out-of-the-way harbour on August 23rd, 1519. They took on board pigs, cassava bread and water, and showed the man in charge part of the gold they were carrying, which so deeply impressed him that he subsequently declared on oath that he thought the caravel was ballasted with it. When Velázquez heard this, "after seven months of so much anguish awaiting news," (12) his fury knew no bounds. He tried to intercept the ship, and sent two swift caravels in pursuit of her, well provided with artillery; but Alaminos knew those virgin waters well, and turning aside from the beaten roads, sailed through the Lucayas and the Bahama Canal and finally reached Sanlúcar in October 1519. (13)

* * *

They fell in the midst of a bureaucracy torn by personal feuds and separate allegiances. The Casa de Contratación, a kind of Colonial-Office-Board-of-Trade contrivance, was mostly manned by Bishop Fonseca's creatures, all, like their chief and patron, anti-Colonites, i.e. enemies of Christopher Colón and therefore of his heir the new "Admiral" Don Diego. As a logical consequence of this position they were in favour of Velázquez, because Velázquez, for reasons of his own, was on the worst possible terms with Don Diego Colón, whose hereditary claims as Governor General and Viceroy of

all "the Indies" were an obstacle to his own ambitions. Velázquez
had nursed this natural predisposition in his favour by judicious
grants of Indians to officials high and low, both in the Casa de
Contratación and in the Consejo de Indias, and Bishop Fonseca
was so fond of him that it was said he planned to marry him to one
of his nieces. (14) Logic being the tyrant of man's action, for, after
all, he is a rational being, it follows that, since Fonseca and his creatures in the Casa de Contratación were pro-Velázquez, being anti-
Colón, they were anti-Cortés, being pro-Velázquez. So that when the
two procurators of the Rich Town of Veracruz reached Seville, they
found that they had to pass muster before their enemies ere they
were allowed to present their case to the King.

Benito Martín, Velázquez' agent, was then in Seville, and he presented a petition to the King, claiming that the ship (as belonging
to Velázquez) should be dry-docked, remanned, loaded and sent
back to Cuba; the officers, more papist than the pope, took all:
ship, royal present, and even the three thousand Castillians the two
procurators brought for Cortés' father and the three thousand Castillians they brought for their own expenses. (15) Benito Martín,
meanwhile, wrote to Bishop Fonseca who was then in La Coruña,
busy preparing the fleet in which Charles, elected Emperor, was to
return to Flanders after a two-year visit to his Spanish Kingdoms;
and Fonseca lost no time in writing to the King. He was a warlike,
executive bishop, and his advice smacked more of gunpowder and tar
than of holy water. He said to the King, says Las Casas, that he
"should have the two procurators hanged, and that Cortés was a
traitor, and other similar things"; but Fonseca himself was not having it all his own way, for at the time Las Casas was busy at Court
defending the right of the Indians to live in peace and though he was
no less an enemy of Cortés than of all the other conquerors—indeed,
he seems to have felt a particular passion against Cortés—he was an
uncompromising accuser of Fonseca's own callous exploitation of
the New World natives. His dramatic speech before the King in
Council on the sufferings of the Indians took place when the King
and his Court were staying in Molin del Rey, in the suburbs of
Barcelona, during the epidemic which afflicted the capital in December 1519. (16) It was precisely in Molin del Rey that the King
signed an order dated December 5th, 1519, to have Cortés' present

registered by his Keeper of the Jewels. (17) He was then, as usual, full of other preoccupations, more urgent and far closer to him than the outlandish fairy-tales which Cortés' letter and present revealed. But despite Fonseca's efforts, the stupendous achievements of the Conqueror did not fail to impress the Court. "While in Barcelona," writes Sandoval of Charles V, "he heard the happiest news which a Prince ever received, that of the discovery of New Spain and of the great city of Mexico, by Hernán Cortés, a man worthy of eternal fame." (18)

Thus crowned with fame and deprived of money, Puertocarrero, Montejo and Alaminos left Seville for Medellín, to visit Cortés' father, "and all of them with much poverty," they took the road towards Barcelona to see the King. While on the way, they learnt that the King had already left for La Coruña. Finally, Martin Cortés and the emissaries of his great son were received by the young monarch in March 1520 in Tordesillas, where Charles had come to take leave of his mother the Queen Juana. They were not yet able to present the gorgeous jewels and the load of gold but, as living witnesses of Cortés' victory, they brought before the King two caciques and two Indian women, brightly dressed. Charles was by now able to speak that Castillian language which, though utterly foreign to him when he had landed two years earlier in his Spanish realms, was to become the true language of his heart. But he must have listened unattentively to the detailed requests which the messengers put before him, distracted by his European problems and bewildered by the plot-counterplot of Spanish intrigues and schools of thought on Indian affairs. Later on, at the beginning of April, he received the messengers again, in Valladolid; this time, the present and royal fifth had arrived: the delicate workmanship of the pieces, cotton wraps and curtains, "which looked richer than if they had been made of silk," feathers, precious stones, silver, gold, impressed the Court even more than the intrinsic value of the metals and stones, considerable though it was; and Las Casas, who was an eyewitness of the presentation, says: "All those who saw these things so rich and so beautifully wrought and lovely, things never heard of nor seen [. . .] were wrapped in astonishment and admiration." (19)

But the King was in a hurry and after a glance at all these splendours, he took to the road again towards La Coruña, where,

after much delay, and legal questions and answers, all that the procurators could obtain was that their expenses should be refunded
them out of the gold brought over in their ship. The delaying tactics
of Fonseca had won. Nothing was decided on the chief point raised
by the Chapter of the Rich Town, namely: in whom was constitutional authority legally vested in Mexico, or in other words which of
the two, Cortés or Velázquez, was in New Spain the authentic representative of the anointed King of Old Spain. Charles, the anointed
one, left La Coruña on May 16th, 1520, without having answered
that question. (20)

*   *.   *

While Cortés' messengers in Spain went from pillar to post,
Velázquez was venting all his wrath in the preparation of an avenging
fleet. He had on his hands an epidemic of smallpox which was deci-
mating the island. (21) Nothing daunted by this formidable obstacle,
he was moving heaven and earth to ensure his revenge, calling it
justice, duty and all those wonderful names men have invented for
their passions and interests. The Audience of Santo Domingo, looking at things more coolly, tried to calm down the irate Governor, and
a man of law, the Licentiate Lucas Vázquez de Ayllón, was appointed
by the Audience to prevent the dispatch of Velázquez' fleet in order
that the Spaniards should not give the natives the sorry sight of a
civil war amongst Christians. (22) He went to Cuba, parleyed with
both Narváez and Velázquez, whom he found in Guaniguanico, at
the westernmost point of the island, and finally agreed to let the fleet
sail on condition that definite instructions were given to Narváez to
seek a peaceful arrangement with Cortés.

The fleet left Guaniguanico at the beginning of March; but
Ayllón, feeling somewhat uncertain about the sincerity of Velázquez'
newly declared pacific intentions, remained on board. Their crossing
on towards Yucatán and the coast of Culúa was stormy, and they
lost six ships and fifty men; finally, part of the fleet, including
Ayllón's ship, arrived in San Juan de Ulúa, the very port in which
Cortés had landed a year earlier. A Spaniard came on board and
gave Ayllón a summary of the situation, the gist of it being Ayllón's
own words that Cortés "holds sway over a very large part of the
country and the Indians do whatever Cortés orders them to do."

Ayllón instructed the Spaniard to explain to the natives that "they were all sent by Your Highness and that all were the same people, those who were already there and those that were now arriving." (23)

Next day, Narváez arrived in San Juan de Ulúa with the rest of the fleet. He found it an excellent spot for founding a town, in which he was paying Cortés the compliment of imitation. There was a method in this mania of Spanish captains for founding towns, for a town needs a chapter, and a mayor and councillors, and all these magistrates can, if need be, depose any other magistrates who may be in the offing. So, after explaining to Ayllón the excellent reasons he had for founding a town there, and overruling the objections of the honest lawyer, Narváez did found a town, which means that he appointed some magistrates; and, this done, the new magistrates having felt doubts as to the powers of Ayllón, the Licentiate and his secretaries and inkpots were forced to re-embark and sent back with a good wind to the Audience of Santo Domingo. (24)

Three of Cortés' soldiers were in the neighbourhood in search of mines—one of them, Cervantes, the jester, whose jokes have a way of turning up at every bend of this story—and they lost no time in boarding the ships, happy to have shaken off the authority of a hard master. "See whether it is not better," they said while sprawling on board ship in a holiday mood, "to be here drinking good wine rather than a captive in the power of Cortés, who kept us so much enslaved by day and by night that we dared not speak, and awaiting death under our eyes from one day to the next." And Cervantes, in his jesting, familiar way, said to the general: "Oh, Narváez, Narváez, what a lucky fellow thou art, coming just when that traitor Cortés has put together over seven hundred thousand gold pesos and all the soldiers are against him because he has taken most of what was due to them!" (25) These three soldiers had picked up enough of the language to act as "tongues" for Narváez, and by this means Moteçuçuma was informed by the second Spaniard that the first Spaniard and his companions were evil persons and thieves who had run away from Castille without permission from the King and that he, Narváez, would soon come and free the Mexicans from Cortés' tyranny. Moteçuçuma would have been more than human if he had not felt gratified at this news. He gave orders to provide the newcomers with all they might need and sent Narváez presents of gold and wraps. He seems even to have made him a fair offer to send him Cortés dead or alive, made moreover through one of his prominent local chiefs known as "Cortés" (possibly that Quintalbor whose likeness to Cortés had been noticed a year earlier by Moteçuçuma). This episode suggests once more the magic bent of the Uei Tlatoani. (26)

Narváez meanwhile was informed by the three soldiers that a few leagues away there was a Spanish settlement known as Veracruz, garrisoned by Sandoval with about seventy Spaniards, mostly of the older and weaker sort. Had Narváez been Cortés, he would have gone there straightway and taken Veracruz. As it was, he sent a priest, Juan Ruiz de Guevara, a notary, Alonso de Vergara, and one of Velázquez' kinsmen known as Pero de Amaya together with three other men to act as witnesses. This deputation went to Veracruz, where Sandoval, having sent away the oldest and least able-bodied part of his population, awaited a more spirited attack. The streets, by Sandoval's orders, were deserted; the six men went to the Church and prayed, then called on Sandoval. After the usual dialogue, first formal, then more and more heated, as to their respective powers, Sandoval who was inclined to strong measures, hearing Guevara say to his notary, "What are you doing there with all these traitors? Produce your papers and let them see them," burst forth: "You lie, you low-down cleric," and had the lot arrested and sent to Cortés.

The cleric, the notary and the gentleman were suddenly "fished" by a number of natives in hammock-nets and, before they had recovered, they were on their way to Mexico, carried on the shoulders of patient and powerful tlamemes. "They went on astounded, seeing so many villages and cities [. . .] and they wondered whether they were enchanted or dreaming." (27)

CHAPTER TWENTY-ONE

The Defeat of Narváez

$\mathbf{C}$ORTÉS, meanwhile, had passed a bad fortnight of doubt and anguish. He had sent several messengers to enquire who the newcomers were and to warn Juan Velázquez de León, who was exploring Coatzacoalco, in search of a good river; Narváez had written to Velázquez de León, who was the Governor's kinsman, and this influential captain chose to side with Cortés—a move which may well have been decisive in Cortés' life, since it so happened that at that critical time Velázquez de León, in effective command of nearly half of Cortés' army, was on the coast, closer to Narváez than to Cortés. This, however, can hardly be counted as mere luck, for Velázquez de León fully aware of all the circumstances, including the vast superiority of Narváez in men, horses and artillery, chose to remain faithful to Cortés.

Cortés' messengers did not return, and he was reduced to whatever information he could get from Moteçuçuma. He learnt that his men had been detained by Narváez and that the new army consisted of eighty horses, eight hundred men and ten to twelve guns. He was neither rushed into action nor cowed into submission. As was his wont, he chose to negotiate, yet with a strong and commanding voice. He sent Father Olmedo, with letters from him and also from the alcaldes and councillors of Veracruz, whose *togae* were suddenly produced from under the dust their *arma* had covered them with; these letters asked the newcomers who they were, offered help if needed, forbade landing with arms and even threatened punishment if obedience was not instantly given to the duly elected magistrates of His Highness, in whose royal service, of course, as well as in that of God, everything was being done. (1)

305

A few days after Olmedo's departure Guevara, Vergara and Amaya, the three men taken prisoner by Sandoval, arrived in Mexico, under a guard of twenty men commanded by one Pedro de Solís, called "Solís-behind-the-door", because he would watch from his house unseen, those who passed by.(2)Solís brought more than a hundred letters sent by Narváez to the Spaniards in Veracruz urging them to rise against Cortés; and almost at the same time a Spanish courier came from Velázquez de León, informing Cortés of his loyal decision to abide by his former and only chief. (3) Despite this accession of strength, Cortés acted with his usual tact and diplomacy. Before they had even arrived in Mexico, he sent out three horses for the three prisoners, so that they could enter the town as free men, and wrote to them expressing regret at Sandoval's high-handed action (which, no doubt, had pleased him very much indeed); he himself came out to meet them; and in short, what with the great city, the wealth and splendour of Cortés' establishment, his winsome ways and his generous presents of gold, the three messengers of Narváez, who had come to curse, remained to admire and soon went back to bless the Conqueror of Mexico.

Narváez received the first letter of Cortés with contempt and, in the picturesque language of Bernal Díaz, "did not think a chestnut of us." (4) But soon the camp began to take on a different aspect. Guevara and his two companions back from Mexico, happy and prosperous, spoke marvels of Cortés and of his conquest and made many a mouth water and many an eye gleam with their gold chains and nuggets; Guevara spoke blandly of dividing the land, for it was big enough for all; Olmedo, in his turn, showed Narváez a second letter of Cortés, aggrieved at Narváez' warlike attitude, affable and diplomatic; and, while Narváez read and pondered it, went about quietly recruiting friends for the side which had the gold. For it is known that

> The best captain to obey
> Is he who gives the best pay.

Thus Cortés' ability to keep his purse always open was doing wonders; particularly as Narváez, lacking that divine gift, was a most jealous guardian of every present he received from Moteçuçuma and never gave a single wrap to his soldiers; "rather would he, in his high-sounding, under-a-vault sort of voice, say to his steward: 'See that no wrap is missing, for they are all set down on record.' " (5)

Further letters informed Cortés that Narváez had moved to Cempoal, where, if we are to believe Bernal Díaz, he despoiled the fat cacique of all the presents of gold and wraps which Cortés had sent his Cempoalese friend from Tlaxcala, and even took possession of the girls whom the Cempoalese caciques had given the Spanish captains, and who had been left behind "in their parents' houses, because they were daughters of lords, and too dainty to go to our wars." Cortés, however, paints a different picture and informs the Emperor that the coast natives "were in revolt and on Narváez' side, particularly those of Cempoal and its district"; Sandoval had thought it wiser to seek a stronger position higher up on the hill; Cortés did not like the news, and reluctantly, for he felt the risk he was running in leaving Mexico, he decided to go straight towards what, for the moment, was the chief danger. (6)

He went to take leave of Moteçuçuma. He had never taken notice of the fact that Moteçuçuma was helping Narváez. Moteçuçuma seems to have enjoyed a moment of quiet humour to which he was well entitled. "Malintzin," he said, "I see you and your captains coming and going very much put out, and you come to see me less often than usual; Orteguilla, the page, tells me you intend to march against those brothers of yours who came on those ships, leaving here Tonatiuh to keep watch on me; tell me all, in case I can help you in any way, which I will do with pleasure; and I am anxious that nothing untoward should happen to you, for you have but few *teules* and those who have come are five times more numerous, and they say they are Christians like you and vassals and servants of that Emperor of yours and they have images and they set up crosses and have mass said to them and they publicly say you are people who came running away from your King and that they have come to seize and kill you. I do not understand you. So, see what you can do."

It must have taken Cortés all his admirable self-control to answer "with a joyous face" this delightful, but in the circumstances, cruel persiflage. He began with words in which there lurks perhaps an irony just as cruel: "if he had not told him earlier it was because he loved him so much that he did not want to sadden him with the news of our departure"; he explained that both his men and the men of Narváez were indeed Christians, but, for lack of anything further to say on this score, left it at that; he simply denied that he had run away from Spain and repeated that he had been specially sent by the King-Emperor to visit the Uei Tlatoani of Mexico; and as for Narváez' forces, he said he did not fear them because Jesus Christ and St. Mary, His blessed Mother, would protect his arms, for Narváez and his soldiers were bad men; and he then, by way of explaining this puzzling situation, informed Moteçuçuma that his King had many Kingdoms, so that he and his men were Castillians, while Narváez and his soldiers "were Biscayans who speak [a different language] like the Otomies in Mexico." It was a pretty way of getting out of it, this bringing in of the Biscayans, just because they spoke another, and a most recondite, language, when Narváez was even more Castillian than he! But Cortés was not overscrupulous in his choice of arguments.

Having shaken off Moteçuçuma's doubts as well as he could, and assured him that he would soon return victorious, Cortés explained that he was leaving Alvarado in Mexico with eighty Spaniards and warned Moteçuçuma in dead earnest against tolerating any trouble or revolt during his absence; then "he enjoined him to keep the image of Our Lady always well provided with flowers and with wax candles burning before it day and night"; and after embracing each other twice, the Mexican Emperor and the Spanish Captain parted in apparent good friendship, with an exchange of promises and presents in which Cortés gave back some jewels and wraps to Moteçuçuma and his son. (7)

Before leaving Mexico, Cortés provided most carefully for the safety of the small force which he left in the capital. He happened to be well stocked with food, for, as the year's crops had been poor in Mexico, he had imported large quantities of maize from Tlaxcala; (8) he strengthened the defences of Axayacatl's palace, till it became a real fortress and garrisoned it with five hundred men, eighty of them Spanish, including fourteen musketeers and five horsemen. (9) They were left in a most perilous situation, for if Cortés came to grief in his hazardous expedition against a vastly superior adversary, the garrison left behind in Mexico would not stand a very good chance of salvation. It is therefore quite natural that Cortés should have left Alvarado in command, for, according to the code of honour of those days, his senior captain could not have been passed over when selecting the chief for the most dangerous position. Yet, as events were to show, Alvarado's judgment was by no means on a level with his new responsibilities—and the most tragic event of the whole conquest was to be due to this unfortunate appointment.

* * *

Cortés left Mexico soon after May 4th, 1520. He was beginning again the journey which he had undertaken about six months earlier, in the opposite direction, yet in circumstances which fate had designed to be curiously similar. On that fateful November, he had started from Veracruz leaving behind a small force of some seventy men, to face the unknown dangers which Velázquez' anger brewed for him, while high up on the lofty tableland of Mexico the mysterious power of Moteçuçuma was for him and his men a magnet, a lure, an inspiration and a challenge. Bold to the point of foolhardiness, he had led his men up the steps of that gigantic teocalli which was the Mexican land, till they had established their hold over the Empire of Anáhuac, beyond reasonable expectations and even beyond their wildest dreams. And now, leaving behind a force equally small under Alvarado, there he was again, leading his army all the way back, down the steps of the huge teocalli, to meet the Cuban danger, at last materialised, and, if still lucky, to begin the ascent of his dramatic fortunes from the very bottom once more. Truly could the stout-hearted captain think that Fate's challenge to him was as hard as any man had had to meet. But he met it without a murmur.

On leaving Mexico, Cortés made straight for Cholula. He had seventy men in all, less than a tenth of Narváez' contingent. While on his way to Cholula, he sent messengers to the Tlaxcatecs asking for five thousand warriors, but his one-time friends answered that had it been against Indians they would gladly have sent five thousand and even more men; but as it meant fighting against other *teules* and guns, they would be content with sending a present of twenty loads of hens—which in the circumstances may have struck the Spaniards as not devoid of humour, albeit subconscious. As a

L.*

compensation, Cortés was reinforced by two important contingents:
Velázquez de León with one hundred and fifty Spaniards came back
from Coatzacoalco, and Rodrigo de Rangel with one hundred and
ten came from Chinantla. Both met him in Cholula. He sent back
to Mexico a few of the men who were wavering in their allegiance,
and without tarrying took the road again. Sixty miles out of Cholula,
he met Father Olmedo who brought him the latest news of Narváez'
camp: the founding of the town; the imprisonment and despatch
home of Ayllón; the close contact which had been established between
Narváez and Moteçuçuma; and Narváez' determination to take
possession of the land. (10)

The little army went on its way and presently, between Tepeyac
and Quecholac, their scouts came upon one Alonso de Mata, who
said he was a notary and came loaded with papers and flanked with
witnesses to reduce Cortés by ink. Cortés was always most reverent
before an inkpot, and so he alighted from his horse and before
allowing Mata to read his papers summoned him to show his own
credentials as royal notary, which thoroughly shattered the legal
serenity of the improvised man of law. "Let them have something
to eat," said the general, and they all sat down to their meal. When
they had been refreshed, he took them aside and, carefully refrain-
ing from uttering a single derogatory word against Narváez, he took
their hands in his and did not let them go till "their fingers were well
smeared with gold." "And as many of our soldiers out of smartness,
were wearing gold jewels on their armour and chains and necklaces,
these persons who came formally to read their papers to us went to
Cempoal telling marvels about us, and there were many prominent
persons in Narváez' camp who wanted to bring peace-proposals and
deal with Cortés." (11)

On they went to Ahuilizapan (which the Spaniards turned into Orizaba). where they were detained by rain for two days. Here Cortés
drafted and despatched a letter to Narváez, offering him any province
he might choose for himself and his men to "settle"; summoning him
to present his despatches, and if he had none, to return to Cuba without upsetting the country, and threatening him with the power of the
law if he resisted the authority of the only Captain General and
Chief Justice of New Spain recognised as such by the said Chief
Justice and Captain General. Signed, Cortés; and underneath sev-

eral captains and soldiers. "And my signature went there," proudly adds Bernal Díaz. This letter was taken to Cempoal by Father Olmedo, with a soldier named Usagre who was a brother of Narváez' artillery master. Both Olmedo and Usagre were well provided with gold. (12)

In Cempoal the friar began by sowing gold judiciously here and there; he worked so well that Narváez grew suspicious of him and made up his mind to arrest him; but, by then, Father Olmedo had won over Andrés de Duero, who, despite his record as one of those who had originally advised Velázquez to appoint Cortés to command the fleet, was Narváez' secretary. Duero easily bamboozled Narváez into asking Olmedo to lunch instead of putting him in jail. Olmedo presented himself as Narváez' best friend, assured him that it would be easy to get hold of Cortés, for many of his men wanted to get rid of him and told him that the stiff letter he had been asked to deliver Narváez was just one more trick of Cortés' men to undo him altogether. The letter was read; it infuriated Narváez and his clan. Duero feigned to be nonplussed by it. One Bermúdez—*alguacil mayor*, or chief constable of Narváez' camp—joined in the astute friar's comedy and assured Narváez that Father Olmedo had secretly told him that Cortés would be sure to seek an interview with him if messengers were sent to his camp to negotiate it. The serpent, at a distance, was already curling himself round his huge prey. (13)

The eagle, meanwhile, was by no means idle. He had been thinking about his armament. He sent one of his men, Tovilla, who had been in the Italian wars and was an excellent spearman, to the Chinantecs with a request to have three hundred spears made of the exceptional length this tribe used in battle, but with spearheads of copper, according to a design they were given, instead of their native obsidian. While Tovilla went on his quest, Cortés continued his march towards his stay-at-home adversary and reached Cuautochco (now Huatusco, in the State of Veracruz), where he received another embassy from Narváez, composed of Guevara, a cleric known as Juan de León and his old friend and accomplice in the conspiracy to have him elected captain general, Andrés de Duero. They brought him Narváez' proposal; it was elegant and simple: Narváez was to have the land and Cortés and his men whatever ships and supplies they might want to take to clear out of Mexico altogether. (14)

These proposals were not of the kind that could be made to Cortés, but the men who brought them were of the kind he could talk with and win over. It was therefore agreed that Narváez and Cortés should meet, each with ten men, after exchanging safe-conducts, which, so far as his was concerned, Cortés prepared and signed there and then. But at the following stage in their march, in Tampecanita, when Narváez' safe-conduct arrived, there came with it a message of caution from Olmedo and Duero: the interview was a trap to have him assassinated. (15)

Cortés thereupon mounted his legal high horse and sent a regular summons to Narváez to abstain from exerting any authority in the land, and to all his followers to abstain from obeying Narváez' authority; but when Rodrigo Alvarez Chico and Pero Hernández, his secretary and notary, arrived in Cempoal with this summons, they were immediately granted by Narváez an unlimited time to meditate in jail on authority and its true fountain and origin. (16)

In Tampecanita, Cortés found Sandoval with those amongst his soldiers who were not too old or too infirm to put up a fight, and on the way to Mictlancuauhtla (humanised by Bernal Díaz into Mitalaguita) he met Tovilla back from Chinantla with the three hundred long lances, "extremely good"; Cortés started practising at once; their chief advantage in his mind was that they allowed his infantry to keep the horsemen at bay—an improvised way of neutralising his rival's superiority in cavalry. (17) Cortés was negotiating and sending to Cempoal wave after wave of gold-scouts, but meanwhile he prepared his army for a fight; he mustered his men and found he had "two hundred and sixty-six counted by drum and fife, without the friar"; this included five horsemen and two small guns, very few muskets and crossbows. He made up his mind to attack Narváez; and this is the way he imparts his decision to the King: "And seeing that I could in no way prevent so much damage and evil, and that the natives were daily rising and revolting more and more, commending myself to God, and leaving aside all fear of the harm which might follow, considering that from our death in the service of the King and in the defence and protection of his lands and to prevent their usurpation, there would follow much glory for me and for my company, I gave my order to Gonzalo de Sandoval, my Chief Constable, to whom I gave eighty men, to seize the said Narváez, and I, with another one hundred and seventy, for, in all, we were two hundred and fifty men, without firearms nor horses, just on foot, followed my Chief Constable to lend him support." (18)

So much for the eagle. As for the serpent, he was busy conquering Andrés de Duero, who, under the mask of negotiations, had come again to see Cortés, this time to remind him of their pact and to claim his share in the spoils. Cortés promised a brilliant share, and loaded with gold two Cuban Indians whom Duero had brought in his service, in exchange for a fresh promise of help to undo the power of Narváez, not only on Duero's part but also on behalf of Bermúdez, Narváez' Chief Constable. Duero mounted his horse and came to take leave of Cortés: "What is your worship's pleasure?" he asked. "For I am leaving." "Go with God," answered Cortés, "and see that all comes above as we have talked it over, or else, upon my conscience, in less than three days I shall be in your camp and you will be the first at whom I will thrust my spear." Duero laughed and said: "I shall not fail in anything which may be in your worship's service." (19)

Cortés must have felt by now that Narváez was a poor match for him. He had come all the way from Mexico while the newly arrived general, with his fresh and still untired troops, remained enjoying the delights of Cempoal for no reason other than his usual indolence and carelessness; he was well informed about happenings in Narváez' camp from his own men who came and went, as well as from the men of Narváez who came and sometimes remained, like one Villalobos who, with seven other soldiers, deserted to Cortés as a protest against Ayllón's imprisonment. In this state of mind, he called Juan Velázquez de León. "And as Cortés spoke sometimes very honeylike, and with laughter in his mouth, he said to him half laughing: I had you called because I am told by Andrés de Duero that Narváez says, and it is a general rumour in this camp, that if you go there, I am done with and destroyed, for they believe that you will go over to him; and so, I have decided that, if you love me, you should go thither straightway on your good dapple mare, with all your gold, and your Swaggerer [a thick gold chain to which the soldiers had given this picturesque name] and other small trifles I will give you; and you will wear the Swaggerer round one shoulder and arm, and round the other one another chain still heavier, and you will see what Narváez wishes of you, and as soon as you come back, I shall send Diego de Ordás, whom they also wish to see in their camp." (20)

This scene, vividly recorded by Bernal Díaz, is of the purest Cortés: a flower of free, spontaneous, humorous and slightly swaggerish life, grown out of a root of coldly calculated caution. It was essential for him to test the loyalty of these two captains, one-time leaders of the Velázquez group, *before* the battle and not *during* the battle. If they were to abandon him, it was best that they should do it by themselves, as individuals, albeit important, than as commanders of important forces in his none too numerous army. The right—though bold—decision was therefore to trust them to the limit and even beyond the limit of danger, by giving them every opportunity to desert, thus putting them on their honour. And that is why Cortés was so insistent in sending Velázquez de León to Narváez with all his gold and even with some of his own. The shrewd generosity of Cortés worked on Velázquez de León at once: he accepted to go, but refused to take his gold with him. Cortés gave him one of his servants as an escort—just in case.

Velázquez de León, on his good mare, pulled up at dawn before the house of the fat cacique; the Cempoalese recognised his genial, bulky figure, and told the Spaniards; Narváez came upon the scene very much elated, and took Diego Velázquez' kinsman to his own quarters, reproaching him for not having gone there of his own accord; to which Velázquez de León answered that he was going back soon because he had only come to kiss his hands and to try to make peace between him and Cortés. "Peace with a traitor?" asked Narváez, incensed; but Velázquez retorted: "Not a traitor but a good servant of His Majesty." Narváez then altered his tactics and tried to win him back, offering him the highest grade in his army next to his own, but Velázquez declared his firm intention of remaining loyal to Cortés.

By this time many of Narváez's captains had come to greet Velázquez de León, "embracing him with great courtesy for he was very much of a Palace man, and of good body, thick-limbed, and a good presence and face and the beard very well set, and he wore a very big gold chain over his shoulder, which went twice around his arm, which suited him very well as a smart and good captain."

Egged on by some of the more eager anti-Cortés group, Narváez made up his mind to arrest him; but Duero, Bermúdez and the two clerics, who had all had "their fingers smeared with Cortés' gold," argued with great cogency that Cortés received all Narváez' messengers very well (didn't they know it?) while Narváez put all Cortés' messengers in jail, and they suggested that Narváez invite Velázquez de León to dine.

Narváez took his advice; he took also the advice of Olmedo, who seems to have been a bit of a wag, and who suggested that the troops should file past the visitor so as to impress him with his host's power. "Great is the power you bring," said Velázquez de León. "May God increase it." "That will show you," retorted Narváez, "that if I had wished to march on Cortés, I would have brought him back a prisoner and all of you who are with him." "Take it from me that he is such a man," the Captain retorted, "and that we, his companions, are such men that we shall give a good account of ourselves." Despite which, the dinner took place next day; or at least such was everybody's intention. But it so happened that one of the guests was a nephew of the Governor General of Cuba and his namesake, a young captain in Narváez's army. This Diego Velázquez junior lost no time in declaring that Cortés and all his followers were a lot of traitors, words which Velázquez de León hotly declared he would not tolerate in his presence; whereupon Diego Velázquez junior retorted that he who backed a traitor was a traitor himself and could not be a good species of Velázquez; this brought Velázquez de León to his feet, declaring that he was a better Velázquez than either young Diego or his uncle, and ready to prove it with his sword there and then if their mutual host gave him leave thereto [. . .] It was finally decided to send Velázquez de León back to Cortés, together with the Father of the Mercy. Cortés' ruse had been an unqualified success. (21)

Cortés meanwhile had advanced towards Veracruz and Cempoal leaving Mitalaguita at dawn. It was hot and sultry, and the army had halted for a rest by the River of Canoes where, later, the second Veracruz was built; there Velázquez de León came to join them; and while Olmedo diverted the soldiery with his merry stories of the Narváez camp, the captain reported to Cortés on the military position. Narváez had brought his army rather more than a mile

out of Cempoal. It rained hard the whole day and his captains, bored
and somewhat humiliated to have to wait for a force they held in
contempt, prevailed upon him to return to Cempoal and, after placing
his twenty-three guns in readiness before the teocalli, to wait for the
enemy in his own headquarters. "What are you doing there," asked
the fat cacique, no doubt struck by the contrast between this indolent
army and the high-strung force of Cortés, "what are you doing there,
so carefree? Do you think that Malintzin and his *teules* are like
you? I must tell you that, if you do not look out, he will be here
and kill you." He was laughed at, though Narváez did take some
precautions and had his crier promise two thousand pesos to whosoever would kill Cortés or Sandoval. Then, having well garrisoned
the steps of the teocalli which led up to his own quarters, and given
the army *Santa Maria* for its password, the carefree and easy-going
Narváez went to sleep. (22)

That same afternoon which Narváez had wasted, Cortés having
heard Velázquez de León's report, moved on to a river (Chachalacas)
just four miles out of Cempoal, and as soon as he had chosen his
camp and set his scouts and sentinels, he called the army together,
and, from his horse, he addressed them: "a speech of so pretty a
style and reasoning, and so well said, truly quite another thing and
more tasty and full of offers than I here could write down." He began
by reminding them how they had made up their minds to "conquer"
and "settle" instead of merely "bartering," which was Velázquez's
plan, and how they had elected him their leader and Chief Justice;
then came the vivid narrative of their hardships, battles, wounds,
losses, and final victory; the night was falling; he must be brief;
here is now this Narváez, calling us traitors, writing to Moteçuçuma
words unworthy of a wise captain; arresting one of His Majesty's
Oidores, a crime which in itself deserves a severe punishment; pro-
claiming open war against us, "as if we were Moors." So far, he
went on to say, you have fought to save your lives; now you must
fight to save both your lives and your honour, for if they win they
will prosecute us and say we have killed and despoiled and destroyed
this land (a shrewd sense of the subservience of the law to the
sword!). "So," he concluded, "as good gentlemen that we are, we
must defend our honour and the King's. With this mind, I left

Mexico, trusting God and you. I have put all in God's hands first, then in your hands. Now, what do you say?" (23)

So far Bernal Díaz. But I confess that for once I find a fresher accent, and one more instilled with the spirit of truth, in Tapia's version. Cortés, somewhat disturbed at the news imparted to him by Velázquez de León, said to his army: "I am but one and can do no more than one does. Compromises have been suggested to me which were good for me, but only for me; yet, as they were not good for you, I have refused them. You see what the position is; and since this business touches every one of you, let every man say what he feels about fighting or seeking peace; no one will be prevented from doing what he may wish. See now; these our messengers tell me how in the camp of our adversaries it is said and believed that you are taking me there under false pretences, to deliver me into their hands." They gave him every satisfaction on that point, then they insistently importuned him to give his opinion first; whereupon, as if irritated, he burst forth: "I will tell you; a proverb of Castille says *Let the ass die with him who goads him on*; and that is my opinion." Then the soldiers acclaimed him and raised him on their shoulders till he begged them to leave him. (24)

Both may be right, for both Tapia and Bernal Díaz were present, and the same speech may leave very different impressions on different minds; but whichever version be preferred, one thing is certain: had Cortés left in his army a really objective and permanent impression of meanness at the moment of the distribution of the gold booty in Mexico, neither of these two versions would have reflected the facts, and Cortés would have perished in Cempoal that very night.

These soldiers who acclaimed him were soaked with rain, famished and tired of marching. They set about roasting some venison which the horsemen had killed, but Cortés forbade them to light fires. There was a cool wind, and nothing to do. The general called his men together in the still of night and said: "Gentlemen, you know there is a current saying among soldiers 'At dawn, fall upon your enemy,' and if we have been heard, they are already awaiting us, and if not, since we cannot sleep, we had better use this time fighting and take our leisure after our victory than waste it suffering this cold." (25) He distributed his men carefully. Pizarro with sixty

men was to seize hold of the artillery; Sandoval was to catch Narváez
dead or alive. He addressed them for the last time, with this conclusion: "Better die as good men than live in dishonour." And
Bernal Díaz thought in later life how wise a captain he had been in
keeping quite secret his success in winning over many of Narváez'
followers by quiet intrigues, so that his troops should fight as good
soldiers who hope for no victory but that of their own courage.

They marched on, in the night, and about one mile out of
Cempoal they came upon two of Narváez' scouts, one of whom they
seized, while the other one fled and roused the camp. They hurried
on in the dark, having for their password *Holy Ghost,* so that, in this
curious battle, the Holy Ghost was pitting its forces against St.
Mary. Narváez, suddenly awakened, shouted for his captains. Young
Pizarro, meanwhile, after losing three of his sixty men, who fell,
mowed down by the first onslaught of Narváez' artillery, had taken
the whole battery in a man-to-man fight; Bernal Díaz, who was one
of the sixty, had promised Sandoval to follow him, should he be still
alive after this first operation; Sandoval with his seventy men ran
up the steps of the teocalli, and after some sharp fighting, succeeded
in reaching the top in time to hear Narváez exclaim: "St. Mary, help
me. They have killed me. They have torn one of my eyes!"
Cortés' men, who heard this, shouted: "Victory! Victory for the
Holy Ghost. Narváez is dead!" Martín López, who was a tall man,
set fire to the straw roof of the teocalli. The shouts of victory ran
down the steps and into the still night-covered streets of the garden
city of Cempoal where, in the dark, the glow-worms shone and put
fear into the heart of the dispirited army of Narváez, for they mistook them for so many musket wicks; the eighty horsemen of the
wounded captain galloped away aimlessly, over the countryside. (26)

PART V
THE SECOND CONQUEST

CHAPTER TWENTY-TWO

The Massacre of Mexico

THESE cries of victory, these gallops under the rain, in the dark, spied upon now and then by a furtive glance of the curious moon, were but the forerunners of victory. Several other *cues* had to be taken on top of which Narváez' captains fought valiantly. Cortés, with twenty men he had kept under his direct orders as a reserve, went here and there in the drenched night. He saw a man with a handful of burning straw in his hand: a young gentleman of his company, who had found eight barrels of gunpowder and, believing the Narváez army had made off with the guns, was about to set fire to them; the young man burst open a barrel and as he was going to make it explode, Cortés came upon the scene. "What is that?" he asked; Tapia explained. "Oh, brother," said Cortés to his brave but rash companion, "do not do that, for you would die and many of ours hereby also." And with his own hands and feet he stamped out the fire which was already spreading amongst the gunpowder fallen from the burst barrel. (1) This done, he disappeared again into the night. Here he gave military orders, there he dictated to his secretary-notary legal addresses which were cried in the night by his public crier, summoning all "rebels" to surrender to the "King's" authority and "in his royal name" to his Chief Justice Hernán Cortés. It was hot and sultry, and he was in armour. " 'What about Narváez?' " he asked Sandoval, "sweating and tired, one breath not reaching the next." " 'Here he is, and in good custody,' " answered his loyal *alguacil mayor*; a man came to ask whether he would grant permission for Master John, Narváez's surgeon, to cure his chief's wounded eye, and he gave it readily, then stole towards the spot, and remained there watching unobtrusively, in the circle of onlookers, while Master John operated. Someone whispered in Narváez' ear that his happy rival was present. "Sir Captain Cortés," said the wounded man, "you should hold it a great thing that you have gained this victory over me and taken my person." "I thank God for it," answered Cortés, "and the valiant gentlemen and companions I have; yet I think that to beat you and seize your person is one of the least important things I have done in New Spain. Do you think it right," he asked with his legalistic bee in his helmet, "to have dared take prisoner an *Oidor* of His Majesty's bench?" And without waiting for an answer he disappeared into the night. (2)

He was told the fat cacique had been found wounded in Narváez' quarters, and gave orders to have him well treated and visited by the army surgeon. That cavalry of Narváez, the most precious element in the new army, was very much in his mind. Many had galloped away; about forty of them had been posted out to await Cortés' army and had evidently missed it. Cortés sent two of his captains, Olid and Ordás, to fetch them and win them over, which they did, possibly with the help of the sovereign power of gold. When they returned to the camp, they found it in great noise and confusion. The timbal-master, who was a bit mad, as every man must ultimately become after years of liberty to strike at will on a drum, was raising a glorious roar out of his donkey-skins to celebrate Cortés' victory, though he was a Narváez man (but is not defeat as good as victory to make a noise about?), while a negro jester of Narváez' suite shouted unremittingly at the top of his voice: "The Romans never saw such high deeds!" No objurgations, orders, or good, downright Spanish swearing, could make the negro stop his paeans nor the timbal-master his repeated, rhythmical uproar, till Cortés came upon the scene and had the drum artist put in jail. (3)

The sun had now come out to preside over the events of that May 29th, 1520. The cavalry, won over, was entering the camp; the captains who had carried on the fight had at last surrendered; Juan Velázquez de León had the deep satisfaction of showing his generosity by taking a personal hand in the welfare and comfort of young Diego Velázquez, whom he had beaten and seized during the night. Cortés sitting on an armchair, with an orange-coloured gown over his armour, surrounded by his captains and men, was receiving the homage of his new friends, who filed past him kissing his hand:

"You should see," says Bernal Díaz, "the grace with which he spoke to them and embraced them and the courteous words he said to them, and how gay he was and rightly so, being then so much of a lord and so full of power." (4)

He was a wise victor. Convinced though he was that, had he been caught by Narváez, (5) he would have been hanged, he took no measures against Narváez other than that of keeping him severely guarded, and was meticulously careful in respecting his fallen rival's personal goods and comfort. Pedro de Maluenda, Narváez' steward, was given every facility to that effect and even granted pecuniary help. (6) This action on his part reveals more than a generous disposition towards his beaten rival; it shows that Cortés felt singularly confident about the righteousness of his cause; for Narváez, left to live and ultimately to move in freedom, was to remain an independent and none too friendly witness of events in Mexico. Whatever the motives which determined Cortés' attitude at this juncture, the fact remains that he did not think it worth while to carry his fight with Narváez to the bitter-end by sentencing him to death, as he could easily have done.

Next day, he inspected his troops. When the Narváez army realised that they had been beaten by just two hundred and fifty veterans, poorly clad and worse armed, "they tore their beards off" in anger and humiliation; the fat cacique was enraptured in admiration and had a picture made of the fight to be sent to Moteçuçuma; and ugly Doña Catalina, his daughter, whom he had given to Cortés, and whom Cortés had taken "with a good face," was delighted to hear that the Spanish *teul* was to move to her house and to accept her couch and table during his brief, all too brief, stay. (7)

* * *

There is no light more bright than that of victory. Now, Cortés' soldiers knew that they were prosperous, powerful and respected. Their elation was at this time enhanced by a most picturesque and martial pageant: fifteen hundred Chinantec warriors came to Cortés' summons, under the leadership of one of his soldiers, named Barrientos, and though they arrived on the spot after the event, their smart appearance and good order as they marched through war-scarred avenues of Cempoal, in rows of three men, two spearmen and a bowman, with their wood-drums and shell-trumpets, their small, round bucklers, their feather headgear and banners, shouting, "Long live the King and in his royal name Cortés," gave deep pleasure to the old army and food for thought to the new. Cortés spoke "lovingly" to their captains and sent them back with a few presents of Castillian beads. (8)

But he was not the man to linger in the passive mood of past victories; he set about immediately to attend to the most urgent tasks which his victory demanded of him. He had all the sails, rudders and compasses taken out of the eighteen ships of Narváez's fleet, made all the shipmasters and pilots swear allegiance to him and gave them a new admiral, Pedro Caballero, a man whom he trusted, and whose loyalty he had duly cultivated with gold presents. He sent Velázquez de León with two hundred men to explore the Pánuco region; and Diego de Ordás, with another two hundred men, to develop the colony of Coatzacoalco. Each of these two captains was to have two ships: Velázquez de León, for exploring the coast; Ordás to send them to Jamaica for mares and all kinds of domestic animals. Thus as soon as he was in the saddle as a captain, the statesman in him began without delay the scientific study and economic development of the land he had won. (9) As for Veracruz, a garrison of two hundred men under Rodrigo de Rangel, was left in charge of the remaining ships and on the lookout for further threats from Velázquez.

In order to organise all these expeditions, Cortés needed more captains than he had in his old army. Though victorious in the field, he remained at the head of an ill-assorted army, in a perilous minority within it. He set about to cultivate the new captains, by words of friendship and deeds consisting mostly in appointments to posts of trust and honour and in presents of gold. The old soldiers who had helped themselves to the booty of Narváez' army were made to disgorge their prizes and to return them to the original owners; and Bernal Díaz records, not without a touch of bitterness, that he had to give up a horse which he had ridden, with its saddle and bit, two swords, three poniards and a dagger. The old army resented this wise attitude of their chief as a kind of betrayal, and one of the Captains, Dávila, somewhat proud and unruly, told Cortés what he and his friends thought about it in terms somewhat devoid of deference. Cortés argued patiently that all he had, his person and his wealth, was theirs, but he was bound by circumstances to attract Narváez' men, or else they might revolt: whereupon Dávila answered him back with some insolence. "Those who do not wish to follow me," said Cortés, "let them go. The women in Castille bring forth soldiers." "And captains and governors as well," growled back Dávila. But he was eventually calmed down and won over by his astute chief, and the patient, peaceful second conquest by gold and words of the army already conquered first by iron and bold deeds, proceeded henceforth as his steady will had decided. (10)

Cortés could now at last feel himself the master of Mexico. He had an army of about twelve hundred Spaniards, ninety horse, twenty-five or thirty guns, unlimited supplies, eighteen ships, a chest of just under a million pesos of gold—and the aura of continuous success. (11) He could now at his leisure return to Mexico and organise the Kingdom which he had added to the rich crown of Charles V. But his destiny had not yet taken from him its full toll of hardship. At this hour of his highest triumph, it struck harder than ever, and the conqueror was condemned to lose all his conquest and to begin again from nothing upwards, on a road harder, longer and bloodier than he had ever known.

He had sent a messenger to Moteçuçuma conveying the news of his victory over Narváez. Soon after his departure, two Tlaxcatec messengers came to bring Cortés a verbal message from Alvarado: the city had risen against him; he was besieged and, with all his garrison, in danger of being exterminated. A later letter brought by other Tlaxcatecs and the Spanish messenger who came back from Mexico confirmed this news. (12)

* * *

The gods again had come down amongst men and drowned them in blood. While Cortés went to meet Narváez, the Mexicans were busy preparing their feast of Toxcatl. It was the most important of their religious festivals, in honour of the chief of their gods, Titlacn or Tetzcatlipuca. The central feature of this festival was the sacrifice of a youth specially chosen without the slightest defect in his body. This youth was designated one year in advance. During the last year of his life, the prospective victim lived in the midst of the choicest delights, and was taught to play musical instruments, to sing and to dance. He wore his hair long down to the waist and went about laden with flowers and followed by eight pages richly dressed. He greeted all passers-by gracefully, and they, in their turn, knowing him to be the living image of Tetzcatlipuca, worshipped him as a god. Twenty days before the festival, his hair was cut short in the fashion of captains and four lovely girls, especially trained for the purpose, were told off to accompany him and let him taste of the delights of carnal love for the last twenty days of his life. On the festival day, the four women forsook him; he was taken to the teocalli and there, while he climbed the steps which led up to the eagle-dish where his throbbing heart would soon fall, he broke and threw over each step one of the flutes on which he had played during his divine year. With the last step and the last flute, his last breath was exhaled; five priests seized his perfect body, held it on the sacrificial stone for the chief of them to stab his chest open, and when the living heart had steamed its last before Tetzcatlipuca's ferocious mask, the now empty body was conveyed down the steps and its head, cut off from it, was stuck on a high pole known as *Tzonpantli*. The festival was followed by dances in which the chief nobility of Mexico participated. (13)

Uitzilopochtli was not forgotten either, and the ceremonies in his honour were complicated and numerous, including a procession in which his image was conveyed by many captains and warriors. The maids made up their faces with coloured pastes and covered their arms and legs with red feathers, and with ornaments of reeds and paper; they danced with the priests, whose heads were adorned with white hen feathers, and whose lips and cheeks were shiny with honey. Uitzilopochtli was not, of course, to be fobbed off with mere dancing when Tetzcatlipuca was offered a specially selected youth. Another youth known as Yxteucalli, who accompanied the incarnation of Tetzcatlipuca during the festivals, was sacrificed to the god of war in similar fashion, and his head was stuck on another Tzonpantli next to that of his companion.

Moteçuçuma had asked Cortés first and Alvarado later for leave to celebrate these festivals, and the Spaniards had granted it, with the usual reservation against human sacrifices. This veto was, of course, overruled by the Mexicans, and the two youths were duly prepared in honour of the gods whose help was more needed than ever by their now invaded faithful. It so happened that the preparations for this festival, which in the nature of things, were bound to imply a certain "mobilisation," since captains and warriors were important actors in its chief ceremonies, took place when the credit of Cortés was at its lowest in Moteçuçuma's mind; so that, if we try to visualise things as they appeared to Alvarado, the picture was far from reassuring. He knew that Moteçuçuma had planned to destroy him and his men as soon as he heard that Narváez had been victorious; (14) he saw preparations which might be religious but looked nothing if not military, around him; he knew he was in a hopeless numerical inferiority; and the Mexicans ceased supplying them with food and maltreated their Indian servants (*naborias*) when they sought to procure it. These were not circumstances of a kind to improve a man's good judgment. On this background, when, as the picturesque Spanish saying goes, *his fingers would seem to him so many strangers*, Alvarado observed that some poles had been erected in the yards of the teocalli, obviously the Tzonpantli for the heads of the victims to be offered to the gods. He enquired what they were for: possibly some Mexican priest, hating the sight of the strangers, unwisely answered the inquisitive tongue, "To stick your silly heads on when we have killed you all"; for after all human beings are not always answering questions on oath before a court of law, and, moreover, the priests were then smarting under the irritating Christian veto against human sacrifices. The answer, reported to Alvarado, was accepted by him at its face value, the more readily as it fell on mental soil upset by fear. He seized one of the princes of Moteçuçuma's house, whom the Spaniards, with their quaint habit of applying their national dignities to the Mexicans called the *Infante*; this started the rebellion which evidently was brewing, which in fact, had been announced to Cortés by Moteçuçuma himself. Alvarado rushed to the teocalli; there was a crowd dancing ritual dances, and the two youths, their hair cut short, were awaiting sacrifice. Alvarado seized them and took them over to his headquarters where they were asked what was afoot; the two young men refused to answer. Alvarado had them tortured and assured them that if they spoke out no harm would come to them; they were freed and both said that they were to be sacrificed to their gods, which pleased them much, and that as soon as the festivals were over, which lasted twenty days, the Mexicans would fall upon the Christians. Francisco Alvarez, pro-curator of the Christians, then summoned Alvarado to forestall the Indian attack. A petty officer of Alvarado's army, one Juan Alvarez, happened the next day, Wednesday May 16th, 1520, to be busy col-lecting the meals for his comrades when he saw a crowd of Indians, many of them wounded, rushing out of the teocalli, then the Chris-tians, also running towards their fortified quarters and Alvarado himself, who shouted to him: "Run for safety and let the food go to the devil." "What is all this, sir?" Alvarez asked. And Alvarado answered: "By God, we have fallen on those knaves; as they meant to fall on us, we struck first." Alvarez heard his chief reckon that two or three thousand Indians had been killed, and comment that "as between knave and knave, the first to strike wins." These re-marks are worth noting—first because of the Spanish captains' tendency to exaggerate; Alvarado speaks of two or three thousand, when it is well ascertained that the total number of persons in the temple, many of whom escaped unscathed or wounded, was not more than six hundred to a thousand; then, because of the confession of humiliation implied in Alvarado's phrase "as between knave and knave," he knew he was not behaving up to his standards. (15)

The Christians were instantly besieged, and the first onslaught on their fortress that very day lasted till sunset and was so fierce that they feared not one of them would escape alive; Moteçuçuma spoke to the crowd from a terrace and tried to calm them down; then he advised Alvarado to free the Infante whose imprisonment had caused the trouble. Alvarado followed this advice, but the Infante, instead of calming down his people, came back next day, Thursday the 17th, with a formidable array of power, filling up streets, ter-races and canoes. The fight lasted three or four hours; the Spaniards made Moteçuçuma appear on the terrace again, but the crowd out-side demanded their Uei Tlatoani's liberty as a condition for peace; whereupon, Alvarado, with his usual rashness, drew out his dagger and pointing it at Moteçuçuma's heart, summoned him to keep his Indians quiet or else he and all the Indians would die. From this moment on, things settled down into a siege. (16)

* * *

Moteçuçuma, always well informed of events on the coast, learnt with surprise and possibly with dismay that Cortés had beaten Narváez. He took two decisions: to lessen the pressure put upon Alvarado by his warriors, whom, despite his situation as a prisoner of the Spanish garrison, he seems to have directed and, to a great extent, controlled; and to send messengers to Cortés to complain about Alvarado. Cortés received these messengers somewhat curtly and answered that he would return to Mexico and put things right. Policy? annoyance? self-assurance? arrogance?—time would soon show; but it seems certain that, from this moment on, Cortés' relations with Moteçuçuma took on a shade of contempt on the part of Cortés and of resentment on Moteçuçuma's, which was to prove tragic for the Spaniard and deadly for the Mexican. (17)

Cortés took a number of swift decisions on hearing the lamentable news that came from Mexico; he despatched a messenger to Alvarado announcing his victory over Narváez, and his march by quick stages to Mexico; he called back Velázquez de León and Ordás; and he spoke to the Narváez soldiers urging them to forget past differences and to form a truly united army to march on the common foe. The march on Mexico was marred by hunger and thirst, particularly during the crossing of the long desert before reaching Tlaxcala; though, thanks to the energy and devotion of the two men in charge of supplies, Ojeda and Márquez, and to the friendly cooperation of the Tlaxcatecs, disaster was avoided and the army was able to reach the edge of the lagoon. The siege became less and less severe as Cortés approached; when he arrived in Tetzcuco, the town was practically empty. Alvarado sent him two of his men, who gave him a first report on the fateful events and added that for the last thirteen days there had been no fighting. Cortés wrote cheerfully to the Spaniards in Cempoal, and really believed that his arrival had sufficed to settle the trouble. (18)

He went on more leisurely, and as the horsemen in the vanguard entered the town of Tepeyac, one of them, Solís Casquete, fell in the water, his horse having stuck a foot between two planks of the bridge and broken its leg. "Botello, the astrologer, who seemed to be a good sort of man, and knew Latin, and had been in Rome, and they said he was a necromancer, others said he had a familiar devil, and some called him the astrologer," held it in bad omen, for they were not entering with a good foot. (19) Next day, no native could be found to help with the luggage; all that Ojeda and Márquez, in search of them, would find was a *naboria*, hanging dead from the beam of a deserted house; farther on, a heap of bread and over five hundred hens had been left, obviously for them, in the middle of a square, but no human being was to be seen. Everybody in the Spanish army felt the deepest concern; Cortés did not fail to notice it. He met the facts with a merry face and said: "Gentlemen and friends, our labours are at an end and if there are no Indians to be seen this is due to fear and shame for having attacked our comrades; we shall chastise them and reconcile them with us and you shall all be in good fortune." These words were not merely a mask of good cheer; there are many signs that Narváez' conqueror felt overconfident at the time. (20)

He entered the capital on Midsummer day, having skirted the northern end of the lagoon, to arrive by way of Tepeyac; there were some Indians sitting at the doors of their houses, quiet and motionless, with an enigmatic smile on their thin lips as the Spaniards filed past; Cortés noticed that some bridges had been lifted, but still in his overconfident mood, he thought—as he writes to the Emperor— "that they did it for fear of what they had done and that my arrival would reassure them." He went straight to Alvarado's quarters: the gates were closed; most of the soldiers had climbed to the top of the walls to see the strong army which returned to release them from their siege. After a brief dialogue, in which Alvarado asked whether Cortés returned as free and powerful as he had left (he seems to have feared that Cortés might return as Narváez' lieutenant), the gates were opened and Alvarado, with a deep bow, gave up the keys of the fortress to his chief. (21)

The explanations that ensued between Cortés and his lieutenant must have been somewhat lacking in amenity. Cortés was not in the least satisfied by the version of events which Alvarado gave him. Yet this version was plausible enough and must be accepted as an accurate description of the situation, even though the way in which he met it was inadequate and wild; there obviously was a conspiracy to fall on the Spaniards. Cortés objected, "I am told they asked for your leave to celebrate their dances"; and Alvarado answered: "That is so; but I wished to fall on them when they were off their guard

so that they were not able later to wage war on me." Whereupon
Cortés angrily retorted: "You have made a mistake and behaved
most foolishly." And he left it at that. (22)

Alvarado deserved the rebuke and is rightly considered as the
chief culprit for the events of May 16th, 1520, and all that ensued.
It seemed certain that, had Sandoval, for instance, been in charge,
things might have occurred otherwise; all the narratives moreover
point to the conclusion that, though it is absurd to imagine, as some
have done, that Alvarado deliberately planned the attack on the
temple to secure the wealth of jewels which was worn by the dancers,
once the attack had begun there was much looting of the dead and
wounded by the soldiers, and that Cortés disliked this thoroughly.
In short, in Cortés' stiff attitude towards Alvarado there was an
element of justified resentment at an action both ill considered from
the military point of view and carried out in conditions which were
most dishonourable for the Spanish army.

But when all this has been admitted, it does not in the least
exhaust the complexity of Cortés' state of mind. He was annoyed
with Alvarado, as he had every right to be, but he was also annoyed
with him for less objective reasons. Cortés would have been more
than human had he not seen in Alvarado the instrument of that fate
which had so many times strewn obstacles in his way and which now
threatened to snatch his coveted prize from his hands. He had
vanquished Narváez; subconsciously he must have felt that he was
entitled to a return in triumph. "On the way," says Bernal Díaz,
"Cortés had told Narváez' captains, in self-praise, how much authority and power he had, and how everywhere they would come out to
greet him and to rejoice on his coming and would give him gold, and
that in Mexico he was the absolute master of all, including the great
Montezuma and his captains, and that they would give him gold
presents as was their wont, and on seeing that everything turned out
to be just the reverse of his thoughts, he was very angry and
haughty." (23)

This is the repressed personal resentment which he vented on
Alvarado, along with his legitimate resentment; he was moreover
annoyed also with himself; he was bound to feel the impact of
Alvarado's action on the tender spot left in his memory by the
massacre of Cholula—a day he no doubt would wish to forget. In

this subtle way, he was probably feeling that he himself was the real author of Alvarado's mistake. This was not only galling to his pride; it was also a bitter experience from the point of view of the Cholula events themselves, which now presented themselves to his eyes not, as he might have endeavoured to see them till that day, under the peculiarly favourable light which our own eyes cast on our own actions, but in the sharp and searching light under which he had seen Alvarado's similar deed. He was moreover surely thinking that he had made the wrong choice for the post of trust in which he had left Alvarado. But, most of all, he must have reflected that he had not acted wisely in leaving ninety men in Mexico at all; true he had in Mexico both his gold treasure and the even more valuable treasure of Moteçuçuma's person; but if he was to spare ninety men from the forces he was leading against Narváez, he should have devoted them to guarding both these treasures in some other town safer than the capital itself—even if it meant forcing Moteçuçuma to leave the city, as he had in fact threatened to do.

Finally, there is no doubt that at this stage in his career, Cortés was handicapped by an access of vanity which led him to attribute to his own personal merits what, in harder days, he had always acknowledged to be due to divine protection. His astounding victory over Narváez seems to have intoxicated him, both as a sign of his invincibility and as an increase in his material powers which was to enable him to perform even greater things than those he had so far achieved with far scantier troops. "Gentlemen and friends," Cervantes de Salazar makes him say to the Tlaxcatecs who had related to him the events of Mexico, "if, while I was in Mexico with the men you saw I had, they dared not rise against me, what do you think they can do now when I come with such a powerful army?" Words to which the good canon of Mexico appends a most fitting comment: "Truly, the confidence which Cortés, like David, put in the numbers of his army, was the cause of the misfortune which overcame him." There is a striking consensus of opinion in most chroniclers of the events of this period on the exhilaration of victory which then afflicted Cortés, so that we can give full credit to Cervantes de Salazar when he reports the opinion of Cortés himself on the matter: "he said many a time, and I heard him say so in His Majesty's Court, that, when he had fewer soldiers, he had conquered great victories because he put his trust only in God; and when he saw himself with so many soldiers, relying on them, he lost most of them and the honour and glory previously earned." (24)

*   *   *

We can only conjecture that these or similar reflections were then fermenting in Cortés' mind; but we know for certain that he passed at this moment of his life through a period of bad temper, irritability and overconfidence, which manifested itself particularly in his attitude towards Moteçuçuma. The dealings of the Uei Tlatoani with him were by no means straight. They have been read by most historians with excessive adherence to our own standards of ethical behaviour. Moteçuçuma did not act under impulses dictated by notions of right and wrong, good and evil; but by considerations of immediate expediency, as suggested by magic signs or religious interpretations of sacrifices. This difference in the mental-moral attitude behind the words must have added an all but insoluble obstacle to those due to mere differences of grammar and vocabulary between Spanish and Nauatl. Cortés, in his turn, interpreted Moteçuçuma's actions and words from his standpoint as a Spanish general dealing with a foreign monarch, i.e. a monarch in the European, sixteenth century meaning, a chief of knights. The misunderstanding was bound to be permanent and fundamental.

While still in Tetzcuco, on his way to Mexico, Cortés had received a message from Moteçuçuma intended to placate the anger which Moteçuçuma imagined Cortés would feel at what had occurred. (This, by the way, strengthens the view here maintained that the conspiracy to get rid of Alvarado and his troops had actually existed, and that Moteçuçuma felt insecure about his own responsibility in it.) The Uei Tlatoani assured Cortés that, as soon as the Spanish general entered the city, he would be the master in it, just as he used to be before his departure. Cortés with his usual dissimulation, had answered that he brought no anger against the Emperor and that he meant to do exactly what Moteçuçuma suggested. (25) He knew already that until news of his victory had reached Moteçuçuma, the Spanish garrison had been in daily danger of destruction, and that things had become easier then; which was a sufficient proof of Moteçuçuma's power and therefore of his responsibility; he may

M

not have thought, or if he did, he may not have feared, that Moteçuçuma was deliberately trapping him into Mexico in order to destroy him and all his men.

Yet this seems the only reasonable interpretation of the facts, and the only one which gives consistence to Moteçuçuma's actions from the day he warned Cortés to leave Mexico for good. What had happened since then to alter his mind? Nothing whatever; for the victory over Narváez could in no way alter a decision taken by Moteçuçuma on religious-magical grounds, and the reinforcements which it brought Cortés were not, as events were to show, sufficient to deter the Mexican warriors in trying to fulfill the wishes of their gods. A sentimental approach to the dramatic figure of Moteçuçuma, seen in a grotesque deformation through our European spectacles, should not prevent scholars from realising this fact. Moteçuçuma was not a noble, unfortunate and weak "King," doing his best for the Spaniards; neither was he a treacherous, black villain of a Mexican, plotting against the Spaniards under a smiling mask; he was the archpriest of a magic religion dealing with events as expediently as he and his colleagues in the service of the gods saw fit—ready, if possible, to get rid of the Spanish pest by drastic means; and he would have been utterly unable to see what was wrong with his attitude, since he had no conception of such a thing as "wrong."

Moteçuçuma could not be wrong in the sense in which Alvarado had been wrong. But had he had any inkling of the issue of wrong versus right, he would certainly have found a "moral" reinforcement for his plans in the very fact that Alvarado had massacred several hundreds of his nobility; as it was, he probably thought that Alvarado had acted under some magical inspiration which made it inevitable for him to behave as he did.

Such is the background on which we must try to see Cortés' attitude to Moteçuçuma at this crucial moment of the conquest.

CHAPTER TWENTY-THREE

The Flight from Mexico

T HERE is a curious thread running
through practically all the chronicles of the conquest to the effect that
the attack of the Mexicans against Cortés was due to the haughty
way in which he refused to see Moteçuçuma on his arrival back from
the coast. "Montezuma waited for Cortés to visit him as he used to
do. Cortés, as he came back so powerful, imagining that the whole
Mexican empire was not enough for him, angry over what had
happened, paid no attention to him and refused to visit him, and
this was the main cause of the destruction of his army." So says
Cervantes de Salazar, adding that Cortés sent Father Olmedo to visit
Moteçuçuma, and the Emperor said to him: "If the captain is not
angry, I shall give him a statue of him on a horse, all made of
gold." (1)

This legend came to blossom on a stem of fact: the attitude of
resentment against everything, including Moteçuçuma, and of overconfidence in his powers, which temporarily blinded Cortés; empha-
sized and pointed at as the cause of all the evil by those who would
have been glad to save their gold and let the conquest go, and who
on that account nursed a grudge against Cortés. For it should not
be imagined—contrary to what this legend implies—that what Moteçuçuma had in mind was to atone for his war on Alvarado with
presents of gold and leave it at that; what he had in mind was to
offer more gold to the Spaniards on condition they left at once, not
merely the city of Mexico, but the whole country as well. This was,
we have maintained, the only attitude consistent with the line of
action taken by Moteçuçuma from the day Cortés had attacked the

335

Great Teocalli; it is fully confirmed by the evidence of eyewitnesses and tallies also with the narrative of events as told both by Bernal Díaz and by Cortés himself. (2) Moteçuçuma, says Bernal Díaz, sent two prominent men to Cortés to ask him to call on their master, and Cortés, in a temper, answered: "Let that dog alone, who will not even hold a market and gives us no food." Cortés was of course fully aware of Moteçuçuma's ill will. He realised that the Uei Tlatoani had still enough authority over his countrymen for his word to make all the difference, and he rightly saw in Moteçuçuma's refusal to hold the market in the usual way a blatant proof of the Uei Tlatoani's enmity. Whether this resentment should have led him to the uncompromising and defiant attitude which he adopted is a different matter. In Bernal Díaz' record, the scene continues with some expostulations from four of his captains—none of them, by the way, men who could teach prudence to their chief. Their words greatly incensed Cortés, "as they had a colour of reprimand, and he asked: 'What consideration need I have for a dog who was intriguing in secret with Narváez and now, as you may see, will give us no food?' " Whereupon he sent a kind of ultimatum to Moteçuçuma to hold a market at once or else he would strike. (3)

Yet there are a number of circumstances which must be noted to appraise the situation more accurately. First, the lack of time: Cortés arrived on St. John's day (June 24th) and the Mexicans attacked on the 25th; he had no leisure left during which to consider the situation. Cortés, moreover, was justified in trying with his eight hundred Spaniards and eighty horse to intimidate a monarch he had conquered with four hundred foot and eight horse. Finally, Cortés set free Cuitlahuac. When Moteçuçuma received Cortés' ultimatum, he answered that he was a prisoner and his kinsmen also; he suggested that Cortés should free one of them, who would then take all the measures which Cortés desired. Cortés agreed to liberate Cuitlahuac. He was not conversant with the constitutional laws of the Mexican Empire; Cuitlahuac, brother of Moteçuçuma, called together the *Tlatocan*, or Council, which immediately deposed Moteçuçuma and appointed Cuitlahuac in his stead. Thus was Cortés manœuvred by Moteçuçuma into a position of extreme danger because now the magical powers of the Chief-Priesthood were in the hands of an enemy at large, while the Spanish army held a prisoner the empty shell of power in the body of the deposed monarch. (4)

We must therefore give all its due weight to the observation made by Bernal Díaz, who after laying stress on Cortés' somewhat petulant attitude towards Moteçuçuma, goes on to say: "The prominent Mexicans took in the insulting character of the words which Cortés uttered on their Lord [. . .] and just as they understood it, so they conveyed it to Montezuma, and either because it angered him or because it was already arranged that they should wage war on us, a quarter of an hour had not gone by when a soldier came back in a great hurry, very badly wounded, and [who had been sent to] fetch some Indian women who belonged to Cortés, one of them a daughter of Montezuma, whom Cortés had apparently left in the custody of the Lord of Tacuba [. . .], and the soldier said that the whole city and the way he had come were full of warriors, armed with all kinds of weapons, and that they had taken away the Indian women from him and had he not let them go, they would already have seized hold of him to throw him into a canoe and take him to be sacrificed." (5) Real war had begun.

*   *   *

Cortés sent Diego de Ordás with four hundred soldiers and a few horsemen to find out what was happening; but this captain and his men had not advanced far into the town when they had to beat a hasty retreat, surrounded by enemies who killed a number of them and inflicted three wounds on Ordás himself; when they reached the Spanish fortress, Ordás and his men found it besieged by a furious and noisy multitude of warriors through which they had to hew a way for themselves not without much loss on both sides. As for the plight of the besieged Spaniards, Cortés writes to the Emperor: "The stones they threw with their slings were so many that it seemed as if the sky rained them, and the arrows were so many that the walls and courtyards were full of them so that we could hardly walk." The Mexicans set fire to the building, and in order to stop the flames the Spaniards knocked down part of the wall; this made a dangerous gap in the defences, which Cortés had to hold with his musketeers and artillery. The fight lasted the whole day, and the Spaniards spent the night preparing for the next morning and tending their wounded, who were more than eighty. (6)

Cortés was among the wounded. His left hand was badly injured by a stone. He must have spent a night of heart-searchings, in spite of the feverish activity he had to devote to details; he decided to take the offensive next morning, "so that"—says Bernal Díaz—"they should feel our strength and courage better than on the day before"; but the Mexicans were so numerous that the Spanish artillery shot at them without aiming, and the gaps caused by the huge stone balls were immediately refilled. Against such a sea of absolutely fearless warriors, nothing was of any avail, since the Mexicans could afford an unlimited number of losses and "some three or four soldiers who had been in Italy [. . .] swore many a time to God that they had never seen such fierce wars between Christians nor against the artillery of the King of France nor of the Great Turk." (7)

After yet another day of fighting, Cortés could behold an army which that day had lost again more than ten men dead and fifty or sixty wounded to add to the eighty wounded and four to ten dead of the first day. His position was becoming more precarious every day. He decided to build three battle-chariots in order to meet his enemies in the streets of the town, and in particular to fight against those who attacked his men from the terraces. He devoted the whole night and the following day to this task, taking no heed of the insults hurled at the Spaniards by the infuriated Mexicans because they would not come out and fight. Each of these chariots carried twenty men who, through slits on the sides, shot their muskets and crossbows from a higher level; while, supported by them, other soldiers on foot advanced carrying tools to demolish houses and barricades.

While this work was proceeding in the big courtyard of the fortress, the Mexicans hurled furious assaults against its walls; and though many of them were killed, there were many more ready to follow; the Spaniards, some of whom had already picked up a certain knowledge of *nauatl*, heard their fierce enemies joyfully anticipating the sacrifice of the whites to "Witchywolves" and how the gruesome god's adepts would then feast on their bodies. In the midst of this savage battle, Moteçuçuma appeared on the top of the wall; there was a silence, and the deposed monarch appealed to his countrymen to cease the war. Cortés says, or at any rate, leaves it to be understood, that Moteçuçuma volunteered to do so; this is hardly credible, and Cortés had an interest in lending this role to the ex-Emperor, since his men were inclined to reproach him for his excessive harshness towards Moteçuçuma. Bernal Díaz' account would appear to be nearer the truth. The Spaniards were the hard-pressed party; it was but natural that the idea of making use of Moteçuçuma's influence (which they still thought unimpaired) should have come from them. Though in the language of European institutions, the words which Bernal Díaz lends to Moteçuçuma ring true: "I believe that I will not be useful at all for stopping the war, for they have raised another lord and they are determined that you should not leave this place alive." (8) After some parleying, not directly with Cortés, whom Moteçuçuma refused to see, but with Olid and Father Olmedo, the ex-Emperor agreed to address his countrymen. His words cannot have been very convincing and, in any case, they no longer emanated from a man in authority. Young Cuauhtemoc was amongst the impatient listeners below; he was eighteen, a prince of the royal blood, son of Ahuitzotl, Moteçuçuma's predecessor, and of Tlillacapantzin, a princess who descended from Acamapitl, first King of Mexico. This young man was unable to stand Moteçuçuma's half-hearted objurgations: "What is this Span-iard's wife talking about? He is a vile man and should be punished." And he shot an arrow at him. A volley of stones followed the arrow; Moteçuçuma fell back, covered with blood; three stones had wounded him, one on the head, one in an arm and one in the leg.

He lingered on for three days, possibly weakened more by loss of spirit than by loss of blood. And when he died, "Cortés wept for him and all our captains and soldiers; and there were some amongst us," adds Bernal Díaz, "who knew him and had commerce with him who wept for him as much as if he had been our father, nor should we wonder at this, considering his kindness." (9)

*   *   *

On Thursday June 28th, 1520, the three wooden war chariots sallied forth much to the bewilderment of the Mexicans. Cortés had evidently made up his mind to leave Mexico, and had even selected the way out: the Tlacopan (Tacuba) causeway, leading towards the west, for it was shorter, though narrower than the others. He therefore devoted his efforts, under the protection of the new weapon he had contrived, to securing a number of bridges and terraces along this road; but though the Spaniards, with the help of three thousand Tlaxcatecs, fought the whole morning, they were unable to make much headway against the seething masses of their relentless enemies, and towards midday they "returned in sadness to the fortress." This failure of the Spaniards put so much heart into the Mexicans that by a bold stroke they captured the Great Teocalli, replacing Uitzilopochtli and Tetzcatepuca in the shrines from which Cortés had expelled them; the Great Teocalli rose just opposite the Spanish fortress and was therefore a military position of the first importance; the Mexicans stocked it with abundant provisions of food and water and garrisoned it with five hundred of their leading warriors— "prominent persons," says Cortés, but we know that "prominent persons" in warlike Mexico meant very brave persons since courage in battle was the selective principle for leadership. Cortés felt that both for moral and for military reasons it was imperative to storm the Great Teocalli; he sent there his chamberlain, Escobar, with one hundred men; they tried three times to fight their way to the top and were repulsed by thick volleys of stones and arrows; on hearing which, Cortés, having had his buckler tied to his arm, for his left hand was still useless, put himself at the head of his men and led them up the one hundred-odd steps. "Here," says Bernal Díaz, "Cortés showed himself very much of a man, as he always was." He fought for three hours but won a complete victory and, with his followers, destroyed the garrison and set fire to the towers. "Your Majesty may well believe," Cortés writes to the Emperor, "that this tower was so difficult to take that had not God broken their wings twenty of them would have sufficed to bar the ascent to one thousand; though they fought bravely till they died." (10)

He adds, not without satisfaction, that "they lost some of their pride when we took this fortress from them"; and, with his usual tactics, he tried to drive home his advantage by addressing the Mexican leaders from one of the terraces of his headquarters; but, though impressed, the Mexicans were not depressed, and gave him to understand that they were determined to get rid of the Spaniards at all costs, for even if they were to die at the rate of twenty-five thousand to one, they told him, the Spaniards would come to an end

first; they knew, moreover, that the Spaniards lacked both food
and water. There was nothing left but to fight, and so, that very
night, Cortés sallied forth with a number of his companions and
burnt three hundred houses in one street and many more on his way
back. Meanwhile, during the same night, his much battered war
chariots were repaired, and at dawn Cortés himself, who seems to
have been tireless, was again out fighting to secure control over the
Tacuba causeway which was the only way of salvation left them;
there were eight "bridges" on it, or rather eight gaps over which
bridges had existed; after much hard fighting, he took four of them,
filled up the gaps with the rubble of destroyed houses and barricades,
and burnt down all the houses on both sides of the road from their
headquarters to the last of the bridges won. Next morning, an
innumerable crowd had again taken possession of the road, but the
Spaniards fought so well that not only they won back all the bridges
lost, but some horsemen reached Tacuba, on the mainland, while
Cortés remained to supervise the work on the bridges. He was busy,
with his eye on the job, when Alvarado and Sandoval with eight or
ten more horsemen returned from Tacuba very gay, with flowers
in their hands, much elated by their victories, galloping to the mainland and back. "Roses and nosegays," said Cortés bluntly, "are no
plumes for war-helmets and you'd better be quiet rather than irritate
the enemy with your light-hearted ways." (11) Hardly had he
spoken when a messenger came to announce that the Indians asked
for peace. Cortés left all his men and guns in charge of the bridge
and with two horsemen went to the parley; he was offered complete
peace on condition that two high priests he held as prisoners were
released; he agreed readily and, having seen the Mexicans take
measures which seemed to forecast immediate peace, he went to the
fortress to eat; but he was soon called out to fight again, for the
peace offer had been but a stratagem to obtain the release of the
teotecutli, whose priestly offices were needed for the consecration of
Cuitlahuac. (12)

Out he went again to reconquer the four bridges which had been
lost. With his cavalry he fought over all of them, not only the first
four, but the others as well, till they reached the mainland, but on
the way back he found that his infantry had been unable to defend
them, and all the eight gaps in the causeway had been cut again by

M*

the patient and stubborn Indians, while on both sides, innumerable canoes full of warriors were waiting for them. The riders fought their way back, Cortés having to defend the last bridge single-handed while his horsemen disentangled themselves from the water where they had fallen, then leapt over the gap, "though with much difficulty, for there were nearly six feet across and neither the horse nor we were wounded because we were heavily armed, though we felt it in our bodies." (13)

That night, he left strong garrisons at all the bridges and, with the experience of this continuous fighting for the vital causeway, he struck on the idea of building a portable bridge to be carried by forty men. Botello, the astrologer, went about reminding his companions how four days earlier he had foretold that unless they left that very night, they would all perish. (14) Though there were some who disliked the idea, most of his men insisted on leaving. "All the men of my company requested me many times to leave, and as all or most of them were wounded, and so badly that they could not fight, I decided to leave that very night" (15): so he writes to the Emperor, with the accent of a man who does not like the idea of running away even in desperate circumstances. Nor was the military aspect of the flight his only concern at the time, for he was obviously thinking also of his war-chest, and of the priceless treasure put aside for the Emperor, on which he counted so much for his conquest of the Spanish Court. This preoccupation led him to one of his most fatal errors: he had the treasure brought into one of the halls of the Palace and delivered the King's fifth over to the royal officials, Alonso Dávila and Gonzalo Mexía, to whom he gave, says Bernal Díaz, "seven horses, wounded and lame, and one mare and many Tlaxcatec friends, more than eighty" to carry it out; as for the rest, he let every man help himself as he wished. The scene may be imagined in that tense night which was to be the last of their lives for most of them; the pale faces, till then wan and drawn with lack of food and sleep, most of them swathed in bandages, suddenly flushed with the prospect of instant wealth, the feverish eyes on the heap of jewels and ingots, their eager hands grasping at the fabulous wealth, pockets bulging, shirts, helmets and armour turned into baggage; so that while the wise ones, such as Bernal Díaz, were content with little, "four chalchivitls, which I quickly hid between my breast and my armour, which were most useful later to cure my wounds and to eat their value," for most of them

> All that diabolic metal
> For their bodies proved as fatal
> As it had for their poor souls. (16)

Cortés had put his vanguard under Sandoval and Ordás; he himself, with Olid, Dávila and one hundred young soldiers, was to march in the centre, ready to lend a hand wherever trouble might arise; the rear was in charge of Alvarado and Velázquez de León; while two of Narváez' captains and thirty soldiers would be in charge of the prisoners (one son and two daughters of Moteçuçuma, Cacamatzin and his brother "The Swallow," then King of Tetzcuco by the grace of Cortés), of Doña Marina and Doña Luisa and of the gold. (17)

The night (June 30th, 1520) was black and misty, and it rained enough to make the road slippery for the horses; shortly before midnight Sandoval and his men stole towards the causeway, escorting the forty tlamemes who were carrying the portable bridge; the first gap was passed without resistance, but the Mexican watch gave the alarm and before the unfortunate Spaniards had reached the second, the road and the lagoon were filled with yelling warriors; Sandoval and Cortés broke the resistance and swam across all the gaps to the mainland; hardly had he left the causeway, when he heard some of his horsemen shout: "Sir Captain, do wait, for they say we are running away and leaving them to die on the bridges." "We have escaped by sheer miracle," retorted Cortés and, turning round, he rushed back onto the causeway: Spaniards, Indians, horses, guns, prisoners and gold had fallen into the lake, bridging over the gaps with their bulk and bodies. Cortés gathered together the scanty remains of his army and spurred them forward while he protected their rear, fighting every foot of the way with three or four horsemen and about twenty foot. Alvarado, wounded, a spear in his hand, on foot, having lost his beautiful and famous mare, was the only captain left in the rearguard. Velázquez de León with his golden Swagger, lay, an inert plank of a human bridge, between two sections of the deadly causeway. (18)

*   *   *

Tacuba was not so safe after all; Cortés found his army listless and gregarious, herded together in the middle of the central square, waiting for its leader. He led them to a hilltop where a teocalli would do as a temporary fortress; the march was constantly harassed by the relentless enemy, for "out of the twenty-four horses that remained not one was able to run, not a horseman able to raise an arm, not a foot soldier able to move." "As for eating, not even in imagination," says Bernal Díaz. (19)

Next day he counted his losses. There were about six hundred Spaniards missing, including a number who had remained in Axayacatl's Palace, either, as some say, because they would not leave without first loading themselves with gold, or, as is more likely, because, finding they were unable to fight their way through, they returned to their fortress. They were all finally sacrificed to Witchywolves. (20) "And I forgot to write," adds Bernal Díaz to his tale of woe, "how happy we felt at seeing alive Doña Marina and Doña Luisa, Xicotenga's daughter, and also a woman known as María de Estrada, the only woman of Castille we had in Mexico." (21)

Day after day the broken army wended its way towards Tlaxcala; those who were still able to do some fighting went in the vanguard or in the rearguard; the wounded who could walk, even if lame, marched in the middle; the wounded who could not walk were conveyed on the backs of the horses which were too disabled to fight; in this guise, fighting most of the day, they passed by the lagoon of Zumpango and Xaltocan towards Citlaltepec, which they found empty of inhabitants but, fortunately, well stocked with food. Here they rested from the 4th to the 5th of July, when they reached Xoloc, where, on the 6th, they had to fight with a strong force of Mexicans, and Cortés was twice badly wounded in the head, which he felt less than the loss of a horse, "for"—he writes to the Emperor —"we had no other safety, after God's, than that of our horses"; withal, they were glad to eat it, for they were ravenous, "leaving neither skin nor any trace of it." (22) He felt the enemy was becoming more and more threatening, and so he gave orders that the wounded were to do without the horses, for he was sure he would need all his strength soon; and so it was; for the next day, July 7th, they beheld the plains of Apam, within sight of Otumba, covered with Mexican troops. Cortés addressed his men, gave them his usual tactical instructions cool and matter-of-fact, then his inspiring encouragement, calling forth the help of "God, St. Mary and the name of the Lord St. James." The fight was so close that "we hardly could tell them from us." The situation was saved by Cortés' instinctive habit of striking at the head: he saw a magnificent war chief who, followed by a squadron of captains, carried a brilliant standard made of gold-netting: he was the *Ciuacoatl* or Serpent-Woman, commander in chief, brandishing the great standard or *tlahuizmatlaxopilli*. Cortés, says Bernal Díaz, attacked the Ciuacoatl and made him lower his banner; and another of his captains, Juan de Salamanca, thrusting his spear at the Serpent-Woman, wrenched the plumed crest from his head and chivalrously gave it over to Cortés. All this scene is known to us through Bernal Díaz; Cortés is content to tell the Emperor that "we struggled in this way a good part of the day, till God wished it that one of their army died who must have been a very important person, because with his death all that war came to an end." (23)

Having thus won the day known as the Battle of Otumba, they cast longing glances at the Tlaxcala Sierras which could be seen from the battlefield; their hopes of longed-for rest were mixed with fears lest the friendship of the Tlaxcatecs should break down at the sight of their discomfiture. "He begged us," says Bernal Díaz, "not to annoy the Tlaxcalans nor take anything from them, and this he intended as a warning to the Narváez ones, who were not used to be under the rule of Captains in war as we were and added that he hoped in God we would find them friendly and loyal." (24) The following day, July 8th, they arrived in Hueyotlipan (Galipan in Cortés' letter), in Tlaxcatec territory; they were well received and fed, though they had to pay for their food with gold; and here Cortés was relieved to receive the visit of Maxixcatzin and old Xicotencatl who assured him of their constancy. At their request, Cortés marched on to Tlaxcala on July 12th. He was admirably received and housed in Maxixcatzin's house, while Xicotencatl housed his own son-in-law Alvarado with his daughter Doña Luisa. Here the battered army found a safe rest and was able to lick its wounds. (25)

CHAPTER TWENTY-FOUR

Rise After the Fall

FOR Cortés, this stay in Tlaxcala was a much needed respite for recovery and reflection. He had to attend to his wounds, particularly those in his head which with exertion and neglect had become much worse; Tlaxcala was not abundant in medicines and material for cures; many of his men died or remained permanently disabled, and he himself lost the use of two fingers of his left hand. (1) A strong fit of military temper seems to have contributed to endanger his health, at this point. He had left in Tlaxcala a Captain Juan Páez or Pérez, with eighty men, probably not fit to fight in Mexico; on his return, he learnt that Maxixcatzin had offered Páez one hundred thousand Tlaxcatecs if he dared to go to the help of Cortés; Páez had been content to answer that such a general and such an army would need no help—in which, it must be owned, he was but imitating Cortés himself both in his self-assurance and his caution in the use of Tlaxcatec help inside Mexican territory. Yet Cortés was unable to restrain his wrath and hurled a torrent of abuse at the unfortunate captain, calling him a coward and a captain for hares and not for men and threatening him with the gallows if he uttered a word. This fit of fury made him ill, and the wounds in his head had to be operated upon; which, bearing in mind the state of the surgical sciences in those days, may be considered the deadliest danger this hardy man ever had to face. (2)

Well treated by the Tlaxcatecs, he had leisure to review his situation from that vantage-point of relative security. He had lost many

346

captains and men, and was reduced to a position about equal in numbers to that he had at the outset, though worse in material weapons, for he had no artillery and no gunpowder. He had lost much prestige with the men in his army who had come over with Narváez, though he seems to have kept intact his hold over those whom Bernal Díaz, not without a touch of pride, calls "the men of Cortés." He had lost all the moral authority he once had won over the Mexicans, while, though the Tlaxcalans had remained faithful to him, there was now in their friendship a touch of affection bordering on pity which must have been galling to the one-time "God." But all these losses seem to have thrown him back from his petulant self-confidence to that trust in God which had been the source of his strength in the first phase of the conquest. "And Cortés said to us," writes Bernal Díaz, "that though we were few, for we remained but four hundred and forty, with twenty horses and twelve crossbowmen and seven musketeers and no gunpowder, and all wounded and lame and our arms in slings, we should consider carefully how Our Lord Jesus Christ had been pleased to let us escape alive, wherefore we must always thank and praise Him, and that we had shrunk back again to the numbers which had come over with him and had first entered Mexico." (3)

This reduction of his army to its original numbers must have worked in his mind as a direct hint from on high to signify that divine favours can be withdrawn as easily as they are granted. Such a warning might have discouraged a less brave and a less religious man; he seems to have been spurred to action by it, as if the Lord in Whom he had put his faith had meant to favour him by withdrawing all the military strength which had temporarily led him astray into self-confidence and pride.

* * *

He soon had occasion to draw on his recovered spiritual strength. Despite the sincere friendship of the two old Tlaxcatec caciques, all was not well in Tlaxcala. The once proud *teul* had come back beaten; his men could no longer travel all over the land without fear of attack from the natives, and many had thus been murdered on the roads which Cortés' name had till then kept safe. An expedition which had left Tlaxcala for Mexico, with property belonging to Cortés, worth in all over fifty thousand pesos, had been destroyed and despoiled by the Mexicans. (4) The old spell had vanished. Xicotencatl the Young thought the moment had come to get rid of the Spaniards and seek the alliance of Cuitlahuac. From the point of view of the Indian nations, it does seem the wisest policy which could be followed at the moment, and young Xicotencatl stands out as a spirited and farseeing leader of the type of Cacamatzin. The older men, including his old father, were, however, of another opinion; the matter came to a head upon the arrival of an embassy from Mexico, urging an alliance to liberate their common territory from the whites. The Council received the ambassadors with the usual ceremony and in the presence of Xicotencatl the Young; as was required by custom, the ambassadors withdrew after their message had been delivered, and the Council debated on it. Young Xicotencatl spoke with fire in favor of the Mexican proposal, but Maxixcatzin argued with no less force against it, and the discussion became so heated that the young general was violently hurled down the steps of the platform on which the Council deliberated, with his clothes torn to shreds; nor would his body itself have fared better but for the intervention of his aged father. (5)

This episode vividly shows that Cortés had won a profound ascendancy over the men of Tlaxcala, a triumph due to his political ability. Whatever the effect of this or that action of Cortés on our mind, the general line of his policy, attitude and behaviour, was acceptable, indeed highly commendable, to the natives who were his immediate problem. Two elementary principles determined this attitude: force and justice. They are admirably perceived and expressed by Bernal Díaz in a sentence in which he sums up the fruit gathered by Cortés as a result of his wisdom and spirit during these weeks of recovery: "And from that day Cortés won so much fame among all the people of New Spain, on the one hand as very just in what he did, and on the other as very brave and feared by all [. . .] and such was the authority and 'being' and command which Cortés had acquired that Indians brought their disputes before him from far distant lands, particularly over *cacique-ships* and lordships, for as in those days there was so much smallpox and so many caciques died, the Indians came to Cortés for a decision as to who should be the new cacique and how lands, vassals and wealth were to be distributed, as if he were the absolute lord of all the country." (6)

*   *   *

But the man who had stolen out of Mexico on a night of grief and shame did not rise again to this position of eminence without hard struggle. The first obstacle he had to conquer came from within his own army. After twenty days of rest, he had deemed it necessary to undertake a military operation in order to restore his army's morale; he selected for the purpose the State of Tepeaca in which some of his men had been killed on their way to Mexico, and which, moreover, happened to house considerable Mexican forces. (7) This decision split the army: the well-to-do soldiers and captains who had come over with Narváez, objected violently and longed to be back in their comfortable and safe Cuba. They found a wealth of arguments for presenting this root-wish of their souls, but Cortés argued them down, first "lovingly," then stubbornly, and refused to be impressed even when they put before him a formal summons to give up war and return to the Rich Town, drafted in verbose legalese by the King's Notary. In his usual style, he engineered a powerful opposition in the ranks of his old soldiers, and although he had but few men and horses and no gunpowder, he made them all accept the idea of new campaigns, though he promised that, if an opportunity arose, he would allow all those who wished it to return to Cuba. (8)

What were his reasons for this stubborn resistance to return to Veracruz? "And I," he writes to Charles V, "bearing in mind that to show little spirit in the presence of the natives, particularly of our friends, would result in their leaving us more readily and turning against us, bearing in mind that fortune always helps the daring and that we were Christians, and trusting in the great kindness and mercy of God [. . .] resolved on no account to march down the Passes towards the sea; but, on the contrary, leaving aside all thought of the hardship and of any dangers which might threaten us, I told them that I would never leave this land unattended; for I should deem it not only shameful for my person, and most dangerous for all of us, but a very great treason to your Majesty." (9)

*   *   *

This campaign of Tepeaca which took place in the summer of 1520, was waged with the help of two thousand Tlaxcatecs who came in beautiful order and magnificent attire, all dressed in white, their helmets and bucklers made of rich plumes, marching to the sound of drums and trumpets, in ranks of twenty abreast, under the several banners of the republic, the chief of which were that of Xicotencatl, a white heron, embroidered in featherwork, and that of Chichime-catecuhtli, an eagle of gold and silver within a circle of green feathers. When this brilliant army, glittering in the sun, arrived in Cortés' camp, he received it with much joy and courtesy and embraced its captains; and they, no doubt grateful, repaid his hospitality with a rare ceremony in which Maxixcatzin's son was admitted as a fully grown warrior, or, in the Spanish idiom, armed a knight. A wide ring was made with the banners of the Tlaxcatec army, round which Tlaxcatecs and Spaniards eagerly gathered, drawn by the riot of colour and by the noise of warlike instruments; richly dressed, with feather-adorned buckler and headdress, the young man waited quietly within the ring, while at the other end of it, a group of chiefs and priests watched the sacrifice of some Mexican spies; one of the chiefs, holding in his hand the gory heart of one of the victims, challenged the youngster to cover his face with his buckler and threw the heart at him; then, crossing the ring, slapped the young man in the face, leaving five gory traces on his cheek; the youth stood unmoved—the ceremony was over and, though Cortés did not like it, it was well meant. (10)

The campaign ended with the complete surrender of Tepeaca and the expulsion of the Mexican forces which occupied it. From the strategic point of view it was most important as an indispensable preliminary to the final operations against Mexico, which Cortés was determined to subdue; but it is more important still for the history of the conquest in that it provided the pretext for the establishment of slavery.

This episode of Cortés' life has not always been understood in its historical setting. We must start from the assumption that, in those days, prisoners of war, unless they were Christians, were automatically considered as slaves. Instead, therefore, of hotly condemning Cortés for having started to make slaves in the Tepeaca campaign, we must praise his originality for not having made any slaves till then. What are his reasons for this change of policy? He gives three to the Emperor: "for apart from having killed the said Spaniards, and rebelled against Your Highness' service, they all eat human flesh [. . .] and also [. . .] to put some fright into the Mexicans, and because they are so many that if some great and cruel punishment were not inflicted on them, they would never mend their ways." (11) None of these reasons sounds very convincing: the first crime was sufficiently punished by the military expedition itself; the second could hardly be counted against the Indians of Tepeaca, when Cortés' own allies, the Tlaxcatecs, feasted on their war prisoners under his eyes; there is abundant evidence to prove that Cortés turned a blind eye on this practice so long as he needed the military help of Tlaxcala. (12) The third motive sounds more plausible, and may have contributed to his decision. But, in my opinion, the real reason why he bethought himself of slavery *at this precise moment* was that his war-chest was at the bottom of the lake in Mexico and that he needed funds for himself and some hope of immediate gain for his grumbling soldiers.

For his chief thought was ever the reconquest of Mexico. In his mind he had come to stay, and he considered himself as the natural founder and populator of a new kingdom for the Spanish crown. In this strategic and political state of mind he decided to found a town in Tepeaca territory, on a spot which held the two roads from the coast, that through Xicochimalco and that through Ahuilitzapan, and the two roads into Mexico, the one between the two volcanoes and the other one through Río Frío. The town was founded at the beginning of September and was named Secure of the Frontier (Segura de la Frontera). (13)

*   *   *

Fortune did come to the help of the daring. A number of ships, one after another, swam into his waters, so to speak, while seeking, somewhat aimlessly, to imitate his exploits, or to come to the rescue of those who had tried and failed. His first care, in Tlaxcala, had been to find out whether his establishment in Veracruz was still safe. He had sent Gonzalo de Sandoval with a few natives to guide him thither keeping out of the beaten roads, and, on the return of his trusted messenger, had been much relieved to find that Veracruz was safe and on friendly terms with the natives round it. (14) His attention was, however, drawn to districts closer to him, for the Indian city-states in the vicinity seemed to prefer his sway to that of the Mexicans. The expeditions to Cuauhquechollan (Guacachula), Ocuituco (Ocupatuyo) and Itzocan (Izzuacan) were thus determined at least as much by the natives' own initiative and desire to get rid of the Mexicans as by Cortés' own plans. Messengers came from Cuauhquechollan to ask Cortés' protection against the Mexicans; they declared themselves ready to fall on the Mexican captains who occupied their city if Cortés sent troops to help them against thirty thousand Mexicans who had camped in the heights outside the city. Cortés sent Ordás with soldiers mostly of Narváez' old army; they returned without fighting because in Guaxocingo they were told the whole story was a trap organised by the Mexicans with the connivance of the men of Cuauhquechollan and of Guaxocingo. Ordás arrested the governors of Guaxocingo, though they had always been the allies of the Spaniards. Cortés' soldiers laughed at him. And Ordás, who was a brave captain and could afford a laugh at his own expense, laughed also and swore he would never go out again with rich soldiers but would take poor ones, such as Cortés' were, who were not afraid of risks. Cortés, whose insight into native affairs was deeper than that of most of his captains and who was also more inclined to trust those he had once conquered, freed the Guaxocingo caciques, went to Cuauhquechollan himself and, not without hard fighting, expelled the Mexicans from the district. (15)

This victory brought the spontaneous submission of Ocuituco, an important city owing to its situation at the foot of the Popocatepetl. Its messengers came with fear and trembling, for the city had been somewhat remiss and had waited till the Mexicans had been banished beyond its horizon to acknowledge the authority of the whites; but Cortés, who could be ruthless with an enemy, never rejected the hand of friendship, however late it might be offered, and he was magnanimous. He wanted, moreover, to settle this town as soon as possible in order to pass on to Itzocan, where there was also a Mexican garrison to be dislodged; Cortés' army marched on the city followed by a crowd of friendly natives whom he reckons at one hundred thousand. He found the city deserted by its population but garrisoned by about five thousand men; and after some stiff fighting, he offered them peace and good treatment under Spanish allegiance. The natives accepted the offer, and Cortés, having heard their opinions on the subject of who should succeed their leader, who had fled to Mexico, chose a boy of ten, direct descendant of the fugitive, with a council of Regency composed of two men of Itzocan and one of Cuauhquechollan. (16)

Cortés was gradually recovering his prestige and driving out the Mexicans from their advanced posts. Now and then he received the encouragement of fresh reinforcements, coming to him, as he might think, from heaven. He was still in Tepeaca when an old acquaintance arrived from Veracruz. This was Pedro Barba, the same hidalgo who, as Velázquez' lieutenant in Habana, had been somewhat remiss in carrying out the Governor's instructions to prevent Cortés' departure for Yucatán. Cortés was pleased to see him, but more so to know that he brought one horse and one mare, not to speak of thirteen soldiers. Barba had come with a letter from Velázquez to Narváez asking him to send back Cortés a prisoner, at once; but Caballero, the Admiral appointed by Cortés in Veracruz, had boarded Barba's caravel with a few well armed sailors and after the usual courtesies and small chat, coolly answered Barba's question: "How is the Sir Captain Narváez, and how is he handling Cortés?" with a "Very well; Cortés is in flight with twenty companions"; and as Barba was content to be taken to land on this news, Caballero had him arrested as soon as he had left his ship. (17) But Cortés quickly healed the wound by promoting Barba to a captaincy of crossbowmen and showing him great favour; within a week another ship sent by Velázquez with supplies for Narváez, was received in similar manner; it brought eight soldiers, six crossbars, string for ropes (a precious necessity in the army) and a mare. Three more ships arrived in succession, all sent by Garay from Jamaica to rescue the first expedition under Pinedo, which apparently had been lost: the first was made up of sixty men, all sick, green and potbellied; the second comprised more than fifty hefty soldiers and thirty-seven horses; the third was well provided with weapons, ten horses, many crossbows and about forty men, wearing thick, cotton-padded vests which no arrow could pass. The army, evidently put into a good humour by these constant accessions of strength, quickly nicknamed the three sets of newcomers, the "green-potbellies," the "heftybacks" and "the donkey-saddles." (18)

* * *

The founding of a town was always for Cortés a welcome opportunity to turn his attention from "arms" to "letters." His pen was for him but a subtler form of his sword. He began by setting up all the machinery of a city, in the Spanish municipal tradition; governor, *alcaldes*, *regidores* and other royal officials were appointed; the crier warned all those who wished to be citizens of the new city to register; and a first set of laws was enacted prohibiting blasphemy and games of cards. But it was not in order to stop the two favourite habits of all soldiers that Cortés had founded a town. He was a statesman, that is, a man of law and order, whose career had begun by an act of anarchy. This contradiction in the inner pattern of his life haunted him; and he was obsessed by the desire to exorcise it by means of legal documents. In the dramatic episodes of his struggle with Mexico, he writes to the Emperor, "all the deeds and writs which I had concluded with the natives of these lands were lost"; Cortés was ever careful that his legal pen should countersign whatever his sword had achieved. (19)

The city of Segura de la Frontera was hardly founded when its archives were nourished with several documents born of this preoccupation of its founder. His agent, Juan Ochoa de Lejalde, asks Pedro de Ircio, alcalde of the town, to hold an enquiry on the question, "Who paid for the expenses of the expedition to Mexico: Cortés or Velázquez?" and another enquiry to prove that Cortés did his best to save the gold and jewels of the royal fifth when escaping from Mexico. They are curious documents. Cortés deems them necessary because "the papers and letters of payment thereon were lost when leaving the town of Temistitán (Mexico)"; he, the undisputed commander in chief and actual source of the power held by all the men who are going to hold this enquiry—alcalde and notary and the rest —seeks the official acquittal of the law, incarnated in his own subordinates, whom he raises to a civic majesty higher than his own. There is, of course, artfulness in this attitude and a kind of legalistic subtlety; yet it is based on the keen civic sense which still animated Spanish life, the decay of which in later years was to prove fatal both to the Mother Country and to her overseas Empire. Cortés the conqueror, appearing before a civic court in this Spanish town sprung overseas from a new-world soil, bears witness to the strength of Spanish municipal institutions. (20) But the episode shows also Cortés' ability to use the said municipal institutions to his best advantage, as will be seen anon. Meanwhile, he organised another plebiscite for himself in the form of a petition sent to the King by all his vassals in New Spain, and signed by five hundred and fifty-four of them in Segura de la Frontera in October 1520. This petition is most inaccurately described as a "Letter from Cortés' Army to the Emperor." It is no such thing. The army could not write otherwise than through its undisputed chief. It was a civic paper, in which his men expressed their opinions not as captains and soldiers but as citizens of the Kingdom of New Spain. If we turn to the signatures, we find the old names, so often men in war, but under a new attire of civilian magistracy: "Pedro de Alvarado, alcalde, Diego de Ordás, regidor . . ." (21)

This letter was one of the documents which he thought necessary to establish his position at Court, since he was still without news of his first embassy, that which had been sent as the outcome of the foundation of Veracruz. The two messengers then chosen, Puertocarrero and Montejo, were not merely his personal agents; they had been invested with the dignity of *procuradores* of the Rich Town, something very similar to English Members of Parliament or American Representatives. This time again, the foundation of Segura de la Frontera enabled him to endow his two messengers Diego de Ordás and Alonso de Mendoza with a similar dignity. (22) They conveyed a long letter or report written by Cortés on the events which had occurred between the foundation of Veracruz and that of Segura, together with another letter in which he begged the Emperor to send "a person of confidence to enquire on everything and report to Your Majesty [. . .] for I shall hold it as great of a favour as to be fully believed in what I write." (23)

In this letter, signed on October 30th, 1520, Cortés proposed to the Emperor that the country he had conquered should be named *New Spain of the Ocean Sea,* owing to "the likeness which all this land bears to Spain both in its fertility and its size and cold weather and many other features." (24) His proposal was eventually adopted by the Emperor. Nor was he concerned merely with the Court and its army of officials, for he knew by experience how important was the colonial administration then centred in Santo Domingo. The King of Spain had sought to purify the government of the Indies from the evils of personal ambition by entrusting it to three friars. Cortés sent Alonso Dávila and Francisco Alvarez Chico to put his case before these three co-Viceroys; he knew that in those quarters he could at any rate count on the indignation produced by Narváez' high-handed action with Ayllón. By this ship, Cortés sent letters to his wife and brother-in-law, with news of his adventures and presents of jewels and gold. (25)

On the same occasion, he sent a ship to Jamaica to buy horses. "I know full well," says Bernal Díaz, "that some curious readers will ask how it is that Cortés, without money, could send Ordás to negotiate in Castille, since in Castille, as in other parts, money is most necessary"; the answer was that a good deal of gold had been saved from the disaster, mostly by the Tlaxcatecs, but also by the soldiery, and as "gold and love are most difficult to hide," Cortés had his criers announce that everyone was to declare what he had, on pain of losing the whole, and he would let him keep one-third. This was very much disliked by the army, but who doubts that Cortés was right? (26)

There was, moreover, another source of income—slavery. Now that he had a city, and therefore an offshoot of the Spanish commonwealth, the time had come to regularise the acquisition of the slaves made in the campaigns against the "rebellious" tribes. Cortés and the King's officers had the crier announce that all slaves were to be presented in a central house to be branded with a *G*, meaning *War* (*Guerra*); this clearly showed the origin of the legal title to the ownership of the human beings concerned. Slavery was general in the whole Anáhuac, and men, women and children, either loose or tied to poles, were on sale in every market. From the point of view of the natives, the whites were by no means innovating. From the point of view of the Christian Faith which the whites professed to bring to the land, this branding of women and children with the stigma of war was a sad spectacle—but only for us. In those days, Christians thought it as natural as we nowadays think many things which will seem monstrous three or four centuries from now. The soldiers brought their women, boys and girls, for, says Bernal Díaz, "as to men, we did not care to have any, for they were difficult to keep and we did not require their services having those of our friends, the Tlaxcatecs." But when the next day the soldiers saw that the pretty young girls whom they had set aside and hidden had disappeared, and that all that was left for the common soldiers was the lot of old and ugly ones "when they had given the fine girl they had hidden *naguas* and chemises" they were wroth. Cortés had to promise that in future the King's fifth (and his own) should be obtained by selling all the slaves by auction for what they could fetch. (27)

He weathered this small storm easily. He felt strong enough by then to release those who still hankered after their Cuban farm-houses; to his faithful soldiers who asked him why he allowed them to leave, he answered with a Spanish dictum: "Better alone than in poor company." Moreover, he pointed out, by way of explanation, "you see that some of those who are going back are not made for war." (28)

*   *   *

This enabled him to concentrate a free mind on his main task— the reconquest of Mexico. It will be noticed that in his letter to the Emperor, when suggesting that the land should be known as New Spain of the Ocean Sea, he quietly assumed without discussion that the land would be his. This simple fact, unobtrusively set in a tacit background, is significant of the steadiness of his purpose. Broken, wounded, hounded out of Mexico by a terrifying crowd, he does not think once of giving up his enterprise. And after recovering his health by rest, and his confidence by the repeated arrivals of providentially timed reinforcements, he thought now of nothing but the reconquest.

He summoned Martín López, his master shipwright. He knew full well that a good fleet was indispensable for his purpose. It was decided to have thirteen brigantines built, of different sizes, so that they should be able to sail in groups of three or four. Cortés gave orders to have them made in Tlaxcala, to be conveyed in parts by tlamemes and mounted on the coast of the Mexican lagoon. He was busy on this work during Christmas, which he spent in Tlaxcala. (29) Here, on December 26th, 1520, he promulgated his famous Regulations to his troops: they differ little from the usual orders given to all armies in his day, yet have a flavour all his own. We find in them his chief preoccupation with the legal basis for his actions: the apparently religious concern which seems to inspire his first article, laying stress on the conversion of the Indians as the most important aim of his campaign and of his soldiers' endeavours, reveals its legalistic root in the words which he appends to it by way of explanation: "for," he says, "if war was waged with any other aim in view, it would be an unjust war and all that would be won in it would be obnoxious and bound to be given back." He therefore loudly protests that his aim is to convert the natives to the holy faith and to the yoke of His Majesty to whom the dominion over these lands "juridically" belongs.

There is moreover a typically Cortesian thought in his preamble; after having recalled that in antiquity such regulations were found necessary to guard against disaster for lack of order and discipline, and before pointing out how necessary they must be for them, being so far from home and severed from any human help, against so numerous and astute an enemy, Cortés puts in this touch of purely intellectual light, like a diamond of thought in his chair of iron reasons: "and because order is so praiseworthy, that it is loved and followed not only in human but also in divine things, and without it nothing can have a complete effect, since it is the beginning, middle and end for the government of all things . . ." (30)

So, in the midst of his military cares, while sharpening the sword which was at last to make of him the real lord of Anáhuac, Hernán Cortés let his mind wander for a brief spell over the sunny halls and squares of Salamanca, which he had haunted in his studious youth.

CHAPTER TWENTY-FIVE

Cortés Prepares the Siege of Mexico and Enters Into Legend

T HE flight of the Spaniards and the surrender of those who had remained in Axayacatl's palace, after a three-day siege, were the signal for a brief civil war between the Mexicans who had favoured the Spaniards and those who had opposed them; this struggle ended in the defeat of the pro-Spanish party and the death of its leaders. (1) The Mexicans believed that the Spanish retreat was final and that, not daring to return, the Spaniards would sail away from Veracruz. They settled down to put their own house in order and formally elected Cuitlahuac as Uei Tlatoani on a day (September 7th, 1520) which in their calendar was dedicated to death (*miquiztli*) of the month of "Sweepings" (*Ochpaniztli*). A cousin of the new monarch, that same Cuauhtemoc, whose harsh words and sharp arrow had been the first signal for Moteçuçuma's death, was raised to the post of High Priest. Other princes of the anti-Spanish persuasion were elected to the thrones of Tepaneca and Tetzcuco. The festivals occasioned by all these royal elections and coronations were particularly brilliant, owing to the abundance of Spanish victims who were offered to the gods, and there is reason to believe that Witchywolves was fully avenged of the insults he had received from the white *teules*. The heads of the victims were stuck on the poles of the Tzonpantli, a Christian head alternating with a horse's head, so as to put fear into the horses, should they ever return. (2)

These festivals, however, were soon followed by disaster. The dreadful scourge of smallpox invaded Mexico with a violence that in about two months devastated the land and inflicted on it worse losses than the Spanish wars. One of the first victims to fall was the new Uei Tlatoani himself, who died in the month of Quecholli after a reign of only eighty days. (3) Man's interpretations of the deity are no doubt as remote from God as His designs are from man; the Spaniards saw in this epidemic a welcome and timely help towards the second and final conquest of Mexico. It is a significant sign of the peculiar relations between the Mexicans and their gods that they gave the new scourge the name of *Teozahuatl* or Divine Spot. .

When Cortés returned to Tlaxcala from Segura de la Frontera, he found to his great grief that his staunch friend Maxixcatzin had fallen victim to the foreign scourge. Cortés was assured by the Tlaxatecs that from the day he fell ill till his death, Maxixcatzin constantly mentioned the name of his great Spanish friend and wished he were near by; hearing which, Cortés could not conceal his emotion. (4) Maxixcatzin's elder son, the one who had been armed a knight in the Tepeaca campaign, had been killed in battle. Cortés conferred the succession on a younger son. "He summoned the boy who might be about twelve years of age and who, in his appearance and demeanour, showed that he was the son of such a father. In the presence of all the nobility, he armed the youngster a knight in the Spanish fashion, which those lords admired very much, praising the good manner and beautiful ceremonial. He was then baptized, so that he could also be a Knight of Jesus-Christ. He was given as a name Don Lorenzo Magiscacin, no other Spanish name being given him out of respect for the nobility and virtue of his father." (5)

Old Xicotencatl followed this example and was baptised in great solemnity by Father Olmedo; but in his case the Spanish habit was followed more strictly and the octogenarian Tlaxcatec became Don Lorenzo de Vargas. Cortés was thus perfecting his spiritual, as well as his material, hold over the land which was to provide him with a solid base for his final onslaught on Mexico. By means of military expeditions under Sandoval, Ordás and Dávila he had widened the field of his authority, so that, while Martín López worked on the brigantines, the Spanish captain could by Christmas 1520 look with confidence on an immense territory over which his authority was unchallenged, covering all the country between the volcanoes and the eastern coast. This impressive result, achieved within half a year of his flight from the capital, was due to his perseverance, combined with his eye for strategy, his winsome ways and the care he always took to reduce to a bare minimum the use of force.

When Moteçuçuma died there remained one son and one daughter who, being legitimate, had some claim to the succession. They were both too young, and Cuitlahuac, their uncle, on being raised to power, had married his niece Tecuichpoch, though the marriage was not consummated, the girl being then ten years of age. Tecuichpoch's brother Axopacatzin, was not fit to reign, being out of his mind and paralytic. On Cuitlahuac's death, Cuauhtemoc, known to the Spaniards as Guatemozin or even Guatemuza, was elected Uei Tlatoani (beginning of December, 1520); and, being of an executive character, he married Tecuichpoch and killed Axopacatzin. (6) His actual accession as monarch took place during the "Empty Days" or Nemotemni, which in that year fell on January 25th–29th. Cuauhtemoc means "The Eagle That Fell," which would suggest an unusual acumen in the magicians who presided at his birth rites. He was, in Bernal Díaz' words, "a youth of about twenty-five, very handsome for an Indian, and very brave, and he made himself so much feared that his men trembled before him, and he was married to a daughter of Montezuma, a very beautiful woman for an Indian." (7)

The youthful monarch lost no time in preparing his forces for the coming onslaught, for the optimistic ideas which had prevailed at the outset as to the plans of the Spaniards had vanished on concrete news from Tlaxcala and from the growing number of territories which Cortés had conquered back for the King of Spain.

Cortés, meanwhile, lost no time either. He gave orders for all the rigging and metal parts for the brigantines to be brought from Veracruz, where a welcome addition to his strength arrived then—a ship this time not thrown ashore by good or ill luck, but actually attracted by the possibility of gain. Cortés was glad to be able to purchase arms, gunpowder, three horses and a number of useful materials, and to attract the thirteen soldiers on board to his service. (8)

On Wednesday December 26th he inspected his army; he found he had forty horsemen, and five hundred and fifty infantry, eighty of whom were crossbowmen and musketeers, and the rest, sword-and-buckler men; he had also eight or nine small field guns and a little gunpowder. It was therefore an army approximately half the size of that which had so disastrously lost Mexico, though somewhat stronger than that which had conquered it first. Obviously, the difference was in the spirit; Cortés addressed his army there and then; he reminded them of the past events and bade them take heart and be joyful because they fought for a just cause and had many native friends on their side. His army promised to conquer or die, and all withdrew to their quarters in the best of spirits. (9)

Cortés had secured the help of a powerful Tlaxcatec army which had been drilled and organised by Ojeda and Márquez. Some of these troops were to accompany him, while the rest would remain as an escort for the brigantines. His plan was to take Tetzcuco first as a base for his operations on the lagoon, and to launch the brigantines from his base. But the choice of a road was a matter of the utmost importance. Cortés, who knew that the enemy were aware of his coming and actively getting ready for it, chose the most difficult and steep of the three possible ways, thinking it would be the most neglected. On December 28th he left Tlaxcala with his army and went to spend the night in Tetzmolocan (Tezmoluca), on the plain to the east of the ridge which separated him from the lagoon. The next day, "having heard mass and commended ourselves to God," (10) they climbed the ridge, and spent a very cold night, already in Mexican territory; and on Sunday the 30th they began a descent which was to tax their patience, horsemanship and courage to the utmost, for the road, difficult and dangerous at its best, was made nearly impassable by barricades of felled trees. There was some hesitation, even in the bravest, seeing that the terrain allowed little or no scope for fighting, but Cortés sent a word of encouragement to the rearguard, and soon they found themselves in the open. It would appear that Cuauhtemoc had not actually expected them to come down through so forbidding and well barred a way, for otherwise it is difficult to see how they could have escaped destruction during the crossing of this pass.

Cortés halted his army, and told his soldiers they were to thank God for having brought them safely so far; they all cast eyes again on the enchanting lagoon with a pleasure tinged with sadness; and out of this contemplation, there came a mood of firmness and a

,promise never to leave that land without victory. "And in this determination," Cortés writes to Charles V, "we all went forward as merry as if we were going on some most pleasurable errand." (11)

After some skirmishes, the army spent the night in Coatepec, twelve miles from Tetzcuco, which they found deserted; and the next day, as they were marching, "the beard on the shoulder," towards Tetzcuco, an embassy of unarmed Indians came out to meet them with a golden banner on a high mast. It was an embassy of peace. Cortés and his men were at first overjoyed, but when, on arriving in Tetzcuco, they found no women or children, they suspected—which was indeed the case—that the embassy was a delaying manœuvre to allow the King of Tetzcuco to leave for Tenochtitlan (Mexico) with his treasure and best weapons. Cortés' tactics were, "whenever they were ready to come on peaceful terms, to receive them, and every time to offer them peace." (12) In this case, he had adhered to these tactics to the bitter end, for he could entertain no doubts about Coanochtzin, the King of Tetzcuco appointed by the Mexicans in defiance of his own decision to hold his brother as King—that Swallow (Cuicuitcatzin) whom he had christened as Don Carlos. Coanacochtzin was his uncompromising enemy and had put to death (in fact, quartered) one of his captains, known as Huitzcacamatzin, merely because this nobleman had accepted to convey to him a message from Cortés. Don Carlos, the Swallow himself, whom Cortés sent as his second messenger to find out what had happened to the first, was treated in like manner by his bloodthirsty brother. (13)

Despite these unfavourable symptoms, nothing disquieting occurred during the stay of the army in Tetzcuco. In fact, some of the minor potentates of the Kingdom came to make submission to Cortés; and when the Mexicans sent them messengers to rebuke them for it, they had the messengers arrested and handed over to Cortés in fetters. Cortés, eager for peace, freed them and sent them back with a message suggesting that bygones be bygones, and that he should be spared the grief of having to lay waste their lands and cities. (14)

By way of encouraging the Mexicans to come to terms, he attacked Iztapalapa. He won his way into the city easily but did not fail to notice as he rushed in, fighting at the head of his troops, how a dyke between the two lagoons had been burst open; "and more than six thousand of them died, counting men, women and children; for the Indians [Tlaxcatecs], our friends, seeing the victory God gave us, would do nothing else but kill right and left." The sun, being mere nature, takes no sides and when, by its departure, it interrupted this spirited episode in the propagation of the Gospel, Cortés called back his men; then, while watching the burning of some houses, "it seems as if the Lord had inspired me and brought back to my memory the dyke I had seen broken on the way in." He had just time to order a hasty retreat; some Indians were drowned and all their booty was lost, but they were miraculously saved from the most artful and dangerous trap the Mexicans had yet laid for them. (15) "And we returned to Tezcuco," concludes Bernal Díaz, "half ashamed of the mockery and trickery of letting that water loose upon us, and also because we gained but little fame in the final battle, for lack of gunpowder." (16)

* * *

Cautious in his strategy, though at times rash in his tactics, Cortés was thus familiarising himself with the new situation in Tenochtitlan. The rulers of Otumba seemed to think that he would be the winner, for they came to offer their allegiance; he sent Gonzalo de Sandoval through to Chalco to wrench the allegiance of that important city, the key of the best road to Tlaxcala, which, he had reason to believe, remained faithful to the Mexican party only out of fear. Sandoval after some hard fighting beat the Mexican garrisons which stood in the way of Chalco's allegiance and achieved the peaceful and permanent conquest of this important land. (17)

But the Mexicans were watching and threatened to come upon Chalco to avenge what, from their point of view, was treason. Chalco appealed to Cortés, who writes to the Emperor: "Beyond our own hardships and needs, the biggest grief we had was our inability to help and support our Indian friends, who were molested and attacked by the men of Culúa because they were Your Majesty's vassals." He had the good fortune to receive the visit of messengers from Cholula, Guaxocingo and Cuauhquechollan, who, without news of their Spanish friend, wanted to be sure that he needed no help, as they had of late seen numerous signs of war, such as mountain fires; he took this opportunity to effect an alliance between the newcomers and the Chalco men and sent them all away, well pleased. (18)

During his stay in Tetzcuco, Cortés went to visit the teocalli; and there he found the skins of five horses, "as beautifully stuffed as anywhere in the world, with their feet and shoes," offered to Witchy-wolves along with clothes and other belongings of the five soldiers sacrificed to the gods in Zultepec. Cortés gave instructions to Sandoval to pass by Zultepec on his way to Tlaxcala to fetch the brigantines, now ready, and to inflict heavy punishment on it. Sandoval found most of the population had fled, and in a hot pursuit killed three or four men and took some women prisoners. In the Cu, he found the faces of two of the Spaniards, tanned, offered to the god of war "with their beards on." But Sandoval had pity on the defenceless people and, as Bernal Díaz says, "what could he do but be compassionate towards those of that town?" He set free all his prisoners and called back the fugitives; the whole town asked to be forgiven, and Sandoval, having exacted no punishment, obtained their allegiance to the King of Spain and left them in peace. (19)

Sandoval went on his way towards Tlaxcala, and on the road was greatly pleased and relieved to find the expeditionary force organised by the Tlaxcatec Republic to bring the thirteen ships to be mounted in Tetzcuco, with the separate parts neatly classified and carried by eight thousand men; "a marvellous thing to see and, it seems to me also, to hear, this carrying of thirteen ships eighteen leagues over land." (20) Ten thousand soldiers marched in the vanguard, and another ten thousand in the rear. They entered Tetzcuco, with much joy and noise of drums, towards the end of February. Their march into the town lasted six hours. Cortés received them with the utmost pleasure and courtesy and had to calm their eagerness to attack their traditional enemies the Mexicans, with promises of early activity. (21)

The leisurely pages of Bernal Díaz allow us to catch a glimpse of other reasons than the merely political for the campaign of raids which began then and was to last several months. "As over fifteen thousand Tlaxcatecs had come to Tetzcuco with the wood for the brigantines and they had been in the city five days without doing anything worth telling, and as they had no food, [. . .] and as their captain was very brave and proud [. . .] he said to Cortés that he wished to sally forth and do some service to our great Emperor and fight against the Mexicans." This puts the matter in a nutshell. So far as the natives were concerned, war was an economic necessity. (22) The expedition organised then by Cortés against Xaltocan (Saltocan) and Tacuba must therefore be considered as a kind of payment for services rendered by the Tlaxcatecs. Cortés led the campaign with a strong force of his own troops, and he entered Xaltocan and Tacuba with a destructive impetus. The army stayed six days in Tacuba, in a kind of continuous day-to-day fighting in which the Spaniards, as connoisseurs, thoroughly enjoyed single combats between Mexicans and Tlaxcatecs. Cortés tried to parley with the natives, but the men of Tacuba hurled back insults at him. "You are starving," a Spaniard shouted at them. And while one of them threw a maize cake over to the Spaniards, other shouted: "We shall soon eat you and the Tlaxcatecs." (23) This sidelight on the economic aspects of the Mexican wars is aptly illustrated by a comment of Bernal Díaz on one of Cortés' later raids: "Since I came over to New Spain, we never had so many war-people of our [native] friends in our company. I have other times said that this was so because of the spoils which they expected and, most certain of all, their hope to eat their fill of human flesh [. . .] and it is very much as when in Italy an army went out and marched from one place to another, it was followed by ravens and vultures and other birds of prey who feed on the dead bodies left on the field, that is why I think we were followed by so many thousands of Indians." (24)

Though free from this gruesome aspect, the Spanish urge for war was no less influenced by economic conditions. Cortés army was not a mere formation of soldiers: it was rather an itinerant community. Every captain and soldier had an establishment of his own, composed of Tlaxcatec *naborias,* or servants, one or more Indian girls who were for him a kind of private home or harem, and a number of slaves, women and boys, for bartering purposes. If we reckon Cortés' military power at six hundred men, three thousand persons would be a moderate estimate of the actual number of persons who composed it. This meant a heavy toll on whichever country the army happened to settle and the easiest way of relieving the economic pressure was to sally forth and raid enemy territory.

Bernal Díaz tells a story which illustrates this point as well as the sly and humorous ways of Cortés. The army had fought hard to conquer an almost inaccessible natural fortress in which a number of Mexicans had taken refuge and, though beaten with heavy losses, had ultimately been able to force the Mexican garrison to come to terms through lack of water. Cortés sent a few captains and soldiers, including Bernal Díaz, to inspect the fortress and what kind of people had taken refuge in it. "Mind, gentlemen," he said, "you do not take a single grain of maize from them." What wink, gesture, inflexion of his voice was there in it which made Bernal Díaz understand that his chief meant the men to have a good harvest out of the beaten Mexicans, we do not know; but when the good soldier arrived at last at that fortress from which so many murderous stones had been thrown at him erewhile and saw "many packages of wraps which were part of the tribute they paid to Guatemuz," he felt justified in seizing his opportunity and began—he says—"to load four Tlaxcatecs, my naborias, whom I had brought over with me and also four of the Indians who were keeping guard over it." But one of the captains, Ircio, reminding him of Cortés' dictum, which he had understood literally, forced Bernal Díaz to leave everything behind; and on their way back told the whole story to Cortés and how he had prevented Bernal Díaz from walking away with the wraps. "Why shouldn't he?" asked Cortés quite annoyed. "I wish you had remained behind with the wraps and the Indians. See how well they understood that I was sending them to seize a good opportunity! While Bernal Díaz who did understand me was deprived of the spoils of those dogs who may well laugh now after having killed and wounded so many of us." (25)

As it happens, at that time a friar turned up straight from Spain who had come to set at ease any qualms which the devout Spaniards might have over this kind of behaviour. Fray Pedro Melgarejo de Urrea, "brought some bulls of the Lord St. Peter, and with this we were set at ease if we had anything on our conscience owing to the war, so that within a few months the friar went back to Castille comfortable and well-off and he left many men badly-off here." (26)

*   *   *

At this time, however, both economic necessities and military convenience made an incessant military activity advisable, for Cuauhtemoc was relentless in his preparations for war; the brigantines, which were gradually being erected in a long, narrow canal dug on the edge of the lagoon, were three times in danger, owing to bold Mexican attempts to set them on fire; from fifteen Indians caught in one of these attempts, Cortés was able to extract information which left him no doubt about the determination and power of leadership of the young Uei Tlatoani; he had struck on the same idea Cortés had had for meeting cavalry, the long spear, and he was having good Spanish swords set on the new spears, for many had fallen into Mexican hands during the night of the Spanish rout; messengers and armed forces were constantly being sent into the surrounding districts, to keep them loyal to the Mexican cause. (27)

These campaigns, led either by Cortés or by Gonzalo de Sandoval (whom since the Mexico disaster, Cortés tended to make his *alter ego*, instead of Alvarado), were all similar; in all, the Spaniards had to steer a cautious course between peace and war; when able to negotiate a peace, they did so promptly and secured the allegiance of the natives by fair treatment and still fairer promises, while, if confronted with war, they fought bravely and often in most dangerous circumstances. And, having won, they destroyed the pueblos, drove away the men or left them to the care of their native auxiliaries and took away the women and boys as slaves.

The chief of these raids was that which Cortés himself undertook just after Easter 1521 in order to see for himself the situation round the whole lagoon while the brigantines were being completed, and to secure the political background for his ultimate siege of the capital. He began, in his usual way, by offering peace to the Mexicans. "I always sought," he writes to the Emperor, "all the ways and means to attract these men of Tenuxtitán to our friendship; first so that they should not give me a motive to destroy them; and secondly to rest from the hardships of our past wars." (28) On Holy Wednesday March 27th, he sent to Mexico some Mexican prisoners he had, with his message of peace; nothing came of it, save that the men of Chalco appealed to him for help again, showing him the picture of all the communities which were marching against them. This clinched his resolution, and on April 5th, 1521, he left Tetzcuco, with three hundred men and twenty horse.

He was followed by a considerable force of natives, who accompanied him for the motives so crudely described by Bernal Díaz. After a first peaceful day spent in Tlalmanalco, at the southeastern end of the lagoon, and a brief visit to Chalco, the next morning (Saturday April 6th) the army marched on in a southerly direction to spend the night in Chimalhuacan, where the massed battalions of friendly natives joined them.. The day after, the army had to cross narrow and difficult passes in which strong troops of Mexicans were awaiting them. They fought and passed, not without serious losses and atrocious thirst; that night the din of native warlike instruments kept them awake. During the rest of the week Cortés fought his way through Huaxtepec, Xiuhtepec and Yautepec, whose chiefs came to ask forgiveness and give allegiance to the King of Spain; "and I received them gladly, for we had already inflicted good punishment on them." (29)

In the morning of Saturday the 13th, the army advanced on to Cuauhnauac (Eagle of the Nauacs), which the Spaniards turned into Cuernavaca (Horn of a Cow) and so it has remained. The spot deserves its proud Aztec, rather than its homely Spanish, name, for it is one of the most beautiful in the world, on the edge of one of the terraces which on the side of the high ridge look down on the hot valleys. It was defended by a strong Mexican garrison and seemed to allow no access even for foot soldiers, being surrounded by a precipitous ravine, which separated it from its aggressors. But while Cortés sent a few horsemen to find a way in, which he was told existed half a league away, a light-footed native succeeded in passing over the ravine on the trunks of some trees which formed a kind of natural bridge, and he was followed by many more natives and Spaniards, like Bernal Díaz, difficult though they found the feat, owing to giddiness. The garrison, taken unawares by this unexpected inrush of enemies, was finally put to flight by the arrival of the horsemen, and Cuauhnauac was looted and burnt. While the Spaniards rested in the grounds of the local magnate, the leaders of the city came to put themselves under the authority of Spain. (30)

It took the army two days to recross the ridge and to come back up the valley of Mexico, and on Monday April 15th, 1521, at eight in the morning, it was facing Xochimilco, on the lake, one of the few parts of the old lagoon still in existence. Fights in the morning, over its causeways and bridges, well barricaded by the natives; still more dangerous fights in the afternoon, when Cortés and his horsemen had some difficulty in beating off the brave Mexicans, who stood their ground well armed with Spanish swords. Cortés' horse fell, out of sheer exhaustion, and his life would have ended there and then, had the Mexicans been less addicted to catching prisoners alive for Witchywolves; but their stubborn efforts to drag him away alive gave time for a brave soldier known as Cristóbal de Olea to rescue him, not without paying for it with three serious wounds. As for Cortés, "he rode on, though badly wounded in the head." (31)

These battles of Xochimilco, which lasted three days without respite, not even at night, with their amphibious attacks and defences by canoes, causeways, bridges and mainland, their ambushes, "foot-to-foot" fighting, deadly perils, and at times, the loss of well-known comrades taken away to dreadful sacrifice, were a foretaste of the incredible siege. Gold and greed proved more dangerous than stone or arrow for some of the humbler brethren of Cortés. A few Spanish soldiers following the scent of some Tlaxcatecs who had looted a house, were helping themselves to some cotton clothes in a rich house when a great fleet of canoes full of Mexican warriors fell upon them, wounding many and taking four of them alive. Cuauhtemozin obtained as much information as he wished from them "how few we were and most of us wounded," and then "he had the feet, arms and heads of our unfortunate comrades cut off to send to many of our [native] friends' settlements, adding that before we arrived back in Tetzcuco, none of us would remain alive, and their hearts and blood were offered to his idols." (32)

They tarried in Xochimilco for three days, leaving it "destroyed and razed to the ground"; (33) on Thursday the 18th they left for Coyohuacán (Cuyoacán in Cortés); while organising his column, Cortés noticed that looting had added to the weight of his army; he appealed to his soldiers to leave the loot behind since it might be in their way for the hard fighting that awaited them; "but we all with one voice answered him that, God willing, we were men who would defend their property and persons, and that it would be meanness to do as he said, and as he saw our purpose and answer, he said he left it in the hand of God," than which no hand ever carried stranger burdens. Cuyoacán was deserted. While his men saw to their wounds and prepared more arrows for the battles they expected, Cortés studied the place with a military eye, and next day, having explored

the causeway and made up his mind that it would be necessary to garrison the spot for the siege, he left for Tacuba on Saturday the
20th. (34)

The Mexican troops, which had withdrawn to the water and the
city while he was in Cuyoacán, came out to harass his exposed flank.
Impatient at this, Cortés, with ten horse and four of his personal
grooms, rode away to lay an ambush for the Mexicans, but things
turned out the other way and it was he and his men who were trapped
into a dangerous position from which he at last extricated himself
not without wounds on all his horses and the loss of two of his grooms
who were taken alive to Witchywolves' sacrificial stone. When, at the
slow gait of the lame horses, Cortés returned to his army, already
uneasy at his long absence, all were able to notice his sad face and his
eyes in tears for his servants lost. In this melancholy mood, they
arrived in Tacuba, and Cortés with several of his captains and soldiers went up to the top of the lofty teocalli. The friar who trans-
muted sins into gold and one Julian de Alderete, recently arrived as
His Majesty's Treasurer, were of the group, and as they saw the vast
blue lagoon seething with life and studded with towns, "they were
astounded and said that this our coming into New Spain was not a
thing of human men, but a work of God's mercy [. . .] and that
they did not remember having read that any vassals ever did bigger
services to their King." But Cortés remained sad, and as he watched
the lovely sight, now rooted in his heart by so many sinews of grief,
he heaved a deep sigh. "Be not so sad, Sir Captain," said a soldier,
the bachelor Alonso Pérez, "for these things are wont to happen in
war and no one shall be able to say of Your Lordship

> "Nero watched from Tarpey Rock
> Rome at his feet flare."

The friendly soldier said no more; but all, familiar as every Spaniard was in those days, with the ballads of Castille, mentally completed the four lines:

> Children, women, screamed and died,
> But he did not care.

"You all know," said Cortés, "that I have begged the Mexicans
ever so many times to come to terms; my sadness is not due to one
reason only; it comes from the thought of the great hardships which

await us before we recover Mexico; but with God's help, we shall
win through." (35)

This scene is not merely one of the most living pictures of Cortés'
life, but also one of the most invaluable for the study of history and
legend as flowers of the human mind. The confluence of emotion
(Cortés' sadness) with form (the ballad quoted) gave rise to at least
two currents of legend which have left their trace in Spanish history;
one is the distortion of the figure of Cortés by transferring the event
to the day of the massacre of Cholula, and by inverting the sense in
which the ballad on Nero had been called to memory. This negative
legend is due to Las Casas, who in his zeal for the defence of the
Indians, forgot all sense of fairness and never had any idea of the
objective duties of a historian. In his pamphlet on the Destruction
of the Indies, he writes that "they say that while the five or six thousand men were being passed by the sword in the yard, the Captain of
the Spaniards was singing

> "Nero watched from Tarpey Rock
> Rome at his feet flare:
> Children, women, screamed and died;
> But he did not care."

Nothing short of all the self-centered hate of the passionate monk
could blind any but a half-witted person to the impossibility of such
a scene. The other branch of the tree of legend born of that scene
in Tacuba is more graceful. Cortés was one of the rare men in later
Spanish history to inspire the popular muse, giving rise to one of the
vivid epic ballads which enrich Spanish literature; and by the time
Bernal Díaz was writing, the scene in which he had himself participated, was already the subject of a popular ballad which he is able
to quote:

> In Tacuba was Cortés,
> With his army sorely tried.
> He was sad and full of sorrow
> Sad and much preoccupied
> With one hand under his chin
> And the other on his side . . . (36)

*   *   *

Lack of supplies, and particularly of gunpowder, forced the Spaniards to give up any idea of exploring Tacuba, and they marched on the same morning, passing Azcapotzalco, the town of the silversmiths, and Tenayocan, both deserted; they ended their march in Cuauhtitlan, also deserted, where they arrived drenched by persistent rain, and the next day (Sunday the 21st) they marched to Citlaltepec, after a similar day of rain, little fighting, and poor food. At twelve midday, Monday the 22nd, the army arrived in Acolman, within the State of Tetzcuco, where Sandoval awaited them. It seemed as if Cortés might then look forward to a few days of quiet rest before the final ordeal which he had set for himself. (37)

But at this point, as had happened more than once in earlier days, he was in danger from a conspiracy within his army. Two days after his arrival, a soldier, privy to the conspiracy, came to unburden his soul before his chief; one of them, Antonio de Villafana, had engineered a plot to have Cortés and his best captains murdered; a brother-in-law of Diego Velázquez, one Francisco Verdugo, who apparently knew nothing of the plot, was to succeed Cortés. A letter shut and sealed, purporting to have just arrived from his father, was to be delivered to Cortés at table; and while he was reading it the conspirators would murder him. Cortés, with his trusted group of captains and soldiers, went to Villafana's rooms and found him surrounded by fellow-conspirators; he was seized, and Cortés, with his own hand, drew out from his chest a paper containing the names of his accomplices; there were so many and among them so many persons of quality, that Cortés spread the rumour that Villafana had swallowed the papers and that the conspirators had remained unknown to all but themselves and him. Cortés set up a special bodyguard of six men under a captain; and as for the conspirators, after Villafana had been hanged, he kept no feeling but outward good will and inward mistrust. (38)

N*

CHAPTER TWENTY-SIX

The Siege and Fall of Mexico

O N SUNDAY April 28th the thirteen ships were launched on the lagoon, after mass and communion; each flew its gay flags to the wind and shot blank salvos which echoed in the aching hearts of the threatened Mexicans and re-echoed in the impassive hills. Cortés inspected his troops: he had eighty-six horsemen, one hundred and eighteen crossbowmen and musketeers, and over seven hundred sword-and-buckler men; three big iron guns; fifteen smaller bronze ones and ten hundredweights of gunpowder. He addressed his men, as he always took great care to do, in order to keep ever alive the communion and comradeship which, despite frequent conspiracies, had always been the chief strength of his small band.

Within a few days, his native allies arrived in force from Tlaxcala, Cholula and Guaxocingo. The Tlaxcatec force in particular, led by Chichimecatecuhtli and Xicotencatl junior, was as brilliant as usual and as boisterous in its warlike enthusiasm. Cortés rode out to meet it with some of his captains on hearing that young Xicotencatl was at the head of the army, a courteous precaution which in the light of later events takes on a peculiar significance. The native army took three hours to file past the streets of Tetzcuco to its headquarters.

Cortes had the lagoon carefully charted so that his ships could navigate without fear of mishap; he seems to have met with some difficulty in manning the oars, for every one wanted to fight but few, if any, wanted to row. He met the obstacle with energy; first all sailors, then all those he had seen fishing, then all who had been born in Palos, Triana, El Puerto, or "parts where there are sailors," says Bernal Díaz with the serenity of a man born in the heart of dry and high Castille—all were made to row, much as they might claim to be hidalgos. He then gave each ship twelve men, six of whom were crossbowmen and musketeers, and twelve oarsmen, (1) and taking the command of the fleet himself, divided the rest of his army into three companies: Pedro de Alvarado, with 30 horsemen, 18 crossbowmen and musketeers and 150 men, backed by over 25,000 Tlaxcatecs, was sent to Tacuba. Olid, with 33 horse, 18 crossbowmen and musketeers and 160 men, plus 20,000 native allies, was sent to Cuyoacán. And Sandoval with 24 horse, 4 musketeers, 13 crossbowmen and 150 men, backed with 30,000 natives, was to walk through Iztapalapa and, having destroyed the city, to advance along the chief causeway towards Mexico and meet Olid coming from Cuyoacán.

On their way to Tacuba, the two captains fell out over the billeting of their troops in Aculman—a typical example of the ease with which Spaniards of all times find time and energy for civil war; Alvarado and Olid had already drawn and some of their soldiers were on the point of imitating them when wiser counsels prevailed; Cortés heard of it and sternly rebuked both his captains for their inflammability. (2) Then Alvarado noticed that Xicotencatl had disappeared. The reasons are obscure and differ from one version to another. Cortés was informed and sent him a message to return. It is obvious that, whatever the cause of the young warrior's absence, Xicotencatl hated the policy of his country, as he had every right to do. Cortés sent Ojeda to Tlaxcala with the significant message that the crime committed by the young chief was punished by death in Spain; to which the republic made answer that it was so also in Tlaxcala. Hearing this, Cortés exclaimed, "There is no mending this cacique; he is bent on betraying us"; and he gave orders to have him hanged. Alvarado begged his chief to be lenient; but Cortés, soothing Alvarado with good words, confirmed his orders; and the young cacique was caught and hanged. (3)

*   *   *

Cortés' plan was simple: to besiege the city. He left one causeway unguarded—that which led towards Tepeyac—in the hope that the Mexicans, hard pressed in their city, would evacuate it. (4) This would have suited him for two reasons which he reveals with his usual candour—for a man's candour will out even through the most watchful caution—in his letter to the Emperor: "Seeing that these men of the city were rebellious and showed so much determination in dying or defending themselves, I gathered two things: the first that we would recover little or no wealth out of what they had taken from us; and the second that they gave us cause and forced us to destroy them." And with words which carry conviction as to the sincerity of his feelings, he adds: "And of his second, I felt most sorry and aggrieved in my soul." (5)

He was, however, quite right as to the determination of the Mexicans to resist at all costs and to perish rather than yield. The issue of war or peace had been put to the *Tlaloc*, or tribal council, by Cuauhtemoc; and the younger men, strongly backed by the priests, had won over a moderate section who urged peace negotiations after a few days' fighting. Cuauhtemoc was, of course, of the war party, and the decision was celebrated with the sacrifice of four Spanish prisoners and a number of Tlaxcatecs which Torquemada puts at four thousand.

In Cuauhtemoc the Mexicans had found a leader of indomitable spirit, but also of a military intelligence not unworthy of that of his enemy. The defence of Mexico against the Spaniards was a masterpiece of prodigious valour and devotion, of dogged perseverance, of ever reborn initiative and adaptability to new circumstances, of technical skill, tactical ability and unsurpassed generalship. The leader directed the siege from the tower of the Great Teocalli by means of a system of signals which seems to have worked with the utmost efficiency. (6)

The siege began by an offensive action carried out by Olid and Alvarado against the water supply which came from Chapultepec; the two earthenware pipes were broken, and, very much elated by their success, the captains led their soldiers along the Tacuba causeway to a dangerous attack on the city. The Mexicans, indignant at the Tlaxcatec auxiliaries, threw at them the arms and legs of the prisoners they had sacrificed and shouted at the Spaniards: "Bad men, your blood shall appease our gods and will be drunk by our snakes, and your flesh will surfeit our tigers and our lions." (7) Throughout the siege, this high pitch of personal, mental war, this shadow of sacrificial death, this cannibalistic threat, gave a grim character to the fighting, which was moreover relentless, never ceasing through day or night, and carried out with incredible courage and stubbornness on both sides.

Tactics on both sides changed as days passed and brought in their crop of dearly won experience. The besieged began on a note of strategic defensive but of tactical continuous attack: the Spaniards adopted at first a purely military strategy, consisting in constant onslaughts along the causeways and offensive action with their brigantines both on the causeways themselves and on the swarms of canoes which attacked them from the water. This period began with the destruction of the Chapultepec water pipes (May 26th, 1521); on May 31st, Sandoval and his army settled in Iztapalapa, hurriedly evacuated by the Mexicans, and Cortés left Tetzcuco with his thirteen ships to lend him a hand. But on the way he decided to take Tepopolco Rock, a natural stronghold which rose in the middle of the Tetzcuco lagoon. He stormed it by sheer spirit and persistence against the heavy odds which nature—let alone the vigorous resistance of the garrison—opposed to the invaders; "they wounded twenty-five of my Spaniards," he writes to Charles V, "but it was a very beautiful victory." (8)

The appearance of the brigantines actually sailing on the lagoons was a great event for both sides; but the spirited Mexicans met it with resolution, and Cortés from his conquered Rock, saw over five hundred canoes rowing swiftly towards his ships; he hurriedly reembarked his soldiers, giving them no respite, but gave strict orders to the shipmasters not to move, so that the Mexican canoes should believe the Spaniards were fearful of their numbers. The fleet of canoes stopped dead at some distance from the brigantines; Cortés wished ardently that the first onslaught of the brigantines should impress the Mexicans with their power, and at this moment, he writes, "as we were looking at them and they at us, it pleased our Lord that a wind from land very favourable for the brigantines should begin to blow . . . we broke through them and destroyed innumerable canoes and we killed and drowned many of our enemies, which was the most notable sight in the world." (9)

These two victories encouraged Cortés to round up the day with a third operation, possibly the most important of the three. It was already well into the afternoon—"Vespers," he says—when with thirty of his three hundred men, he landed in Xoloc, the fort where the causeway from Cuyoacán met the main Iztapalapa causeway; after some stiff fighting, he took it, landed three guns and with their deadly fire swept that beautiful avenue along which, eighteen months earlier, Moteçuçuma had come out to meet him in his golden palanquin. He made up his mind to occupy the fort and teocalli, thereby making the occupation of Iztapalapa unnecessary, since Olid, from Cuyoacán, would take charge of that sector also; this released Sandoval for blocking the Tepeyac causeway, thus completing the blockade of the city. (10)

Xoloc, however, was not secure. Far from it. Indeed, the most typical feature of this singular siege was its fluidity which it seemed to borrow from the liquid element on which the city was built; positions were in a constant state of ebb and flow, and the two amphibious forces attacked each other with the ever recurring inrush of two different tides struggling for the same space. Xoloc was fought over during six days, in fights which nearly always turned into inextricable scrimmages by day and even, contrary to the native custom, by night, from the canoes, the brigantines, the causeways and actually from the water by swimming warriors.

This first phase of the siege culminated in a combined attack made by Alvarado and Cortés on June 9th. The pattern of the two lines of attack was the same: the advance had to be made by sheer persistence in the face of ever recurring obstacles, the most dangerous of which were the gaps opened in the causeways by the lifting or destruction of the bridges, and next to them, the flank attacks from innumerable canoes. The brigantines proved invaluable in meeting these two sets of obstacles and, with their help, Cortés was able to reach the Great Teocalli in the heart of the city, not without long hours of persisent "foot-to-foot" fighting; but sheer numbers compelled the Spaniards to let their Tlaxcatec allies loose on their cordial enemies the Mexicans and a panic movement of withdrawal which set in amongst the Tlaxcatecs might have degenerated into a rout, and the loss of a gun, but for the arrival of three horsemen and the imagination of the Mexicans, who multiplied these three cavaliers into Witchywolves knows how many; this, however, was no *mere* miracle, for the horsemen would have been unable to penetrate into the very heart of the town had not Cortés seen to it, with the utmost determination, that all the gaps in the causeway which he left in his

rear should be instantly filled up. Withal, beyond the destruction of
many houses on the way, as a precaution against side attacks in future
assaults, and a most invaluable experience, this battle led to no permanent result. (11)

*   *   *

The second phase of the siege covers the rest of the month of
June. There was continuous fighting along the causeways, in order
to fill up the gaps with rubble from destroyed houses. The blockade
of the town was tightened by devoting two brigantines to the special
task of pursuing and seizing the canoes which stealthily brought supplies of food and water to the city under cover of the night. "Not a
day went by without the brigantines bringing in a prize of canoes
and many Indians hanging from the masts." (12) Cuauhtemoc devised ingenious stratagems to trap the brigantines and sink them;
but, though he succeeded once in killing two shipmasters, no ship was
lost.

During this phase of the siege, the prestige of the Mexicans began
to decline in the valley of the lagoon. Cortés was most elated at the
arrival of 30,000 well equipped warriors whom "Don Fernando," the
new King of Tetzcuco, had sent him, and even more so at receiving the
allegiance of the city of Xochimilco and of the Otomies—both important factors in the strategic situation, for both were in a position
powerfully to help or to hinder the attitude of the city and district of
Cuyoacán. (13) The movement spread to Iztapalapa, Churubusco,
Mexicalcingo, Culhuacan, Mixquic and Cuitlahuac, cities and pueblos on the lagoon all of which came to offer their allegiance; Cortés
accepted their friendship willingly, but asked that they should help
in the siege with armed canoes, and that they should build him a city-
camp in Xoloc—which they did in a way most satisfactory for
Cortés, but less so for Bernal Díaz who, being away in Tacuba with
Alvarado, drily points out: "*Our* camp never was built, and so we
were living in water, for all who have been in these lands well know
that in June, July and August it rains every day." (14)

The time was otherwise spent in a tedious though dangerous process of fighting over "gaps" in the causeways, filling them up with
rubble and finding them cut open again next morning by the stubborn
and persevering Mexicans. "And Your Majesty may well believe,"

writes Cortés, "that the danger in which we were every time we won
these bridges was without compare, for, to win them, the Spaniards
had to swim across; and there were many who could not or dared
not do this, for the enemy, with swords and spears, prevented them
from reaching the other side." He goes on to explain how there
was no way open to them but to fight over the same ground every
day because he could not lock himself up in the city with his
enemy, and as for guarding the bridges by night, "the Spaniards
were so tired after their day's fighting that they could not stand
guard." (15)

Yet his main difficulty in this respect did not come from the fighting over the gaps, but from the labour of filling them. Those told off
to work as masons "held it in dishonour," says Bernal Díaz, that
others should be fighting while they only worked, and Alvarado had
to keep a strict rotation of his three captaincies to avoid differences. (16) The army, moreover, was getting restive. Several times
it had been possible for Cortés and for Alvarado to penetrate right
into the heart of the town and play havoc in the ranks of their
enemies; this had led to some rivalry between the two armies as to
which of the two would first reach and possibly win the *Tianquiztli*
or market, which, the Spaniards thought, would mean the end of all
resistance. Pressure from his troops led Alvarado to one of his most
rash operations, for, baited by the Mexicans who simulated a hasty
retreat, and forgetting the repeated orders of Cortés never to leave
an unfilled gap in the rear, he was suddenly thrown back into Tacuba
by a strong force held in readiness; the way he had come through
had been blocked, and the only way out led to a most dangerous trap,
a wide, specially opened gap in the causeway across which his men
had to swim, savagely attacked by a swarm of armed canoes. Five
of the Spaniards were caught alive to be sacrificed. Bernal Díaz was
miraculously saved from this fate. (17)

Cortés was most displeased at this, for he held it a disregard of
his repeated instructions about filling up all gaps in the causeways;
he went to Alvarado's headquarters, but was astounded at the advance
his lieutenant had made into the city and the number of bridges he held
permanently. He says so himself in his report to the Emperor. His
displeasure at the mishap all but vanished, and there is little doubt

that the subconscious springs which led him to his next and graver
setback were wound up in his inner self during this visit to the camp
of his successful subordinate. (18)

Success, however, had been dearly paid for, and the relentless
Mexicans were now and then able to offer considerable numbers of
Spaniards—as well as numberless Indians—to Uitzilopochtli. Torquemada mentions eighteen caught from Alvarado's force and fifty-
three from Sandoval's. (19) From their headquarters and barricades,
the Spaniards could see their comrades led up the steps to the sacrificial stone, and, after the ceremony, their bodies distributed to their
captors like butcher's meat. These sights, so gruesome for them,
were but forms of Holy Communion and military victory for the
Mexicans. The priests, guardians of the calendar and interpreters
of the stars, could point to the bodies of the sacrificed whites as
tangible evidence of the recurrence of success, in this month of
Tecuilhuitontli, and in particular on the anniversary of June 30th
which had seen the rout of the Spaniards along that very causeway
now in Alvarado's hands.

When the gods are bent on disaster, they can always rely on men
to open the way for them. Cortés found his camp very much upset
and uneasy, not over Cuauhtemoc's resistance, but over Alvarado's
advance. They were determined to reach the strategic Tianquiztli
before Alvarado's force deprived them of the honour; Alvarado's
men were submitting their chief to a similar pressure and for identical
reasons. Cortés demurred. "I hedged as well as I could," he explains to the Emperor, "though I hid my reasons, which were the
obstacles and dangers which I saw; for between us and the market
there were numberless terraces and bridges and broken streets; so
that every house we had to pass had become an island in the midst
of water." (20)

In the end he yielded. Why? On the surface, he yielded, it is
clear, because he was most sensitive to what we would call "public
opinion"; and also because the spokesman, and maybe leader, of this
public opinion in his army was Alderete, the Royal Treasurer, whom
he was too much of a "politician" to disregard. But though these
factors contributed to his decision they did not determine it, for
Cortés was usually able to resist "public opinion" either openly (as

in the matter of his second attack on Mexico) or by more Machiavellian ways (as in numerous incidents and crises of the conquest).
What determined his decision to attack the city was the strong impression made on him by Alvarado's progress and the fear which it no
doubt engendered that Alvarado might forestall him.

He refused, however, to his lower self the mean pleasures of a
scramble for glory, and he carefully planned a combined attack. He
instructed Sandoval to pass over to the Tacuba causeway with all his
forces, leaving only ten horsemen (with native auxiliaries) in Tepeyac; this enabled Alvarado to send Cortés seventy or eighty men; with
his usual eye on "politics," Cortés gave one of the chief commands
to the treasurer Alderete; he was to weep for it within that fateful
day. The combined attack was fixed for Sunday June 30th after
mass, and the chief order was to "fill up all gaps left in the rear."
The first assault was a success: Sandoval and Alvarado reached the
edge of the Tianquiztli; and the three captaincies of Cortés were
equally victorious. But, in circumstances which neither Bernal Díaz
nor Cortés relates very clearly, a retreat, initiated in the vanguard,
was turned into a disaster by disregarding of Cortés' order to fill up
the gaps; one of these, which had been passed on a light, makeshift
bridge, was found cut open when retreat made its passage vital.
Numerous Spaniards killed, drowned and captured paid for this tragic
mistake; Cortés, who had come to inspect the spot from the rear, was
unable to contain the disastrous rout. "Hold, hold," he shouted,
"hold fast. How could you turn your backs on the enemy?" (21) He
was suddenly surrounded, wounded in a leg, and seized by several
Mexicans, the choicest heart to offer Uitzilopochtli. But Olea, the
same man who had saved his life in Ochimilco, at one stroke of his
sword cut off the hand of a Mexican who was holding him; and after
some fighting, in which Olea was killed, Cortés was able to disentangle himself from the swarm of enemies, from the water and from
the mud. A horse was proffered out of the scrimmage and he rode
away into the thick of the fight. (22)

The lugubrious sound of the *tlapanhuehuetl,* or sacred drum, a
sign too well known to the Spaniards, told them that their companions
were being sacrificed. Alvarado was fighting a spirited retreat against
the Mexicans whipped up into a frenzy by Cuauhtemoc's trumpets
sounding a fight to the death; some of them suddenly hurled at the

Christians the heads of five beheaded Spaniards which they held by the hair or the beard, shouting that Malintzin was dead; the Mexicans who fought against Cortés hurled four heads of Spaniards at them and shouted that Alvarado and Sandoval had been killed. Cortés, deeply moved, put Olid in command of the camp and sent Tapia with three horsemen by land to Tacuba, to find out whether Alvarado and his army were dead or alive; Sandoval meanwhile, wounded three times, was also treated to the same gruesome pelting and news—six heads of Spaniards thrown at his soldiers and shouts of Malintzin's death. This methodical use of terror and false news is a further proof of the systematic—as well as the heroical—spirit which Cuauhtemoc had instilled into the defence.

Sandoval, having extricated his troops, left them in charge of Luis Marín and, "wounded and bandaged as he was," galloped over to Cortés' quarters. "Well, Sir Captain," he said, "where are the good ways and war ruses you always used to teach us? How did this setback occur?" Cortés, who felt a fatherly affection for his youthful captain, said with tears in his eyes: 'O my son Sandoval, my sins have brought it upon me; yet I am not as guilty as our captains and soldiers say; but the treasurer Alderete; for I had relied on him to fill up that gap and he did not do so, for he is not used to wars nor even to receiving orders from captains."

Sandoval left his wounded captain disputing this point with the treasurer, and galloped back to Tacuba where he lent a hand to Bernal Díaz and six other Spanish soldiers, up to their waists in water trying to rescue a brigantine which had been run aground by the Mexicans, then led a difficult retreat—difficult not only because of the fierce attacks of the Mexicans who wounded him twice again and, what was worse, his horse, but because of his soldiers' refusal to retreat till he begged them "for the love of our dear brothers," meaning Alvarado and his horsemen who were in danger while the fight went on. Rest at last? The *tlapanhuehuetl* came again to freeze the blood in many a stout Spanish heart with its lugubrious sound. The crowded day was not over, and enough light remained in its ominous skies for Sandoval, Alvarado and their men to see many of their friends, with plumes on their heads, made to dance on top of the teocalli, then laid on the sacrificial stone, and finally cut to pieces at the foot of the gory steps. The Mexicans meant no harm: they were just doing their duty towards Vixtocioatl, the goddess of salt whose festivals were due that month. (23)

*   *   *

This setback, which a caprice of Fate had timed on the anniversary of the defeat of the previous year, was on the whole a blessing in disguise for Cortés. The Mexicans had hastened to open up again all the cuttings in the causeways, and had sent the heads of horses and Spaniards to the surrounding tribes as eloquent pieces of propaganda. But, partly through war weariness, possibly also through hunger, they abstained from active operations for a few days, which enabled the Spaniards to attend to their wounds, and their captain to take stock of the situation. Cortés began by improving his armoury. (24) The sword was often too short for this amphibious fighting: he had spears made for his infantry. And, at this point, (25) a ship from the ill fated expedition of Ponce de León in Florida sought refuge in Veracruz, and brought welcome relief in gunpowder and crossbows. Tactically, therefore, his situation was not so bad as might have been thought; strategically, in spite of Cuauhtemoc's forcible propaganda, Cortés' hold over the valley seemed unimpaired; for though immediately after his setback the announcement that a number of Spanish and Tlaxcatec prisoners were to be sacrificed to Uitzilopochtli induced many native allies to desert from Alvarado's camp, these defections must have been of less importance than Bernal Díaz asserts, (26) since while the Spaniards attended to their wounds Chichimecatecuhtli led a powerful Tlaxcatec force to a spirited assault on the city. Moreover the men of Cuernavaca and the Otomies chose this moment to seek Cortés' help in their local feuds, and Cortés, though in fear and trembling for the safety of his own army, had the political courage and wisdom to send Tapia with a force to Cuernavaca and Sandoval with another force to the Otomies, and the good fortune of seeing the two captains come back safe and victorious. (27)

This period of rest and recovery was not, however, a period of complete quiescence or of truce. "In order that the men in the city should not gain more pride nor guess our weakness, every day a few Spaniards, both infantry and horsemen, went to fight in the city, though they could only win some bridges." (28) These expeditions grew daily more enterprising as the army recovered its physical health and replenished its arsenal; but Cortés realised that some drastic steps had to be taken in view of the stubborn resistance of Cuauhtemoc. It was necessary altogether to destroy every house as the armies advanced; this decision was most unpleasant to him, for the city, he says to the Emperor, "was the most beautiful thing in the world." (29) He called the heads of his native allies and signified his intention to them so that they should organise demolishing parties to follow in the wake of the soldiers—a suggestion which they, as relentless enemies of Mexico, gleefully prepared to carry out.

A dramatic ambush carefully prepared by Cortés, after an acute observation of the eagerness of the Mexicans in pursuing horsemen whom they believed in danger, led to the destruction of five hundred of the best leaders of Mexico; and that night, writes Cortés to the Emperor with his even, unwavering hand, the Spaniards' Tlaxcatec friends "had a good dinner for they took away all the killed and cut them up to eat them." (30) This episode re-established the prestige of his cavalry to an astonishing degree and was most detrimental to the spirit of Cuauhtemoc's followers though not, as time was to show, to that of the indomitable chief.

Some Mexicans stole away in the night and came over to the Spanish camp, driven out by hunger. The besieged tried to fish at night, and wandered in the dark about the part of the city which was already in the hands of the Spaniards, hoping to find some roots or grass to eat. Cortés attacked these marauders at dawn; he found they were but the more miserable part of the beleaguered population, unarmed, many of them women and children. This is one of the most painful scenes in the whole life of this complex man; for he was genuine in his desire to inflict as little harm as possible, yet, he quietly says to the Emperor: "and we did them so much harm in all the part of the city in which we could move about, that between the dead and the prisoners, there were more than eight hundred persons, and the brigantines took also many people and canoes in which they were fishing [. . .] and so we returned to the camp with many prizes [slaves?] and food for our [native] friends." (31)

Meanwhile, the gaps in the causeways were being permanently filled up. Cortés himself gave an example to all his men by carrying planks and earth with his own hands. Day after day, the siege developed in similar fashion; battles, building of the causeway over the gaps won during the days: destruction of the city right and left of the causeway; and garrisoning of the road up to the limit of what had been conquered. One day the force under Cortés saw smoke rising from the towers of the teocalli in the Tlatelolco; (32) they guessed that Alvarado had taken it though they could hardly believe their eyes, and that day Cortés must have felt the pressure to hurry forward in many of his soldiers. But he had taken his lesson to heart, and though only one bridge and one canal separated them from the market he stuck to the prosaic task of building up his solid causeway. The next day his men had the joy of meeting the vanguard of Alvarado's army, inside the city; and Cortés rode with an escort towards the market close by. It was empty, but the terraces round it were full of enemies, kept at bay by their newly acquired respect for the horses. He then went up to the top of the teocalli. There, he found many Spanish heads, offered to Uitzilopochtli, still perfectly recognizable. "And from that tower," he writes to the Emperor, "I saw all that we had won, certainly seven-eighths of the city; and considering that so many people could not possibly live in so little space [. . .] and above all the very great hunger which they were undergoing, and that we found gnawed roots and bark of trees in the streets, I decided to cease fighting for a day and to suggest to them some compromise so that so many people should not perish; for I felt much compassion and grief indeed at the harm we inflicted on them, and constantly offered them peace; and they answered that on no account would they surrender and that even if one of them only were to remain he would die fighting." (33)

Cortés transferred his headquarters and those of the other captaincies to the Tlatelolco; (34) and from this moment he moves from offers of peace inspired by his compassion at the sight of the streets full of women and children driven out of the city by hunger and the pestilence of the thousands of unburied dead, to orders of war on finding his offers rejected or accepted only as a war ruse for further attack. He had much difficulty in circumventing the cruel ways of his native allies and repeatedly refers to this in his letters to the Emperor: "The dead and prisoners reached twelve thousand, towards whom our friends showed so much cruelty that on no account would they grant life to any one, however rebuked or punished by us." (35) And again: "On that day more than forty thousand were killed or caught; and the women and children cried and wept so much that there was no one who did not feel his heart broken, and we had our hands fuller hindering so much cruelty and killing on the part of our friends than in fighting against the Mexicans; which cruelty was never known to be so hard in any other race of people, nor so much out of the order of nature, as it is amongst the natives of these parts." (36)

*   *   *

Led by a genuine desire to avoid unnecessary hardship, and no doubt also to rescue the treasure which still remained in Cuauhtemoc's hands, Cortés tried his best to obtain a peaceful surrender of the city—for that is what he means when in his narrative to the Emperor he speaks of offers of "peace." (37) His men were equally desirous of it; the bravest of them needed all their spirit to withstand the gruesome sights with which an enemy as cruel as artful regaled them, and Bernal Díaz himself with charming candour tells of his anguishing fear of death at the sight of his own friends sacrificed to Witchywolves under his eyes: "In those days, I thought myself a good soldier and was held as such by all and I felt bound to do as much as the most daring, and as I saw my comrades taken away every day to be sacrificed and how they were sawn open across the breasts, and their hearts plucked out all panting and their feet and arms cut off and that sixty-two of them were eaten [. . .], I feared that some day or other it would be my turn, for I had been caught twice to be sacrificed and God wished that I should disengage myself, and remembering those most ugly deaths and bearing in mind the proverb about *the pitcher that goes so often to the fountain, etc.*, always since then I feared death more than ever, and I say this because before going into battle I always felt a kind of gloom and sadness in my heart and then I fasted once or twice and I commended myself to God and to His Blessed Mother and, as I entered battle, all at once my fear vanished altogether." (38)

He was brave enough to feel that he could afford this confession; nor were most of his companions of a lesser spirit than he; but the strain was terrible and unremitting, the food poor, rest precarious and short, broken time and again by noise, alarms, fires, and in

any case never lasting beyond dawn, when the early rising battalions
of the Mexicans began their new day of battle. As the siege pro-
gressed, the Spaniards were able to settle closer to the Tlatelolco
district, the only one now left to the besieged; but this new advantage had to be paid for by a new and appalling torment: the stench
of the thousands of dead which the Mexicans could not bury and
would not burn. It was therefore natural that the desire for peace
should be predominant in the besiegers.

What about the besieged? Cortés' account would appear to
suggest that the chief obstacle to the surrender came from Cuauhtemoc himself; but Cortés, led to sobriety by his executive, clear-
cut and so to speak "classic" mind, is at times apt to oversimplify
complex situations which we find more faithfully set down in the
picturesque disorder of Bernal Díaz' chronicle. Cortés had sent
Cuauhtemoc three prominent war prisoners to negotiate a peace;
these captains were evidently afraid of appearing before the warlike
Uei Tlatoani on such an errand and were in tears when they delivered
their message; but Cuauhtemoc, after some show of indignation,
summoned his war council, for, says Bernal Díaz, "we came to know
later on that he had been inclined to make peace." (39) Brave in
council as he was in war, the young Emperor put the case for peace
squarely before his captains and priests: the brigantines controlled
the lagoon, the horsemen rode freely over the city; there was neither
food nor water, and they were crowded out by their own dead. But
the war council did not follow him: they argued that the whites
would make them all slaves and that it was best to die; whereupon
Cuauhtemoc declared: "Henceforward, I shall put to death whosoever speaks to me of peace." (40)

This scene explains the attitude of the besiegers towards the
peace efforts constantly made by Cortés. His Spaniards came one
day to him in great elation, to announce that some prominent Mexicans wanted to speak to him across a barricade; Cortés went thither,
only to hear a passionate appeal from his desperate foes: "You are
the offspring of the Sun," they said to him, "and the Sun goes round
the world in one day. Why do you not kill us in one day, and put us
out of misery?" He spoke to them of peace, but failed to break their
indomitable resolve. (41)

The scene impressed him so much that he decided to send one of his most prized prisoners to Cuauhtemoc with an embassy of peace; Cuauhtemoc, true to his word, had him sacrificed to Uitzilopochtli, and answered this peace offer with a spirited attack in which the Christians lost a horse but the Mexicans many men. (42) The next day, Cortés entered the part of the town where the Mexicans were holding out, but gave orders not to fight, in the hope that the enemy would surrender. He rode towards a barricade and called some of the Mexican captains to him; from his horse, he spoke to them: he told them he had the power to destroy them all within one hour; and requested them to bring Cuauhtemoc to him, for he promised no harm should be done to the Emperor nor to any of his subjects. "And I added other points whereby I provoked them to many tears, and they, weeping, told me they would go and fetch their lord and that I was not to move from where I was." Presently, they returned, explaining that it was too late, but that Cuauhtemoc would come the next day to the Tianquiztli. Cortés, with his usual care for detail, had everything prepared for the event, including a meal to be served on the platform which occupied the centre of the market square. But he waited in vain. Cuauhtemoc did not come, and his messengers covered his absence with many excuses. Cortés received them well, gave them a meal and sent them back to Cuauhtemoc with food for him and a renewed request to come to a parley. The deputation came back with a present of cotton wraps—for the Mexicans seem to have guessed the Spanish proverb that "the courtesy is no bar to courage" —and a promise to come the next day. The next day Cortés waited in vain. (43)

His patience was exhausted. He gave orders to attack. In one of these assaults Bernal Díaz and other men of Alvarado's division took a local teocalli in which they found a row of heads of sacrificed Spaniards: "and their hair and beards were much longer than when they were alive and I should never have believed it had I not seen it." (44) This kind of sight, to be met every day as they advanced into the town, and the insufferable stench of the native dead, made it the more imperative to take what remained of the city by a final onslaught. Cuauhtemoc had transferred his quarters to a canoe; there was hardly any room left in what remained of the city for the miserably living whose lives dragged on in the gruesome and pestilential company of their own dead.

On August 13th, 1521, Cortés led his troops to the final assault of this stubborn siege, begun at the end of May. Alvarado attacked from Tacuba; Cortés himself, from the main causeway; Sandoval, from the water. Even at this eleventh hour Cortés endeavoured to save what remained of Mexico from the last disaster of a stormy assault with thousands of fierce Tlaxcatecs at his elbow; he went up to a terrace and addressed his enemies; the *Ciuacoatl* in person answered him that Cuauhtemoc would on no account make peace, and that he preferred to die. "Go back to your people," said Cortés, "and get ready to die." (45)

Noncombatants crowded the streets, fleeing towards the Spanish quarters. Cortés had placed Spaniards at all street corners to prevent the native auxiliaries from killing them; and he had severely forbidden the captains of his auxiliary troops to kill any noncombatants; "Yet," he adds to the Emperor, "we were not able to avoid the death of more than fifteen thousand souls." (46)

The quick progress of the two armies forced the remains of the garrison to take to the canoes: Sandoval noticed it at once and sent his brigantines in pursuit, giving orders to catch Cuauhtemoc and treat him well. One of his shipmasters, García Holguín, noticed a canoe somewhat out of the common, and as his crossbowmen were aiming at it, some of the Mexicans signalled to them not to shoot, pointing at the Uei Tlatoani. Cuauhtemoc was caught; a heated discussion followed between Sandoval and García Holguín as to who was entitled to the prisoner. It was, however summarily solved by a message from Cortés, claiming him without delay.

Cortés was awaiting his prisoner by the edge of the water. Cuauhtemoc landed between Sandoval and García Holguín, with a suite of other princely prisoners, and bowed low. Cortés received him cordially, embraced him and made him sit by his side in the hot sun. "Malintzin," he said to his victor, "I have done all I was bound to do in defence of my city and I can do no more; and since I come to you by force, and a prisoner, take that dirk which you have at your waist and kill me with it straight away." His hand was stretched out towards the weapon, and he wept. Cortés answered gently that he held him in higher esteem than ever for his courage, though he would have wished to save the city from destruction, and that he should put all fear aside. He asked Cuauhtemoc about his wife and the other ladies and had them found and paid every possible attention which the occasion required—then, as it began to rain, he took them all to his headquarters in Cuyoacán. (47)

When they were gone, the army felt an overwhelming silence fall over them, as if they had suddenly grown deaf. They had lived ninety-three days in a continuous noise made up of explosions, calls to arms, orders, knocks, victims' cries, the gruesome, lugubrious beating of the sacred drum; and all at once these vociferations of Witchywolves, the ferocious god of war, had died out; peace hung on their idle hands and overawed them with quietness. The Spanish soldiers were left alone with their thoughts in the silent halls of their souls. (48)

Lagoon of the City of Mexico with Its Several Cities

PART VI
SELF-CONQUEST

CHAPTER TWENTY-SEVEN

The Conqueror Conquered
by His Conquest

THAT night must have been for Cortés the first night of real rest since he had made up his mind to conquer Mexico. Yet, it cannot have been a night of deep, unmixed satisfaction. He had lost many a friend, and the sincerity of his grief is unmistakably expressed even in his cold reports to the Emperor, as when he relates the death of his youthful servant Cristóbal de Guzmán: "whose death caused the whole camp so much sadness, that to this day the grief remains recent in those who knew him." (1) He had been gradually led to harden his feelings by having to tolerate the cannibalistic ways of his native allies, he who had begun his conquest as an untiring crusader against human sacrifices; he had been forced to destroy the lovely city which he had dreamt to conquer by political craft and Machiavellian patience; he had seen entire companies of his own soldiers sacrificed to Witchywolves; and he had worked his way to victory over a sea of dead bodies. Cortés was not the man to rejoice in a triumph bought at such a heavy price; on the night of his second conquest of Mexico, he must have dreamt wistfully of that of his first conquest, when in the splendour of Moteçuçuma's pageantry and in clouds of copal incense, he had impersonated Quetzalcoatl.

He was fortunately saved from the throes of introspection by his vigorous appetite for action and by the calls on it which circumstances never ceased making. His first care was for the health of the stricken town. He instructed Cuauhtemoc to repair the aqueducts and to bury the dead; this done, to repair streets and bridges and to rebuild the houses; and to direct his people to return to their houses in the town within two months, leaving aside certain zones for the Spaniards. (2) He discussed with his captains and men where the chief Spanish city was to be built, and decided in favour of Tenochtitlán itself, mostly as he says because "it has always had so much memory and fame"; and a few months later he was able to write to the Emperor: "The city of Tenuxtitlán is being repaired; it looks very beautiful; Your Majesty may believe that it will become nobler every day, so that, just as erewhile it was the chief and mistress of all these provinces it will be so in the future." (3)

These flights into creative statesmanship compensated him for many a minor quarrel within his army, for the hour of the booty is always a sad hour with men. Cuauhtemoc complained that the daughters and wives of many Mexicans had been stolen by the Spanish soldiers; Cortés gave him powers to search the three Spanish camps and claim them. Bernal Díaz records that the missing women were found but that, with the exception of three, all wished to remain with their captors, which is hardly credible. But the human booty was much easier to apportion than the gold. This was the hour his men had fought for; the hour in which they were to rise from hardship and poverty into comfort and wealth. In the elementary economics of the day, and possibly of all days, for men of prey the symbol of wealth was gold. Every man had dreams of gold. Cortés had offered his army a banquet to celebrate their victory, "for which he had much wine which had come from Castille to the port of the Rich Town, and pigs which had been brought from Cuba." Bernal Díaz is somewhat severe on this banquet, partly because there were not enough seats, partly "owing to many things, not very good, which occurred in it"; there is a long paragraph crossed out in his manuscript, in which he goes into the matter: "for this plant of Noah made some behave most foolishly and there were men who went about walking on the tables, who could not find the way out into the courtyard, and others who said they would buy horses with golden saddles and crossbowmen who said that their arrows and darts would henceforward be made of gold out of their share which they were to receive." (4) This scene, which Bernal Díaz records with a frown, throws a searching light into the underworld of simple desires and naïve ambitions which surrounded Cortés in his hour of triumph.

But the direct and unashamed ambition of his soldiers for wealth and comfort was by no means his only problem at the time; after all, he had always been able to weather the storms which now and then agitated his rank and file, by his able mixture of democratic tactics and autocratic leadership. He now had at his elbow the King's Treasurer, Alderete, whose duty it was to see that the King was not done out of his fifth, and who no doubt interpreted it as meaning also that the King's officials—who could make or unmake him—were not forgotten on the day of sharing. Alderete, moreover, was one of Fonseca's henchmen, and, therefore, sure to be on the lookout for any mistake which Cortés might make. (5) All these factors were bound to weigh on the mind of the leader who, though victorious, had not yet received the formal approval of his actions from the King, and, in particular, the absolution for that revolt against Velázquez which was a kind of original sin of his historic life.

This explains the solemn and formal procedure which he adopted to secure the treasure left behind in Mexico on the day of his defeat. The whole army marched "in much concert and order, in two rows"; then Cuauhtemoc himself, with the kings of Tetzcuco and Tacuba by his side, followed by the Serpent-Woman and a host of other leaders. The Mexican court and the Spanish captains met in the houses of Coyohuehuetzin, the only abode rich and vast enough for such a gathering which remained standing in the ruined city; the terraces had been richly furnished with curtains, awnings and carpets; a dais had been provided for Cortés. The Spanish conqueror bade Cuauhtemoc sit on his right and the two other kings on his left; the terrace was thronged with Spanish captains and soldiers and with Mexican leaders and warriors. Doña Marina stood by Cortés.

The first question put to the King was: what had become of the treasure lost by the Spaniards the previous year? Much wealth in gold and jewels was immediately brought forward and deposited in the middle of the room, under the wary and astonished eyes of the King's Treasurer. But though it was much, it was far short of what had been left behind, and Cortés insisted that all was to be brought; whereupon the Mexicans explained that whatever was missing had oozed away by water or by land during the siege. In the end the

O

Spaniards were not content with the great wealth they had recovered,
because of the still greater wealth which could not be found, but, for
the time being at any rate, they thought better to wait. The meeting
ended with an examination of the methods in use among the Mexicans
for exacting tribute from the provinces towards the expenses of the
State. Cortés decided there and then to divide the province of
Tenochtitlán, leaving Cuauhtemoc in authority over all but Tlatelolco, for which he appointed as governor one Ahuelitoctzin "who was
later called Don Juan." (6)

Cortés began by putting aside all jewels and pieces which had a
distinctive artistic value, and obtaining the consent of his companions of all ranks that these pieces should be sent to the King of
Spain as a present, to be conveyed by the procurators (or deputies)
of the Spanish town councils of New Spain. (7) The bulk of the
rest was smelted, and yielded one hundred and thirty thousand
castillians, a fifth of which was handed over to the eager Alderete;
Cortés took his fifth; there were the usual claims on the part of those
who had lost horses (not unreasonable, considering the value, both
military and economic, of a horse in those days); finally the share
of the ordinary soldier came to sixty pesos each for horsemen, and
fifty for infantrymen.

Disappointment bred disaffection, and two dangerous currents
of opposition threatened Cortés; one came from the common soldier,
who was eaten up with debts, owing to purchases of arms at sixty
pesos a crossbow, fifty a sword, (8) or to medical fees of Master
John, the surgeon, who cured grave wounds only, or of a kind of
"killer of healthy men" who was a barber and an apothecary and
also cured for money; for all the wounded were not as wise as those
who were content to go with their gaping wounds to Isabel Rodriguez,
who just washed the wounds with water, tied them up, and blessed
them in the name of the Holy Trinity, thereby curing them quicker
than the surgeon and the "killer of healthy men" despatched their
patients. (9)

More dangerous still, Alderete, with the Narváez and Fonseca
factions within the army, pointed at Cortés' leniency towards Cuauhtemoc as proof of collusion between them on the matter of gold.
Cortés was not in the habit of executing his conquered enemies; he

had dealt generously with his chief opponents all through the conquest, in particular with Xicotencatl junior, with Narváez himself and even, within the standards of his day, with Cacamatzin. It was therefore natural that, feeling at rest about his hold on Mexico, he should allow Cuauhtemoc to come and go unmolested though technically a prisoner, and should even grant him a more or less nominal authority over Tenochtitlán. But the fact that both his rank and file and the powerful Fonseca group suspected Cuauhtemoc of concealing the treasure of Moteçuçuma, made this liberal behaviour of Cortés most vulnerable, and the astute commander realised it the moment Alderete publicly required him to torture Cuauhtemoc in order to extract the truth about the treasure from the defeated King.

Cortés, nevertheless, demurred; and on the white walls of his residence in Coyoacán the satirical vein of his disgruntled soldiers scrawled abuse and innuendo in blunt prose and sprightly rhyme. "Not conquerors of New Spain, but conquered of Hernán Cortés," said one, and another commented: "Not content with his share as general, he wants a royal share as well." Blunt prose might have passed unnoticed, with at most the pursing of his upper lip, and possibly a slight swelling of the veins in his throat and in his forehead which Bernal Díaz had noticed in him as a sure sign of anger; but those mischievous verses proved too much and, carried away by his literary ability, he made the mistake of answering wit with wit—"with very good rhymes and very aptly," says Bernal Díaz. (10) This gave the duel of charcoal on plaster a powerful fillip, until Cortés still a duellist, not yet a chief, wrote on the wall, "White wall, paper for fools"; to which his anonymous critics retorted: "Paper for wise men and for hard truths, and His Majesty will soon know." He had to put a stop to this "press campaign" by an act of authority.

But the incident made him the weaker to resist the pressure of Alderete, and he consented to have Cuauhtemoc and the King of Tacuba put to torture; their feet were exposed to the fire. The scene has often been told dramatically enough and inaccurately enough. On the strength of Gómara and others, it is believed that the King of Tacuba, glancing with appealing eyes at Cuauhtemoc, brought upon himself the stern rebuke: "Am I in some delight or

bath?" Actual facts are not as neat as this story might suggest, for
it is plain from the evidence that, though the torture of the two
kings did not reveal where the remainder of Moteçuçuma's treasure
was hidden, Cuauhtemoc did provide fresh hints which led to the
discovery of some valuable pieces and in particular a golden circle,
"Sun" or Calendar, which lay at the bottom of a pool in the garden
of his own house. This discovery and others of lesser value must
have contributed to clear Cortés in the eyes of his more suspicious
soldiers.

There is no doubt that he disliked the treatment inflicted on
Cuauhtemoc. "Cortés," says Torquemada, "always argued against
[giving torment to Cuauhtemoc], asserting that they should not
anger God Who had given them victory." But Alderete "importuned,
demanded and even threatened him, implying that he, Cortés, had
hidden all that wealth, and openly demanded that torture should be
applied (and with insolent ways he asked him to do so, for he was
a servant of Juan Rodríguez de Fonseca, Bishop of Burgos, President
of the Council of the Indies, whom Fernando Cortés did not hold as
a friend)." "Cortés, annoyed, gave imperious orders to cease the
torture of Cuauhtemoc, holding it inhuman and avaricious to treat a
King in such a way."

This version tallies perfectly with all we know from Bernal Díaz
and other chroniclers; it enables us to form an adequate estimate of
Cortés' share in this disgraceful episode. Cortés was annoyed because
he had acted not as he wished, but out of the weakness inherent in
his own situation, for his authority was a giant with feet of clay.
Yet we should be committing a moral anachronism were we to imagine
that he objected to Cuauhtemoc's torture on the same grounds of
human sensibility which move us—some of us—nowadays. Had he
felt that way, he would have been in advance of his time to an
inexplicable degree. Cortés felt unhappy not because the action to
which he had consented was not up to *our* standards, but because
it was not up to the standards of the men of his century, even though
all of them, everywhere in Europe, took torture as a matter of course.
What humiliated and angered him was not the physical pain of the
torture, but the insult inflicted on the King, and the reflection on
his own name. This *despecho* (the word is untranslatable, with its
suggestions of disorder or turmoil in all that lies within man's breast)

felt by Cortés at Cuauhtemoc's torture must be counted as one of the stages in his Calvary—that Calvary which was now to begin for him. (11)

* * *

Nor should we imagine Cortés as a man above a material ambition of his own. We know how in his youth he had predicted that he would be hanged or eat to the sound of trumpets; in these crises with his soldiery over the gold there was always, on the part of his men, an element of justified resentment since it was a fact that Cortés kept for himself a fifth of the booty. In our eyes he was entitled to it; we know him and his greatness well enough to feel that he had it in him to make gold fructify much better than his humble soldiers would with their gambling and their wine. But these humbler soldiers who had fought for him would have been superhumanly noble had they not felt embittered at the sight of their chief's almost kingly splendour when all they got for a share in the booty was the price of a crossbow or of a sword. Cortés was ambitious, that is, power-thirsty; he knew therefore the value of gold in terms of power, and it was as power that he wanted gold.

There is an episode in his victory which shows that, generous as he was towards his men, he kept intact his rights to the chief honours of the victory. García Holguín and Sandoval had come to him with their quarrel still open over the capture of Cuauhtemoc. Cortés put them off, says Bernal Díaz, "with a story of a quarrel just like this one which the Romans had between Marius and Cornelius Sulla [. . .] when they entered Rome in triumph over their deeds and exploits; it seems Sulla put Jugurtha in his triumph, with an iron chain, and Marius said it was he who ought to put him in his triumph." He then declared that he would put the case before the King as to which of the two captains would be granted the honours of the event for his coat of arms; but, as Bernal Díaz drily records without comment, Cuauhtemoc was one of the seven kings whose heads were granted by Charles V to figure on the coat of arms of Cortés himself. Nor can it be said that in so doing Cortés had gone beyond the bounds of justice. (12)

* * *

Cortés gradually settled down to govern the country. There was first a programme of exploration and conquest as the natural consequence of his seizure of the capital; to this task he applied his untiring energy, stimulated by the need to keep his soldiers both busy and away. Expeditions, moreover, always opened up vistas of more booty and allowed men to look forward to better days in compensation for past disappointments. These expeditions appealed to him for a number of reasons. He was not thinking merely of rounding out his conquest; he was also concerned with the economic basis of his power, both from the point of view of the general support of the population and from that of some essential supplies. Gold and silver were, of course, always welcome; but he was thinking also of copper for his bronze guns; and of sulphur for his powder. By raising the barter price of copper, he put together enough of it to make culverins; but the tin to turn the copper into bronze had to be purchased at high cost from persons who had pewter dinner services; he noticed that in the province of Taxco tin was in use as coinage; he followed up the clue, found the deposits, and at once sent Spanish workers and masters to obtain it; his prospectors discovered iron ore as well. (13)

The adventures of Montaño and Mesa, whom he sent to the Popocatepetl volcano for sulphur, should stand high in the annals of exploration. (14) Cortés persuaded them to make the ascent and to explore the crater with the final and unanswerable argument that those he had sent before had just come back and avowed their failure "as if there was anything in the world so difficult that men of brain and valour could not achieve it." Who ever uttered a prouder, clearer assertion of Renaissance humanism than these words of Hernán Cortés? (15)

*   *   *

But though as keen a prospector as any one in his time Cortés was fully aware of the value of general economy, and from the first he paid as close an attention to land development and agriculture as when, a youthful settler, he had led the way in cattle farming amidst the Spanish colony of Haiti. We owe to Bernal Díaz a revelation of the efforts he made to show the way of true economy to his gold-obsessed soldiers. "In Moteçuçuma's Income Books," Bernal Díaz explains, "we looked up which were the provinces from which he drew gold tribute and where there were mines, cocoa and cotton wraps, and thereto we wished to go [. . .] and as we saw that the pueblos in the neighbourhood of Mexico had no gold mines, nor cotton, but [only] much maize and maguey fields for their wine, we held it a poor land and we all went away to other provinces, to settle in them, and we were all very much mistaken. I remember how I went to speak to Cortés asking him leave to go with Sandoval and he said: 'In my conscience, Sir Bernal Díaz del Castillo, you live in error, and I should like you to remain here with me; but since you wish to depart with your friend Sandoval I wish you godspeed, though I know you will repent." (16)

His plan was clear. He wanted to develop the natural wealth of the land. This meant: grants of land to the conquerors; grants of land to prominent natives; and some general solution of the labour problem. The distribution of land to the conquerors was carried out as the first civic act of the towns created. A "town" was first and foremost a town council, which meant a State in miniature, an image of the Spanish State. Cortés created several of these immediately after his victory, in particular Mexico, Medellín, in Oaxaca, and a second Segura de la Frontera in Tututepec. (17) In each of the towns, lands were given to the conquerors. In Mexico, the capital, the finest sites were given by the City to Cortés himself, to Alvarado, Sandoval and other captains.

But the prominent natives were not left out. Cortés left a clear statement of his policy in this respect, invaluable for the light it sheds on his economic ideas. He explains to the Emperor how he has always wished to see Mexico rebuilt and how he entrusted the Serpent-Woman, or *Cihuacoatl*, with the task of bringing back the natives scattered by the siege. "And in order that he should have more authority, I gave him back the post which he had in the days of his lord, which is that of *ciguacoat*, which means lieutenant of the lord; and I also gave other governing posts which they used to have to other prominent natives whom I knew; and I gave domains of land and people to this *ciguacoat* and to the others, for their upkeep, though not as much as they used to have, nor enough for them to be dangerous for some time to come; and I have always endeavoured to honour and favour them; and they have worked so well on it that there are now [October, 1524] in the city upwards of thirty thousand neighbours, and its markets and commercial transactions are carried out as they used to be; and I have given them so many liberties and exemptions that its population grows considerably every day, for they live very much to their taste, and the skilled workers, of whom there are many, live on their salaries, among the Spaniards [. . .] and the merchants hold their goods in full safety and sell them; and others live, some as fishermen, an important trade in this city, others on agriculture, for many of them have their allotments and sow them with all the vegetables of Spain of which we have been able to obtain seed. And I certify Your Caesarean Majesty that if they had Spanish plants and seeds, and Your Highness were pleased to have us supplied with them, as I asked Your Majesty in my former report, considering how inclined the natives of these parts are to cultivate their lands and make them bear trees, there would be here much abundance in little time, whereof I believe there would flow no small profit for Your Highness' imperial crown, for it would stabilise these lands and Your Sacred Majesty would derive from them more dominion and income than from all Your Majesty at present owns in the name of Our Lord; and to this end Your Highness may rest assured that there shall be no failing in me, and that I shall work thereto as long as my forces and power will last." (18)

This page was written by no shallow adventurer; it was written by a seasoned statesman and a sound, if intuitional, economist. Cortés saw the development of the country he had conquered as one of healthy economic growth, based on the content and prosperity of the native population. At this early stage he began to be concerned over the two chief problems raised by the economic and social adjustment between the two races: the labour question and the reward to be given to the conquerors for their share in the conquest. There was a close relation between the two, for if the reward was to consist in lands, lands without labour are but a ruinous luxury; on the other hand, it was not easy to ensure an adequate supply of labour as long as it was possible for the natives to evade working for the foreigner by internal migration. The conquerors, moreover, came from a race of frontier fighters who had waged an eight-century war against peoples outside the pale of civilisation. It was still customary for Turk or Moor in the Mediterranean to carry away into slavery any

Spaniard caught by their ships; some of Cortés' soldiers were sure to have relatives in slavery. A victory so hardly won, over a people more heathenish by far than Moor or Turk, should in the normal course of things have resulted in wholesale slavery; and only a complete failure to adjust our historical vision to the century we are observing can explain how the greatness of Cortés' attitude in this respect has not been adequately understood. For there is but one reason why, save for a small number of prisoners who were branded as slaves, the fall of Mexico after so fierce a siege should have led to no loss of liberty for the vanquished. When Málaga fell to Ferdinand the Catholic after a siege, stubborn enough, yet not to be compared with that of Mexico, the Catholic King branded the whole population into slavery. (19) Why did Cortés take a different course? Because he was a different and a greater man.

His wars, however, had produced a number of slaves, which went some little way towards easing the labour question; but, precisely because they were so few, slavery could not be considered a wholesale solution of the problem. Cortés was most averse from introducing any form of compulsory labour amongst the natives, because, as he explains to the Emperor, he held them "much more capable than those of the Islands [. . .] and for this reason I thought it a grave matter to compel them to serve the Spaniards in the manner it is done in the Islands; yet, short of it, the conquerors and settlers would not be able to support themselves." He recalls how he suggested to the Emperor that the Spanish settlers should be subsidized out of the Crown's rights on the conquest; then he paints a picture of the situation which led him to accept a solution similar to the *repartimiento* which he knew well from his Haiti and Cuba days: the many expenses of the Spanish Crown; the long services and heavy debts of the conquerors; the delays which would indefinitely postpone his alternative plan for a subsidy, "and above all the constant importunity of Your Majesty's officials and of the Spaniards here." His vocabulary was new: he neither "distributed" (*repartimiento*), nor "entrusted" (*encomienda*); he "deposited" the natives, which meant that they were to "serve and give the Spaniard with whom they were deposited all that he might need for his support." (20)

He defends the scheme, one might think, as a necessary evil; for

O*

on the one hand he explicitly declares that he was "practically compelled" to adopt it, while on the other he argues that "it was not possible to find a better way to ensure both the support of the Spaniards and the survival and good treatment of the Indians." And in his fourth letter, he gives an earnest of his concern for the native population in words which carry conviction: "As it is in my interest to seek all the best possible means for populating these lands, and for ensuring that the Spanish settlers and the natives remain and propagate, [. . .] I enacted some laws. The Spaniards who dwell in these parts are not very pleased with some of them, in particular with those which bind them to strike root in the land; for all, or most, of them intend to deal with these lands as they did with the Islands first populated, namely to exhaust them, to destroy them, then to leave them. And as I believe that it would be a grave guilt for those of us who have experience of the past not to remedy the present and the future by forestalling the evils which caused the loss of those Islands, particularly as this land is so great and so noble [. . .] and where God Our Lord may be so well served and Your Majesty's income so much increased, I beg Your Majesty to look into it." (21)

* * *

These lines convey an attitude of statesmanlike responsibility. The conqueror has been conquered by his conquest. Sitting in Coyoacán, in the spotless white native palace which he had chosen for his residence, or later in Mexico itself, in the sumptuous palace which the bilious eyes of envy were to see bigger and more sumptuous still, the master of New Spain cast a political eye over his domains, not to take them in and enjoy them passively in a self-satisfied contemplation, but to detect in their vast landscape the new avenues of action along which he was to pour his still youthful energy. Even in the days of his first sway, when he was the true power behind Moteçuçuma, he had sought to explore the coast for good harbours, and studied the native maps painted, without much sense of distance or perspective, on cotton cloths Now, in fuller possession of his means of action, he devoted much attention to his point, and not content with organising an expedition to Pánuco, the only part of the northern coast on which he believed good ports could be found,

(22) he sent two different expeditions to discover the Southern Sea. "Discover" was a manner of speaking, for the Southern Sea, the dream of all discoverers, had been sighted by Balboa in 1513, as Cortés was bound to know, and by Magellan in November, 1520, which probably he did not know yet. What he meant was to discover a way to the Southern Sea from Mexico, rightly thinking that "in discovering it a great service was done Your Majesty." (23) He was most happy to receive home the two expeditions he had sent, one of which had taken possession of the Southern Sea in the name of His Majesty, in sign of which they erected crosses on its coast. This discovery spurred his imagination to seek that of the Straits which man seemed somehow or other to expect nature to have provided in the neighbourhood of the present Panama Canal, and he was preparing his untiring energy for this noble task when the usual futile interference from the Court officials came to waste his time and energy with yet another domestic crisis.

Cortés received news from Veracruz that one Cristóbal de Tapia, *Veedor* or Overseer of His Majesty's Gold Foundries in Española, had arrived in the Rich Town with authority to take over the government of New Spain. He was well acquainted with Cristóbal de Tapia and knew him to be a weak official without military talents, and not above the temptations of gold. He therefore adopted legalistic tactics and opposed Tapia's claims with an imposing array of *procuradores* or representatives of town councils. The technique was well tried and had stood him in good stead more than once. He knew that the papers which Tapia brought, though written in the name of King Charles and his mother Queen Juana, really emanated from his relentless enemy Fonseca; it was therefore necessary to meet them with that republican passive resistance which the democratic institutions of Spain permitted, particularly when ably handled by an astute autocrat. Poor Tapia was nonplussed before the arguments and quibbles of all these captains—Sandoval, Alvarado and the rest —turned magistrates. Father Melgarejo, the alchemist of sin, argued with him in his subtle and wise way; and even Narváez (against whom no less than against Cortés, by a Machiavellian stroke of the bishop, Tapia's powers had been drafted) with his voice "under-a-vault," made more solemn by dire experience, said to him: "Methinks, Sir Cristóbal de Tapia, you shall fare no better than I have done.

See what I have come to, though I had such a great fleet. Watch your person and waste no time, for Cortés' good fortune is not yet over. Try to get some gold out of him and go to Castille and appeal to His Majesty, for you will not lack fervour, having the bishop on your side." So, Cortés' friends "bought from him a few negroes and three horses and one ship" and he went away rich though disappointed. The friars who governed in Santo Domingo and who had discouraged his interference in the affairs of New Spain looked askance at his newly acquired wealth, and the episode no doubt contributed to the final discomfiture of the Fonseca-Velázquez faction. (24)

* * *

Cortés had beaten off Tapia, as he had Narváez, Garay and the rest; but his victory remained purely a matter of force, without that sanction of law which, for a mind such as his, was indispensable for the enjoyment of power. His legalistic tricks, his summonses, and his notarial deeds were but tokens of the real anxiety with which he lived in the wilderness of rebellion, tainted with the "original sin" of his conquest, until the only source of legitimate power in Spain, the King in person, recognising his merits, should wash him clean of it. He knew that no man had ever rendered his King a more glorious service, and he would have been justified had he felt a bitter disappointment at the royal silence after two years of hard fighting and of incredible victories. His fame had spread far and wide, but all he received back from the country which he had covered with power and glory was, every now and then, a petty attempt at superseding him with men whose poor quality was an added insult to the prolonged injury he was sustaining.

Faithful, however, to his two-edged tactics, one edge of gold, one edge of steel, he persevered at court with messengers well provided with funds and presents, and in New Spain with an ever awake activity bent on extending and consolidating his hold over the land. From the very first he had attached a considerable importance to the region of Pánuco, and had tried to maintain friendly relations with the local caciques. It was a coast in which he thought he would find good anchorages; and, moreover, a zone on which Francisco de Garay had made persistent claims and to which he had sent repeated if unsuccessful expeditions. When Cristóbal de Tapia came to upset his plans, he was preparing one himself to establish his own authority there. (25) The expedition was adjourned while Tapia was in the offing, but was taken in hand again as soon as the intruder had gone. Cortés heard that Don Diego Colón, Diego Velázquez and Francisco de Garay were conspiring to prevent his penetration in the Pánuco region; and, though Don Diego Colón does not seem to have been a party to such a conspiracy, the power of his enemies, real or imaginary, had the usual stimulating effect on Cortés, who took the field in person and entered again on one of those hard and dangerous campaigns for which he was an incomparable leader. He fought like a lion, negotiated like a fox, and conquered like an eagle, leaving the district in effective possession of his lieutenants. As a mark of his success, he founded a Spanish city Santisteban del Puerto, adorned with its *alcaldes* and *regidores* and all the regalia of Spanish municipal life. (26)

*   *   *

Cortés had now in hand everything that was needed for sending an effective embassy to Spain: he had the booty of his second conquest, which, though not as rich as they all had expected, did amount to 44,979 pesos, leaving aside priceless works of art made of gold, precious stones, silver and featherwork; he had a number of Spanish towns, each of which stood in the hazy background of distance as a stately basis of authority for his—or rather their—*procuradores*; he had also two excellent nominees for the post, chosen with his usual solicitude for the opposition and with his usual skill in the handling of men: Antonio de Quiñones, captain of his bodyguard, and Alonso Dávila, "a forward man and one with whom he was not always in good terms so that he always wished to keep him far away." Quiñones needed no special attentions, but Dávila, just back from another mission to Santo Domingo, was granted lands and Indians enough to ensure his loyalty to the party which made him wealthy; and both left for Spain invested with their democratic dignity of procuradores of New Spain and well provided with funds. (27)

They were of course well provided with arguments also, both in Cortés' own clear, intelligent and executive style and in the more mixed style of his soldiers, to the effect that Cortés should be left in charge and that certain privileges should be reserved for the conquerors. One request must have enlivened with a fleeting smile the careworn face of the youthful Emperor; Cortés' soldiers begged him "not to send lawyers over, for on entering the land they would upset it all with their books and there would be lawsuits and discussions." (28)

The procuradores left Veracruz on December 20th, 1522; they sought refuge against pirates in the Island of Santa María, in the Azores, where Quiñones was seriously wounded in the course of a duel over a lady though, contrary to what Prescott says on Bernal Díaz' authority, he did not die of his wounds. There the two procuradores met their predecessors Ordás and Mendoza, held up for lack of a safe conveyance to Spain; the *Casa de Contratación* knew of their plight and sent two caravels under Don Pedro Manrique; but Fonseca seized the opportunity to lay an embargo on all the gold and jewels the procuradores brought, with the charitable intention of depriving Cortés of his chief tools at Court.

A bishop is a powerful man, but Providence's ways are inscrutable even for bishops; and in this case they led, though deviously, to a much bigger recognition of the splendours of Cortés' treasure than the Bishop had tried to avoid: a French corsair, Jean Florin, who was a loyal Protestant, objected on strictly religious grounds to any gold on which he could lay his hands reaching those of the King of Spain, thought it his duty to fall upon the caravels conveying the treasure, killed Quiñones, took Dávila to La Rochelle, and delivered the gorgeous treasure into the delicate hands of Francis I. (29) "All is won, save honour," the gallant King no doubt thought, and he kept the goods.

This mishap brought Cortés to the direct attention of the Emperor as nothing else could have done; but when the Dávila expedition left Veracruz Cortés had already won a political triumph of which he was unaware. Charles V had arrived back in Spain from his German dominions (July 16th, 1522). Juan de Ribera, Cortés' secretary, who, with Ordás, had left the Azores in advance of the others in a Portuguese caravel, brought news and encouragement to Cortés' father and to the two first procuradores, Puertocarrero and Montejo; the powerful Duke of Béjar, a relation of Puertocarrero's, was an active ally; but the best ally was the very splendour and scope of the conquest itself, an afterglow of which was to be the astonishment which Moteçuçuma's treasure had produced in the brilliant court of Charles' chief rival.

During that summer the Emperor referred the case to a strong committee, presided over by his own chief chancellor Gattinara, and composed of the most prominent men of his public service, both Flemish and Spanish. The very fact that such a body was set up was in itself a grave setback for Bishop Fonseca. The outcome of their labours was a complete vindication of Cortés. Fonseca walked out of the world stage which he had trodden with such an overbearing mien, and soon afterwards died a disappointed man. (30)

CHAPTER TWENTY-EIGHT

Captain General and Governor of New Spain

ON OCTOBER 15th, 1522, Cortés obtained at last what he had so long desired: he was officially recognised as the legitimate ruler of New Spain. He, the fearless adventurer, the pioneer in the wilderness, on the edge of a New World in which everything might seem to be permitted to the strong and to the daring, was, more even than he realised, a citizen of that ghostly Roman Empire, a child of that spiritual Christendom which everywhere rose in men's souls to exact respect for form, order, law, a common inheritance of generally accepted rules. Despite his triumphs, Cortés had felt an outcast until that day towards the end of 1522 when he at last held in his hands the two royal letters, one official, appointing him Governor and Captain General of New Spain; the other one personal, showing the interest with which the King-Emperor had returned to the examination of the affairs of New Spain as soon as he had arrived in the Peninsula, and acknowledging the good services of the Conqueror. (1)

These letters arrived just in time to undo the harm done by the last of the pinpricks with which Fonseca tormented him—the visit of one Juan Bono de Quexo, whom the Bishop had sent to reinforce Tapia in sowing disaffection in his army. (2) The letters of the Emperor acted, in the Spanish saying, "as the hand of a Saint"; and Cortés reports the incident to the Emperor in words which throw much light on his own character: "With the favour which Your Majesty was pleased to confer on me with your royal letters, they [his soldiers] are so happy and serve with so much good will, as the fruit of their services witnesses; for which, they deserve that Your Majesty should grant them favours, since they serve you so well and show so much good will to serve; and I myself most humbly beg Your Majesty to do so, for I will hold any favour done to them as if it were done to me, since without them I should never have been able to serve Your Majesty as I have done." (3)

Fortunate Majesty! Theirs had been all the toil and all the danger. He, in his golden halls of Flanders and stately palaces of Castille, had just waited in blissful ignorance of those far-off lands he was never to see, for his adventurous subjects to come and lay them at his feet; and upon a word of his, a bare recognition and acceptance of services, the loyal hearts of the conquerors poured forth profuse thanks. But he was not merely a lord, and a sovereign; in their eyes he was, above all, the law, the community incarnated; a law and a community the more desired as their unruly selves indulged in a riot of anarchy in the wilderness in which they wandered.

The royal favours to Cortés were somewhat mixed. The Emperor surrounded his new Governor and Captain General with officials chosen from his own royal household: Alonso de Estrada went as Treasurer; Rodrigo de Albornoz, as chief Accountant; Alonso de Aguilar, as *Factor,* or Chief Agent; and Peramil de Cherino, as *Veedor,* or Overseer—all names which are to fill the pages of one of the most turbulent periods in the history of the new colony. (4)

But that was still to come. Meanwhile the new Governor, now at rest on the legitimacy of his powers, set about to organise the country he was to govern. The royal officials had brought him a set of instructions which he was to follow in his governorship; Cortés dealt with them in the manner which had become classic amongst Spanish overseas governors and conquerors: he "obeyed" them but, as to "applying them," he first appealed to the Emperor against most of them. His famous *Ordenanzas,* dated March 20th, 1524, are wholly independent and, more often than not, incompatible with the instructions which he had received from Spain. But there was no indiscipline in his mind. On October 15th, 1524, he discusses the matter point by point in a circumstantial report to the Emperor, a true program of government, capable, bold and wise.

Most of the letter is a refutation of the royal instructions, for he frankly says: "Things examined and seen to from afar cannot be fittingly handled." The first point on which he differs from the King is that of the relations between natives and Spaniards: the instructions require that there shall be the freest possible intercourse, so as to stimulate the conversion of the natives; but he maintains his decision which severely prohibits Spaniards from leaving the Spanish cities without a special permit on the ground that "most of the Spaniards who come over are of low condition and manner, and vicious with various vices and sins, and if they were to be free to move about in Indian pueblos, they would sooner convert them to their vices than attract them to virtue."

He then goes on to examine the *repartimiento*. This was a point on which the Spanish Crown was most sensitive, for the personal responsibility of the King before God, a truly living force with the dynasty from Ferdinand and Isabel to Philip IV, was deeply engaged in it, as the pro-Indian clerics, such as Las Casas, were constantly repeating. In his instructions to Cortés, the Emperor reminds him that he has ordered a committee of theologians to examine the matter and they have come to the conclusion that, "since God our Lord has made them [the Indians] free, their freedom could not be taken from them." Cortés frankly says that the ban on repartimientos which the Emperor has pronounced as a sequel to this opinion has not only remained in abeyance but has been kept strictly secret on his own responsibility, since the effect on the settlers would have been disastrous and the land would have been lost for Spain and for the Holy Faith, as the repartimiento is the only economic basis of the colony.

Cortés argues his case very well, but his case, under the circumstances, is also very good. As to liberty, his point is that under their own social system the natives were not free, but on the contrary lived under the yoke of their masters, and this yoke was so hard that "it has happened and it happens every day that, in order to frighten some pueblos into serving well to Christians with whom they are deposited, they are told that, if they do not behave, they will be put back under their ancient lords: and they fear this more than any other threat or punishment."

He is equally ready to meet arguments based on the deplorable precedent of the Islands, for he says, "as I have experience of the damage done and of its cause, I am most careful not to stray into that way and I endeavour to lead matters along the very opposite road; for I believe that I should be more guilty were I to fall into those errors, which I know, than were those who first committed them." In short, his plan consists in prohibiting the use of "deposited" natives for mining; and also the use of Indian labour on lands other than that in which they live; he therefore attaches the peasants to the land, and in order to ensure a better treatment of them by their masters, he proposes that the "deposit" be made perpetual.

As his Ordenanzas show, he was organizing the land on a feudal system. Every Spaniard who received fewer than five hundred Indians was to keep a certain set of weapons enabling him to serve in the infantry; if he received more than five hundred, he was bound to keep a horse. The Spaniards were to be responsible for the conversion and Christian life of their Indian labour; they had to bind themselves to a minimum residence of eight years; if married, they had to bring their wives over within eighteen months; if unmarried, they were to get married within the same time "for the health of their conscience, for the sake of the population and for the ennobling of their lands"; within the same period, they were to build and occupy their houses; they were to plant one thousand vines for every hundred Indians as well as all the plants from Spain available in their district; these Spaniards to whom Indians were entrusted were, in his mind, to act as leaders in the economic, religious and military development of the country. Nor did his system necessarily set up one race above the other, since all reliable native leaders received "deposits" of Indians in exactly the same conditions as the Spanish conquerors; this was particularly the case with the Cihua-coatl, or Serpent-Woman, and the other Mexican magnates whom Cortés mentions in his letter to the Emperor, and with Moteçuçuma's daughters, who received extensive repartimientos in Tula and Tacuba. (5)

* * *

In the summer of 1522, when Cortés was residing in Cuyoacán, his lieutenant Sandoval, who was exploring, "pacifying" and "populating" Coatzacoalco, received news that a ship had arrived in

Ayagualulco, "a harbour though not good." It brought a number of
women, amongst them Catalina Xuárez, Cortés' wife. Sandoval and
his companions went immediately to Ayagualulco, and gallantly
escorted their captain's wife to the capital. Bernal Díaz records a
rumour to the effect that Cortés was not pleased at her arrival, yet
points out that he received her with great pleasure and much public
rejoicing. He had not asked her to come and was not expecting her.
It is plain that he was not interested in her at all, and that, but for
a brief spell before their marriage, she had never succeeded in
captivating his fancy.

Doña Catalina settled down to enjoy her exalted position, and
obtained Indians from her powerful husband; but she was jealous,
and had often occasion to suffer on that account from Cortés, who
had remained throughout a gallant Don Juan. Her health was not
good. She suffered from asthma, and no doubt found some difficulty
in adjusting her precarious breath to the altitude of Mexico, after
so many years at sea level. One day in October, about three months
after her arrival, she had a scene with her husband and felt most
unhappy about it. Her brother, who had come over with her, seems
to have been the instigator of the trouble, and the cause to have
been some light-hearted love affair of Cortés. The trouble was
patched up, and no trace of it marred the dinner to which many
guests of both sexes had been invited. While at table, Doña Catalina
said to Captain Solís: "You, Solís, think of nothing but making my
Indians work on things other than those I order them to do; and
what I wish never gets done." "It is not I, madam," retorted Solís,
"who make them work. Here is His Lordship who gives them his
orders and keeps them busy." Whereupon Doña Catalina, somewhat
aggressively, it would seem, aiming at her husband, answered Solís:
"I vouch that within a few days, I shall see to it that no one meddles
with what belongs to me." "Madam," said Cortés, half in jest, half
in earnest, "I will have none of what belongs to you." The ladies
present tried to laugh it off, but only made it worse; Doña Catalina
blushed crimson, rose, bowed low to her husband and left the room
in silence.

Cortés kept the conversation going for a while and, when his
duties as host had been fulfilled, withdrew. When he passed to his
bedroom, he found his wife was still in her private chapel, where

she had taken refuge; she was praying in silence, and tears ran down her cheeks.

"Why do you cry?" he asked.

"Let me alone. I feel like letting myself die."

He comforted her as well as he could, and called her maids, who undressed her. All was presently plunged in silence and darkness.

One or two hours had gone by when one of the Indian maids who slept in the room next to theirs heard Cortés' voice calling; on his orders, she went to wake up the two Spanish maids Ana Rodríguez and Violante Rodríguez. "Bring some lights," said Cortés. "I believe Doña Catalina is dead." The maids brought candles and found Doña Catalina's body lifeless on his arm. A necklace of golden beads she was wearing was broken and there were some dark spots on her neck.

Cortés rose from bed and withdrew to his dressing-room where some of his grooms and pages found him in a frenzy, knocking his head against the wall and screaming. Diego de Soto, his steward, sent for Father Olmedo; he also sent word to Xuárez, Doña Catalina's brother, informing him of his sister's death and requesting him not to call since his importunities had been the cause of it. Cortés wore black for years (6)

*   *   *

He was now living as monarch, both in the splendour and comfort of his household and in the power and scope of his undisputed will. He was, for the time being, incarnation of success. Now the Spanish character has many a fine feature, but it is afflicted with one of the saddest diseases of the human soul: it cannot bear success—in someone else. The Spaniard is in nearly everything the opposite of the German; the German is usually afflicted by *Schadenfreude,* or joy at his neighbour's fall; the Spaniard suffers from sadness at his neighbour's rise. Cortés had risen. He was doomed.

The evil spirits raised by his sleepless envy cannot be exorcised by generous, kind, genial ways; Cortés, however, was genial, kind, and generous because he had it in him, and not as a mere matter of policy; even though, like most men of action, he knew how to turn his qualities to good account. He was living like a prince, and behaving like one, because he had a natural greatness, combined with

a keen sensitiveness for beautiful things. His ambition and his sense
of beauty led him to rebuild Mexico as a handsome Spanish capital
—in such a grand manner that to this day it ranks even above Lima
as the most beautiful old city of the American Continents. He built
a palace for himself, of which Bernal Díaz, with his pawky humour,
remarks: "Cortés was having his houses and palaces built, and they
were such, and as great and of as many courtyards as the labyrinth
of Crete." (7) There is just a dash of envy, however slight, in these
words of the otherwise fair-minded soldier-writer; but other men
round Cortés were not as well balanced as Bernal Díaz; and the
conqueror of New Spain had to struggle the rest of his life with the
poisonous envy of the passive, incompetent and weak, and with the
aggressive envy of the strong, dashing and adventurous.

Narváez is a typical example of the first. A less generous enemy
than Cortés would have hanged him the very night of his defeat,
or otherwise disposed of him, for a battle in the night is full of
opportunities. Cortés had kept him a prisoner in Veracruz till 1522,
when he sent for him while still residing in Cuyoacán. Narváez was
dumbfounded at the sight of the lagoon and its cities, and his mind
was even more deeply impressed by Cortés' fortune and greatness.
Cortés was magnanimous and received him with much deference.
Narváez fell on his knees and tried to kiss his hands, but Cortés made
him stand up, "embraced him and showed him much love," making
him sit by his side. Narváez then said: "Now, Sir Captain, I truly
say that the least of your deeds was to defeat me, even had I brought
over bigger forces; for I have seen so many cities and lands which
Your Lordship has conquered and subjected to the service of God
and of the Emperor, that Your Lordship may well hold himself in
higher esteem than the most illustrious men in the universe." "We
are not big enough," answered Cortés, "to have done all we have
done; but God's mercy always helped us and the good luck of our
Emperor." (8)

These modest feelings were no doubt sincere in Cortés; yet no
more sincere than the pride which he at times manifests in his
achievements; they welled up on this occasion because his instinct
warned him of all the repressed envy which dwelt within Narváez'
humility; and he guessed perhaps that this envy of his defeated
opponent was to simmer and ferment with more bitterness when

Narváez' bilious eyes wandered over the splendours of the new Capital rapidly rising above the ruins of the old. (9)

*   *   *

This forlorn figure, wandering aimlessly in the very world which might have been his, was destined to be a living mirror in which more than one of the men who tried to wrench from Cortés the coveted prize of New Spain saw their doom before it overtook them. He had already played this part with Cristóbal de Tapia; he was soon to play it again with Francisco de Garay.

Cortés was preparing two expeditions which occupied his mind above all others: one, under Alvarado, to explore Guatemala; the other, under Olid, to explore Honduras, then known as Las Hibueras. His chief aim was to discover the straits which, in the opinion of many pilots, existed there between the two seas, "the thing in this world which I desire most to find, for the great service which I imagine Your Caesarean Majesty would receive by it." (10) But, when all was ready and the two captains on the point of leaving, the usual intruder came to disturb his plans: Francisco de Garay arrived in the region of Pánuco with thirteen ships and two brigantines, one hundred and twenty horse, four hundred infantry and much artillery. (11) This was, by the standards of Spanish conquerors, a most powerful force. Cortés was in bed with a broken arm, the result of a fall from his horse, and had not slept for two months; but he made up his mind to go and see to it himself, sending Alvarado in advance. His baggage was already on the way—including his bed, for Spaniards then in bedless America transported their beds with them—when a messenger arrived from Veracruz, bringing papers from Spain; and amongst them a letter from the King enjoining Garay to keep away from the parts of New Spain which Cortés had subjected. (12)

This paper was as good as an army for Cortés. He had kept intact his capacity for avoiding bloodshed by the skilful use of ink. He decided to remain in bed, and dispatched his Alcalde Mayor, or Chief Magistrate, Diego de Ocampo, not merely because he was, so to speak, the Chief Inkpot of New Spain, but because he happened to be the brother of one of Garay's most influential lieutenants. (13) The usual tragi-comedy ensued. Garay does not seem to have been capable of winning the loyalty of his officers and men; many left him, either to come over to Cortés, as "the sun which gave the more heat," or to break loose in the countryside and forage for themselves. Cortés' lieutenants, Vallejo, Alvarado and Ocampo, dealt with Garay most skilfully, now threatening, now parleying, now putting on a most judicial earnestness and producing a barrage of legal papers, summonses, enquiries and notarial deeds. Cortés was well posted on the course of events and sent instructions to come to terms if possible; and after some bloodshed and much inkshed, Garay agreed to come to Mexico as the guest of his rival and to strike a bargain with him. Cortés saw to it that he was well treated; and, of course, the very size and wealth of the land which unfolded itself before his astonished eyes, as he proceeded towards his rival's capital, impressed him both with the power and with the magnanimity of Cortés. In a letter dated Otumba, Sunday November 8th, 1523, this feeling of admiration for the conquest oozes out of every word, and he addresses Cortés as "Very Magnanimous Lord." (14)

Cortés *was* magnanimous. He gave orders to have Garay treated with the utmost deference on the way, and had a big banquet given him in Tetzcuco; he rode out himself with a brilliant retinue of his captains to meet the newcomer in his domains and showed him round the palaces and houses he was building for himself. Garay was more and more impressed. Negotiations started at once and, within a few days, led to a treaty in virtue of which Cortés kept Pánuco and gave Garay the Río de las Palmas as his sphere of influence. In the manner of monarchs, the two potentates contracted for a marriage between Garay's son and a daughter Cortés had had by a Cuban native, and whom he had given his own mother's name: Doña Catalina Pizarro.

Garay, loafing about Mexico, had leisure to meet the other loafer, Narváez; the unemployed captain came to see him and, in his solemn, intoned voice, he commented on Cortés' fortune. "I hear," he said half in jest, half in earnest, "that you warned your soldiers: 'See that we are not caught napping, as they caught Narváez.' Now, Sir Don Francisco de Garay, they broke me this eye and burnt and stole all I had and killed my *alférez* and many of my soldiers, before they beat me; but you must know that there never was a luckier man in the world than Cortés; as happy in his enterprises as Octavian; in victories, like Julius Caesar; and more active and brave in battle than Hannibal." Whereupon Garay remarked that he needed no reports on it, for his eyes sufficed to show the splendour of Cortés' achievement. A delightful scene, vividly set down by Bernal Díaz, in which we see the two failures bowing with gaping mouths, before success. (15)

There is a kind of freemasonry in failure, at any rate when it relates to the same object. Garay, in the honeymoon of his agreement with Cortés, begged him to allow Narváez to return to Cuba, to his rich wife, his mines and his Indians; and Cortés granted this readily and gave Narváez two thousand pesos of gold as a parting gift. "Narváez humbled himself before Cortés and made him many promises that he would always be his servant," says Bernal Díaz. Like most men with a bent forward, towards action, Cortés lost all interest in the ashes of past events. (16) He saw in Narváez but the ashes of his adversary; he was too bored with him to detect under the ashes the fire of the old resentment, ready to burn again.

Meanwhile, the treaty between Garay and Cortés was destroyed by fate. It was an essential part of the treaty that Cortés should use his authority to force those of Garay's men who had deserted to return to him; but this measure defeated its own ends, for many of them, determined never to serve under Garay, were overrunning the countryside and inflicting so much harm on the natives that these revolted and not only destroyed all Garay's bands but attacked Cortés' establishment in Santisteban del Puerto, which, more firmly held and more disciplined, resisted the onslaught. (17) Cortés received the news with the bitter disappointment of a man who saw his patient efforts threatened by destruction time and again through the interference of lesser men. As for Garay, he was so deeply upset that, having caught cold on Christmas night after a dinner with Cortés, he developed pneumonia and died within three days.

This was the second dramatic death on Cortés' path in the course of a little over a year; envy had now something to talk about; bilious eyes winked, and bitter tongues wagged; Garay had been poisoned by his victorious rival. (18)

*   *   *

Cortés was probably the last man to notice it, for he was always active and his eyes and thoughts dwelt on higher things. On December 6th, he had dispatched Alvarado with one hundred and sixty horse and three hundred infantry to Guatemala; on January 11th, 1524, he despatched Olid to Las Hibueras, with five big ships and a brigantine, four hundred men and eight thousand gold pesos for horses to be bought in Cuba on the way. "And I hold for certain," he writes to Charles V, "according to the news and charts of that land which I possess, that Pedro de Alvarado and Cristóbal de Olid will meet, unless some straits separate them."

He thought constantly of those straits. He was endeavouring to wrench that "secret" from nature with all his tireless perseverance. "And many secrets will be discovered," he writes to Charles V. (19) His language here is singularly like that of Colón, who also speaks of discovering the secrets of nature: it is the language of the Renaissance man; for the "discovery" of navigators and explorers was only one of the forms of that all-round urge for discovery in all the realms of experience which kindles with a light of steel the eyes of the fifteenth century and with a light of gold the eyes of the sixteenth.

Cortés' eyes shone with both the golden and the steely lights. He was hard and he was imaginative. As soon as he had set foot on the Southern Sea, he had begun to build a fleet there, with his typical perseverance for conquering nature's obstacles; for everything but the wood had to be brought from the northern coast over nearly a thousand miles of broken country and different roads. When everything was ready, a fire devoured it all; but he had forestalled even Fate and fire and had ordered from Castille a spare supply of all that had been lost except pitch, which he expected to find locally; and the fleet was ready in the summer of 1524. (20) It was his ambition to discover a better passage than that which he knew by then Magellan had discovered. (21) But the ships he had put together in Zacatula for that purpose were, after much delay, sent on other errands. He remained, however, alive to the claims of exploration and discovery, and more than once expresses his intention to explore the American coast from the extreme north, which he calls "los Bacallaos" to the extreme south, or the Straits then discovered by Magellan. Thus: "Nothing remained for me to do to that end except to know the secret of the Coast to be discovered between the Pánuco River and Florida [. . .] and from the coast of Florida northwards to the Bacallaos." (22) In that sentence he swept over all that is now the eastern coast of the United States. As for the west, he reports to the Emperor how the expedition he has sent to the Southern Sea has brought news of pearls, of a good harbour and of "an island all populated by women without any male . . . very rich in pearls and gold." Cortés puts down the story but adds, "I shall endeavour to find out the truth about it and report at length to Your Majesty." (23) This "island" was no other than California, whose name and legend came from a Spanish book of chivalry published in 1510. It is still legendary. Some males have crept into it since, and it has become the home of the modern books of chivalry which are no longer written but thrown on a screen.

*　　*　　*

Cortés was now in fact, though not in name, the most important by far of the Spanish colonial viceroys. The scope of his conquest had thrown the establishments of Santo Domingo and of Cuba into relative insignificance; Peru was not discovered yet; and the coast was but beginning to emerge from chaos. Mexico was the biggest and the best organised of the new Spanish acquisitions. Cortés could proudly write to the Emperor that, once Olid and Alvarado returned from their respective conquests, Charles V would have under his sway a land measuring over four hundred leagues on the "northern" (or eastern) and over five hundred on the "southern" (or western) coast, save the broken regions inhabited by the Zapotecs and Mixtecs, against whom he was then organising a campaign under Rodrigo Rangel. (24)

He had every reason to complain that the scope of his achievements and the value of his services were not adequately realised at Court, despite Fonseca's fall. The four officers sent him by the Emperor on behalf of his imperial treasury refused to let him draw on the royal fifth to pay back debts he had incurred in organising his expeditions: he put himself in the hands of the Emperor about it—rather incautiously, it would seem; (25) and having heard that the gold and jewels he had sent through Quiñones and Dávila had been lost to the King of France, he put together another set of presents, less brilliant, of course, than the first, among which he sent the Emperor a culverin made of silver, the metal alone of which cost him, he says, twenty-four thousand five hundred golden pesos. It was highly elaborate and decorated on the theme of the Phoenix,

and bore a proud, perhaps too proud, inscription, addressed to the
Emperor: (26)

> Peerless this bird is by birth
> Peerless you are on the Earth
> Peerless is my service's worth.

Poor culverin! Poor Cortés! The Emperor, aloof, indifferent
to a strange degree towards the epic adventure of the greatest by far
of all his subjects, gave the culverin-phoenix to his Secretary-Treasurer Francisco de los Cobos, who smelted it and pocketed over
twenty thousand ducats of silver and gold from the proceeds.

And who can say whether this sad, utilitarian end of the silvery
phoenix was not after all more favourable for Cortés than a continued
existence of his proud present, with its constant reminder of the
Conqueror's success and outstanding services? There was no lack
of dukes and marquesses at Court who took offence at the verses
and could think of subjects who had better served the Emperor than
Cortés, though they grew silent when challenged to mention names
by the three stout and powerful advocates whom Cortés had now at
Court: the Admiral of Castille, the Count of Aguilar and the Duke
of Béjar, who were already planning the marriage of their daughter
and niece Doña Juana de Zúñiga with the conqueror of Mexico.
The arrival of the silvery phoenix and of sixty thousand pesos of
gold for the King came then to lend support to both friends and
enemies of Cortés; among the last were two of the failures whom
Cortés had sent back from Mexico—Cristóbal de Tapia and Narváez
himself, who now gave vent to his bilious envy without having to
cover it up under thick layers of obsequiousness. (27)

Another storm was brewing against Cortés in Spain. But he knew
nothing about it and went on his business of governing, enlarging and
organising a new country. He was conscious of his superiority—both
moral and intellectual—and writes to the King on the tendency
evinced by the four officials sent from Spain to overstep the bounds
of their respective functions and usurp his. This page is an admirable
illustration of his wise and balanced mind; he explains how he pays
the four officials as much honour and deference as they have a right
to expect and how, so far, they perform their duties satisfactorily;
and when pointing out that they must not be allowed to meddle in

the government, he begs the Emperor to send royal orders to that effect for, realising how important it was that all should remain on friendly terms, he does not wish to create bad blood by doing so himself. (28)

The situation was the more delicate as, by some obscure meanness which had crept into the very royal papers acknowledging his great services, the salary fixed for him as Governor was only just over three hundred thousand maravedís while each of the four royal officials by his side was given five hundred and ten thousand. As he rightly points out, he should have received at least four times as much as any of the others. It is indeed an eloquent proof of his self-control and of his magnanimity that at no time does he complain of these irritating pinpricks otherwise than in the most dignified and objective terms. (29)

He does not seem to have a good opinion of the men he governs from the political point of view. Charles V has instructed him to appoint the *alcaldes* and *regidores* of the towns on lists of nominees presented by the towns themselves; he begs the Emperor to let him keep to his own system which is to appoint them freely himself. For, he argues, the towns would present whomsoever suited the personal interests of the local authorities and not "the good of the republic," while "the Governor, since all order and harmony in the councils redounds to his honour, and the reverse to his infamy, obviously will pay more attention to what is fitting." As a measure adapted to the conditions of the still budding colony, this plan may be defended; but Cortés goes on to provide a second argument which shows that he was no democrat: "And there is a further point which I fancy is a more serious drawback, namely that since the Governor represents your royal person and jurisdiction, in allowing the towns and other persons to take a hand in this matter, your royal pre-eminence would appear to be derogated, and time might extend this and make of it a use and a custom." (30)

There are other opinions of Cortés more in harmony with our way of thinking. He objects to Charles V's claim to have a tax laid on every individual native. He rightly thinks it a ruinous form of service, since the King receives a fifth on all gold, silver and yield of metals and the natives have already to work for the Spaniards so that the Spaniards can ensure the safety of the land. (31) He advocates free trade between the Islands and the mainland, for the Islands have prohibited the export of female animals to New Spain, so as to hold the settlers at their mercy; and rightly points out that the development of New Spain has contributed in no small degree to the prosperity and welfare of the Islands. (32) In all the correspondence of this period, we find him objective, sensible and always bent on the welfare of all concerned, a liberal in economics if an autocrat, however enlightened, in politics.

* * *

He calls to mind one of those enlightened despots who illustrate the eighteenth century—in all but his deep-seated faith. He repeatedly asks the Emperor to send good men in religious orders to New Spain. There is a page in his letter of October 13th, 1524, in which he explains his views on this point with an earnestness not devoid of subconscious humour; he first, he says, asked for bishops; but he now asks for friars, for he says: "Bishops and prelates would not break the habit, which for our sins they now have, of disposing of the wealth of the Church for luxury and for leaving entails to their children and relations; and there would be a worse evil, to wit, that as the natives of these parts used to have religious persons in charge of their rites and ceremonies who were so well behaved in their honesty as in their chastity that, if anything were known there against one of them, he was punished with death, were they now to see Church affairs in the power of canons and other dignitaries, and to know that they were ministers of God, and saw them addicted to the vices and profanities which in our days are usual in those realms [i.e., Spain], this would belittle our faith and lend to its being held in derision: which would do so much harm that no other preaching would be of any avail." (33)

We possess an eloquent testimony of the depth of this conviction in him. On May 13th, 1524, the first mission, composed of Franciscan friars, arrived in San Juan de Ulúa. (34) They were twelve, like the apostles, and they came animated with the holiest zeal for the conversion of the natives. Cortés was very happy to hear the news and at once dispatched a gentleman of his household, Juan de Villagómez, to take charge of all arrangements for their comfort and safety. Villagómez found twelve men who cared nothing for either safety or comfort, and who, after a brief respite to recover from nearly four months at sea, set out for Mexico barefooted, refusing all other favour or convenience.

Cortés had given instructions that all the pueblos on the way, whether of natives or of Spaniards, should receive the friars with the utmost respect and affection; roads were to be swept clean before them, accommodation provided, church bells were to ring for them, "and in those days there were bells [already] in every pueblo," the natives were to come out to meet them with lit candles, and, to impress the Indians, all Spaniards were to kneel before the friars and kiss their hands and frocks. The twelve apostles walked on. They arrived in Tlaxcala and stayed one night to rest. The tian-quiztli was crowded, when the twelve strange figures walked through the native crowd, "marvelling at such a multitude of souls the like of which they had never seen together, they praised God with deep joy at the sight of the most abundant crop which He was putting before them. And as they could not speak to them for lack of knowledge of their language, by signs (as dumb people) they pointed to the sky, meaning to imply that they had come to show them the treasures and greatness which were in yonder height." The natives followed them about like children. They were bewildered at the sight of these strange Spaniards, so much unlike the conquerors, so ill clad, so thin, so humble. They pitied them as half-witted persons, who had no idea of the value of gold or of the use of force. "Poor fellows," they exclaimed. "Poor, poor fellows." For the word "poor," *motolinea* in the Nauatl language, as with us, applies equally to lack of wealth and to lack of wits. *Motolinea! Motolinea!* the crowd repeated behind them, as the good Franciscans wandered about the tianquiztli pointing to the sky and making the sign of the cross. *"Motolinea?"* asked at last one of them, Fray Toribio de Venavente. "What does it mean?" " 'Poor,' " someone translated. "That will be my name for the rest of my life," said the good friar. And henceforward his name was Fray Toribio Motolinea—by which he is still known, for he wrote, and wrote well.

On they walked, barefooted, to Mexico, a march no less victorious, yet more pacific, than that of Cortés and his companions five years earlier. Cortés had called together all his captains and all the Mexican leaders, headed by Cuauhtemoc himself, for, with his

keen insight into the value of dramatic scenes, he wished to impress
the whole Mexican nation which he was creating, both the Spanish
and the native roots of it, with the power of the spirit. Cortés was
no emotional bigot: he was a calculating statesman. The value of
the historical scene he was preparing is the higher for the fact that
it was carefully thought out.

He rode out to receive the twelve dust-covered pilgrims at the
head of a brilliant squadron of Spaniards and natives. "And when
Cortés knew that they were coming," says Bernal Díaz, who was
present, "he alighted from his horse, and when we met the reverend
friars, the first one who knelt down before Fray Martín de Valencia
and tried to kiss his hand was Cortés himself; and Fray Martín did
not consent and he kissed his frock and also that of all or most of
the other friars and so did we all, captains and soldiers present, and
Guatemuz and the other Mexican Lords; and when Guatemuz and
the other caciques saw Cortés kneeling, trying to kiss Fray Martín's
hands, they were astounded and as they saw the friars barefooted
and thin, and their frocks torn, and no horse, but on foot, and very
yellow-skinned, and Cortés whom they held to be an idol or something like their gods, thus kneeling before the friars, they took example and always from that day they receive them with similar marks
of respect."

This scene was the first spiritual stone of the Christian church in
Mexico. "This most memorable act," says Mendieta, "is painted in
many parts of this New Spain, as a perennial remembrance of such
a high deed, the highest Cortés ever did [. . .] for in other deeds
he conquered other men, while in this one he conquered himself."
It was moreover a deed in which the conqueror, the man of force,
laid force at the foot of the spirit; this beautiful scene is to be set
beside that in which Cortés, leaping "supernaturally" with an iron
bar in his hand, rose to attack the hideous face of the God of Blood.
Forcible acts, carved out of the living rock of history with the
clear-cut lines of a masterly, creative character, this rise and this
fall are the two most intense moments in Cortés' life: by their
singular rhythm, so powerful outwards and upwards in the first, so
powerful inwards and downwards in the second, and even more so
by the combined effect of their two spiritual movements, these two
deeds of Cortés, the rise of force to strike the spirit of hate, the fall

of force to serve the spirit of love, bring to mind as a haunting memory the mystic lines of St. John of the Cross:

> And I fell so low, so low
> That I rose so high, so high
> That I overtook my game. (35)

CHAPTER TWENTY-NINE

Cortés Goes to Las Hibueras and Loses Mexico

W HEN, in October 1524, Cortés sent his fourth letter-report to the Emperor, just four months after the arrival of twelve friars of St. Francis, he had every right to look forward to a long period of peace in the enjoyment of an office most suitable for his creative genius. There was enough danger and prospective war and exploration in it to attract the soldier in him: but there was a much greater scope for his gifts as a statesman. A nation had to be created. He was already threatened by yet another of the storms which his envious rivals engineered against him at Court, but he did not know it yet; the imperial letters which recognised his outstanding merit were a solid basis for his power. For the rest, he could trust his ability to handle men.

Yet, at this point, by far the most severe blow to his career came seemingly from one of his captains, actually from his own self. Cristóbal de Olid, whom he had sent to Las Hibueras, rebelled against his authority. Cortés was then so strong that he could easily have sent another more trustworthy captain, such as Sandoval, with a sufficient force to punish the rebel. He, in fact, sent a kinsman of his, Francisco de Las Casas, who, as Bernal Díaz says, and events were to prove, "was a man to face anything"; yet he repented, and decided to go there himself. The gesture, the "style" is the same as in his reaction towards Narváez' arrival; yet what, in the struggling captain still in the wilderness of an adventure of dubious legal origin, was an action as wise as it was courageous, was bound to be a most imprudent action on the part of a kind of Viceroy, enjoying unlimited

430

authority and prestige, but surrounded by officials as ambitious as petty.

In deciding to go in person at the head of a punitive expedition against Olid, Cortés made the most tragic mistake of his life. He deserted his true post, that of Governor General and creator of a new country; he came down to the level of Olid, instead of remaining on the apex of power, ready to punish him through one of his captains, and even to forgive him; he provided fuel for the fires which his enemies were kindling in Spain against him, by allowing them to present him as still and always an adventurer; he finally exposed his person to dangers and hardships which were to try his health far more searchingly than the whole conquest had done.

He was too keen not to have realised some of these facts. Why did he yield so readily to his warlike impulse? First, no doubt, because his soldierly vocation pulled him that way. In his comfortable palace, he felt homesick for the military camp. He explains to the Emperor that he decided to go against Olid "because it seemed to me that my person had been idle for a long time and done nothing new in Your Majesty's service, owing to my disabled arm"; (1) and this explanation is, no doubt, sincere. Bernal Díaz confirms it: "He was so stout-hearted that he was sorry he had sent Francisco de Las Casas instead of going himself in person." And he adds that Cortés wanted to go because the land was renowned for its wealth in gold mines.

But men have a way of using reasons, even genuine reasons, as pretexts; and the deepest motive for this most unwise of Cortés' actions may well have been that inner sense of his own original guilt which, even when absolved by the Emperor, surged again in his political conscience as soon as his own authority was threatened. This deep motive appears on the surface in his covering letter to the fourth report, when, after enumerating all the reasons why he had been so much upset by the news of Olid's revolt, he says: "And yet another thing aggrieved me more: that those who know but little about the previous business between Diego Velázquez and me, will say this is *pena peccati;* and would to God it were so, for I would not have reason for complaining; but it is the other way about, for Velázquez did not speak the truth when he denied that I had come at my expense, nor would Olid, were he to say that in this he has put any money of his own." (2) The subconscious connection between the two events—Olid's rebellion against him, his rebellion against Velázquez—is apparent. And its part as the chief impulse which drove him to the ill-fated expedition is clear from the fact that the words quoted, *coming at the end* of several other motives, lead directly to the conclusion: "And feeling aggrieved about all these things, I made up my mind to go by land to where Cristóbal de Olid was or might be, to find out the truth of the case and, if confirmed, to punish him according to justice." (3)

*   *   *

It was meet therefore that this expedition, secretly sprung from the root of anarchy hidden under the statesman, should have done more than any other single factor to plunge his lifework into anarchy and confusion. He started on October 12th, 1524, leaving as his deputies Alonso de Estrada, the Treasurer, and Rodrigo de Albornoz, the Accountant, together with a lawyer Alonso Zuazo, recently arrived. He could entertain no illusions about either the Treasurer or the Accountant. Estrada was an ambitious man and boasted that he was the son of King Ferdinand of Aragón; (4) Albornoz was intriguing against Cortés out of spite, because Cortés had not given him as many Indians as he wanted and had refused him the daughter of the lord of Tetzcuco, whom he had married to a person of quality. Cortés knew all this, and warned his friends in Spain about Albornoz' habit of sending untrue ciphered reports. What he did not know was that the same ship which conveyed this warning conveyed also one of these ciphered reports full of slanders about him. (5)

The Agent, Salazar, and the Overseer, Chirino, were not pleased when they found themselves excluded from the government. The obvious solution of the problem as seen from our day, would have been to leave a council of government composed of the five officials and possibly one or more friars, with definite quorum and majority rules. Cortés seems to have acted in this matter with less political acumen than was his wont. Salazar and Chirino tried first to prevail upon him not to leave; but, as he was determined to go, they begged leave to accompany him part of the journey, (6) no doubt with the idea of worming their way to power while on the march.

Cortés travelled in state, with the luxury and even the extravagance of a Renaissance prince; his household comprised a steward, two toastmasters, a butler, a_pastrycook, a larder-master, a man in charge of his gold and silver services, a chamberlain, a doctor, a surgeon, many pages, including two spear-pages, eight grooms, two falconers, five musicians, two jugglers, three muleteers. A huge herd of swine was a kind of marching larder for the army. He rode surrounded by a brilliant group of Spanish captains, including Sandoval; as well as by Cuauhtemoc and many prominent Mexicans—a precaution against any hostile movement on the part of the natives during his absence from the capital. (7)

It was a triumphant progress and every town or pueblo through which the army passed received it, and above all Cortés, with the utmost enthusiasm. Cortés must have tasted then the sweetness of the fruit of power at its best. By his side, Chirino, the Inspector, and Salazar, the Agent, were all honey to him and, with much subservience and rhetoric, pleaded with him for an instant return to Mexico. "Uncle, let us return, for I saw signs of ill omen this morning," sang Salazar humorously, and no less humorously Cortés answered him: "Forward, nephew, put no faith in omens, for it will all turn out as God decrees." (8)

God decreed that Cortés should receive letters from Mexico describing—and possibly exaggerating—a quarrel between Estrada and Albornoz. News to the same effect had of course been received by Salazar and Chirino. This was their opportunity; they worked so well on Cortés that they received two sets of powers from him: one, to be used if they found Estrada and Albornoz were still on good terms, giving them an equal share in the government; the other, to be produced only if Albornoz and Estrada were at loggerheads, conferring the government on Salazar and Chirino exclusively—with Zuazo's cooperation in both cases. The two men, having obtained what they wanted, left Cortés to meet his doom, for so, not unreasonably, they believed. (9)

Cortés was again in one of those phases of lighthearted, irresponsible blindness which afflicted him after success. He let these two men go to Mexico, oblivious of the fact that they were ambitious court intriguers who could only use the formidable powers he had granted them in a way detrimental to him and his lifework. He may even have been relieved at their departure, feeling that, thenceforward, he was free to concentrate on his expedition against Olid. While under the influence of this phase of lighthearted exhilaration he gave away Doña Marina, who married one of his captains Juan Xaramillo, during the stay of the army in Orizaba. (10) He gave her away in more ways than one, for it is obvious that her loyalty to Cortés would cool down on being exiled from the private quarters of the chief in the presence of the whole army.

This was no state of mind from which to expect great success in war. Yet, Cortés had kept his ascendancy over both Spaniards and Indians. In Coatzacoalco, he made every Spaniard join the expedition, despite much resistance, for they were all of the old conquistadores, who wanted some rest from their hardships; "but they dared not say no to him and if anyone did he made him go by force," little knowing that the hardships and dangers of this ill-fated enterprise would surpass anything they had known yet. (11)

He made up his mind to cross from sea to sea by the strip of land which makes Yucatán (an island still for many pilots) a peninsula; and arriving in Espíritu-Santo, a Spanish town in the Coatzacoalco district, he called the local notables and made them draw a sort of map of the land, as they usually did, on cotton cloth. This native attempt at geography proved fatal to Cortés, for it confirmed him in the error, then current, that the strip of land which connected the Yucatán peninsula with the mainland was but about twenty leagues, while it was several times wider and moreover hermetically closed to man by thick forests, labyrinths of rivers and swamps and all but impassable mountains. This was the maze into which he plunged, achieving undoubtedly the most incredible march even in the annals of the incredible Spanish discovery. At the very outset, while still in the relatively easy region of Copilco, on the seacoast, they had frequently to build bridges or pass rivers and marshes in canoes; but one of the rivers was so wide that they had to build a wooden bridge about a mile long—"a thing most marvellous to see." In all, Cortés reckons they had to build over fifty bridges to cross the twenty leagues of marshy land in this region of Copilco. (12)

The army then turned southeast and later south, towards Zaguatán, in the swamps of the Grijalva River valley. The natives in this region never used the land as a means of communication, and they lived on the edge of rivers and lakes. Cortés, who had so far been building bridges, had now to open up roads in the virgin forest. The natives had first to be won over, for the behaviour of Olid's Spaniards in Honduras bay had spread terror far into the country. Cortés, however, was past master in this art. He was stimulated to exercise it by dire necessity, for, more often than not, there was actual hunger in the army, despite the herd of swine; this, though skilfully administered by leaving it four stages behind, out of sight of the main body, had in the end been nearly exhausted. At times, they would be twenty days trying in vain to find a way out of the labyrinth, closed in by virgin forest and swamp. Cortés had taken the precaution of bringing a compass with him, though its utility was very much reduced by the inadequacy of his charts and maps. Still, on one particular occasion, probably through a combination of instinct and luck, Cortés having directed his scouts on a north-westerly course from a place into which the army had strayed and where it thought itself lost for good and all, the scouts arrived right in the central square of the town they were seeking. This success impressed the natives, the Mexican no less than the others, both with the powers of Cortés and with those of his compass, and was to bring forth important consequences before long. But meanwhile the army, after weeks and months of incredible hardships, was still either lost at the bottom of dark forests which had to be opened by hatchet and sword, or sinking in marshes up to the waist, or helpless before wide rivers with treacherous banks; and it was always hungry.

One of these obstacles—a river—was so baffling that even Cortés seems to have thought of retracing his steps to Mexico; but he decided to conquer it. What was it, water? They would make a bridge. He sounded it and, by tying two spears together, he tested the bottom. In the end, despite the grumbles of his exhausted and starved army, he had a bridge made by the Indians, on which no Spaniard worked but himself, as an example to the grumblers. A marvel, not of Spanish, but of Mexican craft, it was composed of more than a thousand beams, the smallest of them, he says, as thick as a man's body and nine to ten fathoms long. In his letter to the Emperor, he gives due credit to his Mexican friends: "And I certify Your Majesty that I do not believe that anyone will ever be able to say, in a way that may be understood, the manner in which these lords of Tenuxtitlán and their Indians made this bridge, which is the strangest thing ever seen." Yet though the skill was Mexican, the impulse, the drive, the spirit, came from the chief. Later, when facing a wide and furious river, breaking its swift passage through mighty rocks, Cortés improvised a rougher bridge by cutting gigantic trees which were thrown over between the rocks. The unconquerable spirit of the man was there. It met with instant recognition on the part of legend: "And I want to say," writes Bernal Díaz, "that [. . .] the Spaniards who in later times, when those lands and provinces were already pacified, passed by those roads and to this day found some of those bridges still in being, despite the many years past, and the big trees we had used for building them, wondered at it and nowadays there is a saying 'Here are the bridges of Cortés' as if one said 'the pillars of Hercules.' " (13)

*　　*　　*

They had at last passed on to Acalan, "very abundant in food and in good honey," (14) and Cortés was advancing somewhat relieved, though only temporarily, and wondering whether Yucatán was an island or not, and whether he would find "the secret of it," when one night Coztemexi of Mexicalcingo, (15) one of the Mexican notables who accompanied him, came mysteriously to see him and, showing him a picture on cloth in the native style, explained that Cuauhtemoc and other Mexican chiefs in his suite had conspired to kill Cortés and his captains, hoping then to organise a native rising against Olid and finally recover their sway over Mexico. Cortés acted with his usual swiftness; he seized Cuauhtemoc, Cuanacoch, lord of Tetzcuco, Tetlepanquetzal, lord of Tacuba, and one Tomilatzin, a general whose title was Tlacatecatl, and interrogated them separately. (16) Each was told that the others had confessed; and most of them, believing that Cortés had been told by his compass, revealed all they knew. Those among them whose guilt did not go beyond having listened to the two chief conspirators appealed to the needle of the compass for proof of their innocence. By a careful handling of the compass for these unforeseen uses, Cortés ascertained that the chief conspirators were Cuauhtemoc and Tetepanquetzal; he had them hanged, "and I set the others free," he explains to the Emperor, "for the enquiry proved no more guilt than that of having listened to them [the two leaders] though this might have justified their death."

This episode is in true Cortesian style: cold and hard only when necessary, and only as much as necessary and no more. Cortés kept Cuauhtemoc by his side so long as the deposed King did not threaten his security; nor did he even then punish the conspirators beyond a bare minimum. (17) This episode brought home to Cortés the gravity of the situation into which he had plunged so rashly. He grew worried and restless and could not sleep. One night he was pacing his room in the teocalli of a village in which he was housed when, not familiar with the shape of the room, he fell to a hall below; he was wounded in the head, but said nothing about it. (18) He went on relentlessly, as was his way in good or bad days; new obstacles had to be conquered; hunger; heat; rivers; marshes; black forests; a mountain of sharp flint, every edge and stone of which cut like a razor, that took them twelve days to cross though the way was no more than forty miles, and cost them the death of sixty-eight horses; (19) but, worst of all, the feeling that all was useless, for they had lost their way and would never come out to life again.

"Our Lord wished that when we had already nearly lost all hope, having no guides, and finding the needle useless, since we were in the thick of the wildest mountains which were ever seen, without any road leading anywhere, we should find a boy of about fifteen years of age who said he could guide us to some settlements in Taniha, which is a place I knew I had to pass." (20) In Taniha, they met two native women who had actually served some Spaniards on the coast, just two days away. The army was saved.

But Cortés had to approach his countrymen cautiously. Who were they? Were they Olid's men, and, if so, would they come over to him or remain faithful to his rebel commander? He sent Sandoval in a canoe. By careful tactics, Sandoval secured four Spaniards who were fishing; Cortés was informed by these Spaniards of the dramatic ending of Olid's rebellion. Francisco de las Casas had arrived with a fleet and an army strong enough to overpower Olid; but a storm had destroyed his forces, dashing ships and men furiously against the coast, and Olid, having made Las Casas his prisoner, had marched against Gil Dávila, another conquistador who was operating on his own in the district, beaten him and taken him a prisoner also. Olid was a lighthearted, brave Andalusian. He kept his two prisoners disarmed but left them free to come and go, and even took his meals with them. "Sir Captain," said Las Casas half in jest, half in earnest, "keep a sharp eye on your person for some day I will try to kill you." Olid laughed. He laughed once too much. Las Casas and Gil Dávila, with sharpened steel paper knives, leapt on him and wounded him badly in the throat, they crying: "For the King and for Cortés against this tyrant!" they called together enough men to establish their authority, passed a judgment on him of sorts and hanged him. (21)

Las Casas had returned to Mexico along the coast of the Pacific, not without first founding a town on the Atlantic coast which he named Trujillo, after his own birthplace in Spain. Dávila had also gone to Mexico, having also founded San Gil de Buena Vista on the river Dulce. The men Cortés had found were of Dávila's company. "When they knew it was Cortés, so renowned everywhere in the Indies and in Castille, they did not know what to do for joy." (22) Cortés found them in a desperate state, sick and hungry. As the Spanish saying goes, hunger was meeting appetite. Fortunately, as it often happened in those days, a ship turned up with men, horses and food. Cortés was considering a return by sea, but found he could not risk it with so many sick, unless he could secure more food. So he left the invalids in San Gil and once more gave way to his love for adventure. He set out to explore the Golfo Dulce, an expedition as rich in incident, danger and hardships cheerfully borne as any he had made yet. It was an amphibious enterprise, in which his ingenious mind was constantly called upon to invent ways out—always with a strong dash of courage and of faith in divine protection; as when, having secured abundant provisions of food after weeks of marching and fighting, he loaded it on four rafts and, sending his soldiers along the banks, went with two crossbowmen down the "ferocious" river in a canoe, protecting the rafts against the current, the trees and the Indians. The natives waited on a bank where they knew the fury of a turn in the river would dash them, and wounded them all, Cortés in the head, the only part of his body which was undefended, for he felt feverish and had just taken off his helmet. But the river itself swept them away from the danger, and next day at midday they arrived in the Gulf (where his brigantine was waiting) having covered twenty leagues in twenty-four hours.

*   *   *

As soon as he was able to look around with some leisure, Cortés sent a number of ships—some that were there, some that "turned up" and that he bought, one even that he built on the spot—with letters and orders to New Spain, giving news of his expedition and of his intention to remain in Honduras for some time; to Cuba and to Trinidad and to Jamaica with money for horses and recruits; and to Española with news and dispatches for Spain. All were either lost at sea or diverted from their errand by storms, but one was able to return from Cuba with news from Zuazo (one of the three men he had left in charge of public affairs in Mexico) of the grave disorders which had broken out there. The blow afflicted him deeply. He wept, locked himself up for a day and ordered masses to be said. (23) He was in deep perplexity. Should he go to Mexico? Should he go on exploring new lands south of Trujillo, where more "secrets" were tempting him? He put it to the Lord, and after several days of prayers, masses and processions, decided to go to Mexico. He sent most of his men by land along the southern coast, a road which Francisco de Las Casas had explored and opened, and took to sea. Three times, terrific storms forced him back to port. He read in this a divine disapproval of his decision and, after more masses and sacrifices, sent a ship with full powers for Francisco de las Casas and remained in Honduras himself. (24)

He was very ill; this expedition, which had consumed nearly a year of his life already, had aged him more than the whole conquest. He explored the vicinity, which he found good for settling and developing, and began negotiations with one Francisco Fernández, a captain of Pedrarias Dávila, with the object of poaching on Nicaragua, which Dávila had a right to consider as his preserve. He was even getting ready to proceed to Nicaragua himself, when a ship came from New Spain bringing news of such a grave character that, this time without masses or sacrifices, he took to the sea on April 25th, 1526, and after a short stay in Habana, due to bad weather, landed at last in Veracruz on May 24th, 1526, twenty months after he had left Mexico on a day fateful for Mexico and for himself. (25)

* * *

When Salazar and Chirino returned to Tenochtitlán with the powers unwisely granted them by Cortés, they were disappointed to find that the quarrel between Albornoz and Estrada had been patched up, but soon recovered and coolly suppressed the powers which they had been granted for use in such an eventuality, confronting the chapter and regidores with those which made them sole governors with Zuazo. Despite the efforts of this man of law, who seems to have been a well-meaning peacemaker, Salazar succeeded in getting rid of Estrada and Albornoz by imprisoning them, and even Chirino by sending him to repress a rebellion of the Zapotecs. Zuazo, an inconvenient witness, was forcibly dispatched to Cuba. Cortés had left his steward Rodrigo de Paz in charge of his household, and had appointed him Alguacil Mayor. This man, somewhat rash and overbearing, was imprisoned by Salazar, who, having him at his mercy, forced him to come to terms as to the wielding of actual power in the colony. An attempt by Estrada and Albornoz to leave Mexico for Spain under the pretext of conveying the gold of the Royal fifth for which they were responsible as Treasurer and Accountant, was forcibly prevented by Salazar and Paz at the head of troops recruited under promises of land and Indians. Francisco de Las Casas turned up then, of course without news of Cortés. By then, the relations between Salazar and Paz had deteriorated, because Paz had won twenty thousand pesos from Salazar and Chirino at the gambling table; they decided to put Paz in prison again, setting Albornoz and Estrada free to secure their help in the operation, the chief aim of which seems to have been to take possession of the house of Cortés, strong in artillery and—so they thought—rich in gold.

Once comfortably settled in Cortés' house, Salazar and Chirino solemnly convened a chapter and had themselves sworn in as Governors, giving out that Cortés was dead. They searched the house for gold and even ploughed the estate after turning out of the house all the Indian noblemen and women and the Spanish women whom Cortés kept at his expense, "which was a painful thing to see"; they found nothing, for the fact is that Cortés was not interested in gold but (apart from a certain extravagance in personal luxury) in ships, artillery, conquest and exploration. They put Paz to the torture, plunging his feet in boiling oil, and as the unfortunate steward could not survive, formally sentenced him to be hanged. Flatterers and weaklings flocked to Salazar's party. "One," says Bernal Díaz, "whom we thought to be an honourable man, and whom I do not mention here, for his honour's sake, told the agent [Salazar] in the presence of many persons that he was ill with fear, for as he was walking by night near Tatelulco, where the great Idol Witchy-wolves used to be and where the church of St. James is now, he had seen how in the courtyard the souls of Cortés, Doña Marina and Captain Sandoval were burning in living flames." (26)

The death of Cortés became the official truth which no one could contradict with impunity. Wives of the soldiers in Cortés' army were advised to marry again. One of them, Juana de Mansilla, who refused to be remarried and declared that Cortés and her husband were alive was publicly flogged as a witch. (27) A funeral mass was said in the church of the monastery of St. Francis, and while the sermon was being preached a number of friends of Cortés who had taken refuge in the monastery were dragged out by force under the personal direction of Salazar and Chirino. The guardian of the monastery, however, happened to wield ecclesiastical powers, and he put an interdict on the city, which he left with all his little community, and Salazar, frightened at the spiritual power, surrendered the prisoners.

The night of Sunday January 28th, 1526, a dusty, tired peasant, whose unkempt beard proved him to be Spanish, knocked at the gates of the monastery. When the gate was shut behind him, he revealed his identity to the monks and to Andrés de Tapia, Jorge Alvarado and the other friends of Cortés who lived there. He was Martín Dorantes, a servant of Cortés. Under his clothes, tied up round his waist, he brought letters for the friars, for his friends, and even for Estrada and Albornoz; "and as they saw Dorantes and knew that Cortés was alive and saw his letters they all jumped and danced for joy, and as for the Franciscan friars, Father Toribio Motolinea and one Father Diego de Altamirano, they leapt in the air for joy and thanked the Lord for it." (28) Caution, however, was necessary. Cortés' letters appointed Francisco de las Casas and

Pedro de Alvarado as joint governors; both were away, Alvarado in Guatemala and Las Casas on his way to Spain, whither he had been sent in irons by Salazar, loaded with false accusations. Cortés' letters further provided that if neither Las Casas nor Alvarado was available, Estrada and Albornoz were to take charge. The friars had them discreetly called, and next day, after some fighting, Salazar was caught and put in jail.

"The first thing," says Bernal Díaz, "which the Treasurer did was to honour Juana de Mansilla who had been flogged as a witch and it was done in this way that he ordered all the gentlemen of Mexico to ride and the Treasurer rode with her on his horse along the streets of Mexico and they all said she had behaved like a Roman matron." Albornoz was not straight. He had warned Salazar from the Monastery, during the night meeting, and enabled him to put up a resistance; and a conspiracy organised by Salazar's party to set him free and kill Estrada was only nipped in the bud because Estrada, on hearing of it, kept the news from his colleague in the government. (29)

* * *

Albornoz's letters had meanwhile reached Spain and were beginning to bear poisonous fruit with their plausible calumnies, among which the most dangerous was that Cortés sent feather presents to Spain but hid the gold. (30) Poor Charles V was, as usual, panting for money. He had written to Cortés pointing out this awkward fact to him, and relying on him to put together as much gold as possible, royal or borrowed, and send it to Spain for his imperial needs. (31) This was a welcome opportunity for Ribera, Cortés' secretary, who was working for his master in Spain. He obtained a kind of agreement or compact (*asiento*) with the King-Emperor, whereby Cortés was to find two hundred thousand pesos of gold. In exchange for this money, Cortés was made Adelantado of New Spain, and was granted the right to call himself *Don,* and "owing to the devotion which [the King] felt for St. James, he would make Cortés a knight of that order."

Cortés was granted arms in honour of his conquest: on the right, above, a black eagle with two heads (the arms of the Holy Roman

Empire) and, below, a golden lion on a field of gules; on the left, above, three gold crowns on a sable field (in memory of the three Kings of the Mexican confederacy which he had beaten) and, below, the city of Mexico, on the water; on a yellow field, seven heads on a chain closed by a padlock under a helmet. (32)

But news poured in with every ship that came from the Indies of the chaotic state into which New Spain had fallen, while no news whatever came from Cortés. It mattered little whether the letters spoke well or ill of Cortés himself; the fact was that the news was bad and that Cortés was away. Cortés had enough enemies at Court to make this moment dangerous. The catalogue of his crimes increased daily: he had murdered his wife and also Garay; he was building ships on the southern coast to slip away into France; he was conspiring to become an independent monarch, counting on his artillery—wholly unnecessary against the natives, his enemies argued —on his immense hidden treasures, and on the unlimited devotion of his Spaniards and of the natives: a curious confession on the part of those who accused him of ill-treating the natives as well. The Emperor and his officials grew uneasy, and it seems that Charles V had in mind to deprive Cortés of his government and to give it to the Admiral Don Diego Colón in exchange for his claims on Española; but Cortés was not altogether deprived of friends, and in particular the Duke of Béjar and the Prior of St. John, Don Juan de Zúñiga, whose niece Doña Juana, daughter of the Count of Aguilar, was to marry Cortés. These friends of Cortés took the offensive and pointed out that the favours and honours granted to him so far had been by no means adequate, considering his splendid services and achievements. (33) Withal, the credit of Cortés could not but be affected both by his prolonged absence and by the anarchical state which it entailed in Mexico, while many other cases of disorder and anarchy, though wholly out of his jurisdiction, contributed to make a bad atmosphere at Court for everything which came from the Indies. Finally, it was decided to "take residence to Cortés" as the phrase went, i.e. to hold a special enquiry during which the enquirer held all the authority previously deposited in the person concerned. But, says Herrera, "as his authority was great and his name was held in great respect, a person of letters and of quality was sought to whom to entrust this mission, and it was thought that the Licentiate Luis Ponce de León would be a good choice." (34)

*   *   *

Cortés' story of his own arrival in New Spain reveals the fact that it was most discreet, but not the reason for its discretion. Owing to bad weather, he was not able to land by day; he landed by night, walked four leagues to Medellín, unnoticed, and went to the church to thank the Lord. But Bernal Díaz, in relating the elaborate, and similar, precautions which Martín Dorantes had taken on Cortés' instructions, reveals that this caution was due in both cases to fear lest the land might be in revolt against him. (35) At dawn the sexton, who saw his church full of strangers, went for help, but when the settled conquistadores arrived and recognised their leader, tired, worn out and aged by two years of privations though he was, there was great joy. Cortés wrote to all the towns, to Estrada and to Albornoz, "although he was not his friend," and after an eight days' rest set out for Mexico.

It was a triumphant journey. Indians and Spaniards vied in their desire to show gratitude to their true leader and Governor. All longed for the rest that comes from fair and dignified authority. Gold, clothes, hens poured in; in Tlaxcala, the whole town came out to meet him with much dancing and rejoicing; Albornoz, frightened, came out beyond Tetzcuco, to meet the man he had betrayed and cover up his treason with smiles; the chapter of Tenochtitlan begged Cortés to stay in Tetzcuco for a night so that an adequate reception could be given to him next day. And that day all the town, Spanish and native, gave itself over to joy, festivities, dances, colour by day and lights on the lagoon by night.

Cortés went to the monastery of St. Francis, in order, he writes to the Emperor, "to thank our Lord for having delivered me from so many hardships and dangers and brought me to this peace and rest and for having let me see this land, which was so sorely tried, brought back to peace and harmony, and there I remained six days with the friars, till I gave God an account of my guilt." (36)

CHAPTER THIRTY

The Marquess of the Valley

CORTÉS was still in the monastery, in a kind of religious retreat, when he heard that Ponce de León had landed. He took immediate steps to have him honoured, housed, and in every way treated as befitted his dignity. But Ponce de León kept all his offers at arm's length and travelled throughout as if he wanted to maintain a distant independence from the powerful governor. (1) This attitude seems to have been due both to an inborn sense of dignity and of self-respect, as the authentic representative of the Crown, and to repeated warnings received in Spain and in Veracruz, against falling into Cortés' wily traps and faring as Narváez, Tapia and Garay had done. (2)

But Cortés was full of courtesy and respect. On the day following Ponce de León's arrival, the Chapter met in church: Ponce de León had his credentials read, and Cortés immediately surrendered his "stick" as Chief Justice of New Spain. Everybody seemed to like the new judge, and Cortés in particular was much satisfied to be in the hands of an upright and disinterested man. Ponce de León brought a few friars with him, at the head of whom came one Fray Tomás Ortiz, "more active for dealing with affairs," says Bernal Díaz, "than for the holy mission on which he had come over." (3) On the very day of his arrival, Ortiz came to see Cortés and "revealed" to him that Ponce de León had definite instructions to have him executed and all his property confiscated. Ortiz worked unremittingly, both directly and through the Franciscan friars, to make Cortés break with Ponce de León. But Cortés was this time determined to have his services vindicated by an independent witness,

445

and despite the friar's intrigues he had the highest opinion of Ponce de León. (4)

At this point, death took the judge away. thus giving an awkward twist to events. It was a severe blow for Cortés. His enemies made it worse by pointing to Cortés himself as the cause of Ponce de León's death, though thirty other persons who had come over in the same fleet died of the same epidemic; Father Ortiz seems to have been the originator of this slanderous rumour. The situation was most awkward. In his will, Ponce de León had delegated his powers to a lawyer, Marcos de Aguilar, an old man eaten up with syphilis, who kept body and soul together alive by sucking milk from a woman's breast. (5) Cortés' enemies wanted the enquiry to proceed; his friends, who had "packed" the chapter, "required" him to take over the government of the country. He refused, no doubt to impress the King with his disinterestedness. He, nevertheless, had the crier promulgate some *Ordenanzas* for the protection of the Indians, an action to which he thought he was entitled as Captain General and administrator of Indian affairs; but Aguilar, set in motion by the opposition, challenged his right to both these posts, and Cortés thereupon resigned them both. He writes to the Emperor: "I believe that Your Majesty will gradually be satisfied on the score of my loyalty for not only did I obey and carry out all the orders of the Judge sent by Your Majesty, but I also obey and carry out all those of a Judge whom I do not hold as competent, nor who was, nor is sent by Your Majesty or Council; whereby I undergo many rebuffs, nor is the treatment meted out such as my services deserve [. . .] What I have desired above all else in the world is to make my fidelity and obedience known to Your Majesty." (6)

This language shows at once the true origin of the access of meekness which seemed to afflict Cortés at this moment of his life. Bernal Díaz says that if Cortés, upon his return from Las Hibueras, had "dispatched" his chief enemies, Salazar and Chirino, no one in Castille would have objected, "and I heard this said by the members of the Royal Council of the Indies, in the presence of the bishop Father Bartolomé de las Casas in 1540, when I went thither on my lawsuits, and that he was remiss and they thought him weak and negligent." (7)

They forgot that Ponce de León's arrival, within four days of

Cortés' own, had deprived Cortés of his powers as Chief Justice. Moreover, Cortés knew that the chief item in a number of accusations, some monstrous, some petty, some silly, which Ponce de León was to investigate, was one which represented him as conspiring to break away from his loyalty to the King. In his fifth letter, he refers to this accusation in that firm, yet moderate style of his, a model of inner simplicity and of unsought elegance. It is clear that he is impressed with the possibility that this accusation may, as he puts it, "have raised some mist or darkness before Your Grace's eyes." (8) Now this reproach touched him to the quick, for he was a profound believer in the divine and sacred character of the Crown. Hence, the steadfastness of his self-denying attitude during this period when the chief purpose before his eyes was to drive out that "mist" and "darkness" from his King's eyes.

Aguilar died also on or before March 1st. (9) His peculiar diet made it difficult for anyone to attribute his death to Cortés; but Ocaña, one of Cortés' most relentless enemies, found a way to solve even this insoluble problem; in a letter addressed to the officials of the Casa de Contratación, he relates how during a banquet in Cortés' house some fried bacon was sent to Marcos de Aguilar, who declined it; but one of Aguilar's servants ate of it and was so ill that he nearly died that night. "I believe that if the unhappy old man had eaten it," concludes Ocaña, "he would have gone the way of Luis Ponce." (10)

This was the atmosphere of intrigue, calumny and hatred in which Cortés had to move. On Aguilar's death, he was again formally requested by the Chapter of Mexico to assume power as Governor and Chief Justice; but, though legally his position was still stronger than at Ponce de León's death, his personal attitude remained unchanged. He refused, and the chapter recognised Estrada, who had been designated by Aguilar in his will. Cortés' friends, however, obtained two concessions; the first was that Sandoval should share in the government; the second, that the two governors should consult Cortés in all matters pertaining to the administration of the Indians and to the office of Captain General. But this régime, which was inaugurated on March 1st, ended on August 22nd when Estrada triumphantly exhibited a royal order, dated March 16th, 1527, in Valladolid, which enabled Estrada to shake off Sandoval and to remain sole and unrestricted Governor. This "royal" decision was due to Albornoz who had gone to Spain immediately after Ponce de León's death to work against Cortés, not to speak of the continuous flow of letters which arrived in Spain accusing Cortés of every notable death which had occurred in Mexico, beginning with that of his wife. (11)

We need not assume that Cortés and his friends made no errors of judgment in the day-to-day struggle of petty incidents; but there is no doubt that during this period Cortés found himself in an unenviable position. Estrada did not give him the respect due to him. One day, for instance, he summarily sentenced one of Cortés' servants to have a hand cut off. Cortés, who wielded enough *real* power on Spaniards and natives alike to destroy Estrada in an hour, stood the affront with great dignity and prevented a revolt; but this self-denial was of no avail, and Estrada exiled Cortés from Mexico. "I thank the Lord," said he, as he left the capital, *his* capital, for Cuyoacán, "for being exiled from the lands and cities I won, by persons who are unworthy of the posts they occupy." Ordás, who was aggrieved to see how his chief's prestige had dwindled, advised him to have himself styled "lord," and "Your Lordship," and "Don Hernando," and to have his seat placed under a dais. He knew better. "I never call him Don Hernando," says Bernal Díaz, "nor Marquess, nor captain, but plain, blunt Cortés, because he prided himself on being known as just Cortés." (12)

By then, he had made up his mind to go to Spain and fight for himself at Court. His letter to his father, written at this time, enables us to measure his transparent sincerity and the loftiness of his motives and ambitions. Written to his most intimate confidant, it tallies perfectly with what he writes to the King. First and foremost, he wants to be vindicated as a great and honest servant of the Crown. He asks that "a strict enquiry should be held, so that I may complain of the disfavours which His Majesty had been pleased to order that I should undergo"; his father is to insist on this most of all, "for I wish His Majesty to know my services and loyalty more than to possess all the States and treasures of the world." Note the subconscious revelation—the *States* and treasures; his secret ambitions are first government, statesmanship; then, wealth. Truly, he says a few lines below: "I hold it better to be wealthy in fame than in property." (13)

He was irritated and humiliated by the constant demands for accounts, as if the man who had conquered New Spain and given it to the King should be treated like a steward. He writes to the Emperor and confirms the statement in his letter to his father, that, since his enemies accuse him of having two hundred millions of income out of New Spain, he would be happy to receive twenty from the Emperor and let him have all he owns in New Spain in exchange; he would, moreover, serve at Court as an adviser on the affairs of New Spain. There is little doubt that he was seriously considering some such arrangement, apart from the ironical context in which he presented it. He was sick at heart of his humiliations in Mexico and dreamt of settling in Spain. (14)

At this time, the Court was thinking precisely of ways and means to induce him to come and settle in Spain. The distrust of the Court was at its highest, owing mostly to the work of Albornoz, coming after Narváez, Tapia and the others; and the colours under which he was presented were so lurid that an energetic nobleman, Don Pedro de la Cueva, had been selected to sail to New Spain with a strong force and, if necessary, have him beheaded; while most elaborate precautions were taken to ensure that a ship with gold-laden messengers from the supposed rebel should not elude the vigilance of the Spanish officials and land in Portugal. The quiet arrival of the ship and the straightforward behaviour of Cortés' messengers did much to allay matters; Alvarado, who arrived soon afterwards, and opened astonished eyes whenever anyone at Court asked his opinion on Cortés' loyalty, improved matters further still; yet, the decision was taken to appoint an Audience, a kind of judicial and administrative college of four lawyers presided over by Nuño de Guzmán, acting Governor of Pánuco since the arrival of Ponce de León in New Spain. This Audience was to enquire into the adminis-tration of Cortés and all the officials and to supersede them in the government of New Spain. (15)

Cortés meanwhile was preparing his voyage. He collected as much gold and silver and as many curiosities as possible, to enchant and impress the Court. Spanish settlers and Mexican caciques

flocked to his house in Tlaxcala, to tempt him with the crown of
New Spain. He spurned the fools who spoke treason to him, and
reported the knaves to the acting Governor. (16) Estrada's wife,
Doña Marina Gutiérrez de la Caballería and Fray Julián Garcés,
first Bishop of Tlaxcala, just arrived from Spain, tried in vain to
patch up the breach between the acting Governor and Cortés. He
was determined to leave. His resolution was clinched by the arrival
of a letter from Fray García de Loaisa, the King's confessor and
President of the Council of the Indies, asking him to come to Spain
as soon as possible: a letter which may have flattered him, for he
could hardly guess that it had been written less in love than in fear
of what he might do if left in Mexico with his immense ascendancy
over Indian and Spaniard. He received letters from his Spanish
sponsors urging him to come and answer for himself all the calumnies
unleashed against him; and at this point he lost his most trusted
agent at Court: his father died. He left for Spain on March 17th,
1528. (17)

*   *   *

While Cortés sailed towards Spain, Charles V was immersed in
his duel with Francis V. This is no metaphor. On Wednesday, January 22nd, 1528, Guienne, King at Arms of Francis I, and Clarenceux,
King at Arms of Henry VIII, presented challenges of war to the
Emperor-King at Burgos. To Guienne, Charles answered verbally
with a dry humour: "Paper is sweet, for you have written on it all
you have wished; I shall answer with another paper which will carry
naught but truth." (18)

Some of these truths were not palatable. Technically, Francis I
was the prisoner of Charles V since the battle of Pavia (1525), for he
owed his physical liberty to Charles' magnanimity and to the fact that,
in order to guarantee the fulfilment of the provisions of the Treaty
of Madrid he had given his own children as hostages. In the correspondence which followed the Burgos challenge, Charles reminded
Francis I that, according to Clause IV, the King of France promised
to return to prison if, within the stipulated delays, he had not complied with the conditions of the treaty; and that, after the signature
of the treaty, the Emperor had told the King that if he failed in this
Charles would claim the right to say that Francis had behaved like

a coward and a knave; to which the King of France expressly acquiesced. Francis had broken his promises as soon as he had crossed the border, and Charles, after a year of patience, had made use of his right while in Granada in a conversation with Francis I's ambassador in September 1526. (19) All these facts were conveyed to Francis I to refresh his memory in a letter addressed to the French Ambassador, and signed in Madrid on March 18th, 1528, when Cortés was getting ready to leave Mexico for Spain. "I have seen the letter you have written to me on the words I told you in Granada," wrote the Emperor, "and gather that you do not wish to remember what I then told you for you to repeat to the King of France [. . .] and it was that [. . .] the King your master had behaved like a coward and a knave, in breaking his faith over the treaty of Madrid, and that if he were to contradict me on this, I would uphold it with my person against his." (20)

This style of life was of course to be expected of a reader of Amadis. Francis answered in similar style. "If you have meant to accuse us of aught which a Knight mindful of his honour should not do, we say that you lie as often as you say it. And since you have accused us against truth, write us no more, but secure us the field and we shall come in arms, for we protest that if, after this statement, you were to write to third parties or to utter words against our honour, the shame of having delayed the fight shall be yours since, once come to it, all writing ceases." (21)

This answer had been despatched, with commendable rapidity, on March 28th, ten days after Charles' own letter, but in his answer the Emperor points out that, even if Paris had been farther away, it should have reached him earlier than June 8th. He was not wrong, for after all, Cortés had come from Mexico in the interval and was already in Palos. Borgoña, Charles V's King-at-Arms, was dispatched on June 28th with the Emperor's answer, proposing as a field of honour the Island of the Pheasants on the Bidassoa between Fuenterrabia and Hendaye. But Francis put obstacle upon obstacle in the path of the Imperial King-at-Arms, who was not allowed to see him till the beginning of September and even then was angrily prevented by Francis from delivering his message. (22)

*   *   *

Francis was one of the two monarchs who had staged the gorgeous pageant of the Field of the Cloth of Gold; Charles was the head of the Order of the Golden Fleece, a monarch austere and simple in his personal attire, but born and bred in the splendours of the Burgundian Court. This was the old world towards which Cortés was sailing in the spring of 1528; and his instinct had guessed right when it led him to organise his home-coming in the most gorgeous style that readers of Amadis, Knights of the Golden Fleece and Kings of the Cloth of Gold could ever imagine.

He landed in Palos with an imposing retinue, at the head of which came Sandoval and Andrés de Tapia. He had promised a free passage and board to all who would accompany him, so his suite was imposing. On the native side, he brought over several magnates, including one of Moteçuçuma's sons, Don Martín by name, a son of Maxixcatzin and a son of Xicotencatl. He took over a kind of floating exhibition of the curiosities and rarities of New Spain, inanimate, animal and human, from liquidambar and rare balms to exotic birds, from tigers to albino men and women, from dwarfs to jugglers who could make a stick turn with wonderful rapidity with their feet; gold in bars, in dinner services, in jewels; precious stones of unheard-of size, cut with an incredible workmanship; clothes, plumes and gorgeous attire of barbarous and colourful splendour. This man who had left his native country when nineteen years of age, penniless and obscure, returned to it at forty-three in a glamour of universal glory which the black clouds raised by his envious enemies made even more striking and dramatic.

Soon after his arrival, he lost his friend Sandoval, who died in the inn, too weak to prevent his landlord from stealing thirteen bars of gold from him. Cortés was deeply aggrieved at the loss of this captain, his right-hand man since his trust in Alvarado had been shaken by the massacre of Mexico. He had settled in the Monastery of La Rábida, the only building in or near Palos large enough to accommodate his establishment, and from La Rábida had sent despatches to the King, to Fray García de Loaisa, and to his friends at Court, particularly the Duke of Béjar and the Count of Aguilar. The Emperor was leaving Madrid for Monzón in Aragón, and Cortés had therefore several months in which to prepare the ground for his longed-for interview with his royal master. He decided to leave

La Rábida for Guadalupe, to hold novenas, which of course implied a long stay. (23) This was a shrewd move, for, over and above the favours he might expect from Our Lady of Guadalupe as a reward for his devotions, he was sure to meet powerful personages in one of the most famous and influential of Spanish houses of religion.

It so happened that Doña María de Mendoza was then staying in the Monastery. She was perhaps the most powerful woman in Spain after the Empress, for her husband Francisco de los Cobos, Chief Commander of León, was the Principal Secretary of State for home and financial affairs in Charles V's Spanish Chancery, an all but omnipotent man. Doña María was accompanied by a retinue of ladies equal in quantity to the retinue of men which surroundered Cortés, and higher in rank. Chief among these ladies was her own sister, Doña Francisca de Mendoza, who was beautiful and unmarried. Cortés paid the utmost attention to the two gracious ladies and lavished presents on them, particularly on the youthful and handsome Doña Francisca. But in this he made a grievous mistake owing perhaps to that invincible modesty towards the fair sex which often afflicts even the boldest of men. He evidently raised hopes which he was not in a position to satisfy, since his marriage with Doña Juana de Zúñiga, niece of the Duke of Béjar, had already been finally arranged. The Mendoza sisters were at first his most ardent advocates at court and must have eased his path during the first months of his stay in Spain. But as it became clear that Cortés remained faithful to his pledged word, the wind of favour changed for him in that powerful sector of the Spanish State: Bernal Díaz vouches for the fact that the situation thus created cost Hernán Cortés the viceroyalty of New Spain. (24)

When at last, in the autumn of 1528, he was received by the Emperor, his presence, his looks, his courtesy, his sincerity, his lucid mind and terse style sufficed to drive out of the royal mind all the mists and clouds that envious enemies had raised over the conqueror of Mexico. Charles, who as a busy man could appreciate clear-minded men, enjoyed Cortés' company, and often consulted him on Indian affairs. The monarch was generous, yet not as much as Cortés had the right to expect; and he did not give Cortés the governorship of the land he had discovered. Despite Bernal Díaz' mischievous innuendoes on Cobos and his womenfolk, it is natural to understand this decision of the Emperor as yet another case of the well-known mistrust of the Spanish monarchy towards its outstanding subjects Gómara puts it drily but aptly, "He asked for the Governorship or Mexico, and [the Emperor] did not give it to him"; and he adds: "For so did King Ferdinand deal with Christopher Colón, who discovered the Indies and with Gonzalo Hernández de Córdoba, the great Captain who conquered Naples." (25)

The King made Cortés Marquess of the Valley of Oaxaca, and gave him huge rural properties in New Spain with twenty-three thousand vassals over which he was to hold extensive feudal rights, lands in Mexico city, and the title of Captain General of New Spain. He had made him Knight of St. James, but Cortés never used the title, for he expected a commandership, which was excusable since a commandership had been granted to Alvarado, his subordinate officer, obviously through the influence of Los Cobos. We have Cortés' own statement to prove that he was disappointed and hurt, and went so far as to refuse the royal favours. (26) The Emperor won him over by kind words and modestly explained that he was like an archer aiming at the target of Cortés' merits, and that if Cortés took what he now gave him as a first attempt he would do better later. Cortés was not content with those merely static honours. Thwarted in his creative ambition by being denied the governorship, he was thrown back on his vocation as a captain-discoverer-conqueror, and he concluded capitulations with the Crown for carrying on discoveries in the Southern Sea, in words which still remind us of the days when the planet kept a generous margin of mystery closed to knowledge and therefore open to men's imagination: he was to be allowed "to discover any island or mainland not yet discovered, on which he would have the title of governor [. . .] with all other prerogatives and advantages which are usually granted to discoverers." (27)

More sidelights on his character are provided at this juncture by his watch over the interests of his companions in the struggle; his care to procure funds for the Church, and in particular for the education of Indian children; and his devotion to the four daughters of Moteçuçuma, whom he richly endowed and some of whom he married to Castillian noblemen. He thought also of his bastards and had them legitimised by the Pope, to whom he had sent a special messenger with presents and an exhibition of Indian jugglery—"of the sight of which," says Bernal Díaz, "the Pope and the sacred cardinals were very pleased." (28)

Cortés was at the zenith of his glory: at last recognised and appreciated by the Emperor. He fell ill in Toledo, and it was even feared that he would die. On the advice of Béjar and Cobos, the Emperor in person went to visit him. This visit seems to have proved a double-edged weapon; for the honour bestowed upon him was so great that it provoked a reaction which his enemies were quick to seize. Gossip and criticism began to attack the newcomer—for some, the upstart. Cortés may not always have been as tactful as he should have been. One Sunday, he arrived late at mass, deliberately, says Bernal Díaz, and when the Emperor was already in his seat—which is simply incredible, but the detail is not essential. "He passed in front of some of those illustrious lords, with his mourning train held up, and went to sit down close to the Count of Nassau who sat next to the Emperor." There was a murmur of disapproval at his daring; but his friends Béjar, Aguilar and the Admiral pointed out that His Majesty had expressly bid him to take that seat to honour him specially. (29)

If we are to believe Bernal Díaz, who received detailed accounts about the Court from his companions, Cortés, strongly backed by the Béjar group, tried again to force the Emperor's hand in the matter of the governorship; but by then the Cobos group had turned against him, and the Emperor, who had moreover made up his mind on political grounds, disliked his importunate insistence. Cortés then tried to work through the Count of Nassau to whom the Emperor, already in Barcelona on the eve of his departure for Italy, pointed out that he did not want to hear any more on the matter, for Cortés had already been given a marquisate with more income than Nassau had in Europe. Charles V did not remember that Cortés had written to him: "I am more ambitious of fame than of wealth." (30)

For the sake of fame, he married Doña Juana de Zúñiga, who was of a ducal family. But she was young and beautiful also; (31) and Cortés, who was susceptible to feminine charms, fell a victim to those of his wife. He lavished presents on her, in particular five emeralds each worth a fortune for their size and for their capricious workmanship: one in the form of a rose; one like a bell, with a pearl for a tongue; one like a fish; one like a trumpet; one like a cup. The

Empress, so runs the story, coveted them, and disliked Cortés for having given them to a mere marchioness-to-be. This does not tally with the lofty character of the Empress, but the gossip is only too much in keeping with the petty ways of Court mischief makers.

All this atmosphere of Court intrigue and envy can hardly have been to the taste of a man of his temper and mettle. News from Mexico, moreover, was none too good. He had fulfilled all he had set out to do in Spain, and the Emperor was in Italy. So, in the spring of 1530, he left for New Spain from Sanlúcar, twenty-six years after his first departure from the same harbour; but this time grey-haired and saddened with many a disillusion, he was no longer sailing towards a virgin future, but towards a thorny present and a stormy past.

*　　*　　*

For the second time, Mexico longed for Hernán Cortés, whose absence had unchained shameless anarchy in its life. The Audience which had been entrusted with the duty of "auditing" Cortés' government had obviously been selected on partisan lines; its President, Nuño de Guzmán, who had gone over with Ponce de León as Governor of Pánuco, was a violent man, inimical to Cortés and the terror of the natives; (32) while the two *oidores* or judges who had survived the change of climate, Matienzo and Delgadillo, were men of a low moral level. The Audience arrived in December, 1528, and was solemnly received by the local authorities and the colony. The members settled first in Cortés' house, in which two of the four *oidores*, Parada and Maldonado, died of pneumonia soon after their arrival —"and had Cortés been there," adds Bernal Díaz, "to judge by what evil-thinking people can say, he would have been accused of having killed them." Matienzo and Delgadillo assumed supreme power, and the fact that they resided in Cortés' house added to their authority. (33)

The new "judges" had but two ideas in mind: to get rich quickly and to ruin Cortés. Every other consideration was brushed aside. This programme brought them immediately into partnership with Salazar, who advised them not to grant perpetual repartimientos, since the basis of their authority over the settlers was their power to grant and take back Indians. This advice (which by the way, illustrates the statesmanlike disinterestedness of Cortés' proposals in favour of immediate perpetual repartimientos) was taken to heart by the members of the Audience, who exploited to the full its opportunities for tyranny and money-making. (34)

Every possible calumny was then raised against Cortés, and every low character produced to witness against him. His brother-in-law Xuárez was prevailed upon to promote a lawsuit against him for the murder of Catalina Xuárez, and a deed was formally presented to the court by Juan Xuárez and his mother María La Marcayda actually accusing Cortés of having strangled his wife. (35)

Fortunately for Cortés, there was an upright man in Mexico who was watching events with the eyes of truth. Fray Juan de Zumárraga, first Bishop of Mexico, had been noticed by the Emperor when the weary monarch had gone to spend a Holy Week in the Monastery of El Abrojo, close to Valladolid. Charles V had been impressed by the Prior even before he had seen him distribute to the poor every farthing of the considerable sum granted as imperial "alms" to the community at the end of his visit. Charles, in search of good and true men for his Indies, no doubt remembered the fears which Cortés entertained on the worldly ways of bishops, and sent Father Zumárraga as the first Bishop of Mexico. On August 27th, 1529, the Bishop wrote the Emperor a long and truthful report on New Spain. His brief passages on the conquest and on the rivalry between Cortés and Velázquez show his independent judgment and his impartial mind; his narrative of the events during Cortés' absence in Las Hibueras is admirable for its concision, clarity and good judgment; so that when he enters into his indictment of the first Audience, his moral authority is unassailable, even when his narrative reaches the edge of the incredible. "And as I believe that nothing should be concealed from Your Majesty, I say that the Lords of Tatelulco, of this city, came to me weeping abundantly, so much that I felt great pity, to complain that the President and Oidores asked for their daughters and sisters and female relatives who were of good looks and another lord told me that Pilar [the Interpreter of the Audience] had asked him for eighty pretty girls for the President." Zumárraga complained to Guzmán who refused to give explanations on what he called his private life; and the good Bishop goes on to say that women of ill repute had a predominant voice in what the Audience decided. (36)

It may well be that the worst mistake made by this reckless trio, Guzmán-Matienzo-Delgadillo, was their attack on Alvarado. He was now Don Pedro de Alvarado, Adelantado of Guatemala, and haa married Doña Francisca de la Cueva, a lady of high rank, and a relation of the powerful minister Los Cobos. On arriving in Veracruz, his young wife had died, and Alvarado went about in Mexico, clad in deep mourning, waiting till it was the pleasure of the Audience to let him depart for Guatemala. But Guzmán and his compeers were not ready to let such a rich man go before they had thoroughly shorn him of all his wealth. Taking as a pretext that he had played prohibited card games during the conquest, they gradually deprived him of all his money, horses, Indians, furniture, till they confiscated his last mule, on which he had come to the Court, "and made him return on foot, without respect for his authority." (37)

But worse was still to come. News came to Mexico of the favours granted to Cortés by the King, and that he was to return to New Spain as a grandee and a Captain General, and Guzmán mentioned the fact in a group including Alvarado, Albornoz, Salazar and many more prominent men. Salazar, much incensed at the news, shouted: "A King who sends us such a traitor as Cortés is a heretic and no Christian." Despite the monstrosity of the remark no one dared to protest, since the President who was present said nothing. But a few days later, on Wednesday August 18th, 1529, Alvarado appeared before the Audience asking leave to challenge Salazar on "those words which he had so heinously uttered against his King and other words [. . .] which, speaking on the subject of Don Hernando's coming, he had said to other persons, particularly that vassals should revolt against a King who decided such a thing." Guzmán did not attend that day, but the next, he gave an answer from his chair: "Pedro de Alvarado lies as a mean Knight, if he is one, for the Agent [Salazar] said nothing of the kind, for he is a good servant of his Majesty, and he could not say such a thing"; and on the next day, the Audience threw Alvarado into prison with irons on his feet. (38)

This news must have disquieted Cobos who remained interested in Alvarado's fortune, for the conquistador married again into his family, a sister of his first wife; but also because of the responsibility which the powerful secretary had in the choice of the first Audience. The Council of the Indies were at some pains to find better men to supersede their disastrous first choice. Cortés was still in Spain when these efforts were being made, and wanted to await the appointment of the new Audience to cross over with it, in order to avoid a clash with his infamous persecutors. But the Emperor wished him to leave as soon as possible, thinking him, no doubt, a stabilising factor in the colony. When he left Spain, the new Audience had not yet been appointed; he lingered in Santo Domingo two and a half months, waiting for it, but the expenses of his numerous household did not allow him to wait longer, and he proceeded on to Veracruz. Yet, while in Española, he had the satisfaction of hearing that the Empress had this time appointed men worthy of their mission. The President of the new Audience was to be the Bishop of Santo Domingo.

Thus comforted with the hope of justice—if not of power—he landed in Veracruz on July 15th, 1530. (39)

CHAPTER THIRTY-ONE

The Marquess vs. the Viceroy

CORTÉS was now "the Marquess." But he was a setting sun. From this time on till the end of his life, "he never was lucky in anything on which he laid his hands, and everything became thorns for him." He had come over in state, as a Spanish nobleman, with an imposing retinue, accompanied by his wife and his mother and with a number of Franciscan friars in his composite train. His arrival was hailed as a deliverance by all, Indians and Spaniards, who suffered from the tyranny of the Audience. Indians and Spaniards complained to him that he had left them without his protection: "without him, they were alone." (1) He tried to put heart into them by promising new discoveries. He had himself proclaimed Captain General in Veracruz. Guzmán and the two oidores had severely prohibited the natives to provide any help or service, and Cortés informs the Emperor that more than two hundred people in his train died of want as a result of this inhuman treatment—including his own mother. (2) The aim of the Audience was to drive him into rebellion. On August 9th, while in Tlaxcala, he received a notary who came to read to him an order from the Emperor forbidding him or his wife to enter within ten leagues of Mexico; he took the royal letter in his hands, kissed it, put it over his head and, contrary to what the notary no doubt expected as the usual ending of all these ceremonies, he scrupulously obeyed it and remained in Tlaxcala. (3) Later he settled in Tetzcuco, to be able to procure supplies from Mexico by water; in this, he profited by the fact that it was not known for certain whether Tetzcuco was eight or ten leagues from Mexico. The oidores feigned to fear that he might revolt, and made ready to defend Mexico with artillery; but Cortés

460

sent them the Bishop of Tlaxcala and the Prior of Santo Domingo
to explain that he had come as Captain General, not to challenge
those in authority, but to keep the land quiet and in the faithful
service of the King. No peace, however, was possible between him
and his despoilers. The three unworthy magistrates were living in
his house, had stolen his money, grabbed his lands and Indians, and
even founded a town in his marquisate in order the better to despoil
him by setting up rival interests to his own. He held his temper and
composure despite incredible hardships and humiliations, but, writing to the Emperor on October 10th, 1530, he confesses that he is
well-nigh at the end of his patience and, if the new Audience were
too slow in coming, he will have to seize the pueblos granted him by
the Crown, so that his household shall not perish. (4)

The new Audience sailed from Seville on August 25th, 1530; its
president was Don Sebastián Ramírez, Bishop of Santo Domingo,
who had been for some time at the head of the Audience in Española,
and there were four oidores: Vasco de Quiroga, a saintly man, who
acquired a great reputation later as Bishop of Michoacan; Alonso
Maldonado; Francisco de Zainos; and Juan de Salmerón, who had
acquired some experience of Indian affairs as Alcalde Mayor of
Castilla del Oro. They were granted very high salaries: six hundred
thousand maravedís plus one hundred and fifty thousand for
expenses; they were forbidden to have Indians or to be served by
more than ten of them. (5) Complaints against Guzmán kept pouring in, particularly on the shameless slave-traffic he had organised in
Pánuco where, the King was informed, he had seventeen ships loaded
with slaves for export. (6) The Council was evidently puzzled, not
knowing what to believe, for while bishops and friars were loud in
their denunciations of the cruel and brutal ways of Guzmán and
his like, Guzmán counter-attacked, accusing the friars of ambition
and disloyalty. The friars were unpopular with the settlers because
they invariably took the side of the natives. When the members of
the second Audience asked the Emperor to increase the number of
friars to at least two thousand they, most impartially, added: "We
are alone in this opinion, for even of the said [fewer than one
hundred] friars who are here, the Spaniards say they are too
many." (7) We can discern a trace of this complexity of the situation
in the way Bernal Díaz, while setting down the crimes and misde-

Q

meanours of the first Audience, is led by his sincerity and impartiality to write: "Towards the conquerors they were ever so good and they carried out what His Majesty had ordered on the giving of Indians to the conquerors, for they never failed to give Indians to them when available and they favoured them in many ways." (8) But the bishops and friars could not countenance the wholesale branding of slaves and the callous treatment of the natives which the Audience permitted and even encouraged. The Audience lived in open revolt against the spiritual power. Two men who had sought asylum in the church were taken out to the Crown prison; the two bishops went in solemn procession to claim them; "they could hear the torture," says Herrera, (9) but were not able to rescue them. They excommunicated the Audience; but the three desperadoes cared nothing, and Guzmán went gaily on with his women, Delgadillo with his gambling and old Matienzo with his bottle.

* * *

All this anarchy and indignity ended with the arrival of the four oidores who (ahead of their President, detained in Santo Domingo) landed towards the beginning of 1531; they made their solemn entry into Mexico, as they had been instructed, riding on either side of a mule covered with velvet, which carried on its back a box with the Royal Seal. (10) They settled in Cortés' houses, which they had instructions to buy from him for the Crown. They were to trust and respect Cortés and Zumárraga and to uphold in every way the welfare and human rights of the Indians, prohibiting all slavery, except as between native and native, a point they were to study. They were to restore all freedom of private correspondence, which had been destroyed by the despotic regime of Guzmán and Salazar. (11)

The new Audience begged Cortés to settle in the capital; but early in the day, differences arose as to their respective rights and duties; the system was clumsy and authority was divided in a way which was unfair both to Cortés and to the Audience. The Audience were soon able to realise that the rift in the colony was impairing the utility of Cortés even as Captain General; a roll-call was once sounded by him as head of the forces of the Crown, but many refused to answer; he complains to the Emperor that the Audience has prevented him from punishing those who had thus withheld their services to the community, but the Audience explain also to the Emperor that many men would lose all they had rather than serve under Cortés; and though they sympathised with him they were bound to take the situation as it was. The new men, precisely because they were clean and upright magistrates, were in a position to stand up to his claims, even though, as we know from Herrera, they had to rely on his authority to keep the Indians quiet and obedient. (12)

They punished crime and graft with a strong and pure hand. Matienzo and Delgadillo were made to pay with their ill-gotten wealth for all their exactions, and thrown into jail; Guzmán, who had chosen to lead an expedition against some Indian "rebels" in Xalisco in order to be out of the way, refused to return to Mexico. These measures were well received by public opinion in New Spain, and the Second Audience established a reputation for good government, clean behaviour and transparent justice.

Cortés, however, was not the man to burden his mind with paying back old scores, as he had proved in his more than lenient way towards Salazar and Chirino on his return from Las Hibueras. This time again, there are documents to show that he forgave Matienzo who had drunk his wine in his house and deprived him of his lands and Indians. (13) Like most creative men, he was bent on the future, ready to let bygones be bygones but keen on the present and the morrow. He was anxious to establish his house as solidly as the great houses of Spain; and to engage in still higher pursuits beyond New Spain. Now, in the first of those two endeavors, he clashed again with the Audience. He had been granted twenty-three thousand vassals by the King; he claimed that this meant twenty-three thousand homes; the Audience, no doubt anxious to reduce his power within the framework of the State, claimed it meant twenty-three thousand persons, which reduced the value of the grant by a considerable amount. The conflict dragged on and was adjourned rather than settled. (14) The Audience wrote a most moderate, wise and statesmanlike letter to the Emperor on this matter, showing how Cortés was seeking to establish a kind of feudal lordship over extensive territories; and how difficult the census of his vassals would be owing to the reserved attitude of the natives, curbed as they were under the tyranny of their own caciques. The oidores granted Cortés part of his claim, some of it (Cuernavaca) as a feudal favour, with jurisdiction, but most of it in trust (encomienda) as to any other Spanish settler. It was a wise compromise, and the report of the oidores makes very good reading. Yet it was bound to be received by the proud Cortés with deep bitterness of heart.

After all, everything was due to him. He had an inherent right not only to this or that land, city, valley, but to the whole of New Spain; the grave oidores who examined his claims with the utmost honesty and the best good-will, were there only because he had fought and led his little band of men to victory. It was not merely a matter of right or wrong; it was a sense of the incoherence of things which placed the chief man in a subordinate place. One day, the first high-mass day after the arrival of the Audience, solemn mass was being sung in Mexico by the Bishop of Tlaxcala. The Audience was present, and the Captain General, Cortés, also. The Bishop when saying prayers for the royal family added one for the Captain General: *et ducem exercitus nostri.* One of the older oidores, Salmerón, strongly objected and reported the case to the Council of the Indies. (15)

But these men who kept him in a secondary place were not the greedy brutes of the first Audience; they were upright men and good governors; they freed the natives from many legal and illegal abuses; declared the Indians as free as the Spaniards and promulgated the King's Instructions punishing with death any Spaniard who branded Indians as slaves; they prohibited forced labour; and organised the pueblos with native *alcaldes* and *regidores* elected on a democratic basis; they developed education, arts and crafts and agriculture. Cortés, in hearty agreement with this enlightened policy, could not complain of them on public grounds.

* * *

He withdrew to Cuernavaca with his wife and family. There were two avenues open to his activity: one was the development of his estates: the other, the Southern Sea. There is hardly any form of economic development to which he did not devote his personal attention. Sugar, silk, vines, cattle, horses, cotton, wood, are only some of the branches of his activity which he mentions in his letters and other documents; in 1532 he is already sending cotton to Spain, and he writes with care and discrimination asking for Merino sheep and ewes to be sent from Spain for his estates. He may be considered the true founder of the Mexican mining industry, particularly of the silver industry. He had also conceived the ambition of developing sea-borne trade on the Southern Sea, and to that end had fought successfully to obtain the port of Tehuantepec as part of his estate, which he used to build ships for both his commercial enterprises and his adventures in discovery. "Your Lordship was not born to be a merchant," wrote one of his agents to him. He was not successful in these commercial endeavours; but then, was it success he was seeking, or rather distraction and relief from a life too sedate and comfortable for his imaginative mind and ambitious heart? (16)

"I was glad," he writes on June 25th, 1532, to his agent in Spain, "to hear of the ruse with which those galleys took that Moorish spot, and I also read the news of the reception given in Avila [to the King?], but that is not the quality of news I should like you to write; in every one of your letters, I should like to receive news as full as possible of the Empress' household and changes in Court people, and the affairs of the Realm, and news about Portugal, and the frontier, and about France and England and of Luther and of the Council [of Trent], and of His Majesty's coming [to Spain] and about the Turk and the Pope, and the Signiories, and of Italy, and of the King of Hungary, and things about the Emperor's household and those of his officers who may be replaced, and grants of commanderships and dignities, and whenever there is news of this quality, let me know at long length." (17) Here is a first-hand revelation of his preferences. He is thinking of world politics. He wants news of those who lead the affairs of Spain; and of the chief nations and problems of Europe. He is above all a statesman. Had Charles V had a more discerning eye towards men, he would have discovered in Cortés a man worthy to be his Spanish Prime Minister. As it was, he did not even see, in the man who had conquered Mexico, the best natural choice for governing New Spain. Cortés, too great to be a mere pioneer landowner in Cuernavaca, and a shipowner in Tehuantepec, sought relief in further discovery. The Southern Sea was still full of mystery—and of danger.

*   *   *

He had begun to dabble in South Sea affairs before his voyage to Spain. On October 15th, 1524, he wrote to the Emperor about the four ships which he was building in Zacatula, on the Southern Sea, and expressed the hope that they would be able to sail by June, 1525; he was evidently thinking of discovery and conquest and proudly concluded that, if he succeeded, "nothing will remain for Your Excelsitude to do to be the monarch of the world." On his return from the ill-fated expedition of Las Hibueras, the ships had not yet left, but he wrote to the Emperor reminding him of the offer he had made to secure all the Spiceland and other islands, if any, near the Molucas, Malacca and China, "and even to see to it that Your Majesty have the spices not by way of mere trade but as Your Majesty's own property, and that the natives of those islands acknowledge and serve Your Majesty as their King and natural lord; for I offer myself, under the said conditions, to send thither an armada, or to go in person, so that they be subjected and we settle there and build fortresses provided with munitions and artillery and to resist any princes of those parts or other ones." (18) The conditions which he demanded were apt to evolve with time. On October 27th, 1529, the Queen grants him a "capitulation" for discovery on the Southern Sea and towards the west in exchange for which he becomes Governor and Chief Constable for life of all lands discovered; but, while he has asked for a twelfth of all lands discovered for himself and his successors, he only obtains the twelfth "for the time which the royal favour and pleasure would consent." (19) Four years later, possibly under the stimulus of Pizarro's achievements in Peru, he presents a much stiffer proposal through Juan de Ribera. Having claimed for himself the honour of having discovered the Pacific, he offers: (a) to provide and arm ships on the southern coast; (b) to explore four hundred leagues of the southern coast; (c) to sail the gulf or gulfs till he shall discover islands or mainland never seen by Spaniards; (d) to sail towards the Equator in order to find Spice-lands "for there are many signs and conjectures which make the said Cortés hope to find the said Spice-lands"; (e) to arm as many fleets as necessary if the first be lost; (f) to carry out this plan within six years from the previous year (1532) when he began to undertake discoveries in the Southern Sea. His conditions are: (a) the Governorship of all the lands discovered to be vested in him and his heirs, with full rights over justice and police; (b) a tenth on gold, silver, pearls, precious stones, other metals and taxes, for him or his heirs; (c) no obligation to subjugate any lands discovered, but he will conquer up to three islands on condition that he and his heirs be granted one of them in total ownership excepting the political sovereignty, which will remain vested in the King; (d) if spice-lands be discovered, Cortés and his heirs to receive one-fifteenth of the royal income gained thereby; (e) one-third of the spice-lands discovered and conquered by him to be his or his heirs', and the Crown to pay two-thirds of the cost of the conquest; (f) during the six years of his service, no one else to be allowed to send ships to the said lands and islands (which of course, are undiscovered!) except by leave of Cortés; (g) the right to barter for gold, paying one-tenth to the Crown; (h) the governorship of New Spain for life; (k) the right to punish Spaniards guilty of ill-treating the natives; (l) arms and munitions as well as craftsmen such as carpenters and smiths to be supplied by the Casa de Contratación; (m) a royal guarantee that all his compacts with and promises to the natives shall be honoured and respected; (n) the waste from gold foundries in the new-discovered lands to be granted by the King to the first hospital founded in them; (o) the King to obtain from the Pope plenary absolution for those who shall die in the discovery, pacification and settlement of the Southern Sea. (20)

This is a most revealing document. Experience, disappointment, even bitterness, can be felt in it like the nourishing juices of the earth which feed the roots; but the stem of enterprise and the flower of imagination rise still in triumph and colour in the full light of life. In spite of the disastrous events which have thwarted his career at every step from 1524 to 1533, Cortés is still longing for adventure and dreaming of power.

His thoughts had probably been drawn to Spice-land by a letter which the King had sent him from Granada on June 20th, 1526, ordering him to send his ships to the rescue of two expeditions which had left Spain for the Pacific through the Strait of Magellan: one, under Loaisa, had sailed from Coruña on July 24th, 1525; and the other, under Sebastian Cabot, in 1526. (21) Cortés had carried out this flattering order with the utmost speed, competence and satisfaction; his instructions to his cousin Alvaro de Saavedra, whom he sent as captain, dated in "Temusticán" (i.e. Tenochtitlán, or Mexico) May 28th, 1527, reveal a universal yet concrete attention; they cover the usual provisions against blasphemy and gambling, against ill-treatment of the natives and, in particular, against insulting their womenfolk; but also crafty suggestions as to how to gain control of any fortress which the Portuguese might have built in the Molucas, in violation of what the King of Spain thought were his rights; not forgetting detailed instructions to secure plants of spices for developing their cultivation in New Spain. (22) Saavedra was given a number of letters—for Cabot, for his men, for the King of Cebu, for the King of Tidore, and for "the King of the Island or land where he might come with his fleet"—all models of lucidity and courtesy, in particular this last, a masterpiece of clear Spanish prose, and a perfect statement of Renaissance humanism: "To you, the honourable and Good King of . . . I, Don Hernando Cortés; It is a universal condition of all men to wish to acquire knowledge . . ." (23)

But in his letter to Cabot, he explained how he had been prevented from giving adequate help to one of Loaisa's ships, which had sought refuge in New Spain, owing to the curtailment of his powers by the arrival of the "Judge of Residence." (24) Saavedra's expedition, owing to these delays, could not leave till Thursday October 31st of that year. This expedition was one of the many efforts wasted by Spain in her long-drawn out duel with Portugal over the spice-trade and the ownership of the Molucas. Upon his return from Spain, writing from Tetzcuco on October 10th, 1530, Cortés reports that the ships he had left in readiness to reinforce the Saavedra fleet had been emptied of all that could be turned into money, all work stopped on them and the hulls allowed to rot, by the first Audience. Once again, his purposeful, creative activities were set at naught by the low ambitions of the mean. With his usual grit, he began all over again and gave orders to build two ships in Tehuantepec and two more in Acapulco, not without having to meet bureaucratic obstacles which led him to suspend all work for a time. (25) But, on January 25th, 1535, he is in Tehuantepec himself, personally supervising the work, and he writes to the Emperor complaining of the obstacles he finds in the Audience, yet reporting on an expedition already out and on another one he expects to send out soon. The first of the expeditions was made up of two ships under the command of one Diego Hurtado de Mendoza; it left Acapulco in May, 1532. One ship came back, probably in revolt against the captain; the other was never heard of again. The second expedition was sent by Cortés in search of the first. It also was composed of two ships under Diego Becerra de Mendoza, who had as chief pilot one Ortuño Ximénez—"great cosmographer," says Bernal Díaz, adding that this Ortuño Ximénez "promised to lead them to most fortunate lands [. . .] and said so many things about all of them becoming very rich that some persons believed it." Despite these happy auguries, the expedition ended in disaster, revolt, the murder of Becerra by his sailors, and a return to Xalisco with more or less fabulous news about an island full of pearls. (26)

"Cortés," writes Bernal Díaz, "heard the news with much grief, and as he was a stout-hearted man who could not rest while such things happened, he decided to send no more captains and to sail himself in person." His immediate aim was the "island" of Santa Cruz, that is the peninsula of Lower California; his ultimate aim, the discovery of another new world. He protests against the prohibition to sail which he then received from the Audience on the ground that it is against His Majesty's interests "to prevent him from discovering another new world for H.M. as the said Marquess is ready to do, and hoped in God our lord he would." (27) His dangers were the unknown and Nuño de Guzmán, his archenemy, who, in rebellion against the Audience, terrorised the coast of New Galicia on the flank of his voyage. As soon as it was known that Cortés in person intended to go out "discovering," recruits flocked to him; he put together three well provided ships and three hundred and twenty persons, including the wives of thirty-four married soldiers and many craftsmen. He first marched on Chinantla, a port in which he had to avenge spoliations committed by Guzmán on a previous expedition and recover a ship which Guzmán had stolen; then the rest of the expedition met him by sea, coming from Tehuantepec, on the Pacific side of the Isthmus. On April 18th, 1535, he sailed ahead with one hundred and thirty infantry soldiers and forty horsemen, leaving the rest, including sixty horses, with Andrés de Tapia; after a good crossing, he landed in Santa Cruz, on the southern point of Lower California; he then sent back the ships to fetch the rest of the expedition. This second crossing was disastrous; one ship succeeded

Q*

in joining Cortés; one was thrown back to Xalisco by the storm; the third had to take refuge in an unknown bay. The lost ships had the food supplies on board; the land in which Cortés was stranded offered but scanty opportunities for securing food. Weeks and months went by, and hunger threatened the small colony with extinction. Cortés took to the sea in search of help, found the two ships, one derelict, the other caught in a labyrinth of reefs; extricated himself from this situation by incredible deeds of endurance, ingeniousness and valour, bought meat and maize on his personal credit for his starved troop and crossed the Gulf for the third time bringing hope and relief to his men in Santa Cruz. He longed to return, yet lingered on in the hope of retrieving the failure with some marvellous discovery like that of Tenochtitlán. One day, as he was still hesitating, two ships appeared in Santa Cruz. They were sent by his loving wife, calling him back to his home and children; the captain, one Ulloa, brought also a letter from a new personage: the Viceroy of New Spain, Don Antonio de Mendoza, affectionately asking Cortés to return. He left the expedition in charge of Ulloa and sailed home. He arrived in Cuernavaca, "where the Marchioness was, with whom he rejoiced very much, and all the citizens of Mexico and the conquerors were much elated at his coming, and the Viceroy and Royal Audience as well, for it was rumoured that all the caciques of New Spain would revolt, on seeing that Cortés was not in the land." (28)

* * *

The appointment of a Viceroy was the outcome of advice tendered by Cortés, by Zumárraga and by the Audience. It was moreover the natural extension of the monarchical principle to the imperial conception of the day; the idea of "colony" in our modern sense was foreign to sixteenth century Spain. Mexico became the Kingdom of New Spain, on an equal footing with the several Kingdoms of Old Spain for which Charles was responsible to God. The King impersonated the people, and the system of government which was then thought best by the best men consisted in putting all responsibility into the hands of an upright man whose prime consideration was his own honour.

"The most illustrious and good Knight and worthy of high memory, Don Antonio de Mendoza," was a scion of one of the most honourable houses in Spain, which had given the country one of its greatest knight-poets, the Marquis of Santillana, and one of its greatest ecclesiastic statesmen, the Cardinal of Spain, Don Pedro González de Mendoza, whose political power under Ferdinand and Isabel had caused him to be known as "the third King." The new Viceroy was eminently fitted for the post, both by his illustrious blood and by his personal qualities. But every Spaniard knows that no bullfight is possible when there are two bulls in the ring. Difficult as Cortés' situation had been while political power in his own New Spain was in the hands of bishops and lawyers, it became more difficult still when his sun had to play satellite to the official sun which had come from Spain. His personal relations with the Viceroy, excellent at first, deteriorated as time went by. The Viceroy was a quiet, moderate, wise and somewhat crafty man. His tactics were based on the time-honoured tricks of the art of government; dilatoriness and balance of power: he applied the first to the census of Cortés' vassals; the second to Cortés' feud with Nuño de Guzmán, whom he screened from the royal prosecutions which this brutal adventurer had so richly deserved. (29)

Bernal Díaz, who records the fact with a priceless wealth of picturesque detail, has left us a long description of the festivities given in the city of Mexico to celebrate the Truce of Aiguesmortes between Charles V and Francis I. Cortés and the Viceroy had come also to some kind of truce, after the difficulties which had arisen between them over Guzmán and over the census of Cortés' vassals. The two magnates vied in magnificence and even in extravagance. The chief square of Mexico was transformed into a forest "with as many and different trees and as natural as if they had grown there"; birds, animals, "savages" who gave an excellent imitation of a fight; followed by a pageant of negroes and negresses adorned with gorgeous jewelry; and another fight. Next day, the square had become the city of Rhodes, defended by one hundred richly dressed commanders and defended by a fleet, sailing in the midst of the square, and commanded by Cortés himself—who possibly cast back longing thoughts to the days when he had sailed, fighting in fact and not in jest, over the lagoon near by; and Indians, and "Turks" and shepherds and bulls, all rushing in and out for the pleasure of the ladies of the conquistadores who looked down from the windows round the square, in their silks and jewels, sipping cool drinks and nibbling at marzipan, coated almonds and other sweets. Then the two banquets, one given by the Marquess to the Viceroy and one given by the Viceroy to the Marquess, with plates of gold and silver, and meals of such Gargantuan proportions that no reader would believe a tenth of the story were it not told by Bernal Díaz, honesty incarnate; with the touching detail that the Viceroy, who had taken the precaution of having an Indian watch over every single gold or silver object on the table, lost nothing but a few salt cellars, while Cortés, who took no such precaution, lost over one hundred marks of silver—which he freely mentioned, says Bernal Díaz, "out of greatness." (30)

This kind of greatness, however is but the façade for a man such as Cortés. He could not remain idle. He was ever faithful to the call of the Southern Sea. "As long as I live," he writes to the Emperor on February 10th, 1537, "I shall not cease to pursue my purpose"; and he announces that he has six ships ready and four in construction. In 1539, he sent Ulloa to explore the Gulf of California, which he did till Cortés, and the world with him, had acquired a fairly accurate idea of the shape of the land and ascertained that it was part of the Continent. (31)

Thus, even if Cortés had not conquered Mexico, he would have a place in history as the man who organised the mapping out of the Pacific coast from Tehuantepec to California. He had also sent two ships to Pizarro, then in difficulties in Peru, with food, ammunition and "silk clothes for his person"; his heart was set on discovery. (32) On September 20th, 1538, he writes to the Council of the Indies informing them that he has nine new ships ready to continue his exploratory work, but that he has no pilots, so he is sending ships to bring some over from Spain. (33) There was great ado at the time over a new fabulous discovery-to-make, the land of Quivira or the Seven Cities. Both Cortés and the Viceroy claimed the right to "discover" this new land. Relations between the two men became so strained that Cortés thought it necessary to appear again in person at the royal Court. He was getting older; he had never recovered the full use of his broken arm and was moreover lame from a spear-stroke received while he took part in a tournament on the festivities over the Truce of Aiguesmortes. (34) But his mind was alert and his heart still attached to power and glory and, though not vindictive, still keen in the pursuit of what was owed to him.

He began to amass gold for his voyage and stay in Spain. His expeditions had cost him three hundred thousand castillians of gold; he lived richly but beyond his means. "He spent most lavishly," says Gómara, "in war, in women, in friends and in caprices." (35) He thought himself the creditor of the royal treasury both on account of the expenses he had incurred in his sea adventures and because of the vassals owed to him. But he knew that gold was a sesame for Court affairs, and he had to travel in state. He was, moreover, taking over two sons, his legitimate heir Don Martín, then eight years of age, and one of his bastards, Don Luis. He sailed in the early spring of 1540. He was never again to see the land he had conquered. (36)

CHAPTER THIRTY-TWO

Beyond the Conquest

THE Spain of 1540 differed from that of 1530 even more than did the disillusioned and battered Marquess of the Valley from the youthful and petulant conqueror who had come over ten years earlier. Charles was no longer thinking of knightly duels with the King of France; he was saddened with personal sorrows and overburdened with European cares. His Castillian subjects were finding him a most expensive monarch. In 1538, he had failed to wrest a grant from the noblemen, one of whom, the High Constable, he had threatened to throw down from a gallery, had quietly answered: "Your Majesty will think it over, for, though small, I am heavy." (1) The Emperor was not more fortunate with the humble. One day early in 1539, he lost his way while chasing a deer in the forest of El Pardo. He had just killed the game, about two leagues from Madrid, when an old peasant turned up with a small ass laden with firewood. The Emperor asked him to unload the ass and take the deer to Madrid, promising to pay him more than the wood was worth. "By the Lord, Brother," answered the peasant, "you must be half-witted. Don't you see that the deer is heavier than the ass and the wood put together? Why don't you carry it yourself who are young and strong?" The Emperor made him talk, and asked him how old he was and under how many Kings he had lived. "I am very old. I have known five Kings. I knew King John II when I was already a bearded young man; and his son King Henry; and King Ferdinand; and King Philip; and this King Charles we now have." "Father," said the Emperor, "tell me by your life, who was the best of them and who the worst?" "The best," said the old man, "there is no doubt it was King Ferdinand. The worst, I can only say the one we have now is bad enough, and he keeps us restless

474

enough, and himself also, always away in Italy, or in Germany or in
Flanders, leaving behind his wife and children and taking away all
the money of Spain, and not only his income and the treasures of the
Indies, which are enough to conquer a thousand worlds, but new
taxes and tribute which he levies on us poor labourers." Courtiers
began to gather round them, and the peasant ended: "After all, you
may perhaps turn out to be the King! By the Lord, had I known it,
I would have told you many more things." (2)

The King who heard these home truths so meekly was only thirty-
nine years of age; but he was already feeling the weight of the years.
Within a few months of this sylvan scene, he lost his lovely wife,
Empress Elisabeth, who died in Toledo on May 1st, 1539. Charles
had loved her deeply and trusted her as he never trusted any other
human being in his life. Her death came at the moment when he was
most in need of companionship and advice. Germany was overrun
with the Protestant heresy, and, in Flanders, the heresy made rapid
progress and contributed to political unrest which was just then
finding expression in the threatening attitude of the burgesses of
Ghent, his native town. In November, 1539, the Emperor left for
Flanders and, despite the advice of many of his courtiers, crossed
France, trusting the word of Francis I. He was in deep mourning.

He had left as regent the Cardinal Archbishop of Toledo, Don
Juan Tabera, and in effective control over State affairs, Don Francisco de los Cobos. Indian affairs were in the hands of Cardinal
Loaisa. These were the men to whom Cortés had to put his case
when he arrived for the second and last time in Spain in the spring
of 1540. His plan was to stay for just as long as might be necessary
in order to settle his affairs at Court, to leave behind his three boys
in the Royal Household and to return to his wife and daughters and
his estates in New Spain.

He was received with the utmost consideration. Bernal Díaz, who
was also in Spain at the time, records that when the members of the
Council of the Indies learnt that Cortés was at the gates of Madrid,
they sent representatives to welcome him and gave him the houses
of the Commander Don Juan de Castilla for his residence while in
the city. Each time he attended a sitting of the council, one of the
oidores came out to receive him and accompanied him to a special
chair beside those of the grave magistrates. There, the weary con-

quistador put his case again and again: his fortune spent in the service of the Crown; the vassals promised him and never actually given; the dilatory ways of the Viceroy; the criminal attacks of Nuño de Guzmán on his privileges and property; all the bitterness accumulated by ten years of petty strife.

But the members of the Council of the Indies were also adepts in the art of dilatoriness, and as the Emperor was abroad, they preferred to wait for his return before deciding on this thorny and important case. (3) The Emperor meanwhile had crushed the rebellion of his subjects in Ghent, had tried again half to conciliate, half to reduce to obedience the rebellious Protestants in Ratisbon, and, in the summer of 1541, crossed the Alps towards Italy with twelve thousand Germans and one thousand horse, for he was determined to storm Algiers in order to destroy one of the chief centres of the power of the Infidels in the Mediterranean.

After an interview with the Pope in Luca, he left for Luni to embark, "loaded with blessings but not with funds." (4) He had thirty-five galleys in the port, which he sent with his Italians and his Germans to Majorca, where, after a most tempestuous crossing and short stays in Corsica, Sardinia and Minorca, he met one hundred and fifty ships with six thousand Spaniards and four hundred light horse under Don Hernando de Gonzaga, Viceroy of Sicily, and six thousand Germans and five thousand Italians under Camillo Colonna. The fleet was in command of Doria.

There came yet another fleet from Spain; "it brought no paid soldiers, but so many adventurers, workers and peasants as well as lords and squires, that it was marvellous." The list of the noblemen who thus rushed to this popular campaign contains nearly every great Spanish name; one of them was: "Don Hernando Cortés, Marquess of the Valley of Huaxaca, with his sons Don Martín and Don Luis." (5)

All this array of Christian forces was mobilized against a Sardinian eunuch, a renegade known as Azan Aga. He had eight hundred Turks, five thousand Moors, many of them Spanish renegades or Moriscoes, Arabian cavalry and a witch who predicted that he would win. On October 23rd, 1541, the sea being calm, the Emperor ordered his Spanish troops to land with food for three days, and, despite some resistance, sent a message to Azan Aga reminding him he was the son of Christian parents and asking him to surrender Algiers to the Christian Emperor with promises of honours for himself and freedom for his subjects. Azan Aga made answer that no one fared well by following the advice of his enemy.

The siege was laid, and the first skirmishes gave rise to no worse events than a few incidents between Spaniards, Italians and Germans as to their respective ardour in battle. But a cold rain followed by a disastrous storm caused the loss of many ships and the slaughter of many Christian troops in an amphibious fight on the murderous coast. One of the ships lost that night was that in which Cortés had sailed. He saved his life and that of his two boys but lost all his property and in particular a number of his precious emeralds.

The Emperor consulted his War Council and decided to withdraw. There were good men around him, but only one who had conquered an Empire with four hundred men and sixteen horse. That man went about from tent to tent, sad and forlorn; not because he had lost his precious emeralds valued at one hundred thousand ducats, but because the Council of War had met and he had not been asked to share in its debates. He felt certain that the situation could be retrieved; he proposed to those who would consent to listen to him that the Emperor should re-embark leaving him in command, and he pledged himself to win Algiers. "They would not listen to him, and it is even said that there were some who laughed at him." (6)

*   *   *

The time had come for him to taste the bitterest dregs of experience. Of the three aims which he pursued in Spain—wealth, honour, recognition—the first was constantly receding in a never-ending, dusty perspective of legal delays: the second was niggardly granted by a parsimonious Emperor, steeped in medieval prejudices about blood; the third was unattainable, for seldom does a Spaniard attain recognition by his fellow men till he is dead.

Cortés was a keen contester for these three aims. The pursuit of the first led him at times to a passionate partisanship, as for example in his opposition to the Viceroy, after a first period of friendly relations. In 1542, he presented a petition against the Viceroy summing up his grievances with much power and animus. (7) But there is abundant proof that he was free from rancour and from meanness, and that in all this struggle his eyes were on wealth and power, not on the men who, for fair or unfair reasons, stood in his way towards them.

Wealth for him, moreover, as he showed from the earliest days of his public life, was but an instrument for high endeavour. He spent fortunes in his Southern Sea expeditions, and in the social duty of maintaining a house worthy of his achievements and rank. He was conscious of being the creator of a great house, and alive to his responsibilities as such. On January 9th, 1535, in Colima, while preparing his exploration of the Southern Sea, he set up a Mayorazgo or entail, for which he had obtained royal authority in Barcelona on June 27th, 1529; he emphatically provided that his vast estates in New Spain were for ever to remain the property of the Marquisate, and that the heir should style himself Cortés, and use his coat of arms. (8) He was by no means narrow-minded about his succession: if legitimate heirs failed, the marquisate and entail were to pass to his bastards, most of whom were half-caste. Cortés was a loving father to all his children. In a letter to his agent Francisco Núñez written from Santiago of the Southern Sea on June 20th, 1533, he refers to an illness of his eldest son Don Martín, the bastard he had had by Doña Marina: "Now I want you to know that I do not love him less than the one God has given me by the Marchioness." In every way that the law permitted, he treated his children as equals. Thus, by a deed signed on November 27th, 1539, while he was preparing his voyage to Spain, he gives one hundred slaves to his three sons, Don Martín (legitimate), Don Martín and Don Luis (bastards), "which donation I grant you in equal shares." (9)

His sons were more precious to him than his daughters, for he was deeply imbued with the sense of posterity: hence the pathetic tone of his complaint to the Emperor over legal delays: "The most prejudicial thing for me, for I am sixty, and I left home five years ago, and I have only one son to succeed me, and though my wife is young and could give me more, my age will not allow much tarrying; and if I had no other, and God disposed of this one without his leaving any issue, what would it profit me to have acquired all I have? for if daughters succeed, memory is lost." (10)

* * *

But, though wealth and fame were close to his heart, none of his ambitions was so deeply rooted as the thirst for recognition which was the anguish of his whole life. He, an obscure lad, penniless and inexperienced in a new world just emerging from the unknown, had discovered and conquered the biggest and most gorgeous empire which had till then been laid at the feet of any European monarch. Cortés knew enough history to be conscious of the size and import of his achievement. If in the solitude of his meditations he felt the equal of Julius Caesar, no one can reproach him that he was wrong; indeed his conquest has not unreasonably been appraised as a higher achievement than that of the Gauls. (11) With the self-absorbed ingenuity of men who pursue and attain great things, he expected a wave of affection and rewards from a country and sovereign overwhelmed with gratitude. Poor Cortés! As soon as his greatness had set him up high above his countrymen, he became the favourite mark for mud-slinging, calumnies, innuendoes, all the vile weapons of the low and impotent to remove from sight the odious incarnation of outstanding success. Cortés, though genial and simple, was no equalitarian; he would have cut through the wave of smaller enemies with an unmoved heart and an insensitive skin; but he was deeply imbued with a living sense of the symbolic value of the monarch to a degree general then in Spain but unknown today outside England, and he suffered abominably from the indifference, coldness, insufficient recognition, and at times downright ingratitude, which he found in the Emperor.

Throughout his numerous papers, the passages in which he refers to Charles V are always couched in this strong emotional tone. The man-subject is chained to the man-monarch by a deep affection made up of genuine attachment and loyalty but battered and bruised by a desolate experience. In a note to his agent Núñez, written about 1533, he sums up his services, then goes on to enumerate his grievances beginning quaintly with this: "His Majesty was pleased to send Luis Ponce de León to sit 'in residence' over him, a thing which it is not customary to do to captains and conquerors of new lands." The tone is personal. He is deeply hurt. Yet, he is grateful for the "favours and good treatment which he has received from Your Majesty, for he holds ingratitude to be a grave sin"; and "he remembers the favour he was granted in being so kindly received by Your

Majesty when he came to kiss hands and in the loving words Your Majesty said to him and good treatment Your Majesty always instructed should be meted out to his person." And he touches on the fringe of religious worship when he adds: "He says he holds as relics two letters Your Majesty had written to him on his way to Barcelona to embark for Italy [. . .] For truly in all his labours he has no other comfort than to see and read them many times, and to keep his faith in the word of a prince so Catholic that it cannot be broken, and that with this hope God knows how much he has suffered believing what he says." (12)

Ten years later, he was still wandering in Spain, unemployed, he, the chief Spaniard, the most capable Spaniard of his day. This truly great man was reduced to the idle life of a courtier, so aptly described in one of the dialogues, born within his own house, which Pedro de Navarra was to publish after his death. "At Court," says one of the debaters, possibly Cortés himself, "we eat by weight, drink by measure, sleep without rest, and live with so much leisure, that every dot of time is ticked off by a dot of the clock; yet, though our time is so well measured, our life is so empty that we mistake death for life, unlike you [the rustic] whose life is death. At twelve I go to bed and at eight I rise; I transact business till eleven; from eleven to twelve I dine; from twelve till one I pass the time with fools and gossips, or in fruitless talk; from one to three I have my siesta; from three to six I transact business; from six till eight I haunt the Court or go walking round the valleys; and from eight to ten I dine and rest; from ten to twelve I am idle and hold conversations, and from twelve on I sleep, as I said, accompanied rather by ambition and greed, or by fear and mischief than by quietness and content- ment." (13)

This was not the life which a man like Cortés would enjoy. Yet even this life might have satisfied him if the Emperor had admitted him into his inner circle and recognised his merit. But the Emperor though urbane was aloof, indifferent, at times even offensive: Charles V, no doubt under the temporary influence of Cortés' enemies, went one day so far as to say to him that "the conquest was not his," meaning that Cortés had usurped Velázquez' rights. "I also want to bring to Your Majesty's memory," writes the unemployed conqueror and statesman, "what Your Majesty told me in this city, to wit:

'that the conquest had not been mine,' for it is for me a matter of honour. Let Your Majesty be cleansed of this doubt and see that I have always told Your Majesty the truth." (14)

Withal, while still fighting hard for worldly affairs, his thoughts are beginning to turn inwards, and in this letter, written four years before his death, there is already a graver tone even in his reproaches to the ungrateful Emperor. After recalling his grievances, he goes on to say: "I thank the Lord for it all Who wishes to pay Himself back for the many offences I have done Him. Let Him be pleased to count it in my discharge, as I believe He will, for since my services have been such as no vassal ever rendered his King, and since they have been rendered to the most powerful, catholic and grateful of all Kings, this gratefulness and reward could not be possible were it not that the heart of the King is in the hand of God; and from Him flows everything, and He does not allow aught else to happen to me." (15)

The same mood pierces through his worldly complaints in a letter which he wrote to the Emperor from Valladolid, on February 3rd, 1544. "My work profited me in that it brought me contentment for having done my duty, but not in bringing forth its own results, for not only has it failed to secure rest for my old age, but it has brought me labour till death, and God grant it may not go beyond, but end with bodily life and not extend to the perpetual, for he who works so hard to defend his body is sure to offend his soul."

He saw himself always hanging on at Court, with his three sons and a host of costly lawyers, "old, poor and in debt"; so he urges the King to have his business quickly settled for, he says, "were it to be delayed, I would let it go and return home, for I am not of an age to hang about in inns, but rather to retire and settle my account with God, for it is long, and I have little life left to put my case before Him, and it is better to lose one's wealth than one's soul." (16)

* * *

This mood of earnestness was genuine in him from his earlier days. Now that, old, ill and disappointed, he trailed his person and household in the train of the itinerant monarch, it was but natural that it should prevail in him. His mind was always open to the quests which nature and the mysteries beyond call forth in man. He had gathered round him a number of persons of quality and of scholars, who met regularly in his house, making up a kind of informal Academy. Among the members of this Academy were two Italian princes of the Church, Cardinal Poggio, the papal nuncio, and Domenico Pastorelo or Pastorelli, Archbishop of Cagliari. Amongst the grandees, there were two brothers Peralta, Don Bernaldino and Don Antonio, Marquess de Falces, whose son was to be the third Viceroy of Mexico. The last of the members to arrive gave the theme of the discussion, and one of the scholars present was requested to take down the minutes. Pedro de Navarra, who later became Bishop of Comenge, was one chosen for this task. He took so much pleasure in it that he wrote several volumes of dialogues out of his mental experiences in Cortés' Academy. This much may be gathered from his statement: "The subjects discussed by these illustrious men were so notable that if there is aught of good in my rude judgment it had its beginnings in them: so much so that in the two hundred dialogues which I have written there are very few things which this excellent Academy had not discussed."

Navarra's book may therefore not unfairly be considered as a kind of unofficial record of Cortés' Academy; and the subjects of those of his Dialogues which are known, as fair indications of those which Cortés and his friends actually discussed. These subjects vary in depth and substance: "Of the Eternity of the Soul"; "Of the Difference Between Speaking and Writing (an Extremely Subtle and Notable Matter)"; "What Kind of Man the Prince's Chronicler Should Be? (a matter still touched but by few)"; "Of the Difference Between Rustic and Noble Life (a very useful doctrine for the errors of our day)". The language of these dialogues is simple and noble, and the mental air which bathes them is more luminous than our vain epoch might suspect. "Peace to the people and liberty to thy person," one of the debaters exclaims to hail the arrival of his interlocutor. (17)

In May, 1547, Don Francisco de Los Cobos, the powerful minister of Charles V, was on the point of death. The Academy chose for its debate "the way in which every good Christian should make ready to die well." This subject was then sure to be uppermost in Cortés' mind. His health was rapidly failing. He wanted, says

Gómara, "to return to New Spain and to die in Mexico." He left Madrid for Seville. He was at the time expecting the arrival of his elder daughter, Doña María, who was to marry the son of the Marquess of Astorga, to whom he had already paid 20,000 ducats out of the 100,000 of the dowry which had been stipulated. There he dictated his will on October 12th, 1547. It is a document which reveals his three chief preoccupations: his family; New Spain; his conscience and the salvation of his soul. His name and estate are left to his son Don Martín; his legitimate daughters are handsomely provided for; his illegitimate sons and daughters are also generously endowed; and the compact with the Marquess of Astorga for the marriage of his daughter Doña María, especially mentioned and recommended. The Marquess of Astorga is appointed one of three executors, the other two being the Duke of Medina Sidonia and the Count of Aguilar.

So much for his family and worldly ambitions. But his own heart was set on Mexico. It may be said without fancifully distorting the facts that Cortés was the first man who felt a Mexican patriotism. The first clause of his testament stipulates that his remains are to be laid at rest in Cuyoacán. Numerous are the passages of his letters and reports which express his clear vision of a New Spain as a nation in which Spaniards and Mexicans are to live side by side in peace and prosperity. This aim is ever present in his will; he bestows particular attention on the spiritual and intellectual interests of his new country. He was first to found hospitals, monasteries and centres of learning in New Spain; he leaves capital and maintenance for a hospital, a convent and a university college which in his mind was to provide intellectual and spiritual leadership for the natives of New Spain.

His conscience was far from easy at the way the Spaniards dealt with the rights of the natives. He knew that the very basis of the right of the Spaniards to make slaves of the Indians even in war was hotly contested by many a Spanish theologian, and that even if this right were conceded, many natives had actually been branded as slaves in New Spain against the rules which it would sanction. In his will, he orders his heirs to find out the exact position and to act accordingly "in order to unburthen my conscience and theirs." He also instructs them to find out whether any of his lands have been unfairly taken from the natives and, if so, to give them back. In short, as he felt the approach of death, this man sought the peace of his soul in a searching scrutiny of his actions on principles of justice according to his lights. It is in this denuded state of mind that on December 2nd, 1547, in Castilleja de la Cuesta, close to Seville, he left the earth on which he had fought so bravely. (18)

*   *   *

In his last struggle with the Angel in that penetrating twilight of the last day on earth, he must have seen through his unheard-of prowess and found the treble cause of failure which it hid within. He had failed as a man of action, for, though his achievement had been as great as any in history, he had thrown away his conquest, by exposing it once to Alvarado's rashness, once more to satisfy his own impatience towards Olid, once again when he failed to master the intricacies of the Court and to conquer the graces of the Emperor. During his lifetime, the country he had created was being developed by other hands than his. New Spain was taking shape under a Viceroy, while he wandered, sad and idle, in the train of an ever distracted monarch.

If he looked away from this failure and sought a stoic consolation in the thought that his work would be seen by posterity in its true colour and size, the light eternal which on the edge of this earth shone upon him from beyond would soon shatter that dream. For history as a mirror of truth is beyond and above men, and his noble name was to be the target of every insult and the toy of every misunderstanding; while, in his lifetime, his countrymen were bored by his achievements and remained cold and uninterested before this tragedy of his noble life.

And if he looked away again and tried to think that, at least, even if unrecognised, he remained in truth the creator of a new nation born of two races—then his disappointment would be bitterest of all—for that nation has not yet succeeded in finding its soul. A graft of one race upon the stem and root of another, it does not yet know its true meaning and destiny, and lives an agitated life in a perpetual struggle between the two bloods, so that Moteçuçuma dies and Cuauhtemoc is hanged every day, and every day the white man conquers and humiliates the Indian within the soul of every Mexican.

This is the deepest failure of all. Three years before his death, he had written to the Emperor: "This work which God did through me is so great and marvellous . . ." (19) He knew he had been just an instrument. But of what or of whom? Of God, of course, he would have answered unhesitatingly. Yes, of God. But men are not dead instruments, like hammers and saws. They have a freedom of their own, a freedom to err. He had gone over in the name of God, dreaming of a new Christian nation made up of the natives, whom he would save from heathenism, and of the Spaniards who would settle, develop, enlighten and ennoble it. He had started this nation on its new path of economic prosperity, respect for the natives, education of native and white and the "ennobling" of the land by the queen of civic arts—architecture. Within his lifetime, there were enough Latin scholars and theologians amongst the natives to frighten some timorous priests at their progress; and the first printing press of the Continent was at work. Noble buildings had made Mexico the chief capital of the New World. Shortly after Cortés' death, Cervantes de Salazar records the prosperity of Tlaxcala, the beauty of the buildings and the fertility of its lands, the wealth, contentment and well-being of the natives, and tells how one of Cortés' captains, who governed it, had built thirty-three stone bridges in the vicinity to ensure communications. (20) This was the work that he meant to achieve and had undertaken according to his lights, which were those of the best men of his day: the native Emperor, order and faith had to be removed, and in their stead the Christian Emperor, State and faith were to be finally established. It was quite simple. As for the two races, they were both born of Adam and Eve, children of God.

So he thought. So thought everybody in his day. Could he guess that, in the depths of races and nations, there lie hidden oceans of instincts, emotions, obscure memories, and that he was preparing for New Spain centuries of mental and moral storms? Could he guess that a day would come when his ashes, buried by his express desire in New Spain, would have to be protected by secrecy from the infuriated crowds of the nation he had founded, turned in a frenzy of self-negation against the man to whose vision they owed their existence? that Mexico would erect a statue to Cuauhtemoc, less to honour Cuauhtemoc than to insult him? that a painter of that race he did so much to ennoble and liberate would one day smear the walls of his own house in Cuernavaca with so-called scenes of the conquest distorted by a prejudice of which the painter himself is innocent since it comes from the racial depths?

He had risen by high endeavour to be one of the heroes of mankind. But, as such, what could he do but err? Poor mankind, seeking her peace and unity through the tortuous ways of history, groping almost blindly under the feeble light of her reason through the uncharted ocean of her soul, in a world which stubbornly conceals its complex secrets—mankind is a cruel devourer of her own heroes, whom she condemns to throw away treasures of energy and of self-denial in gestures tragically irrelevant to the very aims she seeks.

Cortés, great in his achievement, was greater still in that his tragic life is a fit symbol of the tragedy of man on earth.

NOTES

I. ACKNOWLEDGMENTS

I wish to express my thanks to the Librarian and staff of the Bodleian Library and to the Director and staff of the London Library for their unfailing courtesy and patience; as well as to Don Adolfo Prieto and Don Carlos Prieto of Mexico, Don Federico Gómez de Orozco of Coyoacán, and Don Abel Gracia Azorin of Mexico, for the trouble they have taken in sending me books and other material.

* * *

My thanks are also due to a number of readers who have pointed out misprints and errors in the first edition; notably Mr. W. H. Fellowes, of Beaconsfield; Mr. Viggo Carlsen, of Norwich, Connecticut; Mr. J. R. Edwards, M.A., of the Liverpool Institute; and Mr. J. Cooper Clark, editor of the Codex Mendoza. I agree with the last mentioned that the name of the Mexican Emperor should be Motecuçuma rather than Moteçuçuma. For technical reasons the change has not been made in the text.

II. SPELLING OF NAMES

1. SPANISH.

I have dealt with the spelling of Spanish names in English books in my *Life of Columbus* (p. 410) and explained in particular why I prefer *Colón* to *Columbus* or *Colombo* for the discoverer of America—in agreement, by the way, with *Colón* himself. As for *Cortés*, it is perhaps still useful to say that the form *Cortez* is utterly absurd. It seems to be due to some confusion with the form in *ez* of many Spanish patronymics such as *Rodríguez* or *Fernández*; which is very much as if we turned Washington into *Washingson* on the strength of *Jefferson* and *Jackson*.

I have adopted the form *Hernán* for several reasons: the first is that *Hernán Cortés* is the name by which the conqueror of Mexico is known throughout the Spanish-speaking world; the second is because this form is undoubtedly of a finer sonority than any of the other choices available; the third, that though it is the Spanish way, it fits most other languages better than either *Fernando* or *Hernando Cortés*.

2. MEXICAN NAMES.

I have followed the established tradition of writing Mexican names in a Spanish phonetical (approximate) rendering. An English phonetical script would have led to rendering unrecognisable many familiar names. But the Spanish spelling is by no means uniform. *Cuauhuanac*, for instance, which became *Cuernavaca*, is spelt in a variety of ways: *Quadnavac, Coadnavach, Coadnabaced* by Cortés and *Cuedlavaca* by Bernal Díaz. The sound *Coat* becomes *Guad*, familiar to the Spaniards in names coming from *Wed* (river in Arabic) such as *Guadalquivir=Wed-El-Kevir*; *Coatzacoalco* and *Guazacoalco*; *Huesotzingo, Guaxocingo, Guasocingo* are varieties of the same name. A certain variety must be forgiven, owing in particular to the fact that different authors spell the same names in different ways. Bernal Díaz is the most picturesque of all; in one case, his "translation" of *Uitzilopochtli* into *Huychilobos*, has tempted me to translate his *Huychilobos* into *Witchywolves*.

III. PORTRAITS

There are a number of Cortés, but only three or four with any claim to having been painted in his lifetime and by painters who knew or had access to the original. These are:

1. A picture on canvas belonging to the City of Mexico. Age of Cortés, about 50. He is in armour.

2. A picture on canvas, full length. Belongs to a private collector. A photograph of it has been published in *Archives de la Société Américaine de France*, Deuxième Série, Vol. I. Planche XIX, p. 296.

3. Woodcut published in *Cortés Valeroso* by Gabriel Lasso de la Vega (Madrid, 1568). Represents Cortés in the year of his death.

4. Full-length portrait in the Hospital de Jesús Nazareno of the City of Mexico. A copy of some original painted while Cortés was in Spain during his first visit.

I have not come across any complete study of this matter. The above data are borrowed from an article published in *El Universal* of Mexico, November 16th, 1919, by Professor N. León, of the National Museum of Mexico.

IV. BIBLIOGRAPHY

The list given below contains the books actually used. It has been compiled in the alphabetic order of the abbreviations generally used ·in the notes.

Alamán Disertaciones sobre la historia de la República Megicana desde la época de la Conquista que los Españoles hicieron a fines del siglo XV y principios del XVI de las Islas y Continente americano hasta la Independencia, por D. Lucas Alamán. Mégico, 1844. 3 vols.

A.M.N.M. Anales del Museo Nacional de Mexico.

B.D.C. Historia verdadera de la Conquista de la Nueva España, por Bernal Díaz del Castillo, uno de sus Conquistadores. Unica Edición hecha según el Códice Autógrafo. La publica Genaro García. Mexico, 1904. 2 vols.

Bourne Spain in America, by Edward Gaylord Bourne. 1904.

C.C.S.M. Christopher Columbus, Being the Life of the Very Magnificent Lord Don Cristóbal Colón, by Salvador de Madariaga. London, 1939; New York, 1940.

C.D.H.M. Colección de Documentos para la Historia de Mexico, publicada por Joaquín García Icazbalceta. Mexico, 1858. 2 vols.

C.D.I.A.I. Colección de documentos inéditos relativos al descubrimiento, conquista y colonización de las posesiones españolas en América y Occeanía [*sic*], sacados, en su mayor parte, del Real archivo de Indias, bajo la dirección de los Señores Don Joaquín F. Pacheco y Don Francisco de Cárdenas, miembros de varias reales academias científicas, y Don Luis Torres de Mendoza, abogado de los Tribunales del Reino. Madrid, 1864–84. 42 vols.

C.M. Codex Mendoza: The Mexican Manuscript known as The Collection of Mendoza and preserved in the Bodleian Library, Oxford, edited and translated by James Cooper Clark. London, 1938.

C.S.   Crónica de la Nueva España que escribió el Dr. Francisco Cervantes de Salazar, cronista de la Imperial Ciudad de México. The Hispanic Society of America, Madrid, 1914.

Written in Mexico towards 1560, under the eye of several conquistadores, still living, this work remained in MS. form till 1914. It is therefore both old and new. It was known by Herrera who borrowed from it frequently.

Chaplain   Itinerario de la Armada del Rey Católico a la Isla de Yucatán, en la India; el Año 1518, en la que fue por Comandante y Capitán General Juan de Grijalva. Escrito para Su Alteza por el Capellán Mayor de la dicha Armada.

A Spanish translation of an Italian translation of the original, now lost, in C.D.H.M., vol. I, pp. 281–568. The author can be no other than Juan Díaz, the only priest in Grijalva's fleet.

Conway   The Last Will and Testament of Hernando Cortés, Marqués del Valle. A Facsimile and Paleographic Version, Together with an English Translation of the Original Testament, dated Seville, the Eleventh Day of October, 1547. Edited with an Introduction and Notes by G. R. G. Conway. Privately printed in the City of Mexico, 1939.

Cuevas   Cartas y otros documentos de Hernán Cortés novisimamente descubiertos en el Archivo de Indias de la Ciudad de Sevilla e ilustrados por el P. Mariano Cuevas, S.J. Sevilla, 1915.

Cuevas-D.   Documentos inéditos del Siglo XVI para la Historia de Mexico colegidos y anotados por el P. Mariano Cuevas, S.J. Mexico, 1914.

F.A.I.   Historia Chichimeca, por Don Fernando de Alva Ixtlilxochitl, in K., vol. IX, pp. 197–316.

F.A.I.-R.H.   Relaciones Históricas, por Don Fernando de Alva Istlilxochitl, in K., vol. IX, pp. 317–468.

F.C.   Doña Catalina Xuarez Marcayda, Primera Esposa de Hernán Cortés, y su familia, por Francisco Fernández del Castillo. Mexico (without date).

Gayangos   Cartas y Relaciones de Hernán Cortés al Emperador Carlos V. colegidas e ilustradas por Don Pascual de Gayangos. Paris, 1866.

R

Gómara   Crónica de la Nueva España, con la conquista de Mexico
                  y otras cosas notables hechas por el valeroso Her-
                  nando Cortés, Marqués del Valle, Capitán de su
                  Magestad en aquellas partes. Con mucha diligencia
                  corregida y añadida por el mesmo autor en Çaragoça.

H.C.C.C.   Hernán Cortés: Copias de Documentos Existentes en el
                  Archivo de Indias y en su Palacio de Castilleja de
                  la Cuesta, sobre la Conquista de Méjico. Sevilla,
                  1889.

Herrera   Historia General de los Hechos de los Castellanos en las
                  Islas y Tierra Firme del Mar Occeano, escrita por
                  Antonio de Herrera coronista mayor de su M^D de
                  las Indias y su coronista de Castilla. En cuatro
                  Décadas desde el año de 1492 hasta el de 1531.
                  Madrid, 1601.

Humboldt-Essai Essai Politique sur le Royaume de la Nouvelle Espagne,
                  par Alexandre de Humboldt. Paris, 1811. 2 vols.

Humboldt-Vues   Vues des Cordillères et Monuments des Peuples Indi-
                  gènes de l'Amérique, par Al. de Humboldt, avec 19
                  Planches, dont plusieurs colorées. Paris, 1816.
                  2 vols.

K.   Antiquities of Mexico, edited by Lord Kingsborough.
                  London, 1831. 9 vols.

Las Casas   Historia de las Indias, by Bartolomé de las Casas. Vols.
                  62 to 65 of Colección de Documentos Inéditos para
                  la Historia de España, por el Marqués de la Fuen-
                  santa del Valle y Don José Sancho Rayón. Madrid,
                  1875.

Las Casas-D.   Brevissima Relacion de la Destruycion de las Indias:
                  colegida por el Obispo dõ Fray Bartolome de las
                  Casas o Casaus de la orden de Sãcto Domingo. 1552.

MacNutt   Fernando Cortés and the Conquest of Mexico, 1485–1547,
                  by Francis Augustus MacNutt. New York, 1909.

Maudslay   The True History of the Conquest of New Spain, by
                  Bernal Díaz del Castillo, one of its conquerors.
                  From the only exact copy of the Original Manuscript,
                  edited and published in Mexico by Genaro García.
                  Translated into English with Introduction and Notes
                  by Alfred Percival Maudslay, M.A., Hon. Professor
                  of Archaeology, National Museum, Mexico. London,

printed for the Hakluyt Society, MDCCCCVIII. 5 vols.

Means   History of the Spanish Conquest of Yucatán and of the Itzas, by Philip Ainsworth Means, in Papers of the Peabody Museum of American Archaeology and Ethnology, Harvard University, vol. VII. Cambridge, Mass., 1917.

Means-Main   The Spanish Main: Focus of Envy, 1492–1700, by Philip Ainsworth Means. New York, 1935.

Mendieta   Historia Eclesiástica Indiana, obraescrita a fines del siglo XVI por Fray Gerónimo de Mendieta, de la Orden de San Francisco. La publica por primera vez Joaquín García Icazbalceta. Mexico, MDCCLXX (misprint for MDCCCLXX).

Motolinia   Historia de los Indios de Nueva España por Fray Toribio de Benavente o Motolinia, in C.D.H.M., vol. I, pp. 1–249.

Motolinia-L   Letter to Carlos V, Taxcala, Jan. 2, 1555, in C.D.H.M., vol. I, pp. 253–276.

N.C.D.H.M.   Nueva Colección de Documentos para la Historia de México, publicada por Joaquín García Icazbalceta. Mexico, 1886. 2 vols.

Navarra   Dialogos de la differencia del hablar al escrevir . . . dictados por el Illvstrissimo y Reuerendissimo Señor Don Pedro de Nauarra, Obispo 9e de Comenge, y del consejo supremo del Rey Christianissimo. Tolosa, 1565.

Navarrete   Colección de los viajes y descubrimientos que hicieron por mar los Españoles, por Martín Fernández de Navarrete. Imprenta Real. Madrid, 1825. 5 vols.

O. y B.   Historia antigua y de la Conquista de Mexico, por el Lic. Manuel Orozco y Berra. Mexico, 1880. 4 vols.

O. y B.-G.   Geografía de las lenguas y carta etnográfica de México, precedidas de un ensayo de clasificación de las mismas lenguas y de apuntes para las inmigraciones de las tribus, por el Lic. Manuel Orozco y Berra. Mexico, 1864.

Oviedo   Historia general y natural de las Indias, islas y tierrafirme del mar océano, por el capitán Gonzalo Fernandez de Oviedo y Valdés, Primer Cronista del

Nuevo Mundo, publícala la Real Academia de la Historia [. . .], por D. José Amador de los Rios. Madrid, 1853. 4 vols.

Pereyra   Hernán Cortés, por Carlos Pereyra. Madrid, 1931.

Prescott   History of the Conquest of Mexico, by William H. Prescott, edited by Wilfred Harold Munro, Professor of European History in Brown University, and comprising the notes of the Edition by John Foster Kirk. Philadelphia and London, 1904. 4 vols.

R.G.   De Rebus Gestis Ferdinandi Cortesii (Incerto Auctore), in *C.D.H.M.*, vol. I, p. 510 et seq.

Ricard   La "Conquête spirituelle" du Mexique: Essai sur l'apostolat et les méthodes missionnaires des Ordres Mendiants en Nouvelle Espagne de 1523–24 à 1572, par Robert Ricard. Paris, Institut d'Ethnologie, 1933.

Sahagún   Historia universal de las cosas de Nueva España, por el M. R. P. Fray Bernardino de Sahagún, in *K.*, vol. VII.

Sandoval   Historia de la vida y hechos del Emperador Carlos V. max. fortissimo, rey catholico de España y de las Indias, islas y tierra firme del mar oceano. Al Catholico Rey Don Felipe III deste nombre nuestro Señor. Por el Maestro Don Fray Prudencio de Sandoval su coronista, Obispo de Pamplona. Pamplona, 1634. 2 vols.

Tapia   Relación hecha por el Señor Andrés de Tapia, sobre la Conquista de Mexico, in *C.D.H.M.*, vol. II, pp. 554–594.

Thorne   "The Great Temple of Mexico," by Rosalie Thorne, in Vassar Journal of Undergraduate Studies, vol. XII, May, 1939, p. 1.

Torquemada   Monarchia Indiana con el origen y guerras de las Indias Occidentales, de las Poblaciones, Descubrimiento, Conquista, Conversión y otras cosas marauillo sas de la mesma tierra distribuidos en tres tomos. Madrid, 1723 (first published, 1615). 3 vols.

Tezozomoc   Crónica Mexicana de Fernando de Alvarado Tezozomoc (probably written towards 1589), in *K.*, vol. IX, pp. 5–196.

Waley   The Way and Its Power: A Study of the Tao tê Ching
               and Its Place in Chinese Thought, by Arthur Waley.
               London, 1934.

Wilgus   Histories and Historians of Hispanic America, by Alva
               Curtis Wilgus. Washington, 1936.

V. NOTES TO THE CHAPTERS

CHAPTER I

1 Here is a table providing the corresponding designations of the fifty-two years which ended in the year of the conquest.

A.D.	Mexican (Nauatl)	Mexican (English)
1467	1. Acatl	1. Reeds
1468	2. Tecpatl	2. Flint
1469	3. Calli	3. House
1470	4. Tochtli	4. Rabbit
1471	5. Acatl	5. Reeds
1472	6. Tecpatl	6. Flint
1473	7. Calli	7. House
1474	8. Tochtli	8. Rabbit
1475	9. Acatl	9. Reeds
1476	10. Tecpatl	10. Flint
1477	11. Calli	11. House
1478	12. Tochtli	12. Rabbit
1479	13. Acatl	13. Reeds
1480	1. Tecpatl	1. Flint
1481	2. Calli	2. House
1492	13. Tecpatl	13. Flint
1493	1. Calli	1. House
1502	10. Tochtli	10. Rabbit
1506	1. Tochtli	1. Rabbit
1509	4. Calli	4. House
1519	1. Acatl	1. Reeds
1520	2. Tecpatl	2. Flint

The combination of the figure and the glyph (rabbit, reeds, flint, or house) which determined the year within the "sheaf" was preceded by a number of "sheaf" glyphs which determined the number of "sheafs" elapsed since the beginning of the era. (1091) *C.M.* vol. I, p. 45.   *Humboldt-Vues.*   *O. y B.*, bk. IV, ch. VI, vol. 2, pp. 116–17.

2 *Tezozomoc*, ch. LXXXII, in *K.*, vol. IX, p. 143.

3 *C.M.*, Vol. I, p. 42.

4 10-Rabbit, i.e. 1502, *C.M.*, vol. I, p. 51.

5 *Picietl*, from *piciltic*, small and *yetl*, tobacco. *C.M.*, vol. II, p. 108.

6 *Tezozomoc*, chs. LXXXII and LXXXIII, in *K.*, vol. IX, pp. 143–5.

7 There has been much discussion as to the exact nature of the Mexican Empire and of the dignity and power of Moteçuçuma and his predecessors. It can be seen well summed up in *Prescott*, vol. I, particularly ch. II.

498

I have adopted the words *Empire* and *Emperor* because, though there were considerable differences with the Roman and with the Holy Roman Empires, the Mexican whatever-it-was had the following points in common with them:

1 With the Holy Roman Empire:

    (a) the Emperor was elected (or rather chosen) by a small body of princes and electors (the lord of Tetzcuco, the lord of Tlacopan and four Mexican electors the chief of whom was Tlacoatl). *C.M.*, vol. I, p. 31, n. 5.

    (b) The Mexican Empire was a federation of kingdoms and republics.

2 With the Roman Empire: the Mexican Emperor was above all the *Imperator* or commander in chief.

There is in my opinion too much self-confidence in some modern historians, in their interpretation of Mexican institutions and their assertion that the Spanish chroniclers misunderstood them. Though the difference in outlook and the set character of the European civilisation of the time were certainly an obstacle, these Spanish chroniclers were much closer to the events and often, as is the case with Sahagún, they mastered the local languages. Moreover we should never forget that institutions live often quite differently from what they look on paper. On paper the King of England is absolute. In general it is only reasonable to imagine the Mexican institution as some complex form of life which we have not fully mastered, and which was neither quite the feudal image the Spaniards have presented to us nor the kind of religious-communistic polity which American specialists are apt to visualize.

I have chosen *Moteçuçuma* as the most correct form for the Emperor's name, but other forms may be more suitable in the course of the narrative.

The pen portrait in the text will be found in *C.S.*, bk. IV, ch. III, p. 279.

8 On the four (or five) worlds and their disastrous ends, see *F.A.I.*, ch. I, in *K.*, vol. IX, p. 205; also *C.M.*, vol. I, p. 25, which gives a different version. On the unlucky character of the end-of-cycle year, see also *C.M.*, vol. I, p. 20, and *Sahagún*, bk. IV, appendix, in *K.*, vol. VII, p. 157. On the ceremonies of the new fire: *Sahagún*, loc. cit., and also bk. VII, chs. x–xiii, pp. 191–4; *Torquemada*, bk. X, chs. xxxiii and xxxiv, and *C.M.*, vol. I, p. 25 et seq.

9 See *C.M.*, vol. I, p. 51 and p. 25.

10 *Sahagún*, bk. VII, ch. III, in *K.*, vol. VII, p. 187.

11 I have based my narrative mostly on *Sahagún*. I do not know on what authority the editor of the Codex Mendoza (*C.M.*, vol. I, p. 26) states that this ceremony took place on November 16. Sahagún (end of bk. VII, in *K.*, vol. VII, p. 194) thinks the year began on February 2nd; it is difficult to see how it could end on November 16th. Orozco y Berra has made a masterly study of this point and shown that the beginning of the year oscillated between January and February (*O. y B.*, bk. IV, ch. VI, vol. 2, p. 93 et seq.)

12 There are numerous descriptions of this sacrifice in *Sahagún, Torquemada, Tezozomoc, Codex Telleriano-Remensis, Motolinia, Prescott* and others. Torquemada (bk. II, ch. LXIII, vol. I, p. 186) gives 72,344 victims in one day; Motolinia (letter to the Emperor *C.D.H.M.*, vol. I, p. 254) puts the figure at 80,400. I have reduced it to the figure provided by the Mexicans themselves in the *Codex Telleriano-Remensis*, in *K.*, vol. I. A convenient summary will be found in *C.M.*, vol. I, p. 38.

13 *F.A.I.*, ch. I, in *K.*, vol. IX, p. 206. This tradition was probably of Toltec origin. A similar tradition existed amongst the Mexicans proper, or Aztecs, as shown in *Sahagún*, bk. X, ch. xxix "párrafo" XIV, in *K.*, vol. VII, p. 321.

14 *Sahagún*, bk. VIII, ch. VI, in *K.*, vol. VII, pp. 201–2.

15 *Tezozomoc*, ch. c, in *K.*, vol. IX, p. 177.

16 *Tezozomoc*, ch. cii, in *K.*, vol. IX, pp. 181-2.

17 *Tezozomoc*, ch. ciii, in *K.*, vol. IX, pp. 183-4.

18 *Tezozomoc*, ch. ciii, *loc. cit.* In the two following chapters, this author describes with much picturesque detail this attempt—real or imaginary—of Moteçuçuma to escape from his fate.

19 *Tezozomoc*, ch. cvi, in *K.*, vol. IX, p. 189.

CHAPTER II

1 "Una de las mejores provincias de España." (*C.S.*, bk. II, ch. xv, p. 96.)

2 *Hilaire Belloc*, "A Wanderer's Note-Book: The Tagus," The Sunday Times, London, Aug. 13, 1939.

3 *Gómara*, ch. i, fol. ij.   *Las Casas*, bk. III, ch. xxvii, vol. 65, p. 11.

4 *Don Quixote*, chs. i (First Part), xviii (Second Part).

5 *C.S.*, bk. II, ch. xv, p. 96.

6 *Gómara*, ch. i, fol. ij.

7 *Alamán*, Disertación V, vol. 2, p. 4.

8 *C.S.*, bk. II, ch. xv, vol. I, p. 96.

9 *Las Casas*, bk. III, ch. xxvii, vol. 65, p. 11; *B.D.C.*, ch. cciv, vol. 2, p. 440; *C.S.*, bk. II, ch. xv, p 96.

10 *Gómara*, ch. i, fol. ij.

11 *Gómara*, *loc. cit.*

12 *R.G.* in *C.D.H.M.*, vol. I, p. 511.

13 *R.G.* in *C.D.H.M.*, vol. I, p. 512.

14 *Gómara*, *loc. cit.*

15 *D. Quixote*, part II, ch. xxiv.

16 *Gómara*, *loc. cit.*

17 *C.S.*, bk. II, ch. xv, p. 96.

18 *R.G.* in *C.D.H.M.*, vol. I, p. 515.

19 The alternative explanation given by the unknown author of *Rebus Gestis* (*C.D.H.M.*, vol. I, p. 515)—namely, that out of hatred for Francisco Niño and revenge for having taken from his father the post of pilot of the ship, Quintero misdirected the ship while the pilot slept—is preposterous. How could they bribe sailors to strand their own ship in the dreaded and cruel ocean? Gómara is positive that Niño was responsible, and all we know of the empirical formation of pilots in those days points to the same conclusion (*Gómara*, ch. ii, fol. ij, verso). The dove episode is to be found in all the chronicles quoted (*R.G.*, *loc. cit.*).

20 *R.G.* in *C.D.H.M.*, vol. I, p. 515.

21 "Id ni ita est, inquit, caput nihi abscindite, et corpus, ut coquatur, in istum cacabum qui in foco est, injicite." Quinterus tamen et pater pertinaciter, ut ea in re animo erant obstinatissimo, verum illud non esse contendebant. Ceterum die quarto quam samana se navigantibus videndam obtulit, optatissimum intrant portum, quem jampridem quator illae naves, quarum supra mentio facta est, tenuerant . . . (*R.G.* in *C.D.H.M.*, vol. I, p. 516.)

The author of *R.G.* makes therefore Cortés land in Santo Domingo eight days after Good Friday, for Zorzo saw land eight days after the dove visited the ship and they entered harbour eight days after seeing land. Good Friday in 1504 was on April 5th. (Trésor de Chronologie d'Histoire et de Géographie pour l'Etude et l'Emploi des Documents du Moyen Age, par le Cte de Mas Latrie, Paris, 1889,

p. 379). Therefore Cortés landed on Saturday April 13th. Gómara is not so clear: "y asi luega la mesma pascua descubrieron la Isla Española [. . .] dende a tres: o quatro dias entrarô en Santo Domingo . . ." (*Gómara*, end of ch. ij, folio ij verso.) If by "la mesma pascua" he means Easter Sunday, they saw land on the 7th and landed on the 10th or 11th April.

22 *R.G.* in *C.D.H.M.*, vol. I, p. 517.

CHAPTER III

1 *C.C.S.M.*, p. 300.

2 This was the name he wanted and chose, as I have explained in my Life of Christopher Columbus.

3 *Oviedo*, bk. III, ch. xii, vol. I, p. 89; *Las Casas*, bk. II, ch. iii, vol. 64, p. 17.

4 *Oviedo*, bk. III, ch. xi (entitled "Of the advantage and difference which the author sees in this island Española over the islands of Sicily and England: and the reasons which he gives thereon"), vol I, pp. 84–85.

5 *Oviedo*, bk. V, ch. iv, vol. I, p. 141.

6 After an attempt to settle convicts, organised by Colón, which will be found discussed in *C.C.S.M.*, pp. 306–7, 338.

7 *Motolinia*, ch. xiv, in *C.D.H.M.*, vol. I, p. 77.

8 *Oviedo*, bk. V, ch. iii, vol. I, p. 136.

9 *Oviedo*, bk. III, chs. x and xi, vol. I, pp. 83, 87.

10 *Oviedo*, bk. III, ch. x, vol. I, p. 84.

11 Calderón de la Barca, in *La Vida es sueño*:

> En lo que no es justa ley
> No ha de obedecer al rey.

This free and democratic nature of the Spanish society was a creation of the Crown. The Spaniards who still lived under the sovereignty of feudal lords did not enjoy it. Las Casas tells how, as he was engaged in recruiting farmers for the Indies, seventy men from Berlanga, a town "belonging" to the High Constable of Castille, offered themselves to him through four "regidores" or councillors, who in the utmost secrecy, for fear of the High Constable, told him: "Sir, no one amongst us wishes to go to the Indies for lack of means, for each of us has an income of 100,000 maravedis at least, but we go because we want to leave our children in a country royal and free" (*Las Casas*, bk. III, ch. cv, vol. 65, p. 401).

12 *Oviedo*, bk. III, ch. xii, vol. I, p. 93.

13 "The literary monument of nearly two centuries of its [the Council of the Indies'] activity is the great *Recopilación de leyes de los reinos de las Indias*, a body of law which, in spite of shortcomings as to finance and variances with modern ideas is, in its broad humanity and consideration of the general welfare of the King's American subjects, far superior to anything that can be shown for the English or French colonies." (*Bourne*, p. 226.)

14 There are, however, a few observations to be made in extenuation of this depopulation of the Antilles: (1) The figures given by *Las Casas* are not reliable. His tendency to exaggerate is never more active than when he estimates human beings, whether as warriors in battle or as natives killed or otherwise dead. An objective study on this point, which though arising out of the situation of Mexico applies

also to the Antilles, will be found in *Humboldt-Essai*, vol. I, p. 55. (2) The Spaniards proscribed polygamy, and this acted as a severe check on the growth of population (*C.S.*, bk. I, ch. xxv, p. 47). (3) There were frequent wars and rebellions. (4) There were numerous epidemics. The whole matter is ably discussed in *Bourne*, pp. 211-15, and in *Means-Main*, ch. ii.

15 *Bourne*, pp. 190-91.

CHAPTER IV

1 *Navarrete*, vols. II, III.   *Las Casas*, vol. 64.   *Oviedo*, vol. I.

2 Cf. *C.C.S.M.*, chs. xxix, xxx, xxxi.

3 *C.S.*, bk. II, ch. xvi, p. 97.

A detail in *De Rebus Gestis* would appear to imply that Cortés was not poor when he began his Indian days: "Cortesius, ne exspectato quidem praesidis adventu, cum his famulis quos ex Hispaniâ secum adduxerat, ad effodiendum aurum, cujus ea insula feracissima est, ire parat" (*R.G.* in *C.D.H.M.*, p. 517). These servants brought from Spain would appear to be due to the imagination of the anonymous author. Cervantes de Salazar was in a position to know, and his cloak for three is far more in keeping with the circumstances of Cortés' own family: "Estaba muy pobre y tanto que de una capa se servían tres amigos para salir a negociar a la plaza" (*C.S., loc. cit.*).

This is confirmed by *Sandoval*: "Finalmente se embarcó para Indias solo y sin arrimo de nadie" (bk. IV, par. II, vol. I, p. 161).

4 *Gómara*, cap. iij, fol. ij verso, *R.G.* in *C.D.H.M.*, p. 518, *C.S.*, bk. II, ch. xvi, p. 98, all make Cortés share in the doubtful glory of having subjugated "Queen" Anacaona's subjects by massacring the caciques and hanging the "Queen" herself. *Prescott* (vol. I, p. 302; bk. II, ch. ii) follows suit; but *Oviedo* (bk. III, ch. xii, fol. I, p. 90) is positive that this episode took place in 1503, and therefore Cortés could not have participated in it. Moreover, *Las Casas* (bk. II, ch. ix, vol. 64, p. 50, ch. x, p. 56), who seems to be the man who *lived* closest to the events, unlike the other chroniclers, discriminates between this repressive action, led by Ovando himself, and later, consequential campaigns, one of which was led by Diego Velázquez. It is not impossible that Cortés may have fought in these later campaigns; but it is highly unlikely, not only because the dates would have to be somewhat strained, but also because, had he fought in them, Las Casas or Oviedo would have mentioned the fact.

5 *Gómara*, ch. iij: "Dióle Ovando ciertos Indios en tierra del Daiguao." Also *R.G.* in *C.D.H.M.*, p. 508; and *C.S.*, bk. II, ch. xvi, p. 98: "donde (in Achua) Cortés vivió seis años dándose a granjerías y sirviendo su oficio a contento de todo el pueblo."

6 *B.D.C.*, ch. cciv, vol. II, p. 439.

7 *Las Casas*, bk. II, ch. xl, vol. 64, pp. 204-5.

8 *C.S.*, bk. II, cap. XVI, p. 98.

9 *Oviedo*, bk. X, ch. ii, vol. I, p. 363.

10 *C.S., loc. cit.   Gómara*, ch. iij, fol. ij verso; *R.G.* in *C.D.H.M.*, pp. 318-19. This last adds that Nicuesa and Hojeda waited for Cortés for three months owing to "tanta e dignationis Cortesius ob praeclaram virtutem est habitus," which is hard to believe.

11 *Las Casas*, bk. II, ch. lii, vol. 64, p. 262.

12 *Las Casas*, bk. I, ch. lxxxiv, vol. 63, p. 7.

13 *Las Casas*, bk. I, ch. lxxxii, vol. 62, p. 499.

14 "Por el olor de las nuevas, que de la riqueza della, el Almirante primero que la descubrió había dado." (*Las Casas*, bk. II, ch. LII, vol. 64, p. 263.)

15 *Las Casas*, bk. II, ch. LII, vol. 64, p. 266.

16 "Yo los vide hacer en la villa de Yáquimo y eran de los grandes y hermosos tocinos que en mi vida he visto." (*Las Casas*, bk. II, ch. LII, vol. 64, p. 268.)

17. *Las Casas*, bk. II, ch. LVIII, vol. 64, p. 295.

18. *Las Casas*, bk. II, ch. LIX, vol. 64, p. 298.

19 *Las Casas*, bk. II, ch. LIX, vol. 64, p. 301.

20 *Las Casas*, bk. II, ch. LX, vol. 64, p. 306.

21 "Valía más Hojeda en la guerra que la mitad de todos allos." (*Las Casas, loc. cit.*)

22 "Traía Hojeda en su talega, con la comidilla, una imagen de nuestra Señora, muy devota y maravillosamente pintada, de Flandes." (*Las Casas, loc. cit.*)

23 *Las Casas*, bk. II, ch. LXII, vol. 64, p. 312.

24 "Andá ios al moridero." (*Las Casas*, bk. II, ch. LXVI, vol. 64, p. 338.)

25 On Nicuesa and Hojeda my main authority is *Las Casas* (chs. as in above notes).

26 *C.S.*, bk. II, ch. XVII, pp. 99–100.

CHAPTER V

1 *Oviedo*, bk. IV, ch. I, vol. I, p. 97.

2 *Las Casas*, bk. II, ch. L, vol. 64, p. 256. He miscalculates Don Fernando's age, which he gives as eighteen.

3 "Señor Salcedo, levántate y perdónanos: que caymos contigo, e yremos nuestro camino." (*Oviedo*, bk. XVI, ch. VIII, vol. I, p. 479.)

4 On Ocampo, see *Oviedo*, bk. XVII, ch. II, vol. I, p. 495, and *Las Casas*, bk. II, ch. XLI, vol. 64, p. 210.
  The portrait of Velázquez by *Las Casas* is in bk. III, ch. XXI, vol. 64, p. 462.

5 *Las Casas*, bk. III, ch. XXVI, vol. 65, p. 5.

6 *Las Casas*, bk. III, ch. XXVI, vol. 65, pp. 7–8.

7 *R.G.* in *C.D.H.M.*, p. 324.

8 "Fernando Cortés fué a la conquista por oficial del Tesorero Miguel de Passamonte para tener cuenta con los quintos y hacienda del rey: y aun el mesmo Diego Velázquez se lo rogo: por ser abil: y diligente." (*Gómara*, ch. iiij, fol. ij verso.)
  See also *Las Casas*, bk. III, ch. XXVII, vol. 65, p. 11.

9 *Las Casas, loc. cit.* "Itaque Cortesius postquam in Cubam cum Velázquio venit, nihil antiquius ducere quam modis omnibus gratissimum esse duci." (*R.G.* in *C.D.H.M.*, p. 323.)

10 *Gómara*, ch. iiij, fol. iij.

11 "Y en fin se casó con ella. Aun que primero tuuo sobre ello algunas pendencias. Y estuuo preso." (*Gómara, loc. cit.*)

12 *Las Casas*, bk. III, ch. XXVII, vol. 65, p. 10.

13 "Diego Velázquez era bien acondicionado y durábale poco el enojo." (*Las Casas, loc. cit.*, p. 11.)

14 *Gómara*, ch. iiij, fol. iij; *R.G.* in *C.D.H.M.*, vol. I, p. 327.

15 "Diego Velázquez le riño a Cristóbal de Lagos, diziendo que soltara a Cortés por dineros: y soborno" (*Gómara, loc. cit.*) "Más Cortés entendía las palabras y resistía la fuerça" (*Gómara, loc. cit.*).

16 Catalina Xuárez is only mentioned in connection with this arrest by *C.S.*, bk. II, ch. xviii, p. 101. It seems to me too much in keeping with Cortés' character to be put in doubt; yet neither *Las Casas*, *Gómara*, nor *R.G.* mention her, though they all agree that Cortés was caught while he had gone out of his refuge. My feeling is that, for a man as cautious and astute as Cortés, nothing but a petticoat could suffice to throw him out of his guard.

17 "Desnudóse: y atóse con un tocador sobre la cabeza ciertas escripturas que tenía: como escriuano de ayunta-miento: y oficial del thesorero, y que hazían contra Diego Velázquez." (*Gómara, loc. cit.*)

18 "Cortés se caso con la Catalina Xuárez porq lo hauia prometido y por viuir en paz." (*Gómara, loc. cit.*)

19 My narrative is the outcome of a balanced estimate of the claims of *Gómara* and *Rebus Gestis* on the one hand and of *Las Casas* on the other. *Gómara* and *R.G.* make Cortés arrive in a defiant way, with Xuárez, his accomplice in all this, and, having frightened Velázquez, almost cow him into a reconciliation. *Las Casas*, who was closer to the events than either, pours contempt on *Gómara's* story (the more moderate of the two), arguing with force that Cortés was not then strong enough to allow himself such an attitude; I may add that the part which *R.G.* makes Xuárez play in the events is enough to show that they cannot have happened in the way the anonymous author describes them. Yet, the scene at the farm where Velázquez is reading his accounts, smacks of the truth. The more reasonable view is that Cortés, having come to Xuárez' house on escaping from the boat, got rid of one of his enemies by compromising on marriage, then used Xuárez as his envoy to Velázquez.

20 "No sé si en su mujer." (*Las Casas*, bk. III, ch. xxvii, vol. 65, p. 13.)

21 "La vna obo en una yndia de Cuba q se dezia doña hulana piçarro." (*B.D.C.*, ch. cciv, vol. II, p. 438.)
   "Hulana" is only a token name, meaning that Bernal Díaz did not know or remember her Christian name.

22 "Cortés no se descuidaba nada de serville y agradalle, y no enojalle en cosa chica ni grande, como era astutísimo, de manera que del todo tornó a ganalle, y a descuidalle, como de antes." (*Las Casas, loc. cit.*)

23 "Crio vacas: ouejas & yeguas. y assi fué el primero que allí tuuo hato y cabaña." (*Gómara*, ch. iiij, fol. iij.)
   "Cortesius Hispanorum primus omnium aurifodinas in Cuba invenit [. . .] Pecuriam primus quoque habuit, in insulamque induxit, omni pecorum genere ex. Hispana petito." (*R.G.* in *C.D.H.M.*, vol. I, p. 337.) There is another version which says "Ex Hispania," but it is not likely that Cortés went so far away to provide himself with livestock when he could have it from Haiti.
   Oviedo (bk. XVII, ch. iii, vol. I, p. 496) says, speaking of Cuba: "e llevaronse ganados desta Isla Española."

24 *Las Casas*, bk. III, ch. xxvii, vol. 65, p. 13.
   On Cortés saved by the Indians: *R.G.* in *C.D.H.M.*, vol. I, pp. 335–6, and *Gómara*, ch. iiij, fol. iij verso.

25 *Las Casas, loc. cit.*, p. 12.

26 *Oviedo*, bk. XVII, ch. iii, vol. I, pp. 496–7.

27 *Oviedo*, bk. XVIII, ch. xix, vol. I, p. 538.
   One of the emissaries through whom Velázquez negotiated his appointment as permanent or independent Governor was Narváez. *Las Casas*, bk. III, end of ch. lxxxi, vol. 65, p. 267. See also bk. III, ch. c, vol. 65, p. 371, where Fonseca and Conchillos are named as the chief sponsors of Velázquez in this matter.

CHAPTER VI

1 *Oviedo*, bk. XVI, ch. xi, vol. I, p. 482.

2 "Porq no avia q conquistar q todo estaua de paz que el Vazco nuñ^z de balboa [. . .] lo avia conquistado, y la tierra de suyo es muy corta." (*B.D.C.*, ch. i, vol. I, p. 8.)

3 *B.D.C.*, Preamble, vol. I, p. 3. *B.D.C.*, ch. xviii, vol. I, p. 50.

4 These words of Bernal Díaz are the more valuable in that he, as one of the originators of the scheme, is the only authority strong enough to confute Las Casas, whose narrative (bk. III, ch. xcvi, vol. 65, p. 340) is obviously warped by his mania for seeing nothing in the conquest but slave-trading expeditions—a view which, in this case at any rate, is proved untrue by Bernal Díaz's own words as shown in the text. (*B.D.C.*, ch. i, vol. I, p. 8.)

5 "Y como se aviâ ya pasado tres años, ansi [. . .] y no auiamos hecho cosa ninguna que de contar sea." (*B.D.C.*, ch. i, vol. I, p. 8.)

6 *B.D.C.*, *loc. cit.*

7 *B.D.C.*, ch. i, vol. I, p. 10.

8 "Obo gran fama dello." (*B.D.C.*, ch. vi, vol. I, p. 24.)

9 "Y El diego velasq^z puso los quatro nauios y çierto rrescate de quentas y cosas de poca valia, y otras menudencias de legunbres." (*B.D.C.*, ch. viii, vol. I, p. 26.)
  On Indians and wine, *Oviedo*, bk. XVII, ch. viii, vol. I, p. 504.
  B.D.C. puts the soldiers at 240; both *Oviedo*, *loc. cit.*, and *C.S.*, bk. II, ch. ii, p. 63, say 200.

10 *B.D.C.*, ch. ccvi, vol. II, p. 467.

11 *Las Casas*, bk. III, ch. cxi, vol. 65, p. 430; bk. III, ch. cxiii, vol. 65, p. 439.

12 On Velázquez's address, *C.S.*, bk. II, ch. ii, p. 63. See also *B.D.C.*, chs. cxlii, viii, vol. I, p. 28, and *Las Casas*, bk. III, ch. cix, vol. 65, p. 422.

13 *B.D.C.* says April 8th (ch. viii, vol. I, p. 29). Oviedo and the chaplain say May 1st (*Oviedo*, bk. XVII, ch. viii, vol. I, p. 503; chaplain, *C.D.H.M.*, vol. I, p. 281).
  B.D.C. gives ten days to the crossing; Oviedo and the chaplain, only three.

14 *Oviedo*, bk. XVII, ch. ix, vol. I, p. 505.

15 *Chaplain* in *C.D.H.M.*, vol. I, p. 287.

16 *B.D.C.*, ch. ix, vol. I, p. 32; *C.S.*, bk. II, ch. v, pp. 67–9.

17 *B.D.C.*, ch. xi, vol. I, p. 34; *C.S.*, bk. II, ch. vi, p. 71.

18 *B.D.C.*, ch. xi, vol. I, pp. 35–6.

19 *Chaplain* in *C.D.H.M.*, vol. I, pp. 230, 231, 298–9.

20 "Et el capitaneo li disse que non volevano se non oro." (*Chaplain*, *loc. cit.*)

21 *Chaplain* in *C.D.H.M.*, vol. I, p. 302.

22 "Li manco ventura *p* signoregiar in tal terra." (*Chaplain* in *C.D.H.M.*, *loc. cit.*)
  The description given by Las Casas (bk. III, ch. cxiii, vol. 65, p. 439, and beginning of ch. cxiv, vol. 65, p. 445) of Grijalva's character tallies so well with the Chaplain's disgruntled attitude owing to Grijalva's refusal to settle that Las Casas is more likely to be right than Bernal Díaz on this point.

CHAPTER VII

1 *B.D.C.*, ch. clxv, vol. II, p. 208.

2 Bernal Díaz says of Diego Velázquez: "Si pensatiuo estaua antes q Enbiase a xpvl de oli muy malo estubo despues q lo uio boluer sin rrecaudo y En esta sazon llego El Capitan pedro de alvarado a cuba." (*B.D.C.*, ch. xv, vol. I, p. 44.)
From the instructions of Velázquez to Cortés, discussed below, it is clear, however, that Olid arrived after Alvarado.

3 "Como si le hiciera merced de alguna dehesa para meter en ella a su ganado. . . . que era manera y uso de flamencos cuando querían negociar." (*Las Casas*, bk. III, ch. ci, vol. 65, pp. 370–72.)

4 *Las Casas*, bk. III, chs. cxiv and cxviii, vol. 65, pp. 446, 465.
Prescott (vol. I, p. 316 footnote) following *Herrera* says the title of Adelantado was given Velázquez on Nov. 13th, 1518. (Prescott's reference to Herrera is erroneous. He gives Dec. 2nd, bk. 3, ch. 8. It is Dec. 11th, bk. III, ch. xi, p. 99.) But *Oviedo* (bk. XVII, ch. xix, vol. I, p. 538) says it was in or after May 1519, and, as Oviedo himself was present in Barcelona at the time, he must be right. Oviedo says also that Velázquez was made Adelantado of all he had discovered ("de todo aquello que había descubierto") while Las Casas says his new title applied only to Cuba. The conflicting title given to Garay need not deter us from following Oviedo's opinion, which in the circumstances is the more logical of the two, for the chancery at home had but vague notions of the geography of the discovered lands.

5 *Las Casas*, bk. III, ch. cxviii, vol. 65, p. 466.

6 "Despues que llego a Cuba El capitan joan de grijalba, ya por mi memorado, y visto El governador diego Velasques, que heran las tierras rricas, ordeno de enbiar vna buena armada, muy mayor que las de antes." (*B.D.C.*, beginning of ch. xix, vol. I, p. 52.)
Prescott (vol. IV, app. 5, p. 288) gives a most inaccurate abridgement of these instructions, marred moreover by numerous misprints. The full text will be found in *C.D.I.A.I.*, vol. XII, p. 225; *Alamán*, vol. I, app. 2, p. 1; *C.S.*, bk. II, ch. xiv, p. 86; *H.C.C.C.*, p. 113.

7 *Alamán*, loc. cit., p. 67, and *C.S.*, loc. cit., p. 87.

8 *Alamán*, loc. cit., pp. 21 and 22; *C.S.*, loc. cit., pp. 94 and 93.

9 I have explained in *C.C.S.M.*, p. 450, note 16, why I have adopted the neologism *Jeromites* instead of *Hieronymites*.

10 *Las Casas* (bk. III, ch. cxiv, vol. 65, p. 446) says: "Envio a esta isla Española a un hidalgo llamado Juan de Saucedo, para que pidiese licencia, que enviase a poblar aquella tierra y hacer lo a esto necesario, a los padres de Sant Hierónimo."
But, as *B.D.C.* (ch. xix, vol. I, p. 53) says: "El diego Velasqz enbiaba a rrescatar y no a poblar, segun despues paresçio por las ynstruçiones que dello dio, y avnque publicaua y pregono, que enbiava a poblar."

11 "Porque yo pensaba traer todas las gentes de aquellas partes en el conocimiento de nuestra santa fe y ponerlas debajo la real corona con el menos mal i detrimento dellas que posible fuese." (*C.D.H.M.*, vol. I, p. 401.)

12 "Y alli ouo bien q rreyr y dezir de la burla y del rrescate." (*B.D.C.*, ch. xvi, vol. I, p. 47.)

13 *B.D.C.*, ch. xxx, vol. I, p. 82.

14 "Diego Velazquez diole pocas gracias [. . .] antes riño mucho con el, afrentándolo de palabra, porque asi era su conviccion, porque no habia quebrantado su instruccion y mandamiento." (*Las Casas*, bk. III, ch. cxiv, vol. 65, p. 445.)

15 *Prescott*, bk, II, end of ch. ɪɪ, footnote, vol. I, p. 316.

16 *B.D.C.*, ch. xɪx, vol. I, p. 53.

17 "Tamaño como un codo, pero cuerdo y muy callado, y escribía bien." (*Las Casas*, bk. III, ch. xxvɪɪ, vol. 65, p. 11.)

"Solía yo decir a Diego Velázquez: Señor, guardaos de veintidos años de Italia." This and the rest of the portrait quoted in the text in *Las Casas*, bk. III, ch. cxɪv, vol. 65, p. 447.

18 "El secretario andres de duero hizo las proviçiones como zuele deziros el rrefran de muy buena tinta y como cortes las quiso." (*B.D.C.*, ch. xɪx, vol. I, p. 54.)

19 "Diego Velázquez [. . .] envió habrá un año a Hernando Cortés por capitán de cierta gente, y con siete navios, y todo a su costo y misión . . ." (*Alamán*, vol. I, app. II, p. 27.)

Memorial de Benito Martinez (or Martín), en nombre del Adelantado Diego Velázquez.

"Envíe [. . .] una armada [. . .] en la cual despues de enviarla muy copiosa y proveida de todo lo necesario . . ." (Carta de Diego Velázquez al licenciado Rodrigo de Figueroa, *C.D.H.M.*, vol. I, p. 400.)

R.G. (p. 348) goes to the other extreme: "in his omnibus comparandis, circiter quindecim mille aureos nummos impenderat. (*Cortesius*) Velazquius nuum quidem obolum expendit."

The reasonable view is that the Veracruz letter to the King-Emperor was about correct: two-thirds was spent by Cortés and one-third by Velázquez (*Alamán*, vol. I, app. 2, p. 57). For, though *Prescott* (vol. I, p. 314 footnote) says it "was prepared under the eye of Cortés," Cortés was never in a position to inflict on his proud companions the utterance of obvious falsehoods, still less at the time when he was, so to speak, seeking their votes.

20 *B.D.C.*, ch. xɪx, vol. I, p. 54.

21 "Vn uiejo que se dezia joan millan, q le llamaban el estrologo, otros dezian q tenia rramo de locura." (*B.D.C.*, ch. xxɪɪ, vol. I, p. 60.)

"Y no habia menester mas para entendello de mirar al gesto a Diego Velázquez, segun su astuta viveza y mundana sabiduría." (*Las Casas*, bk. III, ch. cxv, vol. 65, p. 451.)

22 *B.D.C.*, ch. xx, vol. I, p. 57.

23 *Las Casas*, bk. III, ch. cxv, vol. 65, p. 452.

24 It is disquieting to find that this famous episode is not mentioned by Bernal Díaz. Yet the perfect concordance of all other sources, and above all the narrative of Las Casas bind us to accept it as true; particularly since the style of Cortés' share in it is so true to type, as established in numerous well authenticated cases in his later life. On the other hand Bernal Díaz' account shows several traces of the episode, and particularly the beginning of chapter xxɪɪ, vol. I, p. 60.

25 *B.D.C.*, ch. xxɪ, vol. I, pp. 59–60.

26 As Bernal Díaz *explicitly* denies the story told by Gómara about a dinner which Ordás had offered Cortés in order to seize him by treason, and which Cortés, warned in time, dodged by feigning sickness, I prefer to follow Bernal Díaz.

27 *B.D.C.*, ch.xxɪɪɪ, vol. I, pp. 65–66.

28 "Dizquestava tan Enojado el diº belasqz que hazia bramuras." (*B.D.C.*, ch. xxɪv, vol. I, p. 67.)

29 *B.D.C.*, ch. xxɪv, vol. I, p. 68.

CHAPTER VIII

1 *B.D.C.*, ch. xxv, vol. I, pp. 70–71.

2 *B.D.C.*, ch. xxvi, vol. I, p. 71.

3 Bernal Díaz had written "his Indians" ("sus yndias"), then struck out his qualification, leaving only "las suyas," i.e. "his (women)." (*B.D.C.*, ch. cciv, vol. II, p. 443.)

4 *B.D.C.*, ch. cciv, vol. II, pp. 439–44.

5 This was in accordance with general instructions. The text of this extraordinary document, together with some sarcastic comments on it, will be found in *Oviedo*, bk. XIX, ch. vii. vol. III, pp. 27–32. See ch. ix hereafter.

6 *B.D.C.*, ch. xx, vol. I, pp. 55–6.

7 *B.D.C.*, ch. xxvii, vol. I, p. 72.
Aguilar's story is in *C.S.*, bk. II, ch. xxviii, p. 117.

8 "Que el fué ynventor que nos diesen la guerra que nos dieron." (*B.D.C.*, ch. xxix, vol. I, p. 80.)

9 The episode of the two sailors is in *B.D.C.*, ch. xxvii, vol. I, p. 72; that of the altar of the Virgin, *loc. cit.*, pp. 75–6.

10 *B.D.C.*, ch. xxviii, vol. I, p. 77.

CHAPTER IX

1 *B.D.C.*, ch. xxxi, vol. I, p. 84.

2 *B.D.C.*, ch. xxxi, vol. I, p. 84. Text in *Oviedo*, bk. XIX, ch. vii, vol. III, p. 28. Also *Las Casas*, bk. III, ch. lxii, vol. 65, p. 154.

3 *Oviedo, loc. cit.*, p. 31. *Las Casas*, bk. III, ch. lxiii, argues with great force against the very principle of this paper.

4 "Sobre esta posesión la parte de di° velasqz tubo q rremormurar della." (*B.D.C.*, ch. xxxi, vol. I, p. 87.)

5 *Gómara*, cap. xx, fol. xj verso.   *C.S.*, bk. II, ch. xxxiii,. pp. 130–31.   *B.D.C.*, ch. xxxiv, vol. I, p. 94.
The editor of *Prescott* (John F. Kirk) says, "The remark of Bernal Díaz is not to be taken as ironical." This requires qualification. If it means that B.D.'s remark must not be understood as meaning that he was sceptical on miracles at all, well and good. But if it means that B.D. admits the possibility of the miracle having happened that day, we beg to differ. In our opinion he does mean to say that there was no such St. James nor St. Peter, but just Morla on a chestnut horse.
Las Casas gives here one of the clearest proofs of his relentless bias. He gives the Indian dead at 30,000, leaving the responsibility of the figure to hearsay: "Dijose." (*Las Casas*, bk. III, ch. cxx—not cxix as *Prescott* says erroneously, vol. I, p. 355 footnote.) But Bernal Díaz is most positive the Indian dead were 800, and it is to-day generally accepted by the best authorities that the Spanish conquerors in Mexico always put their figures too high. (*B.D.C.*, ch. xxxv, vol. I, p. 96.)

6 *B.D.C.*, ch. xxxv, vol. I, pp. 96–8.

7 Las Casas rants against Gómara for having, he says, invented this act of allegiance of the Indians to the Emperor in which he sees but one of Cortés' tricks. But *B.D.C.* proves him wrong. (*Las Casas*, bk. III, ch. cxx, vol. 65, p. 479.)

8 *B.D.C.*, ch. xxxv, vol. I, pp. 95–8.

9 *B.D.C.*, ch. xxxvi, vol. I, p. 102.

10 Prescott misses the point altogether, partly because he mistranslates Puertocarrero's improvised verse into: "to look out only for the rich lands and the best way to govern them," and so the point of the speech is altogether lost. (*Prescott*, bk. II, ch. v, vol. I, p. 359.)

11 *Tezozomoc*, ch. cvii, in *K.*, vol. IX, p. 191.

12 *Tezozomoc, loc. cit.* Sahagún, bk. XII, ch. viii, in *K.*, vol. VII, p. 420.

13 *Sahagún*, bk. XIII, ch. iv, in *K.*, vol. VII, pp. 418 and 417.

14 *B.D.C.*, ch. xxxviii, vol. I, p. 106.

15 Bernal Díaz calls him Tendile. His name is more likely to have been Teotlili, which is the form to be found in *F.A.I.* (*K.*, vol. IX, p. 286, ch. lxxix). Teutlile is Prescott's version of the name.

16 See these efforts in the admirable reproduction of the *Codex Telleriano Remensis*, pp. 29, 30 of the fourth part, *K.*, vol. I.

17 *B.D.C.*, ch. xxxviii, vol. I, p. 109.

18 *Sahagún*, bk. XII, chs. vi and vii, in *K.*, vol. VII, pp. 419, 420.

19 *Loc. cit.*, ch. viii, p. 420.

20 Sahagún says that these messengers offered the Spaniards "*tortillas* steeped in human blood [. . .] on instructions from Moteçuzuma who held them to be Gods from Heaven." Bernal Díaz, however, says nothing of this scene which would have left a deep trace in his memory had it taken place, since, according to Sahagún, "the Spaniards felt sick, at that food and spat it out, for the bread with the blood had a nasty smell" (*Sahagún, loc. cit.*).

21 "De la pobreza que trayamos." (*B.D.C.*, ch. xxxix, vol. I, p. 112.)

CHAPTER X

1 *B.D.C.*, ch. xl, vol. I, p. 114.

2 *B.D.C.*, chs. xl and xli, particularly p. 116 (vol. I).

3 *Prescott* (vol. II, p. 34) writes Chiahuitzla. His editor, in a footnote corrects: "According to Ixtilxochitl, Hist. Chich. MS. 289, Quiahuiztlan." But *B.D.C.* writes also Quiahuiztlan (see vol. I, p. 113, and others).

4 *Gómara*, ch. xxix, fol. xvj verso. *B.D.C.*, ch. xl, vol. I, p. 113; ch. xli, vol. I, p. 118.

5 *B.D.C.*, ch. xli, vol. I, pp. 118–19.

6 *B.D.C.*, ch. xlii, vol. I, p. 119.

7 *B.D.C.*, *loc. cit.*, p. 121.

8 *B.D.C.*, ch. xl, vol. I, p. 113.

9 My narrative here follows the Letter sent by the Chapter to Charles V (*Alamán*, vol. I, app. 2, pp. 74–79. Also *Gayangos*, pp. 1–34.)

This point—where the community or chapter of Veracruz was set up—is not clear. *Gómara* in a most confused narrative seems to imply that it was close to Quiahuiztlan (chs. xxix, xxx and xxxj, fols. xvj and xvij). *C.S.* (chs. vii and viii, bk. III, pp. 151–3) is definitely of that opinion. This is also the general impression left by chs. cxxii and cxxiii of *Las Casas* (bk. III, vol. 65, pp. 487–99). And yet Bernal Díaz, who was there and records events as they happened, does imply that the "constitutional" changes in Cortés' authority took place in San Juan de Ulúa: now, though we might reject his sequence, well knit though it is, on grounds of bad memory after sixty years, there is one detail which cannot be so easily disposed of: "and then we decided to build, found and settle a town which was called The Rich Town of the True Cross because we had arrived on Last Supper Thursday and had landed on Good Friday" ("y luego ordenamos de hazer y fundar E poblar vna villa, que se nombro la villa rrica de la vera Cruz, porque llegamos jueves de la çena y des Enbarcamos En viernes santo de la cruz," ch. XLII, vol. I, p. 121). These dates refer to San Juan de Ulúa and not to Quiahuiztlan. As, on the other hand, it was but natural that Cortés, brewing his *coup d'état*, should consider the foundation of the new town in the new site he was looking for or had selected as the best moment for his scheme to be produced, my surmise is that he was led to found the town in spirit before he was in a position to found it in body, owing to the pressure of circumstances. This conclusion is corroborated by *B.D.C.*, beginning of ch. XLVIII, vol. I, p. 136 ("acordamos de fundar la villa rrica de la vera cruz, En vnos llanos, media legua del pueblo questava Como En fortaleza que se dize quiaviztlan"), and by *Torquemada*, bk. IV, ch. XXIII, vol. I, p. 405 ("Le pareció a Cortés con acuerdo de el Regimiento que en el Sitio de San Juan de Ulúa se avia nombrado, [. . .] que se edificase la Villa Rica de la Vera-Cruz, en vnos Llanos, medio legua de aquel Pueblo, que estaba como en fortaleza, dicho Chiauitztla"). See also *C.S.*, bk. III, ch. XVII, p. 169: "A quien puso nombre la Villa Rica de la Veracruz, como había determinado cuando en Sant Joan de Ulúa nombró Alcaldes y Regidores." Finally *Gómara* himself: "Como havian acordado quando se nombró el Cabildo de San Juan de Ulhua" (ch. XXXV, fol. XX verso).

10 *B.D.C.*, ch. XLIII, vol. I, p. 123.

11 *B.D.C.*, ch. XLIV, vol. I, p. 125.

12 *Tezozomoc*, chs. CVIII, CIX, in *K.*, vol. IX, pp. 193, 194; ch. CX, p. 196.

13 *B.D.C.*, ch. XLI, vol. I, p. 117.
    Las Casas, bk. III, ch. CXXII (not 121 as *Prescott*, vol. II, p. 26, footnote, says by mistake), denies this and suggests that Cortés made up the complaints of the men of Cempoal, which is thoroughly inconsistent with later indisputable events. But Las Casas on Cortés is always blinded by his passion. See also *Gómara*, ch. xxviii, fol. xv verso.

14 Letter from the Chapter and "Regiment" of Veracruz. *Alamán*, vol. I, app. II, p. 80; *Gayangos*, pp. 22–23.

15 *B.D.C.*, ch. XLIV, vol. I, p. 126.

16 *C.S.*, bk. III, ch. XII, p. 160; *B.D.C.*, ch. XLV, vol. I, p. 129.

17 *B.D.C.*, ch. XLV, vol. I, p. 129.
    Tlamama, plural *tlamamaque* (Icazbalceta in a footnote to *Motolinia* in *C.D.H.M.*, vol. I, p. 139). The Spaniards simplified it into *tamemes*.

18 *B.D.C.*, ch. XLVI, vol. I, p. 130; *Gómara*, ch. xxxij, fol. xix; *F.A.I.*, ch. LXXXI, in *K.*, vol. IX, p. 289; *Tapia*, in *C.D.H.M.*, vol. II, p. 562.

CHAPTER XI

1 *B.D.C.*, ch. XLVI, vol. I, p. 132; *Torquemada*, bk. IV, ch. XXI, vol. I, p. 400.

2 "Pierde amigo" in *Gómara*, ch. xxij, fol. xix verso, and in *C.S.*, bk. III, ch. XIV, p. 165. "Pie de amigo" in *Herrera*. *C.S.*'s editor is, however, wrong as to Gómara (footnote p. 165).

3 *Motolinia*, Tratado Tercero, ch. I, in *C.D.H.M.*, vol. I, p. 143.

4 *B.D.C.*, ch. XLVI, vol. I, pp. 133–5; *Torquemada*, bk. IV, ch. XXI, pp. 399–402; *Gómara*, chs. xxxiij and xxxiiij, fols. xix verso and xx; *C.S.*, bk. III, chs. xv–xvi, pp. 165–9; *F.A.I.*, ch. LXXXI, in *K.*, vol. IX, p. 289.

Torquemada says that the three calpixques were liberated in agreement with the lord of Chiahuitztlan ("con voluntad del señor de Chiahuitztlan"); but this runs counter to Bernal Díaz, who was a witness to the events, and does not tally with the rest of Cortés' action.

5 Cervantes de Salazar makes the fat cacique say that "Motezuma is the richest prince in the world though he is constantly at war with the men of Tlaxcala, Guaxocingo and Cholula"; words not unlike those which the Spanish-Mexican chronicler Ixtlilxochitl attributes also to the Cempoalan fat man, dragging in, by the way, a mention of a famous maternal ancestor of his: "for though great and most powerful, Motecuhzoma had many enemies, especially his nephew Ixtlilxochitl, who was in revolt against him; and the men of Tlaxcalan, Huexotzinco and other powerful peoples waged constant war against him." Despite this concordance, it may well be that this news was made up after the event by a process of induction, for, though the fact was true, it can hardly have been imparted to Cortés by the Cempoalans, since Bernal Díaz does not mention it and since—though the fat cacique wept and lamented his plight—he seems to have been too much afraid of Moteçuçuma to seek to enlist Cortés in a plot against him; *C.S.*, bk. III, ch. xv, p. 162.

This is, however, what *F.A.I.* makes him say: "y que por salir de poder de tiranos se holgaría él y otros muchos de las provincias comarcanas se revelase contra Mexico . . ." (Ch. LXXXI, in *K.*, vol. IX, p. 289.)

6 *B.D.C.*, beginning of ch. XLVIII, vol. I, p. 136; *C.S.*, bk. III, ch. XVII, p. 169; *Torquemada*, bk. IV, ch. XXIII, vol. I, p. 405.

7 *B.D.C.*, ch. XLVIII, vol. I, p. 136. The reader might compare with the attitude of Colón in a similar case (*C.C.S.M.*, ch. XXII, p. 277). Colón would do everything by force and from above. Cortés, a much braver man, was most sparing in the use of force and had a deep sense of comradeship entirely lacking in Colón.

8 *C.S.*, bk. III, ch. XVII, p. 169.

9 *C.S.*, bk. III, ch. XVII, p. 170.

10 *B.D.C.*, ch. XLIX, vol. I, p. 139.

11 *B.D.C.*, ch. XLIX, vol. I, p. 142.

12 Both *Gómara*, ch. xxxj, fol. xxj, and *C.S.*, bk. III, ch. XVIII, p. 172, say that Cingapacingo was taken by force. *F.A.I.* says as much in his ch. LXXXII, in *K.*, vol. IX, p. 290. I hold *B.D.C.* the supreme authority on whether there was a fight or not when he was present. My narrative conforms to his ch. LI, vol. I, p. 143. He explicitly denies Gómara's version at the end of the chapter, p. 148.

13 *B.D.C.*, ch. LI, vol. I, p. 145.

14 *B.D.C.*, ch. LII, vol. I, p. 150.

Gómara (ch. xxxj, fol. xix) and *C.S.* (bk. III, ch. XIII, p. 163) record this present of girls (C.S. says they were twenty) at an earlier stage in the relations between Cortés and the fat cacique. I have followed *B.D.C.* from whom it is not safe to differ in these matters unless there be strong reasons for it.

15 *B.D.C.* (ch. LIII, vol. I, p. 151) does not say that the caravel belonged to Cortés, but *Gómara* (ch. xxxvj, fol. xxj verso) does: "hallo que era ya venido Francisco de Salzedo: con la carauela que el auia côprado a Alonso Cauallero vezino de Santiago de Cuba, y que la hauia dexado dando carena." He puts the reinforcement at 70 men and 9 horses; but on this point *B.D.C.* is a better authority, and *Torquemada* (bk. IV, ch. XXIV, vol. I, p. 406) bears him out. The ship's purchase and its being left behind are the subject of question number 28 of the Enquiry (Provanza) made in Segura de la Frontera (Mexico) in 1520 (exact date unmentioned), to be found in *H.C.C.C.*, p. 158.

16 *B.D.C.*, ch. LIII, vol. I, p. 152.

17 *B.D.C.*, ch. LIV, vol. I, p. 156.

18 "Carta de la Justicia y Regimiento de la Rica Villa de la Veracruz a la reina doña Juana y al emperador Carlos V, su hijo, a diez de julio 1519." (*Gayangos*, pp. 21 and 8, also *Alamán*, vol. I, app. II, p. 46 et seq.)

19 This first letter is lost. *B.D.C.* records that Cortés mentioned it to the soldiers, though he did not read it to them (ch. LIII, vol. I, p. 153, and ch. LIV, vol. I, p. 156).

20 *B.D.C.*, ch. LIV, vol. I, p. 156.

21 *B.D.C.*, *loc. cit.*

22 *Torquemada*, bk. IV, ch. XXIV, vol. I, p. 407. *Las Casas*, bk. III, ch. XXIII, vol. 65, p. 498.

23 *B.D.C.*, ch. LIV, vol. I, p. 156. True he gives on July 6th at the beginning of ch. LVI, p. 159, but this is obviously an oversight since the letter to the King and Queen is dated July 10th.

24 *B.D.C.*, ch. XXXVI, vol. I, p. 100.

25 "Tenia mucho ser." (*B.D.C.*, ch. XXXVII, vol. I, p. 104.)

26 *B.D.C.*, ch. XXXVII, vol. I, p. 104.

27 *B.D.C.*, ch. LXXVII, vol. I, p. 224, and ch. CCLIV, vol. II, p. 438.

28 *Torquemada*, bk. IV, ch. XXV, vol. I, p. 408. See also *B.D.C.*, ch. LVII, vol. I, p. 163; *C.S.*, bk. III, ch. XXI, p. 178; *Oviedo*, bk XXXIII, ch. II, vol. III, p. 261.
There are some minor discrepancies: Torquemada speaks of only one foot cut off to a man, not Umbria, who in his account is flogged; but I follow *B.D.C.*, who knew the pilot well and saw him footless time and again; the Christian name of Escudero is Diego for *Torquemada*, Pedro for *B.D.C.* and Juan for *C.S.* and *Oviedo*, who are right. Cermeño is also Diego for *Torquemada*, *C.S.* and *Oviedo*, Juan for *B.D.C.* Cortés in his second letter to the Emperor (*Gayangos*, p. 53) calls them Juan Escudero and Diego Cermeño. He calls the pilot Gonzalo de Ungria. I do not know why *Prescott* (bk. II, ch. VIII, vol. II, p. 66) says the priest was "probably the most guilty of the whole," unless it be the special importance which most Protestants attach to priests. "Distance lends enchantment to the view." (His reference to *Las Casas*, bk. III, ch. 122, is erroneous for ch. 123, vol. 65, p. 496.) Gómara and Cervantes de Salazar record that Cortés knew of the conspiracy twice; that, the first time, he put everyone in jail and then released them all, though warning them that, if they tried again, he would hang them; but this would appear to be an attempt on the part of these two authors to justify Cortés' severity. There is no trace of this first conspiracy and imprisonment, possibly a rehash of the events of a similar nature which had taken place in San Juan de Ulúa and had led to the winning over of Juan Velázquez de León. Nor is such justification necessary.

29 "Con grandes sospiros y sentimientos." *B.D.C.*, *loc. cit.*

30 H.C. Second Letter to the Emperor, *Gayangos*, p. 52.

31 H.C. Second Letter to the Emperor, *Gayangos*, p. 54.
This was his secret mind; Bernal Díaz, on reading it, less tactfully put, in Gómara's words, exclaims: "It did not happen as he says: for what are we Spaniards like, to refuse to go forward and to remain in places where there is neither profit nor war?" As the brave soldier he was, he felt the slur on his reputation; yet Cortés' narrative rings true for all that, and all the men and sailors in the expedition were not of the same mettle as Bernal Díaz and his captain. (*B.D.C.*, ch. LVIII, vol. I, p. 166.)

32 "Y sobre Ello dixo otras muchas comparaciones y hechos Eroycos de los rromanos." (*B.D.C.*, ch. LIX, vol. I, p. 167.)

See also *B.D.C.*, ch. LVIII, vol. I, p. 165; *C.S.*, bk. III, ch. XXII, p. 180; *Gómara*, ch. xi, fol. xxxiij; *Las Casas*, bk. III, ch. CXXIII, vol. 65, p. 497; *Oviedo*, bk. XXXIII, ch. II, vol. III, p. 262. *Torquemada*, bk. IV, ch. xxv, vol. I, p. 407; H.C. Second Letter, *Gayangos*, p. 54; *F.A.I.*, ch. LXXXII, in *K.*, vol. IX, p. 290.

CHAPTER XII

1 This results from a confidence made by his page Diego de Coria to Cervantes de Salazar (*C.S.*, bk. III, ch. XI, p. 157).

2 *B.D.C.*, ch. CCVI, vol. II, pp. 467–8.

3 *B.D.C.*, ch. LVIII, vol. I, p. 166. I have based my narrative on H.C. Second Letter, *Gayangos*, pp. 54–7, and on *B.D.C.*, chs. LIX–LX, pp. 169–71. On points of fact having no bearing on Cortés' own justification, I have followed Cortés himself, whose narrative was written at a date much closer to the events. For instance, *B.D.C.* says there were four men on land; Cortés speaks only of three; here Cortés is sure to be right, which moreover seems borne out by that fact that *B.D.C.*, who gives the name of these men, cannot provide the name of the fourth. But when Cortés' interests are concerned, I have used my judgment after reading both H.C. and B.D.C. as explained in the text.

4 There are minor discrepancies among the authors. *B.D.C.* speaks of two hundred tamemes. I have adopted the figures of *F.A.I.*, ch. LXXXIII, in *K.*, vol. IX, p. 291. The date is given by *F.A.I.* also, as well as by *Torquemada* (bk. IV, ch. xxvi, vol. I, p. 411) and by *C.S.* (bk. III, ch. xxv, p. 186). *B.D.C.* (ch. LXI, vol. I, p. 172) speaks of the middle of August: "mediado el mes de agosto." Cortés describes the departure in H.C. Second Letter, *Gayangos*, p. 57, but gives no date.

5 Some authors say they came as hostages, but this does not tally either with the excellent relations which prevailed between Cortés and the men of Cempoal, or with the fact that Cortés left in Cempoal one of his pages, aged twelve, to learn the Totonac language "and to make sure that he would be well treated, he said he was his son."
   "Muchos caballeros Cempoalles que traía en su Companía [. . .] a quienes, aunque so color de Compañía llevaba, como por prendas y Rehenes." (*Torquemada*, bk. IV, ch. xxvi, vol. I, p. 411.)
   "Rescibió los rehenes, que fueron muchos, pero los señalados eran Mamexi, Teuch y Tamalli, hombres muy principales." (*C.S.*, bk. III, ch. XXIV, p. 185.)
   Sahagún, bk. XII, ch. x, in *K.*, vol. VII, p. 422, says that their guide was a prominent Indian known as Tlacochcalcatl.

6 *C.S.*, bk. III, ch. xxv, p. 186; *Torquemada*, bk. IV, ch. xxvi, vol. I, p. 412.

7 "Se sumen los caballos hasta la barriga." (*Torquemada*, *loc. cit.*, p. 411.)
   "Había muchas parras de vbas de la trra." (*B.D.C.*, ch. LXI, vol. I, p. 172.)

8 H.C. Second Letter, *Gayangos*, p. 57.
   "Tuvimos falta de comida." (*B.D.C.*, ch. LXI, vol. I, p. 172.)
   "Siempre caminavamos muy apercébidos, y con gran Concierto." (*B.D.C.*, ch. LXI, vol. I, p. 173.)

9 *F.A.I.* calls it Zacatlan (ch. LXXXIII, in *K.*, vol. IX, p. 291): *C.S.* (ch. xxvi, pp. 188–9), Zacatlan or Zacatlani. He corrects *Gómara* for having identified it with Castilblanco, but it is he who is in the wrong. See *B.D.C.*, ch. LXI, vol. I, p. 173; H.C. Second Letter, *Gayangos*, p. 58.

10 *C.S.*, ch. xxvi, p. 188, on the sacrifice. "Nos dieron de comer poca cosa, E de mala voluntad" (*B.D.C.*, ch. LXI, vol. I, p. 173). I follow Bernal Díaz rather than Cortés ("del señor y gente fui muy bien recibido y aposentado," *loc. cit.*) because his version fits the rest of the facts better and is moreover strikingly confirmed

by *Torquemada*: "mandó dar de comer a la Gente, no con abundancia ni con mui buena voluntad" (bk. IV, ch. xxvi, vol. I, p. 412).

11 *C.S.*, bk. III, ch. xxvi, pp. 188–9; *Torquemada*, bk. IV, ch. xxvi, vol. I, pp. 412–13; H.C. Second Letter, *Gayangos*, p. 58; *B.D.C.*, ch. lxi, pp. 173–5.

    Prescott, vol. II, footnote 16, is so impressed by Bernal Díaz' courage here that he promotes him to the rank of captain, which would have pleased Bernal Díaz very much.

12 Details as to embassies and ambassadors amongst the natives of Anahuac in *C.S.*, bk. III, ch. xxxi, p. 198.

13 *Torquemada*, bk. IV, ch. xxvii, vol. I, p. 415; *O. y B.*, vol. IV, p. 197.

14 *B.D.C.*, ch. lxii, vol. I, p. 179.

    Maudslay (vol. I, p. 226) translates "hold their lances before their faces," and though *B.D.C.'s* "q llevasen las lanças por las caras" might justify the error, the meaning of Cortés' advice stands out clear from another text of identical import a few page later (ch. lxv, vol. I, p. 187): "las lanças terciadas sin pararse a lancear sino por las caras y ojos."

15 *B.D.C.*, ch. lxii, vol. I, pp. 178–9. There are some minor discrepancies as to the order of events, but on this I have followed H.C. rather than Bernal Díaz because his report was closer to the facts. Bernal Díaz is certainly wrong about the messengers: he repeatedly says they were two, while it is obvious from many passages in Cortés that they were four.

16 H.C. Second Letter, *Gayangos*, p. 60; *C.S.*, bk. III, ch. xxxii, p. 201.

17 Cortés does not mention this in his letter to the Emperor, and Bernal Díaz is equally silent, though, in his case, it may be due to the fact that when he came upon the scene the horsemen that rode with Cortés had already broken through it.

    C.S., *loc. cit.* He seems to imply, and *Torquemada* (bk. IV, ch. xxviii and xxix, vol. I, pp. 417, 419) actually says that the charms were laid by Moteçuçuma's magicians and on his instructions, which is politically impossible. They overlook the fact that Aztecs and Tlaxcatecs held the same belief and had the same magical powers.

18 *B.D.C.*, ch. lxii, pp. 180–81; H.C. Second Letter, *Gayangos*, p. 61; *Torquemada*, bk. IV, ch. xxix, vol. I, p. 419; *C.S.*, bk. III, chs. xxxii, xxxiii, p. 202. There are the usual minor discrepancies.

19 *B.D.C.*, ch. lxiii, vol. I, p. 181; H.C. Second Letter, *Gayangos*, pp. 62–3; *C.S.*, bk. III, ch. xxxiv, p. 204; *Torquemada*, bk. IV, ch. xxx, vol. I, pp. 420–21.

20 *Gómara* (ch. xliiij, fol. xxvj), *C.S.* (bk. III, ch. xxxv, p. 208), *Torquemada* bk. IV, ch. xxxi, vol. I, p. 422), all give September 1st. *B.D.C.'s* dates would appear more in agreement with the narrative. I have, however, accepted September 1st on the authority of *O. y B.*, bk. I, ch. viii, vol. IV, p. 204, whose study of dates is usually reliable.

21 H.C. Second Letter, *Gayangos*, p. 62; *B.D.C.*, ch. lxv, vol. I, p. 186; *C.S.*, bk. III, ch. xxxvii, p. 211; *Torquemada*, bk. IV, ch. xxxii, vol. I, p. 424; *Gómara*, chs. xliiij, xlv, fols. xxvj, xxvij.

CHAPTER XIII

1 *Tapia*, *C.D.H.M.*, vol. II, pp. 569–70; H.C. Second Letter, *Gayangos*, p. 63; *B.D.C.*, ch. lxx, vol. I, p. 203.

2 Neither of the two soldiers present, whose chronicles we possess, says this; on the contrary, Bernal Díaz asserts that "no harm was done to them," and Tapia that "the Marquess ordered that no Indian should be killed and that nothing should

be taken from them"; but Cortés ought to know better, and moreover his letter to the Emperor was written at a time much closer to the events.

There are a number of discrepancies between the three main sources, all coming from eyewitnesses: Cortés himself (H.C. Second Letter, *Gayangos*, pp. 64-5), Bernal Díaz (*B.D.C.*, ch. LXVIII, vol. I, pp. 196-7), and Tapia (*C.D.H.M.*, vol. II, pp. 568-9). For the reasons given in the text, I have preferred Cortés in case of doubt; Bernal Díaz, for instance, says that there were six horsemen only, but Cortés says that he took with him "los de caballo," which means all of them; this is confirmed by the fact that he himself mentions that he sent back five of them, while Tapia says that those who remained and were led by the rein, were eight.

That Cortés was ill with quartan fever is in *B.D.C.* Both *B.D.C.* and *Tapia* shorten up and simplify the narrative, suppressing the arrival in the two pueblos before dawn.

3 *B.D.C.*, ch. LXIX, vol. I, p. 198; *Torquemada*, bk. IV, ch. XXXIV, vol. I, p. 428.

4 The scene is described in detail in *B.D.C.*, ch. LXIX, vol. I, pp. 198-202; Cortés sums it up in H.C. Second Letter, *Gayangos*, p. 65.

5 H.C. Second Letter, *Gayangos*, p. 65.

6 *Loc. cit.*

7 *Loc. cit.*

8 *Tapia*, in *C.D.H.M.*, vol. II, p. 571.

9 *Torquemada*, bk. IV, ch. XXXV, vol. I, p. 429.

10 Cortés (H.C. Second Letter, *Gayangos*, p. 69) and Bernal Díaz (*B.D.C.*, ch. LXXII, vol. I, p. 208) both mention the Mexican embassy after the first peace embassy of the Tlaxcatecs, though *B.D.C.* relates Xicotencatl's own embassy after that of Moteçuçuma. But Cortés says definitely that he kept the Mexican Ambassadors in his camp during a good part of the war: "y estuvieron conmigo en mucha parte de la guerra hasta el fin de ella" (*loc. cit.*).

11 "Mandó Cortés a los suyos los acarisciasen y tratasen bien, pues eran señores y mensajeros de tan gran príncipe." (*C.S.*, bk. III, ch. XLIV, p. 229.)
"Y los mando regalar mucho." (*Torquemada*, bk. IV, ch. XXXV, vol. I, p. 431.)

12 *B.D.C.*, ch. LXXII, vol. I, p. 209; *Torquemada*, bk. IV, ch. XXXV, vol. I, p. 431; *C.S.*, bk. III, ch. XLIV, p. 229.

13 *B.D.C.*, ch. LXXI, vol. I, pp. 205-6.

14 *F.A.I.*, ch. LXXXIII, in *K.*, vol. IX, p. 292.

15 *F.A.I.*, *loc. cit.*, says that, as Tolimpanecatl Tlacatecuhtli was leaving, Doña Marina called him aside and suggested to him that the Tlaxcatecs should kill the Mexican Ambassador. This story is to be found in no other chronicler that I have read. At first sight it has a plausible air, for, outwardly at any rate, it is in the style of Cortés. But, on reflection, how could Cortés risk so clumsy an action right in the teeth of the native traditions which granted a sacred inviolability to Ambassadors?

16 *B.D.C.*, ch. LXXIII, vol. I, p. 211.

17 ". . . first because he was ill with fever and then because he pondered over those words the ambassadors had said to him, for though he feigned to pay no heed to them, he wondered whether they might not be true, till he was more sure as to the peace, for they were of a kind that made one think about them." (*B.D.C.*, ch. LXXIII, vol. I, p. 212.)

18 *B.D.C.*, *loc. cit.*

19 These are the names given by the national historian of Mexico, Orozco y Berra (*O. y B.*, bk. I, ch. IX, vol. IV, p. 194). *B.D.C.* gives other names, probably mixing up personal names with official titles.

20 *B.D.C.*, ch. LXXIV, vol. I, p. 215.

21 "Y desque oyeron aquella palabra, sintieron tanto plazer, que en los rrostros se conosçio [. . .] y en menos de media ora traen sobre quinientos yndios de carga." (*B.D.C.*, ch. LXXIV, vol. I, p. 215.)

Both *Torquemada* and *C.S.* pass over the arrival of the tlatoanis in camp, nor does *Prescott* (bk. III, ch. v, vol. II, p. 161) give it the importance which it undoubtedly had. *H.C.* Second Letter, *Gayangos*, p. 67.

CHAPTER XIV

1 *B.D.C.*, ch. LXXV, vol. I, pp. 217–18.

2 H.C. Second Letter, *Gayangos*, pp. 67–9. It is generally held that Cortes exaggerated in his comparison with Granada. Such is the opinion of *O. y B.* (vol. IV, p. 232) and of *Prescott* (bk. III, ch. v, vol. II, p. 166).

3 *H.C.* Second Letter, *Gayangos*, p. 69.

4 *Tapia*, in *C.D.H.M.*, vol. II, p. 572; *B.D.C.*, ch. LXXI, vol. I, p. 208; *C.S.*, bk. III, ch. XLVIII, p. 237; *B.D.C.*, ch. LXXV, vol. I, p. 219.

5 *B.D.C.*, ch. LXXV, vol. I, p. 218.

6 *B.D.C.*, ch. LXXV, vol. I, 219.

7 *C.S.*, bk. III, ch. XLIX, p. 239.

8 *Tapia*, in *C.D.H.M.*, vol. II, p. 573.

9 *B.D.C.*, ch. LXXVIII, vol. I, p. 229.

10 *B.D.C.*, ch. LXXVII, vol. I, p. 222.

11 *B.D.C.*, ch. LXXVIII, vol. I, p. 227.

12 *B.D.C.*, ch. LXXVII, vol. I, p. 223.

13 *B.D.C.*, ch. LXXVII, vol. I, p. 224.

14 *C.S.*, bk. III, ch. LIII, p. 247.

15 *B.D.C.*, ch. LXXVIII, vol. I, pp. 225–7.

16 *B.D.C.*, ch. LXXX, vol. I, p. 235. See *C.S.*, bk. III, ch. LII, pp. 243–4. He says that Alvarado came back by Guaxocingo, which cannot be true, for the way to Mexico by Guaxocingo was found by Ordás when he climbed to the volcano, as related by Cortés (Second Letter, *Gayangos*, p. 78). Cortés does not mention this embassy at all, either because it was a failure or because in his mind it was but a scouting expedition. Bernal Díaz places here yet another embassy from Moteçuçuma. But there seems to be no foundation for it, and his memory is apt to mix up Tlaxcala events with Cholula events, as for instance when he relates Ordás' climb to the volcano. This embassy came to Cholula, and there was only one, though some authors (*O. y B.*, vol. IV, pp. 240, 245, for instance) mention two.

17 This narrative is based partly on H.C. Second Letter, *Gayangos*, p. 70, and *B.D.C.*, ch. LXXIX, vol. I, pp. 230–32.

18 *B.D.C.* (ch. LXXXI, vol. I, p. 237) says they did not come, giving as an excuse that they could not be expected to come to the home of their enemies, a reason accepted as fair by Cortés. But Cortés' version must prevail, for he wrote when the events were far more recent (H.C. Second Letter, *Gayangos*, p. 71.)

19 H.C. Second Letter, *Gayangos*, p. 72.

20 *O. y B.*, vol. IV, p. 238.

21 *C.S.*, bk. III, ch. LV, p. 253.

22 *B.D.C.*, ch. LXXXIII, vol. I, p. 242. On the events in Cholula I have collated and carefully weighed: H.C. Second Letter, *Gayangos*, pp. 70–75; *B.D.C.*, ch. LXXXIII,

vol. I, pp. 240–53; *Tapia* in *C.D.H.M.*, vol. II, pp. 572–7; *Sahagún*, bk. XII, ch. XI, in *K.*, vol. VII, p. 423; *Torquemada*, bk. IV, chs. XXXIX, XL, vol. I, pp. 437–41; *C.S.*, chs. LIV–LVI, pp. 249–59.

23 "Having discovered the existence of a plot to exterminate his forces, he simply struck first. The Cholulans had taken measures to annihilate the invaders, which must have proved successful against ordinary foes. Not only the Spanish historians but the native chronicles testify to this fact. The Mexican story is told in the Indian paintings still preserved at San Juan Cuauhtlautzinco. The Cholulans did not regard the Spaniards as Gods. They went to work to trap them and starve them like ordinary human beings [. . .] The Tlaxcatecs knew all the while that treachery was planned. [. . .] The Spaniards thought that the perfuming with incense indicated submission to themselves. They did not know that prisoners of war, destined for sacrifice, were perfumed in the same way." (Prof. Munro in *Prescott*, vol. II, p. 212 footnote.)

CHAPTER XV

1 *B.D.C.*, ch. LXXIII, vol. I, p. 249; H.C. Second Letter, *Gayangos*, p. 75.

2 *C.S.*, bk. III, ch. LV, p. 252.

3 *Torquemada*, bk. IV, ch. XLI, vol. I, p. 441.

4 *B.D.C.*, ch. LXXXIII, vol. I, p. 253.

5 H.C. Second Letter, *Gayangos*, p. 76.

6 *Torquemada*, bk. IV, ch. XLI, vol. I, p. 442.

7 H.C. Second Letter, *Gayangos*, p. 87; *B.D.C.*, ch. XCIV, vol. I, p. 301; *Torquemada*, bk. IV, ch. XLVIII, vol. I, p. 455; *Tapia* in *C.D.H.M.*, vol. II, p. 579; *O. y B.*, bk. II, ch. IV, vol. IV, p. 310; *Gómara*, ch. lxxxiij, fol. xliij; *Oveido*, bk. XXXII, ch. VI, vol. III, p. 287; *F.A.I.*, ch. LXXXV, in *K.*, vol. IX, p. 296; but above all *C.S.*, bk. III, ch. XXVI, p. 180, for it is only by putting together H.C.'s version and C.S.'s narrative that the respective attitudes stand out in mutual clarity; the matter is not without interest owing to its bearing on the important events related in ch. XVII below.

8 H.C. Second Letter, *Gayangos*, p. 77.

9 *Loc. cit.*

10 *Loc. cit.*

11 *B.D.C.*, ch. LXXVIII, vol. I, pp. 228–9.

12 H.C. Second Letter, *Gayangos*, p. 78.

13 *B.D.C.*, ch. LXXXIII, vol. I, p. 252.

14 *B.D.C.*, ch. LXXXV, vol. I, p. 257.

15 *B.D.C.*, ch. LXXXV, vol. I, p. 258.

16 *B.D.C.*, ch. LXXXVI, vol. I, p. 269. *Prescott* (vol. II, p. 222, footnote) speaks of this phrase as a "homely but expressive Spanish proverb," which is hardly correct.

17 *Torquemada*, bk. IV, ch. XLI, vol. I, p. 443.

18 *Torquemada*, bk. IV, ch. XLIII, vol. I, p. 445; *Sahagún*, bk. XII, ch. XII, in *K.*, vol. VII, p. 424.

19 *Sahagún*, bk. XII, ch. XIII, in *K.*, vol. VII, pp. 424–5. The description of drunken people as being possessed by four hundred rabbits comes from the same author, bk. IV, ch. V, in *K.*, vol. VII, p. 129.

20 *Tapia*, in *C.D.H.M.*, vol. II, p. 577.

21 *C.S.*, bk. III, ch. LX, p. 265; *Torquemada*, bk. IV, ch. XLI, vol. I, pp. 243–4.

22 H.C. Second Letter, *Gayangos*, pp. 79–80.

23 *B.D.C.*, ch. LXXXVII , vol. I, p. 264.

24 *B.D.C.*, ch. LXXXVI, p. 261.

25 *B.D.C.*, ch. LXXXVI, pp. 261–2.

26 *Torquemada* (bk. IV, ch. XLII, vol. I, p. 444) says that Cacama's view prevailed. I have followed H.C.'s own report on his interview with Cacama in Ayotzinco (see below, note 28).

27 H.C. Second Letter, *Gayangos*, p. 81.

28 H.C. Second Letter, *Gayangos*, p. 82; *B.D.C.*, ch. LXXXVII, vol. I, p. 265.

29 H.C. Second Letter, *Gayangos*, p. 82; *B.D.C.*, ch. LXXXVII, vol. I, p. 266.

30 Whether this insistence of the Mexicans on taking Cortés to Iztapalapa for the night was due to Cuitlahuac's desire to efface any traces of this opposition in Cortés' mind, or, on the contrary, to some eleventh-hour plot to prevent his entry into Mexico by violence, is not known. The more likely view is the first, for Cortés, never slow in detecting signs of treason, has nothing of the kind to repeat on his stay in Iztapalapa—nor has Bernal Díaz. (H.C. Second Letter, *Gayangos*, p. 82.)

31 H.C. Second Letter, *Gayangos*, p. 83; *B.D.C.*, ch. LXXXVII, vol. I, p. 267.

32 H.C. Second Letter, *Gayangos*, p. 82; *B.D.C.*, ch. LXXXVIII, vol. I, p. 268.

CHAPTER XVI

1 *Torquemada*, bk. IV, ch. XXXV, vol. I, p. 299.

2 *Sahagún*, bk. II, ch. XXXIII, in *K.*, vol. VII, p. 73.

3 *Sahagún*, bk. IV, ch. XXXI, in *K.*, vol. VII, p. 147.

4 H.C. Second Letter, *Gayangos*, p. 84; *B.D.C.*, ch. LXXXVIII, vol. I, p. 269.

5 H.C. Second Letter, *Gayangos*, p. 85.

6 *Sahagún*, bk. V, all chapters, in *K.*, vol. VII, p. 159 et seq., for auguries, and bk. III, pp. 116–18, for Hell, Paradise and Heaven.

7 Arthur Waley's remarks on the evolution of the Chinese in his introduction to his edition to the Tao Tê Ching seem to me to apply most aptly to the Mexicans as Cortés found them. (*Waley*, pp. 17 et seq.)

8 *O. y B.*, bk. I, ch. v, vol. IV, p. 92.

9 *Torquemada*, bk. VII, ch. XIV, vol. II, p. 108.

10 *Sahagún*, bk. XII, ch. XVI, in *K.*, vol. VII, p. 426.

11 *Torquemada*, bk. IV, ch. XLIV, vol. I, p. 451.

12 H.C. Second Letter, *Gayangos*, p. 85. *Prescott* (bk. III, ch. IX, vol. II, pp. 257–8) says the Emperor awaited Cortés in the courtyard of the Temple and offered his necklaces there. *B.D.C.* is vague on the first point ("que alli le estuvo esperando," ch. LXXXVIII, vol. I, p. 271—we do not know who awaits whom); and he describes the presentation of the necklace—not of two—in the "aposento y sala," dwelling and room, destined for Cortés. But the narrative of Cortés is final, and I have followed it.

13 *Torquemada*, bk. IV, ch. XLVI, vol. I, p. 451.

14 *Torquemada*, bk. IV, ch. XLVI, vol. I, p. 451. On the size of the rooms *Torquemada*, bk. III, ch. XXV, vol. I, p. 296, *B.D.C.*, ch. LXXXIII, vol. I, p. 271, *C.S.*, bk. IV, ch. I, p. 275; these last three sources use practically the same words. From a detailed study of this and other cases, I put forward the conclusion that when

Torquemada and *C.S.* coincide they are both borrowing textually from Ojeda's lost Memoriales; I suspect that *B.D.C.* used some MS. of Ojeda's Memoriales to refresh his memory, which might account for the traces of *B.D.C.* to be found in *Torquemada*.

15 H.C. Second Letter, *Gayangos*, p. 85; *Torquemada*, bk. IV, ch. xlvi, vol. I, p. 451; *C.S.*, bk. III, ch. lxiii, p. 274. Here again *Torquemada* and *C.S.* use practically the same words.

16 *B.D.C.*, ch. lxxxviii, vol. I, p. 272.

17 *B.D.C.*, ch. lxxxix, vol. I, p. 273.

18 *B.D.C.*, ch. lxxxix, vol. I, pp. 273-4.

19 *C.S.*, bk. IV, ch. viii, p. 288.

20 I have combined H.C. Second Letter, *Gayangos*, pp. 86-7, and *B.D.C.*, ch. xc, vol. I, pp. 274-8. H.C. speaks only of one visit; *B.D.C.* gives Moteçuçuma's call and H.C.'s return visit. I have preferred *B.D.C.* this time because of H.C.'s well-known tendency to simplify and also because B.D.C. was actually present at the return visit and witnessed such details as Moteçuçuma showing his body, while in H.C.'s version he would not have been in a position to say so. See also *C.S.*, bk. IV, ch. i, p. 277.

21 On troops confined to the teocalli, *B.D.C.*, ch. lxxxix, vol. I, p. 274. On the visit to Tianquiztli, *B.D.C.*, ch. xcii, vol. I, p. 286; H.C. Second Letter, *Gayangos*, pp. 103-4; *C.S.*, bk. IV, ch. xviii, p. 303 and ch. xix, p. 306. On the visit to the teocalli, *B.D.C.*, ch. xcii, vol. I, p. 286; *C.S.*, bk. IV, chs. xx-xxi, pp. 309-10. On the size of temple, there is a useful study of Rosalie Thorne in *Vassar Journal of Undergraduate Studies*, vol. XII (May 1939).

CHAPTER XVII

1 *B.D.C.*, ch. xcii, vol. I, pp. 291-3; H. C. Second Letter, *Gayangos*, pp. 106-7.

2 *B.D.C.*, ch. xci, vol. I, pp. 278-85; H.C. Second Letter, *Gayangos*, pp. 109-13; *C.S.*, bk. IV, chs. iv-xiii, pp. 281-96.

3 On supplies; *B.D.C.*, ch. xciv, vol. I, p. 300. On H.C.'s decision: H.C. Second Letter, *Gayangos*, p. 88.

4 *B.D.C.*, ch. xciv, pp. 299-300.

5 *O. y B.*, bk. II, ch. v, vol. IV, p. 310; *Prescott*, bk. IV, ch. iii, vol. II, p. 339.

6 *B.D.C.*, ch. xciii, vol. I, p. 299; H.C. Second Letter, *Gayangos*, pp. 88-9; *Torquemada*, bk. IV, ch. xlviii, vol. I, p. 454.

7 *B.D.C.*, ch. xciii, vol. I, p. 300; H.C. Second Letter, *Gayangos*, p. 89.

8 The sources are: *Tapia* in *C.D.H.M.*, vol. II, pp. 579-81; *C.S.*, bk. IV, ch. xxvi, p. 321; *B.D.C.*, ch. xcv, vol. I, pp. 297-301, ch. cxiv, vol. I, pp. 301-4, ch. xcv, vol. I, pp. 304-11; H.C. Second Letter, *Gayangos*, pp. 87-92; *Torquemada*, bk. IV, ch. xlvii-li, vol. I, pp. 452-61. See also *Prescott*, vol. III, p. 335.

There is some confusion amongst the authors on several points: some give two battles; others only one. In my opinion, the story is clear thanks mostly to *C.S.*, and had *Prescott* and *O. y B.* known his version they would have written otherwise than they did. These are the stages: Moteçuçuma wishes to receive a "specimen of a Spaniard" (*C.S.*); Quauhpopoca, wishing to please him, traps some Spaniards (H.C. Second Letter, *Gayangos*, p. 88); the two heads are sent to Moteçuçuma (*C.S.*; *B.D.C.*); Cortés receives news of this first battle while in Cholula, but pockets it because it would have ruined his efforts to persuade his men to march on to Mexico (H.C.); he gets news of the second battle on the very morning of Moteçuçuma's seizure (*B.D.C.*). This analysis, moreover, fits the facts and explains the ambiguity in the respective responsibilities of Moteçuçuma and Quauhpopoca.

I am aware of the view that the ease with which Cortés seized hold of Moteçuçuma tends "to prove that the so-called 'Emperor' had no real power, but was only the agent of the tribe" (Prof. Munro's note to *Prescott*, bk. IV, ch. III, vol. II, p. 346). In my humble view, this opinion is, if not altogether untenable, very much exaggerated. The direct impact of events, faces, emotions, ceremonies, which the Spaniards received and faithfully registered, makes of them guides at least as safe as merely bookish investigators; and all the details which we owe to these old eyewitnesses go to prove that the power of Moteçuçuma was real, and his dignity royal.

9 *Torquemada*, bk. IV, ch. LI, vol. I, p. 459; *B.D.C.*, ch. xcv, vol. I, p. 307.

10 *Torquemada*, bk. IV, ch. LII, vol. I, p. 462.

11 On Quauhpopoca's arrival *Torquemada*, bk. IV, ch. LV, vol. I, p. 467. On meeting with Moteçuçuma, *Torquemada*, *loc. cit.*; *B.D.C.*, ch. xcv, vol. I, p. 308; wisely records "y lo que con ellos habló no lo sé."

12 *O. y B.*, bk. II, ch. v, vol. IV, p. 318; H.C. Second Letter, *Gayangos*, p. 91; *Torquemada*, bk. IV, ch. LV, vol. I, p. 468; *Gómara*, ch. lxxxv, fol. xliiij.

13 *Torquemada* (bk. IV, ch. L, vol. I, p. 458) seems to imply the brigantines were ready before Moteçuçuma's seizure. He also implies that the appointment of Grado first and of Sandoval afterwards to govern Veracruz was made before the seizure, this being linked up with the former by the fact that it was Sandoval who sent from Veracruz the rigging and metallic materials for the craft (*B.D.C.* and end of ch. xcvi, vol. I, p. 314); but though Torquemada's presentation fits better the character of Cortés there is no evidence to warrant his view, and whatever evidence there is tends to suggest that Cortés gambled in this episode as in many others. This gambling element must never be lost sight of in him. He was essentially a gambler, though a careful one, and he called his luck "faith." This view is borne out by Gómara (ch. lxxxj, fol. xliij), who definitely says that, though Cortés would have wished to have the ships ready first, he made up his mind to seize Moteçuçuma without waiting.

14 *Tapia* in *C.D.H.M.*, vol. II, p. 584.

15 H.C. Second Letter, *Gayangos*, p. 91; *B.D.C.*, ch. xcv, vol. I, p. 309.

16 *B.D.C.*, ch. xcv, vol. I, p. 309; H.C. Second Letter, *Gayangos*, p. 91.

17 *B.D.C.*, ch. xcvi, vol. I, pp. 311-14.

18 *B.D.C.*, *loc. cit.*

19 *B.D.C.*, ch. ccvi, vol. II, p. 468.

CHAPTER XVIII

1 *Torquemada*, bk. IV, ch. L, vol. I, p. 459.

2 *B.D.C.*, ch. xciii, vol. I, p. 297.

3 *B.D.C.*, ch. xcvii, vol. I, p. 317.

4 *B.D.C.*, ch. xcvii, vol. I, p. 315.

5 *Torquemada*, bk. IV, ch. LI, vol. I, p. 460; *C.S.*, bk. IV, ch. xxviii, p. 334.

6 *B.D.C.*, ch. xcix, vol. I, p. 322.

7 H.C. Second Letter, *Gayangos*, p. 97; *B.D.C.*, ch. c, vol. I, p. 327.
This confirms the view that the advice Cacama always had given to Moteçuçuma in the past—namely, that the Spaniards should be allowed to come to Mexico—was not due to defeatism or cowardice as is written everywhere but to a confident

belief in the capacity of the Mexicans to deal with the strangers adequately if they forgot the faith which Cacama wanted first to be put in them. In my opinion, this young prince seems to have been the most intelligent and brave of the native leaders. That is why I do not attach much value to the story given by *F.A.I.* (XIII Narrative) in *K.*, vol. IX, p. 411, which purports to trace the origin of Cacama's rebellion to the fact that Cortés had put his brother to death. Let alone the fact that the haste and lack of formality in the capital execution of no less a person than a nephew of the Emperor which this story implies on the part of Cortés is most unlike him, and that so notorious an event would certainly have been recorded by Bernal Díaz and even by Cortés, it makes no sense from the point of view of Cacama either, the line of whose action is perfectly consistent until this story comes to blur it—particularly as, on F.A.I.'s own version, Cacama *after* having lost one brother to Cortés gave him another to replace the first one in the gold-seeking operations which are supposed to have provided the background for the tragedy. This is one of the many examples of the tendency in some historians to blacken the Spaniards which, balanced by the equally numerous cases of the tendency to whitewash them in others, makes a reasonable history of the conquest a most difficult achievement for an honest man.

8 *B.D.C.*, ch. c, vol. I, p. 325.

9 *B.D.C.*, ch. c, vol. I, p. 326.

10 *B.D.C.*, ch. c, vol. I, p. 325; H.C. Second Letter, *Gayangos*, p. 97; *Torquemada*, bk. IV, ch. LV, vol. I, p. 470.

11 H.C. Second Letter, *Gayangos*, p. 98; *B.D.C.*, chs. XCVI and c, vol. I, pp. 314, 329.

12 *B.D.C.*, ch. c, vol. I, p. 329.

13 *B.D.C.*, chs. XCVI, XCVIII, c, vol. I, pp. 307, 319, 326.

14 *B.D.C.*, ch. c, vol. I, p. 330.

15 *B.D.C.*, ch. CI, vol. I, p. 332.

16 H.C. Second Letter, *Gayangos*, pp. 98-9; *B.D.C.*, ch. CI, vol. I, pp. 330, 332; *Oviedo*, bk. XXXIII, ch. IX, vol. III, p. 297.

17 *Las Casas*, bk. III, ch. CXVI, vol. 65, p. 456.

18 "O tempo, o mesmo tempo, de si chora." I quote from memory.

CHAPTER XIX

1 *Gómara* (ch. lxxxj—not 83, as stated by *Prescott*, II, 341 footnote—fol. xiij), *C.S.* (bk. IV, ch. XXVI, p. 325) and *Tapia* (in *C.D.H.M.*, vol. II, p. 579), all say that Cortés was pacing the room by himself when he discovered the door and had it opened by his servants. *B.D.C.* (ch. XCIII, vol. I, p. 298) records that the door was discovered by Yáñez the carpenter while looking for a suitable place to build an altar, and it sounds more reasonable than that it should have been discovered by Cortés while brooding over his dangerous situation in Mexico. *Torquemada* (bk. IV, ch. XLIX, vol. I, p. 456) supplies a happy compromise which probably reflects the truth: Cortés was warned of the discovery made by Yáñez while he was pacing the room. The details on the size of the "Jewel Shop" are from *Torquemada*, ch. LI, vol. I, p. 461.

2 "Till we see another time," says *B.D.C.*, ch. XCIII, vol. I, p. 298. "Because all that [gold] was sure to stay at home"—*Gómara*, ch. lxxxj, fol. xliij.

3 This version is given by Torquemada, bk. IV, ch. LI, vol. I, p. 460, and *C.S.*, bk. IV, ch. XXVIII, p. 333, who both say explicitly that they borrow it from

Ojeda's *Memoriales. Tapia* in *C.D.H.M.*, vol. II, p. 580, tells the story in practically identical terms. But *B.D.C.*, ch. CIV, vol. I, p. 340, gives a different version as shown later in the text.

4 *B.D.C.*, ch. CIV, vol. I, p. 340.

5 Thus *C.S.*, bk. IV, ch. XXVI, p. 325; *Tapia*, in *C.D.H.M.*, vol. II, p. 579; *Gómara*, ch. lxxxj, fol. xliij; *Torquemada*, bk. IV, chs. XLIX and LI, p. 461; *B.D.C.*, ch. XCIII, vol. I, p. 298. The most characteristic example is that of *B.D.C.* for, after all, in the others, the mention of the Jewel Shop immediately before the imprisonment might be plausibly explained away on the ground that Cortés was pacing the room thinking over his scheme of getting hold of Moteçuçuma when the discovery was either made by him (*Gómara, Tapia, C.S.*) or announced to him by or from Yáñez (*Torquemada*); but in *B.D.C.* there is no such pacing the room; the discovery is made by Yáñez; Cortés is told; he and some captains first, the other captains and all the soldiers afterwards, visit the treasure just discovered; and then, without any transition at all, in his quaint, uncouth style, the soldier-chronicler goes on to say: "Let us leave off about this wealth and say that as we had so many brave captains . . ." they drew Cortés aside into the church and told him they were all in danger and he had better get hold of Moteçuçuma. This means that in three entirely different sets of narratives, implying three entirely different interrelations between the two events—the *Tapia-Gómara* set which, closely relates them since Cortés discovers the Jewel Shop while pacing the room thinking of how to seize Moteçuçuma, the *Torquemada* system, which connects them though far more loosely, and the *B.D.C.* system, in which there is no connection at all between the discovery of the Jewel Shop and the imprisonment of Moteçuçuma—the only feature that remains unaltered is a direct sequence in the story: in all of them, the writer passes from the discovery of the treasure to the decision and even to the actual execution of Moteçuçuma.

6 *B.D.C.* admits as much in a passage in which he is summing up Cacama's speech before his council, when the young prince is trying to induce his friends to revolt against both Moteçuçuma and Cortés. Enumerating together the sins of the two, Cacama says (according to *B.D.C.*) "and that we had broken into and opened the house in which is kept the treasure of his grandfather Axayaca"; this action, which cannot refer to the discreet opening and subsequent walling up of the door, since the words used by *B.D.C.* suggest a regular housebreaking, may have given rise to the story told by Tapia and others to the effect that Cortés asked Moteçuçuma what he was to do since the Spaniards had taken some gold and other things from the treasure house (*B.D.C.*, ch. c, vol. I, p. 327).

7 On the stolen cocoa *Torquemada*, bk. IV, ch. LVII, vol. I, p. 72, and *C.S.*, bk. IV, ch. XLIV, p. 373, in practically identical words, borrowed from Ojeda. On Cacama's torture *O. y B.*, who discusses this point which I find in none of the usual chroniclers. Yet, despite the bias which the distinguished Mexican historian evinces against the conquerors, his case is well proved and must be accepted. (*O. y B.*, pt. IV, bk. II, ch. v, vol. IV, p. 341, and in particular the footnote.)

8 I take these figures from *Prescott* (bk. IV, ch. v, vol. III, pp. 10–11), who on this question seems to me, as in most other cases, fair and competent.

9 *B.D.C.*, ch. CV, vol. I, 343.

10 H.C. Second Letter, *Gayangos*, p. 100; *B.D.C.*, ch. CV, vol. I, p. 344.

11 *B.D.C.*, chs. CV, CVI, vol. I, pp. 345, 346.

12 H.C. Second Letter, *Gayangos*, p. 95; *Gómara*, ch. lxxxviij, fol. xlv verso.

13 *B.D.C.*, ch. CIII, vol. I, p. 338.

14 H.C. Second Letter, *Gayangos*, p. 94.

15 H.C. Second Letter, *Gayangos*, pp. 95–6, who calls the local chief Tuchintecla;
   B.D.C., chs. cii, ciii, vol. I, pp. 334, 336, who calls him Tochel; *C.S.*, bk. IV,
   ch. xxxix, p. 366, who calls him Tuchintle.

16 See *O. y B.*, vol. IV, p. 346 footnote. His attitude is, as usual, cantankerous
   towards Cortés. He seems to treat these daughters of a man who at one time had
   one hundred and fifty concubines pregnant (*C.S.*, bk. IV, ch. ix, p. 288) as if they
   were the two or three princesses of the blood of a reigning house. The quotation
   is from *B.D.C.*, ch. cvii, vol. I, p. 348.

17 H.C. Second Letter, *Gayangos*, pp. 107 and 106.

18 *Tapia*, in *C.D.H.M.*, vol. II, p. 584. *Prescott* (bk. IV, ch. v, vol. III, p. 16 et seq)
   prefers to follow *B.D.C.* (ch. cvii, vol. I, p. 348 et seq), who relates a story of
   compromise and negotiation between Cortés and Moteçuçuma. But Cortés' version
   should have prevailed in any case, as being closer to the events. On the discovery
   of Tapia's manuscript (unknown to Prescott) Cortés is fully vindicated. The story
   of a compromise told by Bernal Díaz is on the other hand quite compatible with
   the destruction of the chief idols and is in fact confirmed by Tapia (p. 585).

CHAPTER XX

1 *Tapia*, in *C.D.H.M.*, vol. II, p. 586.

2 *B.D.C.*, ch. cviii, vol. I, p. 351; *Gómara*, ch. xcij, fol. xlvij verso.

3 *B.D.C.*, ch. cviii, vol. I, p. 351.

4 *B.D.C.*, ch. cviii, vol. I, p. 350; *Torquemada*, bk. IV, ch. lviii, vol. I, p. 473.

5 *Gómara, loc. cit.*

6 It is almost certain that he would have done so in any case, since when the wind
  of his fortune changed so suddenly, he was thinking of sending an expedition to
  Santo Domingo, to recruit more men and horses for his conquest, "for his were
  few for so great a Kingdom." This fact, which we owe to Gómara, suffices to
  show that Bernal Díaz is right when, discussing another of Gómara's assertions,
  he writes: "What it was that Cortés said to Martín López on this I do not know,
  and I say this because the chronicler Gómara in his history says that he told him
  to put up a show that he was making the ships, but only as a comedy to let
  Moteçuçuma hear about it; I will stand by what they both might say, for, thank
  God, both are alive, but in great secret Martín López told me that they did build
  them and in a great hurry." (*Gómara*, ch. xcij, fol. xlvij and verso; *B.D.C.*, ch.
  cviii, vol. I, p. 352.)
  Sandoval is noncommittal (bk. IV, par. XXI, vol. I, p. 183).

7 Don Quixote, ch. iii of pt. II.

8 A fortnight because: (1) *Gómara* says Narváez' ships arrived eight days after the
  carpenter had left (ch. xciij, fol. xlviij); (2) on *Gómara's* authority, Moteçuçuma
  knew four days later; (3) *B.D.C.* (ch. cx, vol. I, p. 358) says Moteçuçuma knew
  of it three days before he told Cortés.

9 *B.D.C.*, ch. cx, vol. I, p. 358.

10 *Tapia*, in *C.D.H.M.*, vol. II, p. 586.

11 *B.D.C.*, ch. lv, vol. I, pp. 159, 158.

12 This is Velázquez' own version in a letter to Rodrigo de Figueroa, a magistrate
   in Santo Domingo, dated November 17th, 1519 (*C.D.H.M.*, vol. I, pp. 399–403).
   An extract also in Testimonio de una Información hecha en la Audiencia de Santo
   Domingo, 24 de Diciembre de 1519, in *H.C.C.C.*, p. 27. See also his letter of
   October 12th, 1519, probably to Fonseca, in *C.D.I.A.I.*, vol. XII, p. 246. *B.D.C.*,
   ch. liv, vol. I, p. 157, gives another version. A sailor was deliberately sent by

Montejo with letters to Velázquez. This is not impossible, for Montejo, as a man of property in Cuba, would naturally be anxious to keep on the right side of the Governor. But his behaviour in Spain does not seem to lend colour to the story.

13 *Las Casas*, bk. III, ch. cxxiii, vol. 65, p. 498; *Herrera*, Dec. II, bk. V, ch. iv, p. 168.

14 *Las Casas*, bk. III, ch. cxxiv, vol. 66, p. 11.

15 *H.C.C.C.*, p. 5; *C.D.H.M.*, vol. I, p. 407; *Las Casas*, bk. III, ch. cxxii, vol. 65, p. 498.

16 *Las Casas*, bk. III, chs. cxlvii–cxlix, vol. 66, pp. 123–36.

17 *O. y B.*, bk. IV, ch. vi, vol. IV, p. 357.

18 *Sandoval*, bk. IV, par. I, vol. I, p. 159.

19 *Las Casas*, bk. III, ch. cxxi, vol. 65, p. 486.

20 Request of Cortés' father to the King in *Cuevas*—D., I, p. I. Date March 1520. *Sandoval* (bk. IV, par. X, vol. I, p. 170) says they were well received in Barcelona; but I have followed *Las Casas*, bk. III, ch. cxxiii, vol. 65, p. 499, who was more intimate with the facts and persons concerned.

21 Letter to Figueroa already quoted (*C.D.H.M.*, vol. I, p. 399).

22 Ayllón's instructions were to go to Cuba to try to prevent a break between Cortés and Velázquez, and, if the fleet had left for New Spain, to sail there himself and bring about a settlement between Cortés and Narváez (letter of Miguel de Passamonte to the King, Jan. 15th, 1520, *Gayangos*, p. 35).

23 Report of Ayllón, Aug. 30, 1520, *Gayangos*, p. 44.

24 Ayllón, *Gayangos*, pp. 46–9.

25 *B.D.C.*, ch. cx, vol. I, pp. 356–57.

26 This is told by one Diego de Avila, a witness who answers the thirty-first question in an interminable inquiry made in Cuba, July 28th, 1521, under the thumb of Velázquez (*H.C.C.C.*, pp. 163–318). The answer in question is on p. 203. The witness shows how Narváez declined the offer and answered Moteçuçuma "not to kill nor seize Cortés for they were all vassals of the King and friends and brothers"—obviously a concocted answer after Narváez' defeat; on the other hand, *B.D.C.* (ch. cx, vol. I, p. 357) seems to me to lay it on thick on Cortés' side. Truth probably lies between the two though it is clear that Narváez did present himself to Moteçuçuma as the saviour come to free him from a bad man.

27 *B.D.C.*, ch. cxi, vol. I, p. 361.

CHAPTER XXI

1 H.C. Second Letter, *Gayangos*, pp. 114–15. The "text" of Cortés' letters to D.V. given by *C.S.*, bk. IV, ch. lviii, pp. 399–400, though curiously very true to Cortés' style, may be an invention of *C.S.*, for it is much milder than Cortés' own summary to Charles V.

2 *B.D.C.*, ch. cxi, vol. I, p. 361; cf ch. ccv.

3 *B.D.C.*, ch. cxi, vol. I, pp. 361–2.

4 *B.D.C.*, ch. cxii, vol. I, p. 365.

5 *B.D.C.*, ch. cxiii, vol. I, p. 366.

6 *B.D.C.*, ch. cxiv, vol. I, p. 369; H.C. Second Letter, *Gayangos*, p. 119.

7 *B.D.C.*, ch. cxv, vol. I, p. 371.

8 *B.D.C.*, ch. cxiv, vol. I, p. 370.

9 H.C. Second Letter, *Gayangos*, p. 119.

10 H.C. Second Letter, *Gayangos*, p. 120; *B.D.C.*, ch. cxv, vol. I, p. 373; *C.S.*, bk. IV, ch. LXIX, p. 417.

11 *B.D.C.*, ch. cxv, vol. I, p. 374.

12 *B.D.C.*, ch. cxvi, vol. I, p. 378.

13 *B.D.C.*, ch. cxvii, vol. I, pp. 379–82.

14 H.C. Second Letter, *Gayangos*, p. 121. Tampecanita is a place which not even *O. y B.* has been able to identify (p. 387, vol. IV, footnote). On Olmedo's message *B.D.C.*, ch. cxvii, vol. I, p. 382.

16 The order of events is obviously wrong in the otherwise excellent Itinerary given by *Maudslay*, appendix C, vol. II, p. 322, on the strength of *O. y B.* I have followed Cortés, checked by *B.D.C.*; on a detailed analysis moreover, it will be found that the sequence adopted by Maudslay does not make sense, apart from being incompatible with both Cortés and *O. y B. C.S.*, bk. IV, chs. LXII–LXIII, p. 407, says that Motolinia thought the warning on the plot to murder him had been given to Cortés by Alvarez Chico; but *B.D.C.* is positive it was given by Olmedo and Duero. Alvarez Chico was not yet then in Narváez' camp (if my reading of events is correct), and though, in the view of *Maudslay* and *O. y B.*, he was there, he was in jail.

17 *B.D.C.*, ch. cxviii, vol. I, p. 383.

18 H.C. Second Letter, *Gayangos*, p. 123

19 *B.D.C.*, ch. cxix, vol. I, p. 385.

20 *B.D.C.*, ch. cxix, vol. I, pp. 385–6. Also a more elaborate version in *C.S.*, bk. IV, chs. LXIX–LXX, pp. 418–20.

21 *B.D.C.*, ch. cxx, vol. I, p. 387; *C.S.*, bk. IV, ch. LXXII, p. 421.

22 *B.D.C.*, ch. cxxi, vol. I, p. 393.

23 *B.D.C.*, ch. cxxii, vol. I, p. 394.

24 *Tapia* in *C.D.H.M.*, vol. II, p. 588.

25 *Tapia* in *C.D.H.M.*, vol. II, p. 589.

26 On the glow-worms, *B.D.C.*, ch. cxxii, vol. I, p. 402. The whole chapter has of course been useful for the description of these events.

CHAPTER XXII

1 *Tapia* in *C.D.H.M.*, vol. II, p. 591.

2 *B.D.C.*, ch. cxxii, vol. I, pp. 402–3.

3 *B.D.C.*, ch. cxxii, vol. I, p. 404.

4 *Loc. cit.*

5 H.C. Second Letter, *Gayangos*, p. 125.

6 *C.S.*, bk. IV, ch. xc, p. 448.

7 *C.S.*, bk. IV, chs. LXXXVII, LXXXVIII, LXXXIX, pp. 444, 446.

8 *B.D.C.*, ch. cxxiii, vol. I, pp. 405–6.

9 Bernal Díaz says these expeditions were of 120 men (ch. cxxiv, vol. I, p. 408), but Cortés says they were of 200 (H.C. Second Letter, *Gayangos*, p. 125).

10 *B.D.C.*, ch. cxxiv, vol. I, pp. 408–9.

11 *B.D.C.*, ch. cxxiv, vol. I, p. 410.

12 *Sahagún*, bk. II, chs. 4–5, and bk. XXIV, in *K.*, vol. VII, pp. 24–5, 45.

13 H.C. Second Letter, *Gayangos*, p. 125.

14 *Proceso de Alvarado*, quoted by *O. y B.*, vol. IV, p. 413 footnote.

S

15 On the numbers of the persons present, *Oviedo*, bk. XXXIII, ch. LIV, vol. III, p. 550, says 600; *Gómara*, ch. cij, fol. lj verso, "more than 600 and others say more than 1,000"; *C.S.*, bk. IV, ch. CI, p. 462, says "more than 700 (others say more than 1,000)"; *Torquemada*, bk. IV, ch. LXVI, p. 490, gives no figure.

Alvarado's rash and violent personality and the tragic effect of his action on the general pattern of the conquest have told against him more than, in my opinion, he deserves. Responsible as he remains for the blackest day of the conquest, I believe: (1) that he is innocent of the accusation, sometimes levelled against him, that he deliberately planned the massacre to despoil the victims of their jewels—an accusation which seems to me, all the evidence considered, untenable; (2) that he was right in thinking that there was a conspiracy against him and his troops. This follows from: (a) Moteçuçuma gave Cortés an ultimatum to get out; (b) the Spaniards were threatened by this ultimatum even before the Mexicans knew that Narváez' arrival had put Cortés between two fires; (c) the Spaniards were from this day on afraid of being sacrificed to the Mexican gods (*Gómara*, ch. cxiij, fol. xlviij; *C.S.*, bk. IV, ch. L, p. 383); (d) Alvarado's explanation to Cortés (*B.D.C.*, ch. cxxv, vol. I, p. 413)—to wit, that Moteçuçuma, seeing that the Spaniards would not go, even after the arrival of the ships, the lack of which had been given as a pretext by Cortés, thought best to get rid of Alvarado first, then obtain his freedom, then attack Narváez, who by then, he thought, would have beaten Cortés—sounds plausible and reasonable in the circumstances; (e) in view of the wholesale destruction of weapons which Cortés had effected, the Mexicans must have carefully re-armed, for when Alvarado struck they were ready; (f) the siege and fierce attack on Alvarado's fortress immediately upon Alvarado's attack on the teocalli shows the Mexicans were ready to attack him not, as the two victims he rescued and tortured told him, at the end of the twenty days of religious festivals, but at once; (g) Moteçuçuma's bad faith to the Spaniards—what else could the Spaniards expect of him!—is proved by "the Infante" episode, related in the text. For all these reasons, it is obvious that Alvarado not merely must be excused as having *imagined* that there was a conspiracy, but was right in *thinking* that there was a danger and a most urgent one. (3) Yet, his action could not have been worse calculated to help him out of his trouble; he did not strike at the warriors lurking in the city and in the neighbouring townships, but at the unarmed nobility who attended the religious festival; on the other hand it is difficult to see what he could have done and, moreover, he had the Cholula precedent as a guidance.

My narrative is based in particular on Juan Alvarez' answer to question 47 in *H.C.C.C.*, pp. 260–62. The Enquiry in which the answer is given was made in Santiago de Cuba on June 28th, 1521; under Diego Velázquez' thumb; the witness is a rabid opponent of Cortés whom he presents almost as selling human Mexican meat to the Tlaxcatecs. This circumstance makes his narrative on Alvarado more trustworthy, for there is little doubt that, had he been able to blacken the episode, he would have done so. Incidentally this narrative helps to settle the controversy about the date of Alvarado's onslaught, for Alvarez says it was a Wednesday, which would appear finally to fix the day on May 16th.

B.D.C. deals twice with the subject—ch. cxxv, vol. I, p. 413, and ch. ccxiii, vol. II, p. 509; *C.S.*, bk. IV, ch. xci, p. 449, and ch. ci, p. 462; in this second chapter, *C.S.* says of Alvarado: "He killed most of them, took their jewels and valuable things which they were wearing, which gave an occasion for some to think that he had caused so much destruction for greed of that wealth." This is a legend: the story told by Alvarez shows that no sooner had the deed been done than the Spaniards ran to shut themselves into the fortress (*Gómara* chs. cij, and ciij, fols. lj verso and lij). *F.A.I.*, ch. LXXXVIII, in *K.*, vol. IX, p. 300, puts the blame on the Tlaxcatecs, which may have been partly true, and on Alvarado's subconscious tendencies, which certainly played a part. *Sahagún*, bk. XII, chs. XIX and xx, in *K.*, vol. VII, p. 428, obviously transliterating a Mexican narrative, says Alvarado himself requested the Mexicans to celebrate the festivals of Uitzilpochtli; which on the face of it makes no sense, since these festivals were automatically celebrated every year. On the other hand, in spite of the anti-Spanish slant which he gets from his native sources, Sahagún says nothing of looting and speaks exclusively of the deed as a bloody onslaught without any justification whatsoever. *O. y B.*, pt. IV, bk. II, ch. IX, vol. IV, p. 410 et seq., is painstaking but, as usual, too hot-tempered to see things in their true perspective. He quotes interesting papers from Alvarado's trial. As for *Prescott's* "not an Aztec, of all that gay company, was left alive" (bk. IV, ch. VI, vol. III, p. 87), it is belied by the eyewitness herein quoted. I have not mentioned the story that Indian women had already prepared cauldrons with spices for stewing the bodies of the Spaniards though it is mentioned by both *C.S.* and *Torquemada*, and therefore probably comes from Ojeda, an eyewitness, for it does not seem to me well founded. Neither do I think likely that the Indians had arranged to trap Alvarado into the festival and had concealed arms in the teocalli to fall upon him during the festival. These are details which strike one as embroidery on the facts. Nevertheless, it is almost certain that there were armaments stored up, not hidden, in the teocalli; for the city was instantly armed, and thoroughly.

16 *B.D.C.*, ch. CXXV, vol. I, p. 412; *C.S.*, bk. IV, ch. C, p. 460.

17 *C.S.*, bk. IV, ch. XCVIII, p. 458.

18 *C.S.*, bk. IV., ch. XCIC, p. 458; *B.D.C.*, ch. CXXVIII, vol. I, p. 427.

19 *C.S.*, bk. IV, ch. XCIC, p. 459.

20 H.C. Second Letter, *Gayangos*, p. 128; *C.S.*, bk. IV, ch. XCIC, p. 459.

21 On Cortés' conversation with Alvarado, *B.D.C.*, ch. CXXV, vol. I, p. 413; on Cortés' dissimulation with Alvarado, *Gómara*, ch. CIJ, fol. lij.

22 *B.D.C.*, ch. CXXV, vol. I, p. 415.

23 Curiously enough, Cortés seems to have had a foible for Alvarado, for even after this disastrous episode, when in later days he praised his captains and soldiers to the King of Spain, he singled out for special eulogy Alvarado, Olid and Sandoval (*B.D.C.*, ch. CCVI, vol. II, p. 468).

24 *C.S.*, bk. IV, ch. XCVI, p. 454; *C.S.*, bk. IV, ch. C, p. 460.

25 H.C. Second Letter, *Gayangos*, p. 127.

CHAPTER XXIII

1 *C.S.*, bk. IV, ch. C, p. 460. *Torquemada*, bk. IV, ch. LXVIII, vol. I, p. 494, says Olmedo went the same afternoon, not the next day as in *C.S.*'s version. Also *C.S.*, bk. IV, ch. CIV, p. 464.

2 See the answer of Juan Alvarez, the witness already quoted, to question no. 50 of the interrogatory engineered by Diego Velázquez against Cortés—a question by the way in which the resentment of the gold lost is writ large: "the said Fernando Cortés refused to speak to the said Motençuma [. . .] and Motençuma sent him word again to go away from the city and that for his journey he would give him Indians to carry all he should wish by land or by sea, and nothing of any of our comrades was to remain, and the said Cortés would not answer, arguing that the city was his" (*H.C.C.C.*, p. 222). As for the facts themselves, *C.S.*, bk. IV, ch. CIV, p. 465, and *Torquemada*, bk. IV, ch. LXVIII, vol. I, p. 494.

3 *B.D.C.*, ch. CXXVI, vol. I, pp. 415–16.

4 As pointed out by *Prof. W. M. Munro* in his footnote to *Prescott*, vol. III, p. 97.

5 *B.D.C.*, ch. CXXVI, vol. I, p. 416.

6 H.C. Second Letter, *Gayangos*, p. 128.

7 *B.D.C.*, ch. cxxvi, vol. I, pp. 418, 419.

8 *B.D.C.*, ch. cxxvi, vol. I, p. 423.

9 *B.D.C.*, ch. cxxvi, vol. I, p. 424.

C.S. (bk. IV, ch. cxii, p. 477) and *Torquemada* (bk. IV, ch. lxx, vol. I, p. 497) would appear to confirm H.C.'s version (Second Letter, *Gayangos*, p. 130). Both make Moteçuçuma take the initiative through Doña Marina; but their narrative (probably from Ojeda) loses much of its authority since they make M. express views on Cuitlahuac's election wholly at variance both with the facts as known to him and with Mexican institutions. *Prescott's* imaginative description of M. in his "imperial robes" though confirmed by *C.S.* (bk. IV, ch. cxii, p. 477), "adereszado y vestido con sus paños reales," may well be a fanciful interpretation of whatever apparel M. was wearing since M. was deposed and knew it (*B.D.C.*) and had almost certainly been privy to his own deposition as a weapon against Cortés. See, however, *O. y B.*, bk. III, ch. i, vol. IV, p. 468 footnote, on the date of Cuitlahuac's accession.

Torquemada (bk. V, ch. i, vol. III, p. 122) and *C.S.* (*loc. cit.*) weave a romantic tale of deathbed, tears and embracements between M. and Cortés; on the other hand, *O. y B.* (bk. II, ch. xi, vol. IV, pp. 426-7) is led by his anti-Cortés bias to reject altogether the possibility of this last interview because he cannot admit that M. should have entrusted Cortés with the care of his three daughters, though the weight of evidence points to his having done so.

For Cuauhtemoc's outburst see *Codex Ramirez*, quoted by *O. y B.*, bk. II, ch. xi, vol. IV, p. 425.

As to M.'s actual death and its cause *Sahagún* (ch. xxiii of bk. XII) whether in the MS. version given by *Prescott* (end of ch. i of bk. V, vol. III, p. 126 footnote) or in *K.*, vol. VII, p. 431, which is less complete, throws the blame of it on the Spaniards. Prescott has already shown "the absurdity of this monstrous imputation." But it is proved false by the best of witnesses, Juan Cano, the fifth husband of the much married Tecuichpoch, later Doña Isabel, daughter of Moteçuçuma. Cano was a bitter enemy of Cortés and, as is often the case with Spaniards (for instance Las Casas), he became more pro-Indian than the Indians. Cano says definitely of his imperial father-in-law: "M. died of a stone thrown from those outside, which would not have happened had a man with a buckler not covered him, for if they had seen him, no one would have shot at him, and thus, because he was covered by the buckler and [the Indians] did not think he was there, they hit him with a stone of which he died." (Dialogue with Oviedo, *Oviedo*, bk. XXXIII, ch. liv, vol. III, p. 550.)

It is important to find a clear and concrete case in which Sahagún is at fault on the facts, for it helps to estimate his reliability. His personal honesty was above suspicion; but he did no more than transcribe the records of the natives without discussing them. The treatment of this question by *O. y B.* (bk. II, ch. xi, vol. IV, pp. 437-43, footnote) is characteristic. Conscious of his bias, he quaintly declares: "We are not moved by hatred, but by conviction." Qui s'excuse s'accuse. He overreaches himself to the point of asserting that Cacama was murdered in the same circumstances when we know directly from Cortés that he was conveyed as a prisoner out of Mexico along the Tacuba causeway. *O. y B.*'s attitude towards Cortés and Bernal Díaz, whose records on the point are of course in his way, are a pitiful example of bias. The assertion of Cortés that he had Cacama with him is dismissed with a mere: "Es absolutamente falso." Reasons: "We have already established on good authority that he had been assassinated in the barracks" (p. 446 footnote). This way of indulging one's own passions has nothing to do with history. Cortés had no qualms whatever about telling the Emperor when he killed people or did not kill them. *B.D.C.* (ch. cxxvIII, vol. I, p. 433) fully vindicates Cortés to the effect that Cacama died on the causeway.

10 H.C. Second Letter, *Gayangos*, pp. 130-32; *B.D.C.*, ch. cxxvI, vol. I, p. 421.

11 *C.S.*, bk. IV, ch. cxI, p. 475.

12 H.C. Second Letter, *Gayangos*, p. 133.

13 H.C. Second Letter, *Gayangos*, p. 134. Here again *O. y B.* betrays his bias even in this unimportant detail: "if the horsemen," he says, "passed all by the same place, either they all leapt or they all passed by the bridge" (bk. II, ch. xI, vol. IV, p. 436). He overlooks the fact that all the horsemen had fallen into the water.

14 *C.S.*, bk. IV, ch. cxIx, pp. 487-8, says that Cortés asked Botello's advice in public; this is not likely because: (a) *B.D.C.* (ch. cxxvIII, vol. I, p. 428) says nothing of the kind; (b) Gómara (ch. cvij, fol. liiij verso), neither; (c) the impression left by *B.D.C.*'s narrative about Botello's authority does not warrant such a formal consultation; (d) public and so to speak official appeals to necromancers or astrologers were not in keeping with Cortés' devout ways. But it is quite possible that, having made up his mind to leave that very night, he quietly used Botello's influence on his rank and file. There is a faint suggestion of this in Gómara, and it would be, of course, quite in keeping with his character.

15 H.C. Second Letter, *Gayangos*, p. 135.

See also seventh question in *Segunda Probanza de Lejalde* (*C.D.H.M.*, vol. I, p. 423); *Carta del Ejército de Cortés al Emperador* (*C.D.H.M.*, vol. I, p. 429). In all these documents Cortés screens himself behind his men for the two reasons pointed out in the text.

16 *B.D.C.*, ch. cxvIII, vol. I, p. 429.

Und das teuflische Metall
War nicht bloss der armen Seele
Sondern auch dem Leib verderblich:

three lines in an otherwise deplorable poem, "Vitzliputzli," by Heinrich Heine (*Gedichte*, vol. III, p. 97, Hamburg, 1851).

17 *B.D.C.*, ch. cxxvIII, vol. I, p. 428.

18 *B.D.C.*, ch. cxxvIII, vol. I, p. 431.

19 H.C. Second Letter, *Gayangos*, p. 136; *B.D.C.*, ch. cxxvIII, vol. I, p. 432.

20 On this point, and on that of the numbers missing, *O. y B.* is excellent. He is always at best in such as casualties, dates, calendars—when human passions are not involved. (Bk. II, ch. xI, vol. IV, pp. 455-6.)

21 *B.D.C.*, ch. cxxvIII, vol. I, p. 434.

22 H.C. Second Letter, *Gayangos*, p. 138.

23 *B.D.C.*, ch. cxxvIII, vol. I, p. 436; H.C. Second Letter, *Gayangos*, p. 139.

24 *B.D.C.*, ch. cxxvIII, vol. I, p. 438.

25 *B.D.C.*, ch. cxxvIII, vol. I, p. 440.

CHAPTER XXIV

1 H.C. Second Letter, *Gayangos*, p. 142; *C.S.*, bk. V, ch. Iv, p. 515.

2 *B.D.C.* says nothing on this episode. But as it is found both in *C.S.* (bk. V, ch. II, p. 512) and in *Torquemada* (bk. IV, ch. LXXv, vol. I, p. 512) it is practically certain that it comes from Ojeda, an eyewitness of the events.

3 *B.D.C.*, ch. cxxvIII, vol. I, p. 438.

4 H.C. Second Letter, *Gayangos*, p. 141; *C.S.*, bk. IV, ch. cxxxiv, p. 509.

5 *Torquemada*, bk. IV, ch. lxxv, vol. I, p. 503. *C.S.*, bk. V, ch. iii, p. 513; ch. vii, p. 519; ch. viii, p. 521. *B.D.C.*, ch. cxxix, vol. I, p. 442.

6 *B.D.C.*, ch. cxxxiv, vol. I, p. 464.

7 *C.S.*, bk. V, ch. ix, p. 522, says the Tepeaca campaign was undertaken at Maxix-catzin's request.

8 *B.D.C.*, ch. cxxix, vol. I, pp. 444-5; H.C. Second Letter, *Gayangos*, p. 142.

9 H.C. Second Letter, *Gayangos*, pp. 142-3.

10 *C.S.*, bk. V, ch. xii, p. 528.

11 H.C. Second Letter, *Gayangos*, p. 144.

12 *O. y B.*, bk. II, ch. xii, vol. IV, p. 477, quotes the following: Juan de Mansilla, Rodrigo de Castañeda, Bernaldino Vázquez de Tapia, Juan Tirado, all witnesses in Residencia contra Cortés. He would have been delighted to know yet another one: answers to questions 55, 57, 58, 59 in *Información, etc.* (*H.C.C.C.*, pp. 236-7). See also *Torquemada*, bk. IV, ch. lxix, vol. I, p. 495, and *C.S.*, bk. IV, ch. cviii, p. 471, who in almost identical terms, evidently borrowed from Ojeda, record how, after the storming of the teocalli, the Tlaxcatecs and Cempoalese auxiliaries ate the Mexican warrors for dinner.

13 *O. y B.*, bk. II, ch. xii, vol. IV, p. 479; H.C. Second Letter, *Gayangos*, p. 145.

14 H.C. Second Letter, *Gayangos*, p. 142.

15 *C.S.*, bk. V, ch. xix, p. 536, says Dávila was also a member of this expedition. Both were bold captains. This brings Cortés' decision into sharper relief. *B.D.C.*, *loc. cit.* denies Gómara's assertion that Cortés had to take the matter in hand personally, but Gómara is vindicated by Cortés himself. Gómara, by the way, gives three captains: Tapia, Ordas, Olid.
　　Gómara, ch. cxiij, fol. lvij verso; H.C. Second Letter, *Gayangos*, p. 147.
　　B.D.C.. ch. cxxxiii, vol. I, p. 455; H.C. Second Letter, *Gayangos*, p. 145.

16 Itzocan becomes Oçucar in *B.D.C.*, ch. cxxxii, vol. I, p. 457; Izzucan in H.C. Second Letter, *Gayangos*, p. 151. Now Izúcar de Matamoros in the State of Puebla (*O. y B.*, vol. IV, p. 487, footnote iii).

17 *B.D.C.*, ch. cxxxi, vol. I, p. 453.

18 *B.D.C.*, ch. cxxxiii, vol. I, pp. 459-62.

19 H.C. Second Letter, *Gayangos*, p. 141.

20 Documents in *C.D.H.M.*, vol. I, pp. 411, 421.

21 *C.D.H.M.*, vol. I, pp. 427-36.

22 *B.D.C.*, ch. cxxxvi, vol. I, p. 471.

23 H.C. Second Letter, *Gayangos*, p. 156.

24 *Loc. cit.*

25 *B.D.C.*, ch. cxxxvi, vol. I, p. 470.

26 *B.D.C.*, ch. cxxxvi, vol. I, p. 472.

27 *B.D.C.*, ch. cxxxv, vol. I, pp. 467-9.

28 *B.D.C.*, ch. cxxxvi, vol. I, p. 471.

29 *C.S.*, bk. V, ch. xxx, p. 548.

30 *C.D.H.M.*, vol. I, p. 445.

CHAPTER XXV

1 *Torquemada*, bk. IV, ch. LXXIII, vol. I, p. 510.

2 *O. y B.*, bk. II, ch. XII, vol. IV, p. 469.

3 I follow *O. y B.* (bk. II, ch. XII, vol. IV, pp. 468, 493), usually reliable in these matters, rather than *Torquemada* (bk. IV, ch. LXXIV, vol. I, p. 512), who gives him but forty days' reign. Juan Cano, in his talk with *Oviedo* (bk. XXXIII, ch. LIV, vol. III, p. 548) gives him sixty days.

4 *O. y B.*, bk. II, ch. XII, vol. IV, p. 492.

5 *C.S.*, bk. V, ch. XXXII, p. 552.

6 Cortés (H.C. Second Letter, *Gayangos*, p. 153) speaks of two sons of Moteçuçuma, both unfit to reign. But Juan Cano, who was one of the numerous husbands of Tecuichpoch, or Doña Isabel, M.'s daughter, denies this explicitly in his dialogue with Oviedo (*Oviedo*, bk. XXXIII, ch. LIV, vol. III, p. 549). This is indirectly confirmed by *B.D.C.*, ch. XCV, vol. I, p. 307.

7 *B.D.C.*, ch. CXXX, vol. I, p. 452.

8 *B.D.C.*, ch. CXXXVI, vol. I, p. 476.

9 H.C. Third Letter, *Gayangos*, p. 166.

10 H.C. Third Letter, *Gayangos*, p. 167.

11 H.C. Third Letter, *Gayangos*, p. 169.

12 H.C. Third Letter, *Gayangos*, p. 172.

13 H.C. Third Letter, *Gayangos*, p. 177; *F.A.I.*, ch. XCI, in *K.*, vol. IX, p. 306.

14 H.C. Third Letter, *Gayangos*, p. 173.

15 H.C. Third Letter, *Gayangos*, p. 175.

16 *B.D.C.*, ch. CXXXVII, vol. I, p. 486.

17 H.C. Third Letter, *Gayangos*, pp. 177-8.

18 H.C. Third Letter, *Gayangos*, pp. 182-3.

19 H.C. Third Letter, *Gayangos*, p. 183; *B.D.C.*, ch. CXL, vol. II, pp. 8, 9.

20 H.C. Third Letter, *Gayangos*, p. 184.

21 *O. y B.*, bk. III, ch. II, vol. IV, p. 526.

22 *B.D.C.*, ch. CXLI, vol. II, p. 12. *Torquemada* (bk. IV, ch. LXXXVI, vol. I, p. 534) explains this as the result of Cortés' hint to Ojeda and Márquez to take from the Tlaxcatecs the gold they had looted while leaving them the cotton wraps. *C.S.* (chs. LXXVIII and LXIX of bk. V, pp. 608-9) confirms this with vivid details from a note given him by Ojeda. This gives the version considerable force, even though it flatly contradicts *B.D.C.* It confirms Cortés' tendency to let his troops reap a harvest wherever they can. It must also be remembered that Cortés was never very eager to enter Mexico with a great body of Tlaxcatecs, and though he needed them at first, he was oversupplied with auxiliaries soon after he settled in Tetzcuco.

23 H.C. Third Letter, *Gayangos*, pp. 187-8.

24 *B.D.C.*, ch. CXLIV, vol. II, p. 33.

25 *B.D.C.*, ch. CXLIV, vol. II, p. 38.

26 *B.D.C.*, ch. CXLIII, vol. II, p. 31.

27 *B.D.C.*, ch. CXL, vol. II, p. 11.

28 H.C. Third Letter, *Gayangos*, p. 193.

29 H.C. Third Letter, *Gayangos*, p. 196.

30 *B.D.C.*, ch. cxli, vol. II, p. 42. *O. y B.* (bk. III, ch. vi, vol. I, p. 494) says that Cuauhnauac means "near the trees" or "near the forest." Such is also the opinion of Mr. James Cooper Clark in *C.M.*

31 *B.D.C.*, ch. cxlv, vol. II, p. 45.

32 *B.D.C.*, ch. cxlv, vol. II, p. 50.

33 H.C. Third Letter, *Gayangos*, p. 201.

34 See quotation in *B.D.C.*, ch. cxlv, vol. II, p. 50; also p. 51, and H.C. Third Letter, *Gayangos*, p. 201.

35 The scene is pictured by *B.D.C.*, ch. cxlv, vol. II, p. 54.

36 Here is the Spanish text given by *B.D.C.*, *loc. cit.*:

> En Tacuba está Cortés
> Con su escuadrón esforzado.
> Triste estaba y muy penoso,
> Triste y con gran cuidado,
> Una mano en la mejilla
> Y la otra en el costado.

As for Las Casas, here is the text: "Dizese q estando metiendo a espada los cinco o seis mil hombres en el patio, estaua catando el Capita de los Españoles: mira Nero de Tarpeya a Roma como se ardía: gritos dan niños y viejos, y el de nada se dolía." (*Las Casas—D.*, folio 18.)

37 *B.D.C.*, ch. cxlv, vol. II, pp. 54–5; H.C. Third Letter, *Gayangos*, pp. 202–3.

38 *B.D.C.*, ch. cxlvi, vol. II, p. 56.

CHAPTER XXVI

1 I follow Cortés (H.C. Third Letter, *Gayangos*, p. 208) rather than *B.D.C.* (ch. cxlviii, vol. II, p. 61), who speaks of twelve crossbowmen and musketeers.

2 *B.D.C.*, ch. cl, vol. II, p. 69; H.C. Third Letter, *Gayangos*, p. 208.

3 Cortés says nothing on this episode. *B.D.C.* attributes Xicotencatl's flight to political ambition (ch. cl, vol. II, p. 68); *Torquemada*, to a complicated set of circumstances including love jealousy (bk. IV, ch. lxxxx, vol. I, p. 542).

4 H.C. Third Letter, *Gayangos*, p. 215.

5 H.C. Third Letter, *Gayangos*, p. 222.

6 *Torquemada*, bk. IV, ch. lxxxx, vol. I, p. 541; *B.D.C.*, ch. cli, vol. II, p. 78.

7 *Torquemada*, bk. IV, ch. lxxxx, vol. I, p. 542.

8 H.C. Third Letter, *Gayangos*, p. 211.

9 H.C. Third Letter, *Gayangos*, p. 212.

10 H.C. Third Letter, *Gayangos*, p. 213.

11 H.C. Third Letter, *Gayangos*, pp. 216–19.

12 *B.D.C.*, ch. cli, vol. II, p. 81.

13 H.C. Third Letter, *Gayangos*, p. 220.

14 *B.D.C.*, ch. cli, vol. II, p. 89.

15 H.C. Third Letter, *Gayangos*, p. 224.

16 *B.D.C.*, ch. cli, vol. II, p. 89.

17 *B.D.C.*, ch. cli, vol. II, p. 84; H.C. Third Letter, *Gayangos*, p. 227; *C.S.*, bk. V, ch. cxlvii, p. 679.

18 *C.S.*, bk. V, ch. cxlviii, p. 680.

19 *Torquemada*, bk. IV, ch. xciii, vol. I, pp. 552-3.

20 H.C. Third Letter, *Gayangos*, p. 228.

21 H.C. Third Letter, *Gayangos*, p. 232; *B.D.C.*, ch. clii, vol. II, p. 94.

22 H.C. Third Letter, *loc. cit.*; *B.D.C.*, ch. clii, vol. II, p. 95.

23 *B.D.C.*, ch. cli, vol. II, p. 102; H.C. Third Letter, *Gayangos*, p. 234; *Sahagún*, bk. II, ch. vii, p. 26, and ch. xxvi, p. 55, in *K.*, vol. VII.

24 H.C. Third Letter, *Gayangos*, p. 246.

25 H.C. Third Letter, *Gayangos*, p. 240.

26 *B.D.C.*, ch. cliii, vol. II, p. 107.

27 H.C. Third Letter, *Gayangos*, pp. 235, 237.

28 H.C. Third Letter, *Gayangos*, pp. 240-41.

29 *Loc. cit.*

30 H.C. Third Letter, *Gayangos*, p. 244.

31 H.C. Third Letter, *Gayangos*, p. 245.

32 *B.D.C.*, ch. cliii, vol. II, p. 109; H.C. Third Letter, *Gayangos*, p. 247.

33 H.C. Third Letter, *Gayangos*, p. 248.

34 *B.D.C.*, ch. clv, vol. II, p. 123.

35 H.C. Third Letter, *Gayangos*, p. 250.

36 H.C. Third Letter, *Gayangos*, p. 254.

37 *Loc. cit.*

38 *B.D.C.*, ch. clvi, vol. II, p. 134.

39 *B.D.C.*, ch. cliv, vol. II, pp. 114-15.

40 *B.D.C.*, ch. cliv, vol. II, p. 116.

41 H.C. Third Letter, *Gayangos*, p. 250.

42 H.C. Third Letter, *Gayangos*, p. 251.

43 H.C. Third Letter, *Gayangos*, p. 253; *B.D.C.*, ch. clv, vol. II, p. 123.

44 *B.D.C.*, ch. clv, vol. II, p. 120.

45 H.C. Third Letter, *Gayangos*, p. 255.

46 H.C. Third Letter, *Gayangos*, p. 256.

47 H.C. Third Letter, *Gayangos*, p. 257; *B.D.C.*, ch. clvi, vol. II, p. 128.

48 *B.D.C.*, ch. clvi, vol. II, p. 129.

CHAPTER XXVII

1 H.C. Third Letter, *Gayangos*, p. 233.

2 *B.D.C.*, ch. clvii, vol. II, p. 137.

3 H.C. Third Letter, *Gayangos*, p. 282.

4 *B.D.C.*, ch. clvi, vol. II, pp. 132-3.

5 *Torquemada*, bk. IV, ch. ciii, vol. I, p. 574.

6 *Torquemada*, bk. IV, ch. cii, vol. I, p. 572.

7 H.C. Third Letter, *Gayangos*, p. 258.

8 *B.D.C.*, ch. clvii, vol. II, p. 142.

9 *Torquemada*, bk. IV, ch. xcvi, vol. I, p. 558.

10 *B.D.C.*, ch. cciv, vol. II, p. 440.

s*

11 *Torquemada*, bk. IV, ch. CIII, vol. I, p. 574. On Cuauhtemoc's confessions as well as on the details of his torture, in confirmation of the views put forward in the text, see also: *Torquemada*, *loc. cit.*; *Gómara*, ch. cxiiij, fol. lxxij; *C.S.*, bk. VI, ch. II, p. 746; *Herrera*, Dec. III, bk. II, ch. VIII, p. 69 (his text is identical with Torquemada's); *B.D.C.*, ch. CLVII, vol. II, p. 138.

12 *B.D.C.*, ch. CLVI, vol. II, p. 130. *Prescott* (vol. IV, p. 102, footnote) says: "This piece of pedantry savours much more of the old chronicler than his commander." I beg to differ. The old story was sure to come from the well stocked memory of the Salamanca student. Bernal Díaz was too ignorant to think of it.

13 H.C. Fourth Letter, *Gayangos*, p. 311.

14 *C.S.*, bk. IV, ch. VII, p. 753.

15 *Loc. cit.* H.C. Fourth Letter, *Gayangos*, p. 312.

16 *B.D.C.*, ch. CLVII, vol. II, p. 144.

17 H.C. Third Letter, *Gayangos*, p. 261, and Fourth Letter, *Gayangos*, p. 277.

18 H.C. Fourth Letter, *Gayangos*, p. 308.

19 *C.C.S.M.*, ch. XXIV, p. 296.

20 H.C. Third Letter, *Gayangos*, p. 271.

21 H.C. Fourth Letter, *Gayangos*, p. 322.

22 H.C. Third Letter, *Gayangos*, p. 263.

23 H.C. Third Letter, *Gayangos*, p. 269.

24 Official documents on Tapia's mission in *C.D.H.M.*, vol. I, p. 452, also *C.D.I.A.I.*, vol. XXVI, p. 30. From these documents we gather that Tapia's arrival took place on or about Dec. 2nd, 1521. Narrative in H.C. Third Letter, *Gayangos*, p. 263; *B.D.C.*, ch. CLVIII, vol. II, p. 145 et seq.; *Herrera*, Dec. III, bk. III, ch. XVI, p. 130; *Oviedo*, bk. XXXIII, ch. XXXII, vol. III, p. 429.

25 H.C. Third Letter, *Gayangos*, p. 263.

26 H.C. Fourth Letter, *Gayangos*, pp. 281-6. *Oviedo* (bk. XXXIII, ch. XXXV, vol. III, p. 442) denies that the Admiral ever thought of such a conspiracy.

27 Registro del Oro, joyas y otras cosas que ha de ir a España en el navio Santa María de la Rábida, su maestre Juan Baptista (1522). *C.D.I.A.I.*, pp. 253-68 and in particular 265. *B.D.C.*, ch. CLIX, vol. II, p. 157.

28 *B.D.C.*, ch. CLIX, vol. II, p. 158.

29 The agents called at the Azores, where Quiñones lost his life in a brawl (*Prescott*, bk. VII, ch. I, vol. IV, p. 138; *B.D.C.*, ch. CLIX, vol. II, p. 160). As against this version *Herrera*, Dec. III, bk. IV, chs. I (p. 138), III (p. 143) and particularly XX (p. 183) seem to me to carry more authority in the sense of the version adopted in the text.

30 *Herrera*, *loc. cit.*

CHAPTER XXVIII

1 *C.D.I.A.I.*, vol. XXVI, pp. 59, 65.

2 H.C. Fourth Letter, *Gayangos*, p. 279; *B.D.C.*, ch. CLX, vol. II, p. 172.

3 H.C. Fourth Letter, *Gayangos*, p. 281.

4 *C.D.I.A.I.*, vol. XXVI, p. 69.

5 *Alamán*, vol. I, p. 177. Emperor's Instructions in *C.D.I.A.I.*, vol. XXIII, p. 353 (quotation, p. 357); also partly in a copy made on 16-VI-49, published in *C.D.I.A.I.*, vol. XII, p. 213. The Instructions themselves are dated 26-VI-23. H.C. Letter to Charles V dated Tenustitán (Mexico), Oct. 15th, 1524, discussing

the Emperor's instructions, *C.D.H.M.*, vol. I, p. 470, or *Gayangos*, p. 325. Ordenanzas of March 20th, 1524, in *C.D.I.A.I.*, vol. XXVI, p. 135, or *Alamán*, vol. I, app. II, p. 105.

6 I have based my narrative on a critical use of *B.D.C.* (several passages but particularly ch. CLX, vol. II, pp. 169-71) and on the statements of the witnesses in the Enquiry of February, 1529 (*C.D.I.A.I.*, vol. XXVI, pp. 298-352). On H.C.'s mourning, *B.D.C.*, ch. CXCV, vol. II, p. 382.

7 *B.D.C.*, ch. CLXII, vol. II, p. 185.

8 *B.D.C.*, ch. CLVIII, vol. II, p. 149.

9 *B.D.C.*, ch. CLVIII, vol. II, p. 148.

10 H.C. Fourth Letter, *Gayangos*, p. 290.

11 *B.D.C.*, ch. CLXII, vol. II, p. 168; H.C. Fourth Letter, *Gayangos*, pp. 290-91.

12 *C.D.I.A.I.*, vol. XXVI, p. 71. The letter is dated Valladolid, April 24th, 1523.

13 *B.D.C.*, ch. CLXII, vol. II, p. 181.

14 Better than in H.C. Fourth Letter, *Gayangos*, pp. 290 et seq., or even than in *B.D.C.*, ch. CLXII, vol. II, pp. 176-94, this curious episode should be studied in the legal documents reproduced in *C.D.I.A.I.*, vol. XXVI, pp. 77-120. The letter from Garay to Cortés is in the same volume, p. 131.

15 *B.D.C.*, ch. CLXII, vol. II, p. 185.

16 *B.D.C.*, ch. CLXII, vol. II, p. 186.

17 See *C.D.I.A.I.*, vol. XXVI, pp. 111-13, for curious examples of the indignities and ill-treatment which Garay inflicted on his men.

18 H.C. Fourth Letter, *Gayangos*, p. 299. *B.D.C.*, ch. CLXII, vol. II, p. 186.

19 "Y se descubrirán hartos secretos" (H.C. Fourth Letter, *Gayangos*, p. 306). On Colón and the secrets of nature: *C.C.S.M.*, ch. v, p. 44.

20 H.C. Fourth Letter, *Gayangos*, p. 307.

21 H.C. Fourth Letter, *Gayangos*, p. 315. The mention of 1525 instead of 1524 is a misprint.

22 "Saber el secreto de la costa que está por descubrir entre el río de Pánuco y la Florida [. . .] y de allí la costa de la dicha Florida por la parte del norte hasta llegar a los Bacallaos" (H.C. Fourth Letter, *Gayangos*, p. 314).

23 H.C. Fourth Letter, *Gayangos*, p. 288.

24 H.C. Fourth Letter, *Gayangos*, p. 306.

25 H.C. Fourth Letter, *Gayangos*, p. 316.

26 H.C. Fourth Letter, *Gayangos*, p. 317; *B.D.C.*, ch. CLXX, vol. II, p. 259.

27 *B.D.C.*, ch. CLXVIII, vol. II, p. 234, and ch. CLXX, vol. II, p. 260.

28 H.C. Covering Letter of Oct. 15th, 1524, *Gayangos*, p. 335.

29 H.C. *loc. cit.*, *Gayangos*, p. 338.

30 H.C. *loc. cit.*, *Gayangos*, pp. 333-4.

31 H.C. *loc. cit.*, *Gayangos*, p. 331.

32 H.C. *loc. cit.*, *Gayangos*, p. 321.

33 H.C. *loc. cit.*, *Gayangos*, pp. 319-20.

34 See Don José Fernando Ramírez in *C.D.H.M.*, vol. I, p. xlv, in particular the footnote, based on *Torquemada*. He might have added in favour of this date that it is also the one given by *Mendieta*, ch. XI, p. 208, the best authority and the one from whom Torquemada no doubt took his. Cf. "Vno destos Criados de Cortés, que fueron a este recibimiento, era Juan de Villagomez, de quien el

Venerable Padre Frai Geronimo de Mendieta, tuvo esta Relación, y yo la saqué de sus escritos" (*Torquemada*, bk. XV, ch. x, vol. III, p. 20).

35 The narrative is based on *Mendieta*, ch. XII, pp. 210–13 (from whom *Torquemada* took his narrative), and *B.D.C.*, ch. CLXXI, vol. II, p. 262.

CHAPTER XXIX

1 H.C. Fifth Letter, *Gayangos*, p. 396; *B.D.C.*, ch. CLXXIV, vol. II, p. 276

2 H.C. Covering Letter of Oct. 15th, 1524, *Gayangos*, p. 337.

3 H.C. *loc. cit.*

4 *B.D.C.*, ch. CLXXIV, vol. II, p. 280.

5 *B.D.C.*, ch. CLXXII, vol. II, p. 266.

6 *B.D.C.*, ch. CLXXIV, vol. II, p. 278.

7 *B.D.C.*, ch. CLXXIV, vol. II, p. 277.

8 *B.D.C.*, ch. CLXXIV, vol. II, p. 279.

9 Memoria de lo ocurrido en Mexico desde la salida de Hernán Cortés hasta la muerte de Rodrigo de Paz, 1526, by an anonymous writer (*Gayangos*, p. 382). H.C. Fifth Letter, *Gayangos*, pp. 397–8.

10 *B.D.C.*, ch. CLXXIV, vol. II, p. 279.

11 *B.D.C.*, ch. CLXXV, vol. II, p. 282.

12 H.C. Fifth Letter, *Gayangos*, p. 399.

13 The passage on the bridges of Cortés comes from *B.D.C.*, ch. CLXXVIII, vol. II, p. 203. For the rest of the narrative *B.D.C.*'s chapters from CLXXIV onwards, and H.C. Fifth Letter, *Gayangos*. See also *Means*, especially ch. III, p. 24 et seq.

14 "Muy abundosa de mantenimiento y de mucha miel" (H.C. Fifth Letter, *Gayangos*, p. 421).

15 Cortés calls him Mexicalcingo, which seems to have been the name of his country of origin (*F.A.I.—R.H.*, in *K.*, vol. IX, p. 439).

16 *F.A.I.—R.H.*, in *K.*, IX, p. 439. Cortés and Bernal Díaz call him by his title as if it were his name.

17 "Y a los otros solté porque no parescia que tenian mas culpa de habelles oido, aunque aquello bastaba para merecer una muerte" (H.C. Fifth Letter, *Gayangos*, p. 421). It has, nevertheless, been counted against Cortés that he had Cuauhtemoc hanged as well as many others whom he did not hang, mostly because of a phrase in Bernal Díaz: "and this death inflicted on them was most unjust and all of us thought it wrong." But Bernal Díaz here is not thinking but feeling. In the preceding page he has recorded how Cuauhtemoc confessed that there had been a conspiracy; here he says he had pity on Cuauhtemoc and on his cousin and records how they often had honoured him on the way, which had obviously flattered his naïve vanity.

The facts are so clear that I think it hardly necessary to enter into the merits of this episode. There is a good summary of the strange opinions and inaccuracies to which it has given rise in *Pereyra*, pp. 365–72.

See also *B.D.C.*, ch. CLXXVII, vol. II, pp. 295–6; *Gómara*, ch. clxviij, fol. lxxxv verso; *Prescott*, bk. VII, ch. III, vol. IV, pp. 183–8, who misinterprets B.D.C. badly. *F.A.I.—R.H.*, in *K.*, vol. IX, p. 439, spins a wonderful yarn which has no relation to the facts.

18 *B.D.C.*, ch. CLXXVII, vol. II, p. 297.

19 H.C. Fifth Letter, *Gayangos*, p. 433.

20 H.C. Fifth Letter, *Gayangos*, p. 437.

21 H.C. Fifth Letter, *Gayangos*, pp. 457–65. *B.D.C.*, ch. CLXXIII, vol. II, pp. 271–6.

22 *B.D.C.*, ch. CLXXIX, vol. II, p. 309.

23 *B.D.C.*, ch. CLXXXV, vol. II, p. 329.

24 H.C. Fifth Letter, *Gayangos*, pp. 470–71.

25 H.C. Fifth Letter, *Gayangos*, p. 479.

26 *B.D.C.*, ch. CLXXXV, vol. II, p. 332.

27 *Loc. cit.*

28 *B.D.C.*, ch. CLXXXVIII, vol. II, p. 343.

29 The narrative is based mostly on a very impartial account written by an eye-witness and published in *Gayangos*, p. 381; on the report of the Municipal Council of Tenochtitlán, dated Feb. 20th, 1526 (*Gayangos*, p. 341); *B.D.C.*, chs. CLXXXV, vol. II, pp. 329–37, and CLXXXVIII, vol. II, pp. 341–5; *Gómara*, chs. clxij and clxiij, fol. lxxxij; *Herrera*, Dec. III, bk. VI, chs. XI and XII, pp. 247–55; and of course the Fifth Letter in *Gayangos*. A report by Diego de Ocaña to the Royal Council of the Indies (*Gayangos*, pp. 351–67) is an important if unreliable document, for Ocaña seems to have been the evil spirit behind Salazar.

30 *Herrera*, Déc. III, bk. VI, ch. II, p. 225.

31 *Herrera*, Déc. III, bk. V, ch. III, p. 193.

32 *Herrera*, Déc. III, bk. VII, ch. IV, p. 272.

33 *Herrera*, Déc. III, bk. VIII, ch. VII, p. 305; *B.D.C.*, ch. CLXVIII, vol. II, pp. 234–7; *Herrera*, Déc. III, bk. VII, ch. IV, p. 273.

34 *Herrera*, Déc. III, bk. VIII, ch. XIV, p. 321.

35 H.C. Fifth Letter, *Gayangos*, p. 479; *B.D.C.*, ch. CLXXXVIII, vol. II, p. 342.

36 The narrative comes from *B.D.C.*, *loc. cit.* and ch. CXC, p. 350. The quotation comes from H.C. Fifth Letter, *Gayangos*, p. 480.

CHAPTER XXX

1 H.C. Fifth Letter, *Gayangos*, pp. 480–82.

2 *B.D.C.*, ch. CXCI, vol. II, p. 355.

3 *B.D.C.*, ch. CXCI, vol. II, p. 356.

4 H.C. to his agent Núñez (*C.D.H.M.*, vol. II, p. 43); to the Bishop of Osma, January 12th, 1527 (*Gayangos*, p. 495), and to Charles V, Sept. 3d, 1526 (*C.D.I.A.I.*, vol. XII, pp. 483–4).

5 H.C. Fifth Letter, *Gayangos*, p. 482; H.C. to Bishop of Osma, *Gayangos*, p. 495; *B.D.C.*, ch. CXCIV, vol. II, p. 372.

6 H.C. to Charles V, Sept. 11th, 1526, *C.D.I.A.I.*, vol. XII, pp. 476–9.

7 *B.D.C.*, ch. CXC, vol. II, p. 353.

8 As might be expected, these accusations will not be found in the two "Instructions" given to Ponce de León, inserted in *C.D.I.A.I.*, vol. XXIII, pp. 368, 382; but they may be inferred from a document drafted at H.C.'s request on may 8th, 1529 (*C.D.I.A.I.*, vol. XXVII, p. 5; also in *Herrera*, Déc. III, bk. VIII, ch. xv, p. 322); they can also be read in the "Secret chapters to the Instruction given to the Licentiate Luis Ponce de León in *C.D.I.A.I.*, vol. XXVI, p. 376. Quotation from H.C. Fifth Letter, *Gayangos*, p. 484.

9 *Alamán*, vol. I, p. 240.

10 Ocaña's letter, Sept. 7th, 1526, *C.D.I.A.I.*, vol. XIII, p. 355.

11 H.C. to his agent Núñez, *C.D.H.M.*, vol. II, p. 44; *B.D.C.*, ch. cxcIV, vol. II, pp. 372, 374, and *Alamán*, vol. I, p. 248. Also *Herrera*, Déc. III, bk. IX, ch. vIII, p. 343.

12 *Herrera*, Déc. III, bk. IX, ch. vIII, p. 343; *B.D.C.*, ch. cxcIV, vol. II, p. 378, ch. cxcIII, p. 370.

13 H.C. Letter to his father, Sept. 26th, 1526, in *Cuevas*, p. 29. Compare with Fifth Letter, *Gayangos*, pp. 484-9. It is only fair to point out that in the language of the period the word *estados* may well mean estates or worldly situations.

14 H.C. Fifth Letter, *Gayangos*, pp. 487-8; H.C. to his father dated Huejocingo, Nov. 24th, 1527, in *Cuevas*, p. 33; *Herrera*, Déc. IV, bk. III, ch. vII, p. 74.

15 *Herrera*, Déc. IV, bk. II, ch. I, p. 28; *B.D.C.*, ch. cxcIV, vol. II, p. 374; document dated February 26th, 1527, in *H.C.C.C.*, p. 361; on the new Audience, *Alamán*, vol. I, p. 251; document, April 5th, 1528, in *C.D.I.A.I.*, vol. XXVI, p. 280.

16 *B.D.C.*, ch. cxcIV, vol. II, p. 378. Both *C.D.I.A.I.* (vol. XXXII, p. 444) and *H.C.C.C.* (p. 397) show that the editors of these collections mistook this Doña Marina, Estrada's wife, for Doña Marina the Indian interpreter; nor do I find anything in *Cuevas* (pp. 91, 93 and note) to dispel the confusion, due only to the coincidence in the Christian name. Estrada's wife belonged evidently to the La Caballería family, a converso family strongly entrenched in the household of the Kings of Aragón from which her husband had been transferred to his position in New Spain.

17 The date of Cortés' homecoming has given rise to so much confusion that it deserves a little attention. The sources are:
Herrera, Déc. IV, bk. IV, ch. I, p. 72, who says that in May, 1528, Cortés was already in Castile and had seen Pizarro;
Gómara, ch. clxxx, fol. xciij verso, who says that H.C. arrived in Spain at the end of 1528 while the Court was in Toledo;
B.D.C., ch. cxcV, vol. II, p. 383, who says that the crossing lasted forty-two days, and that H.C. arrived in Castile in December, 1527 (an obvious slip for 1528);
Sandoval, bk. XVI, par. XXVI, vol. I, p. 895, who says that in 1528 towards the end, while the Emperor was in Toledo, H.C. arrived in that city.
On the preceding authorities—
Prescott, bk. VII, ch. IV, vol. IV, p. 213: "Cortés [. . .] entered the little port of Palos in May, 1528." To which Prescott's editor Munro adds: "Sandoval (Carlos V, bk. XVI, par. XXVI, I, 895) and Gómara (hist. Mexico, p. 283) make Cortés to have landed in the latter part of the year 1528."
Alamán, vol. II, p. 22, following *Herrera* and *Prescott* against *B.D.C.*, gives May, 1528, as the date of arrival.
The confusion comes from the mixing up of two arrivals: in Spain and at Court. Cortés arrived in Spain (Palos) in May; at Court (Toledo) in December. *Herrera* speaks of the first arrival; *Sandoval*, *Gómara* and *B.D.C.* (when giving dates) of the second. The Emperor was in Toledo on November 10th (*Sandoval*, vol. I, p. 892) and in Madrid on Nov. 11th (vol. II, p. 28); but as he was in Toledo till March 7th, 1529, when he left for Aragón (*Sandoval*, vol. II, p. 25), we may take it that Charles was in Toledo for the end of the year.
Cortés left San Juan de Ulúa on March 7th; this has been proved by *F.C.*, p. 34, on the strength of Villagómez, a member of H.C.'s household, and it is confirmed by the instructions left by Cortés to his steward Santa Cruz for the time of his absence in Spain, which are dated March 6th, 1528 (*Cuevas*, p. 41). As *B.D.C.* records that the crossing took forty-two days, landing took place on or about April 18th.
Moreover we know that Cortés refused to go to Seville (*Herrera*, see note 23 below); probably because the Audience against him was precisely then in Seville on the point of starting for New Spain, for it arrived in December.

Finally I believe *Prescott* has been led astray by a hasty reading of *Herrera*, for he describes a meeting of Pizarro and Cortés in Palos "on the spot consecrated by the presence of Columbus," a meeting which in my opinion never took place. Pizarro landed in Seville, not in Palos (*Herrera*, Déc. IV, bk. VI, ch. III, p. 130) and the meeting to which Herrera refers took place at Court. I do not know on what authority *Alamán* says (vol. II, p. 23) that Pizarro arrived in Palo on his way to conquer Peru. The sequence of chs. IV and v of Déc. IV, bk. VI, of *Herrera*, p. 135, suffices to destroy this view. Pizarro went direct from Seville to Toledo, as shown in *Herrera, loc. cit.*

18 *Sandoval*, bk. XVI, par. XXI, vol. I, p. 841.

19 *Sandoval*, bk. XVI, par. XXII, vol. I, p. 859.

20 *Sandoval*, bk. XVI, par. XXII, vol. I, p. 863.

21 *Sandoval*, bk. XVI, par. XXII, vol. I, p. 867.

22 In Borgoña's report it is said that he left for France "on the same day June 24th" (*Sandoval*, bk. XVI, par. XXII, vol. I, p. 880); but as Charles V's own letter which Borgoña conveyed was signed on the 28th (p. 874) there is a doubt about which of these two dates is the right one. The documents given in detail by Sandoval show dilatory tactics at their best and provide an admirable illustration of the diplomatic-heraldic usages of the day.

23 Bernal Díaz says that he went first to Seville where he stayed with the Duke of Medina Sidonia. But Bernal Díaz was in Mexico, and *Herrera* says definitely that he refused to go to Seville (Déc. IV, bk. VI, ch. I, pp. 72–3).

24 *B.D.C.*, ch. cxcv, vol. II, p. 386. *F.C.* (p. 34) argues that Cortés came to Spain to marry Doña Francisca de Mendoza and changed his mind after his arrival. Though this is backed by actual statements to that effect made by Villagómez, it seems to me that the documents against are stronger still. *Gómara* (ch. clxxxij, fol. xciiij) says that he married Doña Juana de Zúñiga by procuration given to his father. But there is a stronger document still, H.C.'s letter to his father Sept. 26, 1526 (*Cuevas*, p. 30): "As for Doña Juana coming over [to Mexico] I have nothing to say, for I would prefer to take this trouble myself rather than letting her take it." This shows conclusively that the marriage had been arranged before H.C. sailed for Spain.

25 *Gómara*, ch. clxxxj, fol. xciij verso.

26 H.C. to Charles V, Feb. 3rd, 1544, Valladolid (in *Prescott*, vol. III, app., p. 338, or *Gayangos*, p. 568).

27 *Herrera*, Déc. IV, bk. VI, ch. IV, p. 134.

28 *Herrera*, Déc. IV, bk. VI, ch. IV, p. 132; *Gómara, loc. cit.*; *B.D.C.*, ch. cxcv, vol. II, p. 392; *Alamán*, vol. II, p. 28 (with papal bull, vol. II, app., p. 32); documents of imperial grants to Cortés, *C.D.I.A.I.*, vol. XII, pp. 376–86.

29 *B.D.C.*, ch. cxcv, vol. II, p. 387.

30 *B.D.C.*, ch. cxcv, vol. II, pp. 388–9.

31 "Era doña Juana hermosa muger" (*Gómara*, ch. clxxxij, fol. xciij).

32 Bishop Zumárraga to Charles V, *C.D.I.A.I.*, vol. XIII, p. 118.

33 Zumárraga to Charles V, *C.D.I.A.I.*, vol. XIII, pp. 122–3; *Alamán*, vol. I, p. 252; *B.D.C.*, ch. cxcvi, vol. II, p. 393.

34 *B.D.C.*, ch. cxcvi, vol. II, p. 393; *Alamán*, vol. I, p. 257; Zumárraga, *C.D.I.A.I.*, vol. XIII, pp. 123–30.

35 The list of accusations dated May 8th, 1529, in *C.D.I.A.I.*, vol. XXVII, p. 5, and H.C.'s answers to them, in a paper signed by Altamirano, his lawyer and kinsman on Jan. 14th, 1534, in *Cuevas*, p. 141. The deed of accusation signed by his mother-in-law on Jan. 4th, 1529, in *C.D.I.A.I.*, vol. XXVI, p. 298.

36 On Zumárraga's meeting with Charles V, *Alamán*, vol. II, p. 175. Zumárraga's quotation in letter to Charles V, *C.D.I.A.I.*, vol. XIII, pp. 132–3.

37 Zumárraga to Charles V, *C.D.I.A.I.*, vol. XIII, p. 137.

38 On Alvarado's incident Zumárraga to Charles V, *C.D.I.A.I.*, vol. XIII, pp. 176–7. The new Audience had orders to release him if he was still in prison (*Herrera*, Déc. IV, bk. VII, ch. VIII, p. 174).

39 H.C. Letter to Charles V, dated, Tetzcuco, Oct. 20th, 1530, *Gayangos*, p. 499.

CHAPTER XXXI

1 *B.D.C.*, ch. CXCIX, vol. II, p. 393. *Herrera*, Déc. IV, bk. VIII, ch. II, p. 193.

2 H.C. to his agent Núñez, for Charles V, 1535, *Gayangos*, p. 550.

3 *Gómara* (ch. clxxxiiij, fol. xciiij verso) says it happened in Tetzcuco; but the document recording the fact definitely says "la ciudad de Tascaltecle" (*C.D.I.A.I.*, vol. XII, p. 404) and H.C. confirms this in his letter to Charles V (Tetzcuco, Oct. 10th, 1530), *Gayangos*, p. 502. On his settling in Tetzcuco, *Herrera*, Déc. IV, bk. VIII, ch. II, p. 194.

4 Details on Tetzcuco stay, in H.C. to Núñez, *C.D.H.M.*, vol. II, p. 255, or *Gayangos*, p. 550. H.C.'s impatience in letter to Charles V, Tetzcuco, Oct. 10th, 1530, in *Gayangos*, p. 504.

5 Date of sailing, *Herrera*, Déc. IV, bk. VII, ch. VIII, pp. 174, 178. On Audience, same, p. 176, also Déc. IV, bk. VI, ch. X, p. 147.

6 *Herrera*, Déc. IV, bk. VII, ch. I, pp. 157–9.

7 *C.D.I.A.I.*, vol. XIV, p. 342.

8 *B.D.C.*, ch. CXCVI, vol. II, p. 397.

9 "Y oian los tormentos," *Herrera*, Déc. IV, bk. VII, ch. II, p. 160. Also, letters from Zumárraga to the Council of the Indies and to Charles V, Mar. 28th, 1531, Valladolid, 1533, *Cuevas—D*, pp. 8, 17.

10 *B.D.C.*, ch. CXCVI, vol. II, p. 398.

11 On Jan. 25th, 1531. H.C. writes to Queen Juana that the new Audience has not yet begun to work (*Gayangos*, p. 507; *Herrera*, Déc. IV, bk. VII, ch. VIII, pp. 175–6).

12 This alarm and call to the forces is mentioned in a number of documents with different approaches and points of view. The most important are H.C. to Núñez (*C.D.H.M.*, vol. II, p. 48, and *Herrera*, Déc. IV, bk. VII, ch. VIII, p. 177); H.C. to Charles V, Apr. 1532 (*Gayangos*, p. 511); Report by the Audience, *C.D.I.A.I.*, vol. XIV, pp. 338, 342. And *Herrera*, Déc. IV, bk. IX, ch. IV, p. 229, points out that the Audience had to rely on the authority of H.C. to keep the peace.

13 Deed forgiving Matienzo's heirs in *Cuevas*, p. 197.

14 Cortés argues his case in a petition to the Council of the Indies, *Cuevas*, p. 80. An enquiry instituted by the Audience on Feb. 23rd, 1531, is recorded in *C.D.I.A.I.*, vol. XVI, p. 548. The letter from the Audience (1531) is in *C.D.I.A.I.*, vol. XIV, pp. 329–47.

15 *Alamán*, vol. II, p. 34

16 Letter of Juan Zamudio, Panama, July 15th, 1539, quoted by *Alamán*, vol. II, p. 69, in the course of an enlightening discussion of H.C.'s commercial and agricultural enterprises.

17 *Cuevas*, vol. II, p. 69.

18 H.C. to Charles V, Sept. 3rd, 1526, *Gayangos*, p. 490.

19 *C.D.I.A.I.*, vol. XXII, p. 285.

20 *Cuevas*, p. 140. Dated, July, 1530.

21 Document in *Navarrete*, vol. V, p. 440; date of Loaisa's departure, p. 5. *B.D.C.*, ch. cc, vol. II, p. 411, says it was on June 22nd, but Navarrete proves him wrong.

22 *Navarrete*, vol. V, p. 444.

23 *Navarrete*, vol. V, p. 459.

24 *Navarrete*, vol. V, p. 458.

25 H.C. to Charles V, Tetzcuco, Oct. 10th, 1530, *Gayangos*, p. 505; H.C. to Charles V, Mexico, Apr. 20th, 1532, *Gayangos*, p. 515.

26 H.C. to Charles V, Teguantepeque, Jan. 25th, 1533, *Gayangos*, p. 521. *Herrera*, Déc. IV, bk. X, ch. xv, p. 290. *B.D.C.*, ch. cc, vol. II, pp. 412–14. *Gómara*, ch. clxxxv, fol. xcv, calls the pilot Fortún Ximénez. Official document dated Aug. 19th, 1534, in *C.D.H.M.*, vol. II, p. 31, calls him Ortuño Ximénez.

27 *B.D.C.*, ch. cc, vol. II, p. 415. *C.D.H.M.*, vol. II, p. 38.

28 *Gómara*, ch. clxxxvj, fol. xcv verso. *B.D.C.*, ch. cc, vol. II, pp. 416–18. Their dates, however, are wrong, as proved by Guzmán's letter to the Audience, June 7th, 1535, *Gayangos*, pp. 535–7, and to the King, *C.D.I.A.I.*, vol. XIII, pp. 445–9; as well as by H.C. who in his letter to Oñate, dated Bahia de Santa Cruz, May 14th, 1535 (*Cuevas*, p. 171), says he took 16 days in the voyage and that he arrived in Santa Cruz on May 3rd (día de Santa Cruz de Mayo), which tallies tolerably well with Guzmán's date.

29 *B.D.C.*, ch. cxcix, vol. II, p. 409.

30 *B.D.C.*, ch. cci, vol. II, p. 419 et seq.

31 *C.D.I.A.I.*, vol. II, p. 568.

32 *Gómara*, ch. clxxxvj, fol. xcvj.

33 *C.D.I.A.I.*, vol. III, p. 535.

34 *B.D.C.*, ch. cci, vol. II, pp. 426–7.

35 *Gómara*, ch. ccxxxvj, fol. cxiij.

36 Document XXI, in *Cuevas*, p. 196, signed Madrid, May 15th, 1540. In a donation *inter vivos*, done in Cuyoacán on Nov. 27th, 1539, Cortés says of his sons: "Because you are my sons and are, you Don Martín, in the realms of Castille serving his Majesty, and you Don Martín Cortés and Don Luis are coming now with me to the realms of Castille to serve His Majesty" (*Cuevas*, p. 190). This shows that the plan to send one of his sons to join Don Martín (Doña Marina's son) who was already in Spain, which Cortés announced in his letter to the Emperor, Feb. 10th, 1537 (*C.D.I.A.I.*, vol. II, p. 568), did not materialise. He referred to Don Luis, for Don Martín, the heir, was then five years old.

CHAPTER XXXII

1 *Sandoval*, bk. XXIV, par. VIII, vol. II, p. 367.

2 *Sandoval*, bk. XXIV, par. X, vol. II, p. 369.

3 *B.D.C.*, ch. cci, vol. II, pp. 427–8.

4 *Sandoval*, bk. XXV, par. VII, vol. II, p. 402.

5 *Sandoval*, bk. XXV, par. VII, vol. II, p. 403.

6 *Sandoval*, bk. XXV, par. XII, vol. II, p. 411.

7 *Cuevas*, Document XXXIII dated 1542, p. 201.

8 *Cuevas*, Document XXVI, p. 151.

9 *Cuevas*, Document XXII, p. 119; Document XXX, p. 189.

10 Letter to Charles V, Valladolid, Feb. 3rd, 1544, *Gayangos*, p. 571.

11 *MacNutt*, ch. xviii, p. 442.

12 *C.D.H.M.*, vol. II, pp. 43, 49–51. To the arguments adduced by Icazbalceta (*C.D.H.M.*, vol. II, p. xxvii) in favour of 1533 for the date of this document, although in a footnote, p. 61, he seems to accept 1540 (a year when Cortés was in Spain), we may add two: the first is that at the beginning of the paper Cortés writes as if he were speaking direct to his agent Núñez about the Emperor, and so for instance, he says "His Majesty" (S.M.) referring to the Emperor; while later, he writes as if it was Núñez who is speaking for him to the Emperor and so he says: "Your Majesty" (V.M.) This justifies not only that he should speak of *this* Court (esta Corte) though he was in Mexico himself, but also of *these* realms (*estos* reinos, p. 48). Then there is the sentence: "Item, que llegados a España el Presidente y Oidores que ahora residen . . ." which proves that the paper was written between 1530 and 1535.

13 See note 17 below. Letter to Charles V, Madrid, Mar. 18th, 1543.

14 *Cuevas*, Document XXXIV, p. 218.

15 Letter to Charles V, *Cuevas*, p. 216.

16 Letter to Charles V, Valladolid, Feb. 3rd, 1544, *Gayangos*, pp. 569–71.

17 Diálogos de la preparación de la muerte, dictados por el Ilustrissimo y Reuerendissimo Señor Do Pedro de Nauarra Obispo 9 de Comenge y del consejo supremo del Christianissimo Rey de Francia. Tolosa (1565).

18 Text of the will and analysis thereof in *Conway*.

19 Letter to Charles V, Feb. 3rd, 1544, *Gayangos*, pp. 569, 568.

20 *C.S.*, bk. III, ch. li, p. 241.

GENERAL INDEX

Acalan, 436
Acamapitl, 339
Acapulco, 468
Acolman (Aculman), 375
Adam, 485
Aguilar, Alonso de, 413
Aguilar, Count of, 424, 443
Aguilar, interpreter, 110, 111, 116, 122, 202, 213, 247, 257
Aguilar, Marcos de, 446, 447
Ahuelitoctzin, 398
Ahuilitzapan, 310, 351
Ahuitzotl, Emperor, 3, 10, 339
Aiguesmortes, Truce of, 471, 472
Alaminos, Antón de, 74, 75, 76, 81, 83, 127, 299, 301
Alba, Duke of, 57
Albornoz, Rodrigo de, 13, 432, 433, 440, 442, 444
Albuquerque, Duke of, 152
Alcántara, Military Order of, 20, 35
Alderete, Julián de, 371, 381, 397, 398, 399, 400
Alexander, 185
Alfonso, Hernando, 98
Algiers, 477
Almería, 218, 259
Alps, 476
Altamirano, Father Diego de, 441
Alvarado, Jorge, 441
Alvarado, Pedro de, 77, 83, 88, 89, 92, 102, 123, 133, 152, 154, 164, 177, 204, 207, 215, 244, 258, 269, 271, 283, 284, 308, 309, 325, 327, 328, 329, 330, 331, 332, 335, 341, 343, 345, 375, 378, 379, 380, 383, 386, 390, 407, 420, 422, 423, 484
Alvarez, Francisco, 328
Alvarez, Juan, 328
Amadis de Gaul, 451, 452
Amaya, Pero de, 304
Amazón, river, 45
Amecameca, 227, 228
Anáhuac, 217, 225, 233, 256, 279, 288, 309. *See also* Culúa
Anciso, 54, 55
Apam, 344

Aragón, Crown of, 35, 140
Arana, María de, 36
Arcos, Duke of, 137
Argüello, 218
Astorga, Marquess of, 483
Atonatiuh (Water-Sun), 7
Audience, the, 464, 468
Avila, 465
Axayacatl, Emperor, 4, 242, 280, 281, 282, 359
Axopacatzin, 361
Ayacapichtlan, 134
Ayagualulco, 416
Ayllón, Lucas Vázquez de, 302, 303, 313, 356
Ayotzinco, 229
Azan Aga, 476
Azcapotzalco, 373
Azores, the, 410
Azúa, 47, 49

Bacallaos, los, 422
Bacon, Roger, 239
Baeza, 87
Bahama Canal, 151, 299
Balboa, Vasco Núñez de, 28, 54, 55, 56, 72, 105, 407
Baracoa, 66. *See also* Santiago de Cuba
Barba, Pedro, 101, 353
Barcelona, 39, 88, 89, 92, 300
Barragana-barraganía, 152
Bastidas, Rodrigo de, 28, 45
Béjar, Duke of, 410, 424
Benavente, Fray Toribio de. *See* Motolinea
Bermúdez, 311, 313, 315
Bidassoa, 451
Bobadilla, Don Francisco de, 35
Borgoña, 451
Borinquen (San Juan, Puerto Rico), 58
Botello, astrologer, 329, 342
Brazil, coast of, 45
Burgos, 450
Burgundian Court, 452

Caballero, Admiral, 353
Caballero, Pedro, 324

543

Cabot, Sebastián, 467, 468
Cacama, 189, 228, 229, 271, 272, 273, 284
Cáceres, 25
Cacique, fat. See Cempoal, cacique of, 544
Cádiz, 28, 45
Caesar, 479
California, 472
Calmecac, 225
Calpan, 226
Calpixques, 15, 140, 141
Calpulli, 225
Caltanmi (Cocotlan), 168
Camacho, 102
Canoes, river of, 315
Cantar de Mio Cid, 105
Capitulations, 454
Casa de Contratación, 299, 300, 468
Castilblanco, 168
Castilla del Oro, 56, 461
Castille, 35
Castillo, Bernal Díaz del, 23, 24, 47, 68, 72, 73, 74, 75, 76, 77, 79, 83, 84, 87, 89, 91, 93, 95, 96, 97, 100, 101, 102, 103, 106, 110, 114, 115, 116, 117, 118, 119, 124, 130, 136, 143, 148, 149, 150, 151, 153, 156, 177, 185, 186, 191, 193, 200, 201, 202, 203, 206, 210, 212, 220, 222, 227, 230, 231, 242, 245, 247, 253, 254, 258, 259, 264, 265, 269, 274, 275, 276, 280, 281, 282, 284, 285, 289, 295, 307, 311, 314, 317, 323, 331, 342, 344, 347, 356, 365, 367, 369, 380, 403, 416, 418, 430, 431, 436, 444, 461
Catalina, Doña (Cempoal cacique's niece), 147, 148, 153, 323
Catalina, Doña (Moteçuçuma's daughter), 323
Catalina Pizarro, Doña (Cortés' mother), 20, 420
Catalina Pizarro, Doña (Cortés' bastard daughter, 420
Ceacatl, 11
Cebu, King of, 468
Cempoal, 136, 139, 140, 154, 156, 163, 164, 167, 203, 228, 307, 310, 311, 312, 315-318, 323; cacique of, 137, 222, 257, 307, 314, 322, 329
Centzontotochtli, or "four hundred rabbits," 224
Cermeño, 154
Cervantes, the jester, 68, 287
Cervantes, Miguel de, 21, 24, 26, 97
Cervantes de Salazar, 5, 22, 23, 47, 48, 190, 191, 289, 332, 335

Chachalacas, river of, 316
Chalco, 134, 222, 228, 229, 230, 364, 365
Chalco, lake of, 231
Chapultepec, 206, 376, 377
Charles V: 20, 71, 89, 155, 162, 163, 164, 166, 208, 209, 210, 238, 243, 256, 272, 274, 279, 280, 283, 301, 316, 324, 325, 443
  Algiers siege, 477
  Cortés, relations with, 301, 454, 455
  Debts, 88
  Flemish Courtiers, 88
  Francis I and, 450
  Ghent revolt, 476
  Grief and cares, 301, 474
  High Constable and, 474
  Ingratitude, 477
  Inexperience, 70, 88
  Indians, attitude to, 414
  Peasant, meets a, 474
  Spanish language and, 301
  Spanish nobility and, 443, 476
  Travels, 302, 452
  Wife's death, 475
  Zumárraga and, 457
Cherino, Peramil de, 413
Chichimecatecuhtli, 178, 350, 374, 384
Chico, Francisco Alvarez, 356
China, 466
Chinantecs, 287
Chinantla, 312, 469
Chirino, 432, 433, 440, 446
Cholula, 174, 179, 257, 259, 309, 331, 332, 372, 374
Churubusco, 379
Cibao, 38
Cihuacoatl (Ciguacoat, Ciuacoatl or Serpent-Woman), 345, 390
Cingapacinga, 145, 146, 147
Cipango, 45
Cisneros, Ximénez de, Cardinal, 33, 88
Citlaltepec, 344, 373
Ciutla, 115, 117
Clarenceux, 450
Coanochtzin, King of Tetzcuco, 362
Coatzacoalco, 11, 84, 288, 310, 324, 415
Cobos, Francisco de los, 424, 453, 482
Colmenares, Rodrigo de, 55, 56
Colom. See Colón
Colombia, 50
Colón (Columbus), 23, 29, 31, 33, 35, 36, 38, 39, 44, 45, 46, 49, 50, 59, 74, 223, 422
Colón, Don Bartolomé, 57, 59

Colón, Diego de, 50, 57, 58, 59, 69, 71, 88, 89, 91, 409
Colonna, Camillo, 476
Conchillos, King Ferdinand's secretary, 42
Copilco, 434
Cordillera, 292
Córdoba, Hernández de, 73, 75, 76, 79, 81, 87, 92, 110, 111, 118, 151, 246
Coria, Bernardino de, 154
Cortés, Hernán (Hernando or Fernando). See special index
Cortés, Don Luis, bastard son, 478
Cortés, Doña María, legitimate daughter, 483
Cortés, Don Martin, legitimate son, 478, 483
Cortés de Monroy, Martin, father, 20, 21, 301
Cosa, Juan de la, 44, 45, 51
Coyoacán (Coyohuacán, Cuyoacán), 218, 231, 234, 272, 370, 371, 375, 378, 391, 399, 415, 483
Coztemexi, 436
Cozumel, 78, 79, 102, 110
Cuanacoch, 436
Cuauhquechollan (Guacachula), 352, 353, 364
Cuauhtemoc (Quauhtemoc, Guatemozin, Guatemuza, Guatemuz), 359, 361, 362, 376, 382, 389, 398, 437, 485
    Appearance, 361
    Conspiracy against Cortés, 359
    Cortés (relations with), 387, 388
    Death, 437
    Generalship, 362
    Emperor, 359
    Goes to Las Hibueras, 436
    Moteçuçuma (challenge to), 359
    Parentage, 361
    Peace policy, 376
    Prisoner, 399
    Qualities, 384
    Leader of siege, 362
    Tortured, 399, 400
    War policy, 361, 366, 367
Cuauhtitlan, 373
Cuba, 36, 44, 53, 58, 59, 72, 73, 74, 84, 87, 126, 161, 288, 302, 310, 439
Cuernavaca (Cuauhnauac), 134, 369
Cueva, Don Francisco de la, 152
Cueva, Doña Francisca de la, 152
Cueva, Don Pedro de la, 152, 449
Cuicuitzcatl (Cuicuitcatzin, Don Carlos), 272, 363
Cuitlahuac (city), 230

Cuitlahuac (King of Iztapalapa), 134, 189, 228, 231, 271, 272, 273, 336, 339, 341, 359, 361
Cuitlalpitoc (Pitalpitoque, Ovandillo), 120
Culhuacan, 79
Culúa, 81, 220, 286, 364. See also Mexico (country), Anáhuac
Cuyoacán. See Coyoacán

Darien, 50, 54, 56, 72, 114
Dávila, Alonso, 77, 83, 84, 92, 129, 205, 271, 325, 342, 343, 356, 360, 409, 423
Dávila, Gil, 438
Dávila, Pedrarias. See Pedrarias Dávila
Delgadillo, 456, 463
Díaz, Bartholomeu, 45
Díaz, Juan, 154, 177
Don Carlos. See Cuicuitzcatl
"Don Fernando," King of Tetzcuco, 379
Doña Marina. See Marina, Doña
Don Quixote, 24, 26, 27, 297
Dorantes, Martín, 441, 444
Doria, Andrea, 476
Duero, Andrés de, 95, 96, 97, 98, 311, 312, 313, 315
Dulce, Gulf, 438
Dulce, river, 438

Ecatonatiuh (Wind-Sun), 7
El Abrojo, Monastery, 457
El Marién, 299
El Pardo, 474
El Patio (Quauhtechcatl), 223
El Puerto, 374
Elisabeth, Empress of Spain, 475
Elvira, Doña, Xicotencatl's daughter, 205
Encomienda. See Repartimiento
England, 36
Enrique, native cacique, 37
Enríquez, Enrique, 49
Equator, 466
Escalante, Juan de, 129, 156, 164, 165, 166, 195, 222, 259, 265, 266
Escudero, Juan, 64, 154, 155
Española, island, 31, 35, 36, 38, 39, 44, 45, 48, 50, 53, 55, 56, 59, 63, 65, 70
Esquivel, Juan de, 50, 53, 59
Estrada, Alonso de, 432, 433, 444, 447
Europe, 41
Eve, 485
Extremadura, 19, 28, 46

Falces, Marquess of, 482
Feathered Serpent. *See* Quetzalcoatl, Huemac
Ferdinand, King of Spain, 20, 25, 34, 36, 37, 42, 44, 471
Feria, Count of, 95
Field of the Cloth of Gold, 452
Figueroa, Rodrigo, de, 91
Flanders, 53, 475
Flisco, Bartolomé, 46
Florida, 70, 71, 72, 76, 233, 422
Fonseca, Juan Rodríguez de, Bishop of Burgos, 28, 42, 44, 50, 300, 302, 398, 399, 407, 411, 412, 423
France, 451
France, King of, 451
Francis I, 450
Francisca, Doña, 458
Franciscan Friars, 441
Fuenterrabia, 451

Garay, Francisco de, 89, 164, 408, 409, 419, 420, 421
Germany, 475
Ghent, 476
Godoy, Diego de, 113, 176
Golden Fleece, Order of, 452
Good Hope, Cape of, 45
Gómara, 20, 21, 23, 24, 26, 27, 47, 60, 61, 62, 63, 64, 67, 72, 83, 115, 143, 185, 289, 295, 399, 473
Gonzaga, Don Hernando de, 476
Grado, Alonso de, 265, 266
Granada, 35, 62, 199, 451
Grand Khan, 46
Great Cairo, 74
Green Island, 118
Grijalva, Juan de, 77, 78, 79, 80, 81, 82, 83, 84, 87, 88, 89, 90, 91, 92, 93, 94, 99, 113, 118, 151, 246
Grijalva River, 434
Guadalcanal, 76
Guadalupe, 248. *See also* Tepeyac
Guanaxes, Island, 74
Guaniguanico, 100, 302
Guatemala, 422
Guaxocingo (Huesocingo, Guajocingo), 178, 199, 214, 217, 232, 352, 364, 374
Guayacan, 49
Guerrero, Gonzalo, 111
Guevara, Juan Ruiz de, 304, 311
Guienne, 450
Guzmán, Cristóbal de, 395
Guzmán, Nuño de, 449, 471

Habana (Puerto de Carenas), 78
Haiti, 36
Hannibal, 421
Hendaye, 451
Henry IV of Castille, 474
Hercules, 436
Heredia, the Old, 287
Herrera, 443, 462, 463
Hibueras. *See* Las Hibueras; Honduras
Hierro, Island of, 29
High Constable, 474
Hojeda (Alonso de), 28, 44, 45, 49, 50, 51, 52, 53, 54, 55, 92, 105
Holguín, García, 390, 401
Holy Ghost (password), 318
Honduras (las Hibueras), 74, 435
Huatusco, 311
Huaxtepec, 134, 369
Huemac, 10, 15. *See also* Quetzalcoatl
Huitzilhuacan, 192
Hungary, King of, 465

Ilhuicatl tlamatilizmatini (Master of the Science of the Heavens), 8, 9
Illescas, 12
Indies, the, 25, 29, 34, 35, 37, 39, 40, 42, 44, 45, 57
Incarnation, the, 245
Infant (Infante), 328
Ircio, Pedro de, 354
Isabel, Queen of Spain, 20, 25, 33, 37, 44, 49, 471
Island of Sacrifices, 118
Italy, 25, 26, 27, 475
Itzcuin, 7
Itzocan (Izzuacan), 352
Ixtacamaxtitlan (Xalacingo), 170, 177
Iztaccihuatl (White Woman), 219, 222
Iztapalapa, 230, 231, 234, 363, 375, 377, 378, 379

Jamaica, 46, 50, 53, 59, 70, 89, 164, 324, 356, 439
Jewel Shop, 280, 281, 282
John II, King, 474
Jordan, 274
Jovío, 72
Juana, Doña, 301, 443
Julián, interpreter, 75, 81

La Marcayda, María, 457
La Niña, 30
La Rábida, Monastery, 452

Lagos, Cristóbal de, 64
Lares, Amador de, 95, 98
Las Casas, Bartolomé de, Bishop of Chi-
apa, 20, 23, 33, 34, 36, 39, 42, 48, 49,
50, 51, 53, 58, 59, 60, 61, 66, 67, 73,
77, 94, 95, 96, 98, 114, 156, 215, 277,
300, 301, 372, 446
Las Casas, Francisco de, 430, 431, 437, 438
Las Hibueras (Honduras), 422, 430, 446,
466
Laws of the Indies, 113
León, Juan de, 311
Lepe, Diego de, 45
Linares, 87
Lisbon, 45
Loa, Guillén de la, 165, 166
Loaisa, Cardinal, 475
López, Martín, 226, 264, 297, 318, 357,
360
Lower California, 469
Lucayas, the, 299
Lugo, Francisco de, 129, 130, 280
Luisa, Doña, Xicotencatl's daughter, 343,
345
Luni, 476
Luther, 106, 465

Maçatlan, 10
Madrid, 280, 451
Madrid, Treaty of, 450
Magellan, Strait of, 467
Magicians. See Tonalpouhque
Magiscacin, Don Lorenzo, 360
Majorca, 476
Malacca, 466
Maldonado, Alonso, 461
Malinalco, 134
Malinaltepec, province of, 287
Malintzin (or Malinche), 151, 152, 212,
228, 229, 246, 249, 254, 260, 288, 316
Maluenda, Pedro de, 323
Mamexi, 174
Mansilla, Juana de, 441, 442
Marco Polo, 38
Marín, Luis, 148, 383
Marina, Doña, 117, 118, 122, 136, 148, 151,
152, 153, 154, 192, 202, 212, 240, 246,
247, 260, 397, 441
Marius, 401
Márquez, 329, 330, 362
Martín, Benito (or Martínez), 88, 96, 300
Matanzas, 78
Matienzo, 456, 463
Matlatzinco, 271

Maxixcatzin, 196, 199, 205, 208, 345, 348,
350
Mayorazgo, 478
Mecca, 222
Medellín, 19, 20, 22, 23, 25, 28, 29, 97,
267, 301, 403, 444
Medina del Campo, 248
Medina Sidonia, Duke of, 137, 483
Melchior, interpreter, 75, 81, 111, 114
Melgarejo de Urrea, Fray Pedro, 367, 407
Méndez, Diego, 46
Mendieta, 33
Mendoza, Don Antonio de, 470, 471
Mendoza, Diego Becerra de, 469
Mendoza, Diego Hurtado de, 469
Mendoza, Doña Francisca de, 453
Mendoza, Doña María de, 453
Mendoza, Don Pero González de, 471
Mesa, 402
Mexía, Gonzalo, 342
Mexicalcingo, 379
Mexico (city). See Tenochtitlán
Mexico (country). See Anáhuac, Culúa
Michoacan, bishop of. See Quiroga, Vasco
de
Mictlan Cuauhtla (Mitalaguita), 15, 315
Millán, Juan, 97
Minorca, 476
Mixtecs, 423
Mizquic, 134, 230
Molín del Rey, 300
Molucas, 466, 468
Monastery of St. Francis, 444
Monroy, Alonso de, 20
Montaño, 402
Montejo, Francisco de, 77, 82, 83, 84, 92,
127, 129, 132, 149, 163, 299, 301, 355,
410
Montesinos, 33
Monzón, 452
Moorish wars, 476, 477
Moors, 404
Morla, Francisco de, 115
Moteçuçuma (Montezuma and other
forms):
Alvarado (relations with), 326, 327
Appearance, 5
Bernal Díaz (relations with), 269
Cortés: meeting with, 235, 259; pres-
ents to, 120, 127; relations with,
253, 254, 269, 270, 286, 289, 298, 329;
last interview with, 338, 339
Death, 339
Games, 269

Moteçuçuma (Continued)—
Generosity, 261, 268, 270, 271
Harem, 255
Household, 244, 255, 270
Intelligence, 260, 268
Legitimate children, 260
Life while a prisoner, 260, 261, 268
Magic ways, 12, 13, 134, 135
Mode of life, 14, 255
Offspring, 260, 452
Opposition to Cortés' coming to Mexico, 120, 127, 207, 216
Policy towards Spaniards, 120, 144, 189, 190
Prophecies (fear of), 3, 11, 124, 125
Quauhpopoca's incident, 259, 260, 261, 262, 265, 266
Refinement, 275, 276
Religious faith, 6, 10, 11, 13, 225, 254, 256, 273
Seized by Spaniards, 260
Sports, 5, 27
Treasure seized by Spaniards, 283
See also Uei Tlatoani
Motolinea, Fray Toribio (Benavente) or Motolinia, 33, 427, 441

Naborias, 270, 366
Narváez, Pánfilo de, 53, 59, 60, 299, 302, 303, 304, 305, 307, 310, 311, 313, 314, 315, 316, 318, 321, 322, 323, 324, 325, 327, 329, 332, 336, 347, 349, 352, 353, 356, 398, 399, 407, 408, 418, 420, 421, 424, 430, 445
Nassau, Count of, 455
Nauhtla (Almería), 218, 259
Navarra, Pedro de, 480
Necromancers. See Tonalpouhque
Nemontemi, 8
Nero, 371, 372
New Spain, 70
New World, 30, 31, 33, 36, 44, 45
Nezahoalpilli, King of Tetzcuco, 4, 13
Nicuesa, Diego de, 28, 49, 50, 51, 52, 54, 72, 90, 92, 105
Niño, Francisco, 30, 31
Niño, Pero Alonso, 45
Núñez, Francisco, 478, 479
Núñez Valera, Francisco, 23

Oaxaca, State of, 286, 403
Oaxaca, Valley of, 454
Ocampo, Diego de, 419, 420
Ocampo, Sebastián de, 59

Ocaña, 447
Ocotepec, 192
Ocuilan, 134
Ocuituco (Ocupatuyo), 352
Ojeda, Alonso de, 281, 329, 330, 362, 375
Olano, 55
Olea, Cristóbal de, 382
Olid, Cristóbal de, 87, 91, 92, 93, 99, 129, 205, 214, 271, 295, 322, 339, 343, 375, 376, 378, 383, 422, 423, 430, 431, 432, 436, 437, 484
Olintetl (Olintecle), 168
Olmedo, Fray Bartolomé de, 101, 122, 148, 169, 221, 253, 305, 310, 311, 312, 335, 339, 360, 417
Ordás, Diego de, 100, 115, 149, 211, 219, 220, 244, 258, 288, 314, 322, 324, 329, 337, 343, 352, 360, 410
Ordenanzas, 413, 415, 446
Orizaba, State of, 310
Ortega, page (Orteguilla), 247, 269, 270, 294, 296, 307
Ortiz, Fray Tomás, 445
Ortuño Ximénez, 469
Otomies, 172, 379, 384
Otumba, 344, 364, 420
Ovando, Don Frey Nicolás de, 25, 26, 35, 36, 44, 46, 47, 48, 59, 121
Oviedo, 35, 36, 38, 39, 40, 41, 69, 71, 76, 114, 276

Páez (or Pérez), Juan, 346
Palacios Rubios, Dr., 113
Palos, 28, 29, 30, 45, 374, 452
Panama, 45, 50
Pánuco, 408, 419, 420, 422, 449, 461
Pánuco River, 422
Parsifal, 181
Passamonte, Miguel de, 68, 69
Pastorelli (or Pastorelo), Domenico, 482
Patagonia, 143
Pavia, battle of, 450
Paz, Inés de, 23
Paz, Rodrigo de, 440
Pedrarias Dávila, 28, 72, 105, 459
Peralta, Don Antonio, 482
Peralta, Don Bernardino, 482
Pérez, Alonso, 371
Peru, 39, 53, 423
Petlacalcatl, 15
Pheasants, Island of, 451
Philip IV, 414
Phoenix, 423
Piçarro, Doña Hulana, 66

Pilar, 457
Pinedo, 353
Pitalpitoque, 121, 135, 144
Pizarro, 287, 317, 318
Pizarro Altamirano, Doña Catalina (Cortés' mother), 20, 420
Pizarro, Doña Catalina (H. C.'s bastard daughter), 420
Pizarro, Francisco (Discoverer of Peru), 39, 49, 53, 54, 105
Ponce, Johan, 71
Ponce de León, Licenciate Luis, 28, 76, 444
Pope, the, 465, 467
Popocatepetl (Hill That Smokes), 219, 222, 402
Porcallo, Vasco, 95
Portugal, 46
Prescott, 94
Puerto de Carenas (or Habana), 76
Puerto Rico (Borinquen, Island of, San Juan), 58, 70
Puerto de Términos, 81
Puertocarrero, Alonso Hernández, 99, 118, 130, 148, 149, 151, 153, 301, 410

Quahnahuac (Cuernavaca), 134, 369
Quauhpopoca (or Qualpupoca), 217, 218, 222, 259, 260, 261, 262, 264, 265, 266, 295
Quauhtechcatl (El Patio), 223
Quetzalcoatl, 10, 16, 25, 82, 83, 120, 121, 134, 206, 217, 233, 234, 261, 395. See also Huemac
Quexo, Juan Bono de, 412
Quiauitztlan, 136, 138, 139, 140, 143
Quilaztli, 134
Quiñones, Antonio de, 409, 423
Quinsay, 45
Quintalbor, 125, 224, 304
Quintero, Alonso, 29, 30, 31
Quiroga, Vasco de, Bishop of Michoacán, 461
Quivira (Seven Cities), 472

Ramírez, Don Sebastián, 461
Ramos, Martín, 110
Rangel, Rodrigo de, 310, 324, 423
Ratisbon, 476
Reformation, 465
Renascence, 239, 274, 290
Repartimiento, 405, 414, 415
Rhodes, 471
Ribera, Juan de, 410, 442
Rich Island. See Yucatán

Rich Town of the True Cross. See Veracruz
Río Frío, 351
Rodríguez, Ana, 417
Rodríguez, Violante, 417
Roman Empire, 412
Rome, 329, 371, 401
Royal Council of the Indies, 446
Rubicon, the, 161

Saavedra, Alvaro de, 468
Sabana, 59
Sahagún, Fray Bernardino de, 33, 120, 124
St. Christopher, 294
St. Francis, Monastery of, 444
St. Francis, Order of, 28, 430
St. James, 103, 115
St. James, Order of, 152
St. John of the Cross, 239
St. Mary, 29, 74, 103, 308, 318
St. Peter, 21, 22, 103, 115
St. Thomas Aquinas, 239
Salamanca, University of, 22, 23, 24
Salazar, agent, 432, 433, 440, 441, 446
Salazar, Cervantes de, 485
Salcedo, 58
Salcedo, Francisco de (El Polido), 148
Salmerón, Juan de, 461, 464
Samaña, Promontory of, 31
San Antón, point of, 78
San Cristóbal de la Habana, 299
San Francisco, 143
San Gil de Buena Vista, 438
San Juan (Borinquen, Island of, Puerto Rico), 58
San Juan de Ulúa, 120, 137, 144, 151, 302, 426
Sanlúcar de Barrameda, 29
Sandoval, Gonzalo de, 205, 244, 258, 267, 304, 312, 316, 318, 321, 331, 341, 343, 351, 360, 364, 365, 368, 377, 378, 383, 390, 401, 403, 415, 441, 452
Santa Cruz, 469, 470
Santa María, Island, 410
Santa María (password), 316
Santiago de Cuba, 66, 76, 77, 148
Santiago of the Southern Sea, 478
Santillana, Marquis of, 471
Santisteban del Puerto, 409, 421
Santo Domingo, 29, 31, 33, 36, 37, 39, 46, 50, 53, 57, 62, 288, 408, 423, 459
Sardinia, 476
Schadenfreude, 417
Sedeño, Juan, 99, 100, 116
Segura de la Frontera, 354, 360, 403

Serpent-Woman, 345. *See also* Cihuacoatl
Seven Cities (Quivira), 472
Seville, 28, 45, 49, 50, 79
Seville, Isidore of, 239
Socrates, 238
Sorcerers. *See* Tonalpouhque
Southern Sea, 54, 407, 423, 464
Spanish Crown, 33, 44, 70, 91
Spiceland, 466
Spices, Islands, 45
Straits, the, 467
Sulla, Cornelius, 401

Tabasco, 81, 113, 117, 118
Tabera, Don Juan, 475
Tacuba, 337, 339, 341, 344, 366, 371, 375, 379, 383, 390, 397, 399, 415. *See also* Tlacopan
Talavera, Bernardino de, 52, 53
Talavera, Hernando de, Archbishop of Granada, 33
Taniha, 436
Tapia, Andrés de, 290, 441, 452, 469
Tapia, Cristóbal de, 407, 419, 424
Tatelulco, 441, 457
Tecoacinco, 176
Tecuichpoch, 361
Tecuilhuitontli, month of, 381
Tehuantepec, 465, 469, 472
Temilutecutl, 172
Tenantzinco, 134
Tenayocan, 373
Tenochtitlán (Temistitán, Tenuxtitlán and other forms), 4, 214, 231, 234, 242, 354, 368, 395, 398, 440, 467
Teotecutli, 341
Teotlatlzinco, 192
Teozahuatl, 360
Tepaneca, 359
Tepeaca, 217, 350, 353, 360
Tepepolco, Rock of, 271, 377
Tepetzinco, 192
Tepeyac, 248, 329, 330, 375, 378
Tetlepanquetzal, 436
Teuch, 181, 188
Teuhtile (Tendile), 121, 122, 123, 127
Teul (teotl), 142, 145, 174, 309, 316, 323
Tetzcatlipoca (Tetzcatlipuca, Tetzcatepuca and other forms), 13, 120, 135, 217, 225, 249, 254, 289, 295, 325, 326, 340
Tetzcuco, 14, 214, 228, 229, 271, 284, 329, 333, 343, 362, 365, 368, 370, 374, 377, 397

Tezmolocan (Tezmoluca, Tetzmolucan), 192, 362
Tezocuilyoxique (Zenteycxique) 134
Tezozomoc, 120
Tianguiz (or Tianquitzli), 248, 380, 389
Tidore, King of, 468
Tilancalqui, 120
Titlacn, 325. *See also* Tetzcatlipoca
Tlacopan, 214, 271, 339. *See also* Tacuba
Tlalchitonatiuh (or Earth-Sun), 7
Tlalmanalco, 369
Tlaloc, god of rain, 236, 375
Tlalmanalco, 232
Tlamemes, 138
Tlapan, 10
Tlapanhuehuetl (sacred drum), 382, 383
Tlatelolco, 264, 386, 398
Tlatlanquitepec, 168
Tlatoanis, 171, 202
Tlatocan, the (or Council), 336
Tlatonatiuh (or Fire-Sun), 7
Tlaxcala, 152, 167, 170, 171, 172, 174, 175, 176, 180, 183, 185, 195, 196, 197, 199, 205, 209, 210, 215, 218, 221, 232, 257, 268, 279, 307, 345, 346, 348, 360, 361, 365, 374, 427
Tlaxcatecs, 175, 176, 177, 178, 179, 186, 189, 191, 192, 193, 195, 200, 202, 203, 204, 205, 206, 207, 208, 210, 214, 221, 223, 226, 246, 257, 259, 284, 309, 325, 329, 332, 340, 342, 346, 350, 356, 362, 375, 378
Tlehuexolotzin (Temilutecutl), 172
Tlillacapantzin, 339
Tlillan Calmecac, 12
Tocoquihuatzin, lord of Tlacopan, 271, 272
Toledo, 455
Toledo, Doña María de, Vicereine, 57, 62
Tomilatzin, 436
Tonalpouhque, 7, 237
Tonatio, 77. *See also* Alvarado, Pedro de
Tongues, the, 202, 247, 263
Torquemada, 154, 217, 238, 262, 281, 284, 381, 400
Totoloque, 269
Totonacs, 136, 140, 141, 142, 144, 145, 171
Tovilla, 311, 312
Toxcatl, feast of, 325
Triana, 374
Trinidad, 99, 439
Trinity, the, 245
Trujillo, 439
Tututepec, 403
Tzapotlan, 10
Tzicoac, 10

Tzioacpopoca, 223, 224
Tzitzimitles, 8
Tzonpantli, 326, 327, 359

Uaxtepec, 10
Uei Tlatoani, 3, 4, 7, 10, 189, 271, 275, 281,
   287, 296, 297, 298, 304, 308, 328, 333,
   336, 359, 368, 388, 390. See also Mote-
   çuçuma, Cuauhtemoc
Uitzilopochtli, 4, 5, 6, 10, 13, 140, 179, 212,
   217, 233, 236, 248, 293, 326, 340, 381,
   382, 386, 389. See also Witchywolves
Uixachtecatepetl, hill of, 8
Ulloa, 470, 472
Umbría (Ungría), 154, 286
Urabá, 54
Urdaneta, 43
Usagre, 311

Valencia, 26, 105
Valencia, Fray Martín de, 428
Valenciano, Pedro, 285
Valençuela, María de, 299
Valladolid, 299, 301, 447, 457
Vallejo, 420
Vargas, Don Lorenzo de, 360. See also
   Xicotencatl the Old
Vasco da Gama, 45
Velázquez, Diego de, 59, 60, 61, 62, 63, 64,
   65, 66, 67, 68, 69, 73, 74, 76, 78, 87,
   88, 89, 90, 91, 92, 94, 95, 96, 97, 98,
   99, 100, 101, 114, 119, 126, 128, 129,
   139, 148, 149, 150, 161, 163, 193, 267,
   299, 300, 314, 353, 373, 397, 409, 431,
   432
Velázquez, Diego, young, 322
Velázquez de León, Juan, 99, 101, 128, 133,
   205, 244, 258, 260, 270, 271, 280, 285,
   288, 305, 310, 314, 315, 316, 317, 322,
   324, 329, 343
Venezuela, 45
Veracruz (Rich Town of the True Cross),
   132, 138, 143, 144, 146, 148, 150,
   155, 156, 163, 164, 165, 184, 194, 195,
   218, 259, 265, 266, 284, 288, 292, 297,
   304, 309, 311, 315, 324, 349, 351, 353,
   355, 359, 361, 407, 410, 419, 459
Veragua, coast of, 48, 50, 72
Verdugo, Francisco, 100, 101, 373
Vergara, Alonso de, 304
Vespucci, Americo, 44, 45
Vexotzingo, 7. See also Guaxocingo

Victory Tower, 176
Villafaña, Antonio de, 373
Villalobos, 313
Virgin Birth, the, 203, 245

Witchywolves, 123, 135, 253, 254, 271,
   273, 275, 277, 289, 291, 295, 441. See
   also Uitzilopochtli

Xalapa, 167
Xalisco, 463, 470
Xaltocan (Saltocan), 344, 366
Xaraguá, 59
Xaramillo, Juan, 152
Xicochimalco, 351
Xicotencatl, the Old (Xicotenga), 152,
   177, 178, 181, 190, 195, 202, 204, 208,
   344, 345, 360
Xicotencatl, the Young, 177, 178, 348,
   374, 399
Xiuhtecutli, 11
Xiuhtepec, 369
Xiuhtlamin, 7, 8, 9
Xiutl, 7
Xochimilco, 134, 369, 370, 379
Xohuitotc, 134
Xoloc, 344, 378
Xoloco, bridge of, 14
Xuárez, Catalina (H. C.'s wife), 62, 65, 66,
   416, 457
Xuárez, Juan (H. C.'s brother-in-law),
   62, 65, 66, 416, 457

Yáñez, Alonso, 280
Yáquimo, 51
Yauhtepec (Yautepec, Yoaltepec), 134,
   369
Yucatán, 74, 75, 78, 79, 80, 81, 87, 88, 89,
   92, 434
Yztacmichtitlan, 174

Zacatula, 422, 466
Zainos, Francisco de, 461
Zaptecs (Zapotecs), 287, 423, 440
Zenteycxique (Tezocuilyoxique), 134
Zozolla (Zuzulla), 286
Zuazo, Alonso, 432, 439
Zultepec, 365
Zumárraga, Fray Juan de, 457
Zumpango, 344
Zúñiga, Doña Juana de, 424, 455

SPECIAL INDEX ON
HERNÁN CORTÉS

(ALSO HERNANDO, FERNANDO CORTÉS AND
MARQUESS OF THE VALLEY)

Abides his time, 92, 93
Adventures (youthful), 21, 25, 26, 27, 28
Algiers, siege of, 477
Ambition, 23, 24, 92, 280, 448, 479
Appearance, 26, 96, 103
Arms and letters, 24, 25, 103, 119, 274, 276, 354
Arrival
  in Santo Domingo, 31; Cuba, 65; Cozumel, 102; San Juan de Ulúa, 120; Tlaxcala, 198; Mexico City (first time), 231; Mexico City (second time), 330; Mexico City (from Las Hibueras), 444; Spain (first time), 452; Mexico (from Spain), 459; Mexico (from Santa Cruz), 470; Spain (second time), 475

Bastards, 66, 152, 420, 483
Battles
  Tlaxcala, 175
  Against Narváez, 318
  Mexico (first), 325
  Otumba, 344
  Cuauhnauac, 369
  Xochimilco, 370
  Mexico (second), 376
Birth, 19
Boyhood, 19, 20, 21, 22
"Burns his ships," 155

Cabildos (municipal councils) as instruments, 354, 355
Caesar, 479
Calpixques seized, 141
  released, 141
Cannibalism (attitude towards), 351
Capitulations for discovery, 454
Captain General, 310
Character and mind
  Abstemious, 92
  Active, 25, 61

Character (*continued*)—
  Aesthetic sense, 482
  Arms and letters, 119, 274
  Astuteness, 65, 66, 100
  Authoritarian, 154, 183
  Calculating, 145, 154, 155, 258, 279
  Cautious, 61, 103, 150
  Cold, 154, 239
  Commercial attitude, 93
  Complex, 98, 331
  Courageous, 63, 96, 126, 340, 343
  Cunning, 61, 119, 131, 263
  Daring, 65, 98
  Details (attention to), 338
  Devout, 107, 112
  Diplomatic gifts, 60, 61, 147, 204, 216, 258
  Dissimulating, 131, 258
  Eager, 239
  Eaglelike, 25, 94, 265, 276
  Economic sense, 67, 279
  Eloquent, 66, 156, 186, 316, 330
  Energy, 183, 341
  Faith, 22
  Farsighted, 25, 93, 94, 96, 98, 128, 156, 204, 250, 288
  Firm, 104, 111, 133
  Gambler, 22, 104
  Generosity, 29, 96, 103, 239
  Grace, 323
  Greatness, 145, 155, 486
  Guile, 61, 166
  Heroic, 61, 63, 161
  Humility, 260
  Humour, 165
  Imaginative, 472
  Initiative, 177
  Leadership, 102, 103, 143, 173, 430
  Legalistic, 47, 274, 354, 357
  Lighthearted, 323
  Longsuffering, 473, 481, 484, 486
  Love, 455

Character (*continued*)—
Methodical, 199, 205
Ostentatious, 433
Patient, 260
Persevering, 260, 473
Poetic vein, 26, 65
Power thirst, 183, 187, 331, 473
Presence of will, 66, 162
Presence of wit, 66
Prudent, 61, 162
Rebellious, 91, 99
Restrained, 154
Ruthless, 154, 213, 263
Sagacious, 93, 94, 162
Self-control, 307
Sensitive, 278
Serpent, 25, 119, 265, 276
Shrewd, 25, 61, 65, 93, 94, 97, 115, 150
Statesmanship, 67, 100, 116, 288, 354, 465
Steadfast, 25, 357
Strong, 63, 126, 340, 343
Suave manner, 98
Thoughtful, 258
Turbulent, 25
Vanity (accesses of), 332
Winsome ways, 66, 201, 265
Women (fond of), 154
Chief Justice, 310, 316, 321, 447
Childhood, 19, 20, 21, 22, 23
Coat of arms, 401, 442
Commercial enterprises, 454, 464, 465
Compass, use of, 436
Complaints
over Fonseca and others, 461
over privileges, 461
over time lost, 461
Concubines, 153, 154, 420, 478
Conspiracies, 61, 119, 149, 155
Court opposition, 455
Court strategy, 342, 355, 430, 456

Dates
Birth, 19
Salamanca studies, 22, 23, 24
Wanderings in the south, 26, 27, 28
Departure for New World, 29
Arrival in New World, 31
Notary in Azúa, 47
Alcalde in Baracoa, 66
Departure for Yucatán, 99
Arrival in Cozumel, 102; San Juan de Ulúa, 120; Tlaxcala, 198; Mexico, 231
Seizure of Moteçuçuma, 260

Dates (*continued*)—
Departure from Mexico to meet Narváez, 309
Arrival in Mexico second time, 330
Flight from Mexico, 339
Beginning of siege, 375
End of siege, 390
Recognised by Emperor, 412
Departure for Las Hibueras, 432
Return to Medellín (New Spain), 444
Arrival in Mexico, third time, 444
Departure for Spain, March, 450
Arrival in Spain, 452
Departure for New Spain, 456
Arrival in New Spain, 459
Arrival in Mexico City, 470
Departure for Spain last time, 473
Death, 484
Daughters, 478, 483
Death, 36, 484
Deposit of Indians, 405
Disappointment, 49
Distribution of Indians, 404, 405, 414

Education, 22, 23, 24
Electoral methods, 149
Eloquence, 66, 156, 186, 316
Emeralds, 455
Endurance, 183, 341
Errors, 292, 331
Exploration, 435

Faith, 256
Family, 20, 25
Feudal ambitions, 464
Fit of temper, 337, 346
Forward drive, 338, 340
Founder of Mexican nation, 402
Friends at Court, 300, 301, 455

Gambling spirit, 22, 104
Generalship, 313, 329, 345
Generosity, 29, 96, 103, 239
Gold, 149, 151, 163, 284, 335
Governor General, 412
Grace, 277, 323

Harem, 288
Health, 21, 22, 23, 26, 48, 182
Houses in Mexico, 351
Humility, 278
Hunger, 329

Ideas on God, 106
  Government, 149, 274, 354
  Indians
    Indian labour, 404, 405, 414
    Political organisation, 403, 404
Idols (destruction of), 292
Illegitimate children, 66, 151
Impatience, 23
Impulse, 292
Indians (relations with), 348
Industrial enterprises, 464
Ingeniousness, 258
Insight, 25, 128, 204
Insomnia, 182
Instructions from Charles V, 412, 413
  Velázquez, 94
Intuition, 93, 204, 404

Jewel Shop, 280, 281, 282, 283

La Rábida, 452
Las Casas and, 277, 300
Las Hibueras, 422, 430, 446, 466
Latin, 23, 24
Leadership, 102, 103, 143, 173, 430
Legend, 32
Leniency, 463
Letters to Charles V, 155, 166, 182, 183,
  199, 213, 218, 219, 226, 229, 230, 258,
  312, 330, 337, 340, 342, 344, 349, 351,
  355, 363, 377, 379, 405, 422, 430, 447,
  461, 466, 472
Luxury, 433

Marquess of the Valley, 448
Marriage, first, 62, 65, 66; second, 455
Mayorazgo (entail), 478

Medieval feudalism, 463
Mexican patriotism, 483
Mining, 465
Mother-in-law, 457

Name, 19

Ordinañces, 413, 415, 446
Ostentatiousness, 433

Political ideas, 149, 274, 354
Practical sense, 61, 93, 103, 128, 250, 288
Presents given, 116, 269; received, 259,
  270
Prophecies, 56
Proverbs used, 292, 317, 399

Religious earnestness, 106, 147, 182, 188,
  239, 244, 253, 289, 347, 349, 358
Renascence type, 239

Seizure of Moteçuçuma, 257
Ships run aground, 155
Sons, 478, 483
South seas discoveries, 464, 465
Speeches, 156, 316, 330
Statesmanship, 67, 100, 116, 288, 354, 465
Syphilis, 48, 49

Vanity, 331
Vassals, 463, 464

Wife, attitude to first, 62; attitude to sec-
  ond, 455
Will, 478, 483
Women, attitude to, 47, 62, 153, 154, 289
Work, attitude to manual, 143

Youth, 21